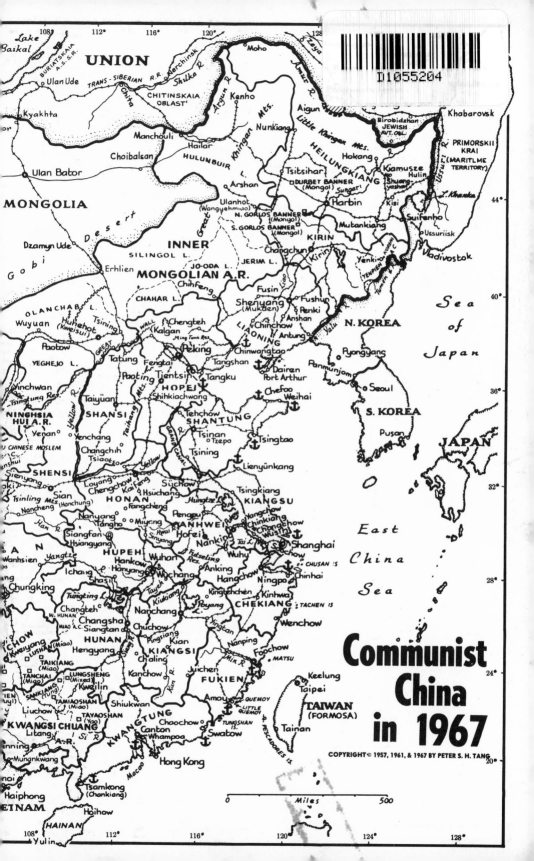

Communist China in 1967

COPYRIGHT © 1957, 1961, & 1967 BY PETER S. H. TANG

Communist China:

The Domestic
Scene
1949-1967

Studies by PETER S. H. TANG

Communist China Today: Domestic and Foreign Politics (1957)

Communist China Today: Vol. II: *Chronological and Documentary Supplement* (1958)

Russian and Soviet Policy in Manchuria and Outer Mongolia 1911-1931 (1959)

Communist China as a Developmental Model for Underdeveloped Countries (1960)

Communist China Today: Vol. 1: *Domestic and Foreign Policies* (2nd ed., revised and enlarged) (1961)

The Training of Party Cadres in Communist China (1961)

Russian Expansion into the Maritime Province: The Contemporary Soviet and Chinese Communist Views (1962)

The Twenty-Second Congress of the Communist Party of the Soviet Union and Moscow-Tirana-Peking Relations (1962)

The Chinese Communist Struggle against Modern Revisionism: Theory and Practice (1964)

Studies by PETER S. H. TANG and JOAN M. MALONEY

The Chinese Communist Impact on Cuba (1962)

√ *Communist China: The Domestic Scene 1949-1967* (1967)

COMMUNIST CHINA:

THE DOMESTIC SCENE
1949—1967

by

Peter S. H. Tang
and
Joan M. Maloney

Introduction
by
John B. Tsu

SETON HALL UNIVERSITY PRESS
SOUTH ORANGE, NEW JERSEY

Research Institute on the Sino-Soviet Bloc Studies

Book Series No. 2

Communist China: The Domestic Scene 1949-1967

The Research Institute on the Sino-Soviet Bloc is a non-profit, academic institution founded in 1959 and dedicated to the study of the world communist movement with particular emphasis on the roles of the Soviet Union and Communist China. It advocates no policies or doctrines, and favors only sound scholarship and scientific objectivity which constitute the real basis of all human knowledge and understanding.

The Institute's publication series has been designed to bring prominent topics to the fore in a manner calculated "to cast a brick to get a gem." The authors of the individual studies are alone responsible for their presentation of facts and analyses.

Published in the United States of America in 1967 by

SETON HALL UNIVERSITY PRESS

South Orange, New Jersey 07079

Printed in the United States of America.

TO
FRANK AND ARLINE MALONEY
AND
THE REVERED MEMORY OF
AN EXCEEDINGLY BENEVOLENT AND RIGHTEOUS MOTHER
(TANG KUO YUN K'UEI)

and to
fighters and martyrs for
justice, whoever, and
wherever they may be

Introduction

With the unleashing of the "great proletarian cultural revolution" in mainland China, the communist regime there has experienced one of the worst crises in its history. With the whole of China engulfed, the area of upheaval is so wide that even a totalitarian and monolithic government cannot restore it to order soon. For the first time in its eighteen years of existence, the regime has been challenged from within, not from without.

The record of the cultural revolution in China offers a rare example of a government functioning without its chief of state. Entirely new machinery, particularly in the body of the Red Guards, has been created to implement a new movement outside the regular government apparatus and Party structure. One can hardly understand how a country with thousands of years of tradition, and molded by Confucian humanism, can produce such a militantly fanatical group as the Red Guards. It is difficult to imagine how the little book, *The Quotations from Chairman Mao Tsetung*, could become a spiritual weapon in China.

A number of questions naturally arise when considering the overall aspects of China's present turmoil. What do the events signify? What is the thought of Mao? What is the ideological and historical background of the regime? Who rules China? Is the government apparatus still functioning? What changes have been wrought in the Party and state organs? What is the character of the leadership? What has happened to the economic structure? Has the military potential been affected?

To answer such pertinent, and indeed vital, questions is the purpose of this book by Dr. Peter S. H. Tang and Dr. Joan M. Maloney. Professor Tang first analyzed the nature and functions of the communist regime in China in his 1957 *Communist China Today: Domestic and Foreign Policies*, which was revised and enlarged by him in 1961. For years, this book has been used as a text by many leading universities and colleges in the United States and Canada. A considerable part of his original research has been incorporated into the present volume entitled *Communist China: The Domestic Scene 1949–1967*, to make this one of the most comprehensive as well as the most up to date of the scholarly works in the field.

Dr. Peter S. H. Tang, Professor of Political Science at Boston College since 1962, is also the Director of the Research Institute on the Sino-Soviet Bloc, which he founded in 1959. He is one of the few scholars who have remarkable command of both the Chinese and Russian languages, a linguistic talent put to excellent use in research endeavors for his writings. He is a genuine scholar and faithful researcher whose solid scholarship can best be appreciated by those who take the time to read his many pioneering contributions. Among Professor Tang's other publications in this field are his *Russian and Soviet Policy in Manchuria and Outer Mongolia 1911–1931*, *Communist China as a Developmental Model for Underdeveloped Countries*, *The Twenty-Second Congress of the Communist Party of the Soviet Union and Moscow-Tirana-Peking Relations*, *Training of Party Cadres in Communist China*, and *The Chinese Communist Struggle against Modern Revisionism: Theory and Practice*. All of these studies are based on original, primary source materials. They have been widely praised and used by several universities as texts or required readings.

Dr. Joan M. Maloney is Professor of History at Salem State College. Before joining the Salem College faculty, she served as a Research Associate for Seton Hall University, where she contributed distinguished in-depth analyses concerning Communist China with Professor C. Y. Cheng. She is Associate Director of the Research Institute on the Sino-Soviet Bloc, and has collaborated closely with Dr. Tang in many research projects, including their coauthorship of the study, *Chinese Communist Impact on Cuba*. She has a solid knowledge of Chinese history and a thorough understanding of contemporary China. This book represents over four years of joint work by her and Professor Tang.

The present volume is one of a series of works on Communist China published by the Institute of Far Eastern Studies in conjunction with the Seton Hall University Press. Other works are in preparation. It is our sincere hope that through these publications we may make a small contribution to understanding modern China. It is gratifying to state that the Most Reverend John J. Dougherty, S.S.D., L.H.D., President of Seton Hall University; the Very Reverend Monsignor Edward Fleming, Ph.D., Executive Vice President; the Very Reverend Thomas G. Fahy, Ph.D., Vice President in Charge of Instruction; Mr. Robert De Value, Vice President in Charge of Business; Reverend Albert Hakim, Ph.D., Dean of the College of Arts and Sciences; and Dr. Joseph Connor, Dean of Graduate Studies—all of whom share a genuine interest in advancing the understanding of China—are endeavoring to further expand the intellectual horizons of Seton Hall University through the work of its University Press and publications such as this one.

JOHN B. TSU, PH.D.
Director,
Institute of Far Eastern Studies
Seton Hall University

South Orange, New Jersey, 1967

Preface

Since its establishment of power on the mainland in 1949, the Chinese Communist regime has constantly attracted and absorbed worldwide attention to an ever-increasing degree. Mao Tse-tung and his followers, with remarkable speed and effectiveness, created a strong central authority that China has rarely known. In 1950, Communist China was able to save its fraternal Democratic People's Republic of North Korea from extinction. For the three subsequent years it discharged its "internationalist" duties to that brother communist state by engaging the United States and United Nations forces with its one million "volunteers." International attention was focused on Peking in 1954 at Geneva, and in 1955 at Bandung. Throughout this period as subsequently Peking continued to challenge the United States via meetings, such as the ambassadorial-level Warsaw talks, and in the never-ending war of words. After 1956, the Chinese Communists, with growing boldness, challenged their former mentor and big brother, the Soviet Union, for the latter's deviation to a revisionist stand. Peking's attitude may be considered as an important contributing factor to Khrushchev's downfall in 1964. But Peking has continued to attack the Brezhnev-Kosygin policies as a type of Khrushchevism without Khrushchev.

This simultaneous struggle against "US imperialism" and "Soviet revisionism" has tended to push Communist China ever closer to a possible confrontation with the world's two super powers. As of this writing, the situation has become more critical, as US bombings of North Vietnam have repeatedly involved targets within ten miles of China's borders, and American planes have been shot down after intruding into Chinese air space. Peking continues to denounce such war "provocation," and to declare that the Chinese people are ready, should they be forced into defensive combat. Meanwhile, its world-wide advocation of people's war against imperialism goes on unabated. At the same time, relations with the Soviet Union have apparently come close to the breaking point on several occasions. Border tensions and incidents involving treatment of citizens of the two countries have been mounting; the Soviets are reportedly preparing a military buildup which includes activities inside Outer Mongolia. The worsening situation with respect to Sino-Soviet relations has also contaminated the atmosphere between Peking and several of the East

European communist countries and Asian Communist Parties. But Mao remains determined to fight against revisionism at home and abroad.

In a similar vein, after years of painstaking cultivation on the declared basis of the Five Principles of Peaceful Coexistence and through considerable economic aid, the once happy relationship which Peking enjoyed with several key "non-aligned" Afro-Asian countries has been destroyed or weakened by circumstances sometimes beyond Peking's control. The disputes over the Dalai Lama and border delineation have estranged relations with India since 1959, and led to the striking armed clash of 1962. Political upheavals, particularly through military coup and take-over in a number of countries in Africa and Asia—notably Algeria, Ghana, Burma (to a degree), and Indonesia—have reversed formerly friendly relations with Peking. Promotion of respect for Mao (e.g., wall posters, Mao's pictures and badges) and the study of Mao's thought (e.g., the little red book of quotations from his works) among Chinese functionaries and residents have inflamed relations with Burma, with the Portuguese over Macau, with the British over Hong Kong, and with several other countries. Nevertheless, established standpoints and traditional patterns remain in force between Peking and some other countries, such as Nepal, Congo (Brazzaville), Guinea, and Tranzania. And Peking continues to stand firm in its pledge to aid the national liberation movement, and in its faith in the anti-imperialist international united front.

Considering its role as a state in the world community of nations, many observers regard Communist China's stand and policies as being peculiar or mysterious. They raise a basic question: How can a country like China, now politically so turbulent, economically so backward, and militarily so unsophisticated or even primitive (a few A-bombs and H-bombs notwithstanding) dare to offer a constant and simultaneous challenge to both the United States and the Soviet Union, and to their friends and allies? Critics question why Peking has failed to play off one power against another in a diplomatic game to assure its own security and derive benefits for its own economic construction. They ask why Peking wastes its limited resources in a hopeless economic competition with the United States and the Soviet Union in Asia and Africa, only to suffer diplomatic debacles there later. A number of these questioners have concluded that Peking's blundering must stem from Mao's sheer madness, probably associated with old age or physical disability.

Mao and his followers, however, view matters quite differently. Regarding themselves as true revolutionaries, they must not fear struggle either at home or abroad. Politically, they are confident that they have constantly streamlined their ideology and strengthened their faith in it. In Mao they find an infallible revolutionary symbol, and they hope to have one Lin Piao after another in the future to assure a correct leadership guided by Mao's thought. Economically, they hope to perform miracles. Taking pride in their advances in the field of synthetic insulin, they intend to conduct similar feats in other areas to overtake and surpass advanced world levels. In all these tasks, they are certain that their fundamental resources are their 700 million hard-working and frugal people. Militarily, they profess that super bombs, like imperialism and reactionaries, are only paper tigers. As revolutionaries, they are certain that victory lies in the strategy of "people's war," which can be conducted successfully and exclusively in one's homeland. Thus, theirs is a confidence born of steadfast adherence to basic ideological principles, and nurtured by past accomplishments.

Yet, there are indeed strong opponents to Mao and his followers in Communist China. Evidently Peking's increasingly difficult international position—in the customary sense of the word—which is described by some observers as isolation, and the economic blunders and failures of the Great Leap period alarmed many within the Chinese Communist leadership corps. Leaders such as P'eng Teh-huai (who were compared by some to such historical figures as Hai Jui or Wei Cheng, who dared to criticize, rebuke, scold, and curse the emperor), began to question Mao's wisdom in foreign as well as domestic policies at least as early as 1958. These critics and dissenters, after years of covert and overt expression, evidently captured not only the ears but also the hearts of many of Mao's associates in the close circles of the leadership. Among the prominent figures who came to doubt or question Mao have been P'eng Chen and Teng Hsiao-p'ing, and even Liu Shao-ch'i, who has been officially called China's Khrushchev, or "the top Party person in authority taking the capitalist road."

It was to cope with this situation of dissension and rebellion within the Party by elements who "raise the red flag to oppose the red flag," that Mao and his close comrade in arms, Lin Piao, launched the far-reaching cultural revolution by which the masses were to cleanse the degenerates within the Party. As a backbone for this work, they reared and nurtured the Red Guards and other revolutionary rebels in schools, offices, factories and communes. These heirs of the revolution have been especially charged with saving its fruits and extending its principles by bringing all Chinese under their scrutiny.

Through daily study of Mao's thought (from his works, and particularly the quotations extracted from them), the 500 million peasants, together with millions of workers, scientific and medical personnel, teachers, and artists, and indeed all persons in China are expected to acquire the communist world outlook. Remolding themselves, they are also to make revolution on others. This work, which essentially constitutes an attempt to transform human nature, is anticipated to be a long and arduous process. The present cultural revolution and similar future endeavors are regarded as necessary stages of a task of unknown duration. As Mao has said, "Without destruction there can be no construction. Destruction means repudiation and revolution. Destruction requires appealing to reason. To appeal to reason means construction. Thus, while destruction heads the start, construction lies in the process."

The formula of the proletarian cultural revolution is to eliminate "private" interest and concepts and to adopt "public" interest and concepts. According to Mao and his followers, only by this fundamental understanding can the revolutionaries rely on and stir up the masses, ceaselessly reform themselves under the supervision of the masses, and persevere in upholding principles and struggling against erroneous thought. Thus, the orientation is to destroy old ideas, culture, customs, and habits of the bourgeoisie, and to establish new ones of the proletariat. The methods, according to Mao, especially in resolving contradictions among the people, scorn curses, fists, and weapons, and embrace discussion, reasoning, criticism and self-criticism. And revolutionaries are taught to use nonviolent means to reveal, repudiate, and defeat their opponents.

Yet, during the "revolutionary seizure of power" "under the proletarian dictatorship," confusion and violence have occurred in numerous organizations, institutions, and local government organs at various levels. The leaders of the cultural revolution have been forced to warn with increasing urgency against the dangers of "anarchism." At present, Peking's future hangs in tenuous balance. In describing Communist China's domestic scene, this volume gives particular attention to the nature of the cultural revolution—in terms of its background, development, and impact on the various aspects of national life, including Party, state, economic, military, social and cultural.

This study was originally undertaken in response to a growing need for a single-volume, systematic presentation of the organizations and operations of the communist system in China. In the present crucial stage of the cultural revolution, more than ever before, events inside mainland China can be considered as a "prairie fire" capable of casting off sparks that can cause conflagration both outside and inside the communist movement. It is, of course, impossible to understand Mao and his followers without a knowledge of their dedication to the internationalist goals of Marxism-Leninism. In this sense, internal events, including the cultural revolution, can be regarded as creating international repercussions both now and in years to come. But to define and correlate both domestic and foreign relations after some eighteen years of communist rule would require a study of epic proportions: to write within smaller dimensions would be to risk minimization or oversimplification. This judgment prompted the authors' decision to confine this volume to domestic affairs, in the hopes that this knowledge will provide some fundamental premises for understanding Communist China, and lead to a later study of Peking's international role.

Any close reading of this text will illustrate that substantial material has been incorporated from the original and revised editions of *Communist China Today: Domestic and Foreign Policies* (1957 and 1961). The warm response accorded that volume and classroom teaching experience of those who adopted it as a text suggest that the sections retained meet the need for a clear, adequately detailed analysis. In every case, despite the rapid shifts associated with the cultural revolution, every effort has been made to document the system and situation as it exists late in 1967.

The chief sources for this study are the variety of publications and official statements of the Chinese Communists themselves. In this country, practically every analyst of the Chinese scene is assisted by the translations of mainland news sources by the American Consulate in Hong Kong. Other information items are based on the authors' translation. This practice of using Chinese Communist sources may be regarded as a "virtue born of necessity." Occasional eyewitness accounts by foreign correspondents or visitors, useful as they may often be, are piecemeal, sometimes biased, and always incapable of substantiation. Moreover, Communist China is a country not only professedly committed to the dictatorship of the proletariat, but, in reality, transformed into a huge ideological school for the entire population. It is a bitter ideological battleground for all concerned for the untiring study and militant implementation of the thought of Mao, which his followers call Marxism-Leninism of the present epoch. Thus traditional ideas, concepts, and value judgments cannot be utilized by outside observers to comprehend the reality of the Chinese scene. Fortunately the Chinese Communists themselves have so far, for reasons of their own, faithfully transmitted or reflected through publications and big character posters their principal ideas, beliefs and activities, whether constructive or destructive. Any objective observer of the Chinese scene can easily be struck by the naked frankness of the Chinese Communists in identifying their objectives and aspirations. Any independent thinker may also be impressed by the remarkable consistency in their line of reasoning and between their words and their deeds.

On the other hand, Peking's economic and statistical information must be scrutinized with the utmost care, and always evaluated with doubt. This is particularly true with respect to statistics, which, as Professor Yuan-li Wu emphasizes, are "at best inadequate, at worst dangerously misleading." Since 1958–59, few statistics have been published. This situation, attributable to the common practice of placing political goals first, also not infrequently reflects the inferior nature of Peking's statistical machinery. The problem for the researcher can be illustrated by one example. A nation's strength is frequently evaluated in terms of its total available manpower. Yet, the population of Communist China can only be estimated roughly. Mao's remark to Edgar Snow (published in the January 9, 1965 *New Republic*) that he didn't really know how many people there were in China is probably as true as it is intended to be disarming.

The authors wish to express their thanks to Most Reverend John J. Dougherty, President of Seton Hall University, and especially to Dr. John B. Tsu, Director of the University's Institute of Far Eastern Studies, and to the staff of the University Press, for their continued interest and assistance. They also want to express their sincere appreciation to Very Reverend Michael P. Walsh, S.J., President of Boston College, Dr. Frederick Meier, President of the State College of Salem, Dr. Edna McGlynn of the latter institution, and Dr. Richard Wraga of the Hoover Institution, for their kind encouragement. It goes without saying that the authors are much indebted to Yvette Forgét, Arline Maloney and Mary C. Tang for their painstaking efforts in preparing the manuscript. The preparation of the index by Barbara Murray and Catherine Newhouse is gratefully acknowledged. Special thanks also go to John T. Ma, Curator-Librarian, East Asian Collection, Hoover Institution, for many photographs used in this book, and to Reverend Brenden C. Connolly, S.J., Director of Libraries at Boston College, and his able assistants, Katherine W. Jaffe and Helen A. Landreth for their generous help.

The gracious and generous assistance received from many sources in no way lessens the authors' responsibility for the presentation of facts, and the analyses, interpretations, and forecasts based thereon. It is axiomatic to add, that given the uncertainty of conditions inside and outside that country, no study of Communist China can be regarded as definitive. The present work represents an attempt, however, to provide the most comprehensive analysis that can be advanced by the authors as of the time of this writing.

PETER S. H. TANG
Professor of Political Science
Boston College

JOAN M. MALONEY
Professor of History
State College at Salem, Mass.

September 10, 1967

Contents

CHARTS, ILLUSTRATIONS, MAP, AND TABLES

COMMON ABBREVIATIONS

ACFDW	The All-China Federation of Democratic Women
ACFTU	The All-China Federation of Trade Unions
ACSF	The All-China Students' Federation
CAS	Chinese Academy of Sciences
CC	Central Committee
CDL	China Democratic League
CPC	Communist Party of China
CPG	Central People's Government
CPGC	Central People's Government Council
CPPCC	Chinese People's Political Consultative Conference
CPR	People's Republic of China
CPSU	Communist Party of the Soviet Union
CPV	Chinese People's Volunteers
CY	League of Communist Youth
CYC	Communist Youth Corps
FFYP	First Five Year Plan
GAC	Government Administration Council
GPD	General Political Department (PLA)
KMT	Kuomintang
NCNA	New China News Agency
NDC	National Defense Council
NDYL	New Democratic Youth League
NMD	National Defense Ministry
NPC	National People's Congress
PA	Peasant Associations
PLA	People's Liberation Army
PRMC	People's Revolutionary Military Council
SC	State Council
SPC	Supreme People's Court
SPP	Supreme People's Procuratorate
YCL	Young Communist League

1. Chairman Mao proclaiming the birth of the People's Republic of China (CPR)

2.   Mao Tse-tung at work

3. Celebration of the 10th state anniversary with guests from over 80 countries

4. Li Chi-shen of the Revolutionary Committee of the Kuomintang speaking at the CPR's 10th anniversary celebration meeting

5. Communist leaders, including Mao, Liu, Chu, and Lin Piao, with representatives of minority nationalities during the celebration

6. Parading masses during the CPR's 10th anniversary celebration

7. Mao reviewing swimmers in the Yangtze near the Wuhan Bridge

8. Mao as the great teacher and supreme commander of the Red Guards

9.   Mao's childhood home: Shaoshan village, Hsiangt'an, Hunan

10.   Mao's former office in the Chingkang Mountains (Chingkangshan)

11.   Mao greeting commune members

12.   Products of the Loyang Tractor Factory

13. Machine turning and drying wheat in the sun at a state farm

14. Minority nationalities using tractors to mow grass in Tsinghai

15. Reform of agricultural tools: sprouts transplanters

16. At a commune mess hall

17. Chemical fertilizers produced by a Lanchow factory

18. One of the short-distance transportation lines in rural districts

19. People's militia

20. A sand fixation belt by the Paotow-Lanchow Railway

21. The second Yangtze bridge at Chungking

22. The Hsinanchiang Hydro-Power Station

23.   A glimpse of the Anshan Iron and Steel Company

24.   A section of the Paotow Iron and Steel Company

25.   The Lanchow Oil Refinery

26.   The new oil field at Yumen

27. Mao, Lin, and other leaders reviewing revolutionary students, teachers, and Red Guards from all over China

28. China's first Marxist-Leninist big-character poster from Peking University praised by Mao

29. A mass meeting for criticism and repudiation

30. Revolutionary workers organizing a command post to "take firm hold of revolution and promote production"

31. Revolutionary students and workers putting up slogans against economism

32. Revolutionary workers of the Shanghai Bus Co. studying Quotations FROM CHAIRMAN MAO TSE-TUNG

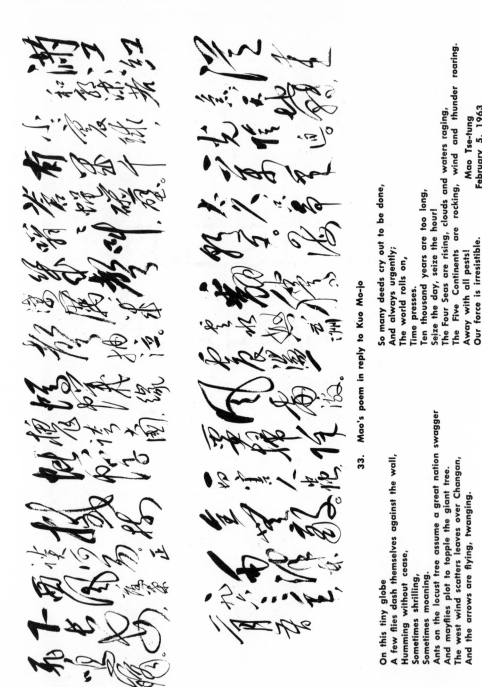

33. Mao's poem in reply to Kuo Mo-jo

On this tiny globe
A few flies dash themselves against the wall,
Humming without cease,
Sometimes shrilling,
Sometimes moaning.
Ants on the locust tree assume a great nation swagger
And mayflies plot to topple the giant tree.
The west wind scatters leaves over Changan,
And the arrows are flying, twanging.

So many deeds cry out to be done,
And always urgently;
The world rolls on,
Time presses.
Ten thousand years are too long,
Seize the day, seize the hour!
The Four Seas are rising, clouds and waters raging,
The Five Continents are rocking, wind and thunder roaring.
Away with all pests!
Our force is irresistible.

Mao Tse-tung
February 5, 1963

Communist Ideology and China: Heritage and Sacred Trust

The ideological impetus for the communist movement in China has come directly from the writings of Marx and Engels, Lenin, and Stalin. In the manner of the orthodox Party faithful in all countries, the Chinese Communist leaders have steadfastly proclaimed their debt and fealty to the so-called Marxist-Leninist body of doctrine.   In observance of the twenty-eighth anniversary of the founding of the Communist Party of China (CPC) on July 1, 1949, Chairman Mao Tse-tung, in his *On People's Democratic Dictatorship*, proclaimed that "the Chinese found the universal truth of Marxism-Leninism, which holds good everywhere, and the face of China was changed."   Two years later, in a widely reproduced article commemorating the same event, Politburo member P'eng Chen declared that the CPC, "since the very day of its birth, has been armed with the theory of Marxism-Leninism."   Hence, "the victory of the Chinese people's revolution is at the same time the victory of Marxism-Leninism in China."

The importance of the communist ideology to the Chinese Communist leaders may be symbolized by the fact that Mao Tse-tung has become the leading theoretician of communism since the death of Stalin, and the first outside the Soviet Union to reach that pinnacle.   The body of his theoretical writing, beginning with his 1926 treatise on *An Analysis of the*

1

Classes in Chinese Society, provides in itself an illustration of the universality claimed for Marxism-Leninism. He has touched upon many aspects of philosophy—logic, epistemology, ontology, and ethics, for example—as well as the laws of social development and the principles of politics and economics. His work thus constitutes a major restatement adapted to the Chinese tradition and Chinese society of the received theory of communism. Whether he has added anything original to the theory itself is open to question. The Chinese Communists themselves initially claimed only to have "discovered" and "applied" Marxism-Leninism to the "people's" revolutionary movement in China. What Mao Tse-tung has done, Ch'en Po-ta has explained in his 1951 essay *On the Thought of Mao Tse-tung*, is to produce a "living synthesis of the universal truth of Marxism-Leninism with the actual practice of the Chinese revolution."

The whole body of communist theory has, of course, many components. Communist theoreticians have retained the general theoretical framework from the work of Marx and Engels, purporting to offer an all-embracing view of the processes and the goal of social evolution. But Lenin particularly, followed by Stalin and Mao, added many specific revisions and even tacit repudiations of Marx. In part these offer an analysis of conditions in the pre-revolutionary societies of Russia and China in terms different from, and in some instances directly opposed to, those Marx had used. But they also constitute a program of revolutionary strategy for the seizure and maintenance of power within such societies, and this program—as will be seen in subsequent chapters—is predominant in the implementation of the theory.

MARX AND THE CLASS STRUGGLE

The universal character claimed for communist theory stems mainly from the Marxian rather than the Leninist component, and in particular from the effort of Marx and Engels, following in the footsteps of the great German philosopher Hegel, to reduce the sweep of history to the operation of certain basic principles of development. Hegel had conceived of a universal principle of development—the dialectic—in the continuous and upward movement or evolution from lower to higher stages; the constant flux of this dialectic stemmed from inherent contradiction or inner conflict. The continuously unfolding inner contradictions—whether in the process of individual human thought (the formation of concepts) or in the evolution of the universe as a whole—were, he held, constantly being overcome or resolved, but only to generate new and more advanced conflicts. Thus every being or concept (thesis) had by its very nature and essence to give rise to its opposite (antithesis); but the contradictions between these two were inevitably overcome in a newly emergent synthesis in which some elements of the original contradiction were conserved, others annulled, and the entire process elevated to a new, higher level. The synthesis in turn immediately became a new thesis giving rise, in a new triadic relationship, to a new antithesis and thence to the "negation of the negation" in another synthesis.

An illustration of the way Mao has assimilated the basic Marxian concepts may be seen from a passage in his treatise of August, 1937, *On Contradiction*, in which he restates the meaning of the dialectic. The "Law of contradiction," as he calls it, ". . . is the basic law of nature and society and therefore also the basic law of thought. . . . According to the viewpoint of dialectical materialism, contradiction exists in all processes of objective things and subjective thought and runs through all processes from beginning to end. This is the universality and absoluteness of contradiction."

Behind this dialectical process, for Hegel, was the motive force of "Reason" or "Spirit," animating the march of history. While appropriating the concept of the dialectic for his own purposes, Marx rejected the Hegelian "idealism." In the oft-quoted words of his preface to *Das Kapital*, he referred to the Hegelian dialectic as "standing on its head" and needing to be "turned right side up again." As he then explained:

> My dialectic method is fundamentally not only different from the Hegelian, but is its direct opposite. To Hegel, the process of thinking, which under the name of "the ideal," he even transforms into an independent subject, is the creator of the real world, and the real world is only the external, phenomenal form of "the ideal." With me, on the contrary, the ideal is nothing else than the material world reflected by the human mind, and translated into forms of thought.

The materialistic form of the dialectic thus became the foundation of the Marxian philosophic system, and as such has been retained by Lenin and his successors. That Mao and the Chinese Communists have fully assimilated the "dialectical world outlook" is shown in Mao's major theoretical study, *On Practice*, dated July, 1937:

> It was not until Marx and Engels, the great men of action of the proletarian movement, made a synthesis of the positive achievements in the history of human knowledge and, in particular, critically absorbed the rational elements of Hegelian dialectics and created the great theory of dialectical materialism and historical materialism, that a great, unprecedented revolution took place in the history of human knowledge. Later Lenin and Stalin have further developed this great theory. Introduced into China, this theory immediately brought about tremendous changes in the world of Chinese thought.

Behind the constant flux, the unceasing becoming and passing away in man's thinking and his social relations, according to Marx, lay the impelling force of changes in the material order.   In particular, the "forces of production," as he called them, provided the ultimate basis for every social order and for every ideological system as well.   In this way the tools, resources, and techniques that men made and used in their work became in turn the instruments shaping their lives.   As Marx explained in the *Poverty of Philosophy*:

> Social relations are closely bound up with productive forces.   In acquiring new productive forces men change their mode of production; and in changing their mode of production, in changing the way of earning their living, they change all their social relations.   The hand-mill gives you society with the feudal lord; the steam-mill, society with the industrial capitalist.

In short, changes in the productive forces of a society give rise to changes in the "relations of production," which in turn become the well-springs of all historical development.   Thus history itself becomes the product of materialistic forces.

More important, however, is the fact that changes in the relations of production and in other social relations also follow the dialectical process of conflict and resolution and renewed conflict.   Thus the underlying and most fundamental social manifestation of Marx's dialectical materialism is the class struggle.   Within any society the inherent contradictions of the dialectic are class contradictions.   Marx thus placed the Hegelian notion of the "negation of the negation"—the continuous process of overcoming these inner contradictions—in the context of his own form of social theory.   The human spirit, the driving force of social history for Hegel, is replaced for Marx by social classes.   In the stark words of the *Communist Manifesto*, "The history of all hitherto existing society is the history of class struggles."

Stemming from Marx's materialism was his view that every political and legal system is merely an outgrowth of the underlying relations of production.   And every form of social consciousness, every ideological system, is determined by these productive relations.   In the preface to his *Critique of Political Economy*, written in 1859, Marx stated the essence of his historical materialism as follows (italics added):

> In the social production of their life, men enter into definite relations that are indispensable and independent of their will, relations of production which correspond to a definite stage of development of their material productive forces.   The sum total of these relations of production constitutes the economic *structure* of society, the real foundation, on which rises a legal and political *superstructure* and to which correspond definite forms of social consciousness.   The mode of produc-

tion of material life conditions the social, political, and intellectual life process in general. It is not the consciousness of men that determines their being, but, on the contrary, their social being that determines their consciousness.

From this distinction between the "structure" and the "superstructure" of society, then, Marx drew his doctrine of revolution as an instrument of social change. Major changes in the means of existence and the relations of production were not automatically and smoothly followed by corresponding changes in the political and legal superstructure. Rather, the privileged classes of one era would attempt to hold on to what had been theirs, while the rising classes of the new era would demand a greater share for themselves, and violence would ensue. In Marx's language:

At a certain stage of their development the material productive forces of society come into contradiction with the existing productive relationships, or, what is but a legal expression for these, with the property relationships within which they had moved before. From forms of development . . . these relationships are transformed into their fetters. Then an epoch of social revolution opens. With the change in the economic foundation the whole vast superstructure is more or less rapidly transformed.

Eventually, in the Marxian view, however, there was to be an end to the dialectical process whereby growing disharmony between economic "structure" and political and legal "superstructure" led to a revolutionary upheaval, followed by a readjustment of the relations among social classes and a renewal of the cycle. Mankind would one day develop the forces of production, through industrialization, to the point where it would be possible to produce enough material things to satisfy the needs of everybody. And in due time, after a final revolutionary upheaval, the masses of the people (who by this time would be for the most part industrial workers and thus members of the proletariat) would gain control of the means of production: the relations of production would then be at last in their favor. Mankind would then be really free, and the long period of struggle which had gone before would be relegated to a "prehistoric" period. The coercive machinery of the state—which had been used to maintain the privileged class in power even after the material basis for their privilege had ceased to exist—would no longer be needed. In a famous passage in his *Anti-Dühring*, Engels wrote of this ultimate stage: "The interference of the State power in social relations becomes superfluous in one sphere after another, and then ceases of itself. The government of persons is replaced by the administration of things and the direction of the process of production. The State is not 'abolished,' *it withers away*."

On the general principles of the economic interpretation of history, Lenin and his successors have followed Marx closely enough, for these principles are alleged to have a universal application throughout history, at least down to the attainment of the ultimate classless society. And the communist theoreticians, whether or not they sincerely believe in all the "universal truths" of Marxism-Leninism, have shown that they recognize the need to be able to encompass all events and developments within a single theoretical framework capable of yielding an interpretation favorable to their cause. They can thus use the Marxian view of history as an ideological weapon, to instill a sense of invincibility in their followers, and to win over the uncommitted and confound the opposition through presuming to represent an inescapable "wave of the future."

In their view of the ultimate goal of the movement, too, the followers of Lenin have retained the Marxian apocalyptic vision of a new world order. It has likewise been very useful to them in rationalizing their own seizure and maintenance of power. They have thus made of Marxism a symbol of a world-wide revolutionary struggle to "emancipate" the downtrodden masses and to achieve a promised utopia. Mao Tse-tung has often invoked this symbol to show that the Chinese Communists have a bolder and more radical program than had any other movement. In his 1945 report *On Coalition Government*, for example, he proudly stated:

> We communists never conceal our political stand. It is definite and beyond any doubt that our future or maximum program is to make China advance into the realm of Socialism and Communism. Both the name of our Party and our Marxist world outlook unequivocally point to this highest ideal of the future, a future of dazzling brightness and unsurpassable beauty.

Notwithstanding the fact that the Chinese Communist leaders have sought to reconcile their every act with orthodox Marxist doctrines, they have deliberately departed from the original meaning of those doctrines in a number of crucial respects. For the inescapable fact is that Marx's "scientific" and historical theories, and particularly his analysis of the stages in the class struggle, are in their original form inapplicable to the Chinese society of the third quarter, just as they were to the Russian society of the first quarter, of the twentieth century. This was indicated by Marx himself in a passage in the *Critique of Political Economy*, in which he revealed what a gap there was, to his own view, between the backward economies of Asiatic countries, such as China, and the advanced industrial countries of his day, such as Germany and Great Britain. He also indicated that such backward countries were far from ready for a revolution of the communist type, but would have to go through a great deal of development first:

> A social system never perishes before all the productive forces have developed for which it is wide enough; and new, higher productive relationships never come

into being before the material conditions for their existence have been brought to maturity within the womb of the old society itself. . . . In broad outline, the Asiatic, the ancient, the feudal, and the modern bourgeois modes of production can be indicated as progressive epochs in the economic system of society.   Bourgeois productive relationships are the last antagonistic form of the social process of production. . . . With this [bourgeois capitalist] social system, therefore, the pre-history of human society comes to a close.

It remained for Lenin and Stalin in Russia and Mao in China to break away from this "scientific" analysis of the progression of social systems, and to revise Marxian thought to apply directly to their less advanced countries.   It was particularly Lenin's contribution to see that a highly disciplined conspiratorial Party, appealing to the Marxian revolutionary ideals of communism, could take advantage of any revolutionary situation (and could even help create such a situation), whether in a "bourgeois" society or not, to seize control of the state machine, with the ostensible purpose of transforming that society into an advanced industrial nation organized along communist lines.   Thus it is not surprising that Mao, himself part of the highly disciplined movement created by Lenin, should pattern his thinking much more upon the Leninist version of Marxism than upon Marx himself.   This fact is tacitly admitted by Ch'en Po-ta, when he remarks: "The spirit in which comrade Mao Tse-tung applies Marxism is precisely [the] spirit of Lenin and Stalin."

THE LENINISTS AND THE WORLD REVOLUTION

It may be noted that where Lenin and his successors have modified or abandoned Marx's formulations, they have done so for very practical considerations growing out of their determination to engineer a successful seizure and development of power, exploiting in the process whatever forces of discontent and upheaval were present or could be activated in any given situation.   While never giving up their reliance upon an all-encompassing theory as a guide to (or a rationalization for) their revolutionary practice, they have stressed the necessity of not letting theory become divorced from practice.   In this way they have achieved a basis for modifying the received theory to fit their practice—that is, to suit the broad requirement of strategy, if not the day-to-day requirements of current operations.

In this vein, Lenin wrote as early as 1901, "Without a revolutionary theory, there cannot be a revolutionary movement."   But, in one of the essays later collected in his *Philosophical Notebook*, he said of theoretical knowledge in general: "Practice should be the first and fundamental view-point of the theory of knowledge," since "practice is higher than knowledge" and "has not only the quality of universality but also that of immediate reality." Stalin's well-known formulation in his lectures on the "Foundations of Leninism" follows this lead: ". . . Theory becomes aimless if it is not connected with revolutionary practice, just as practice gropes in the dark if its path is not illumined by revolutionary theory."

Mao has followed these two theoreticians closely on this point, as the extensive citations in his 1937 work *On Practice* show. In it he attacks the "doctrinaires" in the CPC who deny the fundamental truth that "Marxism is not a dogma but a guide to action." But he had been particularly explicit in demanding that the Chinese Communists take into account, in their study of the orthodox theory, the practical requirements of conditions in China. He sounded this note, for example, in a lecture on "Reform in Learning, the Party, and Literature," delivered at the opening of the Chinese Communist Party School on February 1, 1942: "Theory and practice can be combined only if men of the CPC take the stand-points, concepts, and methods of Marxism-Leninism, apply them to China, and create a theory from conscientious research on the realities of the Chinese revolution and Chinese history."

Applying communist theory to China, Mao suggested in his 1940 work *On the New Democracy* that the feudal system in China began in the Chou and Ch'in dynasties and lasted about 3,000 years. With the opening up of China following the Opium War in 1840, this system began to break down. Thereafter, "Chinese society started to change from a feudal into a semi-colonial and semi-feudal society" in the ensuing century, so that its character had become "colonial, semi-colonial and semi-feudal." [1]

By placing China in this category of feudal societies, the Leninists gained a number of specific advantages for their theory. They could logically claim an interest in the overthrow of feudal society wherever it might be found, as coming one step nearer to the final proletarian revolution of Marxian theory. In plainer terms, this meant there was no longer any theoretical bar to imposing communism in China under the aegis of a Moscow-rooted doctrine. With the establishment of the Soviet Union, moreover, China could then draw upon the aid of this self-styled "advanced socialist state" in carrying out the necessary economic and social transformation to allow it to jump to the stage of socialism. Further, the modified theory provided a useful explanation for the internal forces con-

---

[1] Lenin himself had suggested this position, pointing out that China was in part a "semi-colony," dominated and exploited by foreign powers, while in some places it was a full "colony," formally occupied by these powers.

ducive to a revolution in China—one which was logically compatible with Lenin's theory of "imperialism," the explanation for the external forces. But most important of all, the Leninist interpretation made it possible to assign the Chinese peasant masses, like the Russian peasants before them, a specific role in the world revolutionary movement—a role which previously had been reserved exclusively for the industrial proletariat.

The failure of the Russian Revolution of 1905, more than any other single event, had convinced Lenin that the peasants must be mobilized and drawn into the struggle if the revolution were to succeed. He had first formulated this postulate in his 1905 work on *The Two Tactics of Social Democracy in the Democratic Revolution:* "We [Marxists] must not forget that there is not, nor can there be at the present time, any other means of bringing socialism nearer than by . . . a revolutionary-democratic dictatorship of the proletariat and the peasantry."

Following the successful October Revolution of 1917, in which peasant discontent had been an important factor, Lenin extended his counsel to the communists of other agrarian countries. In his report to the Second All-Russian Congress of Communist Organizations of the Eastern Peoples on November 22, 1919, he explained:

> You are facing a task which has never before been faced by the communists of the whole world: basing yourselves on the general communist theory and practice and adapting yourselves to the peculiar conditions which do not exist in European countries, you must be able to apply this theory and practice to conditions in which the main mass will consist of the peasantry, in which you must solve the task of the struggle not against capital, but against vestiges of the Middle Ages.

Lenin's advice to the communist organizations and Party members of Asia, in the face of these new conditions, was to find the "peculiar forms" of an "alliance of the advanced proletariat of the whole world with the workers and the exploited masses of the East, who often live in conditions which prevailed during the Middle Ages."

Lenin's theory of an alliance between workers and peasants profoundly affected the development of the communist movement in Russia and Eastern Europe as well as in China. Stalin, following Lenin's cue, found in events in China a specific confirmation for the precept. In an article in the June 30, 1925, issue of *Bolshevik*, Stalin had emphasized that the peasant masses of the colonial areas, once drawn into the anti-imperialist struggle, would become a powerful and indispensable ally of the proletariat.[2]

[2] Later, in the summer of 1927, it was evident that Stalin was greatly impressed by the large-scale agrarian uprisings in Hunan, Hupeh, Honan, and other provinces in the early phase of the Chinese agrarian revolution. "The victory of the agrarian revolu-

Mao in turn has had little reason to question the revolutionary role assigned to the peasantry by Lenin and Stalin. His classic *Report on an Investigation into the Peasant Movement in Hunan*, written in 1927, reinforced the Leninist-Stalinist view. Throughout his career—and it has surely been one of the reasons for his dominance in the CPC—he has shown that he regards the peasants as the most reliable ally of the Chinese proletariat and the real core of the revolutionary forces in China. In his 1949 work *On People's Democratic Dictatorship*, for example, he declared: "The transition from New Democracy to Socialism depends primarily upon the alliance of these two classes." [3]

To admit the peasants to an alliance with the industrial workers without proper safeguards, however, would mean that the latter would be completely overwhelmed by the sheer bulk of the peasant population. Thus the high aims of the communist movement would be thwarted by the essentially conservative nature of the peasantry. The Leninists, therefore, were careful to make sure that their worker-peasant formula would in no way admit the rural masses to a dominant or even an equal position in either the Party or the revolutionary movement. Instead they insisted that, at all times and under all circumstances, the proletarian character

---

tion," he declared at the time, "is the victory of the bourgeois-democratic revolution" and "the victory of the revolutionary dictatorship of the proletariat and the peasantry" as well.

[3] A striking example of the importance Mao has assigned to the peasantry as the main force in the Chinese revolutionary movement is found in his 1945 work *On Coalition Government*:

The peasantry are predecessors of the Chinese worker, and in the future millions of peasants will come to the cities and enter the factories. If China needs to build a great national industry and build many modern cities, then she needs a long process of transforming the rural population into an urban population.

The peasantry are a market for Chinese industry. Only they can supply the richest foodstuffs and raw materials and absorb the greatest number of industrial products.

The peasantry are the source of troops. Soldiers are peasants in uniforms. They are implacable foes of the Japanese invaders.

The peasants are the main foundation of democracy in China at the present stage. . . .

The peasantry are the main foundation of the cultural movement in China at the present stage. The so-called liquidation of illiteracy, the so-called universal education, the so-called literature and art for the masses, the so-called popular hygiene would mostly turn into empty talk if they were separated from the 360,000,000 peasants.

When I say that they [the peasantry] are the main foundation, I do not overlook of course the importance of the other 90,000,000 people in politics, economics, and culture. Especially I do not overlook the importance of the working class who are politically most conscious and able to lead all democratic movements.

and leadership of the revolution was to be preserved. Since the Communist Party (as will be seen later) professed to speak for the proletariat, even when the latter were not predominantly communist in belief or sympathy, or were not even politically active for the most part, proletarian leadership of the worker-peasant alliance meant in effect Communist Party control of the whole movement.

The importance of this proletarian leadership was stressed by Stalin in various comments on conditions in China in 1927. In contrast with other Eastern revolutionary movements—in Turkey, Iran, and Afghanistan, for example—Stalin found that "in China there is a well-known basic number of the fighting and active industrial proletariat enjoying enormous prestige among the peasants." He was convinced that without the leadership of the proletariat (that is, without that of the Communist Party) the communist revolution in China was doomed to failure.

Mao, like Stalin, has followed this line consistently. Although he had referred to the peasantry as the main force of the revolution in China, there could be no doubt that, in the words of Ch'en Po-ta, summarizing Mao's views, "the proletariat is the leading force." In 1939, Mao himself had declared, in *The Chinese Revolution and the Chinese Communist Party:*

> In spite of certain unavoidable weaknesses—for example, its small size (as compared with the peasantry), its young age (as compared with the proletariat in capitalist countries) and its low cultural level (as compared with the bourgeoisie)— the Chinese proletariat has nonetheless become the basic motive force of the Chinese revolution.

The effect of Lenin's doctrine of an alliance of the workers with the peasants in so-called feudal agrarian societies was indeed far-reaching. It meant that the center of interest for the revolutionary movement was in practice shifted from the advanced industrial countries, where Marx had looked for proletarian uprisings, to the "backward" and colonial areas of the world. And it meant that one of the mainsprings of the revolutionary upheaval would be the peasants' discontent with long-standing evils in forms of inequitable land tenure and agricultural credit. [4]

But peasant discontent was not the only potential source of revolutionary fervor to be exploited in the non-industrialized areas. Throughout the colonial and semi-colonial territories, feelings were rising against the "im-

---

[4] As David Mitrany has pointed out in his *Marx against the Peasant: a Study in Social Dogmatism* (Chapel Hill, University of North Carolina Press, 1951), "The startling fact is that communism has only come to power where by all Marxist tenets it might have been least expected that it could. In every instance, from 1917 in Russia to 1949 in China, communism has ridden to victory on the back of disaffected peasantries; in no instance has it come near to victory in industrialized 'proletarian' countries."

perialism" of the Western industrial nations, often accompanied by a rising sense of identity and nationalism among the members of a particular ethnic or cultural group. As a master tactician, more than an abstract theoretician, with primary concern for the proletarian world revolution, Lenin saw the opportunities created by this historical development and did not hesitate to alter Marxian theory to take advantage of it. The result of his alteration may be characterized by the new concepts it introduced into the body of Marxian theory. Just as the communists sometimes apply the loose terms "rural proletarians," or "semi-proletarians," to the peasantry, thus keeping up the appearance of adhering to Marx's idea of a class struggle between proletariat and bourgeoisie, so they have also developed the concept of whole "proletarian nations" waging the international class struggle against "capitalist-imperialist" nations. Through his theory of imperialism—his most important ideological contribution—Lenin was thus able to make Marxism-Leninism directly applicable to the Chinese situation in yet another way.

Lenin set forth the main lines of this portion of his theory in 1916. Emphasizing that imperialism was to be regarded as a "development and direct continuation of the fundamental attributes of capitalism in general," he nevertheless regarded it as a distinct stage of capitalism—the highest and last stage before its overthrow and the establishment of a "transition . . . to a higher social and economic system." In economic terms, Lenin defined imperialism as

. . . capitalism in that stage of development in which the domination of monopolies and finance capital has taken shape; in which the export of capital has acquired pronounced importance, in which the division of the world by the international trusts has begun, and in which the partition of all the territory of the earth by the greatest capitalist countries has been completed.

Behind this matter-of-fact definition, however, lay a keen realization of the revolutionary possibilities in the political tensions arising from imperialism. "It is not only in the newly opened-up countries," wrote Lenin, "but also in the old ones, that imperialism is leading to annexation, to increased national oppression, and, consequently, also to more stubborn resistance." To take advantage of this "resistance," Lenin and Stalin developed a new theory of revolution to apply to the colonial and economically backward areas. In place of the mass proletarian movement which was to overthrow the bourgeoisie and establish a socialist state in the imperialist-capitalist nations, they anticipated in the colonial and semi-colonial areas a "bourgeois-national" movement, fostered by the intelligentsia, to drive out the foreign imperialists. Thus Stalin, in a speech on August 1, 1927, on the situation in China as it affected the "International Situation and the Defense of the USSR," clearly distinguished between "the revolution in the imperialist countries oppressing other peoples," such as Russia, and "the revolutions in the colonial and dependent countries suffering imperialist oppression," such as China.

As with the Leninist revisions on the role of the peasant, this addition to the theory again reflected a shift in the center of interest of the communist movement away from the advanced industrial countries where the hope of mass proletarian uprisings was glimmering, to the colonial and economically backward, but politically awakening, areas of the world. To justify this shift, both Stalin and Mao, for one thing, stressed the fact that revolutionary theory must keep abreast of revolutionary "practice." Mao, for example, wrote in his 1937 study *On Practice:*

> In the age of free, competitive capitalism, Marx could not have known specifically beforehand some of the special laws pertaining to the era of imperialism, because imperialism—the last stage of capitalism—had not yet emerged and the corresponding practice did not exist; only Lenin and Stalin could take up this task.

The Leninist innovation was harmonized with the traditional doctrine through extending the concept of the proletariat as a social class to refer to a proletarian camp of nations—even though within many of these nations the actual proletarian class might be only a tiny minority of the total population. In Mao's early work of March, 1926, on *An Analysis of the Classes in Chinese Society*, he followed Lenin and Stalin in developing this concept. The class struggle had now become, he pointed out, a world-wide struggle between the "oppressed classes of the world" on the one hand and the "counterrevolutionary elements of the world" on the other. In this bitter final struggle all classes would have to take sides, for "there is no room for them to remain 'independent.'" Mao's views were thus summarized by Ch'en Po-ta: "Since the October Socialist Revolution, the world has been divided into an anti-imperialist camp led by the general world proletarian-Socialist-revolutionary movement, and an imperialist camp which embraces all counterrevolutionary forces."

Thus the Leninist theory of imperialism carried two major implications for the Chinese Communists. For one thing it allowed them to view their own movement, not as an isolated effort or as an aberration in the worldwide "historical" evolution toward communism, but as part of the "world proletarian revolution as a whole and of the struggle against imperialism as a whole," as Ch'en Po-ta expressed it. More important, however, it gave their own efforts a very special place in this world movement. Following the communist victory in mainland China, Lu Ting-yi, of the CPC Central Committee, described this position in an article on "The World Significance of the Chinese Revolution": "The prototype of the revolu-

tions in imperialist countries is the October Revolution. The prototype
of the revolutions in colonial and semi-colonial countries is the Chinese
revolution."

Like the peasant rebelliousness against the landlords and money lenders
or the state itself, however, the popular resentment against foreign imperialists can not, in the communist view, be allowed to work itself out
spontaneously. The communists must control and lead this reaction, if
their revolution is to succeed. Hence, they must seek allies not only
among the peasantry and the city poor, but among those elements they
believe to be most susceptible to an anti-imperialist and nationalist appeal,
such as the so-called petty-bourgeois intelligentsia and the "national
bourgeoisie" (the latter including the smaller business men, industrialists
not under foreign control, and other employers considered useful to the
communists for the time being). "The problem of allies," Stalin declared
in a speech published in *Pravda* on July 28, 1927, "is one of the principal
questions of the Chinese revolution."

To meet this problem of allies on a broad scale, the communists, under
the original inspiration of Lenin, [5] resorted to the "united-front" device.
Needless to say, the alliances sought under the united-front policy were
to be as far as possible of a one-sided character, in respect to policy determination and joint action. In China, Mao Tse-tung, following the lead of
Lenin and Stalin, advised the Chinese proletariat that they could not
achieve the victory of revolution singlehandedly. Their only hope lay in
"the formation of a revolutionary united-front with all possible revolutionary classes and strata under the given circumstances." The requirement of united-front tactics he called "one of the principal laws verified
by the history of the Chinese revolution."

A single statement of Mao's well illustrates the major adaptations
through which Marxism-Leninism was made applicable to the Chinese
situation. The "bourgeois-democratic revolution" in China (the seizure
of political power prior to the planned transformation of the economic and
social orders and the transition to a socialist society), Mao declared, should
be the work of an anti-imperialist and anti-feudal united-front, and the
subsequent regime should be a "dictatorship of the united-front," in both
cases under the "leadership of the proletariat."

[5] Lenin had initially advocated the use of this device for defeating more powerful
enemies, when in his *Left Wing Communism, an Infantile Disorder*, he had urged the
communists in various "bourgeois" countries to seize all possible opportunities to win
allies of a mass character, no matter how temporary, unstable, unreliable, or conditional.
As early as March, 1927, according to Stalin, the Comintern had instructed the Communist Party of China in the need for conducting a determined united-front policy
through the development of communist-controlled mass movements.

To insist, however, upon winning over as allies under the leadership of the proletariat the bulk of the non-proletarian population in the semi-feudal, semi-colonial areas, would have been relatively futile, unless the proletariat in turn were led by a small core of disciplined and trained revolutionaries. Hence, another of Lenin's major contributions to communist theory is to be found in his concept of the Party itself. Lenin regarded the proletariat, acting on its own, as incapable of effective revolutionary action. As early as 1902, in *What Is to Be Done*, Lenin had stated that the workers themselves through the trade union movement could not spontaneously develop the necessary revolutionary consciousness. Rather, they could only develop what he called "trade union consciousness"—i.e., an awareness of the need to press for better terms from employers and for favorable legislative and other action by the government through trade union action. Revolutionary consciousness, however, "could only be brought to [the workers] from without."

Lenin saw that the main impetus for the revolution would have to come from a small, tightly organized and disciplined *avant garde* of professional revolutionaries (mainly middle-class intellectuals) who possessed a high degree of revolutionary consciousness and could undertake to lead the masses of workers. In effect, then, Lenin completely abandoned the famous Marxian dictum that "the emancipation of the working class is the work of the working class itself." Even more, he took the view that parties, not classes as such, hold the really decisive power in society—thus doing violence not only to Marx's conception of classes as the main levers of historical development but even to his underlying materialist interpretation of social relationships.

To avoid an open repudiation of Marx on this point, however, Lenin adopted the rationalization of viewing the elite corps of professional revolutionaries, who were to constitute the Communist Party, as a "vanguard and organized detachment of the working class." Perhaps the clearest official statement of this doctrine, which has since become a standard text for communist constitutional documents and programs everywhere, is to be found in a resolution adopted by the Congress of the Communist International in 1920:

> The Communist Party is part of the working class, namely, its most advanced, class-conscious, and therefore most revolutionary part. The CP is formed of the best, most intelligent, self-sacrificing and far-seeing workers. . . . The CP is the organized political lever by means of which the more advanced part of the working class leads all the proletarian and semi-proletarian mass in the right direction.

In his lectures at Sverdlov University in April, 1924, Stalin elaborated upon Lenin's vanguard theory of the Party:

The Party must be, first of all, the *vanguard* of the working class. . . . The Party cannot be a real party if it limits itself to registering what the masses of the working class feel and think, if it drags at the tail of the spontaneous movement, if it is unable to overcome the inertness and the political indifference of the spontaneous movement, if it is unable to rise above the momentary interests of the proletariat, if it is unable to elevate the masses to the level of the class interests of the proletariat.

This Leninist-Stalinist concept of the vanguard Party has always been echoed in the official directives and programs of the Chinese Communist movement, as well as in its other propaganda. The 1945 Constitution of the CPC, for example, states that the Party "is the organized vanguard of the Chinese working class and the highest form of its class organization." And the 1954 Constitution of the Chinese People's Republic (CPR) reaffirms this position. While Article I speaks of the CPR as "led by the working class," the preamble is more explicit. It notes that in 1949, "the Chinese People, led by the Communist Party of China, finally achieved their great victory in the people's revolution against imperialism, feudalism, and bureaucrat-capitalism." And P'eng Chen, writing in 1951 on "The Victory of Marxism-Leninism in China," adopts the standard phraseology. The CPC, he states, "has been the vanguard and organized detachment of the Chinese working class, armed with the theory of Marxism-Leninism, organized in accordance with the principles of party construction of Lenin and Stalin."

P'eng's mention of the principles of Party construction introduces the final element in Lenin's tactical revision of Marxian doctrine to make it the instrument of revolution anywhere. Leadership by the Party was not enough, Lenin realized; the Party itself must be highly centralized and hierarchical in structure, so that the effective leadership is in the hands of the few key people at the top of the hierarchy. Under such a principle, there can be no real freedom of thought or criticism within the Party's ranks. Lenin himself set the pattern in vigorously upholding the universal validity of the Marxian philosophy and denouncing all alleged "revisionists," "deviationists," "eclecticists," and "opportunists" who in any way questioned its sacred authority (as interpreted by himself and his own followers). Such elements were to be purged from the Party, which must at all times preserve its purity and solidarity.

For this rigid principle of "monolithic" centralization and discipline, Lenin invented the "dialectical," if contradictory, designation of "democratic centralism." [6] During the dispute with the Mensheviks in 1904, his

[6] More will be said in later chapters about the pervasive way the principle of democratic centralism has been applied in Communist China, not only in the realm of Party

One Step Forward, Two Steps Back presented a clear and dramatic statement of this organizational principle which has since played so important a role in the Communist Parties throughout the world:

. . . It is the organizational principle of revolutionary political democracy as opposed to the organizational principle of the [Menshevik] opportunists of Social-Democracy. The latter want to proceed from the bottom upward and, consequently, whenever possible and to the extent that it is possible, they support automatism [the autonomy of the lesser parts] and "democracy." The former proceed from the top, and advocate the extension of the rights and powers of the center in respect of the parts.

Needless to say, the actual effect of the CPC's faithful adherence to the Leninist-Stalinist principles of Party organization and mission has been far different in practice from the leadership of the proletariat which Lenin was supposedly advocating. In China the proletariat formed a numerically small and politically insignificant element to begin with, while the Party, moreover, maintained its centers of strength for a long period in the countryside, in the form of rural soviets. There was thus no substantial link between the proletariat and the CPC, despite the continuing efforts of the Party theoreticians to insist upon such a link. Their insistence, as a result, served chiefly, at the theoretical level, to reconcile Lenin's revolutionary tactics with the traditional Marxian class analysis. At the practical level, however, it meant placing the cause of the revolution in the hands of a tiny group of professional agitators, organizers, and revolutionaries, rather than in the hands of the proletariat as a class. And under the Leninist principles of Party construction, this tiny group, armed with ultimate control in the top organs of the Party, could lead the Party and non-Party masses in a "two-stage" ("bourgeois-democratic" and "socialist") revolutionary struggle and make the Chinese revolution a part of the communist world revolution.

CHINA: THE SEIZURE OF POWER

The body of basic theory drawn from Marx and modified (or "developed") by Lenin has proved extraordinarily useful to the Chinese Communists. It has provided them with: (1) a rationale or goal for their action—the attainment of a classless society and an economy of abundance; (2) a broad strategy for accomplishing this goal—the mobilization of mass

---

construction, but in the government and the mass organizations, and wherever Party control of an organization is desired.

discontent for the seizure of power, followed by the transformation of the material forces and the relations of production; and (3) an organizational weapon—the centralized and tightly disciplined Communist Party, spearheading a united front of other parties and organizations. But the Chinese Communists looked to Lenin and Stalin for specific guidance on the detailed approaches and techniques for seizing and exercising power. [7]

From the outset, the appeal of the theories of Lenin and Stalin in China was not due simply to the skill and persuasiveness of these leaders as theoreticians. The conditions of political instability and extraordinary intellectual ferment in China itself, as will be seen in the next chapter, made the Chinese intelligentsia receptive to new ideas from many quarters—and the teachings of Marx and Engels were still "new" in China for all practical purposes prior to 1917. But perhaps the decisive factor was the success of the Communist Revolution in Russia, enabling the Communist Party of the Soviet Union (CPSU) to give concrete aid and supervision to a similar movement in China. The great importance of the Russian Revolution as a precipitating factor in China was attested to by Mao Tse-tung in his 1949 work *On People's Democratic Dictatorship:*

> Before the October Revolution, the Chinese were not only unaware of Lenin and Stalin but did not even know of Marx and Engels. The salvos of the October Revolution awoke us to Marxism-Leninism. The October Revolution helped the progressives of China and of the whole world to adopt the world outlook of the proletariat as the instrument for perceiving the destiny of the country, and for considering anew their own problems.

During the first years of the CPC, as will be seen in the next chapter, the Russians took an especially active part in directing its policies and actions. In his *Pravda* article of April 21, 1927, on "The Problems of the Chinese Revolution," Stalin called attention to the importance of the continuing role of the Soviet Union:

> There is a . . . characteristic of the Chinese revolution that should not be overlooked: By China's side stands the Soviet Union, which by virtue of its revolutionary experience and its assistance, cannot but facilitate the struggle of the Chinese proletariat against the imperialism and the survivals of the medieval feudalism in China.

In these early years, Stalin himself took a particular interest in the situation in China. In the article just cited, he extended Lenin's theses

---

[7] For a more detailed treatment of Stalin's influence on the strategy and tactics of the Chinese Communist revolution, see Peter S. H. Tang, "Stalin's Role in the Communist Victory in China," *The American Slavic and East European Review,* vol. **XIII,** no. 3 (October, 1954), pp. 375–88.

to China in an analysis of the factors which would determine the character of the Chinese revolution.[8] At the same time, he also directed the attention of the Chinese Communists to a number of principles to follow in carrying out a successful revolution, and these remained the guidelines for CPC action down to their final victory in 1949.

Three of these tactical principles have already been discussed, and need not be further elaborated here: (1) The leadership of the proletariat and its Communist Party; (2) the alliance with the peasantry; and (3) the united-front tactics. A fourth, however—the reliance on the armed revolution—played a crucial role in the final Chinese Communist victory; and a fifth—the insistence on a two-stage revolution, with an allegedly transitional regime leading toward socialism—provided the pattern for the form of regime finally established after that victory. These require closer examination.

Stalin's great emphasis on force in a successful revolutionary struggle was based upon, and rationalized by, the Marxist-Leninist insistence upon the intransigence of the bourgeois capitalists in the face of a challenge to their power. In a letter to American workers in 1918, Lenin had written that "in all countries, the violent resistance of the bourgeoisie against the socialist revolution is inevitable," and that "it will grow in proportion to the growth of the revolution." Echoing this view, Stalin stated in 1928: "There never was and never will be a case of the working class in a class society advancing toward socialism without having to resort to violence." It was ostensibly for this reason that Stalin, in November, 1926, offered his often-quoted characterization of the Chinese Communist movement as "an armed revolution fighting an armed counter-revolution." He felt that "a peaceful transition [from the "bourgeois democratic" revolution] to the proletarian revolution should be considered excluded." He recalled that, in the unsuccessful Russian Revolution of 1905, the unarmed people were opposed by the armies of the old regime. In China, on the other hand, he observed that there was now "an armed people represented by its revolutionary army." Stalin therefore concluded that "the revolutionary armies in China are the most important factor in the struggle of the Chinese workers and peasants for their own liberation."

[8] These were: (1) the semi-colonial status of China; (2) the internal oppression of feudalist remnants, intensified by warlordism and bureaucratism; (3) the rising revolutionary struggle of the millions of workers and peasants against the oppression of the imperialists, the feudalist officials, and the warlords; (4) the political weakness of the national bourgeoisie and its dependence on imperialism; (5) the increasing revolutionary activity of the Chinese proletariat and its growing leadership of the masses; and (6) the existence of the powerful neighbor and ally in the proletarian dictatorship of the Soviet Union.

In line with his emphasis on armed struggle, Stalin urged the Chinese Communists to "pay special attention to the work in the army"—not only to intensify political work in the Red Army, but also to put military affairs first, to study military science, and to assume positions of military command in order to "guarantee that the revolutionary army in China [will] go along the right way, directly to the goal." More important, it was under Stalin's direction that the Comintern, in February, 1927—a month and a half before Chiang Kai-shek's drastic purging of the communists from the Kuomintang—instructed the CPC to arm the workers and peasants and turn the various localities where peasant committees had been organized into bases of revolutionary power "with armed self-defense."

Hence, when the Chinese Communists credit Mao Tse-tung with having created a "people's revolutionary army," with establishing revolutionary bases in the villages, and with achieving the final great victory of the revolutionary war, their praise is based on his having "developed Stalin's teachings on armed struggle into a complete and integral theory of the peasants' revolutionary war under the leadership of the proletariat in semi-colonial and semi-feudal China."

Another specific lesson on the seizure of power which Lenin and Stalin drew from the Russian revolutionary experience, and for which they adapted Marx's concept of "stages" in economic development, was that of the double revolution. In Western societies, the Industrial Revolution had been accompanied by a "bourgeois democratic" revolution, with the extension of the suffrage to the masses, the popular election of officials, and the guarantee of constitutional and civil rights and liberties. Marx had viewed these democracies as largely the creation of the middle class, which effectively dominated the political life of the capitalist era.

In pre-revolutionary Russia and China, where they claimed to find many vestiges of "feudalism," the communists recognized that there would have to be a bourgeois democratic revolution before there could be a proletarian one. In Russia, Lenin and his followers adopted the view that the bourgeois revolution had been accomplished by the February Revolution which brought Kerensky to power briefly in 1917, so that the subsequent October Revolution had been genuinely proletarian in character. But in China and elsewhere, the Leninist position was that even the bourgeois democratic revolution must be carried out by the Communist Party; once in power, it would then proceed to carry out the second, or socialist revolution. As Mao explained, in his 1940 work *On the New Democracy*, "the historical course of the Chinese revolution must be divided into two steps: first, the democratic revolution, and secondly, the Socialist revolution." Although the first stage was to be essentially a bourgeois-democratic phase, Mao went on to say:

. . . yet it is no longer one of the old type led by the bourgeoisie with the aim of establishing a capitalist society and a state under bourgeois dictatorship; it is a new type of revolution led by the proletariat with the aim of establishing, in the first stage, a New Democratic society and a state under the joint dictatorship of all revolutionary classes.

Mao's implicit contrast in this passage between a dictatorship of the proletariat and a joint dictatorship of all revolutionary classes draws attention to a major theoretical distinction between two phases of the communist revolutionary development, as exemplified in the Soviet Union and China. Following Lenin and Stalin, Mao has built his program for China, in its initial stages, on a multi-class rather than a single-class basis. Hence his emphasis on a "new democracy" and a "people's democratic dictatorship" rather than on a full "proletarian dictatorship."

In communist theory, a political party is considered to represent a social class or some part of it. The Communist Party itself is, of course, the party of the proletariat (and in some cases, of the allied peasantry as well); other parties may represent the peasants, the middle class intellectuals, the capitalist entrepreneurs, and the like. In Russia, according to Leninist theory, the communist seizure of power *followed* the bourgeois democratic revolution and presumably represented the victory of the proletariat, allied with the peasantry and led by the Communist Party. Hence, the new regime was considered to be, in a term Marx had introduced, a "dictatorship of the proletariat," and the sole political party allowed under the regime was the party of the proletariat.[9] As Stalin suggested in his historic interview with Roy Howard in 1936, in a country with only a single economic class, there is no need for more than one party.

In China, on the other hand, the communist victory was intended to *coincide* with the bourgeois democratic revolution, and bourgeois political parties were to be included—though strictly subordinate to the Communist Party—in the united front bringing about the revolution. The so-called revolutionary classes represented in this united front—the proletariat, peasantry, petty bourgeoisie, and national bourgeoisie—were to remain in existence *after* the seizure of power. Hence, the term "people's democratic dictatorship" rather than "dictatorship of the proletariat" was regarded as more appropriate to the actual class situation.

[9] Two other parties—the Socialist Revolutionaries and Mensheviks—participated, it is true, in the victory of the October Revolution. But they, too, were theoretically parties of peasants and workers, and in any case they were forced out of the new government within a few months after the communists took over.

By capturing the power of the state machine in the *first* of the two revolutions, the communists hoped to bring about the second peacefully, through a period of transition to a socialist society. The preamble of the 1954 Constitution of the Chinese People's Republic expresses this hope: "The system of people's democracy—new democracy . . . guarantees that China can in a peaceful way banish exploitation and poverty and build a prosperous and happy socialist state." But the possible necessity of violence to suppress any opposition to the regime is openly admitted in the name of the sharpening of the "class struggle" as the former "exploitative elements" make their last desperate efforts to thwart the revolution. Thus, the preamble also states: "This people's democratic united front will continue to play its part in mobilizing . . . the whole people in common struggle to fulfill the fundamental task of the state during the transition and to oppose enemies within and without."

In practice, of course—as the subsequent chapters will show—there is no substantial difference between the "proletarian" and the "people's democratic" dictatorships. But the theory of the two-stage revolution in itself is of more than passing interest because it represents still another inversion of the original Marxian analysis. To Marx, changes in the political superstructure followed, and were adapted to, changes in the economic structure; in other words, changes in the relations between ruler and ruled followed changes in the "relations of production." But what the Leninists now proposed was to make the political revolution *precede* the transformation in economic structure, instead of the other way around. Thus in his *New Democracy*, Mao warned against being "misled by the 'theory of a single revolution,' by the purely fanciful notion of 'accomplishing both the political revolution and the social revolution at one stroke.' " He added: "It is correct, and fits in with the Marxist theory of revolutionary development to say that, of the two revolutionary stages, the first provides the conditions for the second, and that the two must be consecutive without allowing any stage of bourgeois dictatorship to intervene."

Having developed an elaborate theoretical structure to justify putting the Leninist cart before the Marxist horse—the revolutionary seizure of power before the development of an economic basis for a new order— communist leaders in both the Soviet Union and China, once in power, have been faced with a further tremendous task. Under their theory, they must make over a semi-feudal or agrarian society as quickly as possible into a modern industrial and urbanized society—and one, moreover, supporting the strongest and most modern military establishment possible, in order to strengthen the proletarian camp of nations and advance the world revolution. Calling for nothing less than the enforced reconstruction of the entire social order, this effort is bound to produce major strains and dislocations within the society. Hence, the communists are faced with a double problem in social engineering: In order to put through a ruthless program of social, economic, and cultural transformation and advance the cause of world communism, they must build up the power of the state machine in every way possible, while keeping it strictly subordinate to the Party as the center for final policy decisions. At the same time, they must keep the resentments and disappointments of segments of the people from finding expression in organized opposition, through diverting these feelings to targets other than those associated with the communist system. The Chinese Communists appeal as strongly as possible to the sentiments of "patriotism" and community spirit. They seek to enlist as much popular support as possible for their regime's domestic and international goals and policies—particularly strategies and tactics leading to the triumph of the world communist revolutionary movement.

MAO AND THE CONTINUING DEDICATION TO PROLETARIAN INTERNATIONALISM

After more than eighteen years of control over the entire mainland, the Chinese Communists have in no way diminished their dedication to Marxism-Leninism. Rather, as applied to Chinese conditions through the thought of Mao Tse-tung, these Marxist-Leninist principles continue to provide both the *raison d'etre* and the *modus operandi* of communist rule in China. Just as this dedication to orthodox communist theses enabled Mao and his followers to ride to power, so too, only a continued dedication to these same principles is expected to achieve the stage of socialism for China and hasten the world victory of communism. For this reason, in recent years Mao and his followers have emerged as ardent defenders of what they regard to be the ideological purity of Marxism-Leninism. Although Peking did not originally assume the initiative in publicizing certain variations in interpretation and approach that presently trouble the international communist movement, the Chinese Communists have become outspoken critics of those they deem guilty of "modern revisionism." Thus they have denounced a number of interpretations attributed to Khrushchev and apparently accepted, at least initially and to some degree, by his successors. [10]

An in-depth analysis of Sino-Soviet disputes over doctrinal questions— which date at least from Khrushchev's 1956 secret speech to the 20th

---

[10] For a detailed analysis of this question see Peter S. H. Tang, *The Chinese Communist Struggle against Modern Revisionism: Theory and Practice* (Chestnut Hill, Mass.: Research Institute on the Sino-Soviet Bloc, 1964), pp. 1–50.

CPSU Congress in denunciation of Stalin—does not fall within the scope of this study. However, the challenge from the post-Stalin Kremlin leaders in their theoretical innovations, as embodied in the 1961 CPSU Program, has helped Mao tremendously in systematizing his own theory and practice against modern revisionism. Since Peking's position in the present epoch does illustrate her continuing devotion to Marxism-Leninism, several main questions at issue may be elaborated briefly. This analysis begins with the kernel problem of the nature of the traditional proletarian Party and proletarian dictatorship, moves to inter-Party and inter-state relations which are at the heart of the international communist movement, and concludes with the nature of the proletarian revolution in the non-communist world, with an inquiry into the possibility of peaceful transition, the issue of the national liberation movement in Asia, Africa, and Latin America, and the problem of war and peace, or peaceful coexistence with the developed world.

To Mao the proletarian Party and the proletarian dictatorship are mutually "indispensable"; and both must exist together until the world's entry into the classless, communist society. According to his logic, along Marxist lines, since no "non-class or supra-class political party" exists, there cannot be a "party of the entire people," as suggested by Khrushchev and the 1961 CPSU Program. The CPC makes it abundantly clear that the transformation of the proletarian Party into a "party of the entire people," intermediate to entering the classless society, disarms the proletariat ideologically and organizationally, and is tantamount to helping restore capitalism. Similarly, Mao's followers charge that the CPSU's anti-cult campaign has an "ulterior motive" to defame the proletarian Party and the proletarian dictatorship, by counterposing Stalin to the Party and the proletariat to pave the way for revisionist schemes.

According to Mao's thought, the development and victory of a revolution depend on the existence of an internationalist, revolutionary, proletarian Party—not a revisionist, nationalist, bourgeois reformist party representing the interests of the labor aristocracy. The CPC even warns: "If the leading group in any Party adopts a non-revolutionary line and converts it into a reformist party, then Marxist-Leninists inside and outside the Party will replace that group and lead the people in making revolution."

Mao has stressed that, to deny the existence of class struggle during the period of transition to communism, and to announce, halfway through, that the proletarian dictatorship is no longer necessary is fundamentally in conflict with the theory of Marx and Lenin on the state of the proletarian dictatorship. He explains that, since Marxist-Leninists recognize no non-class or supra-class state, but do believe in the withering away of the state in a classless society, there cannot be a "state of the whole people." Thus, the CPC questions whether Khrushchev's calling the Soviet Union the "state of the whole people" is designed to replace the Marxist-Leninist theory of the state by the bourgeois theory of the state. According to the CPC, the proletarian Party, following the revisionist-opportunist path, can degenerate into a bourgeois political party, and the proletarian dictatorship, into a bourgeois or even fascist dictatorship. Communists can become bourgeois nationalists or reactionaries. In fact, Mao and his followers consider that the degeneration of the proletarian Party and proletarian dictatorship in Yugoslavia typifies such a "peaceful evolution."

Mao and his followers have registered strongly against any attempt to violate the approved standards of inter-Party and inter-state relations. On the basis of the 1957 Moscow Declaration and the 1960 Moscow Statement, the CPC declares that all "fraternal" Parties, large or small, new or old, in or out of power, are independent and equal. The CPC denies the right of any leadership in the international communist movement to lord it over other Parties, as this obviously contradicts the principles sanctioned by these statements to guide inter-Party relations. The CPC insists that the intra-Party principle of the minority submitting to the majority cannot be applied to inter-Party relations, because each Party maintains its independence, and unanimity should be reached through consultation. The Chinese Communists charge that the CPSU leaders' insistence on the formula that "the minority should submit to the majority" disguises their desire to violate the Declaration and the Statement by denying the independent and equal status of all "fraternal" Parties, abolishing the principle of unanimity and engaging in sectarian and divisive activities. The CPC maintains that true Marxist-Leninists and Marxist-Leninist Parties must support those communists who oppose revisionism.

According to Mao's thought, inter-State relations within the communist camp, as "international relations of a new type," require that "socialist" countries, large or small, developed or less developed, adhere not only to the principle of "complete equality, respect for territorial integrity, sovereignty, and independence, and non-interference in each other's internal affairs," but also to the principles of mutual support in accordance with "proletarian internationalism." Thus, "socialist" countries should respect one another's observance of the "principle of self-reliance in construction." They should do this without manifesting national egoism or greater power chauvinism in the name of an "international division of labor" or "specialization," and without following capitalist practices of profiteering at the expense of others.

The leaders of the CPC have also been staunch in their defense of the Marxist-Leninist interpretations of the necessity of violent proletarian revolution. Adhering to Marx's 1870 dictum that "force must serve as the lever of our revolution," and Lenin's 1919 remarks that "revolutionary violence gained brilliant successes in the October Revolution," Mao suggests that violence is integral to proletarian revolution. Violence is said to serve as the "midwife to socialist society" because the key to proletarian revolution is the seizure of state power by force. Emphasizing Lenin's thesis that the "view of violent revolution lies at the root of all the teachings of Marx and Engels," Mao concludes that the unquestioned assumption of peaceful transformation within the framework of bourgeois democracy is an open repudiation of the proletarian revolution.

As early as 1938, Mao Tse-tung wrote that "political power grows out of the barrel of a gun" which is placed "under the direction of the Party." This dictum is said to be drawn from the Marxist-Leninist theory of violent revolution and reinforced by the new experience of the proletarian revolution, and the proletarian-led people's democratic revolution. Mao further stresses that "revolutions and revolutionary wars are inevitable in class society" and "in their absence no leap in social development can be accomplished, the reactionary ruling classes cannot be overthrown, and the people cannot win political power."

The CPC has supported Mao's advocation of the need for Marxist revolutionary war in insisting that Khrushchev betrayed Marxism-Leninism and violated its fundamental tenet on violent proletarian revolution when he advanced the "parliamentary road" at the 20th CPSU Congress in 1956. As early as December, 1956, the CPC was "positively" upholding the road of the October Revolution and criticizing Khrushchev's parliamentary road as being antithetical. At the 1957 Moscow meeting, the CPC delegation headed by Mao sharply debated with the CPSU delegation on the question of the transition to socialism. In November, 1957, Mao emphasized:

It is advantageous from the point of view of tactics to refer to the desire for peaceful transition, but it would be inappropriate to overemphasize the possibility of peaceful transition. It is necessary to be prepared at all times to repulse counter-revolutionary attacks and, at the critical juncture of the revolution when the working class is seizing state power, to overthrow the bourgeoisie by armed force if it uses armed force to suppress the people's revolution (generally speaking, it is inevitable that the bourgeoisie will do so). The parliamentary form of struggle must be fully utilized, but its role is limited.

According to the thought of Mao, revisionists peddle legalism, reject armed struggle, and confine the Party's activities and mass struggles within the framework allowed by the ruling classes. Thus the Party's basic program is debased and discarded and revolution renounced. Although urging that the proletarian Party should take part in parliamentary struggle to accumulate revolutionary strength, Mao has repeatedly warned against the illusion of the revisionist "parliamentary road" as a substitute for proletarian revolution. This stand explains in large measure Peking's dedication to the national liberation movement.

As the CPC distinguishes, "the Marxist-Leninists firmly side with the oppressed nations and actively support the national liberation movement, while the modern revisionists in fact side with the imperialists and colonialists and repudiate and oppose the national liberation movement in every possible way." The CPC accuses the CPSU leaders of advocating revisionist theories of "the disappearance of colonialism" and a "new stage" of the central economic task. It points out that the revisionist objectives are to cover up contradictions and to paralyze and negate the national liberation movement. The prescriptions of "peaceful coexistence" and "peaceful competition" are equivalent to telling the oppressed nations not to rise up in resistance and revolution, but to wait for the natural collapse of imperialism.

Under the guidance of Mao's thought, the CPC has consistently maintained that the national liberation movement should be considered in the total perspective of Marxism-Leninism and the proletarian world revolution. It holds that the national liberation or the democratic revolutionary movements in Asia, Africa, and Latin America, and the international communist movement constitute two mutually supporting historical currents, with the former being an important component of the latter. Thus, the victorious development of the national liberation movement is of tremendous significance for the "socialist" camp and the international communist movement, since the revolutionary struggles of all peoples support one another. Referring to the CPSU Central Committee's Open Letter of October 22, 1963, the fourth comment of the editorial departments of *People's Daily* and *Red Flag* stated:

> According to Marxism-Leninism and proletarian internationalism, every socialist country which has achieved victory in its revolution must actively support and assist the liberation struggles of the oppressed nations. The socialist countries must become base areas for supporting and developing the revolution of the oppressed nations and peoples throughout the world, form the closest alliance with them and carry the proletarian world revolution through to completion.

Mao and his followers warn revisionists against taking the path of nationalism and degeneration by putting an end to the proletarian world revolution and subordinating the national liberation movement to their own national interests.

According to Mao's thought, the Marxist-Leninist line on the question of war and peace is diametrically opposed to the current revisionist line and practices. Marxism-Leninism warns against the "bourgeois pacifist" approach of lumping just and unjust wars together and opposing all of them indiscriminately. The CPC affirms that "Marxist-Leninists take the abolition of war as their ideal and believe that war can be abolished." But the abolition should be based on Lenin's prescribed conditions, reiterated in the 1960 Moscow Statement. These include abolishing the "division of mankind into classes" and "all exploitation of man by man, and of one nation by other nations." In other words, war can be abolished only by the attainment of a communist world society. In November, 1957, at the Moscow meeting, Mao depicted the world situation as reaching a new turning point with a metaphor from a classical novel—"The East wind prevails over the West wind"—to indicate that "the forces of socialism have become overwhelmingly superior to the forces of imperialism." As the CPC suggests, while pointing to the possibility of preventing a new world war—due to communist parity or superiority in strength— Marxist-Leninists must also call attention to the possibility that imperialism may unleash such a war at any time. To ignore either possibility is to be caught unprepared. Thus it attacks Khrushchev and his followers for willfully disregarding the possibility of a new "imperialist-inspired" world war. The CPC bases this charge on Khrushchev's preaching the possibility of preventing all wars, and "holding that the Leninist axiom that war is inevitable so long as imperialism exists is outmoded."

Mao and his associates have vigorously denounced Khrushchev's theses that the emergence of nuclear weapons has changed the laws of class struggle, and that permanent peace or a "world without weapons, without armed forces and without wars"—which can only be a world without states—can be realized while imperialism still exists. According to the CPC, world peace can be won only through the tit-for-tat struggle against the "imperialist policies of aggression and war." The CPC blames the CPSU leaders for relinquishing the struggle against the "imperialist policies of aggression and war," denying the anti-imperialist united front, isolating the peace forces, and liquidating the task of defending world peace, hence following "not the road to world peace but the road leading to greater danger of war and to war itself."

At the same time the CPC prides itself on its consistent application of Lenin's command that socialist countries conduct their relations with countries having different social systems according to the formula of peaceful coexistence. It affirms that Communist China has from the outset consistently pursued this Leninist policy, especially as evidenced in its initiation of the Five Principles of Peaceful Coexistence. The CPC suggests that the correct application of this Leninist policy of peaceful coexistence by the socialist countries helps to "develop their power." This is because peaceful coexistence aids to "expose the imperialist policies of aggression and war" and, above all, to form an anti-imperialist international united front "in harmony with the interests of the people's revolutionary struggles in all countries."

To the leaders of Peking the Leninist policy of peaceful coexistence is diametrically opposed to Khrushchev's dangerous "anti-Leninist" general line of peaceful coexistence, because the former is only for formal relations between countries of different social systems, and is transitory, discriminatory and limited in nature. The Leninist ideal is rooted in the international class struggle, and supports world revolution. However, the formula Khrushchev claims to be "the supreme principle governing the life of modern society" is said to be based on "all-round cooperation with imperialist countries," hence absolute, unconditional, and all-embracing in nature with the purpose of abolishing world revolution. The CPC thus concludes that by making peaceful coexistence the general line of foreign policy, Khrushchev and his successors have been placing the socialist countries and oppressed nations "on a par with the capitalist countries," which amounts to "liquidating the socialist camp" based as it is on the proletarian internationalist relations of mutual assistance. According to Mao's standpoint, it is wrong and impermissible to apply the socialist countries' policy of peaceful coexistence to relations between oppressed and oppressor classes and between oppressed and oppressor nations. It is equally wrong and impermissible to make it the policy of the Communist Parties and the revolutionary people in the capitalist world, thus subordinating the revolutionary struggles to it.

Under Mao's guidance, the CPC's deliberation of the above-mentioned closely related issues involving cardinal principles of Marxism-Leninism has been well focused, unequivocal and strong. Thus the Chinese Communist theory and practice of the contemporary anti-revisionist struggle is a call to battle for the professed purpose of rescuing and advancing the international communist movement at a critical moment.

It should be apparent from this brief analysis that the Chinese Communists publically attribute their political successes and other progress to the correctness of their Marxist-Leninist principles as refined and applied by Mao Tse-tung. Having tested these principles and found them adequate, both pragmatically and intellectually the Chinese Communists believe in the absolute effectiveness of this ideology for all areas of national and international programs and policies. In the present epoch, the followers of Mao have perhaps become the most ardent proponents of an interpretation that could prove the most formidable trend to invigorate Marxism-Leninism in its challenge to the non-communist world.

CHAPTER 2

Communist Revolution
in China:
Road to Victory

ESTABLISHING THE COMMUNIST PARTY AS A
REVOLUTIONARY WEAPON (1915–23)

The years preceding the formal creation of the Communist Party of China in July, 1921, were years of political and social flux, and of extraor-. dinary intellectual ferment in China. Under the circumstances, the wonder is not that a Communist Party was formed (for under Lenin's policy of setting up the Communist International with affiliated parties in each country, some version of a Communist Party would undoubtedly have been organized), but rather, that so few Chinese joined the Party in its first few years. It is not surprising, however, in view of the veritable revolution in the cultural life of the country in these few years, that the charter members and early leaders of the new Party were drawn largely from the intelligentsia, and particularly from the young intellectuals, rather than from the ranks of industrial labor, the armed forces, or the peasantry.

By 1915, a strong reaction had set in against China's traditional philo-sophical and religious systems, most notably Confucianism, Buddhism, and Taoism. The Chinese intelligentsia turned more and more to the Western world for their ideological inspiration. The search for new first principles spread rapidly to the realms of ethics, political philosophy, science, literature, and the arts. Among those in the forefront of the search was Ch'en Tu-hsiu, a professor at the National Peking University. [1] In 1915, he founded a review called *New Youth* (*Hsin Ch'ing-nien*), which soon became one of the principal vehicles of expression for the cultural renaissance. Among its contributors were Li Ta-chao, Hu Shih, Ts'ai Yüan-p'ei, Fu Ssu-nien, Chou Tso-jen, and others prominent in the movement.

Ch'en shared with his colleague at Peking, Li Ta-chao (who later accompanied him into the newly formed Communist Party), the view that Chinese civilization was decadent and Chinese institutions and ideas moribund. Hence, he turned for inspiration to the vigorous culture of the West, which he felt had fully awakened to the possibilities opened up by the growth of science and the spread of democracy. Among the writers who particularly influenced his thinking were Montesquieu, Rousseau, Adam Smith, Comte, John Stuart Mill, Darwin, Spencer, and John Dewey. His interest in Marx did not come until somewhat later. Three features of Western thought particularly attracted him: the concept of "struggle," as compared to the ethical norm of "peace" in the East; the idea of "individualism," as contrasted to the Eastern emphasis on family status and filial piety; and the "practical" outlook of Western society in contrast to the empty "formalism" of Chinese civilization, as he saw it.

Finding in the younger and newer thought of the West so much that was challenging, it was characteristic of Ch'en that he turned to the youth of China to bring about the cultural reawakening of his own weak and languishing country. In the first issue of *New Youth*, he cried out:

> Oh, young men of China! Will you be able to understand me? Five out of every ten whom I see are young in age but old in spirit; nine out of every ten are young in health, but they are also old in spirit. . . . When this happens to a body, the body is dying. When it happens to a society, the society is perishing. . . . We must have youth if we are to survive. We must have youth if we are to get rid of corruption. Here lies the only hope for our society.

There were many evidences that the youth and the intellectuals of China were ready to respond to his plea. One of the dramatic signs of readiness for change was the rapid spread of the so-called *pai-hua* movement for a written vernacular. Hu Shih's initial proposal for this innovation was published in Ch'en's *New Youth* organ on February 1, 1919, and Ch'en welcomed it as opening a way "to destroy the pedantic, unintelligible and

---

[1] Standing alone is the invaluable study of the career and political thought of Ch'en Tu-hsiu made by Julie Lien-ying How under the title, *The Development of Ch'en Tu-hsiu's Thought, 1915-1938*. This unpublished study is available at the Columbia University Libraries.

obscurantist literature of the hermit and the recluse, and to create the plain-speaking and popular literature of the living society." The new style of writing quickly became standard in the nation's schools and colleges. It thus became possible to bring the contributions of Western philosophy and science to a much larger audience in China.

At the same time, a new movement in education was helping the Chinese youth to break out of old molds, by placing emphasis on the development of the total personality, including physical as well as intellectual training, and the teaching of practical skills. These movements in literature and education, taken with their counterparts in political philosophy, ethics, science, and religion, indicated that Chinese intellectuals and Chinese youth were not only receptive to new ideas but were actively seeking a system of ideas which would better meet the needs of the new day.

Although Ch'en's *New Youth* review was not a political organ, Ch'en's own political views, in the formative years preceding 1919, were primarily those of a liberal democrat;[2] they centered around a democratic core of constitutionalism and republicanism, and eschewed the one-party rule which had come to characterize Chinese politics. As late as December, 1919, when Ch'en was already turning toward Marxism, he wrote an article on "The Basis for the Realization of Democracy" in which he embraced Dewey's conception of democracy and proposed that the Chinese Republic had failed only because it had been imposed from above. At the same time, he called for a new type of political party, bearing little resemblance to the Communist Party he eventually helped to found:

> We advocate a mass movement to reform society, different from past and present political parties. . . . We believe that true democracy can distribute political power to the people and it is necessary to build a new era, a new society. Political parties are necessary instruments but they must be different from those parties which work for the interests of an exclusive minority or class.

The Armistice of 1918 and the promulgation of Wilson's Fourteen

---

[2] The term "democracy," like so many others, has of course been differently interpreted by the communists. There is need for a non-invidious term to cover that range of political systems sometimes designated by the too narrowly regional term, "Western democracy." For the sake of exactness, "liberal democracy" would seem a better choice, if it be taken in a historical rather than a programmatic sense. The supporters of a liberal democratic system would include conservatives as well as modern liberals, revisionist socialists as well as laissez-faire individualists and workers as well as middle class capitalists or members of the professions. What is "liberal" in this spectrum is the belief in those basic political and civil rights and freedoms associated historically with nineteenth century liberalism and stemming from British constitutionalism and the American and French Revolutions. Excluded would be the totalitarianisms of right and left, and extreme variants such as anarchism, syndicalism, or corporativism. In this book, therefore, "liberal democracy" will be used for emphasis and precision. Where "democracy" is used without a qualifying adjective such as "people's," it will also refer to this historically liberal version as it has been adapted to modern conditions.

Points brought to a new high the faith of the Chinese people in the liberal democratic ideals of the West. The Chinese began to hope that foreign domination of their country—and particularly the encroachments of Japan —would soon be brought to an end. In his own comment on the Wilsonian principles, Ch'en wrote in December, 1918:

Now that justice has triumphed over force, all people should clearly realize that force cannot be relied on and that justice cannot be ignored. The speeches of the American President, Woodrow Wilson, are noble and just. He is the best man in the world. His most important principles are national sovereignty and the sovereignty of the people over the government.

Within half a year, however, the Chinese faith in the West, and to some extent in its democratic ideals as well, was subjected to the cruel disillusionment of the Paris Peace Conference. The Chinese delegation there had demanded the abrogation of foreign privileges in China, including the recovery of the former German rights in Shantung Province. But the secret agreements prevailed, and the German rights were granted to Japan. The result was an unprecedented upsurge of protest within the newly awakening China.

When the bitter news of the defeat at the Paris peace table reached China shortly before May 4, 1919, the reaction was immediate. On the latter day, some five thousand students from National Peking University and other institutions of learning in Peking staged a demonstration against the Versailles settlement. The demonstrators demanded that the Chinese delegation to the Peace Conference refuse to sign the treaty and that the Twenty-one Demands imposed upon China by Japan in 1915 be abrogated. They petitioned the office of the President of-the Republic to mete out punishment to the "national traitors" who had bartered away China's rights and national integrity. And they stormed the residence of the Foreign Minister and administered a beating to one of the high government officials there. The next day, in protest against the police action in arresting thirty-two of the demonstrators, the students stayed away from their classes.

In the days following, this campaign of protest spread to other parts of China, being taken up not only by students but by workers, shopkeepers, and other patriotic citizens. On June 4 and 5, between sixty and seventy thousand workers in Shanghai went out on strike, and large numbers of merchants closed their shops. Similar demonstrations followed in Nanking, Tientsin, Hangchow, Wuhan,* in Shantung and Anhwei provinces, and

* The Wuhan cities of Hankow, Wuchang, and Hanyang, separated by the Yangtze and Han Rivers, were not formally incorporated as a single municipality until after the communists came to power. For the sake of convenience, however, the name is sometimes used here to refer to the three-cities area (or to Hankow alone) throughout the earlier period as well.

elsewhere. Thus the May Fourth Movement became the first major instance of a nation-wide mass movement, and more especially, the first occasion on which Chinese labor had shown its strength in a national and political role.[3] Indeed, it may be said to mark the birth of the Chinese labor movement. It is not surprising, then, to find the May Fourth Movement regarded, in the official Chinese Communist interpretation, as laying the basis for the founding of the Communist Party of China. In his 1940 work *On the New Democracy*, Mao Tse-tung referred to the year 1919 as the turning point at which the Chinese revolution "was transformed from a democratic revolution of the old type [i.e., under bourgeois leadership] into a democratic revolution of the new type [i.e., under proletarian leadership]."

Within a year after the May Fourth Movement, according to an officially approved history of the CPC,[4] "Communist groups" had been formed in such major cities as Peking, Shanghai, Canton, Hankow, Changsha, Hangchow, Tsinan, and others. But the more exact origin of the Party is to be found in the Society for the Study of Marxism set up by Ch'en Tu-hsiu and Li Ta-chao in the spring of 1918. Ch'en's own conversion from liberal democratic to Marxist-Leninist views was a gradual one, becoming definite only in the early part of 1920. Some elements of his thought (such as his emphasis on unceasing struggle) had been from the start compatible with the Marxist system. The setback for Chinese aspirations and for Wilsonian principles at the Paris Peace Conference contributed to his disillusionment with democratic methods, and the police repressions in the May Fourth Movement only reinforced this process. At the same time, the role of the urban workers in that movement had directed his attention to the possibilities of relying on the proletariat for political action. Hence, where he had once looked to the enlightened minority to awaken and lead the majority in the democratic exercise of power to bring about reforms, he was now ready to accept the idea that the minority should seize power directly and exercise it in the "name" of the majority, as in the "dictatorship of the proletariat."

Despite this change in Ch'en's thinking, the communist movement in China might have remained academic and theoretical had it not been for

[3] For a thorough treatment of this significant movement see Chow Tse-tsung, *The May Fourth Movement: Intellectual Revolution in Modern China* (Cambridge, Mass.: Harvard University Press, 1960) and Chow Tse-tsung, *Research Guide to the May Fourth Movement* (Cambridge, Mass.: Harvard University Press, 1963).

[4] Hu Ch'iao-mu, *Chung-Kuo-Kung-Ch'an-Tang ti San-shih-nien* (*Thirty Years of the Communist Party of China*) Peking, 1951. Versions in English and other languages are available. The author was the Vice Director of the Propaganda Department of the CPC Central Committee.

the intervention of the Communist International (the Comintern) at this time. As indicated in the last chapter, Lenin saw clearly the importance of the anti-colonial revolutions for the victory of the communist world revolution. Under his guidance, the Comintern had decided upon a policy of promoting revolution in colonial and semi-colonial areas, and had been following very closely the development of an interest in Marxism in China. Thus in the spring of 1920, the Comintern sent a mission from the Far Eastern Secretariat of its Executive Committee—consisting of a Russian, Grigori Voitinsky, and an overseas Chinese, Yang Ming-chai, as his assistant—to establish contact with the Ch'en Tu-hsiu group in China.

Under Voitinsky's guidance, the Ch'en group eliminated from its ranks the anarchist and trade union elements whose aims did not square with Lenininist principles of organization and strategy, and proceeded with the task of organizing as a political party. In May, 1921, the Ch'en group met in a conference at Shanghai to make the necessary arrangements and to create a League of Communist Youth to serve as a recruiting organ and training center for the new Party, with a Comintern representative, G. Maring, acting as its instructor. The formal establishment of the Party came at its First Congress, held in Shanghai on July 1, 1921. The delegates to this congress numbered only twelve, including Mao Tse-tung and Tung Pi-wu, but not including Ch'en himself, and the total membership in the communist groups in the various localities did not exceed fifty or sixty. This congress deliberated over the organic structure of the CPC and set up the central organs of the Party, following Leninist lines. Ch'en Tu-hsiu was named the first Secretary General of the Party.

A Second Party Congress was held in West Lake in Hangchow and Shanghai in May and July, 1922, attended by twelve delegates representing about one hundred twenty members. As a propaganda instrument, this congress adopted a Party Manifesto, laying down the Party's minimum program of overthrowing the feudal warlords and imperialism and maximum program of abolishing private ownership and gradually heading toward communism. The Manifesto also criticized the various "bourgeois reformist ideologies" of the day, and stated certain "basic tasks" for the Chinese people. It further made the formal decision to join the Communist International, although the First Congress, according to an official communist account appearing in the *Communist International* in March, 1929, had already provided in fact for a "permanent and systematic connection" with the Comintern.

The intervention of the Russian communist leaders, through the Comintern, in every step of the organization of the CPC was quite evident. The official history of the CPC says only that at the First Congress, "a representative of the Communist International was present." But the twenty-one "Conditions of Admission to the Communist International" laid down by the Second Comintern Congress in July-August, 1920, made clear the degree to which the CPC would have to remain subordinate to the wishes and directions of Moscow. Each member Party, according to these regulations, was to be unconditionally under the control of the Third International, and its programs were to be confirmed by the Congress or the Executive Committee of the Comintern. All the resolutions of the latter bodies were to be binding upon the member Parties, who were to see that their own propaganda and agitation efforts corresponded to the line laid down in the Comintern programs and decisions.

It was evident to the Russian leaders, however, that the CPC, in its embryonic state and with its tiny membership, was not at the outset an effective instrument for capitalizing on the revolutionary ferment of the times to bring a communist victory in China. Hence, following Lenin's strategy, they sought to expand communist influence there through a program of alliances between the communists and other elements. One avenue of influence they attempted to use was that of the labor movement. Following the May Fourth Movement, the trade union movement had shown remarkable growth, and in 1922 and 1923, there were important strikes among the seamen and dockers, textile workers, railway men, and others. Following the program of the Comintern, the Chinese Communists attempted to dominate these unions whenever possible. The degree of their success is subject to dispute, but the official history of the CPC admits a decisive check to their efforts with the so-called "February Seventh Massacre" in 1923, when one of the war lords in the North, Wu P'ei-fu, used troops to suppress the strike of railway workers at Hankow and Ch'anghsintien. The Russian leaders—and Stalin in particular—recognized that the labor movement alone was not a satisfactory revolutionary instrument, even under communist leadership, because it lacked a military arm of its own to advance the revolution.

At the First Party Congress in 1921, however, a second course in the search for allies had been suggested. This congress, according to the previously cited account in *Communist International* in March, 1929,

. . . made the essential change in policy which was afterwards confirmed by the Second Congress . . . consisting in the transference from propaganda work and the organization of trade unions to active participation in the political struggle, to the struggle of the proletariat for hegemony in the national bourgeois-democratic revolution.

By the time of the Second Party Congress, the Russian leaders, influenced by the reports of the Comintern representatives in China, had decided that the Kuomintang (the KMT or Nationalist Party) of Sun Yat-sen represented the leading element and best hope of the "national bour-geois-democratic revolution" in China. This view was made official by a Comintern Resolution on the Chinese Revolution of January 1, 1923, which acknowledged the KMT as the only major force of the national revolution in China. The KMT thus became the target of the communists' drive for "hegemony."

During this period, Dr. Sun's position in China was relatively precarious. After setting up a provisional government in Canton in 1921, he was driven out by one of the local war lords, Ch'en Chiung-ming, in August, 1922, and went into exile in Shanghai, returning to Canton in February, 1923. But to the Russians, his movement seemed to have the greatest potentiality for mass appeal, and offered as well a vehicle for armed struggle against the assorted war lords and factions then in control of the rest of China. By allying themselves with this movement, the Chinese Com-munists would be able to utilize the prestige of the KMT and operate openly in the KMT-controlled areas, thereby broadening their contacts with the masses and strengthening their own power. At the same time, by influencing the policies adopted by the KMT regime, the communists could lay the foundation for a "socialist" revolution, once they had gained the hegemony they sought. Hence, the strategy of the Russian leaders took a double form: to promote some form of united front between the CPC and the KMT; and to advance Soviet military aid directly to the KMT government, while maintaining official relations directly between the Kremlin and the KMT.

In pursuit of the first aim, the official Comintern representative at the Second Congress of the CPC proposed that the Party enter into a formal alliance, or a united front, with the KMT. Although the Comintern representative engaged in direct talks with Sun Yat-sen following this Party congress, there was little progress until Sun's temporary exile from Canton, when the idea of cooperating with the communists and receiving aid from Russia became more attractive to him. The KMT founder and leader had, of course, followed the events of the Russian Revolution with interest, realizing that it might well serve as an example to be followed by China in her own struggle. He had also been favorably impressed by the diplomacy of the new Russian regime in apparently renouncing Russia's claims under the former secret and unequal treaties and advocating a seemingly genuine equality of nations. And he was inclined to welcome the support of the Chinese Communists, as long as they subscribed to the theory and principles of his own party and supported its leadership. For this reason, he insisted that as a condition for allying with the KMT, the Chinese Communists would have to discard their own Party organiza-tion and activities, coming into the KMT only as individuals.

The negotiations between the Soviet representative—who at this time was Adolf Joffe—and Dr. Sun finally reached a successful conclusion with their joint statement of January 26, 1923. On the surface it was apparent that agreement had been reached only through some major concessions on the part of the communists. To remove any suspicion of communist aims in Dr. Sun's mind, Joffe was forced to declare in the statement that "the communistic order or even the Soviet system cannot actually be introduced into China" because of the absence of the necessary conditions. Sun also agreed to allow communists to join his party only as individuals, and to participate in the cause of the national revolution simply because their anti-imperialist aims happened to coincide with those of the KMT. This policy, which came to be known in KMT circles as that of *yung-Kung* (let the communists join as individuals), did not, strictly speaking, imply cooperation between the KMT and the CPC as equals. To Dr. Sun, such a concept would have been meaningless, since he did not recognize the communists as an organized unit within the KMT, but only as a collection of like-minded individuals in the radical wing of his own party. In effect, the Chinese Communists instead agreed, under the *yung-Kung* policy, to allow the leadership of the revolution in China to be in the hands of the KMT rather than their own Party as an independent unit. Late in 1923, in the *Ch'ien-feng (Vanguard) Monthly*, Ch'en Tu-hsiu expressed this idea in an article on "The Bourgeois Revolution and the Classes in Chinese Society": At present, he argued in effect, China requires a national revolution under the leadership of the KMT. Hence, the Chinese Communists should devote themselves wholeheartedly to the national revolution, putting aside the socialist revolution. It was his view, both then and later, that the communist movement in China was ahead of its time, and that its day for revolutionary leadership would come later.

The CPC accepted these concessions to Dr. Sun for the moment as a matter of necessity, because it had not yet achieved any mass support of its own. Yet the concessions, as will be seen, were more apparent than real. The communists did not give up their own Party organization and activities. And their link with the Russian Party became stronger by virtue of being carried on through the man who was at the same time the official adviser to Sun Yat-sen. What the CPC was attempting to accomplish through the policy of cooperation was plainly stated in the official organ of the Comintern on February 19, 1924:

> The Chinese Communist Party collaborated with the Kuomintang Party with the object of revolutionizing it and converting it (as far as this is possible) into a workers' and peasants' party. In spite of its weakness and its comparatively small membership, the Chinese Communist Party can do a great deal in the matter of influencing the Kuomintang and of revolutionizing its principles and tactics.

After the Sun-Joffe understanding the way was open to work out the arrangements for direct aid and representation from the Russians to the KMT. In August, 1923, Sun Yat-sen sent one of his young military aides, Chiang Kai-shek, to Moscow to study the Red Army. A little later, and possibly at his own request, Sun received a representative of the Russian government to act as his personal adviser on political matters. This man, Mikhail Borodin, arrived in Canton on October 6, 1923, and was forthwith appointed to a key position within the KMT organization, reporting directly to President Sun.[5]

With the adoption of the *yung-Kung* policy by the KMT and with the arrival of Borodin as representative of Moscow, the Chinese Communists were now ready to embark on a period of rapid expansion in size and influence within the KMT—a period which was to be terminated only when, under the direction of Stalin and the Comintern, they overreached themselves in grasping for more power and in trying to convert the Kuomintang from within.

THE ABORTIVE DRIVE FOR REVOLUTIONARY HEGEMONY (1923-27)

Having secured their alliance with the Kuomintang, the communist leaders in Russia and their tiny band of followers in China were ready to implement the revolutionary strategy provided by their theory. This called for them, in effect, to ride to power on the backs of a popular movement against imperialism and for agrarian and "bourgeois-democratic" political reforms, and then take over the leadership of the movement and transform it into a proletarian socialist revolution. The KMT was to be the vehicle of such a movement.

To effect this strategy, the Comintern and the Chinese Communists needed to accomplish three aims in particular: (1) Initially, to give sufficient aid and guidance (from the Comintern) to the KMT to insure its survival and growth; (2) to build up the mass strength of the CPC as a

[5] Although Borodin worked closely with Dr. Sun, his attitude toward him was something less than hero worship. In November, 1923, shortly after Borodin's arrival, a disagreement between the two over a set of radical economic measures which the Russians wanted Sun to promulgate led to a violent personal argument. Documents later seized in the Soviet Embassy in Peking show that in reporting to Moscow, Borodin referred to Sun as a "backward man" and an "unenlightened little satrap." These documents have been published in Chinese as *Su-Lien Yin-mo Wen-cheng Hui-pien* (*Documentary Proof of the Soviet Conspiracy*) (Tientsin, 1928). An abridged version in English with editorial comments is to be found in N. Mitarevsky, *World-Wide Soviet Plots* (Tientsin, 1928). An annotated English translation of the documents, edited by Wilbur and How, has been published by Columbia University Press. Typical of the interest shown in the documents at the time of capture is the fact that the American Chamber of Commerce in Shanghai distributed a small selection in pamphlet form *The Soviet in China Unmasked* (Shanghai, North China Daily News and Herald, Ltd., 1927).

party within a party, through recruiting members not just for the KMT but in reality for the communist wing of the KMT; and (3) to capture certain key positions within the KMT, or at any rate to eliminate the influence of any anti-communist KMT leaders, so that in the end, control of the KMT itself could be taken over by the communists.

Hence, in both the party organization and the military buildup of the KMT, the Russian government and the Chinese Communists played a crucial part.   One of Borodin's first acts as high political adviser to the KMT was to convince Dr. Sun that his party should be reorganized along the lines of the Russian Communist Party.   Thus a hierarchy of party units was set up, linked together through the principle of democratic centralism, so that effective power was concentrated in the executive organs of the party at the top—where the communists could hope, through the support they could obtain from their sympathizers among the Left Wing of the KMT, eventually to gain a preponderant influence.   It was Borodin who actually drafted the Constitution of the KMT, which was adopted by its First Congress in January, 1924.

Borodin's efforts extended also to the organization, training, and supply of the KMT armies.   In an early report to his superiors in Moscow (again according to the captured documents of the Peking Embassy), Borodin suggested shipping military supplies for Dr. Sun's armies direct from Vladivostok to Canton, by-passing Hong Kong and the blockade.   The full amount of such military aid actually furnished by Russia is not known, but it was a substantial factor in winning Dr. Sun's consent to the *yung-Kung* policy in the first place, and in postponing the final break between the KMT and the CPC when that policy had badly deteriorated.   Moreover, as with the party, so with the KMT armies, Borodin introduced the Soviet type of organization, and the system of political commissars in particular.   But it was especially in the training of desperately needed officers that the Soviet contribution was apparent.   The famous Whampoa Military Academy, founded in May, 1924, was staffed by Russian military advisers, operated by Russian funds, and furnished with Russian equipment and supplies.   Its commandant was Chiang Kai-shek, but its political instructor was Chou En-lai, who as a student abroad had been one of the founders of the French branch of the CPC.

If Borodin and the Chinese Communists concealed from Dr. Sun their ulterior motives in supporting the KMT so vigorously, they were quite frank among themselves.   What Borodin had to say publicly on his arrival in Canton, he quickly reinterpreted privately at a local communist meeting, the minutes of which were included in the Peking Embassy documents:

"In the press I spoke of the Kuomintang, but to us it means that I was speaking of the increase, in the end, of the influence of the Communist Party." Further on

Borodin pointed out that while working for the stabilization of the Kuomintang it must never be forgotten that in reality the work is done for the stabilization of the Communist Party. . . .

The results of this stabilization effort become quite apparent in a review of the actual growth of the CPC during the period of cooperation. The Third Congress of the CPC in June, 1923, had been attended by some twenty delegates representing only three hundred members. But once the Chinese Communists were able to carry on their recruiting activities behind the shield of the KMT—and particularly through its all-important Organization Department, which was headed at first by the veteran communist leader T'an P'ing-shan [6]—the increase in their own ranks was indeed startling. At the Fourth Congress at Shanghai in January, 1925, more than 70 delegates were in attendance, representing some 1,500 members. During this period, too, the Chinese Communists were initiating mass movements, which included an All-China Labor Union as well as a Kwangtung Farmers' Union. And in the Japanese textile mills in Shanghai and Tsingtao, they instigated major strikes involving some 80,000 workers. A wave of strikes against the British and Japanese in the spring of 1925 gave the communists further opportunity to extend their influence. Nor was the appeal to the radical sentiments of the Chinese students overlooked, as the Comintern in 1925 founded the Sun Yat-sen University in Moscow for the training of Chinese students. [7]

As an inseparable part of these attempts to capitalize upon and lead the strong waves of anti-imperialist protest and labor unrest, the communists were carrying on a bold recruiting campaign for their own Party. A secret resolution adopted by the CPC Executive Committee in the spring of 1924 called upon Party members to "convince all those who are class-conscious to join our organization." Some of the ablest and most energetic of the young KMT members were recruited to the communist ranks. Within a short period of time after the Fourth Congress, the membership had soared from 1,500 to over 10,000. It was said that within a year after this same congress, the Party rolls had multiplied fifty-fold, reaching what was to be the zenith of Party membership in its first decade.

[6] T'an P'ing-shan was replaced in this KMT post in May, 1926. Subsequently he was among those expelled from the CPC in November, 1927, in the general purge following the final debacle of that year. Thereafter he was for a time a leader of a small group calling itself the Third Party. Eventually he returned to the KMT. After 1945 he formed the Three People's Principles Comrades Association as a group within the KMT. In 1948 he led this group into a merger with other such groups to form the Revolutionary Committee of the KMT—one of the minor non-communist parties permitted to survive under the communist regime.

[7] Founded in an aura of KMT-CPC cooperation, this institution lasted only until the early 1930's.

At the time of the Fifth Congress in Wuhan on May 1, 1927, even though the tide had turned against the CPC with Chiang Kai-shek's dramatic and ferocious suppression of the communists in Shanghai and elsewhere the more than 100 delegates were said to represent 58,000 members.

Equally important to the Chinese Communists in their drive to establish "hegemony in the national bourgeois-democratic revolution" was their attempt to install themselves in key positions within the KMT organization. From the beginning, Borodin had taken care to build up communist cells secretly within the KMT, and the Chinese Communists quickly learned to use the familiar communist tactics and to take advantage of the KMT's "democratic-centralist" organization to make their influence count for far more than their actual numbers. At the First Congress of the KMT held in Canton in 1924, seven communists who had only recently joined on an individual basis were elected to its Central Executive Committee (CEC). Li Ta-chao and T'an P'ing-shan were named regular members, while five others were made alternate members, including Ch'ü Ch'iu-pai, Chang Kuo-t'ao, and Mao Tse-tung. Many other important KMT offices were soon held by communists or their sympathizers, including the already mentioned Organization Department under T'an P'ing-shan.

The League of Communist Youth (CY), as an auxiliary of the CPC, also directed its members to "bore from within" in the KMT, at the subordinate but vital levels. A resolution passed by the Enlarged CEC of the CY in March, 1924, stated in part:

> We have joined and co-operated with the KMT. Our attention should be given to the basic and essential work, such as in the sub-committees and the special urban sub-committees. We should avoid unnecessary competition with the KMT members for the middle and high party posts.

Communist influence was further extended in the KMT at the latter's Second National Congress held in Canton early in January, 1926. The 250 delegates included a large contingent of communists and their sympathizers, who were thus able to shape KMT policy and to elect even more CPC members to high positions within the party. Of the 36 regular members of the CEC, 7 were now communists, as were 7 of the 24 alternates—Mao Tse-tung remaining as one of the latter.[8] Mao also served briefly after the Second Congress as acting head of the KMT Propaganda Department, until May, 1926, when Communist Secretary General Ch'en

---

[8] For a list of the members and alternates of the Second CEC of the KMT, see Ch'en Hsi-hao, *Ko-ch'ü San-Shih-wu-nien chih Chung-Kuo-Kuo-Min-Pang (The Kuomintang in the Past Thirty-Five Years)*, (Shanghai, Commercial Press, 1929), pp. 139–40.

Tu-hsiu accepted Chiang Kai-shek's proposal to replace the communist office holders in the higher levels of the KMT hierarchy.

Needless to say, the rise of communist influence within the KMT did not fail to stir apprehension and opposition elsewhere in the party, and particularly among a number of the senior members who had been with Dr. Sun from the earlier days of his revolutionary movement. The communists did not counter this opposition directly; rather, their tactic was secretly to instigate their sympathizers or supporters among the so-called Left Wing of the KMT to attack the old-guard Right Wing. This tactic was particularly emphasized in the CPC directives of the "co-operation" period.

While he was still alive, Dr. Sun steadfastly discouraged the anti-communist feeling within his party and suppressed any open expression of it. He was willing to welcome individual communists as members, as long as they were loyal to his principles, but was mainly interested in the aid and support of the Soviet Union. Somewhat naively, he believed that it was his party, rather than the CPC as such, which the Russians supported. In fact, he wrote in the spring of 1924: "If Russia wants to co-operate with China, she must co-operate with our Party, and not with Ch'en Tu-hsiu. If Ch'en disobeys our Party, he will be ousted."

Following Sun's death on March 12, 1925, the so-called Right Wing of the KMT became more outspoken about their uneasiness and alarm over the rapid infiltration of the communists and the extension of their influence in the KMT. On December 23 this faction held a conference in Hsishan (Western Hills), a suburb of Peking where Dr. Sun's coffin temporarily rested, to intensify its efforts against the communists. However, the three men who were strongest in Canton after Dr. Sun's departure— Borodin, Chiang Kai-shek, and Wang Ching-wei—were all determined, for their various reasons, to prevent any break in the alliance at this time. The members of the Western Hills Conference group were accordingly forced out of their positions in Canton, and at the Second Congress of the KMT in January, 1926, suffered a decisive defeat in the election of the Second CEC.

While the communists were content to use Chiang and Wang against the Right Wing, Chiang himself did not hesitate to act decisively against the communists in the famous March 20th Incident of 1926. Finding evidence of a plot against himself, led by Li Chih-lung, the communist captain of a KMT naval vessel in Whampoa Harbor, Chiang took matters into his own hands at a time when Borodin was away from Canton. In a series of swift moves, including the virtual house arrest of the Russian military advisers, the closing of trade unions and strike committees, and the arrest of all communist political workers attached to his army units,

Chiang—whether this was his objective or not—in effect demonstrated his power over the Russians, the Chinese Communists, and the rest of the Kuomintang.

The immediate loser from this move, however, was Wang Ching-wei of the KMT Left Wing, whose authority Chiang had particularly bypassed in thus taking the law into his own hands. For reasons of his own, Wang chose to "retire" from his KMT positions after this incident and soon left the country. But Chiang was not yet ready for a showdown with the communists; he needed continuing Soviet aid for his projected Northern Expedition to gain control of the entire country, and as a result, he openly rebuffed the efforts of the Western Hills Conference group to join forces with him. Moreover, in his public speeches following the March 20th Incident, Chiang expressed great admiration for the Comintern, and thus for the Russian if not the Chinese Communists. On May 22 and again on May 31, he insisted that "the Chinese Revolution should be under the direction of the Comintern," whose two identical principles were "to unite the oppressed peoples of the world" and to "unite the proletariat of the world."

The communists on their side were determined to maintain the "alliance" with the KMT at all costs, and outwardly pretended that the events of March 20 were of no real significance. Chiang was not content with a demonstration of power, however, and at a plenary session of the CEC of the KMT in May, 1926, he put through two resolutions seriously curbing the power of the communists. Henceforth, the proportion of communists in the higher executive committees of the KMT was not to exceed one-third, and no "members of any other party" were to serve as heads of departments in the central KMT organization. In the subsequent reassignment of party offices, Chiang himself took over the Organization Department, putting in as his secretary and eventual successor in the department his confidant, Ch'en Kuo-fu, later to be known as the reputed joint leader, with his brother, of the so-called CC Clique.

Although this reshuffling was a setback for the communists, it also indicated how far they had come on the road to power since the beginning of the alliance. Initially, the CPC had not even been recognized as a party within the KMT, and it was thus strictly subordinate to the KMT. Now, however, it was recognized as a party in its own right, and as a partner of the KMT. The *yung-Kung* policy had thus given way to one of *lien-Kung* —that is of cooperating with the CPC as a party.[9]

---

[9] For an exhaustive treatment of this question and of the events of the crucial years before 1927, see the highly informative work of Te-kong Tong, *Kuomintang-Communist Relations and the Russian Influence, 1924–27*. This study is available at the Columbia University Libraries.

In June, 1926, one month after these measures to strengthen his position in the party, Chiang launched his controversial expedition against the militarists of the North. From the time it was initially proposed, the Comintern and the CPC had voiced strong opposition to this campaign denouncing it as an adventure and insisting that the KMT forces were not yet ready to face the new situation in the North. As late as August 4, when the Northern Expedition had already scored some early successes, the official organ of the CPC Central Committee, the *Hsiang-tao (Guide) Weekly*, revealed (and the Mitarevsky documents confirm) that the Comintern's Commission of Chinese Affairs was still insisting that the KMT troops should not be moved out of Kwangtung. The communists changed their view only after it became apparent that they could not reverse the course of events.

During the Northern Expedition, the Communist Party workers devoted their full energies to the peasant and labor movements. Communist-led labor unions in Shanghai and Hankow successfully carried out major strikes in those areas. In Shanghai, which was virtually under their control, they even tried to prevent Chiang Kai-shek's Nationalist Revolutionary Army from occupying the city. In Hunan the peasant movement carried out a bloody agrarian revolt in which a large number of landlords and rich peasants lost their lives.

But the Chinese Communists and their Russian mentors throughout this period were facing an increasingly urgent problem in strategy: whether to turn to the worker and peasant movements, arm them, and organize them into soviets in order to carry through a successful revolutionary seizure of power independently of the bourgeois KMT, or to maintain instead the policy of "co-operation" with the KMT, hoping to take over the leadership of the revolution from it at the proper moment. It is known from a secret communist document later captured that a policy of separate and independent action of CPC units, presumably in the peasant and labor movements, had been decided upon as early as October, 1925, at an enlarged conference of one of the Party central organs. But the tactics of this "independent" action would necessarily be influenced by a decision to continue the alliance with the KMT, since even the KMT Left Wing contained many landowners, merchants, and businessmen who would be alienated by any extreme program.

The decision was taken by Stalin and Bukharin, and adopted by the Executive Committee of the Comintern in November, 1926, to maintain the alliance with the Left Wing of the KMT, and through it to work for a "Chinese October"—a seizure of revolutionary leadership comparable to that of the Russian Bolsheviks in 1917. Under this policy, verbal emphasis was given to the fostering of revolt among the workers and peasants, but in practice their actions were to be subordinated to and if necessary held in check by the need to carry on the struggle for leadership within the KMT. In the latter, the communists were to work to remove the KMT Right Wing from any power or influence. They also regarded Chiang Kai-shek, despite his conciliatory gestures toward the communists in the past, as a neo-Rightist, more dangerous than the old-guard Rightists because he had the Revolutionary Army under his command. Hence, Chiang's growing power had to be checked, and he became the first target of this Stalinist strategy of dividing and weakening the KMT.

Under Borodin's influence, the KMT Left Wing prevailed upon the Central Executive Committee of the party to move the capital from Canton to the Wuhan cities in December, 1926. Chiang, who was then on the Northern Expedition, would have preferred a move to Nanchang, where his own forces were centered and where the communists, in contrast to Wuhan, were relatively weak. At the next session of the CEC, in March, 1927—which Chiang did not attend—the Left Wing went a step farther by adopting a resolution instituting a presidium system for the government councils. Chiang, who had been chairman of both the Political and the Military Councils since the March 20th Incident and the retirement of Wang Ching-wei, was thus made subordinate to a collective leadership dominated by the Left Wing and the communists. Meanwhile the communists, who had control of military supplies and arsenals in both Canton and the Wuhan area, began to sabotage the supplying of Chiang's troops.

To meet this challenge to his own position, Chiang rushed his armies eastward, capturing Shanghai on March 22, 1927, and Nanking two days later. On March 26 Chiang's supporters, in a Provisional Emergency Session of the KMT's Central Supervisory Committee, adopted a resolution to the effect that the communist activities (which they said constituted evidence of a planned communist insurrection) should be held in check by armed force, and authorized Chiang to order the arrest of the important communists said to be involved.

At this stage, on April 1, Wang Ching-wei reached Shanghai after returning from abroad by way of Moscow. He had hopes of reuniting the contending factions of the KMT under his leadership. Chiang made the nominal gesture of recognizing Wang's leadership, while making clear that the direction of the Revolutionary Army remained in his own hands. But Wang and Chiang were unable to agree on the treatment of the Chinese Communists within the KMT. On April 6, therefore, Wang left secretly for Wuhan, accompanied by Ch'en Tu-hsiu, the leader of the CPC, after having issued with Ch'en a joint statement to the Chinese people assuring them of the continued co-operation between the two parties.

Chiang thereupon proceeded on his own course, determined to disarm the communists, particularly in the well-equipped Communist General Labor Union of Shanghai, and to go ahead with plans to set up a new KMT government at Nanking. In a bloody struggle which began on the morning of April 12 and lasted for four days, Chiang ordered the arrest of all communists in the area under his control and the execution of the more important leaders. The purge quickly spread from Shanghai to other cities, including Hangchow, Nanking, and Canton. Among the executed communists was the son of Ch'en Tu-hsiu. Chou En-lai, who was arrested in Shanghai, managed to escape with the aid of a Whampoa cadet. The incident has since been bitterly denounced by the communists as the "April 12th massacre."

Shocked and alarmed by this open break with the communists, the KMT government of Wuhan, headed by Wang, expelled Chiang and the other Shanghai leaders from the party. Chiang's arrest was ordered and on April 17 the Wuhan government offered a reward of $250,000 for his head. Chiang countered these hostile moves on April 18 by formally establishing a "Nanking government" in direct opposition to that of Wuhan. Thus, the split between Wuhan and Nanking, which was master-minded and precipitated by the communists, was now a *fait accompli.*

In the interval before the schism in the KMT became final, and before the news of Chiang's drive against the communists had reached Moscow, the Comintern under Stalin's leadership continued to insist on co-operation with the KMT as the right path to a "Chinese October." As for Chiang himself, Stalin still hoped to use him toward this end. As late as April 5 (according to Harold Isaacs in *The Tragedy of the Chinese Revolution*), Stalin was saying of Chiang and his Right Wing supporters that "they have to be utilized to the end, squeezed out like a lemon, and then flung away."

In accordance with the Comintern's instructions, therefore, the Fifth Congress of the CPC, meeting in Wuhan on May 1, 1927, officially adopted a program of continued co-operation with the Left Wing KMT headed by Wang Ching-wei. According to the Comintern's directive, the CPC was also to work out a program of its own for taking over the revolutionary leadership from the bourgeois elements within the Wuhan KMT.

One major obstacle, however, blocked their path. It arose from their effort to "carry water on both shoulders"—to maintain the link with the KMT and at the same time to advance their own cause through promoting revolutionary activity among workers and peasants. In particular, the heart of the communist program was the nationalization of land, which was bitterly opposed by the KMT leaders, supported as they were by many landowners. Hence, Borodin and Ch'en Tu-hsiu decided to modify the communist agrarian policy in order to make concessions to the KMT Left Wing. This retreat seems to have been supported even by Mao Tse-tung, who was then directing the peasant movement in Hunan. Although Mao, a decade later, said that he had opposed this decision, the fact is that as Chairman of the All-China Peasants Association, he did issue an order at the time aimed at preventing any excessive action on the part of the peasants.

The communists' efforts to maintain the KMT link led them to even more drastic modifications of their own revolutionary program, as they endeavored to hold in check the "direct action" undertaken by the workers and peasants in the communist-controlled mass movements. Communist uprisings in Hunan Province, for example, had led to the May 21st Incident (*Ma-jih Sse-pien*), in which the trade union and peasant association centers in Changsha and the surrounding territory were occupied, and the communists and their supporters were slaughtered wholesale by the Wuhan KMT forces headed by Hsü Ke-ch'iang, a regimental commander. A peasant army gathered to march against Hsü in Changsha, but again the CPC Central Committee in Wuhan decided not to risk an open break with the KMT Left, and to wait patiently for a "committee of inquiry" from the Wuhan government to settle the whole matter. That committee, however, failed to accomplish its mission. In the outcome, then, the communists could only petition the Nationalist government of Wang Ching-wei to send a "punitive expedition" to deal with the "rebellious" KMT officials in Hunan. But the Wuhan officials took no such action, accepting the view that the whole incident was the result of an initial "reign of terror" in the rural areas of Hunan, imposed by the communist-led workers-and-peasants movement.

In an effort to get Wang to throw in his lot with the communists and turn against the KMT officials and military leaders responsible for the May 21st Incident, M. N. Roy, an Indian representative of the Comintern then in Wuhan, precipitated the final break between the two parties. Shortly before, Stalin had issued a set of instructions which carried to extremes his policy of carrying water on both shoulders. The land policy of the communists and the program of direct action by the peasants were to be further toned down in order to retain the now tenuous link with the KMT Left. But at the same time, a huge new army of peasants and workers was to be created, apparently outside the control of the KMT and its "unreliable generals," and the CEC of the KMT was in effect to be brought under communist control. Roy, apparently hoping that the threat of withdrawal of Comintern support would prove persuasive, showed these instructions directly to Wang on June 1, 1927. The latter, of course, realized that further co-operation with the communists could now lead only to the complete displacement of his own faction from leadership.

Shocked by this conspiracy, Wang secretly convened the loyal KMT leaders. After a month of preparation, the CEC of the KMT on July 13 formally ordered the communists to withdraw from the Wuhan KMT and from the Wuhan Nationalist Government, although the CPC was still recognized as a legal political party. Shortly thereafter, at about the time of the communists' August 1st uprising in Nanchang (to be discussed shortly), the Political Council of the KMT voted formally to outlaw the CPC as a party. This action and the expulsion from the KMT of the remaining communist leaders, including T'an P'ing-shan, Lin Tsu-han, Chang Kuo-t'ao, and Mao Tse-tung, were confirmed by the Fourth Plenum of the Second CEC of the KMT on February 6, 1928.

The CPC at this juncture was not only isolated from the "ally" on which it had depended for so long, but was also badly demoralized. One of its first reactions to the debacle—again prompted by Stalin and the Comintern—was to fix the blame and punish the culprits "responsible" for the bankruptcy of its policies. At an emergency meeting of the CC of the CPC in Hankow [10] on August 7, 1927, the Secretary General of the Party, Ch'en Tu-hsiu, with whom the communist movement in China had been identified from the very beginning, was singled out as responsible for the total failure of the CPC, and was condemned for his "rightist opportunism." Hu Ch'iao-mu's official Party history notes that "this conference thoroughly rectified Ch'en Tu-hsiu's capitulationism and removed him from leadership," but complains that he "did not admit his mistakes." His failure to do so led to his final expulsion from the Party in 1929, along with T'an P'ing-shan and other former leaders. [11] Yet on leaving the Communist Party, he did admit one "mistake"—which was to have been a faithful lieutenant carrying out Stalin's policies, instead of adopting the more promising line of action then being advocated within the Comintern by Trotsky. His parting words, in a letter addressed to all members of the CPC on December 10, 1929, suggest another view of the final "responsibility" for the utter defeat of the CPC:

I, who was not clear in perception or decisive in upholding my opinions, sincerely carried out the opportunist policy of the Communist International, and became the instrument of the narrow Stalinist faction. I could not save the Chinese

---

[10] A few sources locate the meeting at Lushan, in the mountain resort area north of Nanchang, in northern Kiangsi, or at Kiukiang, north of Lushan.

[11] Ch'en subsequently was identified with the Trotskyites in China, and for a time attempted without success to form an oppositionist party to the CPC. He was arrested by the KMT government in 1932, imprisoned for five years, and then allowed to live under guard in retirement until his death in 1942.

Communist Party nor the revolution. For this, the other comrades and I are responsible. . . . We should recognize . . . that all opportunist policies at present and in the past come from the Communist International, which should bear the responsibility.

Aside from parceling out blame, the historic August 7th Conference (which some say was presided over by Lominadze, the Comintern representative) faced the problem of deciding upon the immediate course of action to save the revolution. To this end, an important resolution was adopted (and confirmed by an Enlarged Plenary Session of the CC in November, 1927) "to organize armed uprisings in all the important provinces." In short, in its effort to carry out a "Chinese October," the CPC could no longer hide under the banner of the KMT; now it was forced to put to the test its claim to leadership of the proletariat and the peasant masses.

There were three broad elements to which the communists could look for support in the new policy of armed uprisings; the army, the peasants, and the workers. The latter two particularly had at one time flocked into the mass movements organized by the communists and provided them with a source of great potential strength. But now all three in turn failed completely as revolutionary instruments.

Typical of the army response was the revolt attempted in Nanchang even before the August 7th Conference. Under the secret instigation of Chou En-lai, Chang Kuo-t'ao, and other communist leaders, between 20 and 30 thousand troops of Chiang's National Revolutionary Army (then engaged in the Northern Expedition) staged an uprising in that city on August 1, setting up a Revolutionary Committee. Commanded by Yeh T'ing and Ho Lung, they were joined in the revolt by Chu Teh, then a regimental commander, and two companies of his troops. But by August 8, the city had been recaptured for the KMT by General Chang Fa-k'uei, and the rebellious troops were forced to flee southward, where they were defeated and dispersed in northeastern Kwangtung Province.

A series of peasant uprisings also followed the decision of the August 7th Conference. The most significant of these revolts was that in Hunan Province led by Mao Tse-tung. Sent back to Hunan by the Central Committee to direct the reorganization of the Provincial Committee and to carry out the so-called Autumn Harvest Uprising, Mao gathered a main force of some 2,000 men and on September 8 opened his attack in an area which included Pingkiang, Liuyang, Liling, and Chuchow. After a bitter defeat, Mao was forced to retreat with remnants of his followers, numbering about 400, to Chingkangshan in neighboring Kiangsi Province, where he established a rural soviet that was to be the base for his own later rise to power. But at the moment of defeat, he was rewarded with a severe reprimand for his conduct. In a resolution adopted by the Central Committee on November 14, 1927, he was formally charged with the responsibility for the mistakes committed by the Hunan Provincial Committee and for failure to reorganize it properly. Mao was thereupon dismissed from reserve membership in the Provisional Politburo of the CC as well as from the Hunan Provincial Committee. [12]

In the ranks of urban labor, too, the drive for a "Chinese October" based upon an upsurge of the masses failed miserably. In Canton, where the communists had built up a strong labor movement in the earlier days of the cooperation period, they now thought they saw a favorable opportunity for an uprising. But in the attempt, on December 11, the workers were apathetic and failed to rally to the side of the insurgents, while the Nationalist troops were forewarned. Hence, the effort collapsed, and several important Chinese Communist leaders, together with a number of Russian comrades, lost their lives.

A bitter critic of the Stalinist policy of this period, Harold Isaacs, in his work on the Chinese Revolution has spoken of the Canton uprising in terms that might well apply to the entire program of direct action undertaken after the final split with the KMT:

This program, launched in an hour of hopeless desperation, was its own comment on the whole previous course. In the days of sweeping mass power, the communists had confirmed themselves to the limited and timid reforms approved by the Kuomintang and had in the end suffered disastrously from their lack of boldness. Now, when they were a handful venturing in the presence of an inert mass to attack well-armed and well-entrenched reaction, they were ready to speak in bold terms that went unheard amid the din of bloody repression.

Once more, the "correctness" of Stalin's policy had to be saved by finding local scapegoats for its failures. This time, the chief victim was the energetic young Russian-trained communist, Ch'ü Ch'iu-pai, who had

[12] The resolution of the Central Committee was published in the *Kuo-wen* (*National News*) *Weekly* and *The Communist International* in 1927. The story of Mao's demotion from the Politburo has remained obscure. But Karl A. Wittfogel has drawn the authors' attention to a record of this event in a secret communist document seized by the Wuhan Garrison Headquarters on December 5, 1927, and subsequently published in the *Kuo-wen Weekly*, vol. 5 no. 3 (January 15, 1928), pp. 5–7.

There is also a discussion of the "Resolutions of the November Plenum of the CC of the CPC" in the publication of the Sun Yat-sen University in Moscow, *Materialy po Kitaiskomu Voprosu* (*Materials on the Chinese Problem*), 1928, no. 10. Though containing no explicit reference to Mao's demotion, it stressed that in the series of peasant uprisings in Hunan, Hupeh, and Kiangsu Provinces, the Party leadership had exhibited shameful vacillation and indecision, which was the principal cause of the Party's failure. The resolution called for all Party organizations to institute drastic measures to rid the Party leadership of all "opportunistic elements."

succeeded Ch'en Tu-hsiu. Where Ch'en had been guilty of "rightist capitulationism," Ch'ü was now criticized for "Left putschism." Wherever the error, however, the result was disastrous for the Chinese Communists. After the break with the Wuhan Government, the CPC had been forced to remove its headquarters to Shanghai, where it could operate under the shelter and aegis of the foreign concessions. And the Sixth Congress of the Party, meeting in July, 1928, symbolized the utter rout of the communist efforts for hegemony in the revolution—in being held completely off Chinese soil, in far-away Moscow. Symbolically, too, Mao Tse-tung, who was re-elected to the Central Committee, was not among the 170 delegates present, but was nursing his small forces in the mountainous region between Hunan and Kiangsi Provinces, remote not only from Moscow but also from the new central Party headquarters in Shanghai.

DEVELOPING REVOLUTIONARY BASES:
THE RISE OF MAO (1927–35)

The Sixth Congress in Moscow, at which Bukharin represented the Comintern, elected as the new Secretary General, Hsiang Chung-fa, a former boatman still scarcely able to read and write. The new Central Committee included Li Li-san, Chou En-lai, Chang Kuo-t'ao, Hsiang Ying, Mao Tse-tung, and others. Because of the intellectual incompetence of the new Secretary General, the actual direction of the Party Central[13] in Shanghai and the implementation of the Party line fell to Li Li-san, a member of the Politburo and head of the Party's Propaganda Department.

Li's policy, known as the "Li-san Line," was essentially a continuation of the bankrupt policy of armed uprisings. However, the emphasis was no longer on local guerrilla actions throughout the country, but on large-scale military campaigns directed toward capturing the urban centers, and especially Wuhan. Li's armies succeeded for a time in occupying the cities of Changsha and Kian, but on the whole, his campaigns failed miserably and only intensified and inflamed anti-communist feelings among the Chinese people. Within the rank and file of the Party, too, there was open opposition to Li's policy, headed by Ch'en Shao-yü (Wang Ming), a Russian-trained young communist intellectual. Pavel Mif, the Comintern representative in China, gave the decisive blow to Li's efforts in his unfavorable report to Moscow. In March, 1931, Li was ordered to Moscow for "consultations." He thus disappeared from the Chinese scene until

---

[13] The term, Party Central, is familiar to Chinese intellectuals as an abbreviated reference to the Party Central Committee or the leading members acting in its name. It is also sometimes referred to as the Party center.

the last days of World War II, when he accompanied the Soviet forces into Manchuria just prior to the surrender of Japan.

The new leader of the Party, Ch'en Shao-yü, officially succeeded to the post of Secretary General in June, 1931, when Hsiang Chung-fa was arrested and put to death by the Nanking government of Chiang Kai-shek. His accession marked the dominance, in the Shanghai Party Central, of the so-called "returned students group" of young Chinese Bolsheviks recently returned from Moscow. This group included Liu Shao-ch'i, Wang Chia-hsiang, Chang Wen-t'ien, Ch'en Yün, Jen Pi-shih, Ch'in Pang-hsien (Po Ku), Li Fu-ch'un, and others who were later to become prominent in the Chinese Communist regime. But Ch'en himself was more a Marxist dogmatist than an energetic revolutionary organizer, and his associates were ambitious but inexperienced idealists. Whatever the brilliance of their theoretical discussions, the failure of their several military uprisings left the Shanghai Party center with little real power to direct communist activities in China. Moreover, it had no significant resources apart from the support provided by the Comintern. The only important source of funds within China lay in the soviets which had developed in Kiangsi Province and were under the control of Mao Tse-tung.

The general powerlessness of the Party Central in Shanghai, stemming from its continued efforts to promote revolutionary seizures of power in the cities and to challenge the KMT armed forces directly, coupled with the rising power of Mao in the Kiangsi Soviet Area, led to sharp differences of opinion within the Party and a new crisis in its leadership. As a result, in 1932 Ch'en Shao-yü was in effect exiled to Moscow, as the CPC representative to the Comintern. His successor, Ch'in Pang-hsien, had little if any real power in his own right, and even less when, in 1933, the Shanghai Party Central finally agreed to transfer its activities to Juichin, the capital of Mao's "Chinese Soviet Republic" in Kiangsi. In January, 1934, the Central Committee in turn replaced Ch'in by Chang Wen-t'ien, who was even more of a figurehead. It was not until the Tsunyi Conference in January, 1935, after the Long March was under way, that an enlarged session of the Politburo united the nominal and the actual leadership of the Party in the hands of one person, Mao Tse-tung. In a sense, this act symbolized the final liquidation of the policy which had led to the debacle of 1927 and the confused and futile efforts at sporadic revolutionary uprisings which followed. It also signalized the full emergence of a more realistic policy, embodied in the leadership of Mao Tse-tung.

In the official Party history of Hu Ch'iao-mu, the leadership of the CPC during this period after the Sixth Congress is criticized for its failure to "understand that tactically the Party should conduct a retreat, and especially that the key question was the necessity of shifting the center of the Party's activity from the cities, where the enemy was comparatively strong, to the rural districts, where the enemy was comparatively weak." Li Li-san is characterized as a "Left opportunist," and his successors, Ch'en Shao-yü and Ch'in Pang-hsien, as members of a "new Left faction" whose error was that they "continued to carry out the adventurist policies which isolated them from the masses," while they "thrust aside" Mao's leadership even after the move from Shanghai to Juichin. (Liu Shao-ch'i, it should be noted, was carefully excepted from this charge of Left adventurism.) Meanwhile, Hu notes, "the problems that had not been correctly solved by the Sixth Party Congress were solved later by Comrade Mao Tse-tung," whose "completely reliable" leadership was finally secured with the removal of the last "Left opportunists" at the Tsunyi Conference.

The essence of Mao's policy, Hu noted, was the recognition that "for the time being there was no way to win victory in the cities." Hence, it was necessary "to encircle and subsequently to seize the cities occupied by the counterrevolution, by means of armed, revolutionary rural districts." The implementation of this policy took two major lines: the development of a disciplined, trained, and equipped Red Army able to withstand the attacks of the KMT troops with their bases in the cities and in command of the main communication lines; and the organization of state power in whatever areas could be brought under communist control, in the form of soviets following the model of the Russian Revolution. The hope was that eventually all these soviets could be brought together in a single government for all China (through a congress of soviets with its executive committee), supported and defended by a unified Red Army.

After the failure of his peasant uprising in Hunan in September, 1927, Mao had fled with his remaining forces to Chingkangshan in southern Kiangsi. There he managed to bring into his ranks certain gangs of local bandits under Wang Tso and Yüan Wen-ts'ai, and devoted himself to the organization and strengthening of his military units in the secluded and mountainous Hunan-Kiangsi border region.[14] To the men under his command he gave the designation of the First Division of the Chinese Workers' and Peasants' Red Army, thus officially establishing what was to be the basis for the communist drive to final victory over the next two decades.

In April, 1928, Mao was joined by the remnant troops which Chu Teh had managed to salvage from the original uprising in Nanchang. He thus had an army of more than 10,000 men with a total of some 2,000 rifles. These he later reorganized and reconstituted as the Fourth Chinese

---

[14] A "border region," as defined by Mao, was an area between two or more provinces, where the military and administrative control of the provincial authorities was at its weakest. Such military "vacuums" proved extremely useful to the communists as bases of operation.

Workers' and Peasants' Red Army, with himself as political commissar and Chu Teh as military commander. In all, between 1927 and 1931, more than twenty-six "Red Armies" were organized by the communists in various provinces of China.[15]

By 1930, according to Hu Ch'iao-mu, the Red Army as a whole had grown to 60,000 men, half of whom were in the area controlled by Mao, and the others in "revolutionary bases" which had extended to Fukien, Anhwei, Honan, Shensi, Kansu, Kwangtung, and other provinces. The growth of the Red Army, needless to say, did not go unchallenged by the forces of the Kuomintang. In July and August, 1928, a joint "annihilation campaign" was directed against Mao's forces in Chingkangshan by the provincial forces of Kiangsi and Hunan. In January of the following year, the three provinces of Kiangsi, Hunan, and Kwangtung joined in a campaign against Mao, and the following month sent another attack against his new capital at Juichin. In November, 1930, the forces of Chiang's Nationalist government at Nanking began the first of a series of "extermination drives" against the so-called Central Soviet Area controlled by Mao. It took five such drives, extending over a period of four years, to break the power of the communists in the Central Soviet Area. According to communist sources, the first three—engaging respectively one hundred, two hundred, and three hundred thousand KMT troops—were "decisively repulsed by Red Army forces, with the capture of great numbers of KMT troops and supplies." The fact that much more massive KMT attacks were finally necessary to break the communist defensive and retaliatory strength was a sufficient testimony not only to the size and quality of the Red Army at this time, but also to the strength of the soviet regimes which had been set up in the communist-occupied areas.

The same Enlarged Conference of the CC which in November, 1927, disciplined Mao Tse-tung for his failure in the Autumn Harvest Uprising in Hunan Province, also proclaimed that henceforth the policy of the CPC would be "to organize soviets in place of the former peasants'· committees." The first soviet had indeed been established on November 1, 1927, in Haifeng and Lufeng counties (Kwangtung Province), by the main body of troops driven out of Nanchang following their unsuccessful insurrection there. The Hailufeng Soviet was short-lived, as was the Canton

[15] Among the more notable of these, in addition to the Fourth Army under Chu and Mao, were the First Red Army in the Honan-Hupeh-Anhwei border region, under Chang Kuo-t'ao and Hsü Hsiang-ch'ien; the Second Red Army led by Ho Lung in western Hupeh; the Third, under Lo Ping-hui in western Kiangsi; the Fifth, under P'eng Teh-huai in Hunan; and the Twenty-Sixth, under Liu Chih-tan and Kao Kang in northern Shensi. Of these the Fourth and Fifth Red Armies were the largest units; the smaller ones never exceeded a few hundred men in the period down to 1931.

Commune which followed it in December, 1927. But from 1927 on, as the Red Army began to increase in size and power, its growth was paralleled in every area under its control by the formation of soviets.

The growth of these soviet areas was not entirely a matter of conquest by the Red Army units. The communists also made a much more direct appeal to the peasants through their land reform program than they had allowed themselves to do during their "cooperation" with the KMT. In the Hunan-Kiangsi border region, for example, Mao carried out a radical land reform in which there was no more equivocal talk of "confiscation with or without compensation," or "sparing the land of military officers," or checking the "overzealous action" of the peasantry. Landlords and rich peasants by the thousands lost their lives, and their land and other holdings were confiscated outright by the soviet.

At first these soviet areas were essentially local in character, though some of them spread over several counties located in more than one province. Their progress from local to provincial to ostensibly a national level may be illustrated by the organizations under the control of Mao Tse-tung. In August, 1929, Mao and Chu created the Northeast Kiangsi Soviet regime, embracing several counties of the province. On February 7, 1930, the Red Army in southwest Kiangsi convoked a conference at which a Kiangsi Provincial Soviet was set up in T'ungku. At the same time the conference established a nation-wide Chinese Worker-Peasant Revolutionary Committee with Mao as chairman. The Provincial Soviet, however, by no means held unchallenged control of the entire Kiangsi Province. It was not until 1931, when the Japanese invasion of Manchuria had effectively diverted the attention of the Nanking government, that Mao succeeded in organizing a large-scale soviet in the Hunan-Kiangsi border region. Finally on the fourteenth anniversary of the Russian October Revolution, November 7, 1931, the First National Congress of Soviets was convoked in Juichin, the capital of Mao's Kiangsi Soviet. It formally proclaimed the establishment of a Chinese Soviet Republic, embracing all the soviet areas throughout China proper.[16]

[16] The early history of the soviets includes such short-lived examples as the Hailufeng and Jenhua soviets in Kwangtung, the Liling and Pingkiang soviets in Hunan, and the Lungchow soviet in Kwangsi. At the First National (All-China) Congress of Soviets in Juichin, the following were the principal soviet areas represented: the Kiangsi (or Central) Soviet Area, the West Fukien Soviet Area, the Hunan-Hupeh-Kiangsi Border Soviet Area, The Northeast Kiangsi Soviet Area, the West Hupeh-Hunan Soviet Area, and the Hupeh-Honan-Anhwei Border Soviet Area.

By the time of the Second All-China Congress of Soviets, meeting in January, 1934, the Red Army had withdrawn from the Hupeh-Honan-Anhwei Soviet Area. (One of the authors had an opportunity to visit this area in 1933, shortly after the withdrawal of the communists.) In its place were the Eastern Szechwan Soviet Area and the Shensi-Kansu Soviet Area—both created in 1932–33.

Over six hundred delegates attended this congress; more than 90 per cent represented workers and peasants. Before its adjournment, it adopted a Draft Constitution, a land law, a labor law, and resolutions on economic policies and other matters. It also elected a 64-member Central Executive Committee, which included Mao, Chu Teh, Chou En-lai, Hsiang Ying, Liu Shao-ch'i, Jen Pi-shih, Ch'ü Ch'iu-pai, Wang Chia-hsiang, and Ch'en Shao-yü (the last not yet removed from his post as Party Secretary General). The CEC of the Republic in turn, on November 27, elected Mao Tse-tung Chairman and Hsiang Ying and Chang Kuo-t'ao as Vice Chairmen.

At the time of this First Congress of Soviets and at the conclusion of the third KMT "annihiliation campaign," the territorial bases of the CPC comprised about 300 counties, scattered through 11 of the 18 provinces of China proper and making up roughly one-sixth of the area of China proper. The total population of the soviet areas, according to communist sources, was over 60 million. Of these areas, the most important by far was the Central Soviet area, with a total population of 15 million and a territorial extent of 45 to 50 counties altogether—about 30 'in the southern half of Kiangsi Province, 10 in southwestern Fukien, 5 in northwestern Kwantung, and 7 in Eastern Hunan. Another area of later significance was formed only at the end of 1931 when, as a result of the peasant uprising in Suiyuan Province, the Shensi-Shansi Soviet was created.[17]

It was chiefly against the Central Soviet Area that the KMT annihilation campaigns were directed. The third campaign, in July, 1931, even with 300,000 troops and under the personal supervision of Chiang, had been unable to defeat the communist power. For the fourth campaign starting in June, 1932, Chiang and Ho Ying-ch'ing were reported to have employed a total of 500,000 men, broadening the scope of the attack beyond the Central Soviet Area. Although this campaign lasted until March, 1933, the decisive break came in October, 1932, when the Red Army was compelled to withdraw from both the Hupeh-Honan-Anhwei Soviet Area and

---

In these areas the communists maintained their own army, police, and bureaucracy. In addition, they had their own currency, with banknotes bearing the images of Marx and Lenin, and their own Red Post Office and postage stamps.

For a detailed description of these soviet areas, see G. Erenburg, *Sovetskii Kitai* (*Soviet China*), 2nd ed., (Moscow, Partizdat, 1934), and P. Mif, ed., *Sovety v Kitae* (*Soviets in China*) (Translated from the German and issued by the China Research Institute of the Communist Academy) (Moscow, Partizdat, 1933). For an authorized interpretation concerning the background and activities of the soviet areas in general, see P. Mif, *15 Let Geroicheskoi Bor'by* (*Fifteen Years of the Heroic Struggle*) (Moscow, Partizdat, 1936).

[17] According to one report, a predecessor of this soviet, the so-called Wu-tzu Soviet Area, had been formed in Shensi Province in 1927.

from the Hunghu Soviet Area in southern Hupeh. These forces first evacuated to Hsich'uan and then on January 23, 1933, entered Szechwan from the north through Chenpa in southern Shensi Province.

Chiang's fifth campaign began in October, 1933, reportedly employing a force of one million men and 200 planes. Moscow, meanwhile, was not neglecting the situation in China and the increasing threat to the communist position there. The Executive Committee of the Comintern in mid-1933 issued a directive to "consolidate and extend the domain of the Chinese Soviets." In response to this directive and in an effort to mobilize their full resources to meet Chiang's fifth campaign—which included a tight economic blockade as well as the powerful military effort—the Chinese Communists held their Second National Congress of Soviets at Juichin on January 22, 1934. Mao was said to have presented a report to this congress calling for a more aggressive policy, with stepped-up mobilization and production to meet the dual threat of the Nationalists. In addition, the Congress proclaimed, apparently under the influence of the Moscow-directed central leadership and the Returned Student group, that the "Republic" would maintain its "pure proletarian" [i.e., worker-peasant] character.

This policy of proletarian purity had already been applied just prior to the Second Congress of Soviets, when a group of KMT Left-Wingers, with the support of the famous anti-Japanese 19th Route Army, broke away from Nanking and organized a People's Government in Fuchow, the capital of Fukien. Had the communists reached an agreement to co-operate with and support the Fuchow government, they could have strengthened their own position considerably, receiving very valuable assistance in their fight against the Nationalist encirclement. But instead, they chose to maintain the "pure proletarian" line, rejecting the Fuchow regime because it lacked the necessary proletarian base and was too Rightist in orientation. As a result, the Fuchow People's Government soon collapsed, and Chiang was free to concentrate his forces in the campaign against the communists. Years later, in his interviews with Edgar Snow (published in *Red Star over China*), Mao spoke of this decision of the CPC as an error in strategy, but placed the responsibility for the error on the official Party leadership, which at that time still centered in Ch'in Pang-hsien and the Returned Student group.

The official leadership of the Party Central also comes in for blame, in Hu Ch'iao-mu's treatment, for the military disasters leading up to the Long March, because of its "completely wrong military line of remaining solely on the defensive and other wrong policies." In March, 1934, the KMT campaign was intensified against the Central Soviet Area, resulting in the capture of Shahsien, T'aining, Kweihwa, and Lungyen. Throughout the spring and summer, the KMT forces continued to tighten their encirclement, taking such strategic county capitals as Yungting and Liench'eng. In the autumn, with the Nationalists ready to draw the noose still tighter, Moscow radioed instructions for the Chinese Communists to evacuate their forces and seek safety elsewhere—as far distant as Outer Mongolia, if necessary. Ch'in Pang-hsien and Chou En-lai, Director of the CPC Political Department, hastily formulated plans for an immediate effort to break through the Nationalist blockade, even though no specific destination had been decided upon. The immediate issue was one of survival. Thus on October 15, 1934, the principal body of the Red Army, totaling nearly 130,000, along with the Party officials in Juichin, moved out on the now famous Long March. Elsewhere, except in the soviet areas of northern Shensi Province, the Red Army units likewise abandoned their territorial bases and fought their way to join the main force.

The main body of the Red Army followed the desperate route along which a revolutionary general of the T'aip'ing Rebellion, Shih Ta-k'ai, had traveled and vanished nearly seventy years before. At first the Nationalists drove the communists toward Kwangsi province, hoping that the local war lords in southwestern China would thus be weakened or destroyed in trying to stop the communist encroachments. This plan failed, allegedly because the Kwangsi generals reached an agreement with the Reds. The Nationalists then attempted to divert the Red column toward Szechwan or Kweichow with the same goal in mind—a move which proved advantageous to the Reds in allowing an easier escape route to the north. By December, 1934, the principal Red forces had entered Kweichow Province. The following month, after fierce fighting at the Wu River, they captured Tsunyi on January 13.

By this time it had become imperative to make some decision about the ultimate destination of the march. At Tsunyi, as already noted, an Enlarged Session of the Central Politburo was held, not only to remove the "Left" adventurists and the "Returned Students" from power and elect Mao Tse-tung to the leading position, but also to consider the question of destination. Northern Shensi, then under the joint control of Kao Kang and Liu Chih-tan, was selected as the terminus of the long trek. It was an area relatively remote from the Nationalist center of power and nearer to the outposts of the invading Japanese. Apparently the Chinese Communists hoped, through resisting the Japanese and even provoking them into a general war, to win popular support for themselves and secure relief from the unremitting KMT pressure. The proximity of northern Shensi to the Soviet Union and its satellite, Outer Mongolia, may also have been a consideration in its favor. Kao Kang had restored Red Army rule in the area in December, 1933, and was carrying on in the surrounding areas the kind of guerrilla and mobile warfare of which Mao Tse-tung had become the chief exponent.

For the next few months, the Red force marched and counter-marched in the Kweichow-Yünnan region. In April, however, it headed westward nearly to Huili in Sikang Province, and then north toward the Tatu River. At the end of May it reached the Luting Iron-Chain Bridge across the upper Tatu in eastern Sikang. Ascending and crossing over the Chiehchin Mountains, and skirting the Tahsüeh Mountains it penetrated the remote northwestern part of Szechwan, marched north through mountainous regions, and early in July reached Maoerhkai, near the Szechwan-Sikang border. Here the troops were joined by Hsü Hsiang-ch'ien and Chang Kuo-t'ao, who had moved toward this rendezvous since their defeat in the Hupeh-Honan-Anhwei Soviet Area in October, 1932.

At Maoerhkai a second historic conference took place, in which the question of the final destination was again raised. At Tsunyi, Chang Kuo-t'ao—through telegraphic communication—had thrown his support to Mao on the leadership question. But at Maoerhkai, he proposed that the new Red Army base should be set up in Sikang Province, which borders Tibet, or in Sinkiang Province, directly adjoining the Soviet Union. Mao held out for the original decision for Shensi, and his view carried. The rift opening between Chang and Mao at this conference later led to an open break between the two and to Chang's defection from the Party in 1938.

Finally on October 22, 1935, having separated once more from Chang's column, Mao's forces reached their destination in northern Shensi. There they were later joined by the troops of Jen Pi-shih, Ho Lung, Hsü Hsiang-ch'ien, and Chang Kuo-t'ao. In the full year of the trek, according to Hu Ch'iao-mu, they had marched 25,000 li (over 8,000 miles) and had crossed almost impassable mountains and steppes. At the end of their journey, they settled down for a time around the small town of Wuch'icheng in Paoan County. But after the seizure of Yenan, they transferred their headquarters to that city in December, 1936, where it remained until the city fell to the Nationalist troops in 1947, during the civil war.

THE "UNITED FRONT" AND WARTIME EXPANSION (1935–45)

Throughout the Long March, and particularly after the Maoerhkai Conference in July, 1935, the Chinese Communist leaders apparently realized that their military position was badly deteriorating, and that a prolonged civil war in China would mean their eventual extermination. Perhaps for other reasons as well, they began to see the desirability of an outward reconciliation with Chiang Kai-shek, in order to be able to capitalize once more on a great popular movement which would allow them to make another bid for the support of the broad masses. In the words of Hu Ch'iao-mu, "the tide of the revolution was once more on the rise." The increasing encroachments of the Japanese against China, which Chiang's regime had been forced to neglect to some extent while trying first to suppress the communists and win a degree of internal solidarity, offered the desired opportunity for such a broad national movement.

Hence, while they were still at Maoerhkai, and at a time when Japanese action in Suiyuan Province was being intensified, the communists decided upon a new policy. On August 1, 1935, the CPC leaders inaugurated their historic policy of an Anti-Japanese National United Front, in an official proclamation urging all countrymen, in spite of differences of political opinions and interests, to "unite as one man" against the common enemy. To Chiang, they made a special appeal, promising full co-operation with him, if only he would halt the fight "against his own people." More concretely, they called for the organization of a National Defense Government and an anti-Japanese allied army for national salvation.

It is probably no mere coincidence that just at this period radio communication was re-established between the Chinese Communists and Moscow. The Seventh World Congress of the Comintern had opened on July 25; and on August 2, Georgi Dimitrov had advocated before that body a policy of a global united front. While the Chinese announcement anticipated Dimitrov's by one day, the two probably reflected a parallel development, or more likely the simultaneous implementation of a policy previously agreed upon by the Moscow leadership. Certainly the new line was an abrupt change for the CPC. When the Fukien People's Government had first proposed an anti-Japanese United National Front to the communists in 1933, they rejected it on the grounds that even in an anti-Japanese campaign they would work only with the proletariat, not co-operating with any "bourgeois" factions. Early in 1934, it is true, in the "April 10th appeal," the communists had themselves called for an Anti-Imperialist United Front. But in reality they were using anti-Japanese slogans in order to attack the Nanking government for "capitulating" and selling out to Japan as in the Tangku Agreement. Following this anti-Nanking bent, the "Chinese Soviet Government," even as late as June 15, 1935, had "sentenced Chiang Kai-shek to death."

To give effect to the new policy, a United Front Work Department was set up within the CPC. And once the communists were established in northern Shensi, toward the end of 1935, the Central Politburo reconvened and issued another appeal for a united front. Again in January, 1936, the

"Chinese Soviet Government" sent out a circular telegram urging the convocation of an Anti-Japanese National Salvation Delegates' Congress. During this period, however, pending a favorable response from the Nationalists, the communists were still anti-Chiang as well as anti-Japanese. It has even been suggested that they wished, through fighting the Japanese, to provoke them into extending their invasion of northern China, thus creating a national crisis which would engage and weaken Chiang's forces, causing the Nationalists to relax their anti-communist efforts. If so, this stratagem was initially defeated when the communist commander Liu Chih-tan was killed by the KMT forces while on his way "to fight the Japanese."

With Japanese and puppet Manchoukuo troops allegedly creating disturbances along the borders of Outer Mongolia and the USSR as early as February 1, 1936, and with the expression of Japan's hostile intentions in the Anti-Comintern Pact of November 25, 1936, the Soviet Union found it to her interest to promote, for the time being, a united China capable of resisting Japan effectively. Accordingly, the CPC shifted its emphasis to stirring up anti-Japanese feeling among the Nationalist troops, particularly among the Manchurian troops under the "Young Marshal," Chang Hsüeh-liang. Out of this agitation for a more vigorous Nationalist effort against the Japanese came the Sian Incident.

The son of Chang Tso-lin, the former anti-communist Manchurian war lord, General Chang in 1936 was one of Chiang's deputies and Commander-in-Chief of the Bandit [Communist] Suppression campaign in the Northwest. But as the Japanese invasion became more serious toward the end of 1936, Chang became increasingly bitter against Chiang's anti-communist policy, and charged his superior with being too old-fashioned and "rightist." On December 12, 1936, therefore, he "kidnapped" Chiang, holding him prisoner in Sian. Through the intervention of Moscow,[18] Chiang's life was spared and he was released—but on condition that the anti-communist war was to be terminated and a new truce between the KMT and the CPC was to be worked out.

---

[18] Moscow made its position known through the official communist press. An editorial in *Pravda* and an "International Observation" in *Izvestiia*, both of December 14, 1936, denounced Chang's "insolent rebellion." His demand for cooperation between the Nationalists and communists they saw as "mere camouflage" to mask the undermining of the anti-Japanese National Front in China. The rumor that the Soviet Union would set up a military alliance with Chang as an independent ruler in his region was vigorously denied.

Moreover, according to Molotov, in a remark to Patrick Hurley in Moscow during World War II, the USSR had extended its political and moral support to the effort to bring about Chiang's release. Hurley's testimony is given on pp. 71–72 of the *United States Relations with China*, issued by the U. S. Department of State in 1949.

The terms of the truce were proposed by the communists and adopted by the Central Executive Committee of the KMT in February, 1937. The Red Army was to be reorganized as a government army under Chiang's overall command; land confiscation was to be brought to a halt; and most important, the Chinese Soviet Republic was to be disbanded; the former soviet area government was now to be organized into special area governments within the Republic of China—as, for example, the Shen-Kan-Ning Special Border Government. In promising to cease communist agitation in China, the communists also paid tribute to Sun Yat-sen's doctrine of the Three People's Principles as "an urgent necessity for modern China," and declared their willingness to "fight for its full accomplishment." The action of the Nationalists in accepting this overture at its face value brought the decade-long Chinese civil war to a temporary halt.

When the Marco Polo Bridge Incident, on July 7, 1937, touched off a nation-wide war of resistance against Japan, the truce terms between the KMT and the CPC were quickly put into effect. On August 22, the Red Army was officially reorganized as the Eighth Route Army of the National Revolutionary (or government) Army under Chiang's supreme command. It was later renamed the Eighteenth Army Group (18AG) and divided into three divisions. The government appointed Chu Teh and P'eng Teh-huai as Commander and Deputy Commander, with Lin Piao, Ho Lung, and Liu Po-ch'eng as the three division commanders. Similarly, before the fall of Nanking on December 13, 1937, the government commissioned Yeh T'ing and Hsiang Ying as Commander and Deputy Commander of the New Fourth Army (N4A), made up of their old Red Army units, and intended to consist of four detachments with the strength of one division.

It is possible that the Nationalist government hoped, by commissioning these communist forces within its own military establishment, to keep a firm rein on both their size and their activities, as well as to utilize them effectively against the Japanese. They were to be paid by the Nationalist government, which also prescribed both their area of operations and their mission. The 18AG was assigned to the Second War Zone to operate in Northern Shansi under Zone Commander Yen Hsi-shan, first in holding off the Japanese and then in conducting guerrilla warfare behind the Japanese lines. The N4A was assigned to the Third War Zone under Ku Chu-t'ung and given the task of waging guerrilla warfare in the area between Nanking and Wuhu south of the Yangtze.

Both Communist and Nationalist forces were left behind the Japanese lines to conduct guerrilla or partisan operations. The communists, however, made use of their own considerable experience in guerrilla warfare not only to harass the Japanese, but even more to overrun the areas where Nationalist troops were operating; they adopted the policy, in fact, of attacking, defeating, and then incorporating the Nationalist troops in adjacent areas, meanwhile replacing the Nationalist governments in the unoccupied areas behind the Japanese lines.

In this process, they first would defeat the local Nationalist partisan units, taking over their armaments and retraining their troops, in order to strengthen their own ranks. When they had become sufficiently strong, they then began to absorb the provincial security forces of the Nationalists in the same way and to wipe out the Nationalist provincial governments or force them to withdraw. After sporadic campaigns against local troops and administrative units in 1938 and 1939, the communists were able, for example, to displace the provincial government of Hopei (whose governor, Lu Chung-lin, was concurrently the commander of the Hopei-Chahar War Zone); in a series of actions from January to March, 1940, they forced its removal to Shansi. Similarly, in August, 1940, after liquidating the Nationalist local units over a period of time, forces of the 18AG attacked the center of the Shantung provincial government at Luts'un, southeast of Tsinan, and forced Governor Sheng Hung-lieh to withdraw. At about the same time, units of the N4A, which had crossed to the north of the Yangtze, were seizing strategic points in Northern Kiangsu held by Han Teh-ch'in, concurrently Governor of Kiangsu Province and Deputy Commander of the Shantung-Kiangsu War Zone. Co-ordinating their efforts (or so the Nationalists charged) with the Japanese advance in the area, the communists were able to render untenable the position of the Kiangsu Provincial Government in Northern Kiangsu.

The constantly rising tempo of these aggravations wherever communist troops were operating led the Nationalist government in Chungking to make a special effort to work out a new arrangement for defining and limiting the activities of the communist forces. In an exchange of proposals entered into on July 16, 1940, the Nationalist government sought to have the communist forces withdraw into a single consolidated area (a subsection of the Second War Zone) under a single command (that of Chu Teh, as Deputy Commander of the Second War Zone); the new command was to cease all operations outside this area. Some increase in the total size of the communist forces was also to be allowed, though by no means approximating the total strength claimed by the communists. The communists in turn, through Chou En-lai, their representative in Chungking, insisted that the Nationalist government should pay their troops up to the full strength claimed for them, and that their units be allowed to remain in the various war zones. They conceded only the need for some "operational demarcations" within each zone.

A deadlock developed between the two sides, while the number of clashes between their forces kept mounting. Finally, on October 19 and December

9, 1940, the Nationalist government issued orders for the communist forces to withdraw to the north of the Yellow River—the 18AG in one stage and the N4A in a two-stage movement. A further clash during the period for carrying out this order led to the so-called Southern Anhwei Incident of January, 1941. The Nationalists struck at the communist units, purportedly to discipline and dissolve the N4A because it "had marched in a direction counter to the orders and attacked friendly units." The communists, of course, denied this and charged a deliberate and unprovoked Nationalist attack. In the ensuing action, the N4A Commander, Hsiang Ying, was killed in action, the Deputy Commander, Yeh T'ing, was captured by the Nationalists, while the central units of the organization were largely destroyed.

Needless to say, the effect of these clashes (which continued unabated after the Southern Anhwei Incident) was to hamper and reduce to a minimum both Nationalist and communist war efforts against the Japanese. The communists charged that the Nationalist government by late 1940 was tying up over 200,000 men (by 1945 the alleged figure was 500,000) to maintain a military and economic blockade of the Shensi-Kansu-Ninghsia border region. But on the other side it was charged that the military slogan of the communists was to devote 10 per cent of their strength to resisting Japan, 20 per cent to dealing with the KMT, and the remaining 70 per cent to expanding and consolidating their own areas.

Whatever the relative distribution of their effort, the communists certainly gave first priority to the development of their own strength in the War of Resistance against Japan, as was well illustrated by the example of Ch'en Shao-yü. The onetime Secretary General of the CPC, now returned from Moscow, seems to have made the mistake, in his public statements, of taking seriously the anti-Japanese propaganda of the CPC, to the extent of being willing to sacrifice the interests of the CPC, if necessary, in the prosecution of the war. Hu Ch'iao-mu gives the orthodox criticism of the "Right-opportunist line" of Ch'en and those who shared his views:

> They . . . demanded that the communists make concessions to the anti-popular policy of the Kuomintang by confining their activities within the scope permitted by Chiang Kai-shek's Kuomintang, and demanded that the Eighth Route Army and the New Fourth Army be completely integrated with the Kuomintang army. . . . They were opposed to . . . the expansion of the Liberated Areas and people's armed forces in the Japanese-occupied areas. They feared that such actions would "frighten away" Chiang Kai-shek's Kuomintang from the anti-Japanese united front.

Inevitably, the Southern Anhwei Incident had a profound repercussion on the political relations between the KMT and the CPC. Had they been in a coalition government with the KMT, the communists would certainly have withdrawn. As it was, they refused to attend the meeting of the People's Political Council (PPC) scheduled for March, 1941, to which they were entitled to send seven delegates, one of whom would have been Mao Tse-tung. The demands put forward by the communists as a condition for re-entering the PPC were unacceptable to the KMT, since they would have increased the authorized strength of the communist forces and granted recognition to the communist-sponsored "democratic regimes" behind the enemy lines.

To these demands Chiang Kai-shek was unalterably opposed. In his statement to the communist-boycotted PPC on March 6, 1941, he compared them to the demands of the Japanese enemy, and added: "There can be only one regime—there cannot be two regimes—within a country." Likewise, with regard to the armed forces, he insisted that "our military command can be one only; there cannot be two commands."

The presentation and rejection of these demands was followed by a political stalemate between the two parties which lasted for the next several years. There were occasional communist military encroachments upon the Nationalist-held areas behind the Japanese lines, and Nationalist actions against the communists, but for the most part a military stalemate likewise prevailed. Nevertheless, in the period of active communist expansion, from 1937 to 1941, the bargaining power of the communists *vis-a-vis* the Nationalists had increased tremendously. Finally, in May, 1944, negotiations were renewed for a political settlement between the KMT and the CPC, with a new set of communist demands. Again no progress was made, and on September 15, 1944, a communist delegate to the PPC, Lin Tsu-han, increased these demands by calling for a "coalition government of all anti-Japanese parties and groups." His proposal was repeated later by other communist spokesmen including Chou En-lai and Mao himself. It was given its fullest expression in Mao's report *On Coalition Government* to the Seventh Congress of the CPC on April 24, 1945. It was symbolic of the extent of the wartime expansion of the CPC that Mao demanded in effect a coalition government in which the communists would eventually have control, with the other parties included mainly as "window dressing" to present an impression of national unity.

The growth of the CPC forces and the communist-controlled areas during the wartime period was indeed phenomenal. Yeh Chien-ying, the Chief of Staff of the 18AG stationed in Chungking, stated in a press conference on June 22, 1944, that by the end of 1943 the "liberated areas" already included a population of 80 million. In North China, the five large "anti-Japanese bases" of the communists included 50 million—51 per cent of the total population. In Central China, 30 million people, or one-half the population in the Japanese-occupied areas, were under communist rule in the eight "anti-Japanese democratic bases." South China had two additional guerrilla areas behind enemy lines, on Hainan Island and near Canton along the Canton-Kowloon Railway. Several months later, on October 10, 1944, Chou En-lai revealed in a speech in Yenan that the total population under communist control had increased to 90 million. There were now 591 county governments in the "liberated areas." A year later, on the eve of the Japanese surrender (according to Hu Hua's 1950 publication, *History of the Chinese New Democratic Revolution*), there were 19 "liberated areas" in all, distributed among 19 provinces, with a total population under communist control of 100 million. [19]

The growth of the communist armed forces was equally striking. The total Red Army strength in 1937 was 80,000, according to figures given by the communist delegate, Lin Tsu-han, to the People's Political Council in Chungking on September 15, 1944. But by the end of 1943, the communists claimed an army of 470,000 and a militia force of 2 million. Chou En-lai reported an increase, before the end of 1944, to 570,000 regulars and 2.2 million militia. By the end of the Japanese War in 1945, the regular forces, according to Hu Hua, had reached a total of 1 million.

The factor of sheer size and weight of numbers was not the only element of strength developed by the communists during the period of wartime expansion. The political indoctrination of the Party and the Army and the maintenance of Party discipline had kept pace with the unprecedented growth of both organizations. At the same time, the communist leaders in the "liberated areas" were able to add further experience in military command and the art of government to what they had learned in the former Chinese Soviet Republic.

As the areas under their control expanded, the communists proceeded to ignore the political terms of the 1937 united front with the Nationalists. They engaged in political agitation among their own troops and among

[19] The governments of these border regions and "liberated areas" were in turn supervised by five regional bureaus of the CPC Central Committee: North China (with three sub-bureaus), Northeast China, Northwest China, Central China, and South China. Among others, the Northern Bureau had under its jurisdiction the Shansi-Chahar-Hopei border region, the Shansi-Hopei-Shantung-Honan border region, and Shantung Province; the Northwest Bureau included the Shansi-Suiyuan border region and the Shensi-Kansu-Ninghsia border region; and the Central China Bureau supervised the Kiangsu-Anhwei border region, the Hupeh-Honan border region, and the administrative structures for the Central Anhwei and the South Yangtze areas. The 19 "liberated areas" were as follows: Shensi-Kansu-Ninghsia, Shansi-Suiyuan, Shansi-Chahar-Hopei, Hopei-Jehol-Liaoning, Shansi-Hopei, Honan, Hopei-Shantung-Honan, Shantung, northern Kiangsu, central Kiangsu, southern Kiangsu, north of Huai River, south of Huai River, central Anhwei, eastern Chekiang, Kwangtung, Ch'unai (Hainan Island), Hunan-Hupeh-Kiangsi, Hupeh-Honan-Anhwei, and Honan.

any KMT troops they captured in the areas behind the Japanese lines. Further, they created an "Anti-Japanese University" through which thousands of lower-level Party workers were trained. And on the issue of agrarian reform, Mao broke a two-year silence in his 1940 work *On the New Democracy*, where he reinvoked the slogan of land redistribution as a key principle of the communist program.

In the international arena, too, the Chinese Communists were not neglecting their "internationalist" duty in coordinating with the world communist center by making their position known. This step was probably also in preparation for the course of diplomacy they were to follow after their ultimate victory. With the signing of the Hitler-Stalin Pact in 1939, they faithfully echoed the Soviet position. Mao viewed England and France as potentially more dangerous to the course of "progress" than Hitler, and declared that certain of the "so-called Western democracies" were worse than Nazi Germany. In particular, he asserted that "the center of world reaction now lies in England." Chou En-lai, then the unofficial Chinese Communist foreign minister, echoed Mao's condemnation of the West. In an article in the April, 1940, issue of the *Communist International*, he attacked the "three biggest imperialist powers"—England, France, and the United States—as warmongers and instigators of a new world war.

But the hard core of Chinese Communist strength lay within the Party itself. During the wartime period, Mao completed the consolidation of his own leadership of the Party. In October, 1938, the enlarged Sixth Plenary Session of the Central Committee confirmed the action of the Tsunyi Conference in acknowledging Mao's leadership as head of the Party Central. The dispute between Mao and Chang Kuo-t'ao, which had come to the surface at the Maoerhkai Conference in 1935, was now brought to a close with the expulsion of Chang from the Party. The 1938 Plenum of the CC also upheld Mao's tactics for the united front, in which the CPC would, in the words of Hu Ch'iao-mu, "organize the people's armed struggle against Japan without restrictions and independently" of the KMT. However, differences of opinion within the Party on this question continued, with Ch'en Shao-yü and others, as previously noted, misinterpreting Mao's line. For these views they were now charged with "Right opportunism" (in his earlier service as Party Secretary General Ch'en Shao-yü had been accused of "Leftist" errors). Mao was able to capitalize on this internal difference to pin the full blame for the "Southern Anhwei Incident" on Hsiang Ying, as one of the alleged "Rightists" influenced by Ch'en Shao-yü.

To insure the complete unity of the Party behind Mao's leadership, a thoroughgoing "Party rectification" movement, known as the *Cheng-feng* movement, was articulately carried out from 1942 to 1944. Basic documents were made required reading; sessions of "criticism and self-criticism" were held on an extensive scale, and undesirable elements were weeded out of the Party. Hence, when the Seventh Party Congress convened on April 23, 1945, Mao's leadership was stronger than ever. He was re-elected Party chairman, and a Politburo of his loyal and hand-picked lieutenants was also designated. The Party Constitution adopted by the Congress provided the basis for a tightly organized and disciplined organization. Thus, the Chinese Communists were now ready to seize the opportunity presented them by the entry of the Soviet Union into the war with Japan, the sudden termination of hostilities, and the accompanying demoralization of the already hard-pressed Nationalist regime in China.

THE FINAL CONQUEST OF POWER (1945–49)

On August 8, 1945, while the Japanese people were still feeling the shock of the atom bomb dropped on Hiroshima, the Soviet Union formally declared war on Japan. Two days later, with the Japanese announcement of willingness to surrender, Chu Teh, commanding the 18th Army Group, ordered his troops to rush into and take over the areas under Japanese occupation. The following day, Chiang Kai-shek ordered Chu to hold back his troops and await further orders. Chiang's command was completely ignored, and Nationalist and communist troops were soon in open conflict in the newly liberated areas. Thus was touched off a struggle to the finish between the two now distinct political forces.

The struggle was waged alternately on the political and the military front. The initial aim of the CPC, politically, was to enter a coalition government with other parties, which the communists would be able to dominate in due time. Though they had greatly increased in power down to 1945, and though the influence of the Kuomintang had been greatly weakened by the long years of protracted war, the Chinese Communists were not yet strong enough to engulf the whole country. Under these circumstances, the demand for a coalition government was an extension of their classic strategy of the united front: it would give them a chance to compete for support from outside the government while engineering to control it from within. Thus in his 1945 report *On Coalition Government*, Mao emphasized the need for free competition in politics. Four years later, however, with complete power within his grasp, Mao said no more about free competition, and stressed instead the need for a "democratic dictatorship."

The goal of reaching a settlement between the KMT and the CPC and of bringing them into a coalition government became for a time after 1945 the chief aim of United States diplomacy in China. Under pressure from Washington, the Nationalist government invited Mao to Chungking for negotiations which began on August 28, 1945. An agreement was finally signed on October 10—the so-called Double Tenth Agreement— calling for the convening of a Political Consultative Conference to which the communists and all minor political parties and many important non-partisan individuals were to be invited by the KMT.

Even while these negotiations were in progress, however, the armed clashes between the two forces in the liberated areas were becoming more serious. On September 10, the government troops suffered their first major defeat at the strategic city of Kalgan in Chahar Province. Seven weeks later, on October 31, the communists again attacked government troops moving into North China, inflicting damage and capturing General Ma Fa-wu, the Deputy Commander of the First War Zone. The Nationalists thereupon undertook a large-scale reprisal against the communists, who at this time were still not strong enough to withstand an all-out Nationalist campaign.

It was at this stage, on December 15, 1945, that President Truman intervened more actively, by announcing he was sending General George Marshall to China to mediate between the two parties. Arriving on December 19, Marshall went right to work. On January 10, 1946, the two parties signed a cease-fire agreement, just in time for the opening of the projected Political Consultative Conference. Because of its representative composition, the resolutions of this body were taken at face value by the Chinese public, and its apparent success was cause for national rejoicing.

In actuality, however, the PCC had solved nothing. The legal status of the communist armies, and of the administrative structures in the communist-occupied areas, was still unsettled. Despite the tireless efforts of the American mediator, the negotiations between the government and the communists reached a stalemate. Meanwhile, both sides were stepping up their preparations for an impending clash. The communists in Manchuria, particularly, intensified their training under the protection of the Soviet occupation forces there. Fighting broke out again in June, 1946, and on August 10, General Marshall and the American ambassador, Leighton Stuart, issued a joint statement admitting their inability to bring about a settlement. Marshall remained, however, until the following January, when he was recalled to become the US Secretary of State. Shortly after, on January 29, 1947, the American delegates were officially withdrawn from the tripartite Military Mediation Group. With the withdrawal of the communist delegation as well on February 21, 1947, the effort at mediation had failed completely, and the country was once more in the throes of a full-scale civil war.

Although the communists at first had to evacuate many areas, they were able to win key battles in Shantung, Shansi, and Hopei, where Chiang had concentrated some of his forces. Chiang captured Yenan, the Chinese Communist capital, on March 19, 1947; but by July, the communists were able to go over to the offensive in many areas. Their effort was made easier by the fact that the United States, despite repeated appeals from the Nationalist government, refrained at this time from giving any substantial military aid to the Nationalists. The communists, on the other hand, benefited from considerable quantities of Japanese military equipment turned over to them in Manchuria by the Soviet occupation forces, and from the action of the latter in delaying the landing of Nationalist forces in Manchurian ports until the Chinese Communists had extended their own occupation to most of northern Manchuria. Actually, the Soviet forces had stayed on in Manchuria longer than provided for by the Yalta Conference and the Sino-Soviet Treaty of 1945, though it was later pointed out by the communists that they did so at the invitation of the Nationalists. The result was that in time Manchuria became an invincible base for the Chinese Communists.

On the political front, the communists at this time were making another bid for popular support, capitalizing particularly on peasant discontent. In a declaration issued by the "People's Liberation Army" (as the former 18AG was now labeled) on October 10, 1947, they called upon all the Chinese people to overthrow the Chiang regime and build a new China. At the same time, the Central Committee of the CPC published the Basic Program of the Chinese Agrarian Law, and proceeded to carry out a land reform program in the "liberated areas," liquidating the landlords as a class. In so doing, the communists were able to appeal to Dr. Sun's principle of "giving land to the tillers"—which had remained an unfulfilled promise of the KMT. Their purpose. however, was quite different from that which had animated Dr. Sun. The economic program of the CPC was further elaborated by Mao Tse-tung in a conference of the CC of the CPC in Northern Shensi in December, 1947; he called for the confiscation not only of the landlords' holdings but also of the business empires of the "bureaucrat capitalists"—men like T. V. Soong and H. H. Kung who had enriched themselves through their government positions and connections. Along with these popular measures, however, Mao emphasized the need of preserving the "national industry and commerce," made up of those who had built up their firms by their own efforts. He referred to the situation of the moment as "the turning point from the growth to the extinction of more than 100 years' rule of imperialism in China."

The military campaigns of 1948 were of decisive importance for the communists. The whole of Northeast China fell into their hands in the Liao-Sheng campaign in the fall. Chingchow, the strategic point linking Manchuria with the Peiping-Tientsin area, was captured on October 15, and Changchun fell four days later, with the surrender of some 100,000 crack government troops. The final collapse of the government forces in Manchuria three weeks later meant the loss altogether of 470,000 KMT troops and their American equipment. With this victory, the communists could boast an armed force of over 3 million men, while the government ground forces had dwindled to less than 2.5 million.

This pattern was repeated elsewhere in the northern half of the country. In the Huai-Hai campaign in Kiangsu Province from November 7, 1948, to January 10, 1949, the government forces lost another 550,000 men, according to communist sources. In the North, somewhat later, Kalgan, Tientsin, and Peking all fell to the communists, with an alleged loss to the Nationalists of another 520,000 men. And on January 10, 1949, General Tu Yü-min, one of the top Nationalist commanders, was taken prisoner by the communists, along with 200,000 of his well-trained troops, in an area less than 300 miles north of Nanking.[20] Soon all of China north of the Yangtze was in the hands of the communists.

At this point, the communists paused to prepare for the next stage in their conquest. At the Second Plenary Session of the Seventh Central Committee of the CPC in March, 1949, the new situation was registered in the decision to shift the emphasis in the work of the Party from the countryside to the cities. Further attention was given to economic problems and the need to restore industrial production after long years of war. Then on April 20, Mao and his top military commander, Chu Teh, ordered the resumption of the drive south of the Yangtze. Nanking fell on April 23, and the drive quickly fanned out to reach Hankow, Shanghai, Canton, Chungking, Chengtu, and the important cities across the country, as well as penetrating into the remote territories of Yünnan, Suiyuan, and Sinkiang provinces. With complete control of the mainland virtually assured, the communists proclaimed the establishment of the People's Republic of China and its Central People's Government on October 1, 1949.

The final victory of the CPC over the KMT on the mainland may be ascribed largely to the efforts of the Chinese Communists, during long

[20] In justice to the many loyal and dedicated KMT troops and field commanders, it must be pointed out that this pattern of mass surrender was not everywhere followed. Some units fought with grim determination against great odds. For example, General Huang Po-t'ao died in a suicide pact with his aides and deputies rather than surrender.

years of political struggle, to develop Party strength, expand their territorial holdings, and build up their armed forces. But the sudden turn of fortune which brought the communists to power in a few short years after World War II must also be attributed in part to the disintegration and demoralization of the Kuomintang regime following the long years of war against foreign and domestic enemies. The capitulation of the Japanese had presented China with the best chance in over a century to achieve a national resurgence in a unified country no longer threatened by foreign penetration and domination. In the presence of this golden opportunity, the shameful record of the irregular and self-enriching conduct of a number of government officials during the taking over of the occupied areas from the Japanese enemy was only symptomatic. Behind it lay a more general lack of efficiency, zeal, and conscientious concern for the welfare of the country—to say nothing of outright corruption—in high places in the ruling bureaucracy, which had widespread repercussions throughout the whole administrative and military structure. This sorry record was not righted—and perhaps not even comprehended—in time to save the regime, whatever efforts the Nationalist leadership may have made subsequently to avoid such conditions on Taiwan. These defects, and the accompanying popular discontent and lack of confidence in the government, all helped defeat the Kuomintang regime from within and make it possible for the communists to take over. In the end, the sharp axe forged by the communists easily felled the rotten tree of the Kuomintang, and therewith brought China onto the communist world stage.

CHAPTER **3**

The Chinese
Communist Leadership:
Its Character and Perspective

The nature and destiny of Communist China are integrally linked to the character of its leadership. For nearly half a century now, a seasoned and dedicated band of Chinese Communists have labored arduously, first to establish the People's Republic and then to ensure the construction of socialism and the ultimate victory of communism on a world scale. At the top of the elite power pyramid is the figure of Mao Tse-tung—a man who in his own lifetime has become a world legend. Regardless of who succeeds Mao as the helmsman of Communist China's Party and state, the thought of Mao Tse-tung will have great impact on Peking's policies for decades to come. Mao and his chosen associates enjoy a longer and more intimate common experience than perhaps any power elite in modern history. Having labored long to win victory on the Mainland, they are acutely aware that both the reason for and the means to achieving their success is contained in the principles of Marxism-Leninism, especially as enunciated and defined in terms of the Chinese experience by Mao himself. Thus the leaders of Peking have jealously guarded the tenets of Marxism-Leninism: they have been zealous, too, in trying to keep the inner circle of the power structure small and free of the influence of any form of "deviation." The following pages analyze Mao's role as a revolutionary leader, the relation-

74

ship between his thought and the Party leadership, the problem of internal solidarity of the power elite, the use of the purge to promote solidarity, the promotion of the present phase of socialist education and cultural revolution to guarantee the correctness of the leadership, the preparation of heirs of revolution in the form of the Red Guards, and the question of succession to Mao's singular position of authority.

MAO TSE-TUNG: THE MAN AND HIS LEADERSHIP

For a man who has come to be regarded as a leading—if not the leading—philosopher of orthodox communism since the death of Stalin, Mao Tse-tung's background, especially his childhood and youth, shows a surprising penchant for "unorthodox" and "un-Confucian" behavior, combined with an apparent lack of any inclination toward philosophy or abstract thought. At the same time, his inclination to rebellion and non-conformity, which might have made him an isolated and ineffectual individualist, was apparently balanced by a drive for some degree of reconciliation, or some bond of communion with his fellows. This caused Mao to accept and to mold to his own purposes the dominant realities of the society he was rebelling against. These two strains of "rebel" and "conservative" have combined not only to make up the contradictory elements of his enigmatic personality, but also to give him an extraordinary talent for attaining practical results through political action.

Born in Hsiangt'an county, Hunan province, in 1893, Mao was the elder son of parents who had themselves received little formal education, but were relatively well-to-do. From his early years, the young Mao seemed to have rebelled against the dominant male authority figures in his life. He ran away from school, and eventually from his home, in protest against the traditional type of moral and intellectual discipline imposed on him by his teachers and, more importantly, his father. The crowning imposition came at the age of fourteen, when Mao was married in the traditional manner, and without his consent, to a girl of twenty. He refused to live with her. His real marriage, which might be counted his second, took place in 1920, to Yang K'ai-hui, the daughter of a Peking University professor. After her execution by the Kuomintang during the campaign to suppress the Communist Party, Mao first married Ho Tzu-chen, a student from a neighboring province, and then his present wife, Nan P'ing. Nan P'ing, who apparently pursued and married Mao out of admiration for his accomplishments, is better known by her maiden name, Chiang Ch'ing. As First Lady of Communist China, until the recent cultural revolution, she was carefully sheltered from the extraordinary fanfare which has constantly surrounded her husband. Unlike the wives of Liu Shao-ch'i and Chou En-lai, Chiang Ch'ing was not associated with any Party or state activities officially until 1965, when she was elected as a delegate to the Third National People's Congress. Her appointments as first vice chairman of the CPC CC's Cultural Revolution Group and as advisor to the PLA's Cultural Revolution Group (discussed later) amply demonstrate her vital role as a guiding force in the cultural revolution. This dramatic promotion of Chiang Ch'ing as a figure of national importance will doubtlessly stir further efforts on the part of Mao's foes, who have labored throughout his career to exploit his marriages to attack his personal character. [1]

As a youth, both at school and at home, Mao showed a preference for reading popular novels, instead of the Confucian classics urged upon him by his father. *All Men Are Brothers*, for example, meant much more to him than the *Analects*, and is reported to have been a strong influence in turning him against tradition and established authority, and in awakening in him a sympathy for the socially and economically underprivileged and the political underdogs. His anti-traditionalist and generally rebellious temperament necessarily compelled him to seek out and support, sometimes even blindly, a variety of new social and intellectual movements. According to Edgar Snow, writing in *The Reporter* for January 3, 1950, Mao had changed his ideological stand at least seven times before he finally became a convinced communist in 1920—progressing from Buddhist, through monarchist, republican, pacifist-idealist, democrat and anarchist to socialist. [2] Such frequent changes, while bespeaking the fermenting and chaotic conditions in China at the time, also reveal in Mao something of a paradoxical drive to reject one orthodoxy only to embrace another, which made him particularly susceptible to the appeal of new or unfamiliar doctrines.

Mao's final choice of communism necessarily suggests that in its radical authoritarianism—or what he called its "revolutionary thoroughness"—he found a solution to his search for doctrinal certainty combined with extreme non-conformity. "Following the path of the Russians" seemed to him less troublesome, if not necessarily more inviting on other grounds, than re-

---

[1] Sources differ as to the number and fate of Mao's children. It is believed that he had four or five children by Ho Tzu-chen, and it is rumored that he has had two children by Nan P'ing. Some reports indicate that his son was killed during the Korean War, and others that the son now holds an obscure army post. For a recent discussion of Mao's family life see Richard Hughes, "Mao at 70 Tries a 'Big Leap' in the World," *New York Times Magazine*, Feb. 2, 1964.

[2] To date, Mao's only lengthy autobiographical account of his early years was given to Edgar Snow during the Yenan period. (See Snow's *Red Star Over China*.) Since, at the time, Mao was seeking a united front, he doubtlessly orientated his remarks to create a favorable impression. However, his statements concerning his childhood and youth are probably authentic and, in any case, this account is the most authoritative available.

maining enmeshed in the endless whirl of arguments over competing doctrines. Besides, he saw in his own country conditions "similar" to those which had accelerated the October Revolution in Russia, the success of which now became a source of real inspiration to him. Among his other motives, his unstable relationship with his father, his irregular opportunities for study, his uncertainty over being able to make a living, and a short-lived and disillusioning experience of direct participation (as a soldier in a local army) in the aftermath of the Double Ten Revolution (October 10, 1911) against the Manchus, all doubtlessly played a part. During these years of rebellion, Mao was often thrown into close association with such members of the "proletarian class" as unemployed workers and disbanded soldiers. All these personal factors and experiences led him to seek "compensation" in the communist movement. His own later success in that movement amply confirmed him in that decision.

The choice of the nascent Communist Party of China meant also a choice of orientation toward the Soviet Union. Whatever the interest which Mao may have felt toward the world outside China, it is noteworthy that he apparently took no opportunity to visit other countries until 1949.[3] His state visit to Moscow in that year not only marked the victory of his efforts in China, but also affirmed the Soviet orientation implicit in his joining the Party in its earliest days, nearly thirty years before, and in his Comintern membership after 1935.

It is significant, however, that Mao's Soviet orientation did not go to the extremes advocated at one time or another by some of the other Chinese Communist leaders. Rather, it was tempered by the "conservative" side of his nature, which led him to keep his major attention focused on the problem of adapting the communist revolutionary doctrine to the realities of the condition of China. During his early years in the Party, this conservative streak was illustrated by Mao's decision to take a library job in Peking University, instead of studying in France, by his visits to the grave of Confucius and the birthplace of Mencius, and by the fact that his own revolutionary activities were confined to his native area—at least partly due to personal wishes. More important, it may be seen also in his emphasis on the role of the peasants in the strategy of communism in China—an

---

[3] Mao did not elect to join the "overseas student movement," popular among his generation after World War I. Yet he has apparently read widely concerning the world outside China. For example, the *Chung-kuo Ch'ing-nien Pao* of August 14, 1959 quotes Mao on the six months he spent in 1912 reading the works of Rosseau, Montesquieu, Huxley, Darwin, etc. as "I read greedily, desperately, like an ox that has rushed into a vegetable garden. . . ." During his 1947 interview with Mark Gayn of the *Toronto Daily Star*, Mao noted: "I study the [New York stock] market reports very closely." And in January, 1965, Mao told Edgar Snow that he had recently read Maxwell Taylor's *The Uncertain Trumpet*. However, his knowledge of the world outside China has remained bookish.

adaptation to the realities of the Chinese society which seemed to over-shadow for the time being, without neglecting, the more familiar doctrine of the leadership of the proletariat in the communist movement. (Mao's early insistence on capitalizing on the revolutionary potential of the peasants was not, it should be stressed, in conflict with orthodox Leninism. Rather it was in accord with what Stalin himself, in articles and lectures, was saying about the situation in China during this period, and represented an application of Stalin's ideas to the Chinese local scene.) Indeed, it may be said that the conservative strain in Mao's character runs consistently throughout his career and has contributed to his pre-eminence, especially in his ideological, political and military leadership.

Apparently a shrewd Party organizer, Mao had a comparatively swift rise in the Party ranks in the first few years of his membership. After participating in the First Congress of the CPC in 1921, he was elected a member of the Central Committee and a candidate member of the Politburo by the Third Congress in 1923. Early in his Party work, he became involved with the peasant problems in his native province. In March, 1927, at the request of the Central Committee and following an on-the-scene study, Mao prepared a *Report of an Investigation into the Peasant Movement in Hunan*. The major part of this report was published in the same year in both the Party central organ, the *Hsiang-tao (Guide) Weekly* and the *Communist International*, marking Mao's debut as an author. His initial successes within the Party received a strong check toward the end of 1927, when, as noted previously, he was removed from his Politburo position following the ill-fated Autumn Harvest Uprising, of which he had been the principal leader.

This temporary setback in his Party advancement did not prevent Mao from developing his capacities as a revolutionary leader. In his work with the Hunan peasants and with the organization of the All-China Peasants Union, as well as in the abortive Autumn Harvest Uprising, he was learning lessons which were afterwards to be put to good use. Thus, while the CPC as a whole was being crushed and driven underground by the KMT campaigns of suppression, Mao was working out the application of one of Stalin's key principles for the revolutionary strategy of communism in China—namely, the reliance on armed struggle carried on from a "liberated" rural area.

Mao's tactics in this respect not only conformed with Stalin's suggestions, but also corresponded with age-old Chinese ideas about the role of a "man on horseback" in overthrowing an established regime and seizing state power. Chinese tradition had impressed upon Mao that "if victorious, one becomes a king; if defeated, one becomes a bandit." For the moment, in his mountain retreat, he was a "bandit" consorting with "bandits." The

Chinese history and Stalin's strategy confirmed to him that the way to power was through armed struggle. And agreeing with Stalin, he saw that this struggle has to be carried on from solidly established bases in the countryside, rather than through sporadic uprisings in the urban areas. Hence, in contrast to Li Li-san, Ch'en Shao-yü and others who over-emphasized the role of the proletarian uprising, Mao followed a program of building revolutionary bases analogous in its conservatism to Stalin's notion of constructing "socialism in one country."

The failure of the Li Li-san line, demonstrated in Changsha in 1930, reflected an increase in strength in Mao's position. Having meanwhile created and consolidated his position in a revolutionary base of his own in Chingkangshan, he was chosen in 1930 as the Chief Political Commissar of the Chinese Workers-Peasants Red Army. His political star was definitely in the ascendancy when, in November, 1931, the First All-China Congress of Soviets of Peasants and Workers Deputies elected him chairman of the Chinese Soviet Republic at Juichin in Kiangsi province. In January, 1933, Mao was made a member of the Party Central Committee's Politburo. And he had definitely "arrived" as a top leader of the Party when, in January, 1935, he conducted the Party Conference in Tsunyi and was at the same time elected Chairman of the CC and member of the Comintern. From then on, as noted in Chapter 2, Mao's primacy in the Party was less and less subject to challenge. In March, 1943, the CC elected him its Chairman and the Chairman of its Politburo. He was re-elected to these positions at the Seventh Party Congress in 1945, which named a Politburo of his own supporters. Since then, Mao has been represented as the CPC's infallible leader.

In the military as well as the political field, Mao's dual tendencies to conservatism and rebellion manifested themselves and played a part in his rise to pre-eminence. In the effective tactics developed during the KMT Extermination Campaigns, his conservatism was demonstrated in his willingness and ability to utilize the military teachings of Sun Wu, one of the greatest strategists and military geniuses of ancient Chinese history. His skill in parrying these KMT onslaughts and his conduct of the military aspects of the Long March helped establish his military fitness and ingenuity.

Mao's program for the Party and his solutions to some of the fundamental problems of the Chinese revolution have revealed the same blend of rebel and conservative elements. His blueprint of the so-called New Democracy, while following Stalin's interpretation of Marxism-Leninism, kept in mind the underlying forces of China's historical development. Likewise, the first Party reform movement of 1942–44 symbolized Mao's efforts to apply Communist principles to Chinese historical conditions, rather than to emphasize doctrinal points for their own sake, or to disregard "theory" altogether in favor of the trial-and-error lessons of "practice." In essence, the New China envisaged by Mao could be described as a development of historical China along Leninist-Stalinist lines. In his Soviet orientation Mao displayed a rebel strain in adopting an essentially foreign ideology and program in preference to the traditional forms and alternatives of Chinese society; but in insisting on adapting the ideology to local conditions his conservative tendencies are also apparent.

The enigma of Mao's personality is thus in part clarified by viewing it as a fusion of apparently contradictory elements in the service of a single goal. The "unity of opposites" of the communist dialectic is manifest in Mao's character, as well as in his political programs and public activities, in the form of a wide range of dualisms which sometimes seem irreconcilable. Some of the more familiar examples include his attempt to embrace subjectivism as well as objectivism, the cognition of the relative and the absolute, the double-edged moral standard of utility and propriety, and such other "integrated opposites" as quality and quantity, love and hatred, criticism and self-criticism, nationalism and internationalism, and the combination of centralism and democracy. Over all these dualisms Mao has maintained an extremely flexible standard of adjustment subject only to his own inner control. His over all concern, it may be said, is not merely with following theory and understanding reality as an onlooker, nor with taking action for its own sake and for immediate goals. Above all, Mao is concerned with securing practical results which ideally combine long range theory with immediate action.

Between 1959, when he retired from his office as Chairman of the People's Republic to concentrate on ideological and Party work, and the mid-1966 inauguration of the cultural revolution, Mao Tse-tung displayed himself only infrequently to his people. He disappeared from public view several times for long months and made only a few public speeches. [4] Instead, Mao has increasingly preferred to speak through the voice of the collective leadership, often in articles prepared by the editorial boards of *Jen-min Jih-pao* (*People's Daily*) and *Hung-ch'i* (*Red Flag*), or in resolutions issued in the name of the CPC Central Committee. Field Marshal Montgomery reported that, as late as 1961, Mao continued to observe a daily schedule of working until 5 A.M., sleeping until 3 P.M., and eating sparingly. As rumors

---

[4] Included in these rare public utterances were his August, 1963 remarks on the American civil rights movement and the worsening situation in Vietnam.

Given the reverence which surrounds Mao, it is surprising that he has apparently never recorded any of his earlier dramatic speeches. It may be supposed that Mao suffers from the problem associated with his age of projecting his voice—a problem complicated by his habitual chain-smoking.

circulated that Mao was rushing to complete a massive ideological tome on the course of international communism since the death of Lenin, his semi-retirement was taken as a sign that he was trying to conserve his waning strength. It was to combat the stories that Mao was suffering from the effects of advanced age, and to renew confidence in the vitality of Communist China's revolutionary leader, that his swim in the Yangtze was so widely publicized. According to the official reports, on July 16, 1966, at Wuhan Mao swam nearly 15 kilometers down stream in rapid currents in about 65 minutes—a considerable feat for a man less than 72! Similarly, photographs of Mao, radiantly healthy and vigorous, have flooded the Chinese Communist press, and his schedule of public appearances has been greatly increased. For example, during the month of July, 1966, Mao received the delegates to the Afro-Asian Writers Emergency Meeting in Peking, Nepalese Crown Prince Birenda Shah and his party, and the foreign delegates to the Peking Summer Physics Colloquium. On August 18, 1966, he personally presided over the first Peking mass rally of the Red Guards—a function that was repeated several times. Nevertheless, it is very likely that Mao Tse-tung will again disappear from the public limelight for an extended period of time. These disappearances serve at least two useful purposes, in addition to conserving Mao's strength. They allow his trusted subordinates additional top level experience, under his vigilant eye, and they heighten the enigma or mystique which has always shrouded him.

Although there have been variations in type and intensity, at least from the time of the Long March, Mao Tse-tung has benefited from the adoration and exaltation of his comrades and followers to enhance his own prestige and further the cause of Marxism-Leninism. Until about 1960, and particularly during the time of Khrushchev's violent denunciation of Stalin, the laudation of Mao was relatively low keyed. Since then, and especially in the period beginning late in 1965, the veneration of Mao and his thought has been advanced by all possible avenues. Such a glorification has left an impression abroad that Mao has gone further than Stalin in creating a new super-human religion centered on himself to incorporate supposedly all that is true and all that is good.

In his January, 1965 interview with Edgar Snow, Mao observed that each generation judges for itself, according to its own conditions. Therefore, he speculated, a thousand years from now Marx, Engels and Lenin may well appear ridiculous. But it is very apparent that Mao seeks by a variety of means to ensure his place in history. His image is everywhere, in the form of pictures that usually represent him at about the age of fifty. Noting that the travelling projectionist teams try to stop film reels when Mao's picture appears on the screen, the Canton *Yangch'eng Evening Paper* of October 21,

1965, concluded that this is "because the people want to contemplate his countenance." Mao's boyhood home and the room where he worked in the library of the Peking University have been made into national shrines. Similarly, the site of the Autumn Harvest Uprising in Hunan is now a national monument replete with a display of shotguns and spears used by Mao's followers. The caves inhabited by Mao and his followers at Yenan have been renovated as national landmarks and the desk used by Mao when he wrote "On Contradictions" and "On Protracted War" is a prized arti-fact.[5] Numerous other instances could be cited, for the fact is that rever-ence for Mao is frank and open.

The advancement of Mao as a revolutionary symbol was not always so blatant. The downgrading of Stalin and the call for a return to the principle of collective leadership at the Twentieth Congress of the CPSU in February, 1956, inevitably produced repercussions—often serious ones—in Commu-nist Parties throughout the world. Mao himself remained aloof to the frenzy against cultism. In major reports to the CPC Eighth Congress, Liu Shao-ch'i and Teng Hsiao-p'ing continued to boldly defend Mao's leader-ship and credited him with advancing the mass line and the principle of collective leadership in China. Apart from the fact that Mao's contribu-tions were not referred to by name in the 1956 Party Constitution, his stature was actually strengthened. For example, the Eighth Congress demoted Wang Chia-hsiang and Chang Wen-t'ien, who had preceded Mao as secretaries general of the Party in the 1930's, from regular membership in the Politburo.[6] The effect of the Party's choices for the top central leadership positions was to provide Mao with a team of long-standing faithful subordinates. If anything, the implementation of the collective leadership theme, then, further consolidated Mao's own position.

Although Khrushchev's denunciation of Stalin's mistakes must be re-garded as one of the major keys to understanding the present troubled status of Sino-Soviet relations, any adequate analysis of this vital issue would require a separate volume. Here, however, several of the ramifica-tions of this ideological debate may be suggested as they have specifically affected Mao's own position. Perhaps as much as any other leader of the international communist movement, Mao suffered from Stalin's mistakes

[5] In his article "Peking Has a Yenan Complex," *New York Times Magazine* (Jan. 30, 1966), Mark Gayn insists that this national shrine reveals a nostalgia on the part of Communist China's leadership for "the good old days," and shows a resistance to change as well as anti-urban and anti-intellectual sentiments.

[6] Wang and Chang may have been scapegoats for deviations some twenty years earlier, which were allegedly similar to those of Stalin at a later date, in order to conform formally to the attack on cultism.

in judgment, particularly in the 1920's and early 1930's.[7] Yet Mao has consistently and often praised Stalin as a great revolutionary leader and faithful heir to Lenin. As phrased in his eulogy on the occasion of Stalin's death, "The Greatest Friendship" (China News Agency, March 10, 1953): "Comrade Stalin's contribution to our era, through his activities both theoretical and practical, is beyond estimation."

It is understandable that Mao should have saluted Stalin as "the greatest genius of the present age, the great teacher of the world communist movement," in his March, 1953 praise of "The Greatest Friendship." But Chinese Communist pronouncements have continued in the same tone, even after Khrushchev ordered Stalin's reputation to be destroyed. For example, even the first major statements to follow in the wake of the judgment of the 20th CPSU Congress carefully distinguished between Stalin's "faults" and his "great merits." This distinction is clearly summarized in the September, 1963 article "On the Question of Stalin," prepared by the editorial departments of *People's Daily* and *Red Flag* and representing the ultimate judgment of Mao and his chosen fellow leaders:

. . . Stalin's life was that of a great Marxist-Leninist, a great proletarian revolutionary. . . . [He] also made certain mistakes . . . some could have been avoided and some were scarcely avoidable at a time when the dictatorship of the proletariat had no precedent to go by . . . His merits outweighed his faults. . . . We have the inescapable duty to come forward and defend him in the interests of the international communist movement.[8]

It may be said that Mao Tse-tung is too mindful of the complexities of history to assume that the burden of all mistakes committed within the communist movement from the 1920's to 1953 can be placed on the shoulders of one man. Regarding Stalin as a true Marxist-Leninist of major stature, Mao understandably resented criticism coming from Khrushchev—whom Mao does not regard as a true Marxist-Leninist. Moreover, the statements of the CPC have emphasized the inconsistency of Khrushchev, who capitalized on the work of Stalin and should therefore share in the guilt, in later castigating his predecessor in order to promote his own image. Essentially since Stalin was a "faithful practioner" of Marxism-Leninism,

---

[7] For details, consult Chapter II, concerning the failures of the "united front" policy toward the KMT, the Li Li-san line, etc.

[8] The English text of this major policy statement was reprinted in *Peking Review*, No. 38, Sept. 20, 1963. This analysis was prepared to answer the CPSU and is full of polemic accusations against assumed Soviet revisionism. For example: "When Stalin did something wrong, he was capable of criticizing himself. For instance, he had given some bad counsel with regard to the Chinese revolution. After the victory of the Chinese revolution he admitted his mistake. . . . Khrushchev . . . simply doesn't know what self-criticism is."

Khrushchev, in his detraction, is said to be rejecting Marxism-Leninism itself. But Stalin's unscrupulous imposition of the cult of personality in violation of the principle of collective leadership and the role of the masses, a contrast to the style of Mao, has been duly denounced by him and his trusted associates.

The leaders of Communist China, from the beginning of the debate over Stalin, have been careful to distinguish between the valid exercise of the Party leadership and the abuses of personality cult. This distinction is manifest in the article on "Why the Cult of the Individual Must be Opposed," which represents the judgment of Mao and his associates. It appeared in *Cheng-chih Hsüeh-hsi* (*Political Study*) on June 13, 1956, as one of a series of articles explaining the decisions of the enlarged session of the CPC Politiburo convened to discuss the question of Stalin. Among the errors associated with cultism are:

First the cult of the individual tends to worship one's power and prestige, consider one's ability the greatest, negate or belittle the role of the masses, and thus suppress the zeal of the people. . . . Second, the cult of the individual is bound to give rise to arbitrariness and despotism in violation of the Party principle of collective leadership. . . .

But this judgment is tempered by other considerations. Thus, "the emergence of an outstanding person results from the needs of the time and the society" and, more importantly, "we are badly in need of advanced personalities who can represent the interest and demands of the masses and who can organize and lead the masses to march forward. We need more 'heroes of the people' of this type."

The leaders of Peking are fully mindful of the advantages to be gained from promoting the image of a popular hero, such as the Stakhanovs in the Soviet Union and their counterparts in China. By popularizing Mao as a revolutionary hero or teacher, they can strengthen a central leadership deriving its authority from Mao's revolutionary thought. Moreover, this process can considerably hasten the eradication of the old traditions. Thus Mao is hailed as China's greatest philosopher, military strategist, scientist, statesman, poet, or master of any other category of human endeavor.

Quite unlike Stalin's imposition of personality cult, promotion of deep respect for Mao Tse-tung has probably worked to strengthen the confidence of the masses and simplify the assignments of the Party cadres. This conception has been strengthened by the fact that even those officials who seek to undermine Mao's thought have to proceed with their programs in the name of Mao. Thus, Mao's slightest pronouncement tends to become the immediate basis for a mass movement, and by inducing a blind acceptance of his proclaimed wish, Mao is able to lead the people on many occasions without resorting to harsh disciplinary measures. Two examples, discussed elsewhere in detail, might be cited here concerning this stimulation of mass devotion. In June, 1958, while on an inspection tour through the villages of Shantung and Honan, Mao declared for the first time that "it is better to establish the people's communes." Although the CPC, in any case, would have carried out this program, Mao's inspiration helped greatly to accelerate the reorganization in the rural areas. After his return from an inspection tour along both sides of the Yangtze in mid-1958, Mao pointed out the need to organize militia divisions throughout China. The "Everyone a Soldier" movement was launched immediately, and within three months the ranks of the militia had been increased from tens of millions to 200 million. Therefore, it may be said that the vitality and zeal deriving from ardent admiration for Mao and his thought has helped the CPC to enforce its decrees with the least resistance and in the shortest span of time.

THE THOUGHT OF MAO TSE-TUNG AND THE PARTY LEADERSHIP

In Communist China, just as the person of Mao Tse-tung has become the revolutionary symbol of the "bright future of communism," the thought of Mao Tse-tung has been glorified as the revolutionary "wisdom" which applies and refines the "truths" of Marxism-Leninism to advance China and the rest of the world to new levels of progress and toward the ultimate goal of true communism. In fact, the basis of Mao's leadership in the Party since 1935 has been founded on his thought, or his ability of ideological reasoning, interpretation and application, rather than on his sheer political maneuvering, economic power, or military supremacy. Most likely, Mao's thought will continue to be the guiding spirit for the future Party leadership. This possibility is evidenced in the current PLA and Red Guards activities to propagate Mao's thought and purify Party leadership through cultural revolution.

Mao's prestige and influence as a theoretician, which date back to his early days in the Party, have grown in at least direct proportion to his acquisition and solidification of power on the Mainland. Beginning with his debate with Khrushchev over the interpretation of Marxist-Leninist principles in the present epoch, Mao's role as the international communist movement's leading theoretician has enjoyed an enormous increment of prestige. By 1967, according to the leaders of the cultural revolution, in China one's fidelity to orthodox communist tenets has come to be measured by the degree of one's allegiance to the thought of Mao. Once confined largely to the place and problems of Mainland China, this thought of Mao is now a powerful factor in the international communist movement and, of necessity, has come to be studied seriously by revolutionaries throughout the world.

At the 1945 Seventh Congress of the CPC, Liu Shao-ch'i described the thought of Mao Tse-tung as "the teachings that unite the theories of Marxism-Leninism with the practices of the Chinese Revolution." The Party Constitution adopted at this congress on June 11, 1945, specifically and prominently included this definition in its general program, again stressing that the Party guides its every action according to the thought of Mao. Hailing Mao as the "creative genius of Marxism," the congress credited him with the successes of the revolution and predicted that the continuing revolution would succeed or fail according to the degree of fidelity given to his thought.

Mao's first endeavors to apply Marxism creatively to the realities in China, as noted previously, resulted in a skillful adaptation of or integration with Stalin's dictums which were credited with the 1949 victory.[9] All major policy decisions since then have been attributed to his ideological guidance. Thus, the agrarian reforms and cooperativization, the socialist transformation of industry and commerce, the Great Leap and the communes, the various phases of Blooming and Contending or anti-revisionist struggle, to mention but a few areas, have represented the concrete application of Mao's theories. His theory of contradictions among the people, first announced in 1957, represents one of Mao's principal contributions to the body of communist philosophy.

The ascendancy of Mao as a theoretician can be attributed in part to the accidents of history. With Lenin and Stalin gone, the Soviet Union has had no theoretician of major stature. Khrushchev's fate is too well known to be documented here. Thus, in a sense, it may be said that Mao's prestige has come through default of other communist leaders throughout the world, and not initially as a reward for his own original interpretations of communist ideology. Analysts have pointed out that few, if any, of his theories can be termed original;[10] and that, if Mao's lucidity and logic

---

[9] For a detailed discussion on this specific question see Peter S. H. Tang, "Stalin's Role in the Communist Victory in China," *American Slavic and East European Review*, Vol. XIII, No. 3 (October, 1954), pp. 375–388.

[10] For example, Mao's foreign policies have been termed nothing more than an adaptation of Trotsky's theories, and his programs for the Great Leap and communes merely a logical extension of Stalin's ideas on control and utilization of the masses.

For a more detailed analysis of this question, the reader is referred to Arthur A. Cohen's "How Original Is 'Maoism'?" *Problems of Communism* (Vol. X, No. 6, Nov.–Dec., 1961). Cohen mentions that Mao has done little more than paraphrase Lenin, and questions his authorship of *On Practice* and *On Contradictions*. In this latter respect, Mao informed Edgar Snow in January, 1965, that he had indeed written these two works in 1937, spending weeks to prepare these lectures for the Anti-Japanese Academy.

remain undiminished, his language and mode of expression have become terribly coarse.[11]   Yet, it is difficult to deny Mao a degree of creativity, beginning with his treatment of the peasant aspect of the communist revolution at the village level.   His works on military tactics, particularly in the field of guerrilla warfare, have become world classics.   And it should be emphasized that Mao himself regards his work as one of "creative application" of the ideas contained in the body of Marxist-Leninist works.

The importance which the Chinese Communist leadership attaches to the thought of Mao Tse-tung has continued to reach new heights of glorification.   In his article published in the July 16, 1958 issue of *Red Flag*—at the time when the CPC was preparing for the massive Great Leap and communalization programs—Ch'en Po-ta, then a vice director of the Central Committee's Propaganda Department, stressed: "If the thought of Mao Tse-tung were not victorious in the struggle against erroneous thoughts of all kinds and if the Chinese revolution did not march forward under the banner of the thought of Mao Tse-tung, then there would be no victory of the present Chinese people's revolution and socialist construction."   Literally millions of praises or warnings in a similar vein could be abstracted from the Chinese Communist press or from Peking radio broadcasts.   Several more recent statements can illustrate selectively the fact that this sort of laudation has continued to increase, despite certain setbacks to Mao's programs.

The *People's Daily* editorial prepared for the celebration of the 16th anniversary of the establishment of the Chinese People's Republic, on October 1, 1965, proudly proclaimed China's two biggest assets to be her 650 million population and "the great thought of Mao Tse-tung."   But of these two assets, the paper observes, "Mao Tse-tung's thought is the guarantee of victory for our cause."   Associated with socialist education and cultural revolution since 1966 mass fidelity to the thought of Mao has become an imperative.   For example, the June 7, 1966 editorial of the now most influential *Liberation Army Daily*, having credited Mao with "the gifts of genius, creatively and comprehensively developing Marxism-Leninism," advances this stern test:

The attitude towards Mao Tse-tung's thought, whether to accept it or resist it, to support it or oppose it, to love it warmly or be hostile to it, this is the touchstone to test and the watershed between true revolution and sham revolution, between revolution and counter-revolution, between Marxism-Leninism and revisionism. He who wants to make revolution must accept Mao Tse-tung's thought and act in accordance with it.   A counterrevolutionary will inevitably disparage, distort, resist, attack and oppose Mao Tse-tung's thought.

[11] The series of open letters to the CPSU, which doubtlessly reflect Mao's handiwork, are said to be illustrative of this degradation of linguistic expression.

It is not surprising that the greatest crime associated with the ideological deviationists of the "Three-Family Village," as encouraged by the "anti-Party" factions at the Peking University and within the ranks of the Peking Municipal Party Committee, was that of rejecting Mao's thought. "Putting it plainly," the *People's Daily* editorial of June 4, 1966 charged the "anti-Party" conspirators, "what you meant was opposition to Mao Tse-tung's thought. . . ." From a negative viewpoint, then, as the editorial emphasizes, anyone who "dares to oppose Chairman Mao" must expect denunciation "whoever he may be." As will be noted subsequently, Party officials up to the level of Liu Shao-ch'i have suffered exposure, vilification, humiliation and loss of authority for their failures to learn from and practice Mao's thought.

The exaltation of Mao's thought, however, is more usually approached from a positive standpoint. Thus, tremendous collective or individual feats are said to be possible if one correctly studies and applies Mao's teachings. The accomplishments attributed to the correct understanding of Mao's thought range through the whole gamut of human experience. Some of these achievements, similar to the report from Peking's Jishuitan Hospital that the Department of Traumatology had successfully treated a patient who was burnt over 96 per cent of his body, only after studying the thought of Mao, are mentioned elsewhere throughout these pages. Meant to be particularly appealing to the masses is the often repeated notion that, by studying the thought of Mao, "workers, peasants and soldiers have set foot in the domain of philosophy which for thousands of years was the monopoly of the intellectuals." Or as expressed in the unintentionally ironic statement of the Canton *Yang-ch'eng Wan-pao* of January 18, 1965: "In some places, illiterates and semi-illiterates study Chairman Mao's works better than the intellectuals do."

Given all these factors, it is not surprising that there is an enormous demand for Mao's works in Communist China.[12] According to official Peking sources, 57 million copies of Mao's *Works* in "A" and "B" collections with large type suitable for peasant readers, were sold in the rural areas alone in 1965. Following orders from the CPC Central Committee, the Ministry of Culture announced plans in August, 1966, to print and distribute some 35 million copies of Mao's *Selected Works* in 1966–67, as well as innumerable pamphlets related to his thought.[13] This target was

[12] Peking news sources frequently report evidence of a similar popularity of Mao's works outside China. These works have been translated into many languages to meet what the Chinese Communists deem to be a tremendous demand. For example, the first 5,000 copies of the *Selected Works* to be translated into Arabic were reportedly sold out shortly after they appeared in Syrian bookstalls; to meet the need, serialized versions were then carried in the newspapers.

[13] According to an NCNA dispatch of August 7, 1966, the "black gang" in the Ministry of Culture was accused by Chang P'ing-hua, deputy director of the CPC CC's Propaganda

apparently oversubscribed. According to *Peking Review* (no. 25, 1967), between January and June, 1967, more than 29 million copies of the *Selected Works* were printed. The PLA's General Political Department has also issued an enlarged edition of the *Selected Works*. Its *Selected Readings from Chairman Mao's Works* was expanded from 80,000 to 230,000 words to provide basic political reading for the troops. At the same time, some 300,000 "culture rooms" have been opened in the rural areas to make copies of Mao's works more readily available to commune members and to sponsor discussion of his thought.

Early in 1966, the Ministry of Culture announced that year's primary goal to be that of "bringing politics to the fore" through increased study of the thought of Mao. With the troops of the PLA providing models, all people were urged to imitate their example of diligent study.[14] Since the inauguration of the cultural revolution, soldiers have assumed the responsibility for conducting group discussions of Mao's works. For example, by September, 1966, ten million peasants were participating in group discussions in Hunan; in Kwangtung, one out of every four peasants had joined a study group; and in Shansi, 80 per cent of the peasants were studying Mao's writings. As NCNA observed (on September 29): "As a movement for ideological revolution and for the popularizing of Marxism-Leninism, this mastering of Mao's thought by hundreds of millions of peasants is without precedent."

It remains to summarize briefly some of the contents of Mao's thought. The key to Mao's political thought is contained in his differentiation of China's various social classes and an analysis of the contradictions that exist among them. Before the second plenum of the Seventh Central Committee in March, 1949, Mao pointed out that China's principal international contradiction was between the people and imperialism. The principal national contradiction, he declared, was between the landlord and bureaucratic capitalist classes, on the one hand, and the Chinese people on the other. Hence, as soon as the landlord class was liquidated in 1952, Mao formulated the general line for the transitional period, calling for the gradual transformation of capitalist ownership of the means of production.

Department, of deliberately restricting distribution of Mao's works. The conspirators used the excuse that paper was in short supply. However, in 1962, when only 50,000 copies of Mao's *Selected Works* were published, 140,000 copies of *Dream of the Red Chamber* were distributed. The publication of Liu Shao-ch'i's *How To Be a Good Communist* in revised form in the same year has been judged part of this plot to minimize the circulation of Mao's works.

[14] This drive which introduced the cultural revolution was similar to, although it surpassed in intensity, the drive that developed from the decision of the eighth plenum of the CPC Central Committee meeting in Lushan in August, 1959. In this former instance, Party members were urged to study Mao's thought to combat the rightists. Lin Piao was extremely active in carrying out this directive. See, for example, Lin's article, "March Ahead Under the Red Flag of the Party's General Line and Mao Tse-tung's Military Thought," in the September 30, 1959 *People's Daily*.

In February, 1957, when this stage was substantially completed, Mao initiated a further program for the correct handling of contradictions among the people. He suggested again that progress required a distinction to be made between two different types of social contradictions—those between the enemy and the people, and those among the people themselves. On the basis of this distinction, Mao indicated in his famous speech of February 27, 1957, at the Eleventh Session (enlarged) of the Supreme State Conference, that different and more effective means could be employed:

> Contradictions in a socialist society are fundamentally different from contradictions in old societies, such as a capitalist society. Contradictions in a capitalist society find expression in acute antagonisms and conflicts, in sharp class struggle, which cannot be resolved by the capitalist system itself and can only be resolved by socialist revolution. Contradictions in a socialist society are, on the contrary, not antagonistic and can be resolved one after the other by the socialist system itself.

It may be assumed that the Party's suppression of counterrevolutionaries prior to 1953, the Blooming and Contending campaign and its resultant anti-rightist struggle, and all subsequent rectification drives have originated in Mao's theory of class differentiation and his analysis of social contradictions. Mao's distinctions on the nature of contradictions continue to be an essential element. As phrased in the June 2, 1966 editorial of *People's Daily:*

> It is erroneous, contrary to Marxism-Leninism and at variance with dialectics to say that there are no contradictions in socialist society. How can there be no contradictions? There will still be contradictions after 1,000 or 10,000 or even 100 million years. Contradictions will exist in the universe even after the destruction of the earth and the extinction of the sun. All things are in a flux of contradiction, struggle and change. This is the Marxist-Leninist outlook.

In the economic field, Mao's outstanding theoretical contributions have been in accord with his belief that China's vast population is one of its greatest assets. As he pointed out in the first issue of *Red Flag*, the enlistment of China's 500 million peasants in the promotion of the national economy encourages success since "the more people . . . the higher the spirit, and the greater the capability." The announcement at the second session of the CPC's Eighth Congress, in 1958, of the "walk-on-two-legs" economic policy reflects Mao's belief that industry must foster both large and small scale projects and utilize western and native methods. The Great Leap and the communalization movements illustrate his theory that the productive forces must be liberated in order to achieve full use of China's human resources.

In military affairs, Mao has been given credit not only for formulating the detailed strategy of the revolutionary victory, but also for the subsequent establishment of the various military units and organizations. In military theory, too, Mao's chief approach has been to emphasize the factor of the human person. While he regards weapons as important elements, he holds that men, not weapons, are the decisive factor. The "human sea" tactics and the "everyone a soldier" movement are both traceable to this thought, as is the concept of the "paper tiger." The theory reflects in such emphasis as that of a NCNA dispatch of February 14, 1966 that "courage and not being afraid of death is more important than shooting with accuracy," and in Peking's attitude toward nuclear weapons (discussed in Chapter 8). Naturally, in keeping with his basic principles, Mao stresses that the military is subordinate to the political, and the political to the ideological. Or, as the February 18, 1966 issue of *Liberation Army Daily* put it, "the relationship between politics and arms is one between the whole and a part."

Among the more famous of Mao Tse-tung's works of a military nature are his *Strategic Problems of China's Revolutionary War* (December, 1936), *Strategic Problems in the Anti-Japanese Guerrilla War* (May, 1938), *On the Protracted War* (May, 1938), and *Problems of War and Strategy* (November, 1938). But all of Mao's works, not just those of a strictly military character, are obligatory reading for the troops of the PLA. The army's official organ has termed the thought of Mao "the highest directive for all kinds of work throughout the PLA" and insisted that "facts show that those armed with Mao Tse-tung's thought are the bravest, wisest, most united, most steadfast in class stand and have the sharpest sight."

The fields of art and literature have been strongly influenced by Mao's thought. As discussed in more detail in Chapter 10, Mao's 1942 speech to the Yenan Forum articulated the general line that art and literature must serve political aims and appeal effectively to the workers, peasants and soldiers.

The importance assigned to Mao Tse-tung's ideological contributions and the wide attention given them by the Party leadership have served to promote his general stature. Thus, as suggested previously, the thought of Mao underlies and reinforces the reverence for Mao as the Communist revolutionary symbol, thereby strengthening his position of power and adding to the prestige of the leadership specifically, and the Party and state generally. Whoever succeeds him, it is most reasonable to anticipate that the thought of Mao will continue to serve as the backbone of the Party leadership and to dominate the policies and programs of Peking.

THE PROBLEM OF INTERNAL SOLIDARITY

In Communist China, as in the Soviet Union, the strength of the regime varies directly with the internal solidarity of the leadership corps of the

Communist Party. The CPSU, in the course of its longer history, has been torn by a number of serious cleavages within the top leadership: these struggles have at times shaken the Party from top to bottom and claimed untold numbers of victims. The rarity of similar high level shake-ups in the ranks of the CPC before its advent to power led some observers to believe that the CPC would be able to avoid the path of the CPSU, resolving its internal dissensions without resort to open strife or the ruthless instrument of the purge.

The sudden, dramatic announcement on April 4, 1955, of the purge of Kao Kang and Jao Shu-shih—both figures of high prominence in the Chinese Communist Party—at once shattered this view and raised serious questions concerning the internal solidarity of the CPC leadership. Kao, reputed to be fifth-ranking in the Party hierarchy, was a veteran member of the Politburo, onetime Party boss of Northeast China or Manchuria, a Vice Chairman of the Central People's Government Council before the adoption of the 1954 Constitution, and the first head of the State Planning Commission. Jao was a member of the Central Committee, director of the CPC's Organization Department, and former Party boss of East China.

Virtually all that the Peking regime chose to reveal about the purge, including a report of Kao's suicide, was given in the resolution adopted by the Party National Conference on March 31, 1955, and published in *People's Daily* on April 5. Borrowing from Soviet example, the resolution told the familiar cloak and dagger story of high placed leaders suddenly discovered to have been secret conspirators and wreckers throughout much of their long and seemingly honorable Party careers. It noted that over a year earlier (in February, 1954) the Fourth Plenary Session of the Seventh Central Committee had established that "from 1949 Kao Kang engaged in conspiratoral activities aimed at seizing the reins of leadership of the Party and the state." The details were enumerated as follows:

In Northeast China and other places, he created and spread many rumors slandering the Central Committee of the Party and lauding himself, to sow discord and dissension among comrades and stir up dissatisfaction with the leading comrades of the Central Committee . . . engaged in activities to split the Party and in these activities formed his own anti-Party faction. . . . [This] faction violated the policy of the Central Committee . . . in the work in the Northeast area, tried its utmost to belittle the role of the Party, undermined Party solidarity and unity, and made the Northeast area the independent kingdom of Kao Kang. Kao Kang's anti-Party activities became even more outrageous after his transfer to work in the central organs in 1953. He even tried to instigate Party members in the army to support his conspiracy. . . .

Jao Shu-shih's duplicity was of even longer standing, according to the CC:

. . . In the ten years between 1943 and 1953, Jao Shu-shih on many occasions resorted to shameless deceit in the Party to seize power. During his tenure of office in East China, he did his utmost to adopt a rightist policy of surrender to the capitalists, landlords and rich peasants in the cities and countryside. At the same time, he did everything possible to protect counterrevolutionaries in defiance of the Central Committee's policy of suppressing them. After his transfer to the Central Committee in 1953, he thought that Kao Kang was on the point of success in his activities to seize power in the Central Committee. Therefore he formed an anti-Party alliance with Kao Kang and used his office as Director of the Organization Department of the Central Committee to start a struggle aimed at opposing leading members of the Central Committee and actively carried out activities to split the Party.

The CPC National Conference voted unanimously to expel Jao and Kao from the Party and to remove them from all posts within and outside the Party. In the case of Kao, the gesture was superfluous, since it was revealed that he had taken his own life following the CC plenum of February, 1954. Therefore, the resolution seemed to bespeak aggravation at plans going amiss: not only had Kao failed to admit his guilt, he had "expressed his ultimate betrayal of the Party" by suicide. In the case of Jao, the punishment might be regarded as less than severe, since he "has never shown any signs of repentance and now persists in an attitude of attacking the Party." Since his expulsion, the CPC has remained silent on the whereabouts or ultimate fate of Jao Shu-shih.

The episode of the Kao-Jao purge, and the charges of anti-Party activities against high placed CPC officials, has been recited at some length. It suggests several pertinent, indeed vital, questions concerning the internal solidarity of the Party leadership. Subsequent sections on "the Purge as an Instrument of Leadership Solidarity," "Socialist Education and Cultural Revolution for Correct Leadership," and the "Problem of Leadership Succession" examine the period following the Kao-Jao purge in terms of the actuality and potentiality of plots against Mao or failure to honor his thought. Here the discussion is confined to the general question of factionalism developing through the assumed formation of "pro-Soviet" or "pro-military" cliques bent upon seizing power.

For about ten years following its assumption of power in China, the CPC incessantly and proudly acknowledged its "Moscow orientation." In its second decade of power, the CPC has, first covertly and then overtly, attacked what it called modern revisionism or "Khrushchev's phony communism" espoused by the CPSU. These two phases must be carefully distinguished, for the mark of loyalty to the CPC leadership was characterized as much in the first stage by "Moscow orientation" as it has been in the second by attacks on the Soviet general line of indiscriminate "peaceful coexistence," or selling out to the forces of capitalism.

It should be understood at the outset that the term "Msocow orientation," when applied to particular Chinese Communist leaders, does not necessarily imply that they were trained in the Soviet Union, or spent any considerable time there. Mao himself, as has been noted, apparently never was in Russia before 1949, yet his pro-Soviet policy certainly had its origins before that visit. In point of fact, several categories can be distinguished. Some of the future leaders of Communist China did go to Moscow at one time or another with the outlook of a pilgrim or student. These were disposed to join the communist movement either before or soon after their arrival in the Soviet Union; hence they consciously undertook training there with the announced purpose of returning to China to apply what they had learned. Others found themselves in Moscow more or less by accident or under circumstances not of their own choosing, as in the case of a forced exile. Once there, they nevertheless took advantage of the opportunity to equip themselves with the Soviet type of applied revolutionary education. Still others became associated with the Russian capital mainly through their activities in the international communist movement. Conferences of the Comintern and Profintern (the international trade union arm of the Communist International) for example, brought many Chinese Communists to the Soviet Union. Special mention might be made of those who were in Moscow for the CPC Sixth National Congress in 1928, when the Party had been driven underground in China. After the CPC gained power in China, many were sent as delegates or representatives (and in the junior echelon, of course, for advanced training). Finally, there are those who have never set foot in the USSR, but who have been so immersed in Marxism-Leninism and so taken by the Soviet experiment and experience as to necessarily be termed "Moscow orientated." Moreover, these categories are not mutually exclusive: several of the leaders of Peking fit into several of the classifications.

Among the inner circle of the CPC leadership, Liu Shao-ch'i went to Moscow twice for intensive training, in addition to his visits in the service of the Comintern and Profintern, and subsequently as a representative of the Chinese People's Republic. Chou En-lai had some experience in the Soviet Union prior to his frequent visits since 1949. Lin Piao spent several years in Moscow. In fact, the number of Chinese Communist leaders who have acquired a Moscow orientation is too lengthy to permit further citation.[15] In any case, it must be concluded that until the inception of the present Moscow-Peking ideological debates, no leader could hope to

---

[15] The list would include the CPR's grand old marshal, Chu Teh, and his fiercest aide, Liu Po-ch'eng, the now purged P'eng Teh-huai, and the demoted economic planner Ch'en Yün, as well as the following full members of the CPC CC; Hsiao Ching-kuang, Nieh Jung-chen, Ch'en Shao-yü, Wang Chia-hsiang, Chang Wen-t'ien, Ch'en Po-ta, Yeh Chien-ying, Lu Ting-yi, Wu Yü-chang, Li Fu-ch'un, Ts'ai Ch'ang, Teng Ying-ch'ao, Liao Ch'eng-chih, Hsü T'e-li, Li Wei-han, and several others who have at least made brief visits.

count for very much in the Party and government hierarchy of Communist China unless he was well versed in Soviet theory and practice.

The Kao-Jao purge was interpreted in some circles as a sign that a pro-Soviet clique within the CPC was seeking to undermine the authority of Mao Tse-tung himself. In fact, several members of the Central Committee at the time had risen to prominence independently of Mao or before he consolidated his power. A few of these men once belonged to the Moscow-trained "return students group," which was prominent in central Party headquarters in the early 1930's. However, any potential factional power of this group was broken in the first large scale Party reform movement of 1942–44, known as the *Cheng-feng* movement. This drive was intended to clarify the CPC's basic position on matters of doctrine, organization and discipline and to correct deviations of the right or the left. Mao's position was consolidated beyond all challenge at the Central Committee meeting of March, 1943, and reaffirmed by the Seventh Party Congress in April, 1945. Hence, it may be said that all the members of the Central Committee at the time of the Kao-Jao purge held their office with Mao's consent.

The target of the Kao-Jao plot was not Mao himself. Rather, the real crime of Kao and Jao was to fail to give sufficient weight to the position of the subordinates Mao himself had chosen. This conclusion is strongly suggested in the official charge against Kao that he set forth an "absurd theory" distinguishing a "Party of the revolutionary bases and the army and a Party of the white areas" within the ranks of the CPC. The "white areas" refer principally to those parts of China that were under the rule of the Nationalist Government after the founding of the armed soviets in the border regions, from the late 1920's on. Both Liu Shao-ch'i and Chou En-lai served in those areas. Throughout the eight year war with Japan, for example, Chou was emissary of Mao at the KMT headquarters in Hankow, Chungking, and later Nanking. During the same period, Liu served as Party secretary in various regional bureaus away from the Party base in Yenan, though in 1943 he did return as a Party secretary to help Mao conduct the CPC reform movement. It is to be assumed that in advancing this theory Kao—whose own service was always within the areas under communist control—sought to belittle the position of the other top leaders and enhance his own standing. If indeed this was his intent, Kao failed miserably, since certainly the purge itself promoted Liu's prestige.

Had the Kao-Jao plot been the work of a pro-Soviet faction, Mao's position at the time would have to have been that of a sort of Far Eastern Tito. Instead, contemporary Soviet sources carefully pointed out that it was his critics, not Mao himself, who were guilty of ideological deviation.[16]

[16] Even before he became the official leader of the CPC, Soviet writers of the middle 1930's, such as G. Erenburg and P. Mif, acknowledged Mao's successful role in the establishment of

Moreover, the dubious hypothesis that the plot was the work of a Moscow-orientated faction would be supportable only if Kao Kang could be cast in the role of the leader of such a faction. Some observers have sought to do this by suggesting that Kao had especially close ties with Moscow, and may even have been hand-picked by Stalin to be the Kremlin's man in the CPC. Two grounds have been advanced for drawing this conclusion. The first is that during the period just after World War II, Kao held a series of important posts in Manchuria while Soviet influence there was at its height; thus he had an opportunity to maintain close contact with the Soviet occupation forces prior to their withdrawal in May, 1946. The second is that in July, 1949, Kao headed a trade mission to Moscow from the so-called "people's democratic authorities" of Manchuria, and that on his return he was made chairman of the newly formed Northeast People's Government. These items must be evaluated in a larger context. Kao had no record of any direct contact with the Soviets before his assignment to Manchuria in 1945. Despite his membership in the Politburo, most of his service in Manchuria was as deputy to Lin Piao, in a number of military, administrative, and Party posts. His own advancement seems to have followed the general rise in the CPC's fortunes, rather than to have resulted from any Soviet intervention on his behalf. As the communist military offensive against the KMT reached its final stages at the end of 1948, the CPC had an urgent need for experienced leaders in the conquered areas. Kao's senior colleagues in the Northeast were consequently called away to other assignments; only then did he attain the top post in the region. At the end of 1948, Kao was made Party chief and military commander in the area, and in August, 1949, was appointed chairman of the regional government. Other high ranking Party officials, such as Lin Piao, Ch'en Yün, Li Li-san and Li Fu-ch'un, had much closer contact with the Soviet occupation forces. Since Ch'en and Li Fu-ch'un were also confidants of the central leadership in Peking, they could have easily checked any efforts of Kao to maintain independent relations with the Soviets.

---

the Soviet areas and the formation of the Chinese Soviet Republic. Other Chinese leaders whose names have been associated with a pro-Soviet clique, such as Li Li-san, Ch'en Shao-yü (Wang Ming) and the late Ch'in Pang-hsien (Po Ko) have, as a rule been attacked as "deviationists" in official Soviet literature. Li Li-san, who in some quarters was regarded as a "Moscow man" on his return to China in 1945 with the Soviet troops occupying Manchuria, is actually charged with "leftist" deviations in the 1934 and 1953 first and second editions of the *Bolshaia Sovetskaia Entisklopediia*. Both editions speak of Li as having "inflicted great harm to the revolutionary movement." Similarly, Ch'en Shao-yü and Ch'in Pang-hsien are singled out in the second edition for their deviations and mistakes from January, 1931 to January, 1935, which "brought the Party and the revolution especially serious damage." Volume 38 of the first edition of the BSE, published in 1938, credits Mao with "waging uncompromising struggle against counterrevolutionary Trotskyism and other deviations."

Internal circumstances, rather than any preference or scheming on the part of Moscow, also explain the choice of Kao to head the 1949 trade mission. At the time, the USSR still recognized the Nationalist Government, since the Peking regime was not yet established. The Soviets undoubtedly preferred to negotiate with an established communist regional government, and Kao's choice was logical.

The historic position of Manchuria as a sensitive border region between China and the Soviet Union probably contributed to speculations that Kao once enjoyed special favor with the Soviet leaders. But had Kao been a tool of Moscow, the USSR would hardly have accepted his downfall without protest; it would have to regard the purge as a unilateral action by its Chinese ally threatening the vital Soviet interest in Manchuria. Instead, Moscow concurred in the purge. The Cominform newspaper *For A Lasting Peace, For a People's Democracy* (Bucharest, April 8, 1955) hailed the purge as "one of the decisive victories of the Party in the struggle for socialism in China."

The fact that the Kao-Jao plot can hardly be identified with a pro-Soviet clique attempting to undermine the authority of Mao and his chosen associates does not preclude the possibility. that such a faction could have developed subsequently. This possibility has become more likely in direct proportion to the intensification of Sino-Soviet debates over the correct ideological course in the present epoch. As noted in the subsequent sections, as individuals high placed members of the CPC have been associated with an anti-Mao line. The current attacks on Liu Shao-ch'i and others, who "sing the same tune as the Khrushchevs of the Soviet Union," may yet disclose the existence of a new pro-Moscow clique. But the very publicity attached to the present accusations would seem to indicate that Mao and his trusted subordinates are now reasonably confident that they can handle any member of-the CPC inclined to favor the Soviet general line.

The most likely major potential source for the formation of an anti-Mao clique is the arm of the military. Chapter 8 will analyze the ideological outlook of the military in detail, so only a few generalizations are pertinent here. In the 1956 enlargement of the Politburo and of the Central Committee itself, a significant number of the promoted officials were army men. Four of the six elected to the Politburo were military leaders; of the increased CC roster, seven of the twenty-three members also held the rank of marshal. The high position of these military leaders, coupled with their popularity, might therefore give them an opportunity to challenge the regular CPC leadership. It is evident that the inner core leadership, which itself is composed of several men who first became prominent in the military, is aware of such a potential danger. Mao and his trusted associates have carefully and consistently maintained the need for the military's subordination to the Party. And the leaders of the military have themselves so far indicated a willingness to serve as the faithful arm of the CPC. Mao's confident choice of Lin Piao as the next leader of Communist China symbolizes the nature of this unity of interests.

It should be noted that the present leaders of the armed forces in Communist China would have little reason to believe that their interests lie apart from those of the Party, or in conflict with the latter's general line. Even during the course of the civil war, the PLA attached as much importance to its political role as to its field operations. The status of the political commissar was at least equal to that of the field commander. In this generation of leadership practically every figure of stature has a military background and many formed their associations with Mao during the days of the revolutionary struggle. This relationship between the military and civilians among the leadership can be illustrated by the policies being carried out through the present cultural revolution. The "civilian" leadership of the CPC is using the PLA as the vanguard to promote Mao's ideas. Thus, for example, all Chinese are called upon to emulate the "Four Firsts," originally designed by Lin Piao for his PLA troops. But the "Four Firsts" emphasize that ideological work is the vital kernel of all work within the general category of political work, which is itself the highest classification. The "three in one" revolutionary committees symbolize this unity. Rather than representing any threat, the increasing prominence given to the PLA appears to reflect an ideal marriage of interests in which the ambitions of the "civilian" or "military" are indistinguishable.

THE PURGE AS AN INSTRUMENT OF LEADERSHIP SOLIDARITY*

If the use of the purge as an instrument to promote the CPC's leadership solidarity were illustrated by graphs, the process would be seen to be continuous. Nevertheless, and despite the meagerness of details, it might also be shown that high level purges have occurred only infrequently in response to some major threat to Party stability. The first of these purges dates back to the August Seventh (emergency) Conference in 1927, when the CPC successfully deposed the Party's spiritual father and first Secretary General, Ch'en Tu-hsiu. When Ch'en refused to submit to this "discipline," he was formally expelled from the CPC at the Sixth Congress late

---

* For a general account of the use of the purge as part of the CPC's continued vigilance against any form of deviationism, see Chapter 4, especially the subsection on "Party Reform Movements."

in 1928. In addition to being charged with "right deviationism" and "opportunism," Ch'en was attacked for failing to exercise class criticism against revolutionary allies, to develop the agrarian revolution and the class struggle of the masses, and to win over the armed forces. Greater than these crimes was his failure to arm workers and peasants to defeat the self-seeking and limited "revolutionary attempt" of the "temporary ally"— the KMT. In effect, Ch'en was made to serve as the scapegoat for the debacle suffered by the Party in 1927.[17]

The second major leadership purge took place in 1938, following a prolonged dispute over revolutionary strategy. The chief target was Chang Kuo-t'ao, who had been a founding member of the CPC in 1921, and was listed as a Politburo member at various times between 1927 (or ever earlier) and 1938. Chang served as a delegate from the CPC to several congresses of the Comintern and was chairman of the Hupeh-Honan-Anhwei Soviet; he also served under Mao as Vice Chairman of the Central Soviet Government of the Chinese Soviet Republic. But Chang was not in full agreement with Mao on the fundamental program for establishing independent soviets within China, since he regarded them as inapplicable to the Chinese scene. And, as already noted, during the Long March, Chang—then leader of the Fourth Front Army—also disagreed with Mao over the ultimate destination of the marchers. He favored Sinkiang or Sikang in the remote interior to Mao's choice of a more strategic location near Inner Mongolia. After leading his forces to join those of Mao in Northern Shensi, Chang served for a time as Vice Chairman of the Military Council of the Soviet regime. But he saw the handwriting on the wall late in 1936, or shortly thereafter, when his own forces were dispersed or re-assigned. In 1938, Chang managed to escape to an area held by the Kuomintang. He was promptly expelled from the Party, although years later Mao was still charging him with "serious sectarianism," of "clamoring to the Central Committee about independence," and of "rebellion against the Party."[18]

The Kao-Jao purge marked the third instance of action taken against a principal Party leader, and the first to lead directly to a dissident's death. In the light of the March 31 resolution of the 1955 Party Conference, both Kao and Jao were strongly warned of the error of their ways at the February, 1954 Central Committee meeting. This warning was followed by strenuous efforts to tighten Party discipline at all levels, particularly in the

---

[17] The later career and fate of Ch'en are described in Chapter 2.

[18] After his break with the communists, Chang joined the KMT and served for a time on the Planning Board of its Central Executive Committee. Later he was active for a short time in an anti-communist group in Hong Kong called the Democratic Fighting Alliance. Mao treated this episode in a lecture of February 1, 1942, entitled "Reform in Learning, the Party, and Literature."

higher echelons. Corrective measures took the form of a whole series of meetings throughout the country, devoted to "criticism and self-criticism" and "study" of the CC resolution. Parallel measures were taken through the Party press and reinforced by certain administrative measures of the central government.

In delivering the Politburo report to the Fourth Plenary Session of the Seventh Central Committee, Liu Shao-ch'i credited Mao with having initiated a proposal for strengthening Party unity at the Politburo meeting of December 24, 1953. Liu then spoke out vigorously, but without naming names, against the threat of a division within the upper ranks of the CPC. His language was echoed in the resolution of the plenum:

> . . . Among some of our cadres, even certain high-ranking cadres within our Party, there is still a lack of understanding of the importance of Party unity and of the significance of collective leadership . . . [These cadres] exaggerate the role of the individual and emphasize individual prestige. . . . They even regard the region or department under their leadership as their individual inheritance . . . or independent kingdom.

Liu's report and the plenum's resolutions constituted a call to "all comrades in the Party to raise their revolutionary vigilance and strengthen Party unity." The theme was taken up and emphasized in a series of six editorials which appeared in the *People's Daily* over the next two months (February 18, March 22, and April 4, 13, 20 and 23). Although Liu's charges were elaborated, the guilty were not named. For example, the April 20 editorial said that the guilty included "a considerably large portion of our cadres" who "in the areas or work departments under their control, rule as despots." At the same time, innumerable meetings were held at every level of the CPC organization to express support for the CC's resolutions. The "high ranking cadres" were particularly urged to submit themselves to criticism and self-criticism.

While these efforts were providing a kind of psychological preparation for the eventual purge, special attention was given to Kao Kang's former region, the Northeast. Between March 26 and April 24, the CC's Northeast Bureau sponsored a regional conference for "senior Party cadres" on the subject of Party unity. The 517 regular delegates were joined by 190 "observers," who undoubtedly included a strong contingent from Peking headquarters. The speakers included members of the Northeast Bureau—though not Kao Kang himself. The line of criticism stressed that the importance of the individual had been exaggerated while the importance of Party leadership had been "minimized" (that is, disregarded).

The CPC hierarchy also determined to increase its central control and discipline by abolishing all regional administrative areas. Thus the Northeast Administrative Committee, which had replaced the Northeast "People's Government" in the 1952 reorganization, was itself abolished as of August 15, 1954, and the principal officers were dismissed from their posts and assigned elsewhere. As a further sign of the centralization drive, the Peking leadership announced that the regional Party and government organ, the Mukden *Northeast Daily*, would cease publication on August 21, to be replaced by the *People's Daily*, the mats of which were to be airmailed to Mukden daily. Needless to say, the effect of these various measures was to eliminate the possibility of any regionally based support for the personal leadership of Kao Kang. Despite these elaborate preparations, the culminating action of the purge remained a closely guarded secret. Official confirmation that the orders of the Fourth Plenum had been carried out took over a year, coming only at the end of the delayed meeting of the Party's National Conference in March, 1955.

In reviewing the events of the purge, it is evident that the strategic positions held by Kao and Jao within the Party confronted the inner leadership core with a serious problem of control and discipline. This is clear first of all from the very nature of the charges. Although a few instances of failure or misconduct in carrying out policies were referred to in the conference resolution, most of the alleged crimes of Kao and Jao, from rumor-mongering to attempts to split the Party, constituted violations of Party discipline rather than disputes over policy. An April 10, 1955 *People's Daily* editorial suggested that the conspirators "dared not publicly bring forward any program or principle against the Central Committee," because they realized that "all Party members and the people throughout the country have full confidence in the Central Committee of the Party headed by Mao Tse-tung." In the official version, therefore, the motives of the so-called alliance were simply "to seize the supreme power of the Party and the state by conspiratoral means."

To meet this threat, the National Conference, simultaneously with its action on the Kao-Jao anti-Party alliance, approved a change in the machinery of Party discipline to tighten the grip of the central leadership. Under Chapter VIII of the 1945 Party Constitution, "discipline inspection committees" had been authorized as control organs for all membership units. The work of these committees was further defined by the Central Committee in November, 1949. However, the CC neglected to provide for its own supervision of the committees: instead, each of the committees was chosen by, and under the supervision of, the Party committee at its particular level. The new arrangement, which substituted a system of "control commissions" for these "discipline inspection committees," emphatically provided that "higher control commissions of the Party have the right to examine the work of the lower control commissions, and the right to examine, approve and change decisions made by lower control commissions." The Conference resolution was frank as to the motives:

The purpose of this is to strengthen Party discipline and the struggle against all kinds of violations by Party members of law and discipline, and particularly to prevent a recurrence of so serious a case as that of the Kao Kang-Jao Shu-shih anti-Party alliance, which gravely imperilled Party interests.

These measures made it more difficult for an individual or clique to oppose the inner core leadership: they did not solve the problem of eliminating opposition to the directives or wishes of the Central Committee. The anti-rightist drive, which followed in the wake of the Blooming and Contending movement in 1957, included among its victims many Party members with considerable experience. Even amid all the polemics concerning Party and state greatness and solidarity, that accompanied the launching of the Great Leap Forward in 1958, the inner leadership gave indication that pockets of resistance still existed within the ranks of the CPC. In his May, 1958 speech to the Second Session of the Eighth Party Congress, when Liu Shao-ch'i officially inaugurated the Great Leap, he also warned against "some comrades" who persisted in "keeping to the right."

The failures of the Great Leap and the original communalization program, which must be attributed in large measure to the planning errors of the highest Party leadership, are discussed in detail elsewhere in these pages. In 1958, Peking was also thwarted in its ambitions which led to the Taiwan Straits incident and was forced to deal with an increasingly critical and intransigent Soviet Union. The passive, and sometimes active, resistance of the peasants to official directives and the bungling and opportunism of many of the cadres were matters of grave concern to the CPC Central Committee. But these signals of resistance were a lesser threat than that emanating from the inner circle of the military.

The dissatisfaction of certain leaders of the military seemed to stem from their opposition to the Central Committee's directives ordering PLA troops to participate actively in productive labor. In the estimate of some officers, this policy would have an adverse effect on the state of military preparedness.[19] Highest placed among these critics was Marshal P'eng Teh-huai, Minister of Defense and member of the CC Politburo, veteran of the Long March and long a trusted member of the inner leadership core. According to one source, P'eng was probably encouraged to question the commune system and allocation of military manpower by Khrushchev himself, who had at least implicitly regarded the Great Leap and communalization with cynicism from their very introduction. This interpretation is reinforced by the subsequent disclosures made in the growing atmosphere of Sino-

[19] It should be noted that the People's Liberation Army had, from its formation, regularly participated in manual labor. The question here is one of proportional allotment of funds and manpower between military and civilian occupations. See Chapter 8.

Soviet disagreement. For example, the statement prepared jointly by the editorial boards of *Red Flag* and *People's Daily* for publication on September 6, 1963 noted: "In his conversation with the delegation of the CPC, Khrushchev . . . even expressed undisguised support for anti-Party elements in the Chinese Communist Party." [20]

The CPC Central Committee held a series of conferences in the first half of 1959, to analyze the alarming defects of the Great Leap and commune systems, and to deal with the inner challenge to its leadership. The communique issued by the eighth plenum of the Eighth CC, after its meeting in Lushan in August, enjoined Party committees "at all levels" to criticize and overcome "right opportunist ideas." In the following month, several high placed officials were removed from their posts. Marshal P'eng himself was accused of failing to pass the "bourgeois-democratic stage of the revolution"—or of never really being a communist—and was sent into obscurity in a rural commune. Among others, Su Yü was removed as Chief of Staff of the PLA and Chang Wen-t'ien as Vice Minister of Foreign Affairs.

Thus the critics were silenced: as yet there is no proof that the accused were engineering any plans to stage a coup—a fact which may explain the relative leniency of their punishments. But the CC did not forget this threat. At its tenth plenary session, on September 28, 1962, the Central Committee issued a communique which denounced "subversion within our State or our Party" and announced its plan to "strengthen the work of the Party Control Commission." Thus, although the CC itself at least tacitly admitted to errors in its Great Leap and commune policies—in a series of decisions which ordered retrenchment in certain areas of the two programs (see the appropriate chapter)—it did not relax its vigilance against Party dissenters. In fact, given the growing Sino-Soviet discord, this task assumed increased importance. In more recent years, the Central Committee's own Control Commission has been joined by the growing authority of the political arm of the PLA itself to ensure orthodoxy throughout the Party and among the people.

SOCIALIST EDUCATION AND CULTURAL REVOLUTION FOR CORRECT LEADERSHIP

The Essence and Origin of the Proletarian Cultural Revolution

Socialist education and cultural revolution are intimately related to cultivating, upholding, inspiring, and promoting the communist world

[20] From "The Origin and Development of the Differences between the Leadership of the CPSU and Ourselves." One of the earliest remarks indicative of the Central Committee's awareness that certain officers were opposed to its directives was made by Chu Teh on July 31, 1958, when he attacked "tendencies toward an exclusive military viewpoint."

outlook. They are important in a fundamental way to every communist member, cadre or leader in guarding against his possible ideological deviation and behavioral deterioration. Naturally socialist education and cultural revolution are many times more important to members of the Party's leadership corps in insuring its ideological purity and revolutionary vitality. Normally, as Chinese proverbs go—"when the wind blows the grass bends" —that is, the influence of leaders over lesser Party functionaries and rank and file must be overwhelming. Moreover, whatever is preferred by the leaders would usually be anxiously carried out by their followers. Thus, it must be the top priority of the Party to insure the healthy development of its hard core by conducting effective socialist education and cultural revolution to strengthen a correct leadership, especially in a demanding domestic and crucial international environment.

The urgent need for socialist education and cultural revolution to combat deviation in theory and practice among Party leaders is further articulated by the general realization in both the communist and the non-communist worlds of the gradual resurgence of a comparatively easy life in Eastern Europe, together with Peking's repeated reports of a wide-spread trend toward capitalism and corruption in the Soviet Union and its impact on certain CPC leaders in authority. As under any dictatorship, "power corrupts" and "absolute power corrupts absolutely." In Communist China, too, there have been reports concerning some leaders' negative thought and conduct or possible corruption through self-content and self-indulgence as well as inertia and sabotage in carrying out the unfinished communist world revolution. For those in power in Communist China, the only way to avert possible corruption is to confront the errant with the Party's revolutionary challenge, and to compel them to deny any undue, extravagant privileges of body comfort or influence. It is through this approach that the Party can expect to stimulate positive ideas and behavior among its leaders in multiplying further revolutionary struggle.

In fact, as a far-reaching proposition, requiring generations to fulfill—if indeed it can be realized at all—the communist or proletarian revolution demands far more than a political revolution to complete its assumed mission. Victory in political revolution is a firm stepping stone to launch economic, social, and cultural revolutions. To the communists, these revolutions cannot stop halfway. If some or all of the Party leaders were hit by "Sugar-coated bullets of the capitalists," then others must rise to lead the all-embracing revolution. Otherwise, like navigating against the current, not to advance means to retreat. In the case of the communist revolution, any retreat in ideology and struggle is bound to endanger the fruits of political revolutions already achieved in Europe, Asia, and Latin America. Thus the communists must think of these revolutions in global terms for, otherwise, the non-communist world would exert strong influence on and eventually overwhelm the communist world.

The most important and fundamental of all types of revolutions embraced in the communist idea of revolution is the cultural revolution. Dedicated communists, especially their leaders, cannot be satisfied by mere superficial submission to their direction in political, economic, and social arrangements. They must work to create wholehearted support and conscientious fulfillment, which, in turn, requires a cultural transformation. Without the sustaining effect of the all-out, universal belief derived only by a thoroughgoing cultural revolution, neither political, nor economic, nor social fruits of the communist revolution can endure. This type of cultural revolution must reach down to man's fundamental attitude toward himself, his fellow men, and his physical environment. Similar to this approach, Theodore Chen observes in *Problems of Communism* (November–December, 1966):

The communists are not satisfied with building a strong and prosperous China; they must push ahead to establish a new society and a new way of life. For them, it is not enough to have a government exercising effective control, not enough to have a stable and growing economy, not enough to have the piecemeal social reforms that are customarily sought by bourgeois-liberal reformers. Such developments are desirable only insofar as they constitute an advance toward the ultimate goal of establishing socialism and communism. Communism calls for the establishment of a new society, not only with new institutions but also with new social and economic relationships reflecting a new ideology. It demands no less than a new type of man for a new social order. It requires fundamental changes in the minds and hearts of the people.

With the creation of the new social order and the preparation of new socialist or communist man as objectives, Mao and his followers deal with human nature and its transformation in a fundamental way. While exceeding in depth and precision the requirement concerning the reorientation of human ideas and values by the world's sages of ages, Mao's outcry is not entirely unfamiliar to the Christian faithfuls who are urged to bear the cross to follow Christ in man's salvation.[21]

Likewise, Mao and his communists require self-denial. Leaving out Party jargon, their persuasion is hardly distinguishable in this respect from

[21] The messianic nature of Mao's role and direction has been pointed out on many occasions. The point to be emphasized here is that Mao demands of his followers an inner perfection which may be compared to the evangelical counsels of Christianity, however different may be his rationale or goals. In an historical sense, the fervor of the Early Church was responsible for the conversion of Western Europe. Without similar fervor, Mao and his successors cannot hope to convert the world to communism.

In the Christian code, the world will be changed only by the transformation of the individual, who must overcome his own weaknesses to overcome society. This interior labor, ceaseless and difficult, begins with self-denial.

the exhortations and strictures applicable to Christians. For example, the *Hongqi* commentator suggests in June, 1967:

Among the handful of Party people in authority taking the capitalist road who have been exposed so far, some were originally bad elements who hid in the Party. Others have turned bad since China was liberated, because they went counter to Chairman Mao's teachings. They grew conceited and complacent, assumed the airs of a self-styled hero, were unwilling to make progress, loved pleasure and disliked continued hard living. They welcomed flattery from the bourgeoisie. As a result, they were hit by the sugar-coated bullets of the bourgeoisie. What has occurred may help us guard against any future eventuality. This is a historical lesson that we should never forget. [22]

Although aiming at entering into and fortifying an atheistic, classless society, the communists who follow Mao realize an urgent need for a supreme effort, similar to that of the Christians, to change human nature in their proletarian cultural revolution. As responsible leaders, the failure of Liu Shao-ch'i and others, who are "in authority and taking the capitalist road," to join in the determined struggle to transform their own natures makes them more than others a greater target for such a revolutionary struggle. Thus, in "Some Current Problems Raised in the Socialist Education Movement in the Rural Areas," or "the 23-article document," drawn up under Mao's personal guidance in January 1965, Mao was given credit for having put forward for the first time the important dictum: "The main target of the present movement is those within the Party who are in authority and are taking the capitalist road." [23]

In the final analysis, the Communist Party requires, especially among its leaders, socialist education and cultural revolution to change or divert the traditional bourgeois-liberal concept of "human nature" based on "enlightened self-interest." The latter concept, based as it is on "common sense," represents the prominently underlying personal and social motivation in a traditional society and has been, in a sense, mainly responsible for world civilization. But, faithful communists, let alone their leaders, cannot tolerate this time-honored "bourgeois" concept of "enlightened self-interest." They consider it as man's justification for traditional evil practices of "exploitation of man by man and of nation by nation." The communists claim that their revolutionary goal—"to each according to his needs, and from each according to his ability"—has made "enlightened self-interest" obsolete, superfluous, and objectionable. Yet the communists

[22] "Hongqi" Commentator, "Guard Against Corruption by Bourgeois Ideology," *Hung Ch'i* (*Hongqi* or *Red Flag*), No. 10, 1967; reprinted in *Peking Review*, No. 27, June 30, 1967, p. 33. A typical concrete example for this principle of self-denial is found in "Regulations on Seriously Improving Style of Work," adopted by the Shantung Provincial Revolutionary Committee on June 7, 1967; for the text of the Resolutions see *ibid.*, p. 32.

[23] "A Theoretical Weapon for Making Revolution Under the Dictatorship of the Proletariat," (Editorial) *Hung Ch'i*, No. 10, 1967, also in *Peking Review*, No. 26, June 23, 1967, p. 30.

are seriously concerned about the possible impact of the traditional view of "enlightened self-interest" on less dedicated communist leaders or undetermined opportunists. Therefore, socialist education and cultural revolution are critically needed by the Party to strengthen its leading cadres and heirs of revolution in guarding against any moral decay, particularly ideological degeneration.

Not until the celebration of the first anniversary of the cultural revolution did the Chinese Communists clarify the timing of those events which launched it. On June 1, 1967, *Red Flag* pointed out that on June 1, 1966: "Chairman Mao decided to publicize through press and radio the Marxist-Leninist big character poster which was the first to appear in China and had been put up in Peking University." "This great strategic measure," the voice of the CPC continued, "lit the mighty flame of the great proletarian cultural revolution." Other important decisions and incidents had led directly to Mao's action. During the months of September and October, 1965, Mao had suggested that Wu Han be criticized and repudiated. Consequently, "under the direct guidance of Comrade Chiang Ch'ing," Yao Wen-yuan prepared to mold public opinion by issuing his "On the New Historical Drama 'Hai Jui Dismissed From Office.' " After the "P'eng Chen clique" refused to permit Yao's article to appear in the Peking press, on December 21, 1965, Mao pointed out explicitly that Wu Han's *Hai Jui* referred implicitly to the action of the 1959 CPC Central Committee's Lushan Conference and the dismissal of P'eng Teh-huai. Mao further classified P'eng Chen as a type of "Hai Jui."

By February, 1966, two diametrically opposed lines of ideological interpretation had emerged within the ranks of the CPC. On the one hand, between February 3 and 7, the P'eng Chen faction prepared an "Outline Report," later labelled as "a counterrevolutionary program . . . aiming at a restoration of capitalism." In Shanghai, however, members of the armed forces engaged in ideological work were simultaneously meeting at the order of Lin Piao, and under the personal direction of Chiang Ch'ing.[24] Between February 2 and 20, this assembly labored to prepare a "Forum Summary," later personally reviewed by Mao Tse-tung on three occasions. In the words of *Red Flag* (no. 9, 1967), "the appearance of the 'Forum Summary' and the 'Outline Report' . . . heralded the coming of the great storm of the great proletarian cultural revolution." In its October 1, 1965 editorial, celebrating the sixteenth anniversary of the establishment of the People's Republic of China, *People's Daily* emphatically declared:

At present the socialist education movement is continuing to develop on all fronts.

---

[24] At the May 23, 1967 mass rally in Peking to commemorate the 25th anniversary of publication of Mao's "Talks at the Yenan Forum on Literature and Art," Chi Pen-yü noted that "proletarian revolutionaries in Shanghai . . . led by Comrade Chiang Ch'ing had begun the criticism of *Hai Jui Dismissed From Office* in November, 1965.

It represents a profound socialist revolution. The struggle between proletarian ideology and bourgeois ideology, between the socialist road and the capitalist road, is being unfolded in greater depth in the political, economic, organizational as well as ideological fields. . . . The socialist education movement is the key link in all work.

Red Flag's editorial marking the same occasion expressed a portentous warning:

. . . Old ideas in disguised forms often sneak their way into new things, corrode men's minds bit by bit and change the color of new things, thus paving the way for the restoration of the old system. . . . All those old things which are not in the interests of the people must be uprooted without the slightest compromise. The socialist education movement going on in the cities and countryside of China today is primarily a profound movement of criticism and self-criticism in the ideological field.

From its beginnings, the drive for socialist education—later to grow into the cultural revolution—was clear as to general goals, methods and leadership. Employing Party and PLA cadres, Mao Tse-tung and his close associates intended to eliminate any sign of the restoration of capitalist or bourgeois thought and bring the class struggle to a higher stage. This sort of mass indoctrination, together with the usual efforts at rectification through criticism and self-criticism, may be considered as similar to previous drives. The new note injected, however, was to prove to be of major significance. According to the leadership, those individuals most in need of socialist education were often members of the CPC who "waved red flags to oppose the red flag." [25] That is, some Party members, outwardly appearing orthodox, were judged to be secretly conspiring against Mao and his thought. Moreover, some of these class enemies held offices at the highest levels of Party and state power. As the now very influential organ of the PLA, Liberation Army Daily, phrased it in a May 4, 1966 editorial: this new breed of traitors "taking advantage of the functions and powers given them by the Party and Government, have put under their absolute control some departments and units." By virtue of their exalted positions, "those who don't know the truth still look at them with blind faith." In short, for the first time Mao and his friends were inviting the masses to take part in the vital work of Party rectification at the highest level. By participating actively in the exposure and denunciation of Party members, officials, and especially leaders, the masses—whose eye according to Mao, "is most discerning"—would collaborate in the CPC's purge process of the first order.

[25] As stressed by Red Flag (no. 8, 1966), the policy of "waving red flags to oppose the red flag . . . is the most peculiar feature of the representatives of the bourgeois class who infiltrated into the Party."

The Case of P'eng Chen

Socialist education and cultural revolution for healthy leaders and cadres have both theoretical and practical aspects. Not limited to lectures and readings they also include the usual forms of ideological rectification. They are conducted in the manner of revolutionary struggle to unite theory with practice and are accompanied by accelerated purge tactics against deviationists in the leadership corps and cadre elite. When P'eng Chen was the chief target during the initial phase, the finger of guilt quickly began to point to the CPC's Peking Municipal Committee. As early as May 16, 1966, *Red Flag* had inquired "who has been sheltering Teng T'o?"[26] The implication was that he was being protected by P'eng Chen himself. P'eng, First Secretary of the Peking Committee, Vice Chairman of the NPC, and member of the Central Committee and Politburo, also served as the secretary in charge of political affairs in the CC's Secretariat. A frequent spokesman for official Party policies and a first-ranking diplomat often assigned to entertaining prominent foreign visitors, P'eng has been considered as one of the top ranking members of the Party hierarchy. He served as deputy head of the CPC delegation to Moscow in July, 1963, and was prominent in the Party's various anti-rightist movements, particularly that which followed the period of the Blooming and Contending campaign. Although his name had dropped out of the news in March, 1966, and he was not present for the May Day celebrations of that year in Peking, P'eng's stature in the Party seemed assured.

Then, on June 3, 1966, Peking radio dramatically revealed that the subversion of the "Three-Family Village clique" had, in fact, been permitted or encouraged by P'eng Chen. In a terse announcement, confirmed the following day by *People's Daily*, the CPC Central Committee revealed that Li Hsüeh-feng, First Secretary of the CC's North China Bureau, had been concurrently appointed First Secretary of the Peking Municipal Committee. Wu Teh, First Secretary of the Kirin Provincial Committee, was transferred to the post of Second Secretary of the Peking Committee at the same time. Their new assignment was to reorganize the Peking Committee in order to eliminate those revisionists who favored the "Three-Family clique."

This June, 1966 purge of revisionist "careerists and conspirators" of the

[26] Teng T'o, formerly the Editor-in-Chief of the *Jen-min Jih-pao*, was then an alternate secretary of the Secretariat of the CPC CC North China Bureau, a secretary of the Secretariat of the CPC Peking Municipal Committee, and concurrently chief editor of the latter's organ, *Ch'ien-hsien (Front)*. He published in this periodical "The Three-Family Village" with two co-authors—Liao Mo-sha, Director of the United Front Work Department of the CPC Peking Committee, and Wu Han, a Vice Mayor of Peking. See Chapter 10 for further details.

Peking Party committee was an important chapter in socialist education for revolutionary leadership. The purged were also identified as "lackeys of US imperialism." From the Chinese Communist point of view the popularization of socialist education through purge and rectification must be regarded as sign of strength, rather than weakness. The charges indirectly levelled against P'eng Chen in *Red Flag* (no. 9, 1966) are reminiscent of the 1953 Kao-Jao purge, the last previous major instance of the removal of high-placed and trusted Party leaders. The members of the Peking Committee were accused of trying to create an "independent kingdom," while "harboring intense hatred for Mao Tse-tung's thought." Unlike the secrecy which originally shrouded the Kao-Jao purge, the dismissal of P'eng has been given much prominence in the Party press.[27] The ability of Mao and his trusted subordinates to uncover such "plots" near the center sets an example for all Party members that no one is above the watchful eye of the Party. The CPC's persistent testing of the ideological dedication of its members and the threat of harsh disciplinary action are intended to further solidify, purify, and vitalize the Party.

The purge of P'eng Chen and the CPC's Peking Committee marked the transformation of the drive for socialist education to the stage of cultural revolution. This decision to widen and intensify the struggle in the interests of Party purity was motivated by several considerations. The downfall of P'eng proved that there were anti-Mao pockets of discontent within the Party. It was also intended as a warning to other Party officials who had sympathized with or even protected P'eng. In this sense, the Peking purge revealed the scope of the disaffection—a scope which might best be dealt with by employing an enormous force outside the ranks of the CPC, but closely collaborating with its leadership. The Red Guards aptly fit this description.

The Case of Liu Shao-ch'i and His "Black Gang"

Until mid-1966, students of affairs in Communist China had little reason to question that the line of leadership succession had been carefully planned by Mao himself to prepare the way for his trusted associate, Liu Shao-ch'i. Like his superior, Liu Shao-ch'i originally came from Hunan province, where he was born probably in 1898. In 1920, Liu went to Shanghai, where Voitinsky was organizing a communist youth league. Liu joined the Party in Moscow, where he had been sent for training. He probably returned to Shanghai in 1922–23, where he was assigned to organizing the workers.[28]

---

[27] For details on the purge of the Peking Committee see Chapter 4.

[28] Conflicting dates place Liu's first visit to Moscow as early as 1919, and as late as 1923. Similarly, the dates for his return to China range from 1922 to 1925. The second edition of the *Bolshaia Sovetskaia Entsiklopediia* (*Great Soviet Encyclopedia*) (1954) fails to mention either the early visits of Liu or those of the other CPC leaders.

After the abortive communist uprising of 1927, Liu returned to Moscow, where he studied at the Sun Yat-sen University and the Red Army Academy. During this interval he was also associated with the Comintern. At the Sixth CPC Congress in 1928, Liu was named chief of the Party's Labor Bureau and a member of the Central Committee. According to the *Bolshaia Sovetskaia Entsiklopediia*, he was involved in the 1929 Russian expedition against Manchuria, in the undeclared war with China over the Chinese Eastern Railway. From 1929 on, he was Secretary to the Manchurian regional committee. In the summer of 1930, at the Fifth Congress of the Profintern, Liu was elected a member of its executive bureau. Sources differ sharply as to Liu's activities in the 1930's. According to the common version, Liu was smuggled into Kiangsi in 1934, to be commissioner of labor, but was left behind on the Long March in order that he might continue his labor unionization activities underground in the cities. Other sources maintain that Liu returned to Moscow in about 1937. It is certain that he was elected to the CC Politburo by 1931, and that by 1942 Mao was displaying high trust in his assistant by assigning him to direct the CPC's first large scale rectification campaign, the *Cheng-feng* movement. In 1945, when Mao went to Chungking to confer with Chiang Kai-shek, Liu appears to have assumed the direction of the Party in Yenan.

Within the ranks of the CPC, until the disclosures made in the cultural revolution, concerning the all-important work of an ideological character Liu Shao-ch'i's reputation was second only to that of Mao. His services have included drafting of the 1945 Party Constitution, the Common Program of the Political Consultative Conference in 1949, and the Constitution of the People's Republic of China in 1954. He was doubtlessly instrumental in the revision of the CPC Constitution in 1956. As noted elsewhere, among the other honors bestowed on Liu were those of leading the Kao-Jao purge in 1953, and of announcing the Great Leap Forward in May, 1958. Thus his elevation to the office of chief of state in April, 1959, was neither surprising nor unmerited.

The change of fortune of Liu Shao-ch'i in the Chinese Communist movement is of unquestionable historical importance and is, therefore, most instructive. His dramatic reversal elicits various interpretations and much speculation. However, some features of Mao Tse-tung's quarrel with Liu can be established with certitude. Chief among these is the fact that their violent differences of views have reached a stage wherein reconciliation is virtually impossible. New documentation reveals that these differences actually began many years ago, although earlier feuds were neither so sharp nor so vital as to rule out collaboration. Yet it must also be recalled that from 1943 or 1945 until 1958 or 1959, Liu was Mao's first deputy, his right-hand man, and his chosen eventual successor. It was Liu who enshrined the thought of Mao in the 1945 CPC Constitution. Rumors and afterthoughts notwithstanding, Mao's 1958 decision to make Liu his successor as head of state was based upon his personal estimate of Liu as someone like himself in dedication.

Given the record of intimate collaboration between Mao and Liu, what factors changed this relationship? Which of them is fundamentally responsible for the shift? It is generally recognized that, since his ascendency to chairmanship of the state, Liu's position has consistently been one of subordination to the shadow of Mao. While Liu and his associates have enjoyed important Party and state offices, the principal guidelines—the three red flags of the communes, great leap and general line of socialist construction, and the anti-revisionist struggle which presently takes the form of the great proletarian cultural revolution—must be credited directly to Mao. The stature of Mao's thought has risen enormously since his 1957 major contribution "On the Correct Handling of Contradictions Among the People." The present phenomena of the cultural revolution and the Red Guards have their roots in this interpretation of class struggle under socialism and revolution under the dictatorship of the proletariat. In tracing Mao's words and deeds over the decades, the consistency of his logic must be acknowledged. Consequently, if Liu retained the unequivocal dedication to the thought of Mao that he demonstrated in 1945, there would be little reason for opposing Mao's subsequent ideological pronouncements or political programs. Rather, as Lin Piao did in his 1965 theory on "people's war," Liu might have been expected to reinforce or even extend Mao's concepts.

Gradually more involved in state bureaucracy at home and contacts with the Soviets, Liu was noticeably unable to keep pace with Mao in developing ideological precepts. As this gap widened, Liu probably ran counter to Mao's wishes and expectations concerning vital Party and state programs. Were there no ideological gaps or conflicts between them, no change would be warranted in their accustomed working relationship. Change was provoked by Liu's significant omissions and commissions and Mao's corresponding determination to rescue the Communist Party and movement. Since any communist behavior needs to be understood in terms of associated ideological attitudes, Peking's unprecedented leadership crisis in the form of the Mao-Liu feud must be attributed to Liu's deviation from Mao's ideological path.

The crimes of Liu Shao-ch'i are said to be economic, cultural, military, political and personal in character. All are closely related to his ideological deviation. In the economic realm, Liu has been accused of promoting economism by emphasizing the "traitor's theory of survival," that principles are unimportant after one has lost his life. Dating back to 1949, he is said to have favored a capitalistic "production viewpoint" based on material incentives.[29] In the 1950's, Liu opposed Mao's plans for agricultural collectivization which culminated in the formation of the communes. During the economic dislocation of 1959–61, he advocated the widespread reintroduction of capitalism since, in his judgment, the communes were unrealistic and adventurist forms of "utopian agricultural socialism."[30] In cultural work, Liu has been labelled the "back-stage manager of the black line for literature and art" who, as early as 1956, formulated a plan to influence public opinion in favor of a restoration of bourgeois values.[31]

At the personal level, Liu Shao-ch'i's choice of friends is regarded as damning evidence of his bourgeois inclinations. Moreover, his marriage into the family of "feudal bureaucrat" and "blood-sucking hangman of the working class" Wang Huai-ch'ing, and his favoritism toward his in-laws in this "petticoat relationship" have been widely castigated as proof of personal deviation from the goals of socialist revolution.[32] On Liu's orders, his brother-in-law, Wang Kuang-ying, a former capitalist and KMT official, was given a number of state offices, and even became a delegate to the National People's Congress. Liu's wife, Wang Kuang-mei, has not only shared in his guilt, but also been attacked for her own crimes.[33] Both Liu and Wang were criticized for fabricating the so-called "T'aoyüan experience" to challenge Mao's socialist education movement in the countryside and to produce a prototype of the "counterrevolutionary revisionist line," which was "left" in form, but "right" in fact. According to an article in the March 4, 1967 issue of the organ of the "Red Guards of the

[29] According to *People's Daily*, April 15, 1967, following an April, 1949 visit to the privately owned Tungya Woolen Textile Mill (now the No. 3 Woolen Textile Mill) of Tientsin, Liu reportedly said: ". . . exploitation by capitalist is an historical service and no communist will blot out the services performed by the capitalists. . . . Today capitalist exploitation is legal, and the more of it, the better. Dividends should be raised. . . . If you are able to exploit more, you will be benefiting both the State and the people, and everybody will approve of it."

[30] See, for example, the article "The Fallacy Advocated by the Top Ambitionist in Economic Work Refuted" prepared by the Tungfanghung Corps of the Economic Research Institute and published in the April 22, 1967 Peking *Kuang-ming Jih-pao*. Liu is quoted as advocating: "If our economy is not as dynamic and diversified as the capitalist economy, and if ours is planned according to a stereotyped pattern, what socialist superiority is there in it?"

[31] Liu had been identified as the "boss" of Chou Yang and other conspirators from literary and art circles. According to *People's Daily* of April 23, 1967, in March, 1956, Liu personally dictated a program for the Chinese Writers Association aimed at fostering bourgeois values. For details on this phase see Chapter 10.

[32] Wang Huai-ch'ing died in 1956, after having been "paid homage" on a number of occasions by Liu. The latter's attendance at the funeral ceremonies and gifts of flowers and ceremonial scrolls have been called "a big exposure of the bourgeois world outlook of Liu." See Canton's *Pa-erh-wu Chan-pao (August 25 Battle News)*, February 14, 1967.

[33] Wang Kuang-mei was born in the United States, during one of her parents' pleasure trips. After completing postgraduate study at Yenching University in 1945, she worked as an English translator. In 1946, she moved to Yenan. See *Pa-erh-wu Chan-pao, ibid.*

Peking Colleges and Universities," in her field work Wang chided Mao, opposed the propagation of his thought, denied the class struggle, sheltered revisionist members of the Party, and worked to prepare public opinion for her husband's usurpation of Party and state power.

For her crimes, Wang Kuang-mei has been criticized by her children, denounced by the Red Guards and, like her husband, probably forced to issue confessions. According to the January 11, 1967 *Chingkangshan*, Madame Liu signed a confession of her mistakes and those of her husband following an all night criticism session by Red Guard units at Tsinghua University.[34] Liu's "self-investigation,"[35] which may be regarded as a model of personal humiliation, admits his failure to understand the nature of the class struggle or master the thought of Mao. Acknowledging that "Comrade Lin Piao is much more distinguished than I am in every respect." Liu pledged his determination to "learn Mao Tse-tung's thought in the same manner as Lin Piao did."

The political crimes of Liu Shao-ch'i are integrally linked to his alleged betrayal of the Communist Party and its revolutionary goals. Their potential impact is held to be enormous. As a *Kuang-ming Jih-pao* editorial of April 8, 1967, warns: "If we allow him to have his scheme realized, the people's regime will change its political color, millions upon millions will be killed, our Marxist-Leninist Party will become a revisionist party and a fascist party, and the fruit of victory which has been obtained at the cost of so much bloodshed by countless revolutionary martyrs will become nothing." Underlying Liu's errors concerning politics and Party affairs is his repudiation of the nature of class struggle. *Red Flag* (no. 10, 1967) traces the first major manifestation of this deviation to the period following "the socialist transformation of the ownership of the means of production" (e.g., 1956), when Liu reportedly said: "Domestically the major class strug-

---

[34] According to this source, Wang Kuang-mei's daughters were part of the plot to lure her from her residence. After an "open self-examination" before the faculty and students of the Number One Middle School, Liu P'ing-p'ing was detained by Red Guard units. Her mother, informed that Liu had suffered a serious accident, rushed to the hospital, to be seized and taken to the university. After seven hours of criticism, Wang Kuang-mei agreed to submit written statements of her own and her husband's errors every ten days and to come to the university whenever summoned.

[35] Liu's confession is said to have been made at an October, 1966 meeting of the CPC. It was first published by the Tokyo *Daily News*, and translated from the Japanese in the February 19, 1967 Hong Kong *Ming Pao*. In this self-accusation, Liu prefaces his remarks by recognition of the decision of the eleventh plenum of the CPC Central Committee to have Lin Piao become "the first assistant and successor to Chairman Mao." "As a member of the Party, I must abide by Party discipline," he added, "and I am determined not to do anything undecided in front of anybody."

Reportedly, Liu Shao-ch'i then admitted his attempts to thwart the cultural revolution, due to his fear of the masses and desire to avoid turmoil, and his retention of a bourgeois outlook. Summarizing his mistakes in economic policy, he traced his errors back to 1946.

gle has basically come to an end . . . from now on there will be no more revolutionary struggles and no more socialist transformation . . . the more important task of the state is to organize the life of society." But signs of Liu's repudiation of the class struggle are now found in his conduct as early as the eve of the war with Japan.[36] Prior to the nationwide communist victory, according to May 18, 1967 commentary by the editorial departments of *Red Flag* and *People's Daily*, Liu "opposed the dictatorship of the proletariat, opposed the socialist revolution, and wanted to practice capitalism."

In early April, 1967, forces of the cultural revolution launched an all-out attack on Liu Shao-ch'i's major work on Party organization, *"How To Be A Good Communist.*[37] In terms of Party organization, despite Mao's warning that the CPC's organizational line must be subordinated to its political line, Liu is said to advocate the precedence of the former over the latter to obtain "blind and absolute obedience" on the part of the Party's membership. This denunciation of the "slave mentality" raises a certain problem for Mao and his associates. On the one hand, particularly since the leaders of the cultural revolution admit that their forces are often, at least temporarily, in the minority, it is essential to criticize Liu's argument that the minority must always submit to the majority, "even when truth lies with the minority." On the other hand, even while damning Liu's concept of absolute obedience, the forces of the cultural revolution are expected to practice such obedience to the wishes of Mao. Or, as expressed in an article prepared by a Red Guard unit and reprinted in the April 6, 1967 *People's Daily:* "What we accept unconditionally is the correct leadership of the Party's Central Committee headed by Chairman Mao."

With Mao's preparation for the cultural revolution, early in 1966, the

[36] For example, Liu is said to have encouraged some Chinese Communists to "give themselves up to the Kuomintang and turn against the Communist Party" on the eve of the war of resistance against Japan. Later, he promoted these "turncoats" to leading positions in the CPC and persecuted those who "did not absolutely obey his black instructions." See "Bury the Slave Mentality Advocated by China's Khrushchev" in *People's Daily* of April 6, 1967.

[37] The fact that Liu's work has been cited repeatedly in these pages as representing the intent and policies of the CPC, according to Mao's interpretations, calls for a word of explanation. *How To Be A Good Communist* was first published in 1939, during the period of the second united front with the Kuomintang. In August, 1949, the book was reissued in a revised form. Both versions stress the need for self-cultivation on the part of Party members, and minimize questions which might give affront to sympathizers with the communist movement. In 1962, the third edition appeared, again in a revised form. It is this last edition which is being subjected to violent criticism for advocating "blind obedience" on the part of Party members. The "sins" of omission attributed to the third edition are Liu's failure to comment upon the need to oppose imperialism and modern revisionism or the importance of the thought of Mao. In this ex post facto type of criticism, the latter point is probably the most serious. Basically, Liu's guidelines for Party organization probably remain intact. In any case, they were not criticized until the emergence of the present power struggle.

position of Liu Shao-ch'i—and the feud between the two—reached a point of crisis. According to a May 18, 1967 statement of the editorial departments of *Red Flag* and *People's Daily*, "it has now been conclusively proved that the counterrevolutionary revisionist 'February Outline' by P'eng Chen was supported by him [Liu] and was actually his programme as well." Although Liu originally appeared to support the cultural revolution,[38] according to this same source, "he called black white and stood facts on their heads, encircled and attacked the revolutionaries, suppressed opinions differing from his own, and imposed a white terror." Liu is accused of resisting the Red Guards, organizing counterrevolutionary work teams, and inciting the masses to attack all Party cadres and Red Guards indiscriminately.[39] But his most serious crime in the long litany of errors and evils, and the one for which no forgiveness could be forthcoming, was his reported conspiracy to usurp power through a military coup.

Following a 16-day continuous denunciation of Liu Shao-ch'i in Peking, on April 16, 1967, big-character posters there revealed for the first time an account of the abortive "February Coup" of 1966. These posters affirmed charges attributed to Lin Piao and published in a poster of February, 1967, that Liu and Teng Hsiao-p'ing were the genuine backstage manipulators of the attempted power seizure. According to Tokyo sources, the April 16 poster told of the frightened reaction of Liu, Teng, P'eng Chen, Lu Ting-yi, Lo Jui-ch'ing, Yang Shang-k'un and others to Mao's 1965 strictures calling for a cultural revolution in Shanghai literary and art circles. In order to avoid their own demise, these men allegedly conspired to engineer a military coup, set for February, 1966. On February 23, 1966, Liu reportedly flew to Sinkiang to urge Wang En-mao to provide his troops for the coup. At the same time, Teng "disappeared" from Peking and flew to Sian to

---

[38] Liu was absent from Peking in March and April, 1966, when he made visits of state to Pakistan, Afghanistan and Burma. He presided at the May 1 celebrations and the July 22 mass Peking rally for the war in Vietnam. During the eleventh CC plenum, which met from August 1 to 12, the decision was reached to demote Liu from his place next to Mao to probably eighth rank in the CC. He was present in a subordinate place at the Red Guard rallies in Peking from August to November. Although Red Guard criticism of Liu dates back to September, the press did not begin its barrage until January, 1967.

[39] For an example of how Liu opposed the Red Guards see "We Accuse the Top Party Person in Authority . . . of Suppressing Our School's Great Cultural Revolution," prepared by a Red Guard unit attached to Peking Normal University, and published in the April 7, 1967 Peking *Kuang-ming Jih-pao*. According to this attack, Liu sent a work team to collaborate with his daughter (a middle school student) in resisting the Red Guards, and stirring up opposition between them and the faculty. Members of the work team, composed entirely of "children of high-ranking cadres," subjected the Red Guards "to all manner of torture, both spiritually and corporally."

Liu's alleged efforts to have the masses turn against all Party cadres are discussed in detail in Chapter 4.

persuade Liu Lan-t'ao, first secretary of the CPC Northwest Bureau, to take a similar step. P'eng Chen likewise flew to confer secretly with Li Ching-ch'üan in Southwest China. Forces loyal to the Liu group were moved to secure positions in Wuhan, Tientsin and Shansi province, while peasants in the vicinity of Peking were given military training under pretext. As attempts were made to bring colleges and middle schools into the plot, food and clothing were stored, and P'eng Chen's home became the military headquarters. Secret meetings and telephone calls, and the wire-tapping of Mao's office and residence reportedly helped amass intelligence reports. Liu was even said to have installed a phone network in the Ministry of Security to communicate with foreign countries, probably for aid.

It is, of course, impossible to substantiate these Red Guard allegations of an attempted "February coup," in 1966. Other sources claim that both Chou En-lai and K'ang Sheng later denied the existence of such a plot. But, it is certain that the Mao-Lin leadership has accused "the number one Party man in authority taking the capitalist road" of plotting with his black associates to usurp Party and state power. The Party press has identified Teng Hsiao-p'ing as Liu's closest collaborator in this devious power struggle.

Ranked fifth among the members of the CPC CC's Politburo until the beginning of the cultural revolution, Teng Hsiao-p'ing was formerly regarded as an expert administrator and one of Mao's trusted lieutenants. Teng joined the Party during his student days in Paris, and in 1925 returned to China to engage in Party and army assignments. After the Long March he served as a political commissar in several units, and in 1949 he was made Secretary of the CC's Southwest Bureau. In 1950, he was made vice chairman of the Southwest Military and Political Committee, and two years later he became a Vice Premier of the State Council. Selected to announce the Kao-Jao purge publicly in 1955, and to report on the revision of the Party Constitution in 1956, Teng added to his esteem within the Party. On the eve of the cultural revolution, his posts as General Secretary and head of the CPC CC's Secretariat, and as Vice Premier and Vice Chairman of the National Defense Council, and his assignment as head of the CPC delegation to the abortive July, 1963 ideological talks in Moscow enhanced his reputation as the "spider at the center of the web." As late as May, 1966, Teng was selected to join Mao, Lin Piao and Chou En-lai in receiving Mehmet Shehu, Albanian Premier and Politburo member of the Workers' Party, in Peking. Teng marked the visit of the Albanian Party delegation by giving a rare public speech at a Shanghai rally in denunciation of modern revisionism.

Until the disclosures of the Red Guards, Teng Hsiao-p'ing's position of authority and trust in the leadership ranks appeared secure. But, by early

1967, he was identified as the "second" of the leaders of the CPC attempting to revise Marxism-Leninism and the thought of Mao and following "the capitalist road." As a co-conspirator of Liu Shao-ch'i, he has been accused of using his authority in the Party to subvert the cultural revolution, by opposing the general line and backing the P'eng Chen group. Like his mentor, Teng's crimes have been traced back at least to 1956. His 1956 report on the Party Constitution, for example, "basically made no mention of the great role played by Chairman Mao," and "energetically blew the trumpet for the 20th Congress of the CPSU." In 1961, he again attempted to resist Mao's plans for the communes by informing a provincial Party meeting that "any idea which cannot be carried out and does not hold water ought to be rectified regardless of who has originated it." By "consistently monopolizing power" through his post as General Secretary, Teng also is said to have resisted the Party's programs for educational institutions. [40] Working with Liu, Teng is accused of taking advantage of Mao's absence from Peking in early 1966, to organize Party work teams to suppress mass participation in the cultural revolution. On January 23, 1967, one day after the seizure of power there, the CPC Kwangtung Provincial Committee acknowledged that it had "carried out the bourgeois reactionary line of Liu and Teng," and pledged to support the leadership of the cultural revolutionary forces to "make up with practical action for the great damage caused by the errors we have committed." [41]

Teng Hsiao-p'ing is considered to be the organizer of the so-called "black headquarters" or "Petofi club" in Peking to bring together officials of the Party sympathetic to his own revisionist line. In 1961, he directed Wan Li, a former member of the Peking Party Committee who was later exposed by the cultural revolution, to construct a "Higher Cadres Club." This building, constructed with state funds, was the meeting place for Party officials who opposed the general line until April, 1966. Regular visitors included Hsiang Tzu-ming, Wang Han-pin, Hsiao Chia, and other members of the former Peking Party committee; Hu Yao-pang, former secretary of the YCL CC; Hu K'o-shih, vice minister of Chemical Industry; playwright Wu Han, and other officials prominent in state and Party organizations. From this center, the "black gang" hatched their plans to use state funds for personal aggrandizement, [42] and to promote others who favored a

---

[40] In 1961, he personally advocated the revisionist line of the "Sixty Articles for Promoting Higher Education;" in 1963, with Liu Shao-ch'i he approved the new system for awarding degrees "after the fashion of capitalist countries;" in 1964, he resisted Mao's call for struggle in the cultural sphere, particularly the socialist education movement introduced at Peking University; in 1966, he was still resisting the work-study program for higher education.

These and other charges are contained in Canton *Pa-erh-wu Chan-pao* (*August 25 Battle News*), Feb. 14, 1967.

[41] "Message from the CPC Kwangtung Provincial Committee to All Party Members, Cadres, and the People of the Province," in Canton *Kuang-chou Hung-wei-ping*, Feb. 10, 1967.

revisionist line to posts of authority in the Party and state. Among these men who owed their posts to Teng and Liu was Hsiao Wang-tung, who became a Vice Minister of Culture in May, 1965, as part of an alleged conspiracy to resist Lin Piao's call for intensified socialist education.

With the reorganization of the CPC Secretariat in 1966, Teng Hsiao-p'ing doubtlessly lost any trust or authority among the subordinates who surround Mao. Like Liu Shao-ch'i, he has become the target for mass denunciation for his criminal activities.

One of the most unusual cases of meteoric rise to a post of high trust in the CPC, and then an equally swift and dramatic downfall, is that of T'ao Chu. An early subordinate of Lin Piao and member of the CPC Central Committee, T'ao apparently won the attention and trust of Mao and his associates for his work as First Secretary of the CC's Central-South Bureau (1961–66). In February, 1964, *Red Flag* published his praises of the thought of Mao, especially the concept of the communes. In January, 1965, he was named 15th ranking Vice Premier of the State Council. On June 1, 1966, T'ao Chu was called to Peking to take over the direction of the CC's Propaganda Department from Lu Ting-yi; he was simultaneously promoted to the CC Standing Committee and the CC Secretariat, and was appointed an advisor to the CC's Cultural Revolution Group. During the period of the Red Guards' rallies in Peking in the late summer and fall of 1966, T'ao Chu enjoyed an honored position in the leadership preceded only by Lin Piao and Chou En-lai.

By January, 1967, T'ao Chu was being denounced as the "Khrushchev of Central-South China," and "number one loyal executor of the bourgeois reactionary line of Liu Shao-ch'i and Teng Hsiao-p'ing." This reversal of his fortunes is attributed to his collusion with his mentors in opposing the general line and the thought of Mao, and particularly for using his position in the Party to attempt to subvert the cultural revolution. [43] His friendship with Liu Shao-ch'i and his wife was strengthened in 1964. According

---

families in an "inspection" of the Northeast in the summer of 1964, which was actually a pleasure trip. See Peking *Tung-fang Hung,* published by the Revolutionary Rebel Liaison Center of Red Guards of Universities and Colleges of Peking, of Feb. 18, 1967.

[43] Like the other targets of the Red Guards, T'ao Chu's crimes have been traced back at least to 1959. In that year, in his article "The Radiance of the Sun," T'ao insinuated the fallibility of Mao and the CC by stating "the sun itself also has black spots." In 1962, he spoke out, "it is necessary to follow the lead of the Communist Party, but not the lead of that person [Mao]." He is said to have resisted the communes from 1961 on. See *Tung-fang Hung,* Feb. 22, 1967. As Party boss of Central-South China, T'ao was said to have encouraged the mass exodus to Hong Kong in 1961–63. By ordering the borders to be opened, "20,000 to 30,000 persons with full labor capacity" deserted their assignments and "more than 1,500 mou of land were allowed to lie idle." He is also accused of encouraging smuggling activities in the Shumchun border defense area. For details concerning his subversion of literary and art circles see Chapter 10.

to Red Guard reports, T'ao admitted that after his rise to power in June, 1966, "he was mindful only of two persons—Liu and Teng." [44]

T'ao Chu used his power in the Party to protect supporters of the Liu-Teng faction and to promote his own coteries of friends. These latter include Wang Jen-chung, former First Secretary of the CPC Hupeh Provincial Committee and a deputy head of the CC Cultural Revolution Group, who became T'ao Chu's successor as Party boss of the Central-South Bureau. Under T'ao's protection, Wang used his offices to suppress the cultural revolution in the area under his control, and at Tsinghua and Peking Universities. T'ao Chu promoted Chang P'ing-hua, former First Secretary of the Hunan Provincial Committee, to the post of deputy director of the CC Propaganda Department and membership in the CC's Cultural Revolution Group. Chang was quickly transferred to Hunan, when that province evidenced trouble. According to Red Guard disclosures, however, he attempted to thwart mass participation in the cultural revolution there. Among the incumbents whom he protected were Ho Wei and Liu Yang-ch'iao, Minister of Education and Vice Minister of Higher Education respectively.

In his very influential position of director of the Party propaganda network, between June and December, 1966, T'ao Chu was apparently able to further several of his theories concerning mass indoctrination through the press media. One of the most sinister examples of his resistance to the approved line was his permission for the revision of Mao's works to omit certain significant passages. According to the accusations of the Canton Liaison Center of the Wuhan Revolutionary Rebel Headquarters of Red Guards, issued on January 14, 1967, T'ao approved the deletion of Mao's five conditions for judging cadres from the *Quotations from Chairman Mao* prepared by the Hupeh provincial CPC committee. The T'ao Chu case is classical in the proletarian cultural revolution to demonstrate that the tremendous revolutionary torrent stirred up by Mao can raise or thrust aside any individuals according to Mao's sole standard of ideological dedication.

The fate of highly placed Party officials, such as P'eng Chen, Teng Hsiao-p'ing and T'ao Chu illustrates the fact that, in the present most serious challenge to Mao's direction, no one is above suspicion. Nor is anyone exempt from punitive action should the disclosures of the Red Guards indicate any contravention of Mao's plans for cultural revolution. Like the pre-1949 challengers of Mao—Ch'en Tu-hsiu (dropped in 1927), Ch'ü Ch'iu-pai (removed in 1928), Li Li-san (descredited in 1930), Wang Ming (disciplined in 1936 and again in 1942–44), or Chang Kuo-t'ao (denounced in 1938)—P'eng, Teng and T'ao have been found guilty of misinterpreting

[44] See *Chingkangshan*, January 11, 1967.

questions of revolutionary strategy and tactics. Like some of the post-1949 cases—notably those of Kao Kang and Jao Shu-shih in 1953–55, P'eng Teh-huai in 1959, and even Lu Ting-yi and Lo Jui-ch'ing in 1966—they are accused of fostering their own ambitions. Yet, these ambitions are, in a sense, limited. None of the accused was in a position to create an impact similar to the authority wielded by Liu Shao-ch'i.

The case of Liu Shao-ch'i stands in a class by itself. No other official has enjoyed the status of the long-time heir apparent of Mao, or the prestige of a veteran head of state. Nor has anyone else had the same reputation as a communist theoretician and Party organizer, with its related powers over the rank and file workers of the Party and state. Never before has the denunciation of a CPC official caused such turmoil in China or such interest, and even the possible threat of intervention from abroad.

While the subjective and objective conditions of the Liu case are unique historically, the gravest and most significant aspect is the threat of such far-reaching deviation from the thought of Mao. This deviation indicates an inclination to follow present Soviet models, and may reveal direct Soviet influence. Such a conclusion is implicitly contained in *Red Flag's* editorial marking the 46th anniversary of the founding of the CPC. Short of using his name, this CC voice branded Liu as the chief revisionist seeking to destroy the communist revolution in China:

When the socialist transformation of the ownership of the means of production in China was basically completed, the top Party person in authority taking the capitalist road talked a lot about the dying out of class struggle. He alleged that "domestically, the major class struggle has basically come to an end" and that "the question of which will win, socialism or capitalism, has now been settled." Like Khrushchev, he attempted to turn the Communist Party into a "party of the entire people." He advocated pulling a number of representatives of the bourgeoisie into the Party and openly declared that if capitalists joined the Party, "it would be all the better." He also said that "the most important task of the state is to organize the life of society" and that "the main task of the Party is to expand the productive forces at the quickest possible rate." [45]

This accusation against Liu, synthesizing numerous others, must have considerable validity. Liu must have taken a firm stand which is seriously different from that of Mao in regard to the future of the Party and state as well as the basic world outlook. Otherwise he would not have risked his already secure "successor's" position to challenge the supposedly "ailing" and "retiring" Mao by antagonizing his thought to the point of resorting to reported military coup. Liu's long-time Party work, originally recognized leadership role, and international standing multiply the danger of his ideological deviation by throwing the Party into complete confusion.

[45] "Mao Tse-tung's Thought Illuminates the Road for Our Party's Victorious Advance," *Red Flag*, No. 11, 1967.

Mao Tse-tung now confronts the greatest crisis in his career, since his assumption of leadership in 1935. Since 1956, and especially since 1959, he has devoted his energies to the struggle against modern revisionism. He has sought at every turn to inspire his followers, by relying on his own prestige and the power of persuasion. The cultural revolution is itself a kind of persuasion in action. Like any other powerful leader, Mao must know that flattery and lip service are always available. But his determination to disregard past meritorious deeds or close relationships in the interests of safeguarding revolutionary principles indicates the supreme importance he attaches to the anti-revisionist struggle. As Lin Piao has stressed, "cultural revolution is applicable to everyone, especially those in leadership." "We should regard ourselves as part of the strength of the revolution," he added, "and at the same time constantly make ourselves a target of revolution." *Red Flag* (no. 11, 1967) proudly concluded: "the great proletarian clutural revolution has purified the proletarian headquarters and greatly strengthened Party leadership." It remains for the successors to Mao to fulfill this pledge.

THE PARTY LEADERSHIP AND HEIRS OF REVOLUTION: THE RED GUARDS

While the CPC must utilize a variety of measures, such as the currently renewed emphasis on socialist education and cultural revolution, to maintain the correct cohesion and dedication of its leadership, it must also prepare young successors to take up and complete the unfinished revolution. [46] Thus, the questions of the solidity and strength of the present leadership and the potential of the future generation are mutually dependent and, in fact, inseparable. In a responsible Communist Party, such as the CPC, those who today exercise control must inspire and train those who will succeed them tomorrow. The latter, in turn, in the process of being aroused, disciplined and steeled, should give new vigor to the present leadership. Or as the CPC warned in its ninth Open Letter to the CPSU, published in *People's Daily* on July 14, 1964:

> The question of training successors for the revolutionary cause of the proletariat is one of whether or not there will be people who can carry on the Marxist-Leninist revolutionary cause started by the older generation of proletarian revolutionaries, whether or not the leadership of our Party and state will remain in the hands of proletarian revolutionaries, whether or not our descendants will continue to march along the correct road laid down by Marxism-Leninism, or in other words, whether or not we can successfully prevent the emergence of Khrushchevite revisionism in China. In short, it is an extremely important question, *a matter of life and death for our Party and our country.* (italics added)

[46] The importance of the Red Guards in stimulating and stiffening the revolutionary dedication of the youth of Communist China is discussed in Chapter 9.

The 1966 emergence of the Red Guards, or the *hung-wei-ping*, most probably represents the answer of the present veteran leadership to the challenge of renewing their own vigor, while selecting and preparing their successors. As the "one stone" conceived to deal with the "two birds," the emergence of the Red Guards is not without precedent in the history of the communist movement in China. In the 1920's, when the Chinese Communists were operating from their base in the Chingkangshan area, the children and youths were organized to defend and extend Marxist-Leninist goals. The Red Guards, who call themselves the "young, red soldiers of Chairman Mao," are designed to provide the "shock force" for waging the great proletarian cultural revolution. Thus they are at once militant and military, in responding to the supreme command and frank encouragement of Mao himself and his trusted subordinates.

The purpose of the Red Guards is to fight against opportunists, deviationists, or counterrevolutionaries, especially among the communists' own ranks. The need for such a vital purifying force is probably felt in all iron-disciplined organizations demanding self-denial and sacrifice of their members. After a long period of rule, it would be practically inevitable that some of the Chinese Communists would give signs of ideological deterioration, moral decay, or softness, and would need some instrument to quicken their fervor. The creation and use of the Red Guards may be regarded as a determined effort on the part of Mao and his trusted associates to champion ideological purity and disciplinary inviolability.

The work of the Red Guards penetrates into the fields of politics, economics, the military, social reform, and culture, but it is, above all, revolutionary or ideological in character. For this reason, their highest obligation is the "study, dissemination, application and defense of Mao Tse-tung's thought." Politically, the Red Guards are to carry out "courageous and stubborn struggles against those in authority who have taken the capitalist road." Chou En-lai described their economic tasks at the September 15, 1966 rally in Peking's Tien An Men Square as applying "the soaring enthusiasm and energy generated in the great cultural revolution to industrial and agricultural production and scientific experimentation." [47] Social tasks include rousing "revolutionary fervor among the masses" and bringing about "a vigorous mass movement on a still greater scale." Culturally, the Guards are to "eradicate the old ideas, culture, customs and habits of the exploiting classes and to foster the new ideas, culture, customs and habits

---

[47] After informing the Red Guards that they were "not to go to enterprises at the county level and below, or the communes," since the cultural revolution in those areas "is to proceed in a planned and systematic way," Chou reminded the million youths present that they must understand that the workers and peasants "can't take time off to make revolution." He then called upon the Guards to put their talents and energies to work in the fall harvest. As a "shock brigade" on the economic front, the Red Guards will doubtlessly have a substantial continuing role.

of the proletariat." Their primary military task is to "learn modestly from the People's Liberation Army" in accordance with its "three-eight" working style—the Three Main Rules of Discipline and the Eight Points for Attention. In fulfilling their ideological assignments, the Red Guards are expected to carry with them at all times copies of *Quotations from Chairman Mao Tse-tung*. To the extent that these teachings are mastered and applied, the Guards will accomplish the work for which they were created—the continuation and extension of the communist revolution.

Mao Tse-tung has taken considerable pains to prove that he personally regards the Red Guards as his and the Party's ideal revolutionary successors. As the children and heirs of revolution, the Guards have enjoyed direct communications with their "supreme commander," Mao, his "close comrade in arms," Lin Piao, and with "other responsible Party leaders." For example, some eleven million revolutionary youths were brought to Peking to be reviewed personally by Mao, Lin and other leaders eight times between August 18 and November 26, 1966. On these and other occasions, the leadership voiced approval of the Guards' spirit and action in the revolutionary tradition. Like learning to swim by swimming, the Red Guards are "learning to make a revolution by taking part in it," and they have learned well. Thus the leadership emphasizes that "the new-born forces are invincible . . . grow and develop in struggle, and in the end [will] defeat the decaying forces." Lin Piao, speaking for Mao and other CPC leaders, summarized the Party's appreciation and approval in his speech to the Red Guards' rally of September 15, 1966:

Red Guard fighters, revolutionary students, the general orientation of your struggle has always been correct. Chairman Mao and the Party's Central Committee firmly support you! So do the broad masses of workers, peasants, and soldiers! Your revolutionary actions have shaken the whole of society and given a blow to the dregs and left-over evils from the old world. You have scored brilliant successes in the vigorous fight to destroy the four olds [old ideas, old culture, old customs and old habits] and foster the four news [new ideas, new culture, new customs and new habits]. You have created utter consternation among those in power who are taking the capitalist road, the reactionary bourgeois "authorities," and bloodsuckers and parasites. You have acted correctly and done well!

Inspired and sponsored by the Party leadership, the Red Guards, in turn, have a real contribution to make to both present and future leadership strength. In his September 15 speech, Lin Piao tacitly confirmed that a power struggle exists within even the high ranks of the Party by noting that "some people are now going against Chairman Mao's instructions and the 16-point [Central Committee] decision [on cultural revolution]." It appears very unlikely that the post-Lenin power struggle of 1924–27, or the post-Stalin power struggle of 1953–55 that damaged the Soviet Party will be repeated in the CPC with Mao's passing. In this context, the integration of Chinese Communist theory and practice in the form of the Red Guards armed with Mao's thought may prove to be an effective deterrent to the Soviet style of Party power struggle. In the reinforcement of the present leadership and the preparation of future leadership, Mao's authority is symbolized by his thought: the two are virtually indivisible. Yet, the respect for Mao's thought is not due solely to his own prestige, or the power he wields. Presuming that his thought, combining as it does developing communist theory and practical application to Chinese conditions, will continue to possess validity, this will have a great positive effect on the stability and vitality of future Party leadership. The Red Guards' respect for Mao's thought may be regarded as the cement which binds the next generation of leaders to the beliefs and practices of the present generation to insure continuity of the revolution.

The Red Guards customarily refer to Mao as "our great teacher, great leader, great supreme commander and great helmsman." Described in official sources, the one and a half million "revolutionary fighters" who gathered for Mao's fourth review of October 21, 1966, each carried a copy of *Quotations from Chairman Mao Tse-tung* and "recited over and over again passages from Chairman Mao's writings." And other leaders of the CPC have emphasized to the Guards the need to study and emulate Mao's thought. For example, at the September 15, 1966 rally, Lin Piao cautioned them "like the workers, peasants and soldiers, to be ever loyal to Chairman Mao" and to his thought. And Chou En-lai added that "we are convinced you will hold high the great red banner of Mao Tse-tung's thought, learn how to make revolution in the revolution, and temper yourselves to become good soldiers and pupils of Chairman Mao."

Although it is evident that the Red Guards constitute a distinct organization with a definite Party-assigned function, their relationship to existing CPC youth organizations has not yet been clarified. The members of the Red Guards have been drawn heavily from the ranks of the Young Communist League (YCL) and its auxiliary Young Pioneers. The YCL is a typical or customary communist-led youth organization, whose traditional role is to serve as an auxiliary and reserve for the Communist Party in the performance of routine tasks. Thus, about one half of the Party's rank and file members have been trained by the League. The Red Guards, on the other hand, have a far more dynamic and far-reaching mission to conduct anti-imperialist, anti-revisionist, and anti-reactionary struggle. Given the publicity concerning the Young Communist League's shortcomings, since December, 1964, and in view of the absence of reports concerning the activities of the League since the August, 1966 emergence of the Red Guards, it is not impossible that the former organization has fallen into eclipse, if not actual dismemberment. However, there is no essential contradiction which would prohibit the continuation of both organizations, in order to better accomplish their distinct tasks. It is more likely that a reorganized Young Pioneers and Young Communist League will eventually continue to provide routine training for Chinese youth, while selected activist members of these organizations will be rewarded by being allowed to hold dual membership in the Red Guards.[48] This conclusion is reinforced by the June, 1967 NCNA announcement of the reorganization of the YCL Peking committee, by which Li Li-kung was transferred from his post as secretary of the Shansi YCL provincial committee to head the Peking committee.

As of this writing, the Red Guards are still in their infancy, if not the embryonic stage, since no constitution, statutes, rules or regulations have been adopted on a national basis to prescribe their organization, function or official standing. In its August 8, 1966 communique, the CPC Central Committee dictated that "permanent cultural revolution groups" be established by the usual controlled system of elections to congresses in a hierarchal framework based on geo-political divisions. The Red Guards are apparently moving toward a similar type of organization. For example, on March 2, 1967, NCNA reported that three Red Guard college and university units in Peking municipality had allied to form a Red Guard Congress. The day following, Peking's *Kuang-min Jih-pao* noted that this congress would elect its standing committee to exercise the powers of the congress when the latter is not in session. On March 25, 1967, the Congress of Red Guards of Peking Middle Schools was established with the full

---

[48] Both the Young Communist League and the Young Pioneers evidenced signs by mid-1966, that a major transformation was in order. At the Fifth National Conference of the Young Pioneers in December, 1962, Lo Jui-ch'ing and P'eng Chen (both of whom were purged in the cultural revolution), together with Chen Yi, stressed the importance of young children learning to wage the class struggle. Subsequently, the Pioneers began a vast recruitment drive. In 1965, some eight and a half million new members were admitted. When the drive continued into 1966, to "mobilize all children," Pioneer membership reached at least 100 million, according to NCNA, May 31, 1966. In April, 1966, age requirements were lowered from nine to seven, and an apparent division was made between the "children's league" for the 7–12 year olds, and the "adolescent league" for those between the ages of 12 and 15. From these latter ranks have come many if not most of the members of the Red Guard. Thus, their first introduction to Party instruction and discipline was provided by the routine agencies of the Young Pioneers, The Young Communist League, on the other hand, appeared to have failed to fulfill its functions with complete success. Among the most publicized examples of such failure was the case of the cover of the League's publication of December, 1964. This cover reproduced a painting by a Peking art student entitled "You Incite, I Follow," which depicted communist youth marching in solidarity. However, close scrutiny seemed to indicate that the youths were marching over corpses and skulls, while one of the Party's three red flags fell to the ground.

approval of the highest leadership. [49]   Since the Red Guards are constantly urged to emulate the PLA, and since many of their instructors and advisors come from the ranks of the military, it is likely that the internal organization of the Red Guard congresses will follow military lines with "general headquarters," "high commands," and a regimented membership, all under the direction of the "supreme commander," Mao Tse-tung. NCNA of October 11, 1966, noted that the Red Guards in Peking had already been formed into companies, platoons, squads, and specialized "combat teams."

The Red Guards are also expected to employ the usual methods of criticism and self-criticism in order to keep their own ranks pure. For example, as worded by one Red Guard unit: "only when we expose our mistaken ideas and face the masses can we get the help of the masses. If we do not want to wash our dirty linen in public, we shall not get rid of the dirt." [50] Should a Red Guard unit fail to maintain the proper discipline or dedication, the PLA stands ready to intervene. For example, in its May 16, 1967 issue, *People's Daily* reported that PLA troops had been sent to Peking Teachers University to deal with dissident members of the Red Guards.

In addition to the inspirational leadership of Mao, Lin Piao has played a prominent role in the organization and direction of the Red Guards. Chou En-lai has also been active in issuing directives, as have other leaders of the CPC. For example, the Chinese Communist press has identified CC Politburo member Ch'en Po-ta as a "leader of the group in charge of the cultural revolution under the Party's Central Committee," whose duties presumably extend to organizing and advising the Red Guards. Other prominent CPC leaders who share in the work of fostering the cultural revolution through encouraging the Red Guards include K'ang Sheng, recently promoted to the Politburo Standing Committee and named an "advisor to the Cultural Revolution Group," and Chiang Ch'ing, called "first deputy leader" of this group. But with the exception of those members of the Central Committee who are currently suffering as immediate targets of the cultural revolution, all the leaders of the Party have lent their support and prestige by appearing prominently at the series of Peking rallies for the Red Guards.

In terms of tactics, since the Red Guards have been encouraged to follow the example of the PLA, the approach has been militant, if not military. Referring to the necessary tactics to wage a successful cultural revolution, the CPC Central Committee's directive of August 8, 1966, urged the peaceable means of "the fullest use of big-character posters and great debates to

[49] Among the host of Party and PLA officials in attendance were Chou En-lai, Ch'en Po-ta, K'ang Sheng, Hsü Hsiang-ch'ien, Chiang Ch'ing, Yang Cheng-wu, etc.

[50] Red Guard United Corps of Department of Philosophy and Social Sciences of the Thought of Mao Tse-tung, "Don't Be Afraid of Washing Dirty Linen in Public," Peking *Kuang-ming Jih-pao*, March 20, 1967.

argue matters out." But the same order admitted that revolution cannot be "refined," "gentle," or "temperate." Thus, if the Red Guards were encouraged to use reason and persuasion, they were not, at least originally denied more coercive tactics. As suggested in the official communique of the eleventh plenary session (Enlarged) of the CPC Central Committee, which met in Peking from August 1 to 12, 1966, with respect to the question of "raising and training successors in the proletarian revolutionary cause," one must not "be afraid of disorder." This point was reaffirmed even after the outbreak of violence in several of the provinces and municipalities. According to *Wen-hui Pao*, in an editorial much praised by *Red Flag:* "Making revolution comfortably is making sham revolution, but really seeking comfort. . . . Proper limits have to be exceeded in order to right a wrong. . . It is unavoidable that the rebels commit mistakes of one kind or another in the struggle. [51]

Instances of the Red Guards' apparent preference for coercive, rather than "gentle" tactics have been frequently reported in the Western press and need only be summarized here. In August-September, 1966, for example, foreign observers in Communist China reported attacks on churches and harassment of clergy and religious, massive book-burnings in several cities, the ransacking of Soong Ching-ling's (Madame Sun Yat-sen's) residence in Shanghai, extensive destruction to private property, and savage attacks on any individual who wore western clothing or displayed any object of "bourgeois origins." [52] The Soviet Embassy in Peking was encroached upon and members of its staff insulted or abused. In Harbin, Manchuria, members of the Red Guards reportedly attacked the Heilungkiang provincial Party headquarters, while the third secretary of the CPC CC's Northeast Bureau, Ma Ming-fang, looked on in apparent approval.

In many areas of the world, the violence of the Red Guards was greeted with dismay, mixed with a hope that such seeming frenzy would lead to a toppling of the present regime. In Moscow, after the Soviet Foreign Ministry sent several protests over the abuse of diplomatic personnel and property, *Izvestiia* on September 21, 1966, termed the cultural revolution a "tragedy for the Chinese people." Similarly, several foreign correspondents in Communist China reported that many of the Chinese themselves had begun to launch counter-demonstrations against the Red Guards. These reports have been reinforced by admissions in the Chinese Communist press. In its August 23, 1966, editorial, for example, *People's Daily*

---

[51] *Wen-hui Pao*, January 6, 1967. *Red Flag* no. 2 (January 16, 1967) reprinted this editorial in full with high praise, as did *Peking Review* of January 27, 1967.

[52] In the cities, the Red Guards demanded that all of the pre-communist signs be destroyed. Thus, the Peking Union Medical College Hospital was renamed Anti-Imperialist Hospital, and the street on which the Soviet embassy is located was renamed Anti-Revisionist Street.

admitted that "saboteurs" of the cultural revolution had "stirred up a few workers and peasants to struggle against the students."[53] Moreover, young followers of Liu Shao-ch'i have organized their own "Red Guard" units which are counterposed to the cultural revolution. For example, the "United Action Committee of Red Guards" in Peking was denounced repeatedly in January, 1967, as a bogus organization seeking to discredit Mao and his wife and subvert the Red Guards' movement.

In its September 5, 1966 issue, *People's Daily* cautioned the Red Guards to avoid violence, since "force can only touch the skin, but not the soul." The Chinese Communist leadership had anticipated that the revolutionary efforts of the Red Guards might involve excessive fervor, that would have to be controlled. For example, the August 8, 1966 Central Committee communique concerning cultural revolution had predicted that "in such a great revolutionary movement, it is hardly avoidable that they should show short-comings of one kind or another." But while the leadership seeks to eliminate these "short-comings," it has also affirmed its belief that the general approach of the guards is correct. This judgment is reinforced by a statement issued by *People's Daily* on August 23, 1966, during the height of the Red Guard activities in the streets of Peking. The Guards are "lawful organizations," this Party source notes, and "those who oppose them directly contravene the teachings of Chairman Mao and the decisions of the Party's Central Committe."

Similarly, the leadership of Communist China does not fear adverse criticism of the Red Guards. Rather, it finds the international reaction to further distinguish or prove who is the enemy and who is the friend. In the words of the September 23, 1966 *Peking Review:*

Different classes take different views of the revolutionary actions of the Red Guards. The revolutionary classes regard them as extremely good while the counter-revolutionary classes look upon them as extremely bad. . . [the latter] have vilified the Red Guards as "young fanatics" and attacked their revolutionary actions as "violating human dignity," "destroying social traditions," and so forth. . . . Only by destroying the various old traditions of the exploiting classes is it possible to carry on and develop the revolutionary traditions of the proletariat. . . . Chairman Mao has taught us that to be attacked by the enemy is not a bad thing but a good thing. It is still better if the enemy attacks us wildly and paints us in the worst colors and without a single virtue.

With renewed self-confidence in the eventual success of the Red Guards in destroying the "three big mountains"—of imperialism headed by the US,

[53] For example, much has been made in the Chinese Communist press of the heroism of Tsai Yung-hsiang, a young soldier who lost his own life in removing a log from the Chientang River Bridge in Hangchow to save a train of Red Guards on their way to a Peking rally. The strategic placement of the log was called "an act of sabotage by class enemies."

of present day revisionism headed by the Soviet Union, and of all reaction—
the Chinese Communists emphasize that "it is indeed an honor for the Red
Guards that they have been attacked wildly by the class enemies at home
and abroad."

The members of the Red Guards have repeatedly responded to this
praise by massing in Peking from all parts of China—"from the shores of
the South China Sea to the areas north and south of the Tienshan Mountains and from the Heilungkiang River to the plateaus of Sikang and
Tibet"—to pledge loyalty to the leaders of Communist China and fidelity
to their commands:

> Respected and beloved Chairman Mao, please be assured that we will resolutely
> respond to Comrade Lin Piao's call, push forward to a new stage the mass movement
> for the creative study and application of Chairman Mao's works, study in the course
> of struggle and genuinely try hard to apply what we study. We will defend the
> revolutionary line of the proletariat represented by you and be your good soldiers
> and students. We will completely smash whoever opposes you and opposes this
> revolutionary line of the proletariat.

This type of conviction on the part of the next generation of communists,
if it can maintain its fervor and continue to grow, can be generated in a
great and persistent force to survive Mao. If the Red Guards are genuinely
armed with Mao's thought, they will find a congenial spirit in his "close
comrade in arms," Lin Piao. United by loyalty to Mao's thought, the Red
Guards could support Lin tomorrow in the same spirit in which they support Mao today. Lin, who developed Mao's thought in the form of
"people's war," together with the dedicated members of the Red Guards
reassure Mao that his carefully cultivated thought and ardently dedicated
revolution need not be discontinued or weakened after he is gone. Carefully manipulated by Mao and his eventual successor, the Red Guards can
be a powerful tool in the transformation of China into a more advanced
stage of socialism, and a fountainhead of the communist world revolution.

THE PROBLEM OF LEADERSHIP SUCCESSION

Mao Tse-tung has had well over a quarter of a century to consolidate his
position as modern China's greatest leader. Every area of Party, state, and
social activities has come under his firm leadership. Reaping the full
benefits of the popularization of his thought, Mao has enjoyed the same
sort of trust and respect given to Lenin, while avoiding the tarnished image
of Stalin. By solidifying the ranks of his chosen associates and training
the future generation of the Red Guards, Mao can reasonably expect that

his image will be preserved by his successors. In fact, whoever inherits Mao's mantle of Party and state power will doubtlessly need—and therefore further promote—the memory of Mao.

However certain of the power he exercises, or the reputation he enjoys, Mao has himself observed on several occasions that his days are nearing a close. In a 1961 interview with Field Marshal Montgomery (published in the *Sunday Times* of London on October 15, 1961), the aging leader referred to an old Chinese legend that the two dangerous years for a man are 73 and 84. If these are survived, said Mao, a man should live to be a hundred. As for himself, he added, he had no wish to survive past the age of 73. Personally, he hoped soon to be with Marx! In December, 1966 Mao celebrated his 73rd birthday: Western reports indicate that his health is failing rapidly.[54]

The question of easing somewhat the many burdens of his offices was raised by Mao himself in 1958. On December 16, of that year, on the basis of a resolution adopted by the Sixth Plenary Session of the Eighth Central Committee under Mao's own guidance, Ch'en Yi announced that Mao had declined to seek re-election as Chairman of the People's Republic. This action confirmed Mao's previous intimations in conversations with Khrushchev and Nehru, in which he reportedly mentioned that his resignation was intended "all the better to concentrate his energies in dealing with questions of the direction, policy and line of the Party and state," and "to set aside more time for Marxist-Leninist theoretical work." Since Mao retained his chairmanship of the Party, the gesture was doubtlessly intended to relieve him of the ceremonial burdens of chief of state, while in no way diminishing his own power, especially in the form of all-important ideological formulations.

The office of chief of state went to Liu Shao-ch'i. As Chairman of the People's Republic and Chairman of the National Defense Council, and ranked second only to Mao in the CPC's all powerful Politburo, Liu therefore became Mao Tse-tung's designated heir apparent. At the time, the

[54] Especially during his 1965 public appearances, Mao was observed to walk on the arms of his aides. According to observers, the leader was virtually carried up the steps of the Peking stadium for the October 1, 1965 celebration of the anniversary of the People's Republic. By contrast, following a period of several months of apparent retirement from any official appearances, in mid-1966 Mao re-emerged to preside personally over the series of Red Guards' rallies in Peking, various meetings of the CPC CC, and other affairs. In 1967, the tempo and variety of his public appearances increased. For example, on June 6, he received N. Sanmugathasan, member of the Politburo of the Communist Party of Ceylon; on June 9, he welcomed delegates to the Peking seminar of the Afro-Asian Writers' Bureau; on June 24, he entertained President Kaunda of Zambia; on June 22, he attended a performance of the opera "On the Docks;" and on July 7, he presided at the Peking PLA Conference on Military Training.

honor seemed a fit reward to a man who had demonstrated his organizational and other talents to further the cause of communism in China for almost forty years.

Replying to a query from Field Marshal Montgomery in 1961, Mao Tse-tung humorously observed that he neither knew nor cared who might follow Liu Shao-ch'i as the leader of Communist China. He would be conversing with Marx, Mao added, and the Chinese people could work things out for themselves! In fact, with the ranks of the CPC apparently strengthened by the removal of the dissidents associated with the Lushan disclosures, and with Lin Piao now leading the army in a drive to master the thought of Mao, harmony seemed restored. The leadership, confident of the line of succession, could turn its attention to the tasks of economic rebuilding and struggle against the signs of revisionism coming from Khrushchev and the Kremlin.

This assumption of Liu Shao-ch'i's succession to Mao was shattered in August, 1966, when Mao Tse-tung chose the much publicized event of his first review of the Red Guards to appear side by side in army dress with his "closest comrade in arms," Lin Piao.[55] Lin's rise, which spelled the dramatic downfall of Liu as the designated heir apparent, was clearly Mao Tse-tung's personal decision. It reflected the judgment that, since Liu had failed to remain loyal to the Party's general line and Mao's own direction, the future role of directing the Chinese Communists rightfully belonged to a man who had proven his steadfastness under battle conditions. And Mao's reversal of his plans for leadership succession were apparently formally accepted by the ranks of his associates at the August, 1966 eleventh plenum of the CPC Central Committee. The CC's resolution adopted on August 12 mentions only the direction of Mao and Lin Piao, and strongly endorses the latter's study of the thought of Mao.

Lin Piao, born in 1908, is the youngest of the inner circle of men who surround Mao in the ranks of the CPC CC's Politburo. A member of the Young Communist League at the age of 16, he is a graduate of Whampoa with an outstanding military record. Lin played a prominent part in the Nanchang Uprising. In 1928, with Chu Teh he joined Mao in the Chingkangshan Mountains, and later accompanied him on the Long March. Wounded in the battles against the Japanese in northeastern Shansi, while

---

[55] There were forewarning signs. For example, when Mao returned to Peking after an absence of several months to receive a visiting Albanian Communist Party delegation in May, 1966, Lin Piao shared the spotlight, not Liu. On June 19, *People's Daily* took the rather unusual step of publishing a letter Lin Piao had written on March 11 in praise of the industrial and communications departments "putting politics in command" by studying the works of Mao. The practice of publishing an earlier statement has most frequently been used in the case of Mao's own pronouncements.

he was serving as commander of the 115th Division of the Eighth Route Army, Lin Piao recuperated in Moscow, where he also studied at the Red Army Academy. His knowledge of military strategy was put to good use in the latter years of World War II and the ensuing civil war. In 1949, Lin became the regional boss of Central-South China, and in 1954 he was named a Vice Premier and Vice Chairman of the National Defense Council. In 1955, he was promoted to membership in the CC Politburo, and in May, 1958 he became a member of its Standing Committee. In 1959, Lin Piao replaced P'eng Teh-huai as Minister of Defense and First Vice Chairman of the NDC. He also became First Vice Chairman of the CPC Central Committee's powerful Military Affairs Commission. Although Lin Piao has suffered, at least intermittently, from poor health, he served as the leader of the Chinese People's Volunteers in Korea and steadily augmented his reputation as the CPC's leading military strategist, second only to Mao.

Even before the inauguration of the cultural revolution, Lin Piao was probably the only one, among Mao's potential heirs, to enjoy a reputation for theoretical work anywhere nearly equal to that of Liu Shao-ch'i. As early as 1942, Mao chose Lin to reorganize the Yenan Party School.[56] In September, 1965, Lin's place as a theorist was greatly enhanced with the publication of his 20,000 word essay, "Long Live the Victory of the People's War." This analysis, based on Mao's thought, suggests that the socialist-capitalist struggle is analogous to Mao's early formulas for the peasant-bourgeois struggle. Thus, Lin Piao confidently predicts that the "countryside" or underdeveloped nations will "encircle" and defeat the "cities," or the imperialist camp. This piece has been hailed in the Chinese Communist press as an outstanding contribution.

Since the beginning of the cultural revolution, Lin Piao has issued various directives to the PLA, which have also been extolled as models for the masses. Principally, his absolute fidelity to the thought of Mao has ensured a high place for his writings. *Red Flag* (no. 11, 1967) stresses this point:

Comrade Lin Piao holds highest the red banner of Mao Tse-tung's thought, studies Chairman Mao's works with the best results and applies them most effectively. For several decades, he has consistently carried out Chairman Mao's proletarian revolutionary line most faithfully, firmly and thoroughly. The method advocated by Comrade Lin Piao of studying Chairman Mao's works with specific problems in mind, studying and applying his works in a creative way, combining study with application, studying first what must be urgently applied so as to get quick results, and of striving hard to apply what one is studying has proved effective and universally suitable and should be further popularized throughout the country.

[56] Lin Piao's partner in this reorganization was P'eng Chen, later to become one of the first victims of the cultural revolution's purges.

Despite the modifications in the ranking of the Politburo's membership in the process of cultural revolution, one man has managed to hold his position and enhance his reputation as a faithful disciple of Mao. Chou En-lai continues to be ranked third, and is preceded only by Mao's newly chosen heir apparent, Lin Piao. Amid all the vicissitudes associated with the exposures of the cultural revolution, Chou has performed valuable services to Mao and Lin Piao. He has been chosen to give speeches in support of the revolution to the Red Guards, at their numerous Peking rallies, and to address workers and peasants in the name of the Party and state. This present role reaffirms Chou En-lai's adaptability—a characteristic that has stood him in good stead during his lengthy career.

Chou En-lai was an overseas student in France, and returned to China by way of the Soviet Union. He was one of the founders of the CPC branch in France in 1921, and in 1924 he was named Acting Director of the Political Department at Whampoa Military Academy by Chiang Kai-shek. In 1931, Chou was implicated in the Li Li-san schism and lost his post as chairman of the CPC's Organization Bureau. However, he managed to retain enough power to reappear as chairman of the Military Affairs Bureau, which was to become a most important organ in the years ahead. Chou is Premier of the State Council. He has distinguished himself in such top level foreign assignments as the 1954 Geneva Conference, and the 1955 Bandung Conference, and the 1961 22nd Congress of the CPSU. He is probably Communist China's best foreign negotiator. Widely known and respected, Chou's chief following has always been in the state apparatus. He is not considered to be a theoretician of any stature. Yet, the choice of Chou En-lai to voice the pronouncements of Mao and Lin during numerous major meetings, rallies and conferences of the cultural revolution, indicates his correct ideological stand. Should Chou continue to be willing to settle for his role as a respected diplomat and administrator and as a trusted associate of both Mao and Lin—and there is no indication to the contrary—then his position should remain secure. As noted elsewhere, Chou has been extremely active in the cultural revolution, and repeatedly favored by Mao and Lin Piao. At the Red Guards' rallies of August 18 and 31 and September 15, Chou had the honor of delivering the only addresses besides those of Lin Piao. These speeches, and his other labors, must be taken as a strenuous endorsement of the thought of Mao and the direction of Lin. They would seem to preclude Chou being drawn into the adverse current of modern revisionism that sharply contrasts Mao's thought.

From 1949, and the establishment of the communist government, until 1966, and the beginning of the cultural revolution, the CPC's power nucleus—the Politburo—was characterized by the high degree of stability among its veteran close associates. During these years only two members were purged. In contrast, between May and June, 1966, one member and one alternate were purged—P'eng Chen and Lu Ting-yi respectively—and since then several other members have been denounced, discredited, and probably removed from any post of real authority. On the eve of the cultural revolution the roster of the Politburo was ranked as follows: (1) Mao Tse-tung; (2) Liu Shao-ch'i; (3) Chou En-lai; (4) Chu Teh; (5) Ch'en Yün; (6) Teng Hsiao-p'ing; (7) Lin Piao; (8) Tung Pi-wu; (9) P'eng Chen; (10) Chen Yi; (11) Li Fu-ch'un; (12) P'eng Teh-huai;* (13) Liu Po-ch'eng; (14) Ho Lung; (15) Li Hsien-nien; (16) Li Ching-ch'üan; and (17) T'an Chen-lin. In mid-1967, this membership and ranking had already been strikingly altered, by deletions, additions, purges and denunciations.

The purges of P'eng Teh-huai and P'eng Chen and the vilification of Liu Shao-ch'i and Teng Hsiao-p'ing have already been discussed. The position of the above said fourth and fifth ranked members of the Politburo can be summarized briefly. Chu Teh, formerly ranked fourth in the Politburo, has been active in the Party since 1922, and was commander-in-chief of the military until the reorganization under the 1954 Constitution. Chu, who has been with Mao since May, 1928, holds the largely honorary post of Chairman of the Standing Committee of the National People's Congress. Until the exposures of the cultural revolution, he was regarded as an amiable figurehead whose age—he was born in 1886—precluded any more active service. However, the Red Guard posters and press have attacked Chu Teh as a "big warlord," and a "man of vaulting ambition." For example, *Hsin Pei-ta (New Peking University)* of February 16, 1967, alleged that Chu Teh, who called himself the founder of the Red Army, has long been a foe of Mao.

Ranked below Chu Teh in the Politburo is Ch'en Yün, who began his services to the Party in Shanghai, and who came to enjoy a reputation as one of the Politburo's best experts in the field of finance. Ch'en also formerly served as Director of the CC's Organization Department, but in 1959, he fell into disfavor for his opposition to the policies of the Great Leap. Having lost influence in the Party, Ch'en Yün retained the relatively minor office of Second Vice Premier of the State Council. [57] A target for Red Guard criticism, Ch'en has been denounced for his resistance to the communes and advocation of independent farming. *Ts'ai-Mao Hung-ch'i (Red Flag of Finance and Trade)* of February 23, 1967, termed him "an advanced guard for the restoration of capitalism." The fact that both Chu Teh and Ch'en Yün were present at the May Day, 1967 celebration at-

---

* Although P'eng was removed in 1959, his name continues to be carried on the official rosters. This practice is not uncommon in the CPC.

[57] The first session of the Third NPC, in December, 1964, demoted Ch'en Yün from first to second vice premier.

tended by Mao in Peking would seem to bear out the rumors that Mao has decided to spare the two old Party veterans any more serious attacks, and to permit them to reform through criticism and self-criticism. Neither Chu Teh nor Ch'en Yün represent any serious threat to Mao or his chosen associates.

Tung Pi-wu, who previously ranked eighth in the Politburo, holds the office of Vice Chairman of the People's Republic (an honorary post), and may still retain his office of Secretary of the CPC CC's Control Commission. So far, he has apparently escaped Red Guards criticism, which may be a mark of respect for his many years of faithful service. He occupied his usual place on the rostrum at the May Day, 1967 festivities. In any case, Tung's age—he is eighty—precludes any larger role for him.

Chen Yi, the Minister of Foreign Affairs and Vice Chairman of the NDC, ranked tenth on the Politburo roster. A veteran Party leader, he has a distinguished revolutionary record and was appointed one of the PLA's Marshals. He was elected to the Politburo in September, 1956, but is chiefly known for his services to the state administration. In the first months of the cultural revolution, Chen Yi delivered several public speeches on foreign policy. On July 10 and 12, 1966 he denounced US aggression in Vietnam, and on September 9 he repeated his anti-American accusations at a reception in the North Korean Embassy in Peking. Since then, Red Guard literature has termed Chen Yi "a big rightist and counterrevolutionary element," and a faithful follower of the Liu-Teng line.[58] His presence near Mao and Lin Piao at the May Day, 1967 rally seems to indicate that he has been allowed to correct his errors.

Li Fu-ch'un was listed as eleventh in the power nucleus of the Politburo. A veteran of the Long March, he formerly served in the CC's Organization Department and is a member of the CC Secretariat, and seventh ranked Vice Premier of the State Council. However, Li's most important service to the Party has been as Chairman of the State Planning Commission. His endorsement of the Great Leap and the commune system doubtlessly helped to improve his stature in the leadership ranks. He has been prominent in the meetings and rallies of the cultural revolution and, on May Day, 1967, shared the rostrum with the inner core of Mao's chosen associates.

Another economic planner for the Party, Li Hsien-nien, holds the fifteenth position in the Politburo's ranks. A veteran of Party and state offices at the provincial level, he is a Vice Premier and Minister of Finance, and a

---

[58] See Peking *T'i-yü Chan-hsien* (January 18, 1967), and Hong Kong *Ming Pao* (April 19 and May 13, 1967). The latter paper reports that Chen Yi was the particular target of the Red Guard units from the Foreign Language Institute, and has also been denounced by his subordinates for trying to suppress the cultural revolution.

member of the CC Secretariat. Like Li Fu-ch'un, he has been relatively prominent in the various activities of the cultural revolution.

Liu Po-ch'eng holds thirteenth place in the Politburo. He is second Vice Chairman of the NDC, and was promoted from the fifteenth to second vice chairmanship of the NPC Standing Committee in December, 1964. He has been in attendance at several of the functions associated with the cultural revolution, but is believed to be ill. His advanced age—Liu is over 70—and questionable health would prohibit any more active role.

Ho Lung's 14th ranking position in the CPC Politburo has certainly been jeopardized, and probably has been negated as a result of the disclosures of the cultural revolution. Third Vice Chairman of the NDC, Ho was elevated from sixth to fourth vice premiership of the State Council by the Third NPC, in December, 1964. In the early stages of the cultural revolution, he was honored by being assigned to the same car with Mao and Lin Piao for the August 31, 1966 Red Guards' rally in Peking. Later, however, members of the Red Guards denounced Ho, particularly for his longtime close association with P'eng Chen and Lo Jui-ch'ing—both targets of the current struggle. For example, Peking *T'i-yü Chan-hsien* (*Sports Front*) of January 18, 1967, branded Ho Lung as a supporter of the Kao Kang anti-Party group, who "for a long time engaged himself in vigorously creating an independent kingdom," and a supporter of Wu Han. Since there have been no reports of Ho's attendance at such functions as the May Day, 1967 rally, it must be presumed that he has been disciplined for his errors.

Li Ching-ch'üan, ranked sixteenth, and T'an Chen-lin listed seventeenth, complete the official roster of the CPC's Politburo, as it was publicized up until the cultural revolution. Li Ching-ch'üan was First Secretary of the CPC's Southwest Bureau and First Secretary of the Szechuan provincial Party committee. The first session of the Third NPC named him third Vice Chairman of the NPC Standing Committee in December, 1964, over several veteran members. But the outbreak of violence in Szechuan province, as the Red Guards challenged Li's direction of the cultural revolution there, discredited the Party veteran. Li was accused of following the Liu-Teng line and opposing Mao in a series of Red Guards' posters: after bloody fighting broke out in May, 1967, Red Guard sources revealed that the CPC CC had recalled Li and removed him from his offices. [59] T'an Chen-lin, who is experienced in Party and state administration at the provincial level, holds the office of Vice Premier and is a member of the CC Secretariat. He survived the drastic purge of the latter body, carried out as part of the cultural revolution, and was present at the May Day, 1967 celebrations,

[59] Hong Kong *Ming Pao* (May 15, 1967) reported that Li was relieved of his duties on May 7, and replaced by the appointment of Chang Kuo-hua, First Secretary of the CPC's Tibet committee.

but he has been denounced by Red Guard sources, such as the March 20, 1967 *Chin-Chün pao*.

In the listings of Politburo membership, until the eve of the cultural revolution, six men held the rank of alternate; Ulanfu, Chang Wen-t'ien, Lu Ting-yi, Ch'en Po-ta, K'ang Sheng and Po I-po. Chang Wen-t'ien, who formerly was a Vice Minister of Foreign Affairs and at one time ambassador to the Soviet Union, has been in eclipse for years. He holds no major Party or state office, and was purged with P'eng Teh-huai. Ulanfu, a Mongol whose position reflected the CPC policy for national minorities, held the post of CPC First Secretary of the Inner Mongolia Autonomous Region; he is also a Vice Premier and Chairman of the Nationalities Affairs Commission. Ulanfu also held membership in the NDC and was commander and political commissar of the Inner Mongolia military region. In February, 1967, Red Guard wall posters in Peking attacked Ulanfu for his failure to support the cultural revolution. He has played no active part in the various Party gatherings and mass rallies in Peking, and may have been removed from his offices. Hong Kong *Ming Pao* on May 15, 1967, reported that Ulanfu was relieved of his duties on May 7, and replaced by Liu Hsien-ch'uan, commander of the Tsinghai Military District. Po I-po, who formerly was Minister of Finance, is a Vice Premier, a Vice Chairman of the State Planning Commission and the Chairman of the State Economic Commission. He has been criticized by Red Guards for supporting the Liu-Teng line, and many have been removed from any post of authority. He was not present at the May Day, 1967 rally in Peking.

Lu Ting-yi's purge was one of the first of the cultural revolution. A Vice Premier, he held the important posts of Minister of Culture and Director of the CC's Propaganda Department. His failure to use these offices to adequately promote the thought of Mao, and his inclination toward the Liu-Teng line, have been bitterly denounced by the Red Guards. It was his abuse of the Party's propaganda machine that led to the CC's decision to create the super body of the Cultural Revolution Group.[60] Presumably, Lu's deputy director in the Propaganda Department was largely instrumental in the disclosures of his perfidy: Ch'en Po-ta's rapid rise can be considered one of the "success stories" of those who faithfully wage the cultural revolution.

Until the beginning of the cultural revolution, Ch'en Po-ta was not considered to rank in the highest echelons of CPC leadership. In the state organization, he is First Vice President of the Chinese Academy of Sciences and Vice Chairman of the State Planning Commission. In the Party, he held offices as alternate member of the Politburo, and as deputy director of

---

[60] For details on the upheaval in the CC's Propaganda Department see the conclusion of Chapter 4.

the CC's Propaganda Department. But, he has long been a trusted friend of Mao Tse-tung's, and has served as his personal secretary, and possibly on occasion as his ghost writer. In 1958, he was chosen as chief editor of the Central Committee's newly established voice, *Red Flag:* through its pages he consistently extolled the thought of Mao and the concept of dedication to the Party's goals. Thus, he is considered as a theoretician of some merit.

In his assignment in the CC's Propaganda Department, Ch'en Po-ta was probably instrumental in the decision to remove that body's director, Lu Ting-yi, in May, 1966, just as he doubtlessly had a role in discrediting and removing Lu's successor, T'ao Chu, from the same post later. When the Politburo determined to assume direction of the cultural revolution, Ch'en was named head of the CC's Cultural Revolution Group. He is a close friend of Madame Mao's, and has collaborated closely with her. Ch'en Po-ta is now identified as a member of the Standing Committee of the Politburo, which must be considered as the reward for his faithful service to Mao and his dedication to Mao's thought.

K'ang Sheng, a veteran communist revolutionary at least since 1926, has had a fluctuating role in the leadership ranks until his promotion from alternate to full membership in the CPC Politburo in 1966, as a result of his prominence in carrying out the cultural revolution.[61] An important organizational and theoretical worker, K'ang was once the chief of the Party's secret police. He was elected to the CPC Secretariat in September, 1962, by the tenth CC plenum. One of the few Chinese Communist leaders with substantial international experience, K'ang Sheng worked for the Comintern between 1933 and 1935, and was a member of the CPC delegation to the 21st and 22nd Congresses of the CPSU. He attended the East German Congress in 1956, the Rumanian in 1960, and the Korean in 1961. He was also a member of the delegation led by Teng Hsiao-p'ing to the 1963 Sino-Soviet ideological talks, and, since 1959, he has participated in a host of bilateral talks with delegations of other Communist Parties and states.

In 1966, K'ang Sheng served on a five-man CC committee to carry out socialist education. It was the questionable nature of this committee's Outline Report that led to the crisis unleashing the forces of the cultural revolution. Presumably, K'ang satisfactorily proved his loyalty to the Mao-Lin leadership for, while his fellow committee member P'eng Chen was held solely responsible for the Report's ideological errors, K'ang was given

---

[61] K'ang was a member of the Politburo of the CPC's Seventh Central Committee, 1945–56. Criticized in 1938 for failing to carry out the rectification campaign, he again attracted attention in 1942, for encouraging workers and peasants to write articles. At the CPC's Eighth Congress he was elected only as an alternate member of the Politburo, despite the fact that many others were earning easy promotions.

TABLE I
MEMBERS OF THE CPC CC POLITBURO (1958–67)*

Name	Date of Birth	Rank in 1958	Rank in May, 1967	Education
Mao Tse-tung	1893	1	1	Normal School
Liu Shao-ch'i	1898	2	b	Normal School
Chou En-lai	1899	3	3	University
Chu Teh	1886	4	6	Military School
Ch'en Yün	1905	5	8	Primary School
Teng Hsiao-p'ing	1904	6	b	College?
Lin Piao	1907	7	2	Military Academy
Tung Pi-wu	1886	8	9	College
P'eng Chen	1899	9	b	Middle School
Lo Jung-huan	1902	10	(died in 1963)	
Chen Yi	1901	11	10	College
Li Fu-ch'un	1900	12	7	College?
P'eng Teh-huai	1902	13	b	Primary
Liu Po-ch'eng	1892	14	(ill health)	Military Institute
Ho Lung	1896	15	b	Primary
Li Hsien-nien	1905	16	11	Apprenticeship
K'o Ch'ing-shih	1900	17	(died in 1965)	Normal School
Li Ching-ch'üan	?	18	b	College
T'an Chen-lin	1902	19	12	Private School
Ulanfu	1903	20	c	University
Chang Wen-t'ien	1900	21	d	University
Lu Ting-yi	1904	22	b	University
Ch'en Po-ta	1904	23	4	University
K'ang Sheng	?	24	5	University
Po I-po	1907	25	?	?
T'ao Chu	1906	a	b	?
Hsü Hsiang-ch'ien	1902	a	13	Military School
Nieh Jung-chen	1899	a	14	University
Yeh Chien-ying	1897	a	15	Military Institute
Li Hsüeh-feng	1907	a	16	?
Hsieh Fu-chih	1898	a	17	College

a = promoted to the Politburo during the cultural revolution
b = purged
c = attacked by Red Guards and others; may have been purged
d = probably purged before the cultural revolution

* This information was compiled from various official and nonofficial sources: Rank in 1958 refers to the listing following the second session of the Eighth CPC National Congress; Rank in May, 1967 refers to the lists published for the May Day celebrations in Peking. Dates of birth and level of education have been checked against *Who's Who In Communist China* (Union Research Institute, Hong Kong; 1966).

more important offices.[62]   Named Advisor to the CC's Cultural Revolution Group, K'ang apparently won the warm respect of that organ's head, Ch'en Po-ta.   Since early 1967, K'ang has been identified as a member of the Politburo's Standing Committee, an office he probably received at the CC's eleventh plenum in August, 1966.   By the time of the May Day, 1967 celebrations, K'ang was being listed in the official reports as fifth ranking Party leader (after Mao, Lin Piao, Chou En-lai and Ch'en Po-ta).

The path of K'ang Sheng's career in the CPC stands in sharp contrast, in certain instances, to that of T'ao Chu.   In K'ang's case, he has been able to weather early criticism, unfavorable association, and demotion. His present ascendancy may illustrate that it is K'ang's qualities of seriousness and diligence, and particularly of loyalty to revolutionary goals, that have been judged to be the ideal characteristics for the leaders of the cultural revolution.

Since the beginning of the cultural revolution, several Party officials have been promoted to the Politburo.   The new members include Hsü Hsiang-ch'ien, Nieh Jung-chen, Yeh Chien-ying, Li Hsüeh-feng and Hsieh Fu-chih. All were confirmed as full members of the Central Committee at the first plenum of the Eighth CPC Congress in 1956, and were identified among the "leading members of the Central Committee" in the official dispatches concerning the Red Guard rallies in August-September, 1966.   Hsü Hsiang-ch'ien is a Vice Chairman of the NDC, and was named a Vice Chairman of the NPC Standing Committee in December, 1964.   He is also a member of the Standing Committee of the CC's Military Commission.   On January 13, 1967, *People's Daily* identified Hsü as Head of the PLA Cultural Revolution Group.   However, Hsü Hsiang-ch'ien has not been spared attacks.   Hong Kong *Ming Pao* (April 15, 1967), for example, reported that Hsiao Hua and his associates had taken over Hsü's duties.   Nieh Jung-chen is also a member of the Standing Committee of the CC's Military Commission and a Vice Chairman of the NDC.   He is the Chairman of the Scientific and Technological Commission, and a Vice Premier of the State Council.   Yeh Chien-ying holds several lesser state offices, such as a vice chairmanship of the CPPCC, but he is also a Vice Chairman of the NDC.   He has been attacked by Red Guards, particularly for his association with Ho Lung.

Li Hsüeh-feng, a Vice Chairman of the NPC Standing Committee, member of the CC Secretariat, and First Secretary of the CC's North China Bureau, was recalled to Peking in May, 1966, and named to replace P'eng

---

[62] According to Hong Kong sources, wall posters in Communist China identified the other members of the committee as Teng Hsiao-p'ing, Lu Ting-yi and T'ao Chu.   Should this be correct, only K'ang Sheng survived the attacks on the authors of the Outline Report.   K'ang's immunity from the criticism of his associates is similar to his earlier immunity from his connection with Liu Shao-ch'i and Teng Hsiao-p'ing as a member of delegations led by them to the USSR.

Chen as First Secretary of the newly organized Peking municipal Party committee. His tenure in this post proved short-lived, however. On April 20, 1967, the Peking committee was reorganized in a "three in one" alliance and Hsieh Fu-chih, was appointed to head the new organization.[63] Hsieh Fu-chih, who was appointed a Vice Premier of the State Council in December, 1964, is Minister of Public Security, and Commander of the PLA Naval Headquarters Public Security Force, as well as a member of the NDC. His April, 1967 promotion to leadership of the Party's Peking committee and the new "three in one" alliance indicates that Hsieh Fu-chih has become a member of the inner circle of power that surrounds Mao.

The analysis of the alteration in the ranks of the Politburo contained in the previous pages illustrates the fact that the cultural revolution and the activities of the Red Guards have had a profound effect on the nature of the leadership core in Communist China. The heretofore relatively static rankings have undergone rapid change as a result of the vitalization demanded by the cultural revolution. Liu's fate proves that the line of succession has been re-examined and replaced, and several other members of the higher echelons have shared in his downfall. Appearances notwithstanding, this struggle has been principally ideological, rather than purely factional. To Mao, and those who follow him faithfully, Party status must depend upon ideological dedication. Lin Piao's new position as heir apparent is intended to stress this fact of communist life, and serve as a model for all Party personnel. As Hsiao Hua, director of the PLA's General Political Department, said of Lin Piao in his instructions to the troops:

At every crucial turn in the history of the Chinese Revolution, Comrade Lin Piao has resolutely taken his stand on the side of Chairman Mao and carried out uncompromising struggle against every kind of "left" or Right erroneous line, and has courageously safeguarded Mao's thought. . . . Chairman Mao's closest comrade in arms, his best student and the best example in creatively studying and applying Chairman Mao's works . . . [is Lin Piao].

For this type of ideological dedication, Lin Piao has become the most logical choice as Mao's successor after the master is gone.

---

[63] For details on the reorganization of the Peking committee see Chapter 4.

The Chinese Communist Party Apparatus and Operations

In accordance with Lenin's teachings, the Communist Party is the spearhead of any communist drive to power and the backbone of any communist regime. The basic policies to be applied in every area of society are decided upon by the Party's top leaders. This means that the crucial issues and disagreements over policy and preferment have to be fought out within the Party's leadership corps, with appeal to and aid from the revolutionary activists, such as the Red Guards, if necessary, rather than before the bar of unguided public opinion or the judgment of the uninspired electorate. Detailed implementation of policy, in turn, has to be insured by the militant and disciplined rank and file of the Party operating in every geographical area and every realm of economic and social activity.

The crucial role assigned to the Communist Party places special requirements upon its policies for admitting, training, disciplining and utilizing its members, and special burdens upon its internal organization. But because it is a highly select body, and because it has such an all-inclusive set of functions to perform, it must also depend upon certain auxiliaries and appendages outside its own structure. By organizing the youth of the country, for example, the Red Guards, with their greater pliancy and readiness to welcome drastic social changes, it can obtain not only a recruiting ground for drawing the cream of the new generation into its own ranks, but also the shock troops it needs to carry out some of its essential projects of social engineering. At the same time, even after the Party has seized control in a country like China, and after it has had time to eliminate all vestiges of private ownership and management, it can usefully allow certain strata of society which were politically prominent under the former regime to retain a restricted political outlet, through nominally independent minor parties.

All of these organizations—the Communist Party, its auxiliary youth organizations, and the minor parties—may be thought of as making up the "party apparatus" upon which rests the entire structure of the state and society. Squarely at the center, however, is the Communist Party itself. China, because of its vast size, the generally inadequate state of its communications network, and its previous history of relatively limited control from the central government, offers a particularly spectacular example of the effectiveness of a Party of the Leninist type in fastening its hold upon a country.

COMPOSITION OF THE PARTY

The victory of Mao Tse-tung's forces on the Chinese mainland brought a fundamental change in the size as well as in the major tasks of the Chinese Communist Party. In the early period of cooperation with the Kuomintang, CPC membership had reached a maximum of about 58,000 by 1927. To what low figure it dipped after the break with the KMT, and during the latter's extermination campaigns, it is impossible to say. But, in 1937, when Party fortunes were again looking up, the total membership was still only 40,000.

During the long years of the war with Japan, the Party increased its membership many times over. By 1941, the figure stood at 800,000, and by 1945, at the time of the Seventh Party Congress, it had reached an estimated 1,210,000. The figures thereafter tell the story of the successful drive to power. By 1947, according to Mao, there were 2,700,000 members. In 1949 alone, 1,400,000 new members were admitted, and in 1950, another 1,300,000. At the end of 1950, after nearly thirty years of growth, the CPC had a total of 5,800,000 regular and candidate members, about half of whom had been recruited in 1949 and 1950. Recruitment slowed thereafter; on the occasion of the 32nd anniversary of the Party in 1953, An Tzu-wen, then Deputy Director and now Director of the Central Committee's Organization Department, announced a total membership of 6,100,000.

Recruitment continued on a considerable scale, particularly as the CPC extended its membership among the various national minorities, including the Mongols and other groups in Inner Mongolia, the T'ing, Yao, Miao and other minorities in western Kwangsi, and the various groups in Sinkiang, such as the Uigurs, Kazaks, Uzbeks, and Tadzhiks. With this increment, the Party's total membership reached 10,734,000 by June, 1956.

Although the rate of annual increase was slowed during the 1957–58 rectification campaign, in 1958 the Party conducted a massive recruitment drive. A primary aim of the 1958 drive was to strengthen the Party at the basic levels for the epic tasks of carrying through the Great Leap Forward and commune programs. Recruitment also extended to the intellectual circles to give a further appearance of universal support to these new programs. Thus Party and social inducements resulted in enlistment of such prominent individuals as President of the Chinese Academy of Sciences Kuo Mo-jo, Minister of Geology Li Sze-kwang, Mei Lan-fang, an opera singer regarded as one of China's foremost artists, and Ch'ien Hsüeh-shen, American-trained physicist and director of the Chinese Academy of Sciences' Institute of Mechanics.

As a result of the 1958 drive and subsequent recruitment, *People's Daily* of September 28, 1959, reported total Party membership to have reached 13,960,000. By estimating the 1959 Chinese population to be about 642,000,000, the ratio between CPC members and the general population would be 1:46. Since continuous economic and social programs have further intensified the need for Party cadres, recruitment has continued at a high pitch. According to *People's Daily* of July 1, 1961, CPC membership was roughly 17,000,000 when the Party celebrated its 40th anniversary. Roughly estimating the population in 1961 as 670,000,000, this decreases the Party-population ratio to 1:39. Should the rate of growth for 1961, which was approximately 1,500,000, have been continued, by 1967, CPC membership would be roughly 26,000,000—minus the attrition due to deaths or individual purges.

One important aspect of this tremendous recruitment within the past years is the age factor of the general CPC membership, in terms of Party experience. According to Liu Shao-ch'i's estimate, reported in the July 1, 1961, *People's Daily*, about 80 per cent of the total membership then reported had joined the Party after 1949, and some 70 per cent were admitted after 1953. On October 17, 1961, the same official organ revealed that 40 per cent of the members joined after 1956. Again resorting to rough estimates of the Party membership for 1961 as 17,000,000, only 3,400,000 at most (not discounting normal attrition due to deaths, "retirement" or purges), or about a fifth of the members, could date their membership prior to the seizure of state power. This hard core of members, who have had long Party experience, training, and discipline has thus been responsible for recruiting and educating many times its own number.

The problem posed for the Party leadership by this tremendous influx of new members from widely varied backgrounds, coupled with the simultaneous problem of organizing every aspect of national existence, can well be imagined. Party leaders had to decide what social and economic backgrounds were likely to yield the most reliable Party members. How could the hard core be sure of the dedication of recruits to CPC principles, rather than personal advancement? How could new recruits be quickly and adequately trained in the fundamentals of communist ideology and discipline, to the point where they could be trusted with critical assignments?

The broad lines for meeting such problems had already been laid down for the Chinese Communists by the example of the Communist Party of the Soviet Union (CPSU). But the CPC, of course, has had its own constitution, regulations, and directives geared specifically to meet its own peculiar situation. During the critical years preceding and following the seizure of power on the mainland, the Party was structured by the Constitution adopted by the Seventh Party Congress in April, 1945. This Constitution was framed under the conditions of foreign war and internal strife, prior to the explosion of the communist forces into Manchuria and other Japanese-held or Nationalist-held areas. After the defeat of Japan, in August, 1945, the CPC's nationwide victory in 1949, and the subsequent reorganization of the country, first into administrative areas and then into provincial and municipal subdivisions, the terms of the 1945 CPC Constitution increasingly became obsolete. The change in Party tasks from seizure and consolidation of power to the construction of a socialist economy and a single-class society made the 1945 document an anachronism. This anomaly was remedied at the CPC Eighth National Congress, on September 26, 1956, by the adoption of a new, revised Party Constitution.

Membership Policy, Recruitment, and Indoctrination

In the CPC, as in all communist Parties, the recruitment of new members is one of the regular functions of the basic unit, the Party branch. Becoming a member, according to Article 1 of both the 1945 and the 1956 Party Constitutions, involves meeting the following four conditions: (1) accepting the Program and Constitution of the Party; (2) belonging to and working in one of the Party organizations; (3) observing Party decisions; and (4) paying membership dues. The 1945 Constitution provided the leadership with a variety of entrance requirements for industrial workers, farm workers, middle peasants and other social elements in order that membership composition could be regulated. These provisions were deleted from the 1956 Constitution, which added a new criterion that a Party member must be one who "works and does not exploit the labor of others."

The Party recruits new members from a variety of sources, such as the Young Communist League, the Red Guards, the troops of the PLA, and the host of mass organizations. Any "activist" who gives indication of a high level of "social consciousness" may be solicited for CPC membership.

Because of the composition of the population, the CPC has consistently remained more of a peasant than a worker party. In 1945, Liu Shao-ch'i reported to the Seventh Party Congress that "its members are the peasantry, and the petty bourgeois intelligentsia, with workers occupying a rather small percentage." In 1951, about 80 per cent of the CPC membership was of peasant origin. Statistics released by *Shih Shih Shou Ts'e* (*Current Events*) in its September 25, 1956, issue indicated that over 69 per cent of the total Party membership of 10,730,000 was still of peasant origin. In 1957, Central Committee General Secretary Teng Hsiao-p'ing's Report on the Rectification Campaign testified that almost 67 per cent of the members were of peasant background. But this minor decline was probably reversed after 1958, when communal programs demanded increases of Party membership in the rural areas. It is reasonable to presume that about three-fourths of the total membership now is from the peasant class.

By comparison, of course, the number of Party members of worker origins has remained low. Teng Hsiao-p'ing's reports for 1956 and 1957 gave the percentage of workers in the CPC as 14 and 13.7 respectively. CPC policies have shown an ambiguous reaction to this small representation of workers. On the one hand, particularly in the period prior to the 1949 victory, the leadership insisted that social origin was not a determining factor in recruitment. By implication, the situation was not considered adverse, or as Liu Shao-ch'i mentioned explicitly in his 1945 report: "The social origin of the Party membership alone cannot determine everything." Liu averred, and the CPC has often repeated subsequently, that ideological unity of the members—rather than social origins—should be considered the "prerequisite of the organizational unity of the Party."

Yet, from time to time, Party policy has given special emphasis to recruitment of workers. Following Stalin's precept that the Communist Party must "first of all absorb all the superior elements of the working class," the CPC has called for a systematic strengthening of its proletarian core and taken measures to prevent infiltration of undesirables from classes other than the proletariat. This emphasis was especially marked following the March, 1949, meeting of the CPC Central Committee. In fact, during this period, the CPC's recruitment policy was guided by three principles: (1) greater emphasis on recruitment of workers; (2) a temporary general cessation of recruitment in rural villages; and (3) an increased caution in overall recruitment, aided by intra-Party consolidation efforts.

In his report of June 6, 1950, to the Third Plenary Session of the Seventh Central Committee, Mao Tse-tung again called for "drawing the politically conscious workers into the Party systematically" and "expanding the proportion of workers in the Party organizations." It should be noted that this policy was in harmony with the general trend then to emphasize the role of the worker over that of the peasant. An indication of this trend was found in the 1951 Chinese edition of the *Selected Works of Mao Tsetung;* a passage was deleted from his 1927 report on the peasant movement in Hunan which gave 70 per cent of the credit for "the accomplishment of democratic revolution" to the "achievement of the rural revolution by the peasant."[1] Concentration on worker recruitment had striking results in some urban areas. For example, more than half of the 3,350 Party members recruited in Peking in 1949 were of worker origin. Of the New Democratic Youth League (NDYL) members admitted into the Party in the entire East China area in 1951, one-fifth were workers, as were more than one-half of those admitted in Shanghai in the three years prior to July, 1952.

As noted previously, since the initiation of the Great Leap Forward in 1958 and the concentration on agricultural programs, emphasis has been shifted from worker to peasant recruitment. For example, it was reported in the February 4, 1960, Changsha *Hunan Pao* that, of the 160,000 admitted to Party membership in that area, over 110,000 were peasants. More recently, the orientation of membership recruitment has been directed toward members of the PLA and the Red Guard, model workers, advanced producers and red flag holders. Party membership may be considered in the nature of a reward for special ideological or productive accomplishments to activists demonstrating their fidelity to overall Party programs.

Recruitment of intellectuals has followed a more consistent course. In 1956, according to Teng Hsiao-p'ing's figures, almost 12 per cent of the membership was classified as intellectuals, and by 1957, almost 15 per cent. Despite the rectification drive against the intellectuals following in the wake of the Hundred Flowers campaign, which is discussed elsewhere, the percentage of intellectuals in the total membership continued to grow. For example, in 1956, Chou En-lai pressed for more active recruitment among the intelligentsia. Through such means as the 1961 "meetings of immortals," by 1962, about a third of the intelligentsia had sought or accepted Party membership. This figure represents stepped up recruitment among teachers and other school functionaries. During the 1958–60 period alone, according to *People's Daily* of July 18, 1960, the proportion of Party members in this group rose from 7.3 to 16.47 per cent. As noted elsewhere, campaigns to recruit members from the various national minorities have met with similar successes.

---

[1] This point was first noted by Professor Theodore Hai-en Chen of the University of Southern California.

The recruitment of new members is, obviously, an active and continuous process. Party organizers must be selected and trained for the membership drive; the recruitment plan must be approved by a higher Party committee; lists of activists must be prepared; and the program of propaganda, education and investigation is ceaseless.

The admission procedure is designed to prevent the admission of new members as a matter of routine and without careful check. Qualifications of members recommending the candidate must first be examined; then the local Party organization must approve the admission of the candidate. But, above all, each candidate must be introduced into the Party individually; enrollment of whole groups is not permitted. Furthermore, after the general membership meeting of the local branch has voted admission, the candidate is to be interviewed, investigated, and his qualifications thoroughly verified by the organizers of a higher Party committee, after which this committee is also to approve his application. Finally, the new member is taken into the Party at a solemn ceremony of admission, at which he takes an oath declaring his unreserved loyalty to the Party.

The probationary period for candidates was first standardized in the 1945 Constitution. Prior to that date, the term varied according to the area from two months to one year. The 1945 Constitution, in line with its preferential recruitment policies based on class distinctions (which provided four distinct categories most favorable to urban workers, city poor, farm workers and poor peasants) provided for alternative periods of probation of six months, one year, and two years according to social origins. It also permitted the Party committee to prolong or reduce the length of candidacy for a particular applicant under its jurisdiction. The 1956 Constitution, reflecting the changed recruitment policy, made the probationary period uniform at one year. While denying the local Party committee the right to shorten this term of candidature, it does permit the committee to extend the period, not to exceed one year (Article 8). Similarly, the local CPC committee can annul the candidacy status at any time during the probationary period that the individual is judged to be unfit for Party membership. Under special conditions, Party committees at the county or municipal level are allowed to admit new members directly to the Party (Article 4).

Cautious recruitment policies may increase the reliability and usefulness of new members, but it still leaves the leadership with the problem of making good communists out of the great numbers of relatively recent recruits. The general prescription for the training of Party members was laid down by Mao Tse-tung, who in May, 1941, declared that each member must learn "the spirit of Marxism-Leninism based on the unity of theory and practice." In short, he must learn the principles of dialectical materialism and historical materialism, and how to apply them correctly to concrete conditions.   Other Party leaders have stated the criteria for members in greater detail.   These criteria were stated authoritatively by An Tzu-wen, Director of the Central Committee's Organization Department, in 1952.   They have been used to such effect in the candidate's indoctrination that a member has been known to write on his registration card beside his signature: "I am determined to fulfill the eight criteria of membership.   I will respond to the call of the Party with concrete action." These standards were specified in the 1945 Constitution (Article 2) and reaffirmed in the 1956 document (Article 2).   They hold that a Party member must:

1. Understand the nature of the Communist Party and the principles of Lenin and Stalin with regard to Party building.

2. Understand the ultimate aim of the Communist Party in China—the realization of communism in China.

3. Be determined to fight heroically all his life for communism, never shrinking back, betraying the Party, or retreating, or surrendering to the enemy.

4. Observe strictly the discipline of the Party and obey its unified leadership; take an active part in revolutionary work; resolutely carry out the policy and decisions of the Party and wage irreconcilable struggle against anything detrimental to the interests of the Party, whether inside or outside the Party.

5. Place the general interests of the masses of the people above his own interests.

6. Examine constantly, by means of criticism and self-criticism, the mistakes and defects in his work, and correct them.

7. Serve wholeheartedly the masses of the people, modestly listen to their opinions and demands, report these in due course to the Party, explain the policy of the Party to the masses, and lead them forward.

8. Make an energetic effort to study Marxism-Leninism and Mao Tsetung's theory of the Chinese revolution, in order to raise his own political and ideological level.

It is clear that the Party member who observes these criteria will become, in effect, a transmission belt for enforcing the CPC line among the masses.   To the masses, he will be a model revolutionary worker.

Indoctrination, or cultivation of the political consciousness of the Party member, is a continuous process.   While applicable to all members, this training is particularly stressed for members of non-proletarian origins, in accordance with Lenin's teaching that members of worker origin have the innate qualities of the proletariat, and the logical corollary that those from other class origins carry with them the characteristics of their respective classes. Generally, this indoctrination is more in the nature of on-the-job than of classroom training. It is guided by the thought of Mao and to be conducted within the "practical revolutionary movement of the broad toiling masses." But as *People's Daily* of March 30, 1963, warns: it must not be set aside no matter how pressing the demands of labor since "a surging river is always formed by streams." Rather, indoctrination and labor should complement one another and form the dialectical unity of opposites. Similarly, the leadership has cautioned against overemphasis of political training to the exclusion of participation in labor assignments. The Peking *Ta-kung Pao* of September 14, 1963, for example, after reciting the case of a Party branch secretary in Canton who attended 78 meetings within four months, or an average of 20 a month, asked that the administrative departments curtail their meetings to permit members more time for work.

Ideally, the training for Party members is to be theoretical and practical, general and specialized, political and vocational. The member must have "ethical training" to build the proper moral character. He needs disciplinary training for "intra-Party struggle" to maintain Party unity, training in the "style of work"—that is, in the way of conducting Party business—as well as in revolutionary strategy, tactics, and methodology. But among all the various kinds of training required, ideological training is of paramount importance and priority. It is the foundation stone of all other activity. Mao Tse-tung requires his followers not "merely to read the doctrines of Marxism-Leninism" but "first to master, and then to apply them." This ideological training is expected to help develop the communist philosophy of life and world outlook, while "conquering" and "eliminating" all other philosophies and ideologies.

In his ethical training, a Party member is taught to bear in mind that the Communist Party "does not represent the interests of each individual member" as a "narrow trade union group," but "represents the long-range interests of all workers and the liberation of mankind." He is told that he should "submit completely to the interests of the Party, deny himself, and work for the common good." This self-immolation has been extolled by Liu Shao-ch'i: "To sacrifice the individuals for the sake of the Party, for the sake of the class . . . even to sacrifice one's own life, without the slightest hesitation, with a feeling of happiness—this is the highest expression of the communist morality . . . and proletarian consciousness." In his disciplinary training, which is intended to guarantee Party solidarity as "a unified, organic body," the member comes to give loyal support to the "centralism" features of the principles of democratic centralism—the submission of the minority to the majority, the individual member to the Party organization, and the lower echelons to the higher, all culminating in the authority of the Central Committee represented by Chairman Mao.

Last, but not least, the CPC trains its members in a vocational or management skill. As early as January, 1945, Mao ordered Party members to learn economic work (as contrasted with political work) and develop technological skills within two or three years. The Chinese Communists well understand, as Stalin taught, that the strength of their rule ultimately involves the concentration of economic as well as political power. Mao has warned his followers that, no matter how successful they may be in political, military, Party or cultural activities, "if they are incapable in dealing with the economy, they will be helpless, and will be overthrown and exterminated by the enemy." Liu Shao-ch'i's 1957 call that all Chinese become "red and expert" represents a further stress of this principle (discussed in the section on general education).

Not all Party training takes place within the Party branch. In addition to the schools for cadres—discussed in the next section—there are also training courses given by special cadres, usually at the county seat. Each branch sends a delegation when such courses are offered.

From this brief survey of admission requirements, criteria of performance, and indoctrination programs of the CPC, it does not follow that all Party members are equally loyal, well trained and capable. As will be noted in discussing Party reform movements, the contrary is the case. Thus, the leadership must ever intensify its efforts to raise the membership as a whole closer to the desired "political level."

Selection, Training, and Promotion of Cadres

As in other nations where the communists hold state power, so too in China, the Communist Party, despite its huge membership, contains only a small proportion of the total adult population. It is an elite group specialized for the purpose of ruling the society in all its manifold activities and aspects. But within the Party there are other elite groups, made up of those who are especially active and prominent in Party activities at the lower and middle levels. These are referred to in Party jargon as "cadres." Communist literature leaves no doubt of the importance of the cadres to the movement; but it does leave considerable question as to the definition of the term, which has no recognized constitutional or statutory standing in the CPC Constitution. As familiarly used, it denotes the large number of "backbone" communists ranking below the recognized Party leaders and above the general rank and file. But the term cadre has also been used to include persons at the level of the Central Committee and Politburo as, for example, in the Central Committee resolution of February, 1954, prompted by the alleged Kao-Jao conspiracy. To further confuse the terminology, in most cases Party functionaries at the same time hold official positions in the government hierarchy or economic organizations, but the literature on cadres makes no distinction between Party and non-Party positions or duties. Furthermore, the same term can be applied to non-Party personages or positions. Generally, however, and as used in these pages, a person is a "cadre" if he holds some position of trust in the Party and exercises some degree of leadership over the rank and file membership. Of these Liu Shao-ch'i said simply in his treatise *On the Party:* "The leading bodies of the Party at all levels are composed of cadres."

Those CPC members who Mao has described as "the treasures of the nation and pride of the whole Party" may be thought of, then, as particularly dynamic elements serving as transmission belts between the Party, state and masses. Or, the cadres could be described as the CPC's eyes, ears and mouth among the masses.

The social background of the cadres reflects that of the general Party membership. This is hardly surprising, for in Liu's phrase, the cadres "emerged from the struggle of the masses and, in turn, directed the struggle of the masses." Thus Liu noted in 1945 that the cadres were generally either of worker-peasant origin, or of student and men-of-letters origin. After the 1949 victory, the Party tried to meet its urgent need for large numbers of new cadres by establishing so-called "people's revolutionary universities" in the newly liberated sectors. These centers were to become "furnaces of revolution." In practice, cadres have been drawn not only from the ranks of outstanding veteran Party members, but also from new members accepted from the NDYL (later the YCL) and other progressive youth, from the activists appearing among the peasants after the land reform, and from among the workers and shopkeepers after the "Three-Anti" and the "Five-Anti" and other mass campaigns.

Since the cadres play so vital a role in the Party, the method of their selection, the criteria they must meet, and the training they have to undergo have all been thoroughly analyzed in Party literature. "Without correct selection and training of cadres," Lenin and Stalin warned, "it would be impossible to carry out the political aims of the Party." Stalin laid down two requisites for the selection of cadres: a correct political line and the ability of business management. Mao's basis for selection follows closely these principles of political preparation and professional competence. Liu Shao-ch'i further elaborated these standards in his 1945 treatise *On the Party:*

Our cadres should be imbued with the warmest communist revolutionary zeal combined with cool-headed revolutionary reason. Our cadres should be . . . capable of independent orientation in intricate circumstances, unafraid of shouldering responsibility for making decisions and highly disciplined and well-trained in

Marxism-Leninism both in fighting the enemy and in the inner-Party struggle over principles.

Proper selection of cadres requires careful investigation of prospective candidates, followed by correct placement based upon the individual's abilities. These requirements were pointed out by Stalin at the Eighteenth Congress of the CPSU in 1939. Correct selection, he stressed, requires first of all a psychological readiness to "appreciate, esteem, and respect them [cadres] as the gold fund of the Party and the state." Thus selection should be based upon "knowing the cadres, and studying their good and weak points, thoroughly and individually;" and this must be followed by "placement in such a way that every Party cadre feels himself in the right place and can make his maximum ability available to our common cause." These strictures are further defined by Liu:

> Firstly, a cadre should be examined minutely and intrinsically by the leadership as to his capabilities and limitations, his merits and defects, his whole personal history and his work. Secondly, a cadre should be examined at the place where he does his work and through the rank and file under his leadership. Only by combining both of these can there be a relatively comprehensive and correct appraisal of a cadre, thereby avoiding many deviations.

Adequate training of cadres is also a matter of the utmost importance. Like the ordinary Party members, the cadres are enjoined, in Mao's words, to "work and study simultaneously to old age." Part of this preparation requires the careful study of twelve books listed by the Central Committee,[2] but the greatest emphasis is placed on the theoretical contributions of Mao Tse-tung. Naturally, the cadre must also study all pertinent Party directives and daily newspaper reading is required.

Formal training of the cadres is carried on through a variety of schools and programs. At the lowest level are the network of Party evening

---

[2] These are: (1) *The Communist Manifesto*, by Marx and Engels; (2) *Socialism, Utopian and Scientific*, by Engels; (3) *The Ideology and Methodology of Marx and Engels*, compiled by the Liberation Press; (4) *Imperialism, the Highest Stage of Capitalism*, by Lenin; (5) *Left-Wing Communism, an Infantile Disorder*, by Lenin; (6) *State and Revolution*, by Lenin; (7) *Foundations of Leninism*, by Stalin; (8) *Lenin and Stalin on China*, compiled by the Liberation Press; (9) *Lenin and Stalin on Socialistic Economy* (two volumes), compiled by the Liberation Press; (10) *Political Economy*, by Leontiev; (11) *Short Course of the History of the Communist Party of the Soviet Union*, edited by the CPSU Central Committee; and (12) *The History of Social Development*, compiled by the Liberation Press. Before Stalin's death, the cadres were also urged to read his work on *The Economic Problem of Socialism in the Soviet Union*, as well as the document of the CPSU 19th Congress.

For an analysis of the titles of Mao's works that are required, and the importance attached, see the chapter on the leadership.

schools and the system of "study instructors." These evening schools are a most important agency. As early as 1952, some 100 had been established just in the Northeast region. In Mukden, for example, it was estimated that more than 15,000 cadres were enrolled in these centers. And the number of these schools has undergone constant expansion. In the Swatow district, Kwangtung province, for instance, during the 1958–1959 period, 309 full-time cadres gave instruction to 183,660 Party cadres, members, and prospective candidates. The "study instructors" serve as tutors to assist the individual cadres in analyzing Party documents.

The Party also provides for more advanced training for more promising cadres. This includes intensive middle-school programs as well as instruction at the college level in such special institutions as the People's University. This center opened in 1951, for the specific purpose of training the "intelligentsia of the proletariat."

The most common form of cadre instruction, however, is that of education through productive labor. Each cadre is expected to spend part of his time in work and part in study, according to a Party-determined ratio. During the Winter of 1957 and the spring of 1958, coinciding with the launching of the commune system, cadres were shipped en masse to the countryside to participate in manual labor. In 1959, according to a January 17, 1960, NCNA dispatch, more than 257,000 cadres contributed nearly a full year of physical labor, while another million contributed 72 million man hours. As noted elsewhere, this force included senior as well as junior level Party personnel.

The promotion of Party cadres entails not only the possible improvement of Party status, but also, and far more frequently, the matter of promotion on the job. It is interesting, in this connection, to note the heavy stress placed on political and ideological study and understanding, often to the point of almost ignoring professional qualifications and performance. Yet, a highly flexible promotion system stimulates the cadres to play a more active role in order to attain a higher, and often more privileged, rank. With a good prospect of promotion, according to Stalin, the cadres can be expected "to cherish and accept the political line of the Party as their personal political line, to be ready to carry it out, to answer to it, defend it, and struggle for it." Following this approach, the CPC has offered as the principal yardsticks for promotion boundless loyalty to the Party, high revolutionary spirit, advanced training in Marxism-Leninism, strict observance of Party discipline, intimate connection with the masses, ability to work independently, willingness to work, and unselfishness. As the Canton *Nan-fang Jih-pao* observed on December 25, 1962, ultimately all promotion depends on self-effort.

THE PARTY HIERARCHY

It might well be supposed that the selection, training and advancement of Party members and cadres would result in a highly competent corps of Party workers, loyal and devoted to the cause, for reasons of personal interest as well as ideological sympathy. But loyalty and devotion are not enough. As previously noted, Lenin and his successors have also demanded unquestioning obedience from Party members. And they have also recognized that the organizational structure of a revolutionary party must provide a maximum of maneuverability and striking force during its drive for power, and a maximum capacity for penetration and control of all areas of life once in power. These twin needs for internal discipline and effective organization are met, in any Communist Party, through a hierarchical organization using the principle of democratic centralism to guarantee that all control comes from the top.

Like the CPSU, the CPC represents a power pyramid erected on a combined territorial-production foundation. The basic Party units are usually formed along production lines, while other high and low level units are established along territorial lines. At the base of the pyramid are the Party branches, known in earlier times as "cells." Branches are organized in agriculture, industry, the armed forces, and all state and social institutions, or in any locality. Under the CPC Constitution, there must be at least three members to form a branch; but there may be as many as several hundred. On this base are erected the successive higher layers: rural and urban districts, cities and counties, regions and provinces, each have their own organizations. All these form a spiral leading upward to the Central Committee.

Organizational Principle: Democratic Centralism

In order to regulate this vast pyramid structure effectively, the Party leadership employs the principle of democratic centralism. This involves both the submission of lower to higher units, and the transfer of control at any given level from large, unwieldy bodies to tightly knit inner groups.

Democratic centralism, one of the cardinal principles of Marxism-Leninism, has been employed fully by the CPC. Like Article 14 of the 1945 Constitution, Article 19 of the 1956 CPC Constitution describes this principle as "centralism on the basis of democracy, and democracy under centralized guidance." This order is reflected in the election of all leading agencies of the Party by their respective representative organs, in the accountability of these agencies to their respective congresses, and in the strict discipline by which the minority submits to the majority, and in the binding force which the decisions of the higher bodies have over lesser bodies. In characteristic communist rhetoric, Liu Shao-ch'i has described the process thus:

It means that the leading bodies of the Party are elected by the membership on a democratic basis and enjoy their confidence. It means that the directives and resolutions of the Party are centralized from the rank and file upward on a democratic basis as well as decided by them or their representatives, and are then persistently maintained and carried out by the leadership in conjunction with the rank and file. The authority of a leading body of the Party is given by the Party membership. Therefore, it is capable of exercising the power of centralized leadership on behalf of the membership in managing all Party affairs and of commanding the obedience of its lower organizations and of the Party membership.

Without the "centralist" features of this principle, the "democratic" features could never achieve Party goals. Presumably contrasting the practices of Western democracies, Liu emphasizes that "inner-Party democracy is neither democracy without leadership, absolute democracy, nor anarchy within the Party." His formulation of the role of centralized leadership is quite explicit:

It means that every Party meeting is to be convened by a leading body and proceeds under leadership. The adoption of every resolution or rule is preceded by thorough preparation and careful deliberation. Every election has a carefully prepared list of nominees. The Party as a whole has a unified Party Constitution, and a unified discipline which every Party member should observe, and a unified leading body, which must be obeyed by the entire membership.

Like Mao, Liu's argument against "absolute democracy" is expressed in terms of potential detriment to the Party's organizational fighting power.

From a Western point of view, this emphasis on centralized leadership leads to innumerable restrictions on inner-Party democracy. Many of these strictures are enshrined in the Party Constitution. Thus, for example, although the functions and powers of the central and local organizations are to be appropriately divided, decisions made at the lower level must never conflict with those made by a higher Party organ (Article 25). Similarly, although the lower Party organizations and the members of the Party committees may hold free and practical discussions, they must submit their proposals for the approval of the higher organs and carry out any decision unconditionally (Article 26). The lower organizations are also committed to use newspapers as mouthpieces for their higher organs, including the central apparatus; and the formation or dissolution of any organization must receive prior approval of the higher level body (Articles 27, 28, and 50). At each level, the election and removal of members of the standing committees and secretariats (or the secretaries at the lower levels) must receive similar approbation (Articles 41 and 46).

The higher level organization has the rights of scrutiny over lower units, and also over the opinions and conduct of individual Party members. Thus the structure provides for central and local control commissions. This ability to judge the thoughts and activities of the individual member of the CPC also extends to non-Party activities. In any non-Party group, such as a government agency, trade union or mass organization, a Party fraction or "leading Party members' group" must be formed to strengthen the CPC's influence and see that its directives are observed (Articles 59 and 60). [3]

For the rank and file of the Party membership, the closest supervision is probably exercised through the Party branch. On an average, according to Party statistics, there are about twenty members in a branch. Where the membership is greater, sub-branches may be formed according to place or residence or type of occupation. As provided in the 1956 Constitution, these basic units, by virtue of their small size and consequent intimate contact, have a vital role in implementing discipline and abetting indoctrination (Article 50).

Among the bulk of the membership, the principle of democratic centralism may encourage a sense of active participation in the election, if not actual choice, of leaders. At the same time, it hampers initiative, since all power is concentrated at the top.

The pyramid of Party organs through which the principle of democratic centralism is applied follows the example of the CPSU. At each level of the hierarchy, there is a quadripartite division of authority and responsibility among representative, executive, administrative, and control organs. The following sections explain the four types of structure.

Congresses and Branch Meetings

The highest leading body of the Party at each level, according to the Party Constitution, is the representative organ at that level. From the National Party Congress at the top, the hierarchy descends through the provincial and regional congresses, to the county, city and rural and urban district congresses, and finally down to the general meeting of the Party branch (Articles 19 and 21). However, the Constitution also provides that the Party committee (i.e., the executive body) elected by each of these congresses shall exercise all its functions when the congress is not in session (Article 21).

[3] A Party fraction, it should be noted, differs from a Party branch. It is a group of three or more Party members organized within a non-Party organization to carry out the CPC's policies therein (Articles 59 and 60).

Theoretically, the supreme authority of the CPC is vested in the National Party Congress. [4] This body is convened by the Party Central Committee. As the 1956 Constitution states, it must be convened annually, rather than every three years as stipulated in the 1945 Constitution. However, the Central Committee may postpone or convene the congress according to circumstances. The 1945 Constitution made convocation mandatory whenever lower Party organizations representing more than half the total membership requested such a session. The 1956 Constitution further reduces this proportion; now a third of the delegates to the National Congress or a third of the organizations at the provincial level may request the Central Committee to call a special session (Article 31). The Central Committee retains the right to determine the number and method of election of delegates to the congress.

Outwardly, the functions and powers of the National Party Congress are those of an organ of supreme authority. Included among its prerogatives are the hearing and examination of reports from the Central Committee and other central organs, the determination of the CPC's general line and policy, the revision of the Party Constitution, and election of members to the Central Committee. In reality, effective power lies elsewhere. Despite Constitutional provisions, the Party actually functioned without a congress from 1928 to 1945, and none was held during the momentous period between 1945 and 1956.

The congresses at the lower levels above the branch meeting are assigned almost the same functions for their respective levels as the National Congress for the entire Party (Articles 3, 38 and 43). Whereas the 1945 Constitution required these lower level congresses to meet every two years, the 1956 Constitution provides that they should be convened annually (Articles 38 and 43). The committee at each level has the power to convene its representative congress, and determine the number and manner of election of delegates, subject to the direction and approval of the higher Party committee (Articles 38 and 42). These meetings or the lower Party congresses, like those of the National Party Congress, serve chiefly as a medium for education and training and to put the rubber stamp of approval on leadership decisions.

Under the terms of the 1945 Party Constitution, during the intervals between congresses, conferences could be convened at levels above the branch. Delegates to these conferences were elected by the Party com-

---

[4] Altogether, there have been eight National Party Congresses since the foundation of the CPC in 1921. The first met in Shanghai in July, 1921; the second in Hangchow (West Lake) in May, 1922; the third in Canton in June, 1923; the fourth in Shanghai in January, 1925; the fifth in Wuhan in April, 1927; the sixth in Moscow in July-September, 1928; the seventh in Yenan in April-June, 1945; the eighth in Peking in September-October, 1956.

CHART I ORGANIZATION OF THE COMMUNIST PARTY OF CHINA
(1945 CONSTITUTION)

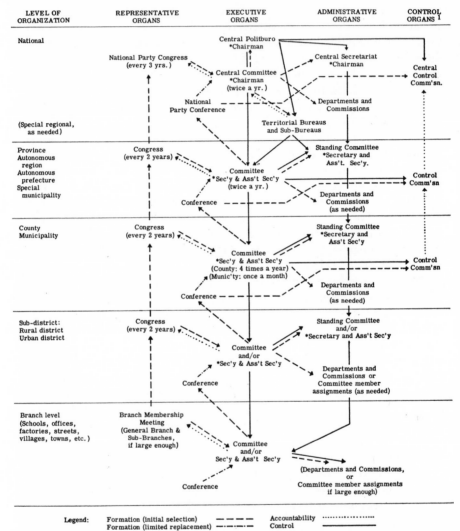

Legend: Formation (initial selection) — — — —   Accountability ··············
          Formation (limited replacement) —·—·—·—   Control ————————

* : Positions at the same level held by the same person.

[1] For the control organs, the lines of formation, accountability and control follow the National Party Conference resolution of March 31, 1954, rather than Chapter VIII of the Party Constitution.

CHART II ORGANIZATION OF THE COMMUNIST PARTY OF CHINA (1956 CONSTITUTION)

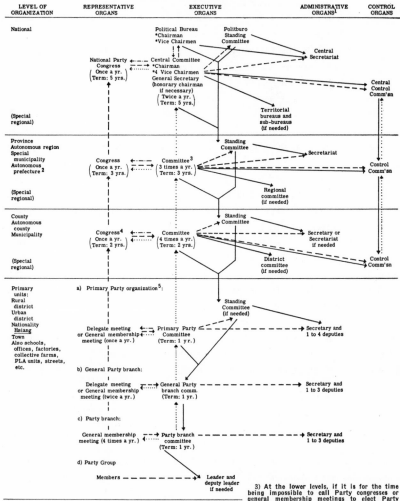

Legend: Election — — — — — Control (decisions binding) ————
         Convocation —·—·—·—·— Accountability ·········

*: Positions at the same level held by the same person.

1) Party committees at all levels may set up departments, commissions, or other bodies to carry on work under their direction.

2) Party organizations in an autonomous prefecture (CHOU) are under the direction of a provincial or autonomous regional Party committee, rather than the Central Committee. The Party congress of the prefecture elects delegates only to the provincial or autonomous regional congress. Both the Party congress and the committee of the CHOU are elected for a two-year term. But the members of the CHOU secretariat and standing committee must be approved by the Central Committee.

3) At the lower levels, if it is for the time being impossible to call Party congresses or general membership meetings to elect Party committees, such committees may be elected at Party conferences (made up of delegates from lower Party committees), or appointed by higher Party organizations. A higher Party committee may also appoint or transfer responsible members of a lower Party organization when its congress is not in session.

4) Within an autonomous prefecture, the Party congresses at the county level elect delegates only to the congress of the prefecture.

5) The members of a primary Party organization may be scattered through a number of production or residence units and sub-units, such as shops or streets. Hence, they may be formed—depending upon their numbers and their dispersion among sub-units—into a "general Party branch," a "Party branch" (both under the primary Party committee), or simply a "group."

mittees. The National Conference's functions and powers included the discussion and the decision of questions concerning Party policy in the current situation; the lower level conferences were to discuss and decide questions within their respective areas. A principal duty of the conferences at all levels was to act in the absence of their respective Party congresses to maintain the membership of their respective committees at full strength. The powers of these various conferences were definitely restricted: decisions with respect to policy or personnel replacement became effective only when ratified by their respective Party committees. When the 1956 Constitution provided for annual sessions of the various congresses, the conferences naturally became obsolete. Just as the CPSU had abandoned its provisions for All-Union Party Conferences in its 1952 rules, the CPC's 1956 Constitution eliminated the previous provisions for convening Party conferences. [5]

The Party branch, as noted previously, is the basic unit of the entire Party organization. [6] Its general membership meeting is a miniature of the Party congress and, like it, it is theoretically the highest body for the branch. The 1956 Constitution provides that a general Party branch shall hold a general membership meeting at least twice a year, while a Party branch shall conduct such a meeting at least once every three months (Article 49). In the branch, as at the highest levels, the representative organ does not play so vital a role in Party work as is indicated by official documents and pronouncements. Its primary purpose is to indoctrinate and familiarize its members with Party decisions and policies, and to mobilize the members to carry out unquestionably and thoroughly all CPC directives at the grass roots level.

---

[5] Under the 1945 Constitution, the convocation of one of the central Party organs was sometimes followed by a succession of Party conferences at the lower levels. As noted earlier, the Fourth Plenum of the Seventh CC in February, 1954, was followed by such a series of conferences to study the CC's report and resolutions and engage in criticism and self-criticism accordingly.

In the Soviet Union prior to 1939, the CPSU had held seventeen All-Union Party Conferences in its history; none was held subsequently. Beginning with the Eighth Congress of the Russian Communist Party (Bolsheviks) in March, 1919, a conference was held in each interim between Party congresses, either just after the congress (from the eighth to the tenth), or just before (from the eleventh on). For the resolutions, decisions and statements of the CPSU conferences, see the *Vsesoiuznaia Kommunisticheskaia Partiia (b) v Rezoliutsiiakh i Resheniiakh S'ezdov, Konferentsii i Plenumov TsK 1898–1935* (Moscow: Ogiz-Gospolitizdat, 1936), vols. I and II.

[6] The number of Party branches has naturally followed the general pattern of increase in the CPC membership. Thus, for example, in 1949, there were 250,000 branches. By 1959, there were 1,060,000 such branches.

The Central Committee, the Political Bureau and Its Standing Committee, and the Lower Executive Bodies

The Central Committee, together with the Political Bureau, the Standing Committee of the Political Bureau, and the Secretariat, is in fact the supreme body within the nationwide hierarchy of the Party (Article 37). During intervals between National Party Congresses, the CC is charged with directing the Party's entire program. Its power to make policy decisions and issue directives to subordinate Party committees and organs is virtually unlimited. Its decisions are binding upon the entire CPC membership.

The Central Committee is elected by the National Party Congress, which determines the number of full and alternate members.[7] The 1956 Constitution provides that alternates fill any vacancy according to an established order of precedence (Article 33), as did Article 31 of the 1945 Constitution. Article 33 of the 1945 Constitution stated that alternates "have the right to state their opinions" in plenary session, but there is no specific mention of alternates' rights in analogous Article 36 of the 1956 Constitution.

The Central Committee, in turn, in plenary session, elects its chairman, vice chairmen and general secretary, as well as the members of the Political Bureau and its Standing Committee, and the Secretariat (Article 37). Mao Tse-tung, CC Chairman, is also *ex officio* head of the Political Bureau, and the CC Vice Chairmen are *ex officio* vice chairmen of the Political Bureau. According to the order of precedence affirmed by the Second Session of the Eighth CPC National Congress, the vice chairmen were Liu Shao-ch'i, Chou En-lai, Chu Teh, Ch'en Yün and Lin Piao. Since the Eleventh Plenum of August, 1966, Lin Piao has become first Vice Chairman, however the roster and rank of the remaining vice chairmen is still uncertain (see the leadership chapter).

[7] In 1945, the Seventh Party Congress elected 45 members and 35 alternates. In April, 1955, there were presumably 43 regulars and 27 alternate members. The Sixth (Enlarged) Plenum of the Seventh Central Committee, meeting in October, 1955, was attended by 38 members and 25 alternates. In September, 1956, the Eighth Party Congress elected 94 members and 73 alternates to the Central Committee. Of the 94 full members, 40 had served as members and 20 as alternates in the previous Central Committee, while 33 were elected for the first time. When the Third Plenum of the Eighth Central Committee met in enlarged session, from September 20 to October 29, 1957, there were 91 regular and 61 alternate members in attendance. The Second Session of the Eighth National Party Congress convened in May, 1958, and elected 25 additional alternate members to the Central Committee. The Ninth Plenum of the Eighth Central Committee, meeting during January 14–18, 1961, was attended by 83 members and 87 alternates. At the September 24–27, 1962, Tenth Plenum of the Central Committee 82 members and 88 alternates were present. The Eleventh Plenum (Enlarged) of the Eighth CC met in Peking from August 1–12, 1966. No figures on the number of members or alternates present were released.

According to the 1945 Constitution, the CC Central Political Bureau was to convoke a plenary session of the Central Committee every six months (Article 33). The Politburo was also authorized to postpone or advance these sessions, and it often did so: between 1945 and 1956 only seven plenary sessions were held. [8] The 1956 Constitution stipulates that the Central Committee is to meet in plenary session, upon the call of the Political Bureau, at least twice a year. However, only eleven plenums were held between September, 1956, and August, 1966. [9] Following the

[8] The Central Committee takes the number of the Party Congress which elected it, and its plenary sessions are numbered serially within the lifetime of the particular committee. Thus the First Plenum of the Seventh CC was held in Yenan in July, 1945. The Second Plenum, held near Shihkiachwang in Hopei province in March, 1949, made the significant decision to shift the focus of the revolution from the countryside to the cities. At the Third Plenum in Peking in June, 1950, Mao Tse-tung delivered a report, "Struggle for a Basic Turn for the Better in the Economic and Financial Situation of the State." The Fourth Plenum met in Peking from February 6 to 10, 1954, to deal with the problem of Party solidarity at top levels. In April, 1955, the Fifth Plenum approved the resolutions of the CPC Conference of the previous month, made appointments to the new control commissions set up in the aftermath of the Kao-Jao purge, and elected two new Politburo members. The Sixth Plenum met in Peking from October 4 to 11, 1955, to discuss and adopt resolutions on the program for agricultural cooperatives and on the convocation of the Eighth Party Congress. The Seventh Plenum met on August 22 and September 8 and 13, 1956, to prepare for the Eighth Congress, which was to examine the Central Committee's Political Report and Report on Revision of the Party Constitution.

[9] The Eighth Central Committee, elected by the Eighth CPC Congress at its September 15–27 session in Peking, held its First Plenum on September 28, 1956, to elect its central bodies and re-elect Mao as chairman. The Second Plenum, meeting between November 10–15, 1956, discussed the current situation in the wake of the Polish and Hungarian revolts and control figures for the 1957 economic plan. The Third Plenum (Enlarged) met on September 20 and October 9, 1957, to hear reports and pass resolutions concerning the rectification campaign. The Fourth Plenum preceded and prepared for the Second Session of the Eighth CPC Congress, which met in Peking between May 5–23, 1958. The CC's Fifth Plenum convened in that city on May 28, 1958. It elected Lin Piao a vice chairman of the CC and member of the Standing Committee of the Politburo. From November 28 through December 10, 1958, the Sixth Plenum dealt with the questions of the people's communes, the 1959 economic plan and Mao's retirement as chairman of the People's Republic. The Seventh Plenum, held in Shanghai April 2–5, 1959, adopted draft plans for the national economy, reviewed the work of overhauling the communes, and heard Mao's report on methods to implement the general line of socialist construction. The Eighth Plenum convened in Lushan, August 2–16, 1959, to set the task of fulfilling the Second Five Year Plan. It scaled down major production goals in view of the over-estimation of 1958 production, criticized "right opportunism" within the Party, and welcomed the exchange of visits between U.S. and Soviet leaders. The Ninth Plenum met in Peking, January 14–18, 1961, to endorse the December, 1960, Moscow Statement of Eighty-One Communist and Worker Parties. It also discussed the 1961 economic plan, ways of combatting natural calamities and continued Party rectification. The Tenth Plenum met in Peking September 24–27, 1962, to discuss further consolidation of the national economy. It also determined to strengthen its Central Control Commission and its branch organizations. The Eleventh Plenum (Enlarged) met in

launching of the Great Leap Forward, the plenary sessions have been marked by increasingly long intervening periods. Thus, the seventh and eighth sessions in 1959, were not repeated until the ninth plenum of January, 1961. Then twenty months intervened before convocation of the tenth plenary session in September, 1962, and almost another four years elapsed between the tenth and the eleventh plenum in 1966.

As in all communist Parties, the Political Bureau (Politburo) is the most powerful single body in the CPC. It is the actual directing organ of the entire Party structure, and functions in the name of the Central Committee when the latter is not in session. As Stalin said in 1925: "The Politburo is sovereign as it is; it is higher than all the organs of the Central Committee, except the plenum."

Until 1956, there was much speculation over the composition of the Politburo, since the communists themselves had never condescended to publish a complete official listing of the members. On the eve of the Eighth Party Congress in September, 1956, there were probably thirteen members in the powerful Politburo. Mao headed the list as chairman, with Liu Shao-ch'i possibly second to Mao as his deputy—although the deputy position had no official status in the 1945 CPC Constitution—followed by Chou En-lai, Chu Teh and Ch'en Yün, in that order. After the "Big Five" the order of rank became rather uncertain, but the list included Tung Pi-wu and Lin Po-ch'ü (Lin Tsu-han)—the two "grand old men" of the Party—K'ang Sheng, P'eng Chen, Chang Wen-t'ien, and P'eng Teh-huai.[10] The two juniormost members were Lin Piao and Teng Hsiao-p'ing, elected at the Fifth Plenum of the Seventh CC in April, 1955.

With the subsequent enlargement of the Politburo's membership by the First and Fifth Plenums of the Eighth Central Committee in September, 1956, and May, 1958, the order of precedence was altered somewhat. Mao remained as chairman, and Liu Shao-ch'i, Chou En-lai, Chu Teh and Ch'en Yün were elected as vice chairmen in September, 1956. Lin Piao was elected to the latter position in May, 1958. Lesser members of the Politburo, in descending order of rank, included Teng Hsiao-p'ing, Lin Po-ch'ü, Tung Pi-wu, P'eng Chen, Lo Jung-huan, Chen Yi, Li Fu-ch'un, P'eng

Peking August 1–12, 1966, to give the highest approval to the "cultural revolution," and the thought of Mao, to reaffirm the CPC's stand against "modern revisionism" and in support of the national liberation movement, and, apparently, to approve the realignment of the Party leadership.

[10] P'eng Teh-huai was apparently elected at the Fourth Plenum of the Seventh CC in February, 1954, to replace Kao Kang, however the communique on the Sixth Plenum which appeared in the Chinese press on October 16, 1955, placed his name before that of P'eng Chen in the list of Politburo members offering remarks at the session. As noted in the section on Party rectification, P'eng Teh-huai was purged in 1959, after he apparently criticized such programs as the commune system while on a mission to Eastern Europe.

Teh-huai, Liu Po-ch'eng, Ho Lung, Li Hsien-nien, K'o Ch'ing-shih, Li Ching-ch'üan, and T'an Chen-lin (the last three having been elected in May, 1958). In 1959, P'eng Teh-huai was purged, and P'eng Chen suffered a similar fate in 1966. With the death of Lin Po-ch'ü in May, 1960, of Lo Jung-huan in December, 1963, and of K'o Ch'ing-shih in April, 1965, the membership of the Politburo was reduced to fifteen. Ulanfu, the first alternate member, was not automatically raised to full Politburo membership, and there is no constitutional provision for such promotion. Instead, NCNA confirmed, on January 14, 1967, that Hsü Hsiang-ch'ien, Nieh Jung-chen, and Yeh Chien-ying—all full members of the CC—had been promoted to Politburo membership. K'ang Sheng, Hsieh Fu-chih and Ch'en Po-ta were also identified as full members of the Politburo early in 1967. It cannot yet be determined with certitude if others have been rewarded with Politburo membership, or if other members have been purged, as a result of their roles in the "cultural revolution." Whatever its precise membership, this power nucleus probably meets several times weekly to regulate Party affairs.

The Standing Committee of the Political Bureau is an innovation of the 1956 CPC Constitution (Article 37). Its creation was probably inevitable, given the fact that the CPC, as the largest communist Party in the world, has need for a nucleus of executive power. In this respect, the Standing Committee not only gives adequate recognition to the remarkably increased prestige of the Party's top leaders, but it also complies with the communist operational code of providing for a hard core center even within the highest organization.[11] Since the Standing Committee is comprised of the chairman, vice chairmen and general secretary of the Central Committee, it may be compared to the CPSU Presidium. However, unlike the Presidium, there is an intermediary body, the Political Bureau, between the Central Committee and the Standing Committee.

The 1956 Constitution also introduced another unprecedented feature in giving the Central Committee authority to "create" its own "honorary chairman" whenever it deemed necessary (Article 37). This post is obviously reserved for Mao Tse-tung, who has served as CC Chairman since January 13, 1935, against the time when the aging veteran can no longer physically or mentally assume active command of Party affairs. Institutionally speaking, this title resembles that of "father of the emperor." Its purpose is to permit the CPC to continue exploitation of Mao's prestige, even after his active service is ended.

The Central Committee directs a number of specialized organs or subsidiary departments, created to handle special types of Party work (Article

---

[11] The members of the Politburo Standing Committee are identified and their roles discussed in detail in the chapter on the leadership.

30). Of paramount importance, since the initiation of the "cultural revolution," is the Military Affairs Commission, with Mao Tse-tung as chairman and Lin Piao as first vice chairman.[12] The CC's Cultural Revolution Group, created in 1966, is headed by Ch'en Po-ta, with Mao's wife, Chiang Ch'ing, as first vice chairman. Among the various CC departments is the Organization Department, with An Tzu-wen as director. This organ is charged with directing the vast hierarchy of Party committees and branches throughout the country. The Propaganda Department, in 1967 directed by Ch'en Po-ta, is responsible for Party propaganda as a whole. Other departments, whose tasks are apparent from their nomenclature, are: the Agriculture and Forestry Political Department, the Finance and Trade Political Department, the Industry and Communications Political Department, the International Liaison Department, the United Front Work Department, and the Nationalities Affairs Section. The Central Committee also directs a number of special agencies. These include the General Office, the Higher Party School, the Bureau for Translating the Works of Marx, Engels, Lenin, Stalin and Mao, and the Administrative Policy Seminar.

Article 27 of the 1945 Constitution provided that the Central Committee might, according to needs, establish central bureaus and sub-bureaus—each having jurisdiction over several provinces or border areas. These bureaus, responsible solely to the CC, could be abolished or merged at its discretion. Following the 1949 victory, until probably 1954 or 1955, the CC directed six regional bureaus and four sub-bureaus. The former included the Northeast Bureau in Mukden, the North China Bureau in Peking, the East China Bureau in Shanghai, the Central-South Bureau in Wuhan, the Northwest Bureau in Sian, and the Southwest Bureau in Chungking. In the latter category were the Inner Mongolia Sub-Bureau in Kweisui, the South China Sub-Bureau in Canton, the Sinkiang Sub-Bureau in Urumchi, and the Shantung Sub-Bureau. These bureaus were mentioned in the Party press until at least mid-1954. At the July, 1955, meeting of local Party officials to hear Mao's major report on agricultural cooperation, however, the above-mentioned organizations were apparently unrepresented among the Party secretaries present. A CC resolution called for abolition of the Sinkiang Sub-Bureau as of October 1, 1955, and it was replaced by the Sinkiang-Uigur Autonomous Regional Party Committee. Late in 1955, there were press references to a CC Shanghai Bureau, although, presumably, it was no longer identical to the former East China Bureau. In the communique of the Sixth Plenum of the Seventh CC, issued on October 16, 1955, apparently only the Shanghai

[12] The function, role and composition of the Military Affairs Commission is discussed in detail in the chapter on the military.

Bureau was represented among the 380 top Party personnel listed as non-voting observers. [13]

The 1956 Party Constitution, in amplifying upon the right of a Party committee to establish representative bodies, made the ability to create bureaus a general principle and, if necessary, a common practice applicable to Party organizations from the level of the Central Committee on down to the municipal and county committees. Article 29 permits the Central Committee to establish a bureau as its representative organ for an area including several provinces, autonomous regions and municipalities. Provincial or autonomous regional committees, when they deem it necessary, may establish a regional committee, or an organization of equal status, as a representative body. Party committees of municipalities and counties may also establish district committees within their areas. The omission of specific provisions for sub-bureaus may be due to the fact that these bodies are no longer deemed necessary since the over-all reorganization of the CPC structure.

Until January, 1961, no effort was made by the Central Committee to establish such bureaus as representative bodies. The communique issued by the Ninth Plenary Session of the Eighth Central Committee on January 20, 1961, declared that, in view of the great progress made in the construction of socialism in the preceding three years, the session had decided to establish six bureaus to act for the CC in strengthening leadership over the various lesser Party committees. With the exception of prefixing Bureau of the Central Committee, these bodies bear the same names as their predecessors, and, like them, they exercise jurisdiction over a specific area.

On the eve of the "cultural revolution" the First Secretaries of the regional bureaus were identified as follows:

[13] Each of these regional bodies, of course, was headed by a hierarchy of Party secretaries, variously titled First, Second, and Third Secretary, or Secretary and Deputy Secretary respectively. There was, however, an extensive transfer of Party officials from the regional offices back to the central headquarters in Peking, especially about the time of the Fourth CC Plenum in February, 1954, when measures were taken to counter the possible emergence of "independent kingdoms" at the regional or local levels. The now obsolete roster of top Party personnel issued at the end of 1952 listed officials in the regional bureaus and sub-bureaus in order of rank as follows: Northeast Bureau, Kao Kang, Li Fu-ch'un, and Lin Feng; North China Bureau, Po I-po, Nieh Jung-chen, and Liu Lan-t'ao; East China Bureau, Jao Shu-shih and Ch'en Yi; Central South Bureau: Lin Piao and Teng Tzu-hui; Northwest Bureau, Hsi Chung-hsün and Ma Ming-fang; Southwest Bureau, Teng Hsiao-p'ing and Liu Po-ch'eng; Inner Mongolia Sub-bureau, Yün Tse (Ulanfu); South China Sub-Bureau, Yeh Chien-ying; Shantung Sub-Bureau, K'ang Sheng; and Sinkiang Sub-Bureau, Wang Chen. After the Kao-Jao purge, most of these officials served in the central apparatus in Peking, many on the Central Committee.

East-China Bureau—K'o Ch'ing-shih (deceased)
Southwest Bureau—Li Ching-ch'üan
Central-South Bureau—T'ao Chu
Northeast Bureau—Sung Jen-ch'iung
North China Bureau—Li Hsüeh-feng
Northwest Bureau—Liu Lan-t'ao

With two exceptions—K'o Ch'ing-shih and Li Ching-ch'üan—the first secretaries came from the second echelon of Party leadership, apparently as a preventative measure to avoid the earlier mistake of allowing too much power to regional chiefs who were also high-ranking members of the Party's centralized leadership. With the death of K'o Ch'ing-shih in April, 1965, and the Party's hesitancy to release the name of his successor, Li Ching-ch'üan, became the only member of the Politburo to serve concurrently as a first secretary of a regional bureau. Li Hsüeh-feng once directed the CC's Industrial Work Department, and Liu Lan-t'ao obtained experience as third in command of the old North China Bureau. Like Sung Jen-ch'iung, Li and Liu have been associated at one time or another with Teng Hsiao-p'ing, the CPC's Secretary-General. With T'ao Chu's increasing prominence in the early months of the "cultural revolution," he was relieved of his post as chief of the Central-South Bureau, and in September, 1966, Wang Jen-chung was named as his successor to that position. T'ao, who apparently worked his way up to the highest echelons of the CC Politburo, had been purged from all Party offices by January, 1967.[14] Although Wang Jen-chung had enjoyed the honor of accompanying Mao Tse-tung during the latter's much publicized swimming feat of 1966, as former second secretary of the Central-South Bureau, he has long been associated intimately with T'ao Chu and his fate is uncertain.

Below the national level, the Party committees at each rung are elected by their corresponding Party congresses to serve as the executive bodies of the CPC at that level (Articles 30 and 44). Party committees of the provincial, autonomous regional or municipal level are to meet at least three times yearly, while those at the county, autonomous county or municipal levels are to meet in plenary session at least four times annually (Articles 41 and 46 respectively).

Apparently in conformity with the structure of the central Party organizations, and possibly because of the great increment of personnel at the various levels and the greatly expanded work load, the 1956 Constitution introduced provisions for the various Party committees at the level of provinces, autonomous regions or municipalities to elect standing com-

[14] For details, consult the chapter on the leadership.

mittees and secretariats in plenary session, subject to the approval of the
Central Committee (Article 41). The standing committees are empowered
to exercise the functions of their Party committees when the latter are not
in session, while the CC's necessary approval may hinder free elections.
This is especially true in the case of Party secretaries at the key political-
geographical levels, where CC approval may approximate designation from
above.

Although there are no specific constitutional provisions governing the
election of secretaries, particularly the first secretaries whose posts are
probably more executive than administrative, election presumably follows
the principles of democratic centralism. This may, in practice, mean
designation from above, to ensure the loyalty of these leaders who serve
as the eyes and ears of the Central Committee.[15] Furthermore, the vast
majority of the first secretaries are drawn from the ranks of the Central
Committee to prevent any sort of rivalry with the CPC hierarchy and
ensure fidelity to its summit leadership.[16]

The 1956 Constitution also provides that the Party committees at the
county, autonomous county or municipal level may elect their own standing committees, secretaries, and, if necessary, secretariats. These personnel must then be approved by the next higher Party committee (Article
46). In key industrial centers and cities with populations of 500,000 or
more, approval must come directly from the Central Committee. In the

[15] In 1960, there were some 210 Party secretaries, including first, second and other, as
well as alternates, serving in 28 major geographical units—the provinces, autonomous regions
and the two special municipalities of Peking and Shanghai. Of these, 36 were appointed in
1960 alone. The Party committees at these levels have an average of six secretaries each, as
well as candidate secretaries. In early 1961, the latter category averaged from one to three
for each unit.

[16] In 1961, for example, the following picture was striking: Three members of the Politburo
were concurrently serving as first secretaries of special municipality and provincial Party
committees: P'eng Chen in Peking; K'o Ch'ing-shih in Shanghai; and Li Ching-chü'an in
Szechwan. Ulanfu, candidate member of the Politburo, was also First Secretary of the
Autonomous Regional Party Committee of Inner Mongolia. Six additional members of the
Central Committee also occupied posts as first secretaries of Party committees at the provincial level: Lin T'ieh in Hopei; Oyang Ch'ing in Heilungkiang; Wang En-mao in Sinkiang;
Tseng Hsi-sheng in Shantung; T'ao Chu in Kwangtung; and Wu Chih-p'u in Honan. Thir-
teen candidate members of the Central Committee were serving concurrently as first secre-
taries of the provincial and autonomous regional Party committees: T'ao Lu-ch'u in Shansi;
Huang Ho-ch'ing in Liaoning, Wu Teh in Kirin; Chang Te-sheng in Shensi; Chang Chuang-
liang in Kansu, Chiang Wei-ch'ing in Kiangsu, Chiang Hua in Chekiang; Yeh Fei in Fukien;
Wang Jen-chung in Hupeh; Chang P'ing-hua in Hunan; Liu Chien-shu in Kwangsi; Yeh
Hung-chung in Yunnan; and Chang Ching-wu in Tibet. The five first secretaries of the
provincial Party committees who, in 1961, were neither members nor candidate members of
the Central Committee include: Chou Lin in Kweichow; Yang Shang-k'wei in Kiangsi, and
Kao Feng in Tsinghai.

primary Party organizations, according to the decision of the next higher committee, the following structures are provided: in organizations with 100 or more members a primary committee may be elected; under special conditions this provision is also applicable to organizations with smaller membership. Primary organizations with less than 50 members may establish a general branch committee; under special circumstances this also applies to units with greater or lesser membership. Primary units with less than 50 members can establish branch committees (Article 48). Members of all these committees are elected for a one year term in a number determined by their next higher Party committee (Article 49).

The Secretariat and the Lower Administrative Bodies

The Secretariat is the top level administrative organ of the CPC; under the direction of the Political Bureau and its Standing Committee, it attends to the daily work of the Central Committee. As noted previously, the members of the Secretariat are elected by the CC at its plenary meeting. Under the 1945 Party Constitution, the Secretariat, then termed the Central Secretariat, was given a role almost equal in importance to, and probably more active than, the Politburo and the Central Committee's Chairman in directing and supervising work of the various specialized agencies under the CC's jurisdiction (such as the departments of organization and propaganda and the commissions for military affairs and the press). The Central Secretariat's position was further enhanced by a provision of the 1945 Constitution that "the chairman of the Central Committee shall be concurrently the chairman of the Politburo and of the Central Secretariat" (Article 34). This body assumed active charge of organizational-executive problems and became a focal point for the control of the Party machinery.

In the process of institutional evolution, the 1956 Party Constitution de-emphasized the Secretariat's functions, although it is still charged with attending to the daily work of the Central Committee. The CC chairman and vice chairmen, while retaining corresponding offices in the Politburo, no longer fill the top positions in the Secretariat. With the exception of two Politburo members, Teng and P'eng, the Secretariat of the Eighth Central Committee originally included only relatively lesser personnel. The Fifth Plenum of the Eighth CC, which opened on May 25, 1958, elected two additional Politburo members to the Secretariat, Li Fu-ch'un and Li Hsien-nien; it also promoted an incumbent member of the Secretariat, T'an Chen-lin, to full membership in the Politburo. Of the ten members of the Secretariat on the eve of the "cultural revolution," five were full members of the Politburo, two were alternates, and the remaining three were full members of the Central Committee. However, even these changes instituted at the Tenth Plenum of the Eighth CC, in September, 1962, did not give the Secretariat the position of prestige of the pre-1956 Central Secretariat. This may have reflected a leadership decision to avoid any overlapping between the Secretariat and the Standing Committee of the Politburo. Such a policy would be motivated by a desire to avoid any usurpation or monopolization of the central Party apparatus and leadership similar to that experienced by the CPSU under Stalin.

The "cultural revolution" has brought great changes to the composition of the Secretariat. By 1966, P'eng Chen, Lu Ting-yi, Wang Chia-hsiang and Lo Jui-ch'ing were purged from their Party posts. T'ao Chu, who was named to the Secretariat in the early months of the "cultural revolution," was himself purged by January, 1967. Liu Ning-i has been identified as a member of the Secretariat, as has Yeh Chien-ying. Excluding the person of Teng Hsiao-p'ing, who may have been removed as Secretary General, it appears that the membership of the Secretariat, as adjusted by the purges and replacements associated with the "cultural revolution," reflects the Party leadership's determination to tie that body more closely to the Politburo and its elite Standing Committee. By March, 1967, all the members of the Secretariat, with the exception of Li Hsüeh-feng, had been identified in the Party press as members of the Politburo.

The 1956 Constitution differs from its 1945 counterpart in one significant respect related to the Party posts of highest esteem. Teng Hsiao-p'ing, as the CC's General Secretary and ranked first in the membership of the Secretariat, in his own person linked the two offices, which are not mutually exclusive by any provisions of the Constitution. The General Secretary, as witnessed by the various reports concerning Teng's activities, has definite executive functions, but in terms of rank and prestige is subordinate to the CC's chairman and vice chairmen. The position cannot be equated with that of similar title in the earlier history of the CPC, nor can it be compared with that of the previous First Secretary and General Secretary of the CPSU and the first secretaries of some other communist and workers' parties.

The Secretariat has counterparts in the administrative organs of the lower Party organizations down to the branch level. Under the 1945 Constitution, each Party committee elected its own standing committee, secretary and assistant secretaries to perform daily administrative work (Article 42). These standing committees and the secretaries performed more as administrative than executive arms. The 1956 Constitution brought their functions into greater conformity with the position of an executive arm. The Party committees on the provincial, autonomous and municipal levels now elect their own standing committees and secretariats in plenary session. These secretariats carry on the daily work of their respective Party committees under the direction of the standing committee (Article 41). The CPC committees at the county, autonomous county and municipality levels also elect their own standing committees and secretaries in plenary session and, when necessary, a secretariat. These secretaries and secretariats then conduct daily affairs for their committees under the direction of the standing committee (Article 46).

As has been described and illustrated, the CPC is meant to be a closely knit and rigidly controlled hierarchy, with all effective power coming from the top. Formerly of an interlocking executive-administrative structure, this leadership is now primarily composed of an executive nucleus, with a subordinated administrative apparatus. It is the executive bodies which dominate; the so-called representative organs provide a symbol of unity and a forum for mobilizing Party membership to carry out decisions which emanate from the leadership.

The Central and Local Control Commissions

In order to enhance its control of the entire Party organization, the CPC maintains a system of control commissions in addition to its executive and administrative organs. The Central Committee, as well as the Party committees at the various levels, establish and supervise these control commissions. The CC elects a Central Control Commission in plenary session, while the various lesser Party committees also elect their local control commissions at their respective plenary sessions, subject to the approval of the next higher Party committee (Article 52). These control commissions then function under the direction of the CPC committees at the corresponding levels (Article 54). Moreover, a higher control commission may examine and modify the decisions of a lower control commission (Article 54).

These control commissions perform the regular task of dealing with any infractions of the Party Constitution, and of administering discipline to any refractory Party member. At the same time, they are charged with hearing appeals and complaints from Party members (Article 53). The 1956 Constitution has placed these control commissions on a uniform basis under systematic direction. While the 1945 Constitution merely stated that such commissions could be formed when the CC or lesser Party committees deemed necessary, the 1956 Constitution stipulates that the commissions shall be organized according to a systematic hierarchial structure. Moreover, unlike the earlier Constitution, the 1956 Constitution has made the lower control commissions responsible to the higher. By comparison, the control commissions, formerly an ad hoc auxiliary of their respective Party committees, are now active agencies taking a proper place within the unified Party hierarchy.

PARTY REFORM MOVEMENTS

The Twin Goals of Party Reform: Quality and Solidarity

Like all communist Parties, the CPC has shown a continuing need to reform its ranks, through renewed emphasis on education and training of members, through reorganization of the Party structure, through timely resort to disciplinary measures within the Party—and even, as the cases of Kao Kang-Jao Shu-shih (1954), P'eng Teh-huai (1959), P'eng Chen (1966), and Liu Shao-ch'i (1967) indicate, through the bloody purge, expulsions, and "cultural revolution" on an undetermined scale. The aim of these continuing reform efforts is twofold: to maintain a high standard of competence and performance for members, lest the Party's hold over the masses be weakened; and to make sure that the differences of viewpoint and direction within the CPC do not reach the point of threatening Party unity. The fact that the CPC, its ranks enormously swollen in a short span of years, provides the only effective outlet for political action in the country gives added importance to the twin goals of high quality membership and organically solid organization. Ironically, it also makes them much more difficult to obtain, since the Party tends to become all the more a hunting ground for the ambitious, the opportunistic, and the self-seeking and a battleground for contending special interests within the society.

The need for maintaining quality standards for Party personnel has been amply recognized by the high echelon leadership. Mao Tse-tung, in summarizing the chief revolutionary experiences of the CPC in 1939, described party-building as an indispensable arm for the future communist victory. This party building, he noted, ultimately depends upon the cultural, ideological, political and moral level of the individual members. When Liu Shao-ch'i in 1951 hailed the CPC as "the greatest, most glorious and most consistently correct party in the history of China," he emphasized that success was and would be contingent upon the long-term, arduous struggle of the individual member.

At the same time, the Chinese Communist leaders, including Mao, have from time to time frankly admitted the various shortcomings of their fellow members. Liu has referred to these unsatisfactory qualities as "rotten and evil," calling those infected "weaklings, bad eggs, and dark forces." The reasons for this concern in the quality of members and cadres are not difficult to perceive. They lie not alone in the phenomenal increase in Party membership from a heterogeneous social background, but also involve the placement of inadequately trained individuals in positions of trust. Furthermore, the problems of excesses and abuses, of complacency, routine, and personal rather than Party concern, can only increase with the passage of time.

In the interests of Party solidarity, the leaders have shown a lively awareness of the absolute necessity for discipline within the CPC. Lenin first laid down the principle that the Communist Party should have a "united, iron discipline." Lenin and Stalin both emphasized that "if the Party wants to maintain its unity, it must put into practice the unified proletarian discipline." Mao has repeated this stricture: "Whoever violates the Party discipline, threatens the unity of the Party." As Liu has pointed out, it is the "duty of all Party members and Party organizations to safeguard and strengthen the unity of the whole Party" by "combatting all factional and double-dealing activities, as well as all breaches of Party discipline."

The need for strict Party discipline highlights the special problem of allowing for differences of opinion in what the communists themselves call the "inner-Party struggle." Since the CPC gained national power, it has prohibited any effective opposition by other parties. Hence, the inevitable conflicts within a society—between urban and rural interests, between capital and consumer goods interests, between extremists and moderates, innovators and conservers, old and new leadership—must be fought out or worked through within the framework of a basic agreement on the nature of the regime.

Needless to say, from the communist point of view, inner-Party struggle does not at all imply that differences of opinion or conflicts of interest are to be fought out openly and democratically at any level of Party organization. Perhaps only in the innermost circles of CPC leadership can the competing claims of various elements be weighed and judged; once a decision is made, it is unconditionally binding upon all lower levels. At the lower levels, the internal strains and conflicts of interest within the Party manifest themselves in tendencies to "deviate" from the CPC line and to fall into "error" in carrying out leadership decisions. Thus the inner-Party struggle is presented in communist literature not as a means of allowing open expression or free play to the claims of multiple interest groups, but rather as a means of detecting and correcting any inclination to stray from the one true path laid down by the highest leadership. The note of adaptability and flexibility suggested by the doctrine of inner-Party struggle is therefore strictly subordinated to the note of rigidity and conformity introduced by the CPC's need for iron discipline to preserve its own power status.

There is, however, a limited recognition that special considerations should govern conflicts within the Party, as compared with the struggle against the enemies of communism outside the Party. These considerations were stressed by Liu Shao-ch'i in counseling "militancy in the fight over principles and ideologies and the least possible militancy with regard to organization and forms of struggle." Liu emphasized that the methods of criticism and self-criticism must be well regulated and conducted in accordance with the Bolshevik yardstick by dealing first with the problem, and then with the person. He warned against confusing the methods of struggle inside the Party with those appropriate with the external struggle, the latter including surveillance, arrest, trial, imprisonment and the like. Liu found that some Party members had fallen into various erroneous and mechanical forms of inner-Party struggle through failure to understand this distinction. Their errors encouraged opposite errors on the part of some Party officials. The communist press frequently refers to these errors of suppressing criticism, avoiding self-criticism, and allowing the inner-Party struggle to degenerate into petty factional strife. Particularly since 1966, the revelations of the "cultural revolution" concerning "the handful" or "the top Party person in authority taking the capitalist road," as well as the Party strictures on the need to vary disciplinary measures according to the nature and degree of the error, indicate that the CPC has by no means yet solved these problems.

Any organization must devote a certain amount of its resources to internal matters; the extent of this concern has a great deal to do with over-all effectiveness in achieving major goals. Although there is no way of measuring precisely the CPC's degree of concern with internal problems of membership quality and solidarity, it must be high given the nature and ambitions of the Party. The wide variety of techniques of internal reform and discipline employed by the CPC, as well as the wide range of abuses which it seeks to correct, substantiate this conclusion.

Techniques for Party Reform

Of all the techniques and organizational measures of reform used by the CPC, some rely on the enthusiasm and voluntary cooperation of the individual member to bring about reform by self-improvement; others involve those characteristic activities of self-scrutiny and group discussion which the communists call criticism and self-criticism. Beyond these lies the possibility of coercive action provided for in the Party's disciplinary framework. But it is well to keep in mind that the CPC does not rely entirely upon coercion or punishment—the "carrot" has a place, as well as the "stick." For example, the 1945 Constitution provided for the commendation of Party individuals or organizations with excellent records (Article 63). This praise was recommended for "absolute loyalty to the cause of the Party in observing Party discipline and carrying out Party assignments." It could be given in person, by public announcement or by publicizing the achievements in question. [17]

One of the most frequently utilized methods of reform is to require the members to undertake a further or renewed program of study concentrating on specified Party documents and reports by Party leaders. This process of "ideological remolding," according to Mao Tse-tung and Liu Shao-ch'i, is in the spirit of "curing the sickness and saving the patient," instead of introducing a penal system of discipline. Hence it is in line with and supposedly capitalizes upon the voluntary efforts of the members. In the *Cheng-feng* movement, or rectification campaign of 1942–44, the CPC Central Committee listed twenty-seven "Documents on the Reform of Party Spirit," for required study. The cadres were called upon, in the spirit of these documents, "to meditate profoundly and reflect on their own work, thoughts and entire past; and then to investigate the work of their departments and draw conclusions about improvements." [18]

Party reform movements, needless to say, have been closely linked to developments in the "inner-Party struggle" to preserve orthodoxy against any challenge from within. Hence the study programs are usually part of a broader reform effort which includes vigorous resort to "criticism and self-criticism." Liu has pointed to Lenin's thesis on Party building "against abandoning strict organization and discipline," against "unprincipled peace within the Party," and "against the denial of inner-Party struggle and fear of self-criticism." Thus, traditionally the CPC has regarded criticism and self-criticism as the chief instrumentality of Party reform. Lenin advocated these practices in 1917, to discover and correct errors and defects within the Russian Communist Party. Stalin called criticism and self-criticism "the genuine weapon in the struggle for communism" and "the law of our development." And Mao has constantly reminded his followers of the absolute necessity of this process. Often, in

[17] One example of this public praise of an individual member was published in the May 10, 1965, *People's Daily*. Despite the normal practice of avoiding personal biography, the death of Liu Ya-lou was noted with several laudatory articles. Yang Ch'eng-wu, alternate member of the CPC Central Committee, member of the NDC, and now Acting Chief of Staff of the PLA, praised Liu Ya-lou, a veteran of the Long March, commander of the PLA air force, and member of the CPC CC, for his love of the Party. Lin Tou-tou, Lin Piao's son, contributed a eulogy entitled "Uncle Liu Ya-lou Will Always Live in Our Hearts," giving details of the Party veteran's last illness and emphasizing his love of Mao Tse-tung.

[18] Specific targets and procedures of the successive ideological reform movements are discussed in detail in the chapter on the cultural system. The present emphasis on the thought of Mao Tse-tung is discussed in the chapter on the leadership.

As noted elsewhere in this chapter, a considerable share of the cadre's time spent in Party activities is given to these study programs carried on individually, in groups, and in regular Party schools.

urging the cadres and members to conduct criticism and self-criticism with more diligence, the highest echelon leaders have given their own practices as examples. The rank and file are endlessly reminded that this technique is the most important weapon of revolution, to be respected as an indispensable part of their Party life.[19]

Educational measures and the technique of criticism and self-criticism complement each other in the arsenal of Party reform. Indeed, Liu Shao-ch'i has pointed out that education within the Party is a kind of inner-Party struggle in a relatively mild form, and inner-Party struggle cannot be divorced from education. But, in the last analysis, these measures depend largely upon the voluntary cooperation of the members, in accord with the CPC's Constitutional provision that discipline "should be conscious and not mechanical." Whenever conscious discipline fails, through incompetence, malevolence, or some other negative factor, then harsher measures must be utilized.

The 1945 Constitution stipulated that measures be taken against individual members or Party organizations who failed to carry out the decisions of the Central Committee or other higher Party organizations, or violated the Party Constitution or Party discipline in any way (Articles 64 to 67). Thus, an entire Party organization could be disciplined by the following measures: (1) a reprimand; (2) a partial reorganization of its executive body; (3) dismissal of its executive body and appointment of an interim body; or (4) dissolution of the entire organization and re-registration of its members.

Until 1956, according to items in the communist press, Party organizations at various levels took disciplinary action against lower organizations and individual members. In 1952, for example, the Kingshi County Party Committee in Kiangsi province and the branch of the Commercial Department of Ninghsia province were ordered to reorganize partially. So was

---

[19] Among the many examples of the continuing need for self-criticism which might be cited, perhaps the best known is the case of Kuo Mo-jo. Kuo, who is respected internationally as well as nationally, is the president of the Chinese Academy of Sciences, a leader in mainland literary and art circles, and extremely active in associations dealing with cultural relations with other countries. He joined the CPC in 1958. As first vice chairman of the NPC Standing Committee, on April 28, 1966, Kuo reacted to a report on cultural work delivered to that body by providing a model case of self-criticism. In his own words, as published in the July 8, 1966, *Peking Review:* "I was elated by this [report on socialist education] and delivered a speech extempore in which I made a frank self-criticism to express my sincere feelings." Comparing his literary efforts with those being produced by the masses, Kuo admitted that his "should be burnt." After considerable speculation outside Communist China, as to whether this confession indicated that Kuo Mo-jo was descredited with the Party, Kuo clarified his own act in a July 4, 1966, speech before the Afro-Asian Writers Emergency Meeting: "It is absolutely normal in our country for a revolutionary writer who is responsible to the people constantly to remold himself and to make serious self-criticism from time to time."

the Wuhan City Party Committee by the directive of the Central-South Bureau of the CPC Central Committee. More severe punishment was meted out to the county committees of Suich'uan, Kiangsi province and of Chiaoho, Kirin province; their leading bodies were dismissed summarily.

In omitting similar provisions, the 1956 Constitution seemed to indicate that the CPC's central control was sufficiently strong as to preclude any mass organizational deviation, or the need to discipline whole Party organizations. However, beginning with the June 3, 1966, announcement of the CPC Central Committee that it had reorganized the entire Peking Municipal Party Committee, and with the later emphasis on the new "three in one" leadership organs in the troubled areas, the events of the "cultural revolution" have proven that, when necessary, the leadership can and will still intervene to modify or replace whole Party committees.

The 1945 Constitution also provided that an individual Party member could be disciplined by any of the following means: (1) admonition or warning in person; (2) admonition or warning in public; (3) removal from assigned work; (4) retention of membership on probationary status; or (5) expulsion from the CPC (Article 64). To combat the low quality of many members, after the seizure of state power these measures were frequently employed. For example, Chang P'ing-hua, Secretary of the Wuhan City Party Committee, was given a warning in public. Li Yü, a former alternate member of the Central Committee and member of the Shanghai City Party Committee, was removed from assigned work. I Chi-kwang, a member of the Wuhan Party Committee, was expelled from the CPC.

Provisions for disciplinary action against individual Party members were reaffirmed in the 1956 Party Constitution, with an added stipulation that the term of disciplinary probation should not exceed two years (Article 13). In 1957 and 1958, the anti-rightist campaign waged within the Party resulted in a great purge. Many leaders in the provincial committees, including first secretaries, were removed from assignments, including at least two alternate members of the Central Committee, Ku Ta-ts'un and P'an Fu-sheng. The first was removed as secretary of the Kwangtung Provincial Party Committee and Deputy Governor of Kwangtung, while the latter was relieved of his position as first secretary of the Honan Provincial Committee.[20] Yet, the Party must still solve the problem of reluctance of members to vote for disciplinary action against a fellow member. Thus Peking's *Pei-ching Jih-pao* of September 3, 1962, preached against a hesitation rooted in passivism or a fear that abbreviated discussion could result in a miscarriage of justice. But as one Party member informed the same paper (September 24, 1962), in five years of discussion

---

[20] The purge is discussed in greater detail in the subsequent section on Party rectification movements.

on disciplinary action, each time he had rendered an opinion it was taken as "a lack of respect for the leadership."

The need for disciplining individual members must increase, rather than diminish, as the CPC increases in size and diversity of tasks, and as the new generation must be trained to the communist mentality—a generalization now substantiated by the "cultural revolution." In any case, the commendation or damnation of an individual member continues to provide the CPC with an educational tool to discipline the membership at large.

Conditions Requiring Reform

The CPC has never lacked for ample evidence of the need to reform both the inferior quality of its members and their errors in "style of work." The shortcomings in quality must be discussed in terms of the cultural, ideological, political or moral levels of the members.

Though it is impossible to ascertain the educational level of Party members, their generally deficient cultural standards have been admitted by many Party organizations. Press reports in 1952, at a time when a concerted effort was being made to raise the level of the members, revealed in general a very low educational level. Despite the enormous efforts at mass education, discussed elsewhere, many of the conditions complained of in 1952 still exist. Even the students in training centers and Party schools, selected because of seniority and promise, have an inadequate background. With the increased emphasis on recruiting members from the lower peasant class, many are barely literate or unable to understand the complexities of their assignments. [21]

Given this low educational level, it is not surprising that the ideological level of the membership leaves much to be desired. As Liu Shao-ch'i admitted, some members fail to regard the Party as "the highest form of class struggle." As late as 1951, the communist press revealed that many members still thought the CPC was a kind of coalition government. In 1962, after noting the large number of persons with inferior knowledge recently accepted as Party members, [22] the Party advocated short-term, off-the-job training when feasible. Otherwise, veteran members were instructed to supervise recent recruits.

---

[21] Incidents reported with respect to the communes, such as the faulty method of bookkeeping, reinforce this conclusion. As noted in the chapter on the cultural system, real achievements have been made in the area of mass education; but the continuance of the half-work half-study programs and other deficiencies still result in inferior education for the vast majority of the population.

[22] According to Peking's *Pei-ching Jih-pao* of March 14, 1962, "certain leading comrades confined themselves to administrative affairs, neglecting or giving up the ideological work and organizational work of the Party."

Aside from the low ideological level, many Party members have also been found to have "mistaken ideologies." As early as 1939, Liu gave examples of types of members who held "fundamentally incorrect ideological concepts." Among these were individuals who joined the CPC for reasons other than the advancement of communism—such as to avoid an unpleasant family situation, to find employment or learn skills. It also included those who retained "comparatively strong individualism and personal egoism," or who still reflected "the ideological concepts of the exploiting class."

The political, as distinct from the ideological, level of the membership may be judged by two criteria: the social composition of the Party (that is, whether the members possess the traits of the proletarian class) and the "style of work" (or the manner and attitude in which the member conducts official business). The question of working style will be reserved for later discussion; the brief treatment of the CPC's social composition, given earlier, needs to be supplemented here. At the time of the victory in mainland China, when between 80 and 90 per cent of the Party membership came from peasant origins, there was some tendency to speak of the peasant members as "proletarians and semi-proletarians of the countryside." But Liu Shao-ch'i, among others of the CPC hierarchy, has often referred to the lax ways, conservatism, narrowmindedness and backwardnesses characteristic of those of peasant origin. Furthermore, an undercurrent of friction within the Party between those of peasant and those of worker origins has caused dissatisfaction among the peasant members and created a serious problem for the Party.[23] The CPC leaders have admitted difficulty in persuading the peasants that they must accept a subordinate role. The peasant complaint has been well summarized by Po I-po: "Since our Party has long existed in the countryside, since the troops are but armed peasants in uniform, and since the greater part of the Party cadres are of peasant origin, while the working classes, though they have been in the cities all this time, only rise up after liberation, how can it be said that the working class leads the peasants?" Since the rural reorganization of the communes, the CPC has ordered that first preference in enlistment of members be given to the lower peasants, but the problem remains and continues to demand remedial action.

Another problem was created by the infiltration of "unreliable and vicious elements of all kinds" into the Party. The CPC leaders have had long experience with the problem of "undesirable elements" entering the ranks in times of rapid expansion. In 1939, Mao reported: "The Central

---

[23] As detailed in the chapter on the leadership, the vast majority of the Central Committee members, and the higher circles of the Politburo and its Standing Committee, do not claim peasant origins.

Committee has emphatically raised the slogan 'Expand the Party far and wide, but let not a single undesirable enter!' Yet in expanding the Party organization in the past, many opportunists and enemy saboteurs did sneak in." In 1957, Mao again reported to the Central Committee:

> Many landlords, rich peasants and scoundrels took this opportunity [of the enormous increase in membership] to slip into our Party. They dominate many Party, government and mass organizations in the rural areas; lord it over, bully and oppress the people; and distort the Party's policies, causing these organizations to become alienated from the masses . . . such serious conditions place before us the task of reorganizing and purifying the ranks of the Party.

The Chinese Communist press continues to cite examples of "undesirable elements" within the Party's ranks and to demand reform. Nor has the CPC leadership been satisfied with the moral level of the membership at large. As revealed in their speeches and reports, the communist victory on the mainland itself contributed to the moral deterioration of many members. The corrupting influences of power and wealth have long pre-occupied the leadership. In 1939, Liu warned against those Party members "who are shaken when they see the glitter of society with its money and women, then commit crimes and even rebel against the Party and the revolution." After the 1949 victory, reports of moral lapses on the part of CPC members became more general. There have been reports of despotism, idle enjoyment, and "mental numbness," sex scandals, drug addiction, corruption, theft of government property and government secrets, fraud, deception, sabotage and non-submission to Party authorities. Despite the "Three-Anti" campaign against waste, corruption and bureaucratism, incidents of moral weakness continue to plague the Party. As noted in the chapter on the leadership, the highest level members have studiously sought to give an uplifting example of personal conduct and to avoid, or play down, the issues of wealth and prestige. But the absoluteness of authority at every level provides the opportunity for personal aggrandizement—and there are those who continue to seize it.

These weaknesses and defects in the cultural, ideological, political and moral levels of the Party membership must inevitably affect the way that members perform their tasks for the Party. The Chinese Communist leaders have repeatedly expressed deep concern about the work style of the membership, particularly at the lower levels where contact with the non-Party masses is closest and makes the deepest impression. Correct "style of work" requires more than a negative avoidance of "error;" it demands effective leadership in whatever task assigned. Ideally, working style is characterized by hard labor, frugality and the ability to improvise with the materials at hand. Conversely, weaknesses in working style range across a vast spectrum from formalism to bureaucratism, and even to anti-Party activities.

Formalism is regarded as one aspect of bureaucratism and is a common defect in the working style of Party members. The most prevalant variety, defined by Kao Kang when he was still an honored member of the Politburo, is the practice of holding meetings in a perfunctory way. Long and unfruitful meetings inevitably cause public complaints. In September, 1962, the CPC Central Committee launched its "New Five-Anti" campaign for Party reform. Strongly urging all members, particularly those at the lower levels, to devote more time to manual labor, the CPC necessarily ordered a curtailment of meetings and desk work. A *People's Daily* editorial of July 21, 1963, stated imperatively that the number of meetings must be minimized. [24]

Allied to formalism is "commandism," which the communists define as "the practice of attempting to carry out Party or government work merely by issuing orders or merely by making use of the administrative machinery, without taking the trouble to mobilize, organize, educate and convince the masses." Commandism implies a concern only for statistical results and reports of compliance, without regard for the reaction of the masses. Hence, Mao has referred to commandism as a political disease of haste; he regards it as "an infringement on the principle of the voluntary will of the masses."

A more general defect in working style, embracing both formalism and commandism is bureaucratism. Jao Shu-shih, when he was First Secretary of the East China Bureau of the Central Committee, enumerated several types of bureaucratism exhibited by Party members: that of standing aloof from the masses and secluding oneself from reality; that of carrying on routine activity and empty talk; and that of leading an easy life, free from cares. Various communist newspapers have frequently reported the greatly varied and endlessly recurring cases of bureaucratism among Party cadres at many levels. For example, the Department of Agriculture and Forestry of Chekiang province, according to a report published in the *Chekiang Daily* in April, 1953, admitted to an undemocratic selection of model workers, issuance of inaccurate and false reports, and fabrication of production achievements. A potentially graver episode was reported in the *Shansi Daily* in the same month. Party cadres in the Department of Civil Administration of that province failed, until late March, to issue instructions at the regional and county levels for a vigorous winter relief program and earlier action to prevent a spring famine. These

---

[24] This decision was prompted by such reports as that of the secretary of a Party branch of the Meihua Sundry Goods Store in Canton that he was obliged to attend 78 meetings between March and June, 1963. See Peking *Ta-kung Pao*, September 14, 1963.

examples, and those mentioned in the discussion on communes, could be multiplied many times over as proof of the prevalence of bureaucratism throughout the country.

A particularly flagrant case of bureaucratism with especially tragic consequences may illustrate the seriousness of the problem. The *Hupeh Daily* in March, 1953, belatedly reported the mass starvation which had occurred in Tsikwei county in the spring of 1951. In the Yanglinch'iao rural district of that county there had been 166 deaths from starvation; in Szuan village, 11 per cent of the population died of starvation. In the Ich'ang rural district, according to the report of the district Party committee, "71 died of outright starvation, 57 died of poisoning from eating argil (white clay) and wild grass; 14 died of other sicknesses in addition to hunger; and 24 died of beatings or other punishments sustained when driven to theft by hunger, or from falling under cave-ins of clay while digging argil to eat or being slaughtered by parents because of hunger." In the Ich'ang rural district the Party committee blamed the acting secretary, Liu Ching-po, saying that if he had not led a corrupt life the disaster might have been averted. In the Yanglinch'iao district, the acting secretary was also blamed for reprehensible conduct. Instead of reporting true conditions, he filed false statements attributing death to causes other than starvation. The local cadres received their share of the blame for continuing to enjoy their own privileged lives even after the first thirty-odd cases of starvation were reported to them. The cadres even convened "idlers' meetings," tied up and beat some of the starving peasants for thievery and pinned on others a red-and-black label inscribed simply "Idler."

Another familiar deviation in working style frequently condemned is that of despotism, or the abuse of official powers for personal gain. Thus the case is reported in the spring of 1953 of a member of a rural district Party committee in Hupeh province who administered severe beatings to at least eighteen peasants, badly injuring several of them. Another Party official in the same province, in his work as town mayor, thwarted the marriage plans of a young couple who then committed suicide, simply because the twenty year old girl had once expressed criticism of him.

The Party leaders have waged a continuous campaign against other errors in style of work, such as "egotistical individualism" and "adventurism." Egotistical individualism, as described by Liu Shao-ch'i, is often expressed in "unprincipled disputes in the Party," and in the errors of clique struggles, sectarianism and particularism, as well as in "actions which willfully damage and show disrespect for Party discipline." Adventurism is expressed in such forms as "war-lordism" and "acting the hero," managing things in an arbitrary fashion, and acting as if "bestowing favors on the masses." To continue this seemingly endless list of "isms," war-lordism is the evil manifested by those who "regard the army as a special power standing outside or above the people, or as an instrument for building up the personal influence or position of a smaller number of people."

The Chinese Communist press has frequently cited cases of the above-mentioned deviations. During the 1957–58 period, conditions listed as demanding reform included sectarianism, subjectivism, political apathy, extravagance, lack of faith in the people and lack of proper planning. Party members still engaged in "tide watching" and "passive resistance," and in many cases the cadres were accused of losing touch with the people. Party functionaries were still practicing "egotistical individualism." Thus, for example, the vice manager of the Sheki Fruit and Vegetable Export Company was disciplined in November, 1960, for keeping products for personal use; while three corrupt cadres in Kanto commune, Kiangsu province, were removed for accepting bribes. At least part of the responsibility for the disastrous harvests of the 1959–61 period, as noted in the analysis of the communalization drive, must be assigned to corrupt and inefficient cadres. The January 18, 1961 communique issued by the Ninth Plenum of the Eighth Central Committee referred to a small number of "bad elements who have sneaked into the revolutionary ranks" and who still remained and called for renewed efforts at reform.

All of these conditions cited as needing reform continue to plague the Chinese Communist leadership. At the first session of the Third National People's Congress, meeting in Peking in December, 1964, although a general decrease in counter-revolutionary activity was noted in President of the People's Court Hsieh Chüeh-tsai's speech, Chou En-lai repeated that "new exploiters" are "ceaselessly generated in society, in the Party and in government organs." The revelations of the "cultural revolution," including such evils as economism and "waving the red flag" to conceal anti-Party activities, prove the correctness of Chou's warning. Ultimately, the elimination or minimization of these elements depends upon the success of Party rectification movements and Party purges.

Party Rectification Movements: 1942-65 [25]

The Chinese Communist leadership, as noted in the previous sections, is ever vigilant against the actions of any Party member which threaten to divide the Party or destroy its solidarity. As phrased in a *People's Daily* article of January 5, 1961: "A rectification campaign is the locomotive in

[25] The effects of the "cultural revolution," beginning in 1966, on Party rectification are discussed in the final section of this chapter, and other related matters are detailed in the chapter on the leadership.

an ideological revolution." It is therefore obvious that Party rectification movements must be regarded as a continuing process, rather than a series of separate disciplinary campaigns. Thus the same article continued: "The rectification campaign, a common Marxist-Leninist ideological education movement, is the principal method for correctly handling contradictions inside our Party." In view of Mao's dictum that contradictions provide life and progress, the rectification campaigns must be continuous, although they may vary in intensity, specific targets or duration.

From time to time the CPC has found it expedient to intensify its continued learning and study program through special campaigns of "ideological remolding" and Party reorganization. The various waves in this movement have followed the description of one of the earlier campaigns given by An Tzu-wen, Director of the CPC Central Committee's Organization Department:

In the course of this movement, all Party members under the unified leadership of the Party are to study certain assigned documents, link these with practice and conduct criticism and self-criticism in a systematic way. The necessary organizational measures are carried out on the basis of the study. In this way problems which occur in the course of Party-building can be effectively dealt with, thus achieving the double objective of raising the ideological level of the Party members and consolidating the Party organizations.

The top leadership of the CPC selects the specific timing and targets for these "reform movements." In 1942–43, the Party conducted a rectification movement directed, in the jargon of the CPC, against subjectivism and sectarianism and aimed primarily at reforming the intellectuals of petty bourgeois origin who had entered the Party without the necessary proletarian outlook. Party membership had increased from 40,000 to 800,000 between 1937 and 1941, and many of the new members were said to retain false ideas of bourgeois liberalism, equalitarianism, absolute democracy, and the like. As a result, they were guilty of subjectivism— or of correctly quoting Marxist-Leninist texts without the ability to apply them to practical problems. The charge of sectarianism was lodged against those members who resorted to the stereotyped jargon of the Party to impress others, or who otherwise turned the attributes of CPC membership into the exclusive mannerisms of a privileged sect, thereby isolating themselves from contact with the non-Party masses.

Outside observers saw in this movement one stage in Mao's efforts to secure his independence from Moscow domination by eliminating the influence of Moscow-orientated leaders in the CPC. But this conclusion would seem unjustified for, as noted previously, the rectification movement served to reaffirm Mao's own orientation toward Moscow. Party documents marked as required reading included a number of Stalin's writings, such as "Leadership and Investigation," "Self-Criticism," "The Principle of Equality," and "The Bolshevization of the Party," along with the conclusion of the official *History of the CPSU (B)* and "The Theories of Lenin and Stalin on Party Discipline and Party Democracy." Mao himself, in a lecture of February 1, 1942, on "Reform in Learning, the Party and Literature," specifically stated that "Marxism-Leninism is the theory that Marx, Engels, Lenin and Stalin created on the basis of actual facts, and it consists of the general conclusions derived from historical and revolutionary experience." In another speech a week later Mao made extensive reference to the conclusion of Stalin's *History of the CPSU (B)* and his speech to the Eighteenth Congress of the CPSU. Thus it would be premature to see this reform movement as an intramural struggle against Soviet influence.

Again in 1947, the CPC launched a rectification movement, with special attention to the cadres and organizations of the lower levels. By this time the membership had reached 2,700,000 and the social composition was said to include a number of landlords, rich peasants and other questionable elements who, in many places, had taken over Party positions at the local level. Since the communists were then conducting an agrarian reform in the areas under their control, the Party reorganization movement was designed to alleviate conditions which were causing peasant discontent and jeopardizing the success of the agrarian drive.

In June, 1950, at the Third Plenary Session of the Central Committee, and after the national victory, Mao Tse-tung called upon the entire Party to launch another rectification movement to raise the ideological and political level of the members. Again, the huge number of new recruits was a factor. The Party's attention was also shifting from the countryside to the cities and industrial areas: alongside the continuing program of agrarian reform were many new problems of urban organization.

After January, 1952, the CPC launched a vigorous "Three-Anti" campaign against waste, corruption and bureaucratism and a Party consolidation movement, which impressed some observers as the grandest purge yet conducted by the Chinese Communists. The work of Party reorganization seems to have been carefully planned, with cadres specially prepared to conduct the movement. As each Party branch was reorganized, the qualifications of its members were reviewed; those found to be undesirable elements were expelled and others failing to meet the standards were allowed or persuaded to withdraw from the Party. The remainder were confirmed in membership. As in the 1950 movement, bureaucratism and commandism seem to have been the chief ideological targets.

The Fourth Plenary Session of the Seventh Central Committee, held in

February, 1954, shifted the emphasis of Party reform from low qualifications of the individual members to the evils of complacency and personal empire-building among the higher cadres. Prompted by the specific case of Kao Kang and Jao Shu-shih, the results of this session were felt at all levels in the year that followed. Titles of articles appearing in *People's Daily* hint in brief at the disciplinary approach: "The Inner-Mongolian Sub-Bureau of the CC of the CPC Holds Enlarged Conference and Seriously Examines Work in Accordance with the Resolution of the Fourth Plenary Session," or "The Sinkiang Sub-Bureau of the CC of the CPC Holds Enlarged Conference and Investigates Deeply into the Problems of Party Unity in the Sinkiang Area," or "The Northeast Bureau of the CC of the CPC Holds an All-Region Senior Cadres Conference to Transmit the Resolutions of the Fourth Plenary Session of the CC of the CPC and to Investigate Work of the Entire Region."

The Party reform movement of 1954–55 may have been more far-reaching in effect, and prompted by a more serious threat to the top leadership, than the previous endeavors. But it was only a stage in the continual process. *People's Daily* itself indicated resignation to the never-ending effort. Recalling its earlier warnings against "the sugar-coated bullets of the bourgeois class," it reported that "the individualist ideology of the bourgeois class nevertheless continues to grow within the Party."

The 1956 Hundred Flowers campaign was originally intended as a mass appeal to solicit assistance in rectification of Party members. During the Blooming and Contending phase and in the subsequent anti-rightist drive the CPC intensified its efforts to discipline refractory members. As Mao announced at the February 27, 1957, Supreme State Conference, the CPC would strengthen its "unified, iron-clad discipline" to secure a universal "surrender of hearts." Among the measures employed to accelerate Party rectification, the CPC ordered intensification of study programs and renewed emphasis on the value of criticism and self-criticism sessions. In addition, and coinciding with the initiation of the Great Leap and communalization, Party members were subjected to a reform-through-productive-labor campaign. Top Party personnel took the initiative in demonstrating the importance of this program. Mao himself, as well as Chou and other high leaders, participated in token form in the construction of the Ming Tomb reservoir. The total number of Party functionaries engaged in productive labor during the 1958–59 period was estimated at 1.3 million. [26]

At the same time, beginning late in 1957, numerous Party members were removed from their posts for disciplinary reasons. As previously

[26] For additional data on the rectification campaigns of 1956–59, see the chapter on the cultural system.

mentioned, Ku Ta-ts'un and P'an Fu-sheng, two alternate members of the Central Committee, were stripped of their leading posts in Kwangtung and Honan. In Chekiang, Sha Wen-han, secretary of the Provincial Party Committee and Governor, was purged for crimes of rightism, individualism and localism; as were the vice governor, provincial public procurator, director of the Party Committee's financial and trade department and nine other members of the provincial people's council. In March, 1958, the governor and vice governor of Yunnan were replaced, while in Tsinghai, Sun Tso-pin, secretary of the CPC provincial committee and governor, was expelled from the Party together with other rightists. In June, 1959, the director and deputy director of the Yunnan Provincial Party Committee's department of organization were accused of attempting to form an anti-Party group. This charge was also levelled against various leading cadres in the CPC Sinkiang-Uigur Autonomous Region Committee. Liu Hung-t'ao, head of the Hopei Provincial Party Committee's United Front Work Department and member of its standing committee for anti-Party affairs, was also removed. In July, an anti-Party group was uncovered in Kwangsi Chuang Autonomous Region; the chairman of the regional government, a deputy procurator, a member of the regional Party standing committee and four members of this committee were expelled from the Party.

In 1960, setbacks in the Great Leap and commune programs indicated the need for intensive Party discipline. The charge most frequently made against CPC personnel was that of failure to understand Party economic programs. Cadres were accused of failure to devote sufficient time to ideological study, and compulsory part-time classes were greatly increased. Disciplinary action against those Party members whose mode of living was superior to the average commune member was centered around the "four together" system of eating, sleeping, working and talking to the peasants to eliminate any sense of superiority. Needless to say, this also promoted peasant informing on the weaknesses of the individual Party members.

In a January 5, 1961, article published in *People's Daily*, Kung Tzu-jung, alternate member of the Central Committee's Control Commission, observed: "The uninterrupted revolution in society calls for uninterrupted revolution in the thought of the individual. It is completely wrong to think that one or several rectification campaigns will settle things for good." In fact, the CPC has continued to stress the value of reform through physical labor to end any "bourgeois" inclinations of its members. Resistance of the members to this campaign and other measures has only reinforced the leadership's conviction that the most important single target for rectification remains that of class struggle. Under slogans such as "take off your shoes and go to the fields," cadres have been instructed to increase the time they spend in non-Party work: those who resist are accused of betraying proletarian (hence Party) standards. Thus, by 1961, all physically able Party members normally assigned to desk jobs were expected to spend the minimal equivalent of one month a year in manual labor.

In September, 1962, at its Tenth Plenary Session, the CPC Central Committee launched a "New Five-Anti" campaign for Party reform, particularly at the local levels. Since then, a barrage of press articles has equated proletarianism with productive labor on the part of the cadres. Singled out for special praise were the Party secretaries of two communal brigades, one in Hopei province and the other in Chekiang. The former contributed 200 days of physical labor in both 1961 and 1962, and the latter labored 308 days in 1962. But while avoiding the Party sin of "earning income by exploitation"—or failing to earn one's own labor points, these and other Party personnel could hardly be expected to function as effectively in their Party assignments of conducting meetings, filling out questionnaires, and the like. And despite the CPC's efforts to reduce these burdens, they still demand a great amount of time in certain areas. For example, one Party secretary of a commune in Kwangsi Chuang Autonomous Region admitted that the commune's third-grade cadres were required to file 64-item reports every third day with the local CPC committee. These cadres complained of insufficient time to fulfill Party assignments and still engage in manual labor. Yet these pressures could not be readily alleviated. Thus, on August 17, 1962, *People's Daily* reported the results of an eight-day cadres' meeting in Suhsien county, Shansi province during which each Party member was obliged to display his "labor book." Those who had insufficient work points for the previous four months were then labelled "members of the exploiting class."

In a January 16, 1965, article in *People's Daily*, Li Ta-chang, Party first secretary in Kweichow province, anticipated the work of the "cultural revolution": "Within this year a deeper struggle and socialist education will be carried out." As Communist China progresses with her Third Five-Year Plan, Party rectification may be expected to intensify. Moreover, Peking's continuing dispute with Moscow over ideological principles increases the need to ensure Party solidarity and correct ideological knowledge among all its members. This continuing rectification campaign will employ every device—including study programs, criticism sessions, reform through labor, etc.—and, as noted in the chapter on the military system, stress the need to emulate the People's Liberation Army in a militant approach. In May, 1965, Huang Huo-ch'ing, First Secretary of the CPC Lianoning Provincial Committee, praised the work of a Party committee in a communal brigade. This brigade prepared an experimental ten-year plan for rectification which calls for a general review of each member's record and committee vote on the individual's level of political and ideological consciousness. Predictably, this sort of action will be carried out on a massive scale at the local levels. At the higher levels—such as the State Council's April 30, 1965, action in removing Vice Minister of Culture Hsia Yen—the purge will continue to be utilized. As the "cultural revolution" has proven, the work of Party rectification is a vital and endless task.

THE PARTY AUXILIARIES:
THE YOUNG COMMUNIST LEAGUE

The Young Communist League (YCL) is to the Chinese Communist Party what the Komsomol is to the CPSU—an instrumentality for extending ideological and political indoctrination to young people at an age when they are awakening to a broader political consciousness and are beginning to make their way in the world, a device for channeling the energy and enthusiasm of youth into the economic and political projects of the Party, and a recruiting ground from which to draw new leaders and willing followers into the membership of the Party itself.

Since its own inception, the CPC has always had close association with a youth organization of some kind. During the years 1920–25, this organization was known as the Chinese Socialist Youth Corps, changing its name in 1925 to the Chinese Communist Youth Corps (CYC). During the period 1936–49, the organ travelled under a variety of names, reflecting the paramount political mission of the day as well as the "popular front" line; for example, the Vanguard of the Chinese National Liberation, the National Salvation Association of Youth, the Vanguard of Anti-Japanese Youth, the Democratic Youth League and the Democratic Youth Corps. In April, 1949, the name was again changed, to the New Democratic Youth League (NDYL), and the present title of Young Communist League was formally adopted in May, 1957.

Efforts to organize and train an auxiliary youth organization were intensified in 1946, when the CPC Central Committee proposed the establishment of such a body for progressive young activists. At that time, the CC instructed its regional bureaus and sub-bureaus to set up such organizations on an experimental basis. In 1947–48, League branches were opened in various centers in the "liberated areas" of the Northeast, the Northwest, North and East. Finally, on January 1, 1949, the CC adopted a resolution to establish the NDYL on a national basis and the League's first national congress was scheduled for the summer of 1949.

The NDYL was fundamentally like the old Communist Youth Corps, but differed in two respects. First, admission to the Youth Corps had required acceptance of the principles of communism; but admission to the new organization originally required only an acceptance of the principles of the "New Democracy." This point of difference was eliminated at the Second National Congress in April, 1953, when the League Constitution was revised. The second point at variance had to do with the social composition of the membership. The former CYC had sought to make the working class and peasant youth the main components of its membership. The NDYL, however, extended its membership base to include young revolutionary intellectuals, in the hopes of uniting the young people of all classes in support of the new regime.

Despite these differences, the organizers of the NDYL were quick to indicate that the basic nature of their organization remained the same as that of the old Youth Corps: both were nucleus organizations to unite young people under the leadership of the Communist Party and to indoctrinate them in Marxism-Leninism and the thought of Mao Tse-tung. As noted previously, differences between the two bodies proved transitory. With the consolidation of the new government, the period of the "new democracy" (a multi-class society) was declared over and a period of class struggle was inaugurated to bring about the reconstruction of Chinese society along the lines of the Soviet Union. In keeping with this planned transition to a single-class society, the League's Representative Congress in May, 1957, changed its name to the Young Communist League (or the same as the Soviet Komsomol). The new League Constitution was also revised at this meeting.

On many essential points, the May 24, 1957, Constitution of the Young Communist League recapitulates the 1953 revised Constitution of the NDYL. The YCL is a mass organization for progressive youth, under the leadership of the CPC. It serves as the lieutenant and the reserves of the Party. Its principal task is "the faithful execution of the resolutions of the Party and the government," and "the strengthening of the people's democratic dictatorship." The League pledges to be "faithful to the principle of proletarian internationalism"—specifically through uniting with "progressive youth" throughout the world to strengthen the forces of socialism.

The League is open to young people between the ages of fifteen and twenty-five, although "overaged" members may remain in the organization for a set period under special circumstances. Procedures for admission very nearly duplicate those of the CPC itself, including recommendation by members of the League and examination into the applicant's social background to exclude undesirable elements. Generally, the leadership has stressed the need to recruit new candidates from the ranks of activists, particularly in areas where no League organization has yet been established. In the communes, youths of poor or lower middle peasant class origins, who work in teams still without League members, are most frequently given preference. According to a typical procedure, a YCL member visits these teams and lectures to the youths regarded as activists, encouraging them to write "histories" of their commune, village or family. These reports are useful in evaluating class consciousness. Likely prospects are then assigned special labor tasks to further demonstrate their proletarian leanings.

The factors of age and sex are also taken into consideration in recruitment of League members. For example, the 27-member YCL branch of the Tungts'un brigade, in T'ungpo commune, Antz'u county, Hopei province, admitted nineteen additional members between December, 1962, and January, 1964. Eighteen of these new members were under age twenty. This preference for teen-aged recruits is designed to give the youth more intensive ideological training and also, perhaps, to counteract the problem of the so-called "over-age" youths. The League Constitution provides that members must resign at aged twenty-five, unless elected to a leading body or assigned a professional duty. In the latter case, they may remain active members until age twenty-eight. The League is regarded as a training-camp and proving grounds for acceptance into the CPC. On a general average, between 1949 and 1959 approximately four out of ten new CPC members were recruited from the antechamber of the League. Thus, many of the twenty-five year old members of the League have requested to defer their resignation lest they be forever bypassed by CPC examiners. Although the official press has repeatedly reminded these "over-age" members that their level of political consciousness—not their League affiliation—is the final determinant in CPC recruitment, the fear apparently persists that resignation forebodes ignominy.

League recruiters have also been warned against discrimination of candidates because of sex. These directives stem from the fact that many branches have been reluctant to train young women who will soon marry, and may abandon an active revolutionary role. For example, in 1963, only two of the fifteen members in the Yungning brigade of Yungan commune, Mishan county, Heilungkung province were women. Yet the CPC professes its eagerness to give suitable representation to China's women. To counteract this form of discrimination, the CPC has stepped up its propagandistic tributes to "model" women Party members. For example, youths are repeatedly reminded of the services of Ch'en Shu-jen, chief telephone operator of the Fohsin Municipal Railway Bureau in Liaoning. In 1948, at the age of seventeen, Ch'en climbed poles during a

KMT bombing attack to keep the lines open, for which she was rewarded with CPC membership. Listed among her subsequent services to the Party are the refusal to accept wage increments and the cleaning of men's latrines! For such proof of revolutionary services Ch'en Shu-jen has been termed a "shining screw" making extraordinary contributions in an ordinary post.

The organization of the League, like that of the CPC, is based on the principle of democratic centralism (Article 10) and presents the same pyramidal structure of representative, executive and—at the higher levels—administrative bodies (Article 11). League branches can be established in factories, farms, mines, business enterprises, offices, units of the armed forces, schools, villages or streets, so long as there are at least three members. Larger branches, of over fifty but under 200 members, may organize general branches. Within a branch, there can be sub-branches (Article 28). Branches usually elect a secretary as the executive officer to carry on the work of the branch; but in the rare instances where a branch has over 300 members it can elect a committee (Article 31).

Above the branch is the usual hierarchy of congresses at the county, municipal, provincial and other levels up to the national congress. The branch membership meetings and the congresses are theoretically the supreme organs of authority at their respective levels. The League congress at the county or municipal level is to meet once a year, and at the provincial level every two years, to examine the reports of their respective committees (Articles 22 and 23). The congresses elect the committee at their particular level and delegates to the congress at the next higher level (Article 23). The League committees presumably exercise authority during the recesses of their respective congresses. But at the county, municipal or provincial level, the committees in turn elect a standing committee, a secretary and a number of assistant secretaries to exercise authority and conduct League work during the recess of the congress and the full committee (Article 26).

With the convocation of the National League Congress, normally every four years (Article 16), and its election of the League Central Committee (Article 17), the hierarchy is completed. Not unlike the CPC Central Committee, the League Central Committee operates through its plenum or full session, supposedly meeting at least twice a year (Article 19), and during its recess through the standing committee and the secretariat (Article 20). In the secretariat, departments are established as needed for such functions as organization, propaganda and education.

Needless to say, under the principle of democratic centralism the submission of the lower committees and secretaries to the directives of the higher committees and the resolutions of the respective congresses is emphatically required. The general membership's rights and duties closely parallel those of the members of the CPC.

Despite its subservience to the CPC in policy matters, the League, like the NDYL before it, maintains an organizational independence. This independence was originally stressed by the NDYL leaders. Jen Pi-shih, founder and first honorary chairman of the NDYL, and Chiang Nan-ch'iang, its organization chief and member of the CC's standing committee, stated that, while following the general policy directives and executing the general tasks assigned by the Party, the League needed its own independent work and activities. It has its own budget to enable it to engage in systematic work according to its own initiative.

However convenient it may be for the League to have its own budget, offices, equipment and personnel, there is no doubt about its subservience to the requirements of the Party. In his report to the First National NDYL Congress, Feng Wen-ping, Chairman of the League Central Committee, affirmed the leadership of the CPC and the duty to unite all youths behind it. In the eyes of the CPC leadership, as Jen Pi-shih pointed out in his political report to the same congress, the League holds a dual significance. On the one hand, the League members have to understand clearly the absolute necessity for accepting Party leadership and resolutely executing its commands. On the other hand, the Party committees at all levels are not to neglect their responsibility for leading the youth movement in their respective areas.

Regarding this relationship—whereby the CPC receives obedience and the League receives direction—the Constitution of the YCL, like that of its predecessor, the NDYL, provides in its general program that all work of the League should proceed under the direct leadership of the CPC. This arrangement is facilitated at the highest level by the fact that Hu Yao-pang, the League's First Secretary, is also a member of the CPC Central Committee. At each level, from the local branch upwards, the League organizations are to accept the direction and supervision of the corresponding Party organizations, in addition to that of the League organs at the higher levels. Moreover, the secretaries at the county level and above are required to be full-fledged CPC members. At the county level, they must have been Party members for at least one year, at the regional level for two years, and at the provincial level or its equivalent for three years. Though these time restrictions are not provided, secretaries at the sub-district or borough level must also be regular or candidate Party members.

In the armed forces, special provisions are made to bring the League units under the supervision and control of Party and state.[27]   A special chapter of the YCL Constitution treats the subject of League units in the People's Liberation Army.   These units are responsible not only to the CPC committee and basic organizations (Article 32), but also to the League Central Committee and the PLA General Political Department (Article 33).   They must also maintain contact with the local League organizations in the area where they are stationed (Article 34).

The League serves as an arm and auxiliary of the Party not only among the young people directly, but also in all the other mass organizations which youths may have occasion to join.   Thus the YCL is able to maintain contact and exert influence in the trade unions, peasant associations, student associations, and countless other mass organizations, in conjunction and with the assistance of the regular Party elements there.   As an indispensable arm of the CPC, the League has organized youths throughout the country to participate in Party programs.   For example, in the first year of the Great Leap Forward, 1958, the YCL organized ninety million youth to collect manure, sixty million young people to aid in water conservancy projects, and thirty million youth into labor shock brigades.   Of equal, if not greater importance, the League has given ideological instruction to millions of members and non-members.   The seriousness with which the League approaches this task of promoting ideological orthodoxy is indicated in the revision of the Constitution of June, 1964.   At this time, the Ninth National Congress added the phrase that all League members must be guided by the thought of Mao Tse-tung, as well as the principles of Marxism-Leninism.

In 1953, after four years of existence, the NDYL boasted of more than 300,000 branches providing instruction and direction for more than nine million League members.   At the time of the League CC session of September, 1955, membership was declared to have reached 14,000,000 divided among 620,000 branches.   In May, 1957, when the NDYL was renamed the Young Communist League, membership was said to have reached 23,000,000 organized into 920,000 basic units.   An NCNA report of May 3, 1959, listed YCL membership at 25,000,000 and stated that some 30 per cent were women.   In keeping with the mass organizational tasks assigned it under the new economic programs, the League declared in a resolution adopted by its Fifth Plenum of the Third Central Committee on July 18, 1959, that basic level organizations would be greatly expanded in the future.   Following 1964 reports that only about 13 per cent of the rural youths had been recruited into the League, in 1965 a major campaign was conducted to increase membership.   In that year alone, some eight

[27] For additional details on PLA advocation of YCL membership, see the chapter on the military system.

and a half million new members were received. This great increment can probably be traced to the Party leadership's plan to use the youth of China as the vanguard of the "cultural revolution."

In April, 1966, the League's Central Committee conducted its plenum in Peking "under the care and guidance of the Party Central." Again giving first priority to learning the thought of Mao Tse-tung, the CC also dictated that the PLA should be the model for the League. With the August, 1966, emergence of the Red Guards, the role of the YCL became less certain. The fact that the Peking Municipal YCL Committee was completely reorganized immediately following the reorganization of the Party municipal committee, and that the League's top leadership was apparently changed, while its organ, *Chung-kuo Ch'ing-nien Pao*, was temporarily suspended in mid-August, 1966, indicates that, at the very least, the YCL is scheduled for a major reorganization to make it a more dynamic vehicle for carrying out the class struggle.

Tributary to the Young Communist League, in much the same way that the League is tributary to the Party, are the young Pioneers. The Pioneers is an organization for children between the ages of nine and fifteen, established under a resolution of the League Central Committee on October 13, 1949, and pursuant to Chapter VII of the Constitutions of both the NDYL and the YCL. Article 29 of the YCL Constitution states that the League is entrusted by the CPC with organizing teams of Pioneers in primary schools, junior middle schools and other places. The establishment of Pioneers headquarters in schools, streets or communal teams is subject to the approval of the appropriate higher League committee at the borough, sub-district or equivalent level. The Pioneer teams, platoons, squadrons and detachments are directly under the control of the local League organizations and have no superstructure of their own, or independent national organization.

The purpose of the Pioneers, as stated in the League Constitution, is to educate and train children through various collective activities. League members are admonished of their responsibility to provide adequate instruction in a variety of ways. The case of the 63-member Pioneer unit in Hsitung brigade, T'anghsi commune, Chinhua county, Chekiang province, may be taken as typical. As reported in *Fu-tao-yüan* (*Instructor*) of May 20, 1965, old peasants are invited to tell stories to the Pioneers of the horrors of pre-revolutionary times. The children are encouraged to understand the nature and importance of proletarianism through voluntary labor assignments. On the *mou* of land assigned them, these Pioneers labor for working points which are kept by their own accountant in a sort of microcosm of the commune system which will prepare them for adult labors.

Organization of children in Pioneer units has been achieved with great rapidity. On the occasion of celebrating the annual Children's Day, on June 1, 1954, following the Second National Conference on Work with Children, the press reported that more than 8,000,000 Pioneers were being trained by some 200,000 supervisor-instructors. A report to the Third Plenum of the YCL Third Central Committee, on June 28, 1958, noted that Pioneer membership had reached 35,000,000. May, 1959, statistics published by the YCL Central Committee's Pioneers and Childrens Work Department listed Pioneer membership at 44,000,000. In May, 1962, NCNA placed Pioneer membership at 50,000,000. Following the reorganization of the communal structure, the decision was made to make the administrative village the basic unit of Pioneer organization. Consequently, the membership drive was greatly intensified early in 1965. One indicator of success may be found in the figures reported for six counties in Hopei province. According to *Chung-kuo Ch'ing-nien Pao* of June 3, 1965, these counties had already organized 80 per cent of the children in Pioneer units, as compared to 40 per cent only a year before. According to official sources, Pioneers membership reached 100 million in mid-1966, as the Party apparently sought to recruit all Chinese children between the ages of seven and fifteen, to reinforce the role of youth in the "cultural revolution." The Party's success in organizing and training these children will, of course, have a profound effect upon its own future. For this reason, the CPC is not likely to relax its vigilance over its citizens approaching adulthood today, and those who will follow them tomorrow.

THE PARTY APPENDAGES: THE NON-COMMUNIST PARTIES

In the Soviet Union only one political party is tolerated—the CPSU. In China, for an unspecified period a number of minor parties are allowed to exist alongside the CPC. To call these "non-communist" parties may be misleading. Although their members are not members of the CPC, they cannot oppose the objectives and controls of the CPC. Nor can they work for a genuinely non-communist form of society. Hence, as will become more evident below, these parties bear little resemblance to the independent political parties characteristic of a democratic system. They are more properly appendages of the CPC, "kept" by it to perform certain useful functions.

Bases for the Existence of Other Parties

The doctrinal basis for the continued existence of non-communist parties has already been alluded to in pointing out that the Soviet Union professes to be a "dictatorship of the proletariat" while Communist China is still in the stage of a "people's democratic dictatorship." More explicitly it is to be found in the ideology concerning the united front as the correct policy for the period of transition from a "new democratic" to a socialist society. This policy was enunciated by Mao in his 1940 speech *On the New Democracy* and his 1945 address *On Coalition Government* to the Seventh CPC Congress in Yenan. In his earlier report, Mao had stressed, in keeping with the needs of the day, the "anti-Japanese, anti-imperialist" nature of the united front, which he referred to as an "alliance of several classes." He added: "We communists never repel the revolutionary people (provided they do not capitulate to the enemy or oppose the communists). We shall persist in the united front with all classes, strata, political parties, political cliques and individuals who insist on fighting against the Japanese to the end, and shall cooperate for a long term with them." Carrying this thesis further in his 1945 speech, Mao pointed out that under a socialist society, with the disappearance of all non-proletarian classes and private ownership of the means of production, a one-party state, such as that in the USSR, would be theoretically justified. Until then, according to Mao, a broad united front of all democratic elements would be essential. He concluded:

> Some people wonder if the CPC members, once in power, will establish a dictatorship by the proletariat and a one-party system, as they have done in Russia. We can tell these people this: a new democratic state of a union of democratic classes is different in principle from a socialist state with a dictatorship of the proletariat. China, throughout the period of her new democratic system, cannot and should not have a system of government of the character of one-class dictatorship or one-party autocracy. We have no reason not to cooperate with non-communist political parties, social groups, or individuals who are willing to cooperate with the CPC and are not hostile to it.

Since minor parties are regarded as useful instruments, the CPC has taken an active part in their establishment and continued operation. These "democratic" organizations have been financed and their personnel designated or approved by the CPC. Their constitutions and programs and all activities are subject to close CPC supervision or formulation. The CPC carries on this work through the Department of United Front Work under the jurisdiction of its Central Committee. As Li Wei-han, the former veteran director of this department, stated publicly, the CPC is the "commonly recognized political leader" of the various "democratic" parties.

The non-communist parties have acknowledged CPC supremacy in various ways. First of all, all of them proclaimed their faithful "acceptance of the leadership of the CPC and close cooperation with it in work" in their constitutions or in the solemn declaration of their congresses or conferences in 1949–50. For example, the China Democratic League, following the lead of the Revolutionary Committee of the Kuomintang a month earlier, included such a proclamation in its revised Charter (Constitution), adopted at the Enlarged Session of the Fourth Plenum of the League Central Committee on December 20, 1949. [28]

From time to time the leaders of the various minor parties separately or jointly have issued statements of support for the CPC. Thus, in a joint declaration for May Day, 1950, these groups affirmed: "We, the democratic parties of China, are unconditionally united under the leadership of the great Communist Party and Chairman Mao Tse-tung for the building of an independent, free, democratic, united and prosperous China." In December, 1954, at the time of the meeting of the Second CPPCC National Committee, individual leaders from these parties were expressing much the same sentiments. The late Li Chi-shen, then Chairman of the Revolutionary Committee of the Kuomintang, promised, for example, that "we will still more closely rally around the Communist Party and march forward under the banner of the great leader Mao Tse-tung."

These expressions are more than verbalizations. In its 1952 platform, the Chinese Peasants and Workers Party officially invited the members of the CPC to accept key positions in its organization to strengthen its leadership. Thus Tung Pi-wu, CPC Politburo member, had reason for satisfaction when he asserted, at the CPPCC meeting just mentioned, that consolidation of the "Chinese people's democratic united front" had been achieved during the previous five years.

The ultimate condition under which these parties are allowed to exist has already been noted: they must forfeit the right to determine their own survival. When the CPC leadership decides that conditions warrant the elimination of nonproletarian organizations, then these parties will be dissolved. At least one such dissolution has already been reported. In December, 1949, the National Salvation Association "voluntarily" disbanded, ostensibly because its historical mission had been fulfilled.

The non-communist parties of China are deprived of the essential attributes of political organizations in the liberal, democratic sense: they are not distinguished by separate ideologies or programs, and they cannot

[28] Similar pledges were adopted by the China Democratic National Construction Association at its First National Conference in 1949; by the China Association for Promoting Democracy at its National Congress in April, 1950; by the Chinese Peasants and Workers Democratic Party at its Fifth National Conference of Party Cadres, exercising the functions and powers of the Party National Congress, in November, 1950; by the China Chih Kung Tang at its Fourth National Congress in April, 1950; by the Chiu San Society at its First National Conference in December, 1950; and by the Taiwan Democratic Self-Government League.

appeal to the general public for support. More importantly, they cannot even struggle for their own survival once the CPC has decided that they are superfluous. Yet, while they continue to exist, they perform a useful function which can be more clearly understood by a consideration of the individual parties.

Nature and Development of the Non-Communist Parties

The various minor parties show a considerable diversity in origin and social composition, if not in their subservience to the CPC. Early in 1951 an attempt was made to formalize the differences between them in a joint declaration on recruitment policy which had been prescribed by the CPC. The Revolutionary Committee of the Kuomintang (RCK) was to recruit former KMT members who had held government posts under the communists and rendered distinguished service in the land reform program or the Resist-America Aid-Korea drive. The China Democratic League (CDL) was to draw its members from the petty bourgeois intelligentsia, particularly educational and cultural workers, college students, technicians, government employees and overseas Chinese. When other parties also drew from these social elements, the potential power of any one group was ensured fragmentation. The China Democratic National Construction Association was to concentrate on the so-called "national bourgeoisie" of industrialists and merchants; the China Peasants and Workers Democratic Party enlisted government employees, specialists and technicians; the China Association for Promoting Democracy, the "progressive" intelligentsia; and the Chiu San Society recruited "progressive" workers in the cultural, educational and scientific fields.

The Revolutionary Committee of the Kuomintang is ranked as chief among the democratic parties by the CPC, although it is numerically vastly inferior to the second ranked China Democratic League. The RCK's superior position is based upon the fiction that it carries on the revolutionary tradition of Dr. Sun Yat-sen's KMT, and thus is far more venerable than the China Democratic League. Actually, the Revolutionary Committee was organized on January 1, 1948 in Hong Kong, under the chairmanship of Marshal Li Chi-shen, reportedly to carry out Mao's appeals for a coalition government within the "new democracy." It had been preceded, however, by the Three People's Principles Comrades Association led by T'an P'ing-shan and Ch'en Ming-shu and the Kuomintang Association for Promoting Democracy, under the leadership of Ts'ai T'ing-k'ai and Chiang Kuang-nai, two military heroes of the anti-Japanese struggle who were politically naive. Other prominent figures in the party include officials or generals who held high posts under the Nationalist government, but afterwards defected or fell in disfavor, such as Shao Li-tzu and Chang Chih-chung, as well as former KMT elders such as Ho Hsiang-ning (Mme. Liao Chung-k'ai) and Liu Yatse. In 1951, independent sources in Hong Kong reported some 100 out of about 800 registered party members to be serving in the government, about 200 in party organs at various levels, and over 400 unemployed. However, the CPC allowed 100 RCK delegates to attend the first CPPCC and to elect forty-four Central Committeemen and twenty alternates for the RCK's own structure. On both these occasions, among others, internal quarrels within the RCK leadership became evident; they were settled by CPC intervention under the guise of "consultation." In December, 1958, the RCK elected 126 members and 43 alternates to its Fourth Central Committee. Despite, or perhaps because of, its continued subservience to CPC policies, the RCK continues to be assigned various propaganda roles, which will be outlined in the next section.

The China Democratic League (CDL), the second ranking minor party, grew out of the "Alliance of Chinese Democratic Political Organizations" (*Chung-Kuo Min-chu Cheng-t'uan T'ung-ming*) organized in Chungking in 1941 from the ranks of the Young China Party, the Democratic Socialist Party, the Third Party, the National Salvation Association, the Rural Construction Group, the Vocational Education Group and others. At first it maintained its base of operations in Hong Kong, with principal branches in Chungking, Kunming, and Chengtu. The party journal *Kuang-ming Jih-pao (Kuangming Daily)* began publication in Hong Kong on September 18, 1941. Three years later, at its First National Congress in Chungking, the organization decided to expand and change its name to the China Democratic League. As its chairman, it chose Chang Lan, military governor of Szechwan at the time of the overthrow of the Manchus, and still a great influence in that province.[29]

From the beginning the Alliance proclaimed itself a middle force between the Kuomintang and the CPC. But according to a confidential report of the Ministry of the Interior of the Nationalist government, which was published in Formosa in August, 1950, the CDL and the CPC had reached an agreement in November, 1944, whereby both undertook not to com-

[29] Tso Shun-sheng was named secretary general and the Standing Committee included, in addition to Chang Lan and Tso Shun-sheng, Lo Lung-chi, Chang Chün-mai (Carson Chang), Chang Po-chün, Shen Chün-ju, Chang Sheng-fun, Huang Yen-p'ei, Liang Shu-ming, Chou Ching-wen, Li Huang, Tseng Ch'i and Tung Shih-ching. Chang Lan died early in 1955. A year later Shen Chün-ju was elected to succeed him. Shen died in June, 1963. Following the secession of the Young China Party and the Democratic Socialist Party and the communist victory over the mainland, Tso Shun-sheng and Li Huang took residence in Hong Kong, Carson Chang, Tung Shih-ching and Tseng Ch'i moved to the United States, where Tseng died. Chou Ching-wen, author of *Ten Years of Storm*, left the mainland in 1956, and has since been an outspoken critic of the CPC from his base in Hong Kong.

promise or cooperate with the KMT. With the outbreak of the civil war in 1946, the CDL moved further to the left, while still presenting itself as a "third force" between the Nationalists and communists. In the KMT-sponsored Political Consultative Council of that year the CDL proposed a "peace program" and attributed the responsibility for the civil war to the KMT. The CDL was outlawed by the Nationalist government in October, 1947. Meanwhile, the Young China Party and the Democratic Socialist Party had seceded from the CDL and joined the Nationalist government then in Nanking. And in January, 1948, at its Third Plenary Session, the CDL Central Committee adopted a declaration, later published in the official communist handbook, *Guide to New China*, proclaiming its "close cooperation with the CPC and its active support for the people's armed revolution."

Following the communist conquest of North China in 1949, the responsible officials of the CDL in Hong Kong went one after another to Peking where they organized a provisional working committee. After the fall of Shanghai, other Central Committee members who had remained in that city—including Chang Lan, Lo Lung-chi and Shih Liang—also made the trek to Peking where the official party organ, *Kuangming Daily*, was now relocated. In June, 1949, the Fourth Plenary Session of the CDL Central Committee met in Peking to arrange for participation in the communist-led CPPCC.

The CDL occupies a special place in communist strategy involving the minor parties. It was regarded as a peripheral organ of the CPC before the establishment of the other "democratic" parties; and, for purposes of manipulation, it was far more pliable than the Revolutionary Committee of the KMT. Many CPC leaders, including Chou En-lai, Li Wei-han and Mao Tse-tung himself, took part in its 1949 convention. Too, since its membership is several times that of the KMT Revolutionary Committee and includes more people from the cultural and educational fields, the CDL's propaganda work for the communists has been far superior to that of the RCK. The *Kuangming Daily's* staff has CPC personnel in key positions. In addition, the CDL operates several smaller papers and publishes books useful to the CPC's cultural and propaganda strategy.

The CPC has overseen the organization of a number of second and third-string "democratic" parties for the transition to socialism.[30] Many of these were carved out of the original China Democratic League, such as the China Democratic National Construction Association, the China Associa-

---

[30] A rule of thumb for determining the importance which the CPC assigns to the individual "democratic" party is that of the relative amount of financial support advanced by the CPC. Second-ranked parties receive less than two-thirds of the allotments given first-string parties.

tion for Promoting Democracy, the Chinese Peasants and Workers Democratic Party and the Chiu San Society (or the September Third Society, so named in honor of V-J Day). A few others have been drawn from reorganized or newly created parties, such as the China Chih Kung Tang, based upon the old "Chih Kung T'ang," a secret Hung Meng organization of the overseas Chinese, and the Taiwan Democratic Self-Government League, established in November, 1947 to rally the Taiwanese against the Nationalist government and the influence of the United States in their homeland.

The Role of the Non-Communist Parties

In carrying out their required task of consolidating political control in the hands of the CPC and facilitating communist policies for the transition to socialism, the non-communist parties perform a number of useful functions. These are generally of two kinds. They join the CPC to give an impressive demonstration of solidarity and support for communist policies and programs. On the other hand, through what might be called their division-of-labor functions, the minor parties carry out indoctrination and leadership for specialized segments of the populace similar to the work the CPC performs among the bulk of the workers and peasants.

The united front functions have proven their value to the communists. By participating in the communist-convoked Chinese People's Political Consultative Conference (CPPCC) in September, 1949, which adopted the Common Program and other basic constitutional documents for the new government, the China Democratic League gave a show of legitimacy to Mao's forces. Subsequently, as already noted, all the minor parties pledged to accept the Common Program—the CPC minimum program in preparation for socialist transformation. The minor parties again participated in the First National People's Congress at which the 1954 Constitution was adopted, thus giving another demonstration of broad-based support. This aura of solidarity has also caused the CPC to place a number of leaders of the minor parties in government positions of high honor, if little actual authority. For example, the Honorary Chairman of the RCK, Soong Ching Ling (Mme. Sun Yat-sen) was named the Third Vice Chairman of the Central People's Government Council (CPGC), preceded only by Chu Teh and Liu Shao-ch'i, and is now First Vice Chairman of the Chinese People's Republic. The Chairman of the RCK, Li Chi-shen, was made the Fourth Vice Chairman of the CPGC. The Chairman of the CDL, Chang Lan, became the Fifth Vice Chairman of the CPGC, while CDL Vice Chairman Shen Chün-ju was named President of the People's Supreme Court.

The policy of naming representatives from the minor parties to state offices continued in the reorganization introduced by adoption of the 1954 Constitution. Thus Soong Ching Ling, the late Li Chi-shen, the late Chang Lan, and the late Shen Chün-ju, among others, were elected to the Standing Committee of the National People's Congress (which, in effect, replaced the CPGC) as Vice Chairmen. Of the sixteen Vice Chairmen of the Second NPC's Standing Committee, six were chosen from the ranks of the minor parties.[31] Membership in the Standing Committee of the Third National People's Congress was announced on January 3, 1965. Among its eighteen Vice Chairmen, the sixth ranked, Ho Hsiang-ning, is also Chairman of the RCK; the seventh ranked, Huang Yen-p'ei, is also Chairman of the China Democratic National Construction Association; the twelfth ranked, Cheng Ch'ien, is third Vice Chairman of the RCK; the sixteenth, Chang Chih-chung, is first Vice Chairman of the RCK; and the eighteenth, Chou Chien-jen, is also second Vice Chairman of the China Association for Promoting Democracy.

Perhaps the most useful and certainly the most noticeable united front function of the minor parties lies in providing a sounding board—or echo chamber—for the statements of the CPC leadership. These leaders appear to believe that reiteration of Party statements by individual spokesmen of the minor parties heightens their effectiveness. Innumerable examples could be cited, but the case of protestations concerning Taiwan is illustrative of the general pattern. For example, on December 9, 1954, *People's Daily* published the official text of Chou En-lai's statement on the Mutual Defense Pact between the United States and Nationalist China. The first two minor parties to support the statement, as might be expected, were the RCK and the Taiwan Democratic Self-Government League. On the following day, the same organ carried the remarks of the late Li Chi-shen, then Chairman of the RCK, accusing the United States of aggression and warning the people on Taiwan that if they did not want "to be national criminals forever and come to the end of the road with the bandit Chiang, they should abandon the forces of darkness and submit themselves to the forces of light." Li Chun-ch'ing, then a vice chairman of the Taiwan Democratic Self-Government League, affirmed opposition to "the sale of Taiwan by the bandit Chiang." In the next three days, the CPC central organ published supporting interviews or articles of the following chairmen of the other minor parties: Chang Lan for the CDL, Huang Yen-p'ei for the China Democratic National Construction Association, Chang Po-chün for the Chinese Peasants and Workers Democratic Party, Ma Hsü-lun for the China Association for Promoting Democracy, Ch'en Ch'i-yu for the China Chih Kung Tang, and Hsü Teh-heng for the Chiu San Society. Like sirens

[31] Li Chi-shen was second Vice Chairman, Shen Chün-ju was fourth, Huang Yen-p'ei was sixth, Ch'en Shu-t'ung the ninth, Ch'eng Ch'ien twelfth, and Ho Hsiang-ning the fourteenth.

sounding one after another, the voices of the minor parties continue to be raised against United States and Nationalist forces on Taiwan. Thus Ch'en Shao-k'uan, 75 years old Vice Governor of Fukien province, and a former admiral under the KMT, who is second Vice Chairman of the RCK, addressed the first session of the Third National People's Congress on December 26, 1964. Chen again called upon all former and present KMT personnel to resist U.S. aggression and help liberate Taiwan.

By far the most important of the CPC's fellow-travellers from the former ranks of the KMT is Li Tsung-jen, Vice President of China under the Nationalist government and interim President between Chiang's flight to Taiwan and the proclamation of the People's Republic. Li Tsung-jen returned to the Mainland in July, 1965, having spent most of the intervening years in the United States. After confessing his "guilty past" and begging to be of service to the government, Li was warmly received by Mao Tse-tung himself, as well as other ranking members of the CPC. His praises of Communist China's accomplishments are added to those of the leaders of the minor parties.

In performing their division-of-labor functions, the minor parties often duplicate, both the organizational features and the membership indoctrination programs of the CPC. This both facilitates CPC control over the key positions in the minor party organizations and extends the Party's indoctrinal efforts to elements not as effectively reached by normal programs. Moreover, it conditions the noncommunist elements to the patterns of democratic centralism and hierarchial organization, thus making it easier for the same parties to vote themselves out of existence when the time comes. Many examples could be chosen, but the case of the China Democratic National Construction Association is representative. The China Democratic National Construction Association, formed by and for members of the "national bourgeoisie," must anticipate its curtailment and finally extinction in the process of socialist transition. *People's Daily* of October 9, 1954, reported an enlarged meeting of the party's Standing Committee under the chairmanship of Huang Yen-p'ei, to clarify policies for and the future of the national bourgeoisie. Here the party leaders were aroused to take the lead among industrial and commercial circles to win "an active acceptance of socialist transformation." The instructions issued by the party headquarters to local branches, summarized in *People's Daily* of October 31, show even more clearly the role of minor parties in preparing certain strata of the society to reconcile themselves to the sacrifices entailed in the CPC program:

Members should clearly understand that our country cannot proceed along the road of capitalism. Apart from the only correct route of socialism, there is no other outlet. Therefore the state should conduct the gradual socialist transformation of capitalist industry and commerce. . . . Private industrialists and merchants can only accept sincerely the socialist transformation. . . . If they dare to resist socialist transformation they would be despised by the people. . . .

The industrialists and merchants should develop a patriotic spirit, abide by the Constitution and laws. . . . In addition [they] should constantly be on the alert to shake off the selfishness characteristic of their class with its consequent negative effect on the national welfare . . . [they] should realize that only by sincerely following the Constitution and the laws [i.e., by accepting the program of socialist transformation] can they really show their genuine support of the CPC and Chairman Mao.

Instructions of this nature indicate that the China Democratic National Construction Association, like other minor parties, faces an ironic reality—organizational and operational effectivenesses mean ultimate extinction.

The division-of-labor role of the minor parties has not diminished, particularly since the CPC has need of the experts and intellectuals who constitute the membership of these organizations. In 1962, the CPPCC, meeting simultaneously with the National People's Congress in Peking, considered the "ten tasks" which Chou En-lai had recommended to the NPC for national economic adjustment. Each of the minor parties then held its own conference in Peking. Their agendas, in addition to the usual items of cooperation with the CPC and ideological reform of the members, called for the formulation of plans to realize Chou's "ten tasks." Thus, for example, the China Democratic National Construction Association pledged to help improve the managerial system—Chou's fifth point. The China Association for Promoting Democracy, the members of which are mostly teachers, established two consultative bodies to assist the government in language and mathematics programs for the primary and secondary schools—in support of Chou's eighth "task." The three intellectual parties, the China Democratic League, the Association for Promoting Democracy, and the Chiu San Society, together with the Chinese Peasants and Workers Democratic Party, were assigned the task of adjusting scientific techniques to aid agriculture, a work carried on among the overseas Chinese centers by the Chih Kung Tang. Thus, the specialized knowledge of the members of these organizations was once again employed advantageously by the CPC.

The authorized organization and the division-of-labor function of the minor parties dissipate and fragment potential opposition to the CPC and its programs. If the national bourgeoisie, for example, were to be accepted into the ranks of the Communist Party, their influence on the CPC could become strong to the point of altering and attenuating such programs as socialist transformation. On the other hand, if members of the national bourgeoisie were free to join intellectuals, labor leaders, rich peasants, or other elements disgruntled with the regime, instead of being confined to a single small party under the CPC control, they might become a threat to the regime. For avoiding these extremes, the multiplicity of non-communist parties provides and ideal solution.

Rectification and Remolding of the Non-Communist Parties

The most striking example of the CPC's effective manipulation of the non-communist parties to promote the general line is the role which the Party has assigned these organizations in the work of rectification and remolding. As witnessed during the 1957–1958 rectification campaign in the wake of the Blooming and Contending campaign (discussed more fully in the chapter on the cultural system), the minor parties represent a highly effective means to control the non-Party intelligentsia, as well as other groups.

Following the May, 1957 CPC Central Committee's persuasive invitation to the "democratic" parties to aid the CPC in its work of rectification, the leaders of the minor parties quickly transformed their initial lethargy and hesitation into a spirit of genuine and enthusiastic cooperation. At a series of forums sponsored by the CC's United Front Work Department these leaders criticized and denounced CPC policies and practices. Chang Po-chün, then Vice Chairman of the China Democratic League and Minister of Communications,[32] called for a limitation to the CPC's monopoly of power. He particularly attacked the united front policies which had reduced the minor parties to a decorative role. Ch'en Ming-shu, then a member of the Standing Committee of the KMT Revolutionary Committee, requested that the CPC abrogate its dominance of educational institutions. Chang Nai-ch'i, then Vice Chairman of the China Democratic National Construction Association,[33] criticized the CPC's sectarianism, doctrinairism and negative attitude toward the bourgeoisie. Lung Yün, who was then a Vice Chairman of the National Defense Council and of the KMT Revolutionary Committee, attacked the Soviet Union for forcing China to bear the costs of the Korean War and to accept unreasonable repayment terms. Other leaders voiced stern criticism of Party policies concerning ideological remolding, secret arrests, failures to enact criminal codes and other major deficiencies. They demanded a sharper demarcation between the powers and functions of the Party (CPC) and State and additional rights for non-Party individuals.

[32] Chang Po-chün remains a member of the Standing Committee of the Third Central Committee of the CDL, but is no longer a Vice Chairman.

[33] Chang Nai-ch'i was also removed from the CPPCC in March, 1963.

These Party-sponsored forums of the Blooming and Contending period provided an opportunity for the CPC to uncover and measure the opposition of the non-communist leadership. The CPC first answered these rebukes in a series of articles which appeared in *People's Daily* beginning in June, 1957. The Party advocated a national rectification drive based on a unity-criticism-unity formula. At the CPC's behest, the various minor parties then launched their own rectification campaigns.[34] The CPC attached considerable importance to these campaigns. As Lu Ting-yi reminded the delegates to the Fourth Session of the First National People's Congress in a speech published in the September 17, 1957 *People's Daily:*

> The struggle with the rightist factions is a struggle between two roads. It is a struggle concerning the life and death of the country and the nation. To reject socialism, to reject proletarian leadership, to reject people's democratic dictatorship and democratic centralism, to reject the alliance with the Soviet Union, the only resort would be the destruction of the country. The rightist programs are intended to ruin our country and to cut off our heads and lay them on the ground.

The bitter revelations of the Hundred Flowers campaign demonstrated the intelligentsia's continued hostility to the CPC and dictated the need for purges within the minor parties. By initiating these purges, the CPC could ensure the future docility of these appendages and provide an indication to the masses that no ideological deviations would be tolerated. For these reasons, the alleged crimes of the rightist elements within the "democratic" parties were given wide circulation. The case of the Revolutionary Committee of the KMT is representative. In a September, 1957 speech, Li Chi-shen denounced Lung Yün for his traitorous attempt to regain his Yunnan kingdom. Ch'eng Min-shu was accused of organizing a reactionary force and publicly denouncing Mao. Huang Shao-hsiung was said to have negated CPC leadership by exaggerating the testimony of hostile witnesses while minimizing Party achievements. The same pattern was followed in the China Democratic League. For example, Chang Po-chün was accused of slandering Party (CPC) leadership by statements that five hundred million Chinese were slaves, eight million were puritans and one was god. Lo Lung-chi was denounced for stating that a principal contradiction of the intelligentsia was that between the higher intellectuals of the petty

---

[34] Decisions to engage in the new rectification drive were made by the minor parties at the following meetings: Kuomintang Revolutionary Committee at the 14th Session of its Standing Committee on July 6; China Democratic League at the final session of its Central Standing Committee on June 18; China Democratic National Construction Association at the 39th session of its Central Standing Committee on June 23; China Peasants and Workers Democratic Party at the 29th session of its Central Executive Bureau on June 19; China Chih Kung Tang at the enlarged session of the Standing Committee on June 8; Chiu San Society at the 17th session of its Standing Committee on June 28.

bourgeoisie and the lower intellectuals of the proletariat. In a September 13, 1957 report to the CDL, Shih Liang declared that Chang Po-chün and Lo Lung-chi were guilty of forming a rightist clique.

The minor parties themselves contributed to this list of "criminals" by labelling members as rightists. For example, the China Democratic National Construction Association and the All China Industrial and Commercial Association branded Chang Nai-ch'i a reactionary for his opposition to the leadership of the proletariat and the CPC and for his declaration that there is no basic distinction between the bourgeoisie and the proletariat. The Taiwan Democratic Self-Government League accused its Chairman, Hsieh Hsüeh-hung, of slandering CPC leadership and showing rightist partiality in united front activities.

Following these disclosures of ideological deviation on the part of leaders of the minor parties, the rectification entered a new phase with the at least temporary removal of these people from positions of supposed trust and authority. At the nineteenth session of its Standing Committee in January, 1958, the KMT Revolutionary Committee voted to remove the following: Lung Yün as Vice Chairman; Ch'en Ming-shu from membership in the Standing Committee and chairmanship of the Ideology and Policy Research Committee; and Huang Shao-hsiung from membership in the Standing Committee and vice chairmanship of the Peaceful Liberation of Taiwan Working Committee. Other members of the Standing Committee, including the vice chairman of the Woman's Committee, T'an T'i-wu, and the vice director of the Organization Department, Li Chen-lun, were also purged. The Standing Committee of the China Democratic League took similar action at its seventeenth enlarged session on January 25, 1958. Chang Po-chün and Lo Lung-chi surrendered their posts as vice chairmen and members of the Central Committee and that body's Standing Committee. Huang Ch'i-hsiang and Ch'ien Wei-ch'ang were also removed from the Central Committee. Yeh Tu-yi, Shen Chih-yuan and Tseng Chao-lun were purged from the Higher Educational Research Committee of which they were vice chairmen. Fei Hsiao-t'ung was removed as director of the CC Education Department, and Yüeh Mien as director of the CC Propaganda Department. Ch'u An-p'ing was purged from editorship of the League organ, *Kuangming Daily*, and P'an Kuang-tan surrendered his post as deputy director of the CC Liason Committee.

The other minor parties conducted their own purges. The China Democratic National Construction Association removed its CC Vice Chairman, Chang Nai-ch'i, and Pi Ming-chih, who was a member of the CC Standing Committee. The China Association for Promoting Democracy purged Vice Chairman Lin Han-ta and several others at its second enlarged plenum of the Fourth CC, meeting in January, 1958. The China Peasants and

Workers Democratic Party, conducting its sixth enlarged plenum of its sixth CC, in the same month removed Chang Po-chün as CC chairman and Huang Ch'i-hsiang as CC Vice Chairman and Secretary-General. This party also purged Li Po-ch'iu from his post as deputy secretary-general, Yang Yi-t'ang as deputy director of the CC Organization Department, and several members of the Central Executive Bureau. At its third plenum of the Fourth Central Committee, the Chiu San Society took similar action: Ku Chih-chung was deprived of all offices and Lu K'an-wu and Tung Wei-ch'uan of their membership in the CC and its Standing Committee. Tung was also removed from his post as vice chairman of the CC's Scientific, Cultural and Education Committee, as was his vice-chairman, Yüan Han-ch'in. The Taiwan Democratic Self-Government League voted, at its representative conference held in Peking in the same month, to expel Hsieh Hsüeh-hung as League chairman.[35]

The minor parties followed their purges by new affirmations of their intention to eliminate all rightism within their ranks. In March, 1958, ten thousand members of the non-communist parties gathered to demonstrate their fidelity to socialist construction and adopt a "charter for socialist self-re-education" which pledged support to Mao Tse-tung. The leaders announced their ambition to "dedicate their hearts to the Communist Party." It should be noted that these efforts were deemed at least partially successful. In December, 1958, for example, Lung Yün was elected to the Standing Committee of the KMT Revolutionary Committee and Chang Po-chün to the Standing Committee of the China Democratic League's Central Committee.

The work of rectification and remolding within the ranks of the appendant parties, however, is a continuous task for the CPC leadership. In 1956 the Party opened its College of Socialism in Peking for the re-education of members of the democratic parties and non-Party democrats. As its vice-president, Nieh Chen, reported in the *Kuangming Daily* of January 5, 1961, the college had already graduated 305 and had an enrollment of 341. Re-education within the minority parties themselves is conducted by bi-weekly forums under the sponsorship of the CPC CC's United Front Work Department. At the same time, the CPC has encouraged the so-called "meetings of immortals" within the minor parties. Described in the *Kuangming Daily* of January 3, 1961, these sessions are intended to convince the bourgeois intelligentsia of the correctness of Mao's thought, particularly as concerns the "united front policy of unity, education and transformation."

The future of the non-communist parties in China is not difficult to fore-

[35] The CPPCC National Committee took similar action at its fiftieth meeting in March, 1958. Chang Po-chün was removed as Vice Chairman and Chang Nai-ch'i, Chou Ching-wen and seven other rightists from membership in the Standing Committee.

see. The CPC has hinted that, when the construction of socialism is completed, these parties of the "new democratic" era will have outlived their usefulness. For the present, however, the CPC finds it advantageous to maintain its united front facade. The 1956 CPC Constitution thus pledged to "strengthen its lasting cooperation with the other democratic parties as well as democrats without party affiliations." But Mao issued a warning in February, 1957. "Whether these democratic parties can long exist," he noted, "depends not merely on what the Communist Party itself desires, but also on the part played by these democratic parties themselves and whether they enjoy the confidence of the people." In reality, the survival of the "democratic" parties is contingent upon their subservience and usefulness to the CPC. The revelations of the Hundred Flowers period almost doomed the minor parties: subsequent rectification, on the other hand, prolonged their existence, at least for a time. Yet another portent of the extinction of the democratic parties is contained in the current "cultural revolution" to eliminate the last vestiges of the bourgeoisie. Foreign sources in Peking noted that, on August 24, 1966, members of the Red Guards demanded that the non-communist parties disband within 72 hours. Although the CPC has apparently ordered no follow-up of this ultimatium, the call of the Red Guards does reflect the Party's long-range thinking. As the CPC continues to consolidate its construction of socialism, and as the leaders of the minor parties die without proper heirs, inevitably the role of the non-communist parties will be reduced, and finally extinguished.

THE INTERLOCKING PARTY–STATE RELATIONSHIP

The Mediating and Controlling Position of the Party

Despite the existence of other parties, the CPC remains the true ruling group in China. To understand its place in the society as a whole, it can best be viewed as one member of the trinity often referred to in communist literature—Party, state and masses. The political theory of liberal democracy, of course, has customarily been preoccupied with only the last two members of this trinity, variously referred to as "state" and "society" or "government" and the "body politic." The superficial resemblance of these two elements of liberal theory, to the "state" and "masses" of communist theory serve to point up the novel and distinctive role played by the other triune member—the Party.

Under a communist regime, the Party stands as a mediating and controlling element between the two realms of "state" and "masses." Party members hold key positions in all the major "private" social institutions—the trade unions, farm organizations, professional societies and other associations in which men gather to enhance some common interest. The Party fraction within each association serves as a particularly active element in determining the policy and conduct of the whole group. On the other hand, Party members also fill the key positions in government, and Party fractions within each administrative section and at every level ensure that state decisions serve the Party interests. Hence the tradition liberal separation between "state" and "society"—between the authoritative and compulsory interventions of government and the private and voluntaristic activities of men in associations—is broken down in a communist regime. The Party stands, so to speak, outside both realms and exerts a directing and controlling influence over each.

A study of the role of the Communist Party as a ruling group, therefore, must be pursued in two directions: one leads out from the Party into all the interest-group associations of the "masses" and illustrates how the Party works through these associations to further its own goals; the other leads in from the Party to all governmental agencies and makes the sovereign government an instrumentality for advancing Party policies and programs.

The "Mass Line" of the Party

The Party's penetration into the associations and activities of the public at large (which is more properly a Party monopolizing of the organization and furtherance of these activities) is referred to in communist literature as the "mass line" of the Party. The theoretical formulations and the implementation of this mass-line policy are discussed in the chapter on the social system. Here it may be pointed out, however, that the CPC has formed a number of "mass organizations" to foster this policy and has seen to it that trusted Party members hold positions of leadership within them. These associations unite people along different lines—some on the basis of the type of work, others according to age, sex, intellectual interests, or support of some professed humanitarian cause. Concrete examples of these categories are the All-China Federation of Trade Unions, the All-China Students' Federation, the All-China Federation of Democratic Women, the All-China Federation of Literary and Art Circles and the Resist-America Aid-Korea movement.

Though there may be special pressures or inducements to join such organizations, the individual is for the most part free to join or not, but under a totalitarian system he is not free to join the organization of his choice. Individual membership is circumscribed by approval and needs of the communist leadership. Consequently, freedom of association is abridged and the supposedly "voluntary" associations take on a compulsory character. More importantly, under the principles of democratic centralism these associations can be controlled effectively by a small inner and self-perpetuating group of leaders. Earlier, the Party loaned even senior officials to this work. For example, Liu Shao-ch'i headed the Sino-Soviet Friendship Association and several members and alternates of the Central Committee (Lin Piao, Ulanfu, Liao Ch'eng-chih, Liu Ning-i, Wu Yü-chang and Saifudin) served as vice chairmen until 1954.[36] The All-China Federation of Democratic Women is headed by Ts'ai Ch'ang, a member of the Party Central Committee in her own right and the wife of another CC member, Li Fu-ch'un.

By controlling these so-called mass organizations and movements, then, the CPC is able to extend its direct leadership over many tens of millions of people representing every facet of society, and to mobilize them at will for its constant stream of political and ideological campaigns. Officially the communist ideology calls upon the Party to do everything for the masses, to assume full responsibility for them, to learn from them, and to have "faith in the people's self-emancipation;" in actuality the mass line is an effective means to keep the masses subservient to the will of the communist leadership.

The Interlocking Relationship between Party and Government

In the same fashion, the assignment of Party functionaries to positions of official responsibility in the government system gives the Party a means for effectively controlling the state apparatus. It is not the governmental hierarchy, then, but the Party which, in Stalin's words, "is the core of political power." Tung Pi-wu, a member of the CPC Politburo, has elaborated on this view: the CPC, in leading the revolution, seizing power, and establishing the people's democratic dictatorship, "has become the directing party of the state organs." He further set forth three principles for defining the correct relationship between the Party and the state organs: (1) the Party issues specific directives to the state as to the nature and orientation of its work; (2) the Party carries out its policies through the state and its apparatus, and oversees its activities; and (3) the Party selects and promotes loyal and competent Party and non-Party cadres to work in the state organizations.

The extent of the Party control of the state apparatus through these in-

[36] Under the state reorganization involved in ratification of the 1954 Constitution, Liu Shao-ch'i was relieved of this post and Soong Ching Ling (Sun Yat-sen's widow) assumed the chairmanship. This change of personnel also extended to the roster of vice chairmen.

terlocking arrangements is indicated by the impressive and bewildering variety of governmental positions held by top Party leaders. Mao Tse-tung, chairman of the CPC Central Committee and its Political Bureau, until April 27, 1959, served concurrently as the Chairman of the Chinese People's Republic, the highest state office. At the same time Mao was Chairman of the Supreme State Conference (the highest body for co-ordinating the various branches of the government), and the National Defense Council (the state's highest organ of military command, formerly called the People's Revolutionary Military Council). Prior to September, 1954, Mao also headed the Central People Government Council (the CPGC), as well as the National Committee of the Chinese People's Political Consultative Conference (the CPPCC) (these organs are described in the next chapter).[37]

The vice chairmen of the CPC Central Committee and its Politburo hold equivalently high posts in the state machinery. Liu Shao-ch'i formerly ranked second on the Party hierarchy, served as Vice Chairman of the original Central People's Government Council, and became the Chairman of its nearest counterpart under the 1954 State Constitution, the Standing Committee of the National People's Congress. Elected to succeed Mao as Chairman of the CPR, on April 27, 1959, Liu became ex-officio Chairman of the Supreme State Conference and the National Defense Council. Prior to September, 1954, with Chu Teh, Chou En-lai and Kao Kang, Liu also served as a Vice Chairman of the People's Revolutionary Military Council.

Chou En-lai, number three leader of the Party, who has been Premier of the People's Republic since its founding, served concurrently as Foreign Minister until February, 1958. Prior to the adoption of the 1954 State Constitution he was Premier of the Government Administration Council and Vice Chairman of the CPPCC. After the constitutional reorganization Chou was given the official title of Premier of the State Council and Chairman of the CPPCC. Chu Teh was made in 1954 the then sole Vice Chairman of the People's Republic under Mao. On April 27, 1959, Chu was elected Chairman of the Standing Committee of the NPC to succeed Liu. He is also a former Vice Chairman of both the PRMC and the CPGC. Ch'en Yün was the first of the State Council's sixteen vice premiers until his assignment to the second position in January, 1965, behind Lin Piao. Since 1958 Ch'en has also served as Chairman of the Committee of National Basic Construction. Formerly he was one of the five Vice Premiers in the Government Administration Council and Chairman of its Committee on Financial and Economic Affairs.

Lin Piao, Mao Tse-tung's new heir apparent, now holds the offices of first Vice Premier, Minister of National Defense and First Vice Chairman

[37] Mao Tse-tung retains the title of honorary Chairman of the CPR and the CPPCC.

of the NDC. Teng Hsiao-p'ing, the Central Committee's General Secretary, who served on the Standing Committee of the Politburo along with the CC Chairman and Vice Chairmen, was ranked as fifth Vice Chairman of the NDC and Third Vice Premier of the State Council.

Other members of the CPC Politburo also hold ranking positions in the state. For example, prior to his death in June, 1960, Lin Tsu-han held the posts of CPGC Secretary General and Vice Chairman of the NPC Standing Committee. Tung Pi-wu, who formerly was a Vice Premier and Chairman of the GAC's Committee on Political and Legal Affairs, under the constitutional reorganization of 1954 served for a time as President of the Supreme People's Court and has been the second of the two vice chairmen of the CPR since April 27, 1959. P'eng Chen, a former member of the GAC and Vice Chairman of its Political and Legal Affairs Committee, in January, 1965, was promoted from seventh to first place as Vice Chairman of the NPC Standing Committee and first Vice Chairman of the CPPCC, and therefore relieved of his duties as the former organ's Secretary General. Both prior to and after the Constitutional changes of 1954 he had served as mayor of Peking, until his purge in the early summer of 1966.

The same interlocking placement pattern holds for the other members of the Central Committee. Prior to the 1954 reorganization, twenty-one members and two alternates were concurrently members of the Central People's Government Council. In its nearest successor, the Standing Committee of the NPC, ten of the eighteen Vice Chairmen are members of the Central Committee (counting the three regular and one alternate Politburo members), and one is an alternate member of the CC. Of the ninety-six other members of the NPC Standing Committee, fourteen are regular and eleven are alternate members of the Central Committee.

The State Council's sixteen Vice Premiers named at the first session of the Third NPC in January, 1965, are all full members of the CC and include ten regular and two alternate Politburo members. Two are Vice Chairmen of the CC and the Politburo and one is the CC's General Secretary. Before the 1954 changes, the other members of the GAC included five members and one former member of the CC. The Ministers and Chairmen of Commissions under the State Council include twenty four regular or alternate CC members (including a CC Vice Chairman and five regular and two alternate members of the Political Bureau). These Party leaders head the ministries of Internal Affairs, Foreign Affairs, National Defense, Public Security, Finance, Commerce, Foreign Trade, State Farms and Land Reclamation, Labor, Culture, Coal, and the Third, Fourth and Eighth Ministries of Machine-Building. State Commissions headed by the above-mentioned CPC leaders include those of State Planning, National Economics, Physical

Culture and Sports, Nationality Affairs, Overseas Chinese Affairs, Economic Relations with Foreign Countries, and Scientific and Technological.[38]

In addition, three regular and one alternate Politburo members and two Central Committeemen also serve as directors of the six offices of the State Council: Political and Legal Affairs, Foreign Affairs, Finance and Trade, Industry and Communications, Agriculture and Forestry, and Culture and Education.

This pattern of relationships at the central level was at first recapitulated at lower levels. A Politburo member and several leading Central Committeemen, who served as chairmen of interprovincial, regional or branch bureaus of the CC, served also as chairmen of the Greater Administrative Areas before the latter divisions were eliminated. Other Central Committeemen and alternates served concurrently as vice chairmen of these areas. Prior to the election of provincial governors in 1954–55, provincial Party secretaries were concurrently provincial governors in Fukien, Chekiang, Hupeh, Shansi, Shantung, Ninghsia and Kwangsi and vice governors in Kansu and Tsinghai. In other provinces the vice secretary of the provincial CPC committee served concurrently as governor. This was also true of the municipal level. In Shanghai, Wuhan, Canton and other cities, secretaries of the Party committee or bureau also served as mayors. In fact, similar relationships were found at the provincial, city, county and rural and urban district levels.

This overly close parallelism in interlocking offices between Party and state functionaries which marked the first years of Chinese Communist rule may have been partially due to the lack of trusted and able personnel and to the needs for immediate and direct action. The danger of an abuse of power was clearly revealed by the tendencies toward bureaucratism and regionalism reflected in the Kao-Jao episode. Shortly after the abolition of the CC regional bureau and greater administrative areas, the CPC began eliminating many of the Party-state "double-hats" in the provinces. Thus Party First Secretary T'ao Chu relinquished his governorship of Kwangtung in July, 1957.[39] In Hopei, First Secretary Lin T'ieh surrendered his post as governor in April, 1958, as did Oyang Ch'ing in Heilungking in September, 1958, and Yeh Fei in Fukien in February, 1959.

By comparing the top Party and state functionaries on the eve of the

---

[38] Since the intensification of the cultural revolution, several ministers and heads of commissions have been subjected to attack and may have been removed.

[39] In addition to his duties as CPC first secretary of Kwangtung province, T'ao also served as First Secretary of the Central-South Bureau. His star rose rapidly in 1966, as a result of his role in the cultural revolution. However, he apparently fell into disfavor, and was obliged to relinquish several of his posts, including that of Director of the CPC CC's Propaganda Department.

"cultural revolution" for the autonomous regions and provinces, and ascertaining their relationship to the CPC Central Committee, certain patterns become evident. In the autonomous regions of Inner Mongolia, Kwangsi Chuang and Ninghsia Hui, the Party first secretary still doubles as chairman. The first-named is a member of the Central Committee and alternate member of the Politburo; the second is a CC alternate; and the third does not belong to either central organ. In the Sinkiang Uigur region, the governor is CPC second secretary and a CC alternate; the first secretary is a regular member of the Central Committee. With the formal establishment of the Tibet Autonomous Region in September, 1965, Ngapo Ngawang Jigme was named as chairman, while Chang Kuo-hua continued as first secretary. Neither is a member of the Central Committee. In terms of provincial leadership, twelve of the Party first secretaries were alternate members and three were full members of the Central Committee. One of the governors was a full member and three were alternates of the CC. This pattern would indicate that the division between Party and state offices at the provincial level, and the high proportion of Party first secretaries who were also CC members is meant to promote Party centralization. Relieved of their civil functions, the Party first secretaries could give singleminded attention to CPC affairs, which include supervision, control and policy-making for their equivalent state officials.

Party control of the state machinery naturally extends to the military arm. In its early years, the CPC sought to build up its own military leadership, especially after its gradual transformation under Mao Tse-tung into a militant Party based on armed strength. In more recent years, it has furnished the leadership for the armed forces. The first session of the Third National People's Congress in January, 1965, confirmed Lin Piao as Minister of Defense and the following as Vice Chairman of the NDC: Liu Po-ch'eng, Ho Lung, Chen Yi, Teng Hsiao-p'ing, Hsü Hsiang-ch'ien, Nieh Jung-chen, Yeh Chien-ying, Lo Jui-ch'ing, Cheng Ch'ien, Chang Chih-chung, Fu Tso-yi and Ts'ai T'ing-kai. The first five named are full members of the CPC Politburo. Hsü, Nieh, Yeh and Lo are full members of the Central Committee. Of the 107 ordinary members of the National Defense Council named at the January, 1965 session, seventeen are full and twenty-one are alternate members of the Central Committee, one (Li Hsien-nien) is also a member of the Politburo.

At the general staff level, the PLA's former chief of staff, Lo Jui-ch'ing, was also a member of the CC. At the command level, practically all the military commanders, commissars, and vice commanders of the various field armies of the PLA, as well as of various military areas throughout the country, are Party leaders of corresponding importance. Similarly, members and cadres of the CPC and YCL form the core of the various military units. Thus the Party is thoroughly integrated with the military forces it has created and nutured.

Through this interlocking relationship between the Party, the mass organizations, and the state apparatus, the men and women of the CPC occupy or otherwise control the key positions in all the manifold activities of China's political, social and economic life. Standing midway between the government and the public, and containing within its own ranks the leading and influential elements from both spheres, the Party can thus extend its control over every segment of society, while avoiding the onus of compulsory or coercive state regulation. By extensive integration and close supervision of personnel in the parallel heirarchies of Party and state, the CPC can reach into the councils and agencies of government to ensure that all decisions forward communist aims and policies. Thus the Communist Party of China dictates every condition of human or national existence.

CULTURAL REVOLUTION AND PARTY REGENERATION

For the CPC, the cultural revolution probably has represented an unprecedented opportunity to utilize the aid of surging masses in carrying out a thorough inner reform of the membership, from lowest to highest levels, once more preparing for the urgent work ahead of combatting the threats of "revisionism, imperialism and all reactionaries" to Marxism-Leninism, thus strengthening the international communist movement. At the same time, the nature of the cultural revolution indicates that, if successful, Party norms and ideals would in turn, permeate to the masses. Having cleansed or rid the country of dissident elements, and solidified its own membership, the CPC could most nearly achieve the Marxist-Leninist dream and fulfill the vision of Mao Tse-tung. However, the disclosures of the cultural revolution, such as the attacks of the Red Guards, also proved to the Party the scope and depth of its opposition. As propagandistic struggles have exploded into violence, even to the brink of civil war, the CPC has realized that it might fully employ all means to restore order and retain its authority. The assistance of the military and the Red Guards have been discussed elsewhere in these pages. Here it remains to analyze the Party's own efforts to discipline its members.

The CPC's Peking Municipal Committee illustrates at once how far the Party will go to rectify conditions disclosed by the cultural revolution and how deeply rooted is the resistance. The first major event of the cultural revolution was the Central Committee's announcement, on June 3, 1966, that the Peking Committee was to be completely reorganized to eliminate anti-Party and anti-socialist personnel. At that time, Li Hsüeh-feng, First Secretary of the North China Bureau, was concurrently appointed First

Secretary of the Peking Committee while Wu Teh, First Secretary of the Kirin Provincial Committee, was transferred as Second Secretary to the Peking Committee. The CC's action in reducing P'eng Chen and his coworkers was heralded throughout the nation as a great victory for the thought of Mao and a warning to those who might oppose Mao. As *People's Daily* put it in a June 4, 1966 editorial: "No one who dares to oppose Chairman Mao . . . can escape denunciation by the whole Party and the whole nation, whoever he may be, whatever high position he may hold and however much of a veteran he may be."

Between June, 1966, and January, 1967, little was heard of the Peking Committee in the press:[40] presumably, Li Hsüeh-feng, Wu Teh and their associates were carrying out the cultural revolution in the capital. Such an assumption was rudely shattered by the decision of the CPC Central Committee and State Council of February 12, 1967, to rush in PLA troops to seize control of the city's internal security forces. Thus, the city's internal security came under the personal direction of Hsieh Fu-chih. Hsieh, in addition to his membership in the CPC Politburo, is a Vice Premier of the State Council, a member of the NDC, Minister of Public Security, and commander and political commissar of the PLA's security forces. His mission in Peking pointed out the failure of the reorgnized municipal committee and the growing authority of the PLA.

On April 20, 1967, amid much fanfare, and with the "solicitous concern of Chairman Mao," the Peking Municipal Revolutionary Committee was created by order of the Party Central Committee as a provisional organ of the "three in one" alliance. Hsieh Fu-chih was appointed Chairman, and Wu Teh, Cheng Wei-san, Fu Chung-pi and Nieh Yuan-tzu as Vice Chairmen.[41] This second reorganization of the Party structure in Peking emphasizes the fact that the June, 1966 action did not eliminate the counterrevolutionary forces. Instead, in the words of the April 22, 1967 *People's Daily*, the Committee directed by Li Hsüeh-feng "completely failed to live up to the trust of Chairman Mao and the Party Central Committee . . . [and] faithfully implemented the bourgeois reactionary line put forth by the top Party person in authority taking the capitalist road."[42] Hsieh Fu-chih

[40] By January, Red Guard organs were denouncing minor officials in the Peking Committee for their failure to wage the cultural revolution. For example, the January 11, 1967 *Ching-kangshan* accused Yung Wen-t'ao, a secretary, of being "T'ao Chu's favorite disciple" and Liu Chien-hsün, another secretary, of similar counterrevolutionary crimes. Yung, formerly First Secretary of the Canton Municipal Committee, and Liu, former First Secretary of the Honan Provincial Committee, had been brought to Peking in the June, 1966 reorganization.

[41] While Fu Chung-pi and Nieh Yuan-tzu were virtually unknown minor officials, it is significant that Cheng Wei-san is deputy commander of the PLA's Peking Military Region.

[42] Some notion of the internal struggle in the Peking committee can be gained from Hsieh Fu-chih's speech at the April 20, 1967 rally. Alluding to the fact that the great majority of

saluted the assistance of the Red Guards in bringing to light the "big traitors' clique within our Party" in his remarks on the establishment of the new Peking Revolutionary Committee. Thus, the action of April 20 may be considered as another victory of the Red Guards and the PLA. But it also illustrates the failure of normal Party processes for organization and rectification. Although, as noted previously, the Party Constitution provides for the replacement of whole committees, the necessity at higher levels seldom arose before the cultural revolution. But the reorganizations of June, 1966 and April, 1967 also show the determination of Mao and his followers to spare no effort to carry out their plans.

As the attacks on Liu Shao-ch'i, Teng Hsiao-p'ing, and later T'ao Chu, have shown, the CPC has been forced to deal with conspirators who formerly occupied some of the most powerful posts in the Party. Able to appoint and protect cadres sympathetic to their own line, these officials collectively represent the greatest challenge to Mao's direction and the most serious threat to the solidarity that must characterize the CPC if it is to carry out its appointed tasks. Thus, the revelations of the cultural revolution have occasioned a massive purge, different, however, both in nature and in kind from the worst excesses of the Stalinist regime. Although all organs of the Party have been affected, two might be used as representative—the Secretariat and the Regional CC Bureaus.

The composition of the CPC's Secretariat, perhaps more than any other Party organ, has been subjected to the storms of the cultural revolution. Under the direction of Teng Hsiao-p'ing, its membership prior to the cultural revolution was as follows: Full members; P'eng Chen, Wang Chia-hsiang, T'an Chen-lin, Li Hsüeh-feng. Li Fu-ch'un, Li Hsien-nien, Lu Ting-yi, K'ang Sheng and Lo Jui-ch'ing; Alternates Members; Liu Lan-t'ao, Yang Shang-k'un and Hu Ch'iao-mu. Of the full members, only T'an Chen-lin, [43] Li Fu-ch'un, Li Hsien-nien and K'ang Sheng have escaped purge; Li Fu-ch'un and K'ang Sheng have been promoted to the Politburo Standing Committee. T'ao Chu, Liu Ning-i and Yeh Chien-ying were appointed to the Secretariat early in the cultural revolution. While T'ao has become a purge victim, Yeh Chien-ying has been promoted to membership in the Politburo. Alternate member Yang Shang-k'un, who was also director of the CC's General Office, has apparently been purged. The Red Guard journal *Mao Tse-tung Chu-i Chan-tou Pao* (No. 2, February 23,

---

cadres in Peking had been found good or comparatively good, Hsieh added: "Many of them, such as Wu Teh, Liu Chien-hsün, and other comrades, have begun to stand on the side of the proletarian revolutionaries."

[43] T'an Chen-lin was under attack by the Red Guards, who demanded his appearance at a mass rally against him, according to a Tokyo dispatch, dated May 26, 1967, appearing in the Hong Kong *Ming Pao* the following day.

1967) termed Yang one of the arch traitors of the P'eng Chen group. Alternate member Hu Ch'iao-mu, who was also the CC Propaganda Department's deputy director for administrative affairs, has been bitterly denounced for his adherence to the Liu-Teng line. Hu has been purged for his resistance to Mao's authority (see Chapter 10). These major changes in the composition of the Secretariat, as well as the fact that no one has been identified as its Secretary-General, illustrate both the instability of this functional organ and its inability to carry out the tasks assigned.

Among the First Secretaries of the CPC Central Committee's regional bureaus, T'ao Chu was transferred from the Central-South Bureau in June, 1966, and apparently purged from all Party posts by early 1967. His successor in the Central-South Bureau, Wang Jen-chung, was bitterly denounced for his association with T'ao, and may also have been relieved of his Party offices. It is certain that Li Hsüeh-feng, formerly head of the North China Bureau, has been purged for his failures to conduct the cultural revolution properly as head of the Peking Municipal Committee. Other Bureau First Secretaries have apparently escaped any violent denunciation, yet their earlier close working relationship with Teng Hsiao-p'ing may be regarded suspiciously.

The shake-up of the CPC Secretariat and the purges in the regional Bureaus point to the fact that the composition of the Party Central Committee itself has undergone drastic change in an attempt to stamp out factionalism, or any threat to the leadership of Mao and Lin Piao. This can be illustrated in the following table:

TABLE II

SECOND ECHELON OF CPC LEADERSHIP: SELECTED FULL
MEMBERS OF THE PARTY'S EIGHTH CENTRAL
COMMITTEE*

Name	Date of Birth	Education	Prominence in Cultural Revolution
An Tzu-wen	1905?	University	None
Chang Chi-ch'un	1899	?	An associate of T'ao Chu; purged
Chang Ting-ch'eng	1897	?	Present at Red Guard and May Day, 1967 rallies
Chang Yün-i	1892	Military Academy	Member NDC; present at 1966 Red Guard rallies
Chao Erh-lu	1905?	Middle School	Died January, 1967
Ch'en Shao-min†	1905	No Formal Ed.	Present at May Day, 1967 rally
Ch'en Shao-yü	1905	University	Holds no offices; probably purged prior to the cultural revolution

TABLE II (*Continued*)

Name	Date of Birth	Education	Prominence in Cultural Revolution
Ch'en Yü	1902	?	A former associate of T'ao Chu; purged
Ch'eng Tzu-hua	1904	Normal School	Member of NDC
Cheng Wei-san	1895	University	Has held no important offices for several years
Chia T'o-fu	1911	Normal School	Has held no important offices for several years; probably purged prior to the cultural revolution
Ch'ien Ying†	?	?	Present at 1966 Red Guard rallies
Hsi Chung-hsün	1912	Middle School	Dismissed from state offices in 1963; attacked as Liu supporter
Hsiao Ching-kuang	1904	University	Vice Minister, NDM; Commander of PLA Naval Headquarters; present at May Day, 1967 rally
Hsiao Hua	1915	?	Director, PLA General Political Dept.; Member, CPC CC Cultural Revolution Group; First Deputy Head, PLA Cultural Revolution Group
Hsiao K'o	1910?	Military Academy	Member, NDC; probably Director of PLA Military Training Subdepartment
Hsü Hai-tung	1899	Trade School	Present at 1966 Red Guard rallies
Hsü Kuang-ta	1901	Military Academy	Vice Minister, NDM; reported purged
Hsü T'e-li	1877	Normal School	Reported in ill health
Hu Ch'iao-mu	1905	University	Purged
Hu Yao-pang	?	?	Reported purged
Huang K'o-ch'eng	1899	Military Academy	Purged
Li Li-san	1896	Middle School	None
Li Pao-hua	?	?	PLA Commissar, Anhwei Military District; CPC First Sec., Anhwei Provincial Comm.
Li Wei-han	1897	College ?	Removed from important state offices prior to the cultural revolution
Liao Ch'eng-chih	1908	University	Denounced by Red Guards, but present at May Day, 1967 rally

TABLE II (*Continued*)

Name	Date of Birth	Education	Prominence in Cultural Revolution
Lin Feng	?	?	Identified as Liu supporter; probably purged
Lin T'ieh	1904	Agric. Institute	CPC First Sec. and PLA Commissar, Hopeh province
Liu Ch'ang-sheng	1904	Apprenticeship	Died January, 1967
Liu Hsiao	1907	University	Present at 1966 Red Guard rallies
Liu K'o-p'ing	?	?	Leader of "3 in 1" revolutionary comm., Shansi province
Liu Lan-t'ao	1904	University	Identified as Liu supporter by Red Guards
Liu Ning-i	1905	Primary School ?	Promoted to CPC Secretariat, 1967; prominent at Red Guard rallies; on rostrum for May Day, 1967 rally
Lo Jui-ch'ing	1906	University	Purged
Lü Cheng-ts'ao	1906?	Military Academy	Member, NDC; attended 1966 Red Guard rallies; fired as Minister of Railways in 1967; probably purged
Ma Ming-fang	1904	Normal School	None
Oyang Ch'ing	1899	?	As former CPC provincial First Sec. and PLA Commissar, bypassed when "3 in 1" comm. established in Heilungkiang
Shu T'ung	1906	Normal School	None
Su Yü	1909	Normal School	Vice Minister, NDM; attended 1966 Red Guard rallies; on rostrum for May Day, 1967 rally
Sung Jen-ch'iung	1904	Military Academy	Member, NDC; CPC First Sec., Northeast China Bureau
T'an Cheng	1903	?	Purged
Teng Hua	1900	Primary School	Held no important offices prior to the cultural revolution
T'eng Tai-yüan	1899	Normal School ?	Member, NDC
Teng Tzu-hui	1893	Middle School	Retired from state offices in 1965; attended 1966 Red Guard and 1967 May Day rallies
Teng Ying-ch'ao†	1903	Normal School	Chou En-lai's wife; attended 1966 Red Guard and 1967 May Day rallies

TABLE II (*Continued*)

Name	Date of Birth	Education	Prominence in Cultural Revolution
Ts'ai Ch'ang†	1900	Normal School ?	Li Fu-ch'un's wife; attended 1966 Red Guard and 1967 May Day rallies
Tseng Hsi-sheng	1909	?	No offices; purged prior to the cultural revolution
Tseng Shan	1904	Apprenticeship	Minister of Internal Affairs; attended 1966 Red Guard and 1967 May Day rallies
Wang Chen	1909?	Middle School?	Member, NDC; attended 1966 Red Guard and 1967 May Day rallies
Wang Chia-hsiang	1907	Studied in USSR	Purged from CPC CC Secretariat
Wang En-mao	?	?	Denounced by Red Guards; may have been purged
Wang Shou-tao	1907	Agric. School	None
Wang Shu-sheng	1909?	?	Vice Minister, NDM; member NDC; attended 1966 Red Guard and 1967 May Day rallies
Wang Ts'ung-wu	1901?	University?	None
Wang Wei-chou	1884	?	Retired; attended May Day, 1967 rally
Wu Chih-p'u	1906	?	None
Wu Hsiu-ch'üan	1909	Middle School	Attended 1966 Red Guard rallies
Wu Yü-chang	1878	Military Academy?	Died December, 1966
Yang Hsien-chen	1899	University	Held no important offices prior to the cultural revolution; his ideological errors denounced in in 1966–67
Yang Hsiu-feng	1897	College	President of Supreme People's Court; called a Liu supporter; probably purged
Yang Shang-k'un	1903	University	Denounced as a Liu supporter; believed purged in January, 1967
Yeh Chi-chuang	1893	?	None

* As noted previously, the membership of the Central Committee is set by the Party Congress under which it serves. The present CC was elected by the first plenum of the Eighth Congress in September, 1956, when 94 full members were

chosen. At its second plenum, in May, 1958, the Eighth Congress brought the number of full members to 99. Since then, several have died. This table shows the composition of the CC on the eve of the cultural revolution and subsequently. Members of the Politburo, who themselves come from the roster of the CC, are discussed in Table I. Biographic data has been compiled from many official and non-official sources. Given the rapidity of change in Communist China during the present struggle, data on the prominence of members in the cultural revolution is in no way complete. It is meant to suggest; not to define. As of this writing, the most current listing of the leaders of Communist China is for the Peking celebrations in honor of May Day, 1967. As in the case of earlier reports of the Red Guard rallies, the omission of a name may or may not be significant, since some members cannot be relieved of field assignments to gather in Peking. When pertinent, a member's assignment in a troubled area has been noted, as have offices connected with the military.

† = female

The data in Table II suggests several points. Although attacks by the Red Guards have invariably been associated with the removal of a Party member, such attacks do not automatically signal the individual's disgrace or purge from any position of trust (the case of Liao Ch'eng-chih, for example, indicates the at least temporary ability to survive criticism or be rehabilitated). Secondly, although connection with the military now means augmented power, it does not necessarily protect from attacks. In fact, members of the PLA, NDC or NDM may be subjected to particularly close scrutiny due to their critical assignments (as suggested by the case of Oyang Ch'ing). Far more importantly, it may be generalized that the ranks of the CC have been greatly depleted by the purges. Second only to the Politburo as a de facto organ of power, the Central Committee might normally be regarded as a sort of school and testing ground to train the leaders of tomorrow. But it is apparent from the table's data that the members of the CC are aging; many are too old to perform any strenuous services, and their membership must be regarded as a recognition of past contributions. Since the CPC has long delayed convening a new Congress to fill the ranks of the CC—possibly to avoid any confrontation between Mao and his followers on the one hand, and his opponents such as Liu and Teng on the other—the role of the CC as a school or proving grounds has been greatly diminished. [44] The effect of this policy born of necessity will

[44] It might be noted that the CPC may have already elevated some members to the ranks of its Central Committee. This would seem most likely, since it is certain that some members of the CC were promoted to the Politburo by the eleventh plenum of August, 1966, although such action would be opposed to the practice of appointment coming only from a Party Congress. Since this would be most irregular, the new members probably would not be identified until such time as a Party Congress could be held. The fact that Yang Cheng-wu, PLA Acting

be apparent in years to come, since the Party has not emphasized grooming men and women in the 30–50 age bracket by giving them experience at higher levels. Mao and his followers, including Lin Piao, apparently prefer to stress revolutionary zeal, rather than the usual approach to the question of training successors. This could lead to a continuing struggle between revolutionary and counterrevolutionary elements as veteran Party leaders die or are replaced. It should also be noted that the CPC does provide a way for a purged member to rehabilitate himself, and it is not unknown for such an individual to be restored to a position of authority. Presumably, some of the CC members denounced before the cultural revolution may be rehabilitated as a result of the downfall of Liu and Teng. But perhaps the most significant generalization that can be made on the basis of this data is that the tendency in the CPC has been toward a greater and greater concentration of power in the hands of a few veteran "revolutionary" members. The "centralism" of democratic centralism has never before been so apparent.

Another far-reaching aspect of the cultural revolution is the complication it has created with reference to the Party membership and the authority of the CPC's cadres. As *People's Daily* acknowledged (on April 24, 1967), "the cadre question is an important and crucial question in the present struggle." The defections of some cadres from the Party line, the misguided purges of other cadres, and especially the mass attacks on the reliability of the cadres point to a new crisis in Party organization, and indicate the weaknesses of the former training programs. In many areas, the attacks on the cadres have perforce meant that power has been placed in the hands of inexperienced and virtually unknown leaders. Displaced and dishonored cadres represent a potential threat to the new "three in one" alliances, and to the PLA and the Red Guards. Thus, the CPC correctly regards the question of cadres as a fundamental issue for the continuation of effective power.

Prior to the inauguration of the cultural revolution, the CPC followed its usual practice of encouraging the cadres to engage in regular criticism and self-criticism. Beginning in October, 1965, the Chinese Communist press frequently alluded to such self-accusation meetings being held at the lower levels of Party organization. For example, provincial committees sponsored "confession" sessions for secretaries from the county committees where many admitted their failure to carry out central directives, their abuse of the peasants, and their inadequacy in waging class struggle. The

---

Chief of Staff and alternate member of the CC, has been listed repeatedly among the members of the CC in reports of official functions indicates that Yang has probably been promoted to full membership. This also appears true in the case of Lo Kuei-po. Among the most likely of those officials who may now enjoy membership unofficially in the CC is Chiang Ch'ing.

CPC offered a suitable model for these cadres in the person of Chiao Yü-lu—an epic figure of the Lei Feng type. [45] With increasing frequency, early in 1966, the cadres met to compare their own efforts to those of Chiao Yü-lu, to confess failures, and to promise greater efforts. Yet, this normal method of encouraging greater responsibility was insufficient. As *Red Flag* pointed out, in the beginning of the cultural revolution, "in some places cadres have not studied as well as the masses and leading cadres have not studied as well as the ordinary cadres." [46]

The subsequent disclosures of the cultural revolution point to some of the more serious defects of the cadres. For example, Public Notice One of the Shansi Revolutionary Rebel General Headquarters, issued on January 14, 1967, two days after the seizure of power in that province, includes among the crimes of the cadres in the CPC provincial committee: spying with secret information networks and wiretapping, refusing to hand over "blacklist" information, opposing the directives of the CPC Central Committee, and using economistic practices to further personal ambitions. In Shanghai, the CPC municipal committee created the Scarlet Guards, as a private tool to sabotage the efforts of the Red Guards. In Shantung, the leading members of the CPC provincial committee, swayed by Liu Shao-ch'i rather than Mao's orders, used the opportunity of the socialist education movement to remove some 60–70 per cent of the cadres, and promote their own followers of the black counterrevolutionary line.

While these and other disclosures indicated a basic crisis for the CPC's organization, they also intensified another contradiction of equally serious dimensions—that between the Party membership and the non-Party masses. This struggle has been termed the work of the followers of the Liu-Teng line to deliberately foster antagonism between the Party and the masses by indiscriminately "hitting hard at many in order to protect a handful." Advocates of this line have been said to encourage mass demonstrations demanding the removal of all Party officials in order to create a sort of power vacuum in which the counterrevolutionary elements can operate freely. Using slogans "left" in form, but "right" in content, they are said to spread anarchistic tendencies as a sinister means to preserve their own status. Whether the result of a deliberate plot, or the manifestation of deep-seated popular antagonism toward the Party, the Chinese Communists have admitted that the masses have risen up against the cadres. *Red Flag* (no. 4, 1967) acknowledges: "In the course of the strong

[45] Just as Lei Feng was intended to become the object of personal admiration and emulation for members of the PLA, Chiao was to represent the ideal characteristics of the loyal Party cadre. This hitherto unknown Party secretary of Lankao county, Honan, reportedly died on May 14, 1964, at the age of 42, of cancer of the liver. His own suffering, of course, was not allowed to interfere with his heroic, although obscure service to the CPC.

[46] *Red Flag*, No. 8, 1966, reprinted in *Peking Review*, June 17, 1966.

counter-offensive . . . a misconception has emerged among some people that all those in authority are no good and unreliable and should, therefore, without exception be overthrown. . . . In some localities, a few persons have proposed that all persons who can be classified as 'leading' cadres should step aside." Other reports testify that cadres have been subjected to harassment and even physical beatings at their self-accusation meetings.

In order to curb threatened anarchy, rehabilitate erring cadres, encourage cadres to join in the denunciation of the Liu-Teng line, and test all members of the Party, the CPC urges that a careful distinction be made between the categories of cadres. The Central Committee's Decision Concerning the Great Proletarian Cultural Revolution, of August 8, 1966, explicitly states that the great majority of cadres fall into the first two categories of "good" or "comparatively good." But it also warns that there are those in the third category who "have made serious mistakes but have not become anti-Party, anti-socialist rightists," and in the fourth category of "anti-Party, anti-socialist rightists." For the latter, the CC directed they must be "fully exposed, hit hard, pulled down and completely discredited and their influence eliminated." Yet the CC also insisted "they should be given a way out so that they can turn over a new leaf."

The CPC has fallen back on its two time-tested methods to promote membership loyalty and discipline. While all cadres are expected to engage in self-criticism, this matter is particularly urgent for those of suspected loyalties. Such cadres are required not only to admit their own mistakes, but also to identify "those who had instructed them to carry out the bourgeois reactionary line." By showing such determination to correct past mistakes, these cadres are then eligible for posts in the Party committees or the new "three in one" alliances. [47] But, it is equally as imperative that the regenerated cadres demonstrate their loyalty by going to and learning from the masses. *Red Flag* (no. 2, 1967) calls upon all cadres who have committed mistakes, but are not anti-Party, to go and "be purified" by the masses. And *People's Daily* (April 24, 1967) demands: "The revolutionary cadres must go among the masses and plunge into the great torrent of revolutionary criticism, repudiation and struggle . . . and really win the confidence of the masses." Time alone will judge whether a more united Party membership, rejuvenated by mass criticism, will emerge, or whether the antagonism between Party members and the non-Party masses will deepen. On this question perhaps hinges the ultimate success or failure of the cultural revolution.

[47] The case of P'an Fu-sheng, former first secretary of the CPC's Heilungkiang provincial committee and now a leading member of that province's new "three in one" alliance, is representative of this approach. P'an criticized his own failure to implement the decisions of the CC's eleventh plenum and pledged total support to the Mao-Lin Piao leadership.

CHAPTER 5

The Chinese Communist Political Order and State Apparatus

The communist-led revolution in China had as its first task the seizure of state power and establishment of the "people's democratic dictatorship." In turn, the "people's democratic dictatorship" would provide the instrument for creating the "dictatorship of the proletariat." With the revolutionary victory, the Communist Party of China had the entire country as its base of operations; but it also had the rich experience first of the Chinese Soviet Republic, then the North-Shensi Special District centered in Yenan, and finally the "liberated areas" behind the Japanese lines during the War, to draw upon. Thus the Chinese Communist leadership set itself to the work of creating a new political order, through the establishment of the necessary state apparatus, first to direct political life, and then to transform the economic, social and cultural life of the country. While, as followers of Marx and Lenin, the Chinese Communists hold that the communist revolution cannot be completed until the whole world is won, the leaders in Peking must continue to exert the utmost control in their "base area," and contribute revolutionary efforts from there, before the "withering away of the state" on earth.

THE CONSTITUTIONAL PROCESS

In order to promote effective control of China and further the international communist cause, the CPC must legitimize its rule. In the long run, only on the basis of such legitimacy can the Chinese Communists muster mass support by persuasion, compulsion, or a combination of the two tactics. Thus, Soviet Russia, later the Soviet Union, adopted Party-inspired Constitutions in 1918, 1924, and 1936, as the fundamental law of the land. These constitutions, in turn, served as prototypes of constitutions for other communist-controlled states. Following their seizure of power, the Chinese Communists therefore turned to this important constitutional phase.

The Constitution and the Social Order

The constitutional process of a given society—if the term be taken to refer to the whole complex of actions and principles by which the basic political structure of a society is defined and kept in operation—is closely bound up with the rate and impetus of social change in the society. In this respect, there is a fundamental contrast between the constitutions of communist regimes and those traditionally associated with Western democratic systems. In the latter, the constitution may be thought of as reflecting the existing balance of social, economic, and political forces within the society. At the same time it provides a framework of rights, duties, and procedures within which these forces can harmonize or adjust their conflicting demands and goals in order to arrive at policies and laws generally accepted and complied with throughout the society. Such a constitution is constantly changing in content and growing in scope, if it is soundly conceived, as the society itself changes. The evolution of the British Constitution as the country progressed from a feudal agrarian society with an established church and a hereditary nobility to a modern urban, industrial, and much more secular society is a familiar case in point. From a democratic point of view, then, the constitution reflects the social order which produces it; in its own growth and evolution, it keeps pace with, while it helps to shape, the process of social change within the society.

Under a communist regime, the situation is otherwise. To date, the communists have been able to seize state power only in the areas that are politically and economically backward, by comparison with the long-established urban and industrial democracies of the West. In these less advanced areas, the Communist Party, armed with an ideology originally intended for countries which had undergone a substantial degree of industrialization, must commit itself to a program of rapid and forced social change; and the constitution adopted by the regime reflects this commitment. The case of Communist China offers an excellent example. As has already been noted in passing, China has had, since the communists came to power, two constitutional documents: the provisional instrument known as the "Common Program," adopted by the Chinese People's Political Consultative Conference in September, 1949, and the present Constitution, adopted by the First National People's Congress in September, 1954. Both these documents have shown the characteristics of the communist, as opposed to the democratic, constitution. They have been programmatic in nature, in that they have reflected, not an existing balance of social and economic forces, but rather one which is to be brought about through the actions of a Party that has seized power and is willing to exercise it ruthlessly. And rather than being instruments to grow and change with the gradual evolution of the society, they have had more the appearance of instruments to be outgrown and tossed aside, as the program of planned social change advances beyond the stage for which the particular constitution was designed.

The extent of the social change to be brought about in China has often been emphasized by the leaders of the CPC. Echoing their views, a Chinese commentator, Wang Hui-teh, in an article in *Hsüeh Hsi* (*Study*), in January, 1954, pointed out that "the revolutionary movement led by the Chinese Communist Party started in a semi-colonial and semi-feudal society, and its ultimate objective is the successful building in China of a socialist society and communist society." Mao Tse-tung, in his 1949 report On People's Democratic Dictatorship, called for the development of those conditions under which "China, under the leadership of the working class and the Communist Party, can develop steadily from an agricultural into an industrial country and from a New Democratic into a Socialist and, eventually, a communist society, when all classes will disappear and universal harmony will become a reality." This emphasis on rapid and forced social change is carried over into the Preamble of the 1954 Constitution, which refers briefly to the two stages through which, according to Mao and the other Party theoreticians, China must pass on its way to the goal of a socialist and eventually a communist society. The first stage, already successfully accomplished, was marked by the "great victory in the people's revolution against imperialism, feudalism and bureaucrat-capitalism," and the founding of the People's Republic of China. In other words, it was the seizure of state power. The second stage, now going forward, is the period of "building socialism," or in the words of the Preamble, the period of transition "from the founding of the People's Republic of China to the attainment of a socialist society." During this period, "the fundamental task of the State is, step by step, to bring about the socialist industrialization of the country and, step by step, to accomplish the socialist transformation of agriculture, handicrafts, and capitalist industry and commerce." In plain language, this "transformation" means the progressive expropriation of the privately owned land and capital of the country.

The Common Program of 1949 and the Constitution of 1954 were thus intended to reflect the stage of social development the country had reached or was approaching. The Common Program reflected the "united front" tactics which the Party had used in its rise to power and was regarded as appropriate to the period of recovery and rehabilitation necessitated by the years of war and civil war. But by 1953 it became evident that the regime was preparing to move ahead from recovery to the active construction of a socialist economy. With the inauguration of the First Five-Year Plan in 1953, communist speeches and editorials began to foreshadow the new "general line" for the Party and the state. Beginning in November, 1953, the Party and the government, assisted by the minor parties and the various mass organizations, inaugurated a program for the study of this "general line." Before many months had passed, this study program was broadened by the appearance of the Draft Constitution embodying the "line." After its approval by the Central Committee of the CPC at its Fourth Plenum in February, 1954, this Draft was the subject of another wave of intensive study at all levels before its adoption in definitive form by the First National People's Congress in September, 1954. As finally adopted, the new Constitution gave formal indication that the regime was ready to move ahead into the stage of full "socialist construction." ' At the same time it specified the appropriate form of government to carry out this task: a "people's democratic dictatorship." The inner contradiction of this term merits a closer examination.

The Nature of the People's Democratic Dictatorship

From what the communists would call a bourgeois liberal point of view, the terms democracy and dictatorship are irreconcilable opposites. The logical contradiction involved in combining them is only part of a larger contradiction in communist theory: the contradiction between the ultimate goal of universal harmony in a society without classes and divisive elements, in which both the Party and the state machinery will have withered away, and the means of achieving this goal, which involves the maximum intensification of state power and authority over the lives of individuals. "Our Party forms the precise opposite to the political parties of the bourgeoisie," proclaimed Mao Tse-tung in his report On People's Democratic Dictatorship. "They are afraid to speak of the disappearance of classes, state power, and parties. We, on the contrary, openly declare that we are striving with all our might precisely to create the conditions that will hasten the end of these things." But the contradiction is revealed in the next sentence: "The Communist Party and the state power of the people's dictatorship constitute such conditions."

The explanation, if not the resolution, of this contradiction is to be found in the dichtomy set up by Mao and his followers between "the people" and all other citizens, who may be called non-people. "Who are the 'people'?" asks Mao. "At the present stage in China, they are the working class, the peasantry, the petty bourgeoisie, and the national bourgeoisie." In short, they are all the elements who may be expected to go along with the policies of the regime without too much trouble, and on whose co-operation the regime must for the time being depend. For them, some of the trappings of democracy are to be allowed; but not for the non-people. The people, Mao adds, "unite to create their own state and elect their own government so as to enforce their dictatorship over the henchmen of imperialism—the landlord class and bureaucratic capitalist class, as well as the reactionary clique of the Kuomintang. . . ." Continuing, Mao wrote:

The people's government will suppress such individuals. It will only tolerate them if they behave themselves, but not if they prove intractable in speech or action. If they are intractable, they will be instantly curbed and punished. Within the ranks of the people, the democratic system is carried out by giving freedom of speech, assembly, and association. The right to vote is given only to the people, not to the reactionaries.

Hence the explanation of the contradiction is simple and stark: "These two aspects, democracy for the people and dictatorship for the reactionaries, when combined, constitute the people's democratic dictatorship." There can be no withering away of the state power so long as there remains opposition to the state. "We want to abolish state power," wrote Mao, "but we cannot yet afford to . . . because imperialism still exists, and within our country reactionaries and classes still exist." In fact, far from abolishing state power, "our present task is to strengthen the people's state machine—meaning principally the people's army, the people's police, and the people's courts."

This was the meaning intended, then, by the Common Program in proclaiming the People's Republic of China to be a "People's Democratic Dictatorship" and by the Constitution in calling it a "people's democratic state led by the working class and based on the alliance of workers and peasants."

The social basis of the regime is spelled out more fully in the Preamble to the Constitution. Within the country, the regime rests upon "a broad people's democratic united front, composed of all democratic classes, democratic parties and groups, and popular organizations, and led by the Communist Party of China." Externally it depends upon its solidarity with an international united front, made up of "peace-loving peoples in all other states." But to say that the regime has the support of these two united fronts does not by any means indicate that its strength is based solely on an unorganized and undifferentiated public opinion at home and abroad. Rather, it maintains its power through the support of certain key organized groups, both domestic and international, dominated by the top leadership of the Party through the principle of democratic centralism. Mao listed these key groups quite explicitly in his report on the nature of the regime: ". . . a disciplined Party which is armed with the theory of Marx, Engels, Lenin, and Stalin, employing the method of self-criticism and closely linked with the masses; . . . an army led by such a Party; and . . . a united front of all revolutionary strata and all revolutionary parties and groups, led by such a Party." Given this tightly controlled regime, devoted to remaking the social order, the question arises: What rights and freedoms are left to individuals and voluntary associations? How is the traditional problem of freedom and authority resolved?

The Position of Individuals, Classes, and Nationalities under the Constitution

"From a bourgeois viewpoint," stated Liu Shao-ch'i in his address to the First Session of the First National People's Congress on the Draft Constitution, "it is impossible to understand the political system of our country." Perhaps in no area is the difference between the democratic and the communist political systems more profound than in the area of human rights and civil liberties. In Chapter III of the Constitution, dealing with the fundamental rights and duties of citizens, according to another Chinese Communist writer, "the superiority of a constitution of a socialist type in comparison with bourgeois constitutions finds striking expression." Under the socialist type, he added, "All citizens in China enjoy equal and extensive democratic rights." The line of reasoning on which this claim of superiority rests will show much about the relation of the individual to the state under the Chinese Communist system.

In part, the reasoning is based on the assumption that rights and privileges ascribed to an aggregate of people must necessarily be enjoyed by every individual within the aggregate. For over a century (one Chinese Communist jurist has written in *People's China* of September 16, 1954) the common people of China engaged in revolutionary struggles to win the rights and freedoms which had been reserved for the reactionary ruling classes. Then, "with the victory of the people's revolution, the people came to power. Freed from slavery and oppression, they are now masters of a new society and a new country." And, being masters, they can now enjoy "their first real democratic rights and freedoms." Similar reasoning is involved in Article 2 of the Constitution: "All power in the People's Republic of China belongs to the people." But from a democratic point of view, power involves the capacity to make choices between realizable alternatives. By this standard, the Chinese people have no power, since they are not presented with any alternatives in top leadership and major policy. They can only approve the single matter put before them, even in the election of their local representatives.

Another facet of the communist reasoning on this question is found in the more detailed assurances of civil rights and personal freedoms given in the Constitution. Wu Chia-lin, the jurist cited just above, takes pride in the fact that under the Constitution, "all citizens 'have freedom of speech, freedom of the press, freedom of procession and freedom of demonstration.' " Yet again this freedom allows the individual no choice among attainable alternatives. To show that there is freedom of association, this commentator cites the great increase in the size of trade unions, and the fact that each line of work now has its own union. Such evidence, while impressive, relates to the fact of association, not to the freedom to associate. There is no evidence that unions or other associations can be freely formed, without prior approval by the Communist Party, and free from domination by its cadres under the principle of democratic centralism.

The communists also take pride in the fact the Constitution not only grants these freedoms but gives assurance that "the state provides the necessary material facilities to guarantee the enjoyment of these freedoms." In part the logic here again assumes that what is attributed to the aggregate is also possessed by the individual. The "people" in some sense "own" the newspaper plants of the country. Therefore, what is communicated by means of these physical facilities must be what the "owners" would choose to disclose and advocate if they could articulate their wishes.

Chinese commentators, like their counterparts in other communist-dominated countries, make much of those provisions of the Constitution which guarantee the economic rights of the individual—the right to work, the right to rest and leisure, to old-age and sickness benefits, and the like. Yet here too, what is presented as a way of securing for the individual an area of freedom and independence in ordering his own life, becomes, in application, a means of strengthening the state. It requires a flourishing economy to secure these economic benefits to the fullest. As a regime bent upon "building socialism," the attainment of economic rights demands that each individual make the sacrifices necessary to carry through the state's plan for economic development. As Liu Shao-ch'i pointed out in his report on the Draft Constitution, "the more prosperous and powerful our motherland, the stronger our system of people's democracy, the more developed our socialist cause, the more secure, the broader and [the more] extended will become the freedoms and rights of the people."

The root assumption in the communist view of individual freedoms and rights is that the interests of the individual are inseparable from and identical with the interests of the state as a whole. In Liu Shao-ch'i's words: "Under the system of people's democracy and socialism, the masses of the people can see for themselves that personal interests are indivisible from the public interests of the country and society; and that they are one and the same." If this were indeed the case, then a "free" individual could in theory want only what his leaders decided he must want. In practice, of course, individuals want other things, and it may be necessary for the state to "force the individual to be free." For this purpose, the Constitution prescribes certain "duties" for citizens, correlative with their "rights" —such duties as bearing arms, paying taxes, and safeguarding public property, upholding labor discipline, keeping public order, and abiding by the Constitution and the laws. The Chinese commentators assume, at least for public consumption, that these "duties" will be performed voluntarily, avoiding the need for undue coercion of the individual. Thus Wu Chia-lin concludes:

> The duties performed by the people create the conditions necessary for the full enjoyment of their rights. The unity of the people's rights and duties reflects the identity of interest of the state and the individual citizen. As a result of this, the absolute majority of citizens can voluntarily and faithfully carry out their sacred duties to the state and to society.

Should voluntary compliance not be forthcoming, however—including willing obedience to laws promulgated by leaders who refuse to submit themselves and their program to the voters for an effective choice among alternatives—the instruments of coercion will not be lacking.

This reliance on coercion was suggested in an editorial in the *People's Daily* of November 3, 1954. It pointed out that one of the important tasks for the Party and state organs following the proclamation of the Constitution was to teach the people to fulfill their duties as citizens in a highly conscientious spirit. It warned that if a person should violate the law of the state, the masses of the people would voluntarily take action against that person, as in the campaigns for the suppression of counter-revolutionaries and agrarian reform, and the Three-Anti and Five-Anti movements. On the ground that exploiting classes still existed in the country and that most of the liquidated element of the landlord class had not yet achieved a thorough reform, the editorial acknowledged that "the obedience to revolutionary law and order as well as the fulfillment of the duties of citizens cannot but be compulsory."

Thus, for the citizens of Communist China, the rights and freedoms guaranteed by the Constitution are conditional, while the duties are onerous and inescapable. Not only are these duties required of each citizen in his own conduct, but the regime has encouraged every citizen to keep an eye on his neighbor and take action against violators in order to defend revolutionary gains and strive for further revolutionary fruits.

A view of the position of the individual in relation to the state under communism in China would not be complete, however, without reference to the lot of the non-people, of whom the Constitution recognizes two categories. The first are the "traitors and counterrevolutionaries," who are to be suppressed and punished. "As for the foreign imperialists and their hangers-on who would like to enslave us," promised Liu Shao-ch'i in his report on the Draft Constitution, "our Constitution and laws will never give them the slightest loophole. Is it not precisely because we have deprived the traitors and counterrevolutionaries of their freedom that the people have genuine freedom?" The second group include those who have committed no overt act but may be likely to do so because of their class background. Under Article 19 of the Constitution, as under the Common Program, "the state deprives feudal landlords and bureaucrat-capitalists of political rights for a specific period of time according to law." This second group of class enemies are not to be treated with the same ruthlessness, but are to be "reformed" through the forced labor system.

The Constitution does not rest content with defining the position of the individual with relation to the state; it is also concerned with the position of various collective entities—economic classes and their instruments, the political parties, as well as nationality groups. The first two, classes and parties, are, of course, to be gradually eliminated during the transition period, leaving only the CPC, formally entrenched in its one-party rule over a single-class society, once the stage of socialism has been finally reached. In its provisions taking away the political rights of two classes, the "feudal landlords and bureaucrat-capitalists," the Constitution foreshadows what will happen to those classes and parties marked for extinction. In the rural areas, Liu Shao-ch'i noted in his report to the First National People's Congress on the Draft Constitution, the "rich peasants" were the one remaining "exploiting class," and they were to be gradually forced to give up their exploitive practices "step by step, through the building of cooperatives and by restrictions on the development of rich peasant economy." In industry and commerce, however, the process of socialist transformation would require, he added, a relatively long period of time, during which capitalist ownership, theoretically, would continue. (In practice, of course, the process of liquidating private business was accelerated.) Thus, "a definite status in political life" would have to be reserved during this transition period for the "national bourgeoisie"— those capitalist elements which "joined the national and democratic revolution in the past" and which have "demonstrated their willingness to accept socialist transformation."

The difficulty is, of course, that not all the rich peasants or bourgeoisie may be willing to accept their removal from the economic scene. Disruptive activity by these elements will have to be punished, according to Liu. Hence under Article 10 of the Constitution, pending the ultimate socialization of industry and commerce, "the state forbids any kind of illegal activity by capitalists which endangers the public interest, disturbs the social-economic order, or undermines the economic plan of the state."

If economic classes and their respective political parties are to disappear under socialism, the nationality groups are not. Their position is defined under Article 5 of the Constitution, which proclaims the equality of all nationalities and prohibits acts of discrimination against any nationality. The Preamble, furthermore, recognizes the special characteristics and needs of different nationality groups. Hence, Liu Shao-ch'i pointed out, "Socialist transformation among certain national minorities will begin rather later and may take more time than in areas where the Han [Chinese] people live." Each nationality group will be allowed to retain its own characteristic language, religion, and customs, provided it does not oppose the policy of socialization. But there can be no doubt of the attitude of the regime toward any nationalist opposition or separatism. What Liu had to say about religious groups would apply equally well to nationality groups: "Safeguarding freedom of religious belief is quite a different matter from safeguarding freedom of counterrevolutionary activities; these two just cannot be mixed up." Hence, the communist leaders will make sure that, as Liu put it, "the building of a socialist society is the common objective of all nationalities within our country."

The Chinese Constitution thus provides the legal basis for a vast program of social change, involving the elimination of entire classes and the industrialization and modernization of even the most backward sectors of the society. In fact it gives to the Party leadership full power to deal with any dissent from or opposition to its policy and rule.

While the regime can eliminate individual and class opposition, it does recognize the need, under the Constitution, to grant a certain status, collectively, to some of the minority economic, political, and nationality groups within the society; in this way it can hope to make sure that the pressures of social transformation will not jeopardize the firm grip of the Party leadership on the state power. The status of these minority groups under the Constitution will be examined more fully in later sections, after a brief review of the structure of the organizational machinery through which the state power is exercised.

STRUCTURE OF THE STATE

The Central Government Apparatus

THE REPRESENTATIVE ORGANS OF STATE POWER

"The state power of the People's Republic of China belongs to the people." So ran the bold pronouncement of Article 12 of the Common Program. "The All-China People's Congress shall be the supreme organ of state power," it further declared; and this body, like the people's congresses at the lower levels, was to be "popularly elected by universal franchise."

But in the fall of 1949, the regime was not yet ready to hold even a limited kind of popular election for an All-China People's Congress. The bulk of the population had not as yet been sufficiently organized into mass organizations under communist control; many parts of the country were still under military rule; hence, conditions were not yet favorable for holding the type of elections—carefully staged for propaganda value, with predetermined outcome—which communist regimes require. Consequently, the communist leaders resorted to a hand-picked representative body to serve briefly as an "organ of state power," even though this body was intended in the long run to have only consultative and advisory functions.

The Chinese People's Political Consultative Conference (CPPCC).—As a sort of ad hoc constituent assembly, the First Plenary Session of the CPPCC, meeting in Peking in September, 1949, served to give a show of legitimacy to the regime by adopting the Common Program, the Organic Law of the CPPCC, and the Organic Law of the Central People's Government, which together provided the constitutional structure of the state, pending the later election of the NPC and the adoption of a definite Constitution. With the adjournment of the First Plenary Session on September 30, however, the CPPCC for all practical purposes terminated its role as an organ of state power. The Plenum did, it is true, elect a National Committee to serve when it was not in session, and this group in turn elected a Standing Committee. Both these bodies were on occasion consulted by the organs of the Central People's Government. But under the

Organic Law of the CPPCC, neither group corresponded as closely in functions and powers to the later Standing Committee of the National People's Congress as did the Central People's Government Council (CPGC), a body of some sixty-three members which the Plenum of the First CPPCC also elected before its adjournment. Once the National Committee of the CPPCC had performed the function of "discussing and submitting the joint list of candidates of units participating in the CPPCC, for the election of representatives to the National People's Congress," under Article 13 of the Organic Law, and once the NPC had been elected, the CPPCC and its committees had no further function as organs of state power. The importance of the CPPCC lies primarily, therefore, in its role, not as an organ of state authority, but as a "representative" body holding a supposedly consultative and advisory status.

The CPPCC has been since its creation the chief united-front organization of the regime, symbolizing the communist "mass line" in action. Its members are drawn, not from territorial units, but from all the communist-led and controlled mass-line organizations, political parties, and nationality groups of the country. The First Plenary Session of the CPPCC was made up of 585 voting members and 77 non-voting alternates who, instead of being elected from the groups they supposedly represented, had been named by a Preparatory Committee set up by the CPC leadership. There were 142 delegates from 14 political parties and groups, including the CPC itself, with the individual party delegations ranging from 5 to 16 in number. In addition, 102 members came from the 9 major political-administrative units of the day, 60 from the 6 army units, and 206 from the 16 mass organizations and groups; the remaining 75 were specially invited individual delegates. The CPC was, of course, much more heavily represented than its own delegation would indicate, since many of the delegates drawn from other organizations and groups were at the same time Party members.

On February 4, 1953, following the call for the elections of the NPC and in preparation for the convocation of the Second CPPCC, the First CPPCC was dissolved by its National Committee. This body in turn selected the members of the Second CPPCC, which was convened shortly after the adjournment of the NPC. The CPPCC was thus not replaced by the NPC but rather reverted to the role originally envisaged for it. In the words of Ch'en Shu-t'ung, a vice-chairman of the first National Committee of the CPPCC, "following the realization of the system of popularly-elected people's congresses . . . the organization of the people's democratic united front [the CPPCC] should not only continue to exist, but should also be augmented and consolidated in order to fulfill its duties."

For the first five years of its existence, the constitutional document for the CPPCC was the Organic Law of the CPPCC adopted by the First Plenum of that body on September 29, 1949. However, on December 15, 1954, according to a NCNA dispatch of that date from Peking, the Standing Committee of the First National Committee met to discuss and adopt the documents to be presented to the meeting of the Second National Committee the following week, among them a set of "Draft Regulations Governing the Chinese People's Political Consultative Conference." This "Constitution" of the CPPCC was duly adopted by the Second National Committee and published in *People's Daily* on December 26. As might be expected, the new document reflects the shift in the aims of the regime as between the Common Program and the Constitution of the Republic. The "General Provisions" of the 1949 Organic Law had stressed the attainment of a New Democracy, and the work of rehabilitation and reconstruction after the war. The new document emphasizes instead the transition to a socialist society. The united-front nature of the organization is reaffirmed. However, the references in the earlier document to the CPPCC as an interim organ of state power no longer appear.

As provided in Articles 11 and 13 of the 1949 Organic Law, the CPPCC Plenary Session may organize various committees as its organs. The principal organ is its National Committee, whose members are elected by the plenary session before its adjournment. But the National Committee in turn elects a smaller Standing Committee, which exercises the real power of the CPPCC, since it can convene or postpone the meeting of the National Committee, and can "take charge of the affairs of the National Committee."

On September 30, 1949, the First Plenary Session of the CPPCC elected a National Committee of 180 members; 18 additional members for the later "liberated" areas were elected by the First National Committee at its third session in October, 1951, with two more seats being kept open for Formosa. Among the 333 members of the National Committee elected at the Second Plenary Session of the CPPCC in December, 1954, according to the *People's Daily* of December 11, 1954, 40 were delegates of the CPC, while the delegations of the non-communist parties ranged from 6 to 25 each. Under the standard communist principle of hierarchical organization, the National Committee is empowered to set up local committees as organs of consultation in the major cities, important areas, and provincial capitals.

Under Article 7 of the 1949 Organic Law, the chief function of the CPPCC, once its duties as an ad hoc constituent assembly had been discharged, remained the submission of "proposals on fundamental policies and on important measures relating to national construction work" to the Central People's Government (CPG), and then later to the NPC. The

National Committee in turn was given the power of "discussing and submitting proposals" to the CPG, along with the task of insuring the implementation of the resolutions of the plenary session and of its own resolutions.

But the real significance of the CPPCC is to be found in the added functions and powers given the National Committee under Article 13 of the Organic Law. Among its tasks are those of "discussing and dealing with other affairs concerning the internal cooperation of the CPPCC" and "directing the work of the local democratic united front." It serves as an agency for coordinating and consolidating the united front. The compulsory nature of this coordination and full consolidation was indicated in Article 5 of the 1949 Organic Law and again in Article 5 of the 1954 Constitution of the CPPCC. Under both documents, if the National Committee decides that a participating unit or individual delegate has violated the Constitution of the CPPCC, it may, according to the seriousness of the offense, warn the offender, or have the individual delegate replaced, or even cancel the representation of the participating unit. Thus the ruling Party with its commanding position in the CPPCC, is given the necessary authority to control the component elements of this united-front organ.

More important, however, is the function of the National Committee in "assisting the Government in mobilizing the people to participate in the work of the people's democratic revolution and of national construction." In this it becomes highly useful as a transmission-belt agency to rally public understanding and support for the policies and programs of the communist leadership. Both of these functions were stressed by *People's Daily*, on December 22, 1954, at the time of the meeting of the Second National Committee. This editorial comment well summarizes, in the language of communism, the essential nature of the CPPCC and its usefulness to the regime:

. . . The present CPPCC does not have to and should not exercise the functions and authority of an organ of state power any longer. But it remains a people's democratic united-front organization for uniting all nationalities, democratic classes, democratic parties and groups, people's bodies, overseas Chinese and other patriotic democrats of our country. It is not an organization with the character of political power or semi-political power: it is an organization of party character. Its task consists in continuously consolidating and developing the democratic united front of our people under the leadership of the CPC and in uniting more extensively, through the unity of democratic parties and groups and people's bodies, the people of all nationalities of our country to oppose in common the enemy at home and abroad in their struggle for peace, democracy, and the great Socialist cause.

In keeping with this interpretation, since its function remains necessary to the CPC, the CPPCC has continued its united-front assignments. The

Third CPPCC was elected in 1959, and the Fourth in 1964. A measure of the Communist Party's approval of the utility of the CPPCC may be gained from the fact that Mao Tse-tung remains as honorary chairman, while Chou En-lai serves as chairman.

The National People's Congress (NPC)—As already indicated, the Common Program and the Organic Law of the CPPCC, adopted in 1949, envisaged the convocation through "universal franchise" of an All-China People's Congress, as well as of people's congresses at the lower levels. Originally it was planned to elect and convene these congresses in 1953. A proposal to that effect was discussed at an enlarged session of the Standing Committee of the CPCC National Committee in December, 1952, and a resolution making it official was adopted by the Chinese People's Government Council (CPGC) in January, 1953. But by September of that year, the elections to the lower-level congresses were not yet under way, and the CPGC was forced to postpone them to 1954. On April 15, 1954, a joint decision of the Central Election Committee and the Government Administration Council (GAC) provided for the holding of county congresses in June, 1954, followed by provincial and special municipal congresses in late July and early August. When this timetable was met, the CPGC decided at its 33rd meeting, on August 11, 1954, to convene the First National People's Congress on September 15, 1954. This body then met in Peking on schedule, with Mao Tse-tung presiding on the opening day, and with 1,141 out of the 1,226 elected delegates reported in attendance.

The election of the delegates to the NPC followed the procedures laid down by the electoral law promulgated by the Central People's Government on March 1, 1953. This law provided for a system of indirect elections, with features of differential and unequal representation. Under its provisions, deputies to each higher-level congress are elected by the congresses at the next lower level. Only the lowest-level congresses are elected directly by the people. The unequal representation features are shown in the differentiation in the ratio of representation between the rural and urban areas. Article 20 of the electoral law provides that for each province the number of NPC deputies to be elected is to be determined on the basis of one deputy for every 800,000 people, while for the municipalities directly under the central government, and for certain other populous industrial municipalities, the ratio is to be one for every 100,000. Suffrage under the electoral law is not really universal. Under Article 5, elements of the landlord class whose status has not yet been changed under the law, as well as counterrevolutionaries deprived of political rights, are denied the right to elect or to be elected. Although representation is for the most part on the basis of territorial units (provinces and municipalities), there are minor exceptions or qualifications providing for representation from

CHART III   THE STATE STRUCTURE OF THE PEOPLE'S REPUBLIC OF CHINA

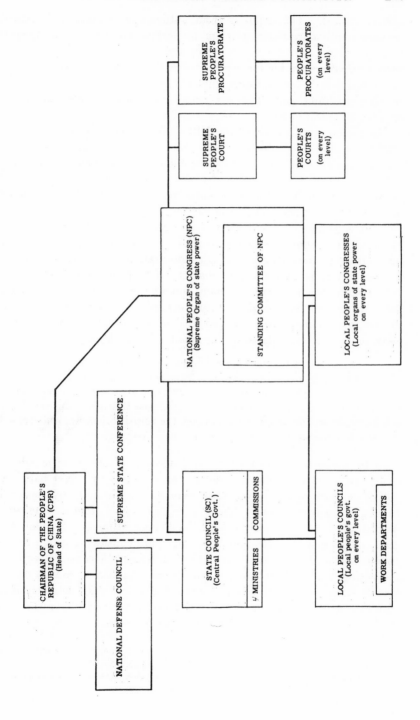

special groups.   The deputies from autonomous regions automatically represent both a territorial unit and a national minority.   But among the delegations of the ordinary provinces and municipalities, 150 seats have been especially set aside for deputies of national minority origin; 60 seats are assigned to the armed forces, and are elected by servicemen's congresses within their units; and 30 are set aside for overseas Chinese, apportioned on a geographical basis. [1]

The election of deputies to the NPC is by no means free.   As in other communist-controlled countries, only one slate of candidates is submitted. In China, the nomination of NPC candidates is controlled by the central authorities through the so-called "consultation" system.   Article 47 of the electoral law stipulates that candidates may be nominated "either jointly or separately" by the CPC, "the various democratic parties, the various people's organizations, and electors or representatives who are not affiliated to the above-mentioned parties or organizations."   In practice, nomination is done jointly through consultation of the leaders of these groups.   In order to make sure that the right people are elected to the NPC, the central authorities actually submit the names of favored candidates to the provincial and municipal congresses for election. An explicit description of this process was provided by the *People's Daily* of July 6, 1954, in an article circulated by the Hsinhua News Agency:

> Lists of candidates for the National People's Congress were discussed and unanimously approved yesterday at the 56th (enlarged) session of the Standing Committee of the National Committee of the CPPCC.   They will be submitted to the people's congresses at provincial and municipal levels throughout the country, and will form part of the candidates' lists which the various congresses will choose for the election of deputies to the National People's Congress.

So far there has been no published account of any case in which a candidate failed of election.   Though the voting is by secret ballot, the voting deputies of local congresses seem to abide strictly by the choice handed down from above.   Thus, a NCNA report from Peking, dated August 22, 1954, and dealing with the Peking Municipal People's Congress, mentioned the fact that the municipal deputies were free to elect anyone not on the list, but "due to the full democratic consultation before the voting, the votes garnered by the elected deputies were very concentrated: 9 (out of 28) received 100 per cent of votes (539); 19 received one vote less than the full vote; 3 received 2 less; 2 received 3 less; while even the lowest one received only 4 less than the full vote."

---

[1] In practice, there are variations from these quotas.   For example, at the first session of the Third NPC, which concluded in January, 1965, representation was on the basis of one delegate for every 400,000 persons in the rural areas, for every 50,000 in the major cities, and with 300 seats reserved for delegates of the national minorities.

Because it is able to control and manipulate the election of all deputies to the NPC, the Communist Party need not worry whether it wins a majority of the seats for its own members. In fact, in the First NPC, the proportion of CPC members was about one-third, with the other two-thirds furnished in roughly equal proportions by (a) the leaders of non-communist parties and mass organizations, and (b) professional workers and labor heroes or model workers. Evidently the communists not only find it advisable to maintain this united-front facade, but also feel it safe to do so. The professional people and model workers are individual proteges of the CPC; the non-communist parties and mass organizations are under the control of the Party; and the selection of candidates from these circles can be only with Party approval. Moreover, the NPC promises to be in session so short a time, and so seldom, that would-be dissident elements would have no time to organize and make the necessary preparations for an effective opposition.

Under the Constitution, the NPC is the highest organ of state power, and the only organ to exercise the legislative power of the state (Articles 21 and 22). It amends the Constitution and supervises its enforcement, enacts laws, and decides on questions of war or peace and the granting of general amnesties. It approves the state budget, "decides on" (i.e., adopts) the national economic plan, and ratifies the status and boundaries of provinces, autonomous regions, and municipalities directly under central authority. It elects and may remove from office the Chairman and Vice-Chairman of the Republic, and the heads of the Supreme People's Court and the Supreme People's Procuratorate. For the other high officials of the central government—the State Council and the National Defense Council—it also decides on appointment or removal in accordance with the recommendation of the Chairman of the Republic or the Premier (Articles 27 and 28). (The actual appointment is then made by the proper official.) But all these actions are formalities only. The NPC, like the Supreme Soviet of the USSR, will apparently be kept too unwieldy in size, and too infrequent and brief in its sessions, to be an effective, deliberative body or to exercise any real power.

To facilitate its work, the NPC may set up auxiliary organs. Article 25 of the Organic Law of the NPC, adopted by its First Plenary Session, stipulates that during its session the NPC establishes the Nationality, the Bills, the Budget, and the Credentials Committees to assist its work. After the adjournment of the full NPC, only the Nationality and the Bills committees continue in existence, and may be called back in session to assist the Standing Committee of the NPC in its work.

In between sessions of the full NPC, it is the Standing Committee which exercises its power and is charged with the conduct of state affairs. This body, as elected in 1965, is made up of a Chairman, 16 Vice Chairmen, a

Secretary General, and 94 ordinary members. Elected by one Congress, it in turn is empowered "to conduct the election" of the next NPC and to convene it into session.

As the permanent body of the seldom-convoked NPC, the Standing Committee is able to wield considerable authority in legislative, executive, judicial, and administrative matters. It may issue decrees having the force of law, and may interpret the laws, or declare null and void any decisions and orders of the Cabinet or the local People's Councils which do not conform to the Constitution, the laws adopted by the NPC, and the decrees of the Standing Committee itself. It supervises the work of the Cabinet, the Supreme People's Court, and the Procurator General. It can exercise the same powers as the NPC in making decisions on appointments and dismissals of high government officials, except for the Chairman and Vice-Chairman of the Republic, the Premier, and the heads of the Supreme Court and the Supreme Procuratorate. It has the power to declare war, to decree full or partial mobilization, to declare martial law, to ratify and abrogate treaties, and grant pardons and amnesties. It also has certain ceremonial and protocol functions, such as creating titles and ranks and deciding on awards of state orders, medals, and titles of honor.

This truly impressive list of powers and functions of the Standing Committee does not mean, however, that the important decisions are made within that body; it can be as much a rubber-stamp organ as is the NPC itself. According to Article 20 of the Organic Law of the NPC, the Standing Committee is ordinarily to meet only twice a month. But the decision to convoke the Committee rests with its Chairman, who may increase or reduce the frequency of the meeting as he sees fit. Furthermore, Article 21 provides that the Chairman and the Vice Chairman of the People's Republic, the Chairman, Vice Chairmen and members of the Standing Committee as well as the State Council can all make proposals to the Standing Committee. Thus the top Party leaders are for practical purposes as much in control of this agency of state power, as they are of the Party and state machines in general; when they choose, they can in effect dictate policy directives in the name of the Standing Committee of the NPC, which in the period between Congresses is constitutionally the supreme organ of state power.

While corresponding in general to the Presidium of the Supreme Soviet of the USSR, the Standing Committee lacks some of the formal power of its Soviet counterpart. In the ceremonial sense of the word, the head of the Presidium is also the head of the state in the USSR, but under the Chinese Constitution, that office is performed by the Chairman of the People's Republic, who need not necessarily be, and is not in fact, the Chairman of the Standing Committee. The Soviet Presidium also has the formal power to decide on the appointment and dismissal of the high command of the armed forces. This power is not explicitly given to the Standing Committee, but seems to have been exercised by it in practice. For example, a report of the Hsinhua News Agency, datelined Peking, November 10, 1954, listed certain military appointments made by Mao Tse-tung, including that of Su Yü as Chief of General Staff of the People's Liberation Army and of other principal department heads. These appointments were said to be "in accordance with the decision passed by the 2nd meeting of the Standing Committee of the First National People's Congress." Finally, under the Soviet system, the Presidium of the Supreme Soviet is the only body intervening between the Council of Ministers and the highest organ of state power, the Supreme Soviet. In China, however, the Standing Committee must share this position with the Chairman of the Republic and the Supreme State Conference, which have no parallel in the Soviet Union. But these are differences of form and convenience. Like the Presidium, the Standing Committee serves as a small and manageable group for giving the necessary legal form and authority to acts of state which are essentially decided upon in the high councils of the Party.

The Executive and Administrative Organs

The Central People's Government Council (CPGC) *and the Government Administration Council* (GAC)—The Central People's Government Council (CPGC) was the supreme organ of the government of the Chinese People's Republic (CPR) from its founding on October 1, 1949, to the adoption of the Constitution on September 20, 1954. Under the terms of the Organic Law of the Central People's Government of September, 1949, it exercised during its existence both legislative and executive powers. Composed of a Chairman (Mao), six Vice Chairmen, and a total of fifty-six members, all elected by the plenary session of the CPPCC, the Council formulated general policy, approved basic laws and regulations, and made appointments and dismissals of senior officials from the national down to the municipal level. In accordance with Article 5 of the Organic Law of the Central People's Government, the CPGC set up in turn the principal operating branches of the government: the Government Administration Council (GAC) as the "highest executive organ for state administration," the People's Revolutionary Military Council (PRMC) as "the supreme military command of the State," and the Supreme People's Court (SPC) and the People's Procurator-General's Office (PPGO) as "the highest judicial and supervisory organs of the country." Later, in November, 1952, the State Planning Committee was added to this group of principal government branches placed directly under the CPGC.

With the adoption of the Constitution, the Central People's Government

Council was abolished. While Chairman Mao was elevated to the chairmanship of the People's Republic, the former legislative and administrative powers of the CPGC went to the Standing Committee of the National People's Congress and to the State Council respectively.

Under the terms of Chapter III of the Organic Law of the Central People's Government, the Government Administration Council (GAC) was to administer the country, to carry out the Common Program, the national laws and decrees, and the decisions and orders of the CPGC. During its five-year life span, it met more than two hundred times. During that time the personnel of the GAC, which was composed of the Premier (Chou En-lai), five Vice Premiers, and sixteen ordinary members, changed only slightly. The same continuity of personnel, be it noted, has thus far characterized its successor, the State Council.

Under the GAC were the specialized executive-administrative agencies: twenty ministries, five commissions, and such auxiliary agencies as the People's Bank of China, the Chinese Academy of Sciences, and a Publications Administration. To facilitate the administrative coordination and control of these agencies, the internal structure of the GAC, under Article 18 of the Organic Law of the CPG, provided an intermediate level of supervision between the ministers and commission heads on the one hand, and the Premier and Vice Premiers on the other. At this level, three super-ministerial committees were set up within the GAC, each one having under it a group of related ministries and commissions, to which it was empowered to issue decisions and orders. This feature was an important innovation of the Chinese Communist regime, going beyond the usual Soviet practice of assigning the supervision of a major ministry or group of related ministries to each of the deputy premiers individually. However, in the changes made in the central government structure at the time of the adoption of the Constitution, the super-ministerial committees were abolished, and all agencies of ministerial rank were formally placed directly under the Premier.

While the system of committee supervision was still in effect, however, the internal structure of the executive-administrative arm was as follows: Under the Premier directly were the Ministry of Foreign Affairs, the Commission of Overseas Chinese Affairs, and the Ministry of Personnel. The Committee of Political and Legal Affairs directed the work of the Ministries of the Interior, Public Security, and Justice, the Legislative Affairs Commission, and the Nationalities Affairs Commission. Under the Committee of Finance and Economics were the Ministries of Finance, Trade, Heavy Industry, Fuel Industries, Textile Industry, Food, First-Machine Industry, Second-Machine Industry, Construction, Geology, Railways, Posts and Telecommunications, Agriculture, Forestry, Water Conservation, and Labor, and the People's Bank. The remaining Ministries of Culture,

Public Health, Education, and Higher Education, along with the Academy of Sciences, the Commission of Physical Culture and Sports, the Commission to Eliminate Illiteracy, and the Publications Administration, were assigned to the Committee of Culture and Education. In addition, a fourth committee of the GAC, the Committee of People's Control, was made responsible for the "supervision of the execution of duties by government institutions and government functionaries."

The State Council—With the adoption of the Constitution, the GAC was replaced by the State Council (SC), now composed of the Premier, sixteen Vice Premiers, and the ministers and heads of commissions. This new executive body, officially designated as the Central People's Government, enjoys a broader authority than did the GAC. It is directly responsible to the NPC, which decides on the appointment of the Premier, after nomination by the Chairman of the People's Republic. On the nomination of the Premier, the NPC similarly approves the appointment of the other members of the State Council, whom it may also remove from office (Article 27). When the NPC is not in session, these powers of confirmation and removal, for members other than the Premier, pass to its Standing Committee (Article 21).

In 1967, the State Council has 40 ministries and 11 commissions as well as 21 specialized agencies, under its aegis. Most of the GAC's ministries were carried over intact, but the Ministry of Personnel was eliminated, along with the Commission on Legislative Affairs and the Commission to Eliminate Illiteracy. The ancillary bodies such as the People's Bank were assigned to appropriate ministries for administration. The general tendency has been toward greater and greater specialization, thus requiring further division of the ministries and commissions. For example, in March, 1965, the Ministry of Building was split into ministries of Building and of Building Materials. The month previous, the Ministry of Light Industry had been divided into First and Second Ministries of Light Industry.

The effect of these changes has been to enhance the position of the Premier in the government. Since the intervening superministerial committees have been removed, he has direct authority, at least in formal terms, over each of the ministries and commissions. The addition of a Defense Ministry to the cabinet gives him a measure of control over military matters which had formerly been kept in the hands of Mao Tsetung as Chairman of the CPGC and the PRMC. And the inclusion of the State Planning Commission under the Premier's authority completes the centralization of economic as well as military affairs within the executive arm of the central government.

Although the former GAC committees were abolished, the Organic Law of the State Council still provides for a smaller "inner cabinet" under the

Premier. Article 4 makes a distinction between a "standing meeting" of the Council, composed of the Premier, the Vice Premiers, and the Secretary General, and the "plenary session" of all the ministers and heads of commissions as well. The authority of the plenary session to issue decisions and orders extends also to the standing meeting.

One other feature of the constitutional provisions concerning the State Council is noteworthy as an innovation by comparison with the Soviet practice. In the 1936 Soviet Constitution, the various ministries were enumerated by name. Later changes in the internal structure of the government thus had the effect of rendering part of the Constitution anarchronistic, and requiring the formality of a constitutional amendment to bring it up to date. Under the Chinese system, the enumeration of cabinet ministries and commissions has been left to a separate Organic Law which can more easily be revised as new departments are created or old ones merged or abolished. The result is a greater degree of flexibility and adaptability.

THE HEAD OF STATE AND THE SUPREME POLITICAL AND MILITARY COUNCILS

The principal executive and administrative responsibilities of the government rest with the State Council, under the Premier as head of government. But the Chairman of the People's Republic, as head of state, must be reckoned as possessing real power. Mao Tse-tung himself held this office until 1958, when his chosen successor, Liu Shao-ch'i, became Chairman. This office is quite different from the largely honorary and titular position of Chairman of the Presidium of the Supreme Soviet in the USSR. In contrast to their roles in some other communist and noncommunist countries, the premier and his cabinet members in Communist China are relatively less powerful, because they are overshadowed to some extent by the head of state.

The formal structure set up by the Chinese Constitution places under the direct control and supervision of the Chairman of the Republic two policy-planning organs of full constitutional status, through which he can exert a dominant influence in political and military affairs. These are the Supreme State Conference and the National Defense Council. Under Article 43 of the Constitution, the Supreme State Conference, consisting of the Chairman and Vice Chairman of the Republic, the Chairman of the Standing Committee of the NPC, the Premier of the State Council, and "other persons concerned," may be convened by the Chairman of the Republic "whenever necessary." He may in turn submit its views to the NPC or its Standing Committee, the State Council, or other bodies, "for their consideration and decision." Thus, as far as formal structure can do

so, the Supreme State Conference offers a means of preventing the development of any differences or rivalries between the various divisions of the
state machine, by bringing together at the top the heads of its various
hierarchies: that of the people's congresses, culminating in the NPC and
its Standing Committee, that of the people's councils leading up to the
State Council, and that of the armed forces, under the supreme command
of the Chairman of the Republic, though with administrative and command channels running through the State Council. In practice, of course,
the Supreme State Conference is responsible to a hierarchy completely
outside the state machinery—and the most important of them all—that
of the Communist Party of China.

On the military side, the Chairman of the Republic, under Article 42
of the Constitution, is given command of the armed forces of the country
and made *ex officio* Chairman of the National Defense Council (NDC).
Replacing the former PRMC, this body has introduced a new arrangement for the control of the armed forces. Under the previous system, the
PRMC had "unified control and command" of the armed forces, while the
Government Administration Council had apparently no powers in the
military sphere. Under the new system, however, the Ministry of Defense,
set up within the State Council, apparently now exercises the "unified
control and command" functions. This was shown in a NCNA report on
the 1954 National Day celebrations in Peking, citing an order of the day
issued by then Minister of Defense, P'eng Teh-huai, "to all commanders
and fighters of the Chinese People's Liberation Army." Such a chain of
command would correspond to that of the Soviet system.

In composition, following the January 4, 1965 appointments, the NDC
includes a Chairman, Liu Shao-ch'i, who is also the Chairman of the
Republic, 13 Vice Chairmen, and 107 ordinary members, making a total
of 121 in all. It is interesting to note that the Standing Committee of the
NPC has no power to appoint and dismiss members of the NDC, this
power being reserved to the full Congress instead.

The NDC, as an organ distinct from the State Council, seems to have
no direct control over the Ministry of Defense. Instead its function seems
to be one of policy making and planning. At the same time, the NDC
has apparently taken on less of a political and more of a narrowly military
and technical character than the former PRMC. Though little explicit
information is available, this change in character has been suggested by
the predominance of military personnel, including a number of ex-Kuomin-
tang generals, on the roster of the NDC, and by the fact that fewer of the
leaders of the present NDC concurrently hold high positions in the State
Council. The three ex-KMT generals reappointed in 1965 as Vice Chairmen of the NDC, Chang Chih-chung, Ch'eng Ch'ien and Fu Tso-yi, were

all members of the former CPGC, but hold no corresponding position within the present State Council. Fu Tso-yi is Minister of Water Conservancy and Power. Of the 11 CPC members appointed as Vice Chairmen of the NDC, all but Chu Teh were members of the former CPGC. Only five of them—Lin Piao, Ho Lung, Teng Hsiao-p'ing, Nieh Jung-chen, and Lo Jui-ch'ing—were also appointed to serve as Vice Premiers of the State Council.

Judging from its personnel, the National Defense Council may be characterized as the repository of the top military men on the mainland. It could thus serve the regime as a brain trust in military strategy. At the same time, by bringing together in one body all the leading CPC and ex-KMT generals, under the control of the Chairman of the Republic, the NDC could be intended to serve as a deterrent to any otherwise ambitious military leaders. It would thus serve to strengthen the Party's hand in the consolidation of its rule and would help relieve the CPC leadership of any worries over the possibility of intrigues and adventures indulged in by the military.

The constitutional provisions for the functions and powers of the Chairman of the People's Republic seem to have been drawn up specially with Mao Tse-tung in mind. With his ideological dedication and acknowledged contributions, the office carried with it both real power and great prestige. Since his succession in 1959, Liu Shao-ch'i has apparently failed to fulfill Mao's expectations. As noted in the leadership chapter, the Chinese Communist supporters of Mao and Lin Piao have questioned Liu's ideological fervor and intimated that he may have become a victim of corruption by power.

COMMUNIST PARTY CONTROL OF THE CENTRAL GOVERNMENT

The dominant theme underlying the whole state structure in Communist China is that whatever power is given, in a symbolic and ceremonial sense, to the people and their representatives must be concentrated, in the practical and efficient sense, in the hands of fewer and fewer individuals, until the ultimate concentration of power is given formal expression in the Supreme State Conference under the Chairman of the Republic. But a subordinate theme, never explicitly stated, may be set off against this dominant theme to give it meaning: as the size of the governmental body decreases, as it becomes further removed from the electorate, and its effective power increases, the proportion of Communist Party members among its personnel becomes much higher. This phenomenon may be described as the "Law of the Vanishing United Front."

Within the First NPC, as noted above, the proportion of Communist Party members was about one-third of the total. But within the Standing

Committee the ratio was more nearly half, with a slight edge to the communists. In the State Council, in 1954, the Premier and all ten of the Vice Premiers (as compared with three out of six under the former GAC) were CPC Politburo or Central Committee members, as were 21 out of the 35 or so Ministers and Commission Chairmen (a gain of five over the GAC). The National Defense Council showed the same pattern, with 11 out of 15 vice chairmanships and 54 out of 81 ordinary members belonging to the ruling Party. Thus, CPC members held a majority in all three of the top governmental organs—legislative, executive, and military. In 1965, the appointments made at the first session of the Third NPC reflected the same general pattern. For example, the Premier and all sixteen Vice Premiers of the State Council are members of the CPC Politburo or Central Committee, as are the Chairman and nine of the thirteen Vice Chairmen of the National Defense Council. Of the 107 regular members of the NDC, seventeen are regular and 21 are alternate members of the Central Committee. Among the Ministers and Chairmen of Commissions under the State Council, twenty-four are regular or alternate members of the Party Central Committee.

It has already been pointed out in Chapter IV that the occupants of the top positions in the state machine at the same time hold the top positions in the Party. The Supreme State Conference, in particular, is in effect a meeting of the top men of the Politburo.

At the summit, then, Party and state machines merge in a common nucleus of leadership, thus giving a hollow note to the constitutional rhetoric about the "supremacy" of the NPC. Communist writers like to argue (as for example in an editorial in the *People's Daily* on July 3, 1954) that the power of the NPC comes from the people, because the deputies are elected by the people and can be replaced by them before their term of office is up. But the electors who chose the NPC deputies (and who were themselves far removed from the voting public at large) are for all practical purposes given no alternative but to choose the Party-approved nominees. Hence, it might better be said that the power of the NPC comes from the Party; it is the Party, rather than the people, which sends its chosen representatives to the Congress and may replace them if they show any disloyalty to it. The same is true of the executive-administrative organs of the government. The so-called "highest organ" of executive authority, the State Council, is in effect under the control of an inner standing committee, the Supreme State Conference, which as it presents itself now is for all practical purposes the inner circle of the Party Politburo injected into the state machine. Whatever the Party leaders decide upon, therefore, the state will be available to carry out, under the cloak of the proper constitutional and legal forms and procedures.

CHART IV   LEVELS OF LOCAL GOVERNMENT IN COMMUNIST CHINA

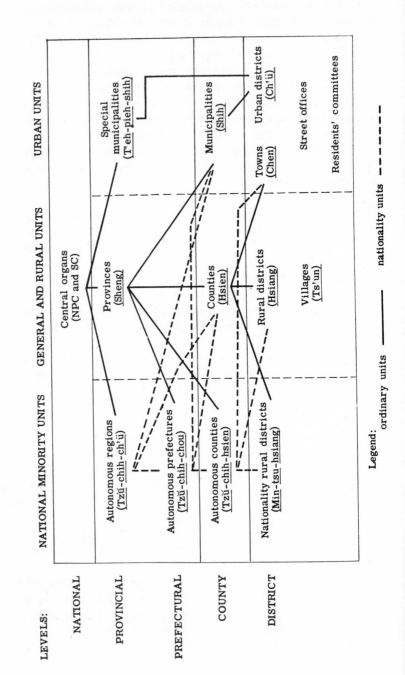

Legend: ordinary units ————   nationality units – – – –

The Organs of Local Government

LEVELS IN THE HIERARCHY OF LOCAL GOVERNMENTS

In its formal structure and operation, the organization of local government—that is, of all units of government below the national or central level—is a model of simplicity and uniformity. At each level of the hierarchy from the most remote rural district up to the largest and most populous province, the same pattern is repeated: A people's congress is elected. It meets, hears reports and speeches, and adopts whatever resolutions, decisions, or proposals are put before it, but chiefly it ratifies the choice of a people's council and a delegation to the higher people's congress, and adjourns. The people's council then carries on the work of government for the unit concerned, under the direct control and supervision of the people's councils at the higher levels, on up to the State Council at the center.

Whatever complexity this system possesses is to be found in the variety of territorial units of which it is made up, and in the way these units are joined together in a multi-tiered hierarchy from the smallest local unit up to the all-inclusive national government.

Basically, there are three levels of government below the national level: the province, the county, and the rural district, urban district, or town. A fourth level, the greater administrative area or region, intervening between province and central government, was abolished in 1954. This very simple three-layer hierarchy, however, is complicated in two ways: by the need to distinguish between urban and rural areas at each level, and by the need to give special treatment to national minorities, who for historical or cultural reasons cannot be fully integrated into a symmetrical hierarchy of local units. The accompanying chart shows in diagrammatic form how each of these needs has been provided for.

In the case of the urban areas, certain cities or metropolitan areas such as Peking, Tientsin, and Shanghai are placed directly under the central government as "special municipalities" (*t'eh-pieh-shih*), holding a rank equivalent to the province. Other municipalities (*shih*) are placed directly under the provincial governments, and are thus the urban equivalent of the counties. The counties (*hsien*) are in turn divided into rural districts (*hsiang*), each comprising one or more villages, and towns (*chen*). The municipalities themselves, whether they are under a provincial government or directly under the central authorities, are further divided into urban districts (*ch'ü*), except for the smallest which remain undistricted.

For the national minorities, so-called "autonomous" units are created. An area the equivalent of one or more provinces may be demarcated as an "autonomous region" (*tzu-chih-ch'ü*). Within such a region, or within an ordinary province, a special sub-provincial division may be set up for another nationality group, under the title of an "autonomous prefecture" (*tzu-chih-chou*). Such a prefecture may be divided up into counties and municipalities, just as the province is. At the county level, whether within a province, autonomous region, or autonomous prefecture, autonomous counties (*tzu-chih-hsien*) may be set aside for particular nationalities. And at the district level, nationality rural districts (*min-tsu-hiang*) may be distinguished from the ordinary rural districts and towns. The basic levels, including the intermediate prefectural level, may thus be listed in descending order:

1. The central government.
2. Provinces, autonomous regions, special municipalities.
2a. Autonomous prefectures within either autonomous regions or provinces.
3. Counties, autonomous counties, municipalities.
4. Rural districts, nationality rural districts, towns, urban districts.

THE DEVELOPMENT OF LOCAL GOVERNMENT, 1949–54

In consolidating its rule, the CPC encountered two major organizational tasks: (1) To establish the effective control of the central government over all levels of local government throughout the country. The need for some degree of central control had often enough been shown by the tendency to "warlordism" in the years since the fall of the Manchu Dynasty, and by the communists' own success in setting up "border regions" cut off from central government control in the days of Kuomintang rule. (2) To make a transition from military to civil control in the local areas, as well as a shift from the outright appointment of local officials from above to a semblance of choice by means of "popular elections," in order to give the local populations a greater sense of participation in the government.

An important step in the direction of greater centralization was taken in December, 1949, with the division of the country into six greater administrative areas, each with its own regional governmental organization. Complete centralization was not considered feasible at the beginning, because of the multiplicity and variety of the separate provinces, the great size of the country, its primitive transport and communications systems, and its general economic backwardness. Hence, as Mao Tse-tung was reported to have said at the time, according to the Hong Kong *China Digest* of December 14, 1949, "Only with the establishment of these strong regional organizations could things be done properly in a big country like China."

The six administrative areas were as follows: the Northeast (the Manchurian provinces and Jehol), with its capital at Mukden; North China (Hopei, Shansi, and Suiyuan), with headquarters at Peking; East China (Shantung, Chekiang, Fukien, Kiangsu, and Anhwei), centered at Shanghai: Central South China (Honan, Hupeh, Hunan, Kiangsi, Kwangtung, and Kwangsi), with its seat at Wuhan; Northwest China (Shensi, Kansu, Ninghsia, Sinkiang, and Tsinghai), with headquarters at Sian; and Southwest China (Sikang, Kweichow, Yunnan, and Szechwan), with its seat at Chungking.

Each region was placed under the leadership of a prominent CPC Politburo member or Central Committeeman. Originally it was apparently intended to organize a full-fledged "people's government" for each region, reproducing at that level the essential features of the central government itself. As a temporary expedient, however, it was necessary to continue to administer the more recently won regions through a system of military-administrative committees, pending the time when military action could be concluded, agrarian reform carried out, and "people of all circles fully organized." By November, 1952, when these preconditions had been largely met, the central government had abandoned the plan to set up full-scale "people's governments" at the regional level, and issued a decree transforming all the regional regimes into simple "administrative committees," which were to serve as the regional administrative agents of the central government. As the process of centralization and consolidation continued, it was decided in June, 1954, to eliminate these regional bodies altogether. Since that time, the provincial governments have reported directly to the central government, rather than going through an intermediate regional administrative committee. The CPGC, in an announcement of this move, reported by the NCNA in a dispatch of June 19, 1954, offered as an explanation the fact that China had "entered the stage of planned economic construction," which demanded "the further strengthening of concentrated and unified leadership of the central government."

From the first, the communists had made clear their intention of establishing "people's congresses" not only at the national level but at all lower levels as well. But just as they had to resort at first to the appointed CPPCC rather than the elected NPC at the national level, so they first set up a system of appointed "All-Circles Representative Conferences" under Article 14 of the Common Program, pending the election of people's congresses at the lower levels. These conferences, according to regulations issued by the government early in 1950, were gradually to "exercise the rights and functions of people's congresses [and] . . . hear and verify the reports of provincial, city, and county people's governments, verify and pass the local government budget, submit proposals and resolutions on the policies of these people's governments, and elect government councils."

At first, the delegates to these conferences were largely selected by the local military control commission. As the various mass organizations were set up, however, some element of local participation was injected into the selection process. Some of the delegates were "invited" by the local government, which also sent its own officials as representatives to the conference; others were chosen through a "consultative" process among the various organizations involved; and still others were elected or otherwise designated by the separate organizations officially entitled to participate.

By the end of 1951, according to communist sources, these representative conferences had been convened at least once in all the provinces and in almost every county and rural district. Furthermore they had assumed the task of electing the corresponding people's government councils in about half of the provinces and municipalities. In the other provinces and cities, as well as at the lower levels, the local government councils presumably still took office by appointment from higher headquarters. In addition, in some of the provinces and municipalities, the military control commissions set up when the communists first took over continued to function side by side with the civil governments during this transition period. It was only gradually, then, that the local "representative conferences," patterned after the CPPCC, moved toward the system of direct or indirect election of a single list of candidates. As this happened, the local government councils likewise moved away from a regime of military control and appointment, toward the system of "election" by and accountability to the people's congresses. Both changes were formalized and made mandatory in the Constitution of 1954.

PEOPLE'S CONGRESSES AND PEOPLE'S COUNCILS

Under the 1954 Constitution, people's congresses and people's councils are set up at each level of local government, repeating, with the necessary adaptations to the particular level, the essential features of the National People's Congress and the State Council.

At each level, the local people's congress is declared to be "the local organ of state power" (Article 55). At the lowest level—the rural district or nationality rural district, the town, the municipal district, or the undistricted municipality—the deputies are elected directly by the voters. But at all higher levels, they are elected by the congresses of the next lower level. Under the present electoral law, the size of the congress at each level varies with the population of the corresponding administrative unit. A rural district or town of 2,000 population would elect a congress of 20 deputies, but the number of deputies in other cases might range as low as 7 and as high as 50. At the county level, the size may range from 30 to

450; a county of 200,000 population would have a congress of 200 members. The provincial congress must have at least 50 members, no matter how sparse the population and how small the number of counties; and the number may not exceed 600, whatever the population. A province of 20 million people would have a 400-member congress. In the case of municipalities, the extreme limits are 50 and 800.

In the allocation of deputies among the sub-units, at any given level, a certain number of seats are set aside for the armed forces of each county, province, or municipality. At the same time, the electoral law in some cases shows marked preference for urban or rural areas. At the county level, the rural districts may average one delegate for every 2,000 population, but for the cities and towns, as well as the important mining and industrial districts within the county, one deputy is allotted for every 500 population. At the provincial level, deputies from rural counties may each represent from 75,000 to over 150,000 people, while provincial municipalities and towns elect one deputy for every 20,000 or less.

Like the NPC, the local congresses are given a wide range of functions and powers. They elect and may recall the members of the people's council and the president of the people's court at the corresponding level; they adopt and issue decisions on their own, and may annul or revise "inappropriate decisions" of their own people's council or of the next lower congresses and councils. In general, under Article 58 of the Constitution, each congress in its area is to insure the observance and execution of the laws and decrees, draw up plans for local economic and cultural development and public works, examine and approve local budgets and financial reports, protect public property, maintain public order, and safeguard the rights of citizens and the equal rights of national minorities.

At all levels, the individual deputies are accountable to and subject to recall by the voters or the lower congresses which elected them.

The process of nominating and electing deputies to the local people's congresses has already been described in connection with the election of the NPC. It involves not only consultation among the various united-front groups at the particular local level, but also the acceptance of suggestions from the congress leaders at the next higher level. In this regard, an instructive account of the election of delegates from the Fukien Provincial Congress to the NPC was carried by the China News Service from Foochow on August 12, 1954. It read in part:

With joint nomination of candidates as the principal method, and through the consultation of the Fukien Provincial Committee of the Chinese Communist Party, the Fukien local organizations of the various democratic parties and groups, the various people's organizations, social figures, and the Presidium of the Congress, a list of candidates was drawn up. The list was discussed by all the deputies in different groups and unanimously accepted. It was then announced before the plenary session, and the elections were held on secret ballot.

When an American politician, for example, seeks a "balanced ticket" of candidates from various territorial, ethnic, or religious backgrounds, he does so in order to attract more votes for his side. The Chinese Communists, on the other hand, can be sure that their version of the "balanced ticket" will attract all the votes there are, because it is unopposed. But it does enable the communist press, after the election, to point out how faithfully the resulting congress represents "the masses of the people of all areas, all strata, and all vocations in the province" or other unit. This kind of "representation" is, of course, purely ceremonial rather than parliamentary. But it presumably allows the ordinary citizens to feel a sense of identification with the delegates. Through such an identification, they can thus be encouraged to have a sense of personal, if vicarious, participation in the work of the government. This use of the balanced ticket for propaganda purposes is well illustrated by an excerpt from an account of the first NPC session in *People's China:*

> Ho Chien-hsiu, the young textile worker from Shantung Province, takes the floor. She stresses how it has come about that an ordinary girl like her, a child of the slums, a "little black devil," had been elected deputy to the National People's Congress. This, she says, bears out the character of the Constitution, a people's democratic constitution.

More important, however, is the way the regime may use the local congresses as a device for informing supposedly influential persons at the grass-roots level about its program and premises, and eliciting not only their support but also their missionary efforts to gain wider acceptance for and cooperation with those programs. In the Kwangtung Provincial Congress, for example, the deputies were treated to a series of forums in which representatives of the government spoke to them about what was in store for people in their particular lines of work. In the forum for peasants' representatives, the directors of the Department of Agriculture, Forestry, and Conservation spoke to the deputies and "brought up future agricultural production-increase plans, afforestation plans, and conservation plans, so that the latter could, on their return home, supervise and assist the authorities in the implementation of the plans." The newspaper account of this congress, in the Hong Kong *Ta Kung Pao* of August 7, 1954, also reported that the representatives of industrial and commercial circles, "following the days of Congress sessions and the hearing of several reports . . . all felt the heavy responsibility of people's deputies, and indicated their desire to make a good job of their task through faithful adherence to the general line during the transition period."

Aside from yielding propaganda and indoctrination benefits to the regime, the people's congresses in China, as in other communist countries, are noted for their prompt and efficient dispatch of business. Meetings last only a few days. The First Kwangtung Provincial People's Congress lasted from August 1 to 14, 1954, while the Fukien congress met from August 2 to 11, and the first national congress met from September 15 to 29. A typical agenda showing the ground covered in such a congress is provided by a newspaper account of the Fukien congress, as given by the China News Service from Foochow on August 13, 1954:

> The meeting examined and approved the report on the work of the Fukien Provincial People's Government during the past five years, discussed and decided on the central task of Fukien Province at the moment as the liberation of Taiwan and the liberation of the islands off the coast, as well as other tasks such as the development of industrial and agricultural production, particularly the guaranteeing of the fulfillment and overfulfillment of the plans for agricultural production increase. The meeting also examined and approved the financial accounts of the province for the 1953 fiscal year, and the budget for the 1954 fiscal year. The meeting further discussed the Draft Constitution of the People's Republic of China and adopted a resolution supporting it. Finally the meeting elected the People's Deputies from Fukien Province to the National People's Congress.

The people's councils, as already noted, are elected by and accountable to their corresponding congresses. But they stand in a double line of authority and responsibility, which is expressed in Article 62 of the Constitution: "Local people's councils, that is, local people's governments, are the executive organs of local people's congresses at corresponding levels, and are the local administrative organs of the state." This is made more explicit in the Organic Law for local people's congresses and people's councils, adopted by the NPC on September 21, 1954, and promulgated by Chairman Mao a week later. Under its terms, people's councils are "responsible to the people's congresses of the corresponding level and to the administrative organs of the state of the next higher level and report to them on their work."

In internal structure, as provided in Article 25 of the Organic Law for local government organs, the councils are much the same at all levels, consisting of a chairman, a number of vice-chairmen, and a number of ordinary members. The titles vary from one level to the next: governor and deputy governor for the province; mayor and deputy mayor for the municipality; magistrate and deputy magistrate for the county; and head and deputy head for the rural district and town. The term of office of each council is the same as that of its corresponding congress—four years for the provincial council and two years for the others.

Local people's councils vary in size according to their level in the hierarchy and the size of the territorial unit they administer. The councils of the provinces and special municipalities directly under central authority will range from 25 to 55 persons in size. County councils range from 9 to 21 persons, with a maximum of 31 for the most populous counties. For ordinary municipalities, the corresponding figures are 9 to 31 with a maximum of 45. Urban districts range from 9 to 21; rural districts, nationality rural districts, and towns may have from 3 to 13 members. At the county and provincial levels, the councils are to meet once a month or oftener; at the district and town levels, twice a month or oftener.

The functions and powers assigned the local councils show clearly that it is they, rather than the local congresses, which are the effective agency of government within their respective territories. Under the Organic Law for local units, the congresses may "adopt and promulgate" resolutions, "approve" or "decide on" plans, "hear and examine" reports, and the like. But the council is given the power to control the work of its corresponding congress. The council "sponsors" the election of deputies to its congress, it "convenes" the congress and "brings forward bills" before it. When the congress is not in session, the council issues decisions and orders and determines administrative measures to carry out not only the resolutions of the congress but also the directives of the higher organs of the state. It directs the work of the people's councils at the lower levels, and may revise or annul any of their decisions and orders it deems inappropriate. It may also intervene to suspend the execution of resolutions adopted by people's congresses at the lower levels.

Under these circumstances, the line of direction and authority coming from the State Council down through the hierarchy of local councils is much stronger in the work of any given council than is the line of direction coming from its congress as the supposed organ of the popular will. The congress serves, not as a source of initiative and innovation, but rather as an echo chamber, to give back to the council what it, or its superior organs, require in the way of authorization for action.

The tightness of the control from the top is to be seen also in the organization and control of "work departments" under the local councils. These correspond to the ministries of the State Council, with the necessary adaptations, omissions, and consolidations into fewer departments at the lower levels. For example, the provincial councils are authorized to set up bureaus, offices, or committees of civil affairs, public security, justice, supervision, planning, finance, food, industry, commerce, communications, agriculture and forestry, water conservation, labor, culture, education, public health, and physical culture, as well as other general offices. Municipalities may add departments of municipal construction and public utilities. The "establishment, addition, reduction, or amalgamation" of these work departments is subject to the approval of the people's council on the next higher level. But more important, the individual departments within any given council, under Article 40 of the Organic Law, are themselves subject to the directives and orders of the corresponding departments or ministries at the higher levels, and in turn issue orders and directives to the competent departments of the lower councils.

Lest there be any doubt about the degree of central control to be exercised through the local people's councils, the section of the Constitution dealing with local government closes with the reminder that "the local people's councils throughout the country are administrative organs of state which are under the unified leadership of, and subordinate to, the State Council."

LOCAL GOVERNMENT CONTROL WITHIN RURAL AND URBAN DISTRICTS

The line of authority from the national government down to the congresses, councils, and individual work departments of the lowest rural and urban districts would be incomplete, and the monolithic hierarchy would be simply a paper organization, unless the effective control extended one step further: from the government organs to the people themselves. Hence, the entire structure of communist local government is based on an intensive indoctrination and direction of the general public at the grassroots level.

The communists, because they first built up centers of power in rural areas long before they were able to seize power over the entire country, gained early training and experience in organizing the peasant masses through the *hsiang*, or rural district unit. On the other hand, the failure of the Nationalist government to pay much attention to village-level organization and administration may have been one of the factors in its eventual loss of power on the mainland. As one of a group of students traveling through the Honan-Hupeh-Anhwei border region in the winter of 1933–34, one of the present writers was greatly impressed by the level of indoctrination and discipline, and the legacy of mass organization and control left behind among the peasants in the villages after the communists had withdrawn on the eve of the Long March. Subsequently the same thoroughness of rural control characterized their administration of the Shensi-Kansu-Ninghsia border region during the Yenan period from 1935 to 1946, and was extended to the "liberated areas" during the civil war. With the establishment of the Peking regime in 1949, the same tight rule of the rural areas was gradually extended throughout the whole country. Without it the communists would have been unable to carry out their agrarian reform program with such vigor and ruthlessness, or to carry on their drive for agricultural collectivization.

There are now more than 200,000 *hsiang* in the entire country, each composed of one or more villages. "The *hsiang* people's government is a very important unit in the government administration," wrote Shie I-yuan in *People's China* of January 1, 1954, "because it is through this governmental organ that the broad masses of the people are drawn into the direction of state administration, and to implement the decisions of the people's government; it is through the *hsiang* that the laboring people are mobilized to participate actively in the work of economic construction." Following the adoption of the Constitution and the inauguration of the period of transition to socialism, the role of the *hsiang* organs of government took on an even greater importance for carrying out the so-called "socialist transformation of agriculture" through organizing the broad masses of the peasants into mutual-aid teams, agricultural producers' cooperatives, and collective farms.

Under Article 28 of the Organic Law of local government units, the *hsiang* people's council may exercise sweeping executive and administrative powers in economic, financial, social, and military-conscription affairs. It may set up, as needed, subsidiary work committees for civil affairs, public security, armed forces, finance and taxation, production and cooperation, culture and education, and mediation, enlisting as members of these committees the deputies to the *hsiang* people's congress and "other suitable persons." (Article 35)   In addition, it has been the communist practice to set up branches of the Party-controlled mass organizations, such as the trade unions, peasants' associations, the women's federation, and the youth federation, at the rural district level, under the leadership of the *hsiang* branch of the CPC.   These so-called people's organizations provide the indirect channel, just as the communist-controlled *hsiang* people's congresses and councils provide the direct channel, through which CPC control reaches each individual in every sphere of his daily life.   The resulting power over the individual—he is dependent upon the communist *hsiang* chief for permission to marry, for a recommendation for getting a job, for approval of his application for an agrarian loan, and even for famine relief—is so great that when this power is abused, the result is an extreme form of despotism.   Various provincial communist organs, notably the *Hupeh Daily*, in the period from January through April, 1953, gave numerous accounts of the tragic effects in the lives of ordinary citizens of the despotic exercise of authority by the *hsiang* chiefs.

At the rural district level, this style of authority could be made effective because of the relatively sparse or small population, its low cultural and educational level, and the lack of diversity in occupations.   But when the fortunes of the civil war brought the communists to power in the great cities, they found a need for a more elaborate set of control organs.   These were provided for in Article 42 of the Organic Law for local government units, which authorized the people's councils of urban districts or undistricted municipalities to set up "street offices" as their accredited organs.

Pursuant to this law, the Standing Committee of the NPC, on December 31, 1954, approved a Regulation on the Organization of Municipal Street Offices, which was promulgated by Chairman Mao on the same day. According to the text of the regulations, as it appeared in the *People's Daily* on New Year's Day, 1955, the purpose in creating these street offices is to "strengthen the work among residents and to tighten the bonds between the government and the residents" (Article 1). In municipalities with a population of more than 100,000, municipal street offices should be set up, as the work of the municipal people's council requires, to serve as the "branch offices" of the council (Article 1 and 2). Municipalities with a population of less than 100,000 but more than 50,000 may do the same if they find it necessary. The expenses of maintaining these offices, including the salaries of their personnel, are to be met by the councils of the province or the directly controlled municipality under a uniform program laid down by the central government. These street offices are to undertake the tasks entrusted to them by the municipal or urban district people's council regarding work among the residents, to direct the work of the residents' committees, and to "reflect the opinion and requests of the residents" (Article 4).

The "residents' committees" just referred to complete the process of transmitting central government control, surveillance, and persuasion into every urban home. Simultaneously with the regulation on street offices was promulgated a second Regulation on the Organization of City Residents' Committees. Like the street offices, these committees are to strengthen the work of the government among the municipal residents and to promote their welfare (Article 1). But in effect, they are to serve as the eyes, ears, and mouth of the municipality or urban district council in "mobilizing the residents to support the government and abide by the law." They are also to lead the work of safeguarding security among the masses (Article 2).

The division of the urban population into residents' committees was facilitated by the earlier subdivision of the city, for census and public security purposes, into "sections." Within each section one or more committees are set up, each containing 100 to 600 families. These are further subdivided into not more than 17 residents' groups, of 15 to 40 families each. Each group elects a delegate to the committee, which thus consists of from 7 to 17 members, most of whom are simultaneously the heads of their respective groups. The committee in turn chooses a director and 1 to 3 deputy directors from among its members. The groups from which these committee officials were originally sent as deputies may then each choose an additional delegate to sit as its representative on the committee. Residents who are under surveillance or who have been deprived of their political rights are to be enrolled in their appropriate residents' groups, but are not eligible to be elected to the residents' committee.

Within a large residents' committee, permanent and provisional work committees may be set up, with the approval of the municipal people's council, if the situation warrants (Article 3). As with the street offices, the public and miscellaneous expenditures of the residents' committee and the living allowances of its members are to be met by appropriations from the competent people's council of the province or the directly controlled municipality, under a country-wide uniform plan (Article 9). Fund-raising drives carried on by the residents' committees on behalf of public welfare projects can be conducted only with the approval of the municipal people's council (Article 10). The main task of the residents' committees, however, is to serve the municipal people's council and its work departments as tentacles and working tools. As Article 8 provides, the various work departments and other organs—including the street offices—of the competent municipal or urban district council can allot tasks to the residents' committee or to its subsidiary work committees, and can give them operating instructions directly, so long as these tasks and instructions are in accordance with the uniform program and have the approval of the people's council.

With the setting up of municipal street offices and residents' committees, paralleling the looser but equally effective organization of the *hsiang* in the countryside, the Chinese Communists gained the capacity for bringing the urban as well as the rural population of the country completely under their control.

THE NATIONALITIES POLICY

The Problem of National Minorities and the Communist Solution

The territory of mainland China, like that of the Soviet Union, includes a variety of national minorities exhibiting a wide range of differences in language, religion, social organization, economic pursuits, and way of life in general. In some cases, cultural and historical factors may serve to a greater or less degree to set these groups apart from the society around them and to give them an internal cohesion or sense of group identity. But the same distinctness and internal cohesion would make these groups, in the eyes of the communist leaders, potential centers of disaffection with and opposition to a regime bent upon a thoroughgoing transformation of the economic, social, and political life of the country. Hence, the problem for the leadership is one of disarming and diverting the potential hostility of these groups, while capitalizing on their latent or active nationalism to build support for the regime.

The dimensions of the problem are not so great, however, for the Chinese leaders as for their Soviet counterparts, since, in Russia, minority nationalities are more varied and constitute a larger proportion of the total population. Although there are more than sixty such groups in China, only twelve have a population exceeding half a million. The largest group, the Chuangs, number over six million, while the smallest are made up of only a few hundred persons. For the most part the national minorities are scattered through the outlying border regions, especially in the huge northwest and southwest frontier provinces. The striking fact is that although they occupy nearly one-half the land area of the country, they account for scarcely 7 per cent of the total population. The other 93 per cent is made up of the Hans, or Chinese. [2]

The theoretical basis for solving the nationality question in China as in

[2] The following table indicates the approximate size of the national minorities in 1954 and 1961, and the location of the principal minority groups in China:

Nationality	1954 Population (a)	1961 Population (b)	Main centers of population
Chuang	6,000,000	7,785,414	Kwangsi Chuang Autonomous Region
Hui	4,000,000	3,934,335	Kansu, Ninghsia, Tsinghai provinces
Yi	3,300,000	3,264,432	Greater and Lesser Liang Mountains on borders of Sikang and Yunnan province
Miao	2,300,000	2,687,590	Miao Autonomous Region of Kweichow province, western Hunan province and many other regions in Central-South and Southwest China
Uigur	3,000,000	3,901,205	Sinkiang province (now Sinkiang Uigur Autonomous Region)
Tibetan	3,000,000	2,775,622	Sikang-Tibet Plateau, Tsinghai province
Puyi	1,100,000	1,313,015	Southwestern part of Kweichow province
Mongolian	1,500,000	1,645,695	Inner Mongolian Autonomous Region and Ninghsia, Tsinghai, and Sinkiang provinces
Korean	1,100,000	1,255,551	Yenpien Korean Autonomous Region of Kirin province
Tung	600,000	825,323	Southeastern Kweichow province and northern part of Kwangsi province
Yao	600,000	747,985	Kwangsi and northern Kwangtung province and southern Hunan province
T'ai	500,000	503,616	Border regions of Yunnan province

(a) *People's China*, June 1, 1954.   (b) *Nationalities of China* (Peking: 1961) the USSR has been taken from Marxist-Leninist theory, as expounded by Stalin in his early work, *Marxism and the National Question.* There are two basic elements to the solution. The first holds that the culture or way of life of the nationality group should be, in the words of the familiar slogan, "national in form, socialist in content." The group should be granted a maximum of cultural autonomy in retaining the national language, customs, traditions, religious beliefs, art forms, and the like. But if their way of life is to be socialist in content—if they are to be taught to think in terms of the Marxist-Leninist ideology and the current line of the Party, and to accept the program of socialist transformation and construction—then a substantial measure of political control and direction from above is required. Hence, the second element of the solution calls for the organization of government wherever possible by national units controlled from the central government.

Local leaders are to be encouraged and trained to take over the responsibilities of administration and government among their own people. Where a minority group is sufficiently concentrated within a given area, it is to have its own "autonomous" government, run by officials of its own nationality. Where minorities are mixed together within the same territory, they are to be proportionately represented in the organs of government. The basic principle in either case is that local rule must be carried out by members of the local minority group—but that their rule must be under the strict control and direction of the central authorities. From the standpoint of the local minority group, it will thus appear, in the words of Stalin, as quoted in an editorial in *People's Daily* on September 9, 1953, that "in all the control organs, there stand your own people, men who know your language, your living customs." What the communist solution requires, therefore, is that the voice of authority shall speak in the language of the local minority group, but that the words shall be the words of the man at the top.[3]

---

[3] Two quotations from Stalin's 1913 essay on "Marxism and the National Question," reprinted in his collection of writings on the subject, will serve to show the essence of the theoretical solution to the question in Marxism-Leninism. The first offers the suggestion of setting up separate governmental units for each territorial concentration of a national minority group (rather than giving autonomy to a nationality group regardless of its territorial concentration or dispersion):

> National autonomy does not solve the problem. What is the way out? The only real solution is regional autonomy for such crystallized units as Poland, Lithuania, the Ukraine, the Caucasus, and so forth. The advantage of regional autonomy consists first in the fact that it does not deal with a fiction deprived of territory, but with a definite population inhabiting a definite territory. Secondly, it does not divide people according to nation, it does not strengthen partitions; on the contrary, it only serves to break down these partitions and unites the population in such a manner as to open the way

Drawing upon Marxist-Leninist theory, the leaders of the Chinese Communist regime have enunciated and have embodied in their constitutional documents a set of attractive principles to guide their policy toward the national minorities—principles of equality, fraternity, cultural freedom, and political unity. Article 3 of the 1954 Constitution proclaims that "all the nationalities are equal," and prohibits any "discrimination against, or oppression of, any nationality." In greater detail, the earlier General Program for the Implementation of Regional Autonomy for Nationalities, promulgated on August 9, 1952, enjoined the governmental organs of the different autonomous areas to "educate the people of different nationalities to respect each other's languages, both spoken and written, customs, traditions and religious beliefs; and prohibit national discrimination and oppression." Under the principle of equality, each nationality with its own regional government is allowed to "exercise autonomy" and "administer" its local finances within the limits of the authority prescribed by the Constitution and the laws, and to organize its own public security forces "in accordance with the military system of the State" (Article 70 of the Constitution).

The principle of fraternity and mutual help is touched upon only in passing in the Constitution, in the Preamble reference to "one great family of free and equal nations." It was illustrated in fuller detail, however, in earlier documents. Article 50 of the Common Program called upon all nationality groups in a given area to "establish unity and mutual aid among themselves . . . so that the People's Republic of China will become

---

for division of a different kind, division according to class. Finally it provides the opportunity of utilizing the natural wealth of the region and of developing its productive forces in the best possible way without awaiting the decisions of a common center— functions which are not proper to national cultural autonomy.

The second argues that this solution, coupled with cultural autonomy, will bring the greatest returns in support and obedience for the least effort in control and direction:

A minority is discontented not because there is no national union but because it does not enjoy the right to use its native language. Permit it to use its native tongue and the discontent will pass of itself.—A minority is discontented not because there is no artificial union, but because it does not possess its own schools. Give it its own schools and all the grounds for discontent will disappear.—A minority is discontented not because there is no national union, but because it does not enjoy liberty of conscience, liberty of movement, etc. Give it these liberties and it will cease to be discontented.—Thus national equality in all forms (language, school and so forth) is an essential element in the solution of the national problem. A state law based on complete democracy in the country is required, prohibiting all national privileges without exception and all kinds of disability and restrictions on the rights of national minorities.

These quotations are found on pp. 64 and 65, respectively, of Stalin's *Marxism and The National Question* (New York: International Publishers, 1942). The Russian source is *Sochineniia* (*Collected Works*) (Moscow: Gospolitzdat, 1946), Vol. II, pp. 361–62 and 363.

a big fraternal and cooperative family comprising all its nationalities."
The 1952 General Program added the requirement that the governmental
organs of autonomous areas help any other minority groups concentrated
within the same area to "practice regional autonomy" (Article 27). Higher
organs of state are likewise required, under Article 72 of the Constitution
as under the General Program, to safeguard the right of autonomous units
to exercise autonomy and to "assist the various national minorities in
their political, economic, and cultural development." In keeping with the
principles of equality and fraternity, no large or numerically dominant
group is to engage in "greater nationalism," or actions tending to oppress
or discriminate against smaller groups in the same area; and no smaller
group is to succumb to "narrow nationalism," or an attitude of fear and
hostility toward the larger group.

The principle of cultural freedom was laid down in Article 53 of the
Common Program, whereby all minorities were to have "freedom to develop their spoken and written languages, to preserve or reform their
traditions, customs, and religious beliefs." The governing organ of an
autonomous region, under the General Program, was to promote the development of the culture, education, arts, and health services of the various
nationalities within its area. The 1954 Constitution once more promised
all nationalities the "freedom to use and foster the growth of their spoken
and written languages, and to preserve or reform their own customs or
ways" (Article 3).

The principles of equality, fraternity, and cultural freedom hold out a
certain hope of real autonomy and self-government to the national minorities; but this hope is effectively removed by the principle of unified leadership and control. This principle emphasizes that each national group is
an integral part of the People's Republic of China and owes its primary
allegiance to the republic. Each group is assigned its own place in the
hierarchy of government and is to accept directives reaching it from the
higher levels, particularly with regard to its financial system, its economic
development, and the role of its military forces. Article 10 of the Constitution, while freely granting the exercise of autonomy, the administration
of local finance and the organization of local armed forces, actually subjects the autonomous units to the close control of the central government
in these matters. It is true, that under Article 67 of the Constitution, as
under the General Program, the various nationality areas are allowed to
retain their traditional forms of local government, at least in name, "in
accordance with the wishes of the majority of the nationality or nationalities enjoying regional autonomy in a given area." But in all essential
respects, these local variants, according to Article 10 of the General Program, were not allowed to deviate from the nationally uniform standard,

which required them to be "set up according to the basic principles of democratic centralism and of the system of people's congresses." And although the local organs are authorized under the Constitution to draw up "special regulations suited to the political, economic, and cultural characteristics of the nationality or nationalities" of their particular areas, such regulations must likewise have the approval of the central authorities (Article 70).

It is apparent, then, that the purpose behind the policy for national minorities is to enable the communist regime to control and utilize these groups in its program of social regimentation and economic transformation. There are various subsidiary means by which this control can be made acceptable and effective. Cultural autonomy, in so far as it is a reality, can be offered as an inducement for support. Manifestations of national particularism can be decried and discouraged, while "Fatherland" nationalism, or identification with the goals of the regime and hatred of its real and supposed enemies, is praised and inculcated. Cadres can be drawn from the minority nationalities for training along political and ideological as well as vocational and cultural lines, and can then be sent back to their native groups to spread the doctrines of communism and Fatherland nationalism among their own people. The central government and its leading personalities, especially Mao Tse-tung, can be held up as shining symbols of Chinese unity and prestige. But however necessary and useful these devices are, the core of the communist solution to the nationality question is to be found in the way in which the so-called "autonomous" units of government, once set up at any particular level, are integrated into a closely knit hierarchy of authority and administration under the control of the central government.

The Autonomous Regions and Organs

The basic principle for the government of national minority groups is that where such minorities are sufficiently concentrated within a given territory they are to organize an autonomous unit of government for that territory. All such units, whether autonomous regions, prefectures, counties, or nationality rural districts, are often referred to in the communist literature as "autonomous regions" or "autonomous areas," and their equivalent of the people's congresses and people's councils as "autonomous organs." But not all minority groups are sufficiently concentrated; hence, special provisions were made for the "scattered minorities," in two sets of decisions adopted by the GAC on February 22, 1952. One provided that where such minorities constituted an appreciable proportion of the population within a given territory, or where the existing relations between the different nationalities might affect local administration in various aspects, representatives of the minority were to be brought into a "democratic-coalition government of nationalities." The other provided that even in cases where the "scattered nationalities" were not brought into a coalition government, their rights and freedoms as citizens, as well as their freedom to "preserve or change their national ways of life," were to be fully respected by the local governments concerned. Special rights of appeal to the local people's government for assistance were provided for members of scattered minorities "faced with insurmountable difficulties in the enjoyment of their right to national equality."

Wherever minority groups are sufficiently concentrated, however, the policy calls for separate "autonomous regions" to be organized for government and administration at the local level. Such areas have been established by negotiations between the spokesmen of the national minorities concerned and the local government authorities of the next higher level. Once an agreement has been reached on the size, the boundaries, and administrative status of an autonomous area, it must be approved by a still higher state organ; for all units of county level or higher, central government approval is necessary.

The resulting autonomous regions are of three types, depending upon their constituent populations. The first includes those regions peopled by one minority only, as in the case of the Tibetans in P'ingwu, in northern Szechwan province. A second type includes those areas inhabited by one large national minority, with enclaves of other minorities of comparatively small population, as in the Inner Mongolian Autonomous Region. The third embraces the "joint autonomous regions" inhabited by several national minorities, as at Lungsheng, in northern Kwangsi province, where people of the T'ung, Chuang, Miao, Yao, and Ling minorities live side by side. Once the type of region has been determined, and provision made for the national minorities-within-minorities (either through a coalition government, or through a separate autonomous unit at a lower level), the structure of government for any given unit follows the system already described for local governments in general. As already noted, however, the Constitution makes special provisions for the use of the local language, and grants limited power to adapt the laws, regulations, and decisions of higher authorities to the requirements of the particular nationality.

In a report to the CPGC on August 8, 1952, Ulanfu, then Vice Chairman (and later Chairman) of the Commission of Nationalities Affairs, stated that as of June, 1952, 130 national autonomous regions of different levels had been established throughout the country, embracing a total of four and a half million members of minority groups. In a later analysis in *People's China* of January 1, 1954, Liu Chun indicated that as of October,

1953, at least 50 autonomous regions with an administrative status of counties or higher units had been established, and that more than ten million people had been brought into autonomous units. [4] Since that date, other units have been created. *People's Daily* of September 23, 1954, carried an account of the formation of a Tash Kurghan Tadzhik autonomous region in Sinkiang province, while a NCNA dispatch from Ining, December 1, 1954, announced the creation of an autonomous prefecture (*chou*) for the Kazak people of northern Sinkiang province. Similarly, an NCNA dispatch from Sining, November 1, 1954, noted the establishment of a Mongolian autonomous region in the southeastern part of Tsinghai province.

The three key areas where national minorities are concentrated, from Peking's point of view, are Inner Mongolia, Sinkiang, and Tibet. The Inner Mongolian Autonomous Region was indeed the first such area to be organized, its establishment dating from May 1, 1947. It was formed by a consolidation of all areas in Northwest China, as well as the western part of Manchuria, containing Mongol populations. This reversed the policy of the Nationalist government, which had tried to bring the Mongols under a system of administration uniform with that of the rest of the country, by dividing the area into several provinces and incorporating them into the regular provincial system. The work of undoing this policy was not completed all at once. In 1950, additional Mongol areas in the former Chahar province were incorporated into Inner Mongolia, the non-Mongol portions being assigned to adjacent provinces. The integration of Suiyuan province into the larger autonomous region followed at a slower pace; however, in 1952, Kweisui in Suiyuan became the capital of Inner Mongolia, and Ulanfu was made concurrently the Governor of Suiyuan. Complete formal integration was finally achieved with the abolition of the province late in 1954.

The Inner Mongolian Autonomous Region, like the provinces, is directly subordinate to the central government in Peking. Within the Region, according to an Organic Regulation approved by the Standing Committee of the NPC and promulgated by Mao on November 11, 1955, a number of special units of local government have been set up to conform to the traditional groupings in the area. At the level of the prefecture or

---

[4] Among the larger units, in addition to the Inner Mongolian Autonomous Region, were the autonomous regions of the Chuangs in Western Kwangsi province, the Tibetans in Sikang province, the Yis in the Liang Mountains of Sikang province, the T'ais in Hsishuangpanna in Yünnan province, the T'ais and Chingpos in Tehhung, Yünnan province, the Miaos in Western Hunan province, the Lis and Miaos on Hainan Island, the Tibetans in Yushu, Tsinghai province, the Tibetans in Southern Kansu province, the Huis in Hsihaiku, Kansu province, and the Koreans in Yenpien, Kirin province.

administrative area (the nearest equivalent to a province within the Region), there is also a league (*ming*). A banner (*ch'i*) is included at the level of the county, the municipality, and the urban district of municipalities directly under the regional government. And alongside the rural district (*hsiang*) and the nationality rural district there are the *sumu* and the *chiach'a* (Mongolian terms not readily translatable).

The authority of the central government (and of the CPC) in the Region has been mainly concentrated in the person of Ulanfu, an alternate member of the CC from 1945 and of the Politburo from 1956, and currently a vice premier and head of the Nationality Affairs Commission in the central government.[5] He holds the usual multiple leading positions as governor, head of the Party committee for Inner Mongolia, and commander and political commissar of the Inner Mongolia Military District. Needless to say, however, the other channels of control, through the centrally directed party and mass organizations, have also been extended into the region. At the same time, the appearance of local autonomy is maintained. Mongolian, which is written with the Russian alphabet, has parity with Chinese as the official language, it is taught in the schools, and is used in local publications.

The second major area inhabited mostly by minority nationalities is Sinkiang, a huge autonomous region (formerly a province) in the northwest on the Russian border, comprising one-sixth of the territory of China. Here the minority problem is more confused, because there are no less than thirteen different cultural or ethnic groups to be taken into account, of which the Uigurs, the Kazaks, and the Moslems are the most important.

When the provincial government of Sinkiang surrendered to the communists in September, 1949, a coalition government was set up which included the East Turkestan leaders who during the Second World War had headed a government of the north border regions under the sponsorship of the Soviet Union. By the end of 1944 this East Turkestan group had formed a Soviet-oriented "Republic of Eastern Turkestan," and in 1948, a "Sinkiang League for the Defense of Peace and Democracy." Its leaders, who had thus actually initiated the "liberation" movement in Sinkiang, proved to be less tractable to Chinese control than the local leaders in other areas (e.g., Inner Mongolia) where the CPC itself had supervised the "liberation" movement. But the chairman and some of the most important league leaders were killed in a 1949 airplane accident, and the less prominent Turkestan figure, Saifudin, who then took over the leadership, proved more amenable to Chinese influence. He joined the CPC in

---

[5] As noted in the chapter on the military, the early 1967 unrest in Inner Mongolia may have been attributed in part to Ulanfu, and may result in a division of his offices and authority.

1950, and the league itself became the "Sinkiang's People's Democratic League" under direct Chinese Communist control. The East Turkestan movement was discredited, and purges of Uigurs and Kazaks followed in 1951 to remove the unwholesome remnants of "narrow nationalism," "Pan-Islamism," and "feudalism."

Even with these changes, the granting of regional autonomy in Sinkiang was slow in coming. The very complexity of the multinational character of the province was undoubtedly one factor in the delay. Another reason, according to Saifudin, was the fact that the East Turkestan revolt had been carried out as a "bourgeois democratic revolution" but not under the direction of the Chinese Communists, with the result that untrustworthy "feudalistic" and "bourgeois" elements had infiltrated the government administration and had to be weeded out. Hence, the major effort to set up autonomous national units did not start until late 1953. By September, 1954, however, according to an article by the Chairman of the Sinkiang Provincial People's Government, Burhan, in the *People's Daily* of September 29, a total of 24 autonomous units had been set up at different levels within the province. Of these, 4 had the status of sub-provincial districts or prefectures (the Mongolian, Hui, Kirghiz, and Kazak units); another 4 were of county level (the Hui, Hsipo, Kazak, and Tadzhik); 7 were equivalent to sub-county districts, and 9 were nationality rural districts. Additional autonomous areas were scheduled to be created in the spring of 1955. A further major step was taken in November, 1954, with the creation of a fifth autonomous prefecture in the region of Ili, called the Ili Kazak Autonomous Chou. According to the *People's Daily* account of December 6, 1954, this area has a population of 770,000, which would make it the largest of the five autonomous chou in Sinkiang.

The final step in the establishment of regional autonomy in Sinkiang came in September, 1955. On September 13, the Standing Committee of the NPC, on the recommendation of Premier Chou En-lai, approved the abolition of Sinkiang Province and the establishment in its place of the Sinkiang Uigar Autonomous Region. At the same time, 6 more autonomous counties were established within the area. The Chairman of the Autonomous Region is Saifudin, who had been Vice Chairman of the Sinkiang People's Government and remains a Vice Chairman of the Standing Committee of the NPC. He is also a member of the NDC and an alternate member of the CPC Central Committee. Wang En-mao, who had been the First Secretary of the Sinkiang Sub-Bureau of the CPC Central Committee (while Saifudin was only the Fourth Secretary) was appointed to the same position in the Party Committee for the new Autonomous Region. Formal inauguration ceremonies for the new region were held in

Urumchi on October 1, the sixth anniversary of the founding of the CPR, with Politburo member Tung Pi-wu representing the Party Central Committee and the central government. [6]

In terms of strategic location and economic value, Sinkiang has increasingly become more important to the Chinese Communists. Through the area run the rail lines which connect Peking to Moscow, while highways lead to Tibet and the Indian frontier. Rich in mineral and petroleum deposits, including uranium and plutonium, Sinkiang also provides the operational base for the development of atomic energy; the test site of Lop Nor is located there. In 1955, however, when the Sinkiang-Uigur Autonomous Region was established, the local national minorities vastly outnumbered the Hans, or Chinese. For example, the 1953 census reported only about 300,000 Hans out of a total population of nearly five million.

Beginning in 1956, and justified by the necessity of developing the economic resources of the area, the Chinese Communists began to encourage or order thousands of Hans to migrate to Sinkiang. [7] By 1957, the Han Chinese already constituted nearly a third of the area's populace, and this policy has been continued, if not intensified, by growing strategic considerations. Included in the latter category are the uprisings of 1957 and 1958, associated with the Hundred Flowers campaign, sporadic incidents between 1959 and 1962, and the turmoil of 1963. In every case, the uprisings seem to have been motivated by anti-Chinese sentiments, although the Chinese Communists have attributed at least the 1963 uprising to Soviet instigation. [8] The outbreak of violence in Sinkiang, early in 1967, again demonstrates that Chinese Communist policies for the region have been unsuccessful in winning the support of the national minorities.

Another area granted regional autonomy directly under the central gov-

[6] It is perhaps significant that regional autonomy was not granted until the process of land reform and agrarian transformation was well along. According to Burhan, the land reform program, begun in September, 1952, had been "victoriously completed" two years later, and one-third of the peasants in the province had been organized into a number of collective farms, 79 agricultural producers' cooperatives, and more than 50,000 mutual-aid teams. In the case of the Kazak Autonomous Prefecture, nearly one-half of all peasant households, according to an official survey, had been organized into mutual-aid teams and agricultural cooperatives by the time of its formation in November, 1954.

[7] As early as 1949, some 200,000 PLA troops were reported to have been sent to Sinkiang as "shock teams" for economic development.

[8] On September 6, 1963, Peking Radio alleged that Soviet agents had lured some 50,000 tribesmen across the border in April-May, 1962, and trained them for the overthrow of the Chinese Communist government in the Ili region. On September 21, 1963, the Soviets charged that the Chinese Communists had systematically violated the common border 5,000 times in 1962 alone. In December, 1966, a Brazilian journalist noted that Chen Yi had informed him that the Soviet Union had already moved 13 army divisions from Eastern Europe to the Sino-Soviet border areas.

ernment is Tibet. The Chinese Communists entered Tibet in 1950 during the Korean War and forcefully reestablished Chinese sovereignty in the region. After token resistance, Tibet in 1951 sent representatives to Peking to conclude an "Agreement . . . on Measures for the Peaceful Liberation of Tibet." Under its terms the Tibetans were permitted to retain the system of monasteries, and the ruler, the Dalai Lama, was kept in office, although the rival pro-Chinese Panchen Lama was allowed to return to Tibet from his retreat in Tsinghai Province, and was given associate status with the Dalai. The Tibetans were granted the right to administer their own internal affairs, but the central government took over control of their foreign policy and demanded integration of the Tibetan army with the People's Liberation Army. To insure these arrangements and to guarantee that internal "reforms" would be carried out, Chinese troops were to be stationed in Tibet.

In the fall of 1954, both the Dalai and the Panchen Lamas journeyed to Peking to add their ceremonial presence to the opening of the first NPC. Their visit turned into an extended stay in the capital city, and it was not until March 12, 1955, that a Hsinhua News Agency dispatch announced the departure of the lamas on the return trip to Tibet, each by a different route. The rival groups backing each Lama were said to have reached an agreement on January 19, 1955, on their long-standing major differences. Apparently the negotiation on this agreement paved the way for regularizing the position of Tibet in the Chinese People's Republic as a full-fledged autonomous region. Other preparations to this end were going on in Tibet itself, where during the absence of the lamas, the conduct of affairs was in the hands of the Vice Chairman of the Tibetan Regional Government, Glenshisu Juimatsejendochi. At any rate, simultaneously with the departure of the lamas for Tibet, the central authorities in Peking announced the formation of a "preparatory committee" to set up the government of a Tibet Autonomous Region. The Dalai Lama was named chairman and the Panchen Lama first vice chairman of the committee; the second vice chairman, significantly, was General Chang Kuo-hua, the Chinese Commander of the Tibet Military District. Anticipating the future relationship of the autonomous region to the central government, this preparatory committee was given the status of a state organ directly subordinate to the State Council. The 51 members of the committee were to include 15 representatives of the already established "Tibet local government," 10 from the Panchen Kanpo Lija, the former ecclesiastical and secular institution of the Panchen Lama, 10 from the "People's Liberation Committee in the Chamdo [Changtu] area," some 380 miles northeast of Lhasa, 5 from among the central government personnel in Tibet, and 11 from the "major monasteries, religious sects, and people's organizations."

The committee was apparently to act as the local people's council pending the establishment of the new autonomous organ, since it was to be organized with two sub-committees for financial-economic and religious affairs, and with ten work departments. The actual organization of this committee was slow. The Preparatory Office for the Preparatory Committee met only on September 50, 1955.

Accomplishments and Limitations of the Nationalities Program

The Chinese Communists, like their Soviet counterparts, take great pride in the achievements of their nationalities program. The absence of racial discrimination and the "successful solution" of the problem of national minorities are among the most popular and effective themes in communist propaganda. There is no doubt that the Chinese Communists, in their own self-interest, are making strenuous efforts to widen the horizons of previously "backward" minority groups, to raise their educational and health standards, to modernize and collectivize their economic activities, and to give them a sense of participation in the life of the country as a whole. But their efforts must be viewed within the framework of the restricting as well as the liberating elements of the program. The famous catchword, "national in form, socialist in content," symbolizes limitations to the concepts of "autonomy" and "national self-determination."

The communist leaders regard the free cultural development of national minorities as one of the key features of their program. In an article on "China's National Minorities" in *People's China*, for June 1, 1954, Tsung Yun stressed the accomplishments of the regime in developing written languages for the minority groups who previously had been forced to adopt the language of the Han or some other adjoining nationality for written purposes, and in translating and publishing books and other materials in the languages of the minority groups. State documents, Mao's writings, literary works, and textbooks are published in many languages by the Nationalities Publishing House. In addition, there are regional publishing concerns, such as the Sinkiang People's Publishing House, which produce textbooks in the Uigur, Kazak, and Mongolian languages. The different minority groups are also encouraged to develop their cultural traditions in folk music and dancing. Performing troupes of different nationalities have been sent throughout the country to acquaint others with these traditions. Writers and artists of minority origin have had their works publicized through translation and movies. Significantly, however, as Tsung Yun says of these publicized works: "The literary productions of the national minorities reflect their warm love for their motherland and their new life."

In the field of education, the Chinese Communists have organized nationality institutes and nationality colleges, to which students from the national minorities are brought for training. Seven nationality colleges were set up in 1950 and 1951—the Central, Northwest, Southwest, Central South, Yünnan, Kweichow, and Kwangsi colleges; other institutes and training classes were organized subsequently. In September, 1954, according to a *People's Daily* article on September 29, the Central Nationality College had an enrollment of 1,206 students from 46 different nationalities, while in the entire period from 1950 on, more than 140,000 cadres from the national minorities had been trained in government schools and courses. At the same time, the number of primary schools within the autonomous areas had been increased, and instruction in these schools is for the most part in the language of the minority group.

These "accomplishments" are presented, of course, in an anecdotal and fragmentary form which makes them seem impressive for propaganda purpose. What is important, however, is not only the language used and the pupils taught, but what the books and newspapers say, and what the pupils learn. In this respect, the phrase, "socialist in content," takes on real significance. Likewise, from the communist point of view, the encouragement of folk music and arts and the exchange of cultural missions and performing artists serve to bind the minority groups all the more firmly in their support of the regime, through giving them a sense of importance and of being appreciated and accepted by others. Up to a point, in other words, the regime can shunt aside the quest for real autonomy and freedom of expression in cultural matters by showing a lively concern over cultural forms and their transmission.

In the economic field, too, the traditional pursuits of minority groups— largely in agriculture, animal husbandry, and hunting—are not allowed to stand in the way of socialist transformation. Under a program that is "socialist in content," the national minorities have been subjected to the same agrarian collectivization drive as the rest of the country, with some delays because of special local circumstances. Scattered indications of the results of the collectivization program among the minority groups have appeared in *People's Daily*. An article by Tan Yin-chi, Chairman of the Chuang Autonomous Chou of western Kwangsi Province, on September 29, 1954, reported the formation of 211 agricultural producers' cooperatives, over 50,000 permanent mutual-aid teams, and over 140,000 seasonal mutual-aid teams. A total of 55.8 per cent of the peasant households were claimed to have been drawn into the collectivization movement. The issue of December 4 gave comparable figures for other minority areas: 85

per cent of all households among the Koreans in Northeast China; only 40 per cent among the Miaos in western Hunan Province. In Inner Mongolia, close to 70 per cent of the households had been organized into 1,300 producers' cooperatives and 118,000 mutual-aid teams. In Sinkiang, according to a *Kwangming Daily* report of September 15, 1955, the number of agricultural cooperatives had increased from 147 in 1954 to 1,700 in 1955. A later report on the Miaos of west Hunan Province foresaw an increase of agricultural producers' cooperatives from 376 in the fall of 1955 to 2,300 in the spring of 1956 and 7,600 by the end of 1957. The proportion of peasant households in the cooperatives alone was expected to reach 48 per cent by then.

The Chinese Communists have apparently met with some resistance on the part of national minority groups against changing their traditional economic pursuits to fit the communist program of modernization and collectivization. This problem came up for discussion at the third (enlarged) conference of the Nationalities Affairs Commission in September, 1953. A brief remark in the report issued by that conference and approved by the GAC, as made public in a Hsinhua News Agency dispatch from Peking on September 9, 1953, reveals the extent to which the "autonomy" of minority groups is restricted in the field of economic activities:

Experience has proved that the appropriate study of the advanced experience is a necessary factor for the smooth progress and development of the various national minorities and the various national autonomous regions. The ideology and work method of resisting advanced experiences and keeping closely to old methods is injurious to the progress and development of the national minorities and the national autonomous regions, and must be properly dissuaded against and rectified.

There is little to say about the accomplishments of the nationalities program in the realm of political autonomy. Liu Shao-ch'i, in his report on the Draft Constitution, praised the liberality of that document in extending special self-government rights to the minority groups, including the control of local finances, the organization of public security forces, and the right to draw up special regulations to suit the characteristics of the local nationalities. But each of these special rights, as already noted, is hedged about with the necessary qualifications to permit the central government to control or veto whatever is done locally. Similarly, Kuo Mo-jo pointed out in September, 1954, that "in the election of deputies to the National People's Congress . . . the national minorities, though forming only one-fifteenth of the whole population, receive one-seventh of the seats." Similarly, *Peking Review* of March 30, 1962, pointed out that 14.6 per cent of the deputies to the third session of the Second NPC represented the national minorities. And NCNA noted on December 19, 1964, that the fifty national minorities, who compose only 6 per cent of the population, were represented by 373 delegates, or 12.2 per cent of the total membership, of the Third NPC. But the manner in which these deputies are selected and discharge their duties indicates that the over-representation of the national minorities in the national congress is most likely for the symbolic purpose of dramatizing the appearance of multi-national support for the regime.

In one sense, the Chinese minorities possess even less of the shadow of political autonomy than do their counterparts in the USSR. In keeping with its federal character, the Soviet state has granted the border republics the theoretical right to secede. The Chinese Constitution, which defines the CPR as "unified, multi-national state," extends no right of secession to its national minorities. It would not matter if it did, for as in the case of the USSR, the Chinese Communist leaders would be sure to interpret any move for national self-determination and separatism as a move, not in favor of national rights and freedom, but in opposition to the goals of socialism and the revolution. On this point, the 1953 report of the Nationalities Affairs Commission already cited is instructive:

Experience has proved that insurrections in the national minority areas had practically in every case been connected with the instigation of the enemy agents and counterrevolutionaries, and that in practically every case, individual persons of the higher ranks in the national minorities had fallen into the trap laid by the enemy whose scheming was thus successfully developed. In dealing with such conditions, the people of the national minorities and their leaders must be made to exercise the highest degree of vigilance, and the sabotage efforts of the enemy must be counteracted . . . through such measures as the exposure of the enemy, punishment of the counterrevolutionaries, and the strengthening of education in patriotism among the people.

The communist nationalities program, therefore, contains within it a number of carefully designed and practically effective limitations on any real autonomy for the minority groups. But, further limitations are imposed by the defects and difficulties in the carrying out of their program, which the communists themselves are aware of and try to correct. Some of these have already been briefly mentioned. The error of "Great Han chauvinism," for example, is constantly pointed out to the Chinese cadres working with national minorities; they are warned against unnecessary aggrandizement of their own posts of power at the expense of the minority cadres, against showing attitudes of condescension and contempt in their dealings with other nationals, or insufficient appreciation of the culture and mores of the people in question. The mechanical copying of methods of land reform or collectivization already applied in the Han areas, without any attempt to adapt them to the needs of the minority group, is another form of this error.

The opposite error of "narrow nationalism" on the part of minority groups is shown when these groups tend to regard themselves as self-sufficient units, rather than as Chinese peoples and as collaborators in the future of the Fatherland. It is particularly shown in an unwillingness to regard the Hans as the "elder brothers" of the other nationalities, whose advanced experience is to be studied and applied where possible.

A related but separate error is that of disunity among the national minorities of a given area, through the perpetuation of a traditional distrust or an inability to solve long-standing conflicts of interest. Where one minority group is dominant in a region, the error of Han chauvinism may be duplicated, if the dominant group neglects the interests of the other minorities in the area. It is partly to minimize the frictions and tensions among different nationality groups that the communist program calls for establishing autonomous regions within other autonomous regions.

These defects and errors lie primarily in the realm of the psychology of cultural contacts and interpenetration. But a warning against another type of limitation in the application of the nationality program was issued in an editorial in the *People's Daily* of September 9, 1953—a warning, one might say, against swallowing too rapidly the rosy propaganda concerning the triumphs and transformations of the nationalities program. It lists as a serious "deviation" the failure to understand

. . . that our country has only just embarked on its economic construction, so that during a long period to come, the state will not be in the position to devote very large resources to assist the national minorities in the rapid development of their economic and cultural enterprises, giving rise to a blind demand for excessive results.

In other words, the promise of the program must not be taken for performance.

In conclusion, it seems fair to say that the nationalities program of the communists, based on Marxist-Leninist ideology and embodying the principles of "national in form and socialist in content," is drawing the national minority groups of China more actively into the economic and political life of the country, and in some cases is making them more accessible to the influences of the more advanced parts of China. At the same time, it offers them the surface attractions of equality and non-discrimination, fraternity, and free cultural development. To the cadres drawn from the minority groups it opens the way to receive advanced training and to rise to positions of responsibility among their own people. All these measures serve to disarm any tendencies to national separatism and prevent the minority groups from becoming centers of opposition to the regime. But if such tendencies and threats develop nevertheless, the regime must take strong action to put down the "counterrevolutionary" influences. And always behind the paper facade of national autonomy runs the spine of Communist Party control. The *People's Daily* editorial cited just above puts it as bluntly and succinctly as could be desired:

> If it is to be considered that by assuming control of one's own household and by establishing one's national identity, there is no further need for the leadership of the Chinese Communist Party, there is no further need to pay heed to the unified laws and systems of the state, there is no further need to submit closely to the unified leadership of the Central People's Government and the leadership of the people's governments at the higher levels, and there is no need for the support of the Han people and cadres—then it will be an obvious mistake which must be prevented and rectified.

SUPPRESSION OF REGIONALISM AND LOCAL NATIONALISM

Events since the Kao-Jao Purge of 1954–55 have continued to show the sensitivity of the Chinese Communist regime to any development of a local center of loyalty and power which might threaten the concentration of communist power in Peking. The July 31, 1958, issue of the *Yunnan Jih-pao* (*Yunnan Daily*) stated quite bluntly the principle on which the CPC reasons and acts: "Wherever there is localism there cannot be communism." Variously termed "parochialism," "local nationalism" and "bourgeois individualism," the concept of local authorities working against rather than for the ultimate victory of socialism has continued to elicit fear, worry and a variety of countermeasures from the communist leaders.

As previously noted, national minority groups constitute less than 7 per cent of the population of mainland China. Their numerical size, however, gives no indication of the importance attached to the assimilation of these groups. In areas such as Sinkiang and Kwangsi, their numbers are actually sufficient to hamper, for instance, the communalization movement. Although the communists profess liberal policies of religious toleration, Hui insistence on the retention of Islamic customs has created other minor crises. Tibet has given a recent example of the dangers inherent in permission of "local nationalism." Moreover, the geographical areas occupied by several of these groups have increasingly gained in importance, and utilization of natural resources in these areas is hampered by minority frictions. As Chou En-lai stated in a March, 1957, speech to the National Committee of the CPPCC in Peking: "We may say, in general, that the future of industry, agriculture, mines and electric power of China lies chiefly in minority lands."

Party policies to promote ideological dissemination and implementation have stressed sending trained Han Chinese cadres in great numbers into minority regions, for rectification movements, educational and propaganda campaigns. This move is coupled with permission for retention of minority customs and, for 90 per cent of the minority groups, the official granting of local autonomy. During the 1958 rectification campaign, large numbers of Hans were sent to the minority areas. As a result, however, parochialism was found to have increased rather than decreased. The minority groups apparently feared that the Hans were sent to take their land and homes, and to abolish their customs. Peking placed blame for this unrest on the Han cadres who were accused of "Great-Han chauvinism"—a worse evil than localism. In a speech to the First Peoples Congress of Kwangsi Chuang Autonomous Region on March 5, 1958, Ho Lung gave the official assessment: "Great-Han chauvinism and local nationalism are both reflections of bourgeois ideas in the nationalities problem and both must be opposed," because of the delay they occasion in the development of socialism.

Despite these unfavorable repercussions, the method of sending large numbers of Han cadres to the troublesome areas has continued. According to the *Kuang-ming Jih-pao* (*Kuangming Daily*) of January 24, 1959, these migrants are minutely instructed in the necessity of mingling with the local population and are told not to bring their families with them. The Young Communist League is said to furnish the greatest number of cadres.

The Communist Party line on the question of national minorities has been to profess acceptance of local customs and culture, to practice patience in educating the national minority to new ways, and to exert an effort to cooperate with the minority group rather than to absorb it. Yuan Po, in a speech on national heritage printed by the *Yunnan Jih-pao*, December 24, 1958, stated that the error of past Chinese leadership had been in the neglect to study national customs and the attempts merely to substitute Han forms.[9] In an October 16, 1958, letter to *Chung-Kuo Ch'ing-Nien* (*China Youth*), a writer inquired if a Han boy might contract a successful marriage with a Hui girl, and was editorially reassured that "all political institutions, customs and habits are super-structures which must change with the development of the economic base." During the May Day celebration of 1959, articles appeared praising the participation of hundreds

---

[9] Expressing the official position of the Party, an editorial in *Nationalities Unity* of February 6, 1959, stated: "It is the set policy of our Party and state toward minority nationalities that each nationality is at liberty to preserve or reform its customs and practices . . . based on free will and the majority decision."

of thousands of minority people in parades and celebrations, and one local official, Wang Chih-chiang, stated: "We minority people know well that only under the leadership of the Communist Party and in the big family of the motherland can we enjoy happiness and prosperity."

Officially, the CPC boasts of the success of its various methods in ending local nationalism. In the Heilungking Olunchun Autonomous Hsiang, the 2,000 people who compose the smallest of the minorities, according to the NCNA, have modernized from a former nomadic existence to living in three villages constructed by the government, complete with clinics, hospitals, schools and libraries. In Yünnan Province, the Yi minority, according to a May 25, 1959, speech of Wang Wei-hsun, has been liberated from slavery. China's largest minority, the seven million Chuangs in Kwangsi, according to the NCNA of March 23, 1959, now boasts a two-thirds literacy rate. In Kwangtung Province, *Hai-Nan-Pao* (*Hainan Gazette*), April 2, 1959, spoke of the blooming of "the flowers of nationalities solidarity and friendship." Vice-Chairman Nusjeti of the Planning Commission of Sinkiang Uigur Automonous Region expressed pride in the fact that the number of Party members of minority groups in Urumchi grew from twenty-seven in 1951 to 608 in 1957. Wang Feng was reported in the January 6, 1959, *Nationalities Unity* as declaring: "During the year [1958] the rectification and social educational movements among the minority peoples, which were centered on fighting against local nationalism, had won a great, decisive victory."

Underlying the note of tolerance and cooperation in official policy, however, runs the threat of coercion, if so warranted. Thus, the Ministry of Public Security has advocated a policy of violence to the enemy and benevolence to the people. Who comprise the "enemy" and who the "people" was indicated by the Chairman of the Inner Mongolia Autonomous Region, Ulanfu, in a speech to the First Session of the Second National People's Congress, April 25, 1959: "Anyone who attempts to split the people of his nationality from the big family of the fatherland, or to oppose the unity and cooperation between the people of his nationality and the Han people within the unified big family of the fatherland will harm not only the common interests of all nationalities in general but also the basic interests of his own nationality in particular."

In addition to the outstanding case of Tibet, there have been other evidences that the members of the "big family" have lacked unity. Disaffection has been found not only among national minority groups, but also in such predominantly Han regions as Kansu and Kwangtung. In an address delivered August 15, 1957, Kuo Ying-ch'iu, Governor of Yünnan, was unusually frank in admitting the existence of those who "exploit the opportunity presented by the rectification of the CPC violently to attack the Party and socialist undertakings." Stating that "national minorities have thoroughly detached themselves from a state of being permanently discriminated against and enslaved . . . and national regional autonomy is being carried out," Kuo went on to mention a number of problems. Some of these were enumerated by the *Tsinghai Daily*, March 11, 1958, as including the expulsion of Governor Sun Tso-pin, thirty-year Party member, because of his advocacy of "letting the people of Kansu rule Kansu;" and the dismissal of Governor Sha Wen-han of Chekiang as an "out-and-out bourgeois, individualistic ambitionist." In May, 1958, the CPC Central Committee branded two of its alternate members, Ku Ta-ts'un and Feng Pai-chu, vice-governors of Kwangtung province, as parochialists.

The problem has been even more acute in Sinkiang, which experienced a popular revolt in 1944, and required the presence of the Red Army in 1949 to elicit the proper submission to Peking. The Moslem people there have also been a major resistive force. Accused of sabotaging Party prestige by claiming "the Party is a Party of Han people only," it is known that the Moslem people resisted the commune system. For example, *People's Daily* on October 1, 1958, reported that, up to September, 90.4 per cent of the Chinese peasants were already established in communes. In Sinkiang this percentage was reduced to eighty.

Cautious in its approach to religious differences, the CPC has been accused of paradoxical behavior in encouraging Arab independence in the Middle East while crushing the independence of the Chinese Moslems. Saifudin, vice-chairman of the Sinkiang Autonomous Region, aware of the religious problem, warned against too rapid advancement of native cadres. The Islam Association of Sinkiang held a meeting to find ways of opposing those who "under the cloak of religion, incite the masses against the Communist Party," and five leading Party members of the area were forced to surrender Party membership. Among them were Ma Sung t'ing, vice-president of the China Islam Association, and Ma Wen-ting, a former member of the Committee for Minority People's Affairs in Tsinghai, who had once stated: "If I had wings I would fly away to some place where I could not see a communist." These two leaders, however, had sufficient religious influence to retain their positions in religious organizations, at least temporarily.

Such instances discount Ulanfu's statement that "more than 95 per cent of the people of the minority nationalities have completed their democratic reform and socialist transformation programs. As a result, they have made tremendous strides in their economic and cultural development." These actions have, no doubt, contributed to periodic evidence of Party moderation, such as the emphasis on autonomy, welcoming of various minority representatives by Mao, Chou, and Liu and inspection trips such as that made by Chu Teh in the fall of 1958.

The revolt in Tibet in March, 1959, dramatized to the world both the resistance of national minorities to the authoritarian policies of Peking and the hollowness of the CPC's avowed liberal policies toward minority nationalities. As mentioned earlier, on October 7, 1950, the Chinese Eighteenth Army, under the command of General Chang Kuo-hua, entered Tibet. The Tibetan Army was defeated in the same month and on May 23, 1951, Peking proclaimed the "peaceful liberation of Tibet from imperialist influences." Nevertheless, because the theocracy of Tibet is the most nationalistic of all the non-Chinese minorities under Peking's control, the Chinese Communists adopted a policy characterized by caution and gentle persuasiveness. The seemingly liberal Seventeen Point agreement signed by the Dalai Lama, Panchen Erdeni, and the communist authorities, allowed the Dalai to retain his official position. Communist control, however, was assured by the presence of Chinese troops under Chang Kuo-hua. The temporarily expedient policy of waiting, while stepping up propaganda and rectification programs, never actually crushed Tibetan resistance—earlier passive and finally active. In the proceedings which paved the way for the 1959 revolt, the Dalai Lama became the symbol of resistance, while the Panchen Erdeni collaborated with the regime.

According to the personal aide of the Dalai Lama in a series of articles entitled "Inside the Tibetan Incident," first published in a newspaper in Hong Kong and then reprinted in the Taipei *Central Daily News* of June 2, 1959, the Tibetan resistance movement began in the autumn of 1954. Opposition to the intolerable communist control tactics—including confiscation of arms traditionally owned by the inhabitants and taxation of lamaseries, even including the gold images of Buddhist gods—chiefly on the part of the Khampa tribesmen led by Kung Telinchesa, was generally successful. By the end of 1958 these armed units had a strength of 25,000–30,000 and had infiltrated the Lhasa area. Regular raids upon the Chinese Communists were staged. The Chinese, unfamiliar with the topography, had reportedly resorted to aerial bombardment in the border areas, destroying many of the lamaseries. By November, 1958, Kung Telinchesa's forces controlled the area south of the Chu River and east of Kiangtse and had won the mass support of the people.

Beginning in the summer of 1958, the Chinese Communists demanded that the Dalai Lama send his local forces and his bodyguards to quell the rebellion. He diplomatically parried these demands, stating that his force was poorly trained and ill-equipped. His delay aroused Chinese skepticism. With the real possibility of assassination of the Dalai, the leading lamas agreed that no one should approach him without the written permission of the People's Assembly. This further infuriated the Chinese. The Dalai was then invited to Peking to participate in the January, 1959, meeting of the National People's Congress. He regretfully declined. On March 10, he was invited to attend a theatrical performance at the headquarters of the Chinese forces in Tibet, but the populace blocked his way and the revolt was in its initial stages.[10]   On March 17, the Dalai Lama set out for the border town of Towang with an escort of 100 rebels.   Two days later, advised that their king was safe, the Tibetans launched an allout attack against the headquarters of the Eighteenth Army.   However, with Mao's orders, the rebels were defeated within two days.   There were reportedly 15,000 deaths in Lhasa alone.   Chinese troops and planes were immediately dispatched to locate the Dalai.

On March 28, 1959, Mao proclaimed from Peking that the government of the Dalai Lama had been dissolved; eighteen members of the Preparatory Committee were removed and the Panchen Erdeni was made acting chairman until the return of the Dalai Lama.   Chou declared a state of martial law and announced that the Dalai had acted under duress.   Chang Kuo-hua was ordered to severely punish the rebels and many of the lamas were sent to forced labor camps.   The Dalai Lama crossed into India on March 31 and confirmed by his presence the most striking example of the forceful suppression of internal revolt.[11]

Following the 1959 flight of the Dalai Lama, another interval of several years elapsed before elections were held to select delegates to county congresses and conferences; these delegates in turn selected the representatives to the Autonomous Region People's Congress, which convened in September, 1965, under the direction of Hsieh Fu-chih, who represented the CPC CC.   This Congress elected Ngapo Ngawang Jigme as Chairman of the Tibetan Autonomous Region, which was officially established on September 9, 1965.   Party leadership in Tibet remained under the supervision of Chang Kuo-hua until his transfer to Szechwan in 1967.   It might be added that the disclosures of the cultural revolution illustrate that the Tibetans have not yet fully accepted Peking's rule.   Following the violence of February, 1967, PLA troops apparently restored order: but Tibet remains a troubled area and a glaring symbol of the CPC's lack of success in its program to win the minor nationalities.

[10] For a detailed description see Peter S .H. Tang, "The Antecedents of the Tibetan Revolt," *Free World Forum*, Vol. I, No. 4, Aug. 1959, pp. 4–8.

[11] On June 5, 1959, Purshottam Trikamdas, General Secretary of the Indian Commission of Jurists, stated in Geneva that the martyrdom of at least 65,000 anti-communist Tibetans constituted a prima facie case of genocide committed by the Chinese Communists.   Indian sources reported that the whole nation of Tibet had been transformed into a vast prison camp and that there were whole villages in which no sign of life was visible.   The International Commission of Jurists found that Peking has adopted a systematic policy constituting an "attempt to destroy the national, ethnic and religious group of Tibetans by killing members of the group and by causing serious bodily and mental harm."

THE JUDICIAL SYSTEM

The Political Nature of Law and Justice

In its program for a drastic and sweeping transformation of the economic and social order, the Chinese Communists do not overlook the laws of the country, its court system, and the administration of justice as useful means for accomplishing their purposes. Mme. Shih Liang, a non-communist then serving as Minister of Justice, in a statement on September 23, 1952, commemorating the third anniversary of the Peking regime, reaffirmed the Marxist-Leninist dogma concerning the role of courts and law, in praising the "people's judicial system of New China" as "one of the fruits of the victory earned by the Chinese people . . . under the leadership of the CPC." "Born of the people's revolutionary struggle," she said, "it is made to serve the people's revolutionary struggle. . . ."

For the attainment of its revolutionary goals, it has been stressed, the Chinese Communist regime finds it necessary to be able to wield virtually total control over the masses. The court system of the country thus provides one more channel or instrumentality through which the regime can exercise the necessary degree of control. The courts make no pretense of being impartial and unbiased, or of standing "above the battle" of the political arena. Instead they are frankly "political" in nature, serving whatever policies and programs are laid down by the regime and fulfilling whatever missions are assigned by it. In the words of the first President of the People's Supreme Court, Shen Chün-ju, himself one of the leaders of the China Democratic League, speaking to the third session of the First National Committee of the CPPCC on October 28, 1951, "Our judicial work must serve political ends actively, and must be brought to bear on current central political tasks and mass movements."

The "current tasks" to which President Shen was referring included that of suppressing "resolutely, sternly, and in good time all counterrevolutionary activities . . . and the resistance of the reactionary classes," and that of protecting "the gains of land reform, production, reconstruction, and democratic order." These or similar "political tasks" have also been prescribed for the courts by the central government. Article 3 of the Provisional Regulations Governing the Organization of the People's Courts, promulgated on September 3, 1951, specifies that in trying criminal and civil cases, the courts are "to consolidate the people's democratic dictatorship, uphold the new democratic social order, and safeguard the fruit of the people's revolution . . ." Earlier, the General Regulations Governing the Organization of People's Tribunals, adopted by the GAC on June 14, 1950, had stated that these ad hoc judicial bodies, set up in order to "pro-

tect revolutionary order" and enforce governmental policies, were to perform their functions "so as to consolidate the people's democratic dictatorship and facilitate the smooth completion of the agrarian reform." What
this practice of assigning political tasks to the courts would mean for the
concept of judicial independence and the tradition of a "government of
laws, not men," was spelled out in blunt terms in an editorial in *People's
Daily* on March 21, 1952: "The law of the people's state is a weapon in
the hands of the people to be used to punish subversive elements of all
sorts, and is by no means something mysterious and abstruse to be controlled by a minority separated from the masses."

In conformity with its aim of using the legal process as a powerful
political instrument, one of the first actions of the new regime was the
sweeping abrogation, under the Common Program, of all the legal codes
of the previous Nationalist government. In the ensuing legal vacuum,
certain basic documents and decrees were laid down by the leaders to
serve as a stop-gap legal system. As listed by Chou En-lai in October,
1950, these included "such basic laws as the Common Program of the
CPPCC and the many laws, orders, instructions, and resolutions of the
Central People's Government Council, Government Administration Council, the Supreme People's Court, and other organs," all of which, Chou
claimed, "were . . . produced out of, and based on, the state doctrines of
Marx and Lenin as well as a concrete analysis of the practical conditions
of China." In addition, under Article 4 of the 1951 Provisional Regulations
on People's Courts, "where no [specific] regulation is applicable, the policy
of the Central People's Government will be adhered to." In the very early
period at least, according to a survey of "people's judicial work" undertaken by the Secretariat of the Peking People's Court and published in
1949, even Mao Tse-tung's 1940 essay *On the New Democracy* was used as
a basis for legal decisions on occasion.

During this early period, it is true, a few basic laws were promulgated,
such as the Marriage Law—to give the government the power of approval
or disapproval in marriage or divorce, with the attendant possibilities of
abuses; the Agrarian Reform Law—to bring the peasants into a position
where they could be swayed by the government; the Regulations for the
Control of Counterrevolutionaries—for the extermination of all undesirable
elements; and the Provisional State Secret Act—for the apprehension of
"spies." But the effective result of the drastic abrogation of the old codes
was to give the government a free hand to rule by means of executive
decrees, security orders, and other prohibitive regulations.

Subsequently, the regime showed no desire to give up this freedom of
rule by enacting a wide range of detailed statutes and comprehensive
codes, although it did set up a Law Codification Committee in the spring

of 1950 to formulate such codes. One year later, however, P'eng Chen, then a member of the Party Politburo and Vice Chairman of the Committee on Legal and Political Affairs of the GAC, in a report to the latter on May 11, 1951, admitted that the laws of the country were still incomplete, but argued that there was no need for hurry in setting forth "complete and detailed" law codes which would be "neither mature nor urgently necessary." He rationalized this position by saying that legislation should proceed from the simple general principles to the complex detailed provisions, and that meanwhile the laws should be issued as needed, in accordance with the central tasks and the pressing problems of the moment. Whatever the rationalization, however, the fact remained that as long as such codes and detailed statutes were not on the books, the regime was free to "legalize" its every political act. It could disregard any limits that might otherwise have been imposed by judicial precedent, or by the popular will acting through freely elected legislative bodies.

At the same time, the abrogation of all previous laws and the substitution of a few basic documents and decrees would have accomplished little to make the court system a useful tool, unless the personnel staffing the courts were also amenable to political influence in administering justice. To accomplish the desired result in this area, the communists have had recourse to two methods: first, placing the courts directly under the political organs of the government, and taking away the last vestige of judicial independence; and secondly, carrying out an extensive reorganization of the personnel staffing the judicial system, weeding out the uncooperative elements inherited from the previous court system, re-educating the more cooperative, and bringing in and training great numbers of new cadres for the system.

From the very beginning, the Peking-regime made sure that the courts at all levels up to the highest tribunal would be subordinate organs in the government machinery. Under the Organic Law of the Central People's Government adopted in September, 1949, the Supreme People's Court, the highest judicial organ, was in effect placed under the control of the CPGC, which appointed and could remove the president, vice presidents, and other members of the court, and which was empowered to enact the Organic Law governing the Supreme Court. The members of the courts, moreover, were appointed for an indefinite tenure, their stay in office being apparently at the pleasure of the CPGC. Later, when the Provisional Regulations Governing the Organization of People's Courts were promulgated, in September, 1951, the subordinate status of the courts was clearly set forth in Article 10: "People's courts of all levels (including branch courts and branch sections of the Supreme People's Court) form organic parts of the people's governments of the corresponding level, and are subject to the leadership and supervision of people's government councils of the corresponding level." At the same time, in a type of subordination similar to that of the work departments within the people's councils, each court was also subject, in its trial work, to "the leadership and supervision" of the court at the next higher level, and in its judicial administration to the next higher organ of judicial administration.

The 1954 Constitution, in Article 79, retains the principle of the subordination of the lower courts to the courts at higher levels, so far as their "judicial work" is concerned, but makes no mention of their subordination to the State Council or the lower-level people's councils. Instead, under Article 80, the courts are made responsible to the people's congresses of their respective levels, and are to report to them. The term of office for the President of the Supreme People's Court and for the presidents of the lower-level courts is fixed at four years. The other court personnel are still appointed for indefinite terms. The other details of organizational structure for the court system have been elaborated in an Organic Law adopted on December 21, 1954, to be examined below.

The absence of judicial independence in the Chinese system is shown not only in the organizational structure but also in the lack of any right of judicial review on the part of the Supreme People's Court. Unlike the United States Supreme Court, for example, it has no power to declare a law or decree unconstitutional. Instead, the highest power of interpreting laws is reserved, under the 1954 Constitution, to the NPC and its Standing Committee—the body which also adopts or approves them—as it was formerly reserved to the CPGC.

By way of insuring the political loyalty and reliability of the personnel of the court system, an intensive judicial reform program was undertaken in the latter part of 1952. By this time, apparently, the regime felt it could dispense with many of the justices and other personnel from the Nationalist days whom it had allowed to re-enlist in their old jobs for lack of an adequate supply of trained replacements. In her report of August 3, 1952, recommending the program to the GAC, Mme. Shih Liang, then Minister of Justice, admitted that because of unsatisfactory personnel, "a number of people's courts had failed to serve actively the central political tasks of the State." The character of the reform program itself was perhaps best described, shortly thereafter, in Mme. Shih's third anniversary statement on the "Achievements in People's Judicial Work," already referred to:

The judicial reform movement is aimed at opposing the former judicial concepts and effecting a complete reform of the judicial organs. Through this movement, depraved elements given to evil habits and law violations have been purged; elite worker, peasant, and women elements emerging from the various mass movements have been selected to consolidate the judicial organs of all levels; all judicial cadres have been educated to recognize still further the harmful nature of the former judicial viewpoint and working style of the reactionary KMT, and to begin to establish a national judicial point of view based on Marxism-Leninism and the thought of Mao Tse-tung.

The political aim ascribed to this reform program in Mme. Shih's statement to the GAC was reminiscent of that attributed to the judicial system as a whole in earlier legislation and policy declarations: namely, "the thorough reform and reorganization of the different levels of people's courts is an important measure for consolidating the people's democratic dictatorship and ensuring the economic construction of the State."

The communists' reliance upon the judicial system as a political tool extends to the indirect as well as the direct consequences of court action. Directly, the court system carries out its political task through enforcing the governmental reform policies and punishing the proclaimed enemies of the regime. Indirectly, however, the system is also intended to have an educative effect upon the political attitudes of the broader masses. In the words of a joint directive of the Supreme People's Court and the Ministry of Justice "On Study and Implementation of Organic Law of People's Courts," published in the *People's Daily* on December 11, 1954: "the people's courts are required not only to deal out punishment but also to educate the people." Mme. Shih, in her 1952 report to the GAC, had stressed this educative function particularly: "We must also conduct systematic propaganda-education on the ideas of law and the State in Marxism-Leninism and the thought of Mao Tse-tung, in order to raise the quality of the cadres and educate the masses." Her concluding sentence left no doubt about the political nature of the judicial process in Communist China: "Only thus will it be possible for the people's judicial organs to become a genuinely powerful weapon of the people's democratic dictatorship." The joint directive of December, 1954, cited just above, gives the definitive sign:

The enforcement of dictatorship and the protection of democracy constitute the two phases of the basic mission of the people's courts which are united and indivisible. Judicial work must be made to serve the political mission of the State. During the transition period, judicial work has the general task to safeguard the smooth progress of the Socialist construction and Socialist transformation of the State. The people's courts . . . should exercise their characteristic functions to serve the Socialist construction and the central work of the State for the various periods through the medium of juridical activities.

Thus, the regime made it crystally clear that law and justice is theoretically based on Marxism-Leninism, as interpreted by Party and state functionaries, for the domination of an important sphere of the Chinese Communist political order.

The Organization and Working of the Judicial Hierarchy

The judicial system in Communist China is closely modeled upon that of the Soviet Union. It is made up of two distinct but intertwined hierarchies: that of the people's courts, culminating in the Supreme People's Court (SPC), and that of the people's procuratorates, leading up to the Supreme People's Procuratorate (SPP). Both are ultimately responsible to the NPC and its Standing Committee, rather than to the Ministry of Justice within the State Council; but as has been pointed out, this line of accountability does not give them any greater degree of actual independence from the political arm of the government. Of the two, it is the people's procuratorates which enjoy a greater freedom from interference by the State Council and the lower-level councils and congresses, but this freedom is given them specifically so that they can check up on the manner in which the executive-administrative and judicial organs perform the political tasks and duties assigned them by the leaders of the regime.

As in the Soviet system, the principle of the separation of powers is rejected in the Chinese constitutional order. As a result, not only is judicial independence lacking, but many of the functions assigned to an independent judiciary in a liberal democratic regime are allocated instead to non-judicial organs under the Chinese system. The judicial review of the constitutionality and propriety of acts of lower-level congresses is given to those of higher level, and ultimately to the NPC; similarly, the higher people's councils may review the decisions and orders of lower councils and the acts of lower congresses. During the agrarian reform movement and the campaign to suppress counterrevolutionaries in 1950–51, moreover, local people's governments and public security organs took an active role in accusing and passing judgment upon alleged offenders, and a category of special "people's tribunals" was set up outside the regular court system to mete out a kind of drumhead justice to landlords and accused counterrevolutionaries. Later, additional emergency powers of arrest and detainment were granted to the public security organs acting independently of the courts and procurators, under regulations promulgated by Mao Tsetung and published in the *People's Daily* on December 21, 1954. Hence, it remains as true today as when it was first pointed out by the Deputy Procurator General in the *People's Daily* of September 5, 1951, that all the judicial and police forces—the courts, the prosecuting organs, the public security forces, and the like—have the same "general political task," with no clearly defined "division of labor" among them.

Within the framework of these overlapping functions and powers, however, the twin hierarchies of people's courts and people's procuratorates merit separate examination. Both have their legal basis in Section 6 of the 1954 Constitution and in separate Organic Laws adopted by the First NPC on September 21, 1954, promulgated by Chairman Mao on September 28, and published in the *People's Daily* the following day. Previously the court system had been established under the set of Provisional Regulations Governing the Organization of People's Courts, adopted in September 1951.

Both the 1951 and the 1954 laws specify that the court system is to be made up of the Supreme People's Court, certain special people's courts, and the ordinary people's courts at the various local levels. The tasks of the people's courts, under Article 3 of the 1954 Organic Law, are to try criminal and civil cases, to punish all criminals and settle disputes among civil litigants, in order to safeguard the "people's democratic system," maintain public order, protect public property, and safeguard the lawful rights and interests of the citizens. The 1951 regulations called for the courts to "conduct propaganda-education among litigants and among the masses in general, concerning the observance of the laws of the State." The 1954 version, in keeping with the general line of Party and state, adds another task: "to safeguard the successful execution of socialist construction and socialist transformation of the state."

Under the 1951 regulations, a two-trial, three-level system was advocated for the judicial hierarchy. A trial started in the first instance in a lower court could ordinarily be appealed once; the decision of the court of the next higher level was final. The three levels were the county, the province, and the national level, or the equivalent levels among municipal and autonomous units. Evidently this system produced considerable congestion at the higher levels, for the 1954 Organic Law calls for four levels, with an intermediate level inserted between the county and provincial courts. The new arrangement thus calls for basic, middle, and higher courts below the SPC at the national level.

The basic courts include the people's courts of a county, an autonomous county, an undistricted municipality, or a municipal district. They may be established at the request of the Justice Department of the next higher level, with the approval of the people's council at that level. The middle people's courts are established for subdivisions of the next higher (provincial) level. That is, several middle courts may be established within a province or autonomous region, within municipalities directly under the central government or other large municipalities, or within autonomous prefectures. A higher people's court, in turn, may be established only for a province, an autonomous region, or a municipality directly under the central government.

In addition, certain special people's courts may be created directly under the State Council, including military courts, railway transportation courts, and water transportation courts (Article 26). Over both the ordinary and the special courts, the Supreme People's Court serves as the highest judicial organ, supervising the trial work of the lower courts (Article 28).

The basic people's courts are the courts of first instance for criminal and civil cases, and perform mediation functions in civil and light criminal cases. Certain cases, however—usually of a more serious nature—are reserved by law or decree to be given first trial in a higher-level court. Moreover, if a basic court feels that the importance of the case so warrants, it may decline to be the court of first instance and request that the original jurisdiction be taken by its superior court. The middle and higher courts receive cases on appeal from the next lower court, as well as cases for retrial when the people's procurator has opposed the judgment of the lower court. In addition, they take initial jurisdiction over certain cases specified by law. Similarly, the SPC has appellate jurisdiction over cases from the higher courts, and original jurisdiction in cases of national importance or cases otherwise referred to it under the laws.

Under the two-trial system, appeals from the lowest to the highest court are ordinarily not possible. There have been occasions—as during the purge of counterrevolutionaries in 1950–51—when no appeal to a higher court was permitted, in order, as was explained in the *People's Daily* of September 5, 1951, to prevent "cunning elements from taking advantage of the two-trial system to delay the settlement of a case." Under "unusual circumstances," too, a third trial (or second appeal) has been allowed. But ordinarily the decision of the second court is final. If the people's procurator feels that the decision is improper or contrary to law, he may protest and oppose the decision, leading to a retrial at the next higher level (Article 11). In addition, once a sentence has been passed the case may be reopened and referred to the judicial committee of the court which rendered the decision, if there is indication that the law has been wrongfully applied. Finally, it may be mentioned that the SPC, as part of its function of supervising the trial work of the lower courts, reviews the decisions taken at the lower levels, not by way of appeal or retrial, but in order to check on the quality of work being done throughout the court system.

Under the Constitution and the Organic Law, certain rights are granted to those appearing before the court. The Organic Law specifies the principle of equality in the application of the laws, regardless of nationality, race, sex, profession, social origin, religious beliefs, educational level, financial status, or period of residence in the area (Article 5). It also grants the right to use one's own national language, the right to an open hearing, and to legal counsel, and provides, except in minor cases, for the adoption of the system of people's assessors (Article 8). [12] Because the members of the court are not always professionally trained, the president of the court may nominate additional persons to serve as a trial committee for the court, with the actual appointments being made by the corresponding people's council. (In the case of the SPC, the appointments are made by the Standing Committee of the NPC rather than by the State Council.) This committee may evaluate the experience of the court's trial work, may discuss important or difficult cases, and take up other related problems emanating from the trial work; but it advises, rather than making decisions for the court (Article 10).

Article 4 of the Organic Law, repeating Article 78 of the Constitution, stipulates that the people's courts are to conduct trials independently, subject only to the laws. In practice, however, the members of the court are subject to other pressures and influences, stemming in part from the manner of appointment and removal of court personnel, and in part from the practices of "mass participation" in the judicial process. Each court is composed of a president (a presiding judge), one or more vice presidents (the number increases at the higher levels), and a number of other judges. A basic court may create a civil and a criminal chamber if necessary; the middle and higher courts may in addition create other chambers as needed. Each chamber has its chief and deputy chiefs. The president of the court at each level is elected, and may be removed, by the corresponding people's congress, and is accountable to that congress. (The President of the SPC is, of course, accountable to the Standing Committee of the NPC in the interim between meetings of the full Congress.) The other officials and members of the courts at all levels below the SPC are appointed and may be removed by the people's councils at the corresponding level. For the SPC itself, appointment and removal are in the hands of the Standing Committee of the NPC.

The qualifications specified for serving on the court reinforce the subordination to political considerations revealed in the manner of appointment and removal of judges. Any citizen over twenty-three years of age

---

[12] The assessors, as lay people chosen to hear the trial, resemble jurors, but in their consultations with the judges over the decision, they are more like lay judges. They are used only for the first trial. In an article entitled "The Masses of the People Participated in the Judicial Work of the State," appearing in the *People's Daily* of September 3, 1954, Lin Hsin reported that the system of people's assessors had already been carried out in the municipal and district people's courts of Peking. Likewise in a companion article on "The Achievements of the People's Judicial Work in the Northwest during the Past Five Years," Ma Shih-wu indicated that 20,745 regular people's assessors had been elected in that area.

and not deprived of his political right to elect and be elected may be chosen a court president. The same qualifications hold for the choice of court assessors, and presumably for the other members of the courts as well. The membership of a court may thus contain a high proportion of non-professional persons without training in or knowledge of the law, with the result that the court may be more susceptible to the views of the people's procurator on the one hand, and to the extraneous influences of "mass participation" on the other.

In the feature of "mass participation" in the court proceedings, noisy spectators often comment on the proceedings as the trial progresses. During the campaign for the suppression of counterrevolutionaries, as will be noted, this audience participation often took the form of denunciations of the accused and the chanting of slogans on the theme, "Shoot the rascals!" Needless to say, due to the hazards of expressing publicly a position contrary to that of the Party and its leaders, such expressions are more likely to be politically inspired than spontaneous.

Finally, there is another principal reason why the independence of the judicial system supposedly guaranteed in Article 78 of the Constitution is largely a myth: namely, the unusually strong powers given the people's procuratorates. The power of these organs to protest the decision of a people's court and bring about a retrial has already been referred to. In addition, the procurators also prosecute the cases before the court, supervise the execution of sentence in criminal cases, and oversee the process of labor reform. But the enforcement powers of the procurators extend not only to the general public and the judicial system, but to government agencies in general. Under Article 81 of the Constitution and Article 3 of the 1954 Organic Law of People's Procuratorates, they are also charged with exercising investigation and prosecution functions over the various ministries of the State Council, the local organs of state at all levels, persons working in the organs of state, and the citizens at large, to ensure the observance of the law. They make sure that the decisions, orders, and measures of the national and the various local state organs are being lawfully carried out (Article 4). If a people's procurator at any level finds a decision, order, or measure of one of the corresponding state organs to be contrary to law, he has the right to ask that the situation be corrected; if the request is not met, he may then report the matter to the people's procurator of the next higher level. While the procurators themselves have no authority to annul, correct, or suspend the decisions protested, their findings may be assumed to carry great weight with the governmental agencies concerned, particularly since, under Article 10 of the Organic Law, they have the right to prosecute government officials and employees for illegal activities and crimes.

As already noted, the hierarchy of people's procuratorates parallels that of the people's courts. The procurator of the province, autonomous region, or municipality directly under central government control may thus set up, with the approval of higher authority, branch procuratorates as needed; these would presumably correspond to the "middle courts" set up within the same territorial-administrative units. Procuratorates are established at each level down to the county or the urban districts. In addition, special procuratorates may be provided for by the Standing Committee of the NPC.

The manner of appointment for procuratorial officials says a great deal about the power they may exercise over the other branches of the government. At each level, there are a procurator general, a deputy procurator general, and a number of other procurators. The only organs of state involved in staffing the procuratorates at any level are the NPC and its Standing Committee. The Procurator General of the Supreme People's Procuratorate (SPP) is elected by the NPC for a four-year term; his deputy is appointed and removed by the Standing Committee. The other procurators within the SPP and at the provincial, autonomous region, and directly controlled municipal level are nominated by the Procurator General or his office, and appointed and removed by the Standing Committee. The personnel of the branch procuratorates, as well as those at lower levels, are nominated by the provincial-level procuratorates and approved by the SPP.

The channels of accountability likewise show the same independence of the other organs of government. Under Article 7 of the Organic Law, the SPP is accountable, and should report its work, only to the NPC or its Standing Committee. At the various lower levels, the procuratorates are to exercise their authority independently, with no interference from the local state organs; instead they work solely under the direction of the higher procuratorates and the overall leadership of the SPP (Article 6).

Unlike the courts, then, the local people's procuratorates are under no obligations of appointment or accountability to the corresponding people's councils or congresses; and even at the top, the accountability of the SPP, for all practical purposes, is only to the Standing Committee of the NPC. As far as formal structure can make it so, therefore, the procuratorial system is independent of the rest of the state machine in a highly centralized hierarchy without lateral lines of responsibility and influence.

In their work of prosecuting cases, and particularly of reviewing judicial decisions, the procurators are to "protect people's democratic rights." But since they share with the people's courts and the public security organs the "same general political task" of "consolidating the people's revolutionary regime," their more important function, as an adjunct of the court system, is to serve as a reinforcement for the judicial weapon of the state, to see that the political tasks of the courts are fulfilled in the trial work. In their broader functions of reviewing and checking up on the actions of other governmental organs, they serve as a backbone to stiffen and strengthen the state machine. Through them the rulers of the regime can make doubly sure that the entire state machine faithfully carries out their will.

EXTRAJUDICIAL SECURITY MEASURES

For the Chinese Communists, the concentration of power achieved through the measures already discussed—the structuring of the Party and state organizations, the penetration of these organs into all the manifold activities of political, economic, and social life, and the consolidation of the reality of central control behind the appearance of national autonomy and mass participation—is still not sufficient to guarantee the attainment and perpetuation of their goals. The possibilities of disaffection, apathy, and passive resistance, as well as outright sabotage and open defiance still exist. The preceding section has shown how the judicial process may be used as a weapon to counter these possibilities. But the rulers of Communist China, like their Soviet counterparts, have found it necessary and advisable to put their trust in a set of extrajudicial protective devices, beyond the reach of the ordinary channels of accountability to popular organs, beyond the scrutiny of their own public and the outside world, and armed not only with the conventional military and police weapons of destruction and coercion, but also with the psychological weapons for spreading among the people a fear of the possible informer, and a terror of the unseen and arbitrary wielder of punishment operating outside the established codes of law. Hence, the secret police system furnishes the principal instrument for enforcing the communist style of public security measures; its chief activity is summed up under the phrase, the "suppression of counterrevolutionaries," and its chief handiwork—which remains for the most part hidden—is the vast system of forced labor to which its victims are consigned.

The Secret Police

The communist secret police system is inspired by Lenin's remark that he would prefer "to put in prison several tens of hundreds of instigators, guilty or not guilty," than to let the communist regime be weakened.

In his work *On People's Democratic Dictatorship*, Mao followed this line in demanding a merciless "dictatorship over the reactionaries," and calling for it "to oppress them" for the protection of the established order. At another point he emphasized that "the army, the police, and the courts are the machinery of the state, the instruments with which one class oppresses another. They are tools of oppression against the hostile classes, and not at all things of mercy." For a regime threatened by "reactionaries," the only course was one of "exposing the intrigues and plots of the reactionaries and arousing the vigilance and attention of the revolutionaries."

To accomplish this purpose, Mao had in mind a system of secret police and public security armed forces to supplement the regular army, police and courts. Such public security units would require extrajudicial powers of investigation, detection, apprehension, and punishment outside the regular channels to suppress "the enemies of the state."

Very little is known thus far about the organization and activities of the secret police in Communist China. They have escaped the world-wide attention and notoriety gained by such Soviet organs as the Cheka, the OGPU, the NKVD, MVD and MGB. The scant materials on hand, however, indicate that the Chinese system, like the Russian, involves a dual hierarchy—one within the Party and one within the state—and that it is the Party organization which effectively dominates the corresponding organs of the state.

The open and publicized organs of the state are the Ministry of Public Security and the public security forces of the People's Liberation Army. Behind the scenes, the CPC Central Committee oversees the entire secret police force. Prior to the Party reform of 1942, the CC carried on this work through its Central Political Defense Bureau. This organ was replaced by the CC Social Department, headed by Li K'e-nung. However, there has been no mention of the Social Department in the Party press since 1950, and Li K'e-lung died in 1962. Thus, it is impossible to establish whether this Department still exists, or, if absorbed by another Central Committee agency, which agency is involved.[13] The Chinese Communists have preferred to focus public attention on the state organ, the Ministry of Public Security, now headed by Central Committeeman Hsieh Fu-chih. By keeping the Party apparatus in obscurity, the CPC may be sparing

[13] It may well be that the work of the Social Department is now being carried out by the CC's United Front Work Department under the directorship of alternate Central Committeeman Hsü Ping. Both before and since 1949, this Department has placed agents in the noncommunist parties and mass organizations. Secret service work outside China may well be under the direction of the CC's International Liaison Department. Almost nothing is known of this agency, although Central Committeeman Wu Hsiu-ch'üan has been identified as its director.

itself from the outwardly damaging spectacle, and influential communists from the disastrous fate, represented in the USSR by the downfall of such secret police chiefs as Yagoda and Beria.

Most of the organizational aspects of the Ministry of Public Security remain highly secretive, which itself bespeaks the secrecy of the operation. The Ministry includes a General Office, an Organization and Education Division, a Political Department, and a Public Security Department. [14] Presumably the directors and deputy directors of these units, together with the Minister and his Vice Ministers, regulate the whole hierarchy of open or public units at the lower levels. In the latter category are the departments of public security at the provincial and special municipal levels; the division, at the prefectoral and sub-provincial levels; the bureau, at the county level; and the station, at the village and city street level. In addition, there are also public security units in factories, schools, and probably in all enterprises. Moreover, the public security organs can draw upon a formidable array of assistants or auxiliary personnel outside their own ranks, including the PLA security forces, the local militia units in the villages and towns, and the host of informers who can be attracted from all walks of life by various kinds of inducements or pressures.

The entire public security system thus constitutes a relatively self-contained structure of security police (public and secret), investigators, and penal institutions; its subordinate units also include such special purpose agencies as the railway public security bureau. And at the grassroots level, there is a whole network of public security committees and security groups. This all-encompassing system is carefully controlled by the Party, and closely coordinated to the military, while it also collaborates with the regular administrative and judicial hierarchies of the state.

While all public security forces are expected to collaborate with the system of people's courts and procuratorates, in special cases they are authorized to act independently. For example, on December 21, 1954, Mao Tse-tung promulgated a new set of regulations governing arrest and detainment. The *People's Daily* editorially hailed this move on January 8, 1955, declaring that "it is entirely necessary for the public security organs to arrest and detain criminals without the prior approval of the people's procuratorates in cases of emergency." Thus, the public security forces are especially dreaded for their ability to conduct trials secretly in their own tribunals.

---

[14] Wang Hai-po's "An Analysis of the Chinese Communists' Secret Service Organizations," in *Tzu-yu Cheng-hsien (Freedom Front)*, vol. XV, no. 1 (July 17, 1953), further indicated the nature of the bureaucratic structure within the Ministry. According to this source, the Bureaus for Political Defense, Economic Defense, Security Administration, Frontier Defense, and Armed Defense were assigned highly specialized tasks by the Ministry.

To maintain such a system requires a tremendous staff of trained personnel, and the public security organs themselves train many of their staff for such duties as intelligence and investigation work, surveillance of suspects or parolees, trial of suspects, the detainment and execution of prisoners, and the running of forced labor camps. The close connection between the Party and the state hierarchies of the secret police system is shown by the fact that the personnel administration of the public security organs of the various levels is under the control of the CPC. Not only the personnel officers of these organs, but also all the security cadres are assigned and transferred by the Party.

In February, 1953, a top-level coordinating agency for all secret police organizations was set up under the name of the Joint Office of Intelligence Agencies of the Central People's Government. Headed by Chiang Chint'ao, a veteran secret service man, the office presumably included special commissioners from several government organs, such as the Ministries of Public Security and Foreign Affairs, the headquarters of the Navy, the Air Force, and the military zones, and the Central Politburo of the CPC, as well as other agencies such as the Commission for Liberation Work in the Asian and Pacific Region. However, it would be logical to suppose that in order to maintain the supreme control of the Party in this very important aspect of its activities, the actual coordination of secret police work at the summit has been kept in the hands of the Central Committee of the CPC.

Particularly since 1964, the Public Security Force of the PLA has served to reinforce, and even inspire, the regular state security forces. The immediate collaboration between the PLA Security Force and the Ministry of Public Security is illustrated by the fact that Hsieh Fu-chih is at once the Commander of the former and the Minister of the latter organ.[15] In addition to performing security functions within the ranks of the military, the PLA forces are stationed throughout the provinces and municipalities and regions to take care of frontier and military defense assignments. Presumably, they are also responsible for regular intelligence work.[16]

The full effectiveness of the public security system in Communist China depends not only upon the secret police and the public security armed forces, but also upon the mass character given it through grass-roots organizations which penetrate into every aspect of life. The authorization

[15] The problem of coordination between the public security and regular armed forces was undoubtedly eased by the adoption of the 1954 Constitution. Under the previous system, the Ministry of Public Security was under the GAC, while the PLA was under a separate body, the PRMC. Now both are under the State Council for administrative purposes.

[16] The PLA Public Security Forces have been saluted repeatedly in the Chinese Communist press for their work in detecting and apprehending secret agents of the "Chiang-US clique," and for destruction of unauthorized planes over Chinese territory. For details see the chapter on the military.

for this extension of the secret police apparatus was furnished by the Provisional Regulations Governing the Organization of Security Committees, as issued by the Ministry of Public Security on August 10, 1952. These committees, under the leadership of the basic-level governmental and public security organizations, were to be set up, in the cities on the basis of such units as factories, enterprises, schools, streets, or public organs, and in the rural areas on the basis of the *hsiang*.   Composed of 3 to 11 members, these committees were also entrusted with the direction of smaller public security teams, to be set up as needed, with the approval of the public security bureaus of the county or municipality, and consisting of "3 to 5 activists selected by the masses" (Article 3).   To these committees were given the duties of maintaining close ties with the masses, carrying on regular propaganda-education among them on "anti-treason, anti-espionage, anti-bandit and anti-arson activities and on the suppression of counterrevolutionary activities," and mobilizing the masses "to help the government and public security organs" in denouncing, supervising, and controlling counterrevolutionaries (Article 5).   They were also given the power and responsibility to arrest counterrevolutionaries and criminals caught in the commission of overt acts, and to investigate, supervise, prosecute, and denounce other counterrevolutionaries, as well as to give other forms of assistance to public security personnel (Article 6).   The committees were to be under the leadership of the lowest unit of the regular public security hierarchy: in the cities the public security department of factories, enterprises, or schools, or the public security station or substation, or the *ch'ü* public security assistant; in the countryside the public security personnel of the *hsiang* government (Article 8).

Scattered reports in the Chinese Communist press have indicated the extent to which these grass-roots units have been used by the regime. Two articles in the *People's Daily* for September 30, 1954, for example, described the work of the people's police of Peking, and of the public security organs in the defense of national economic construction.   The author of the first, Chin Li, asserted that "the tens of thousands of security committees of mass character now established in the streets of Peking and in the rural villages have contributed tremendously to the security of cities and villages."   In the two-year period of 1952–53, he claimed, over 26,000 counterrevolutionary and criminal cases had been dealt with by the masses in the Peking area.   In the article on economic defense, Yin Ning stated that under the leadership of the Party and the administrative organs, public security committees and security groups had been set up on a broad scale within various economic enterprises. [17]

[17] Yin's statistics, based on an incomplete count of the economic, financial, and commercial enterprises of ten large cities, including Peking, Tientsin, Shanghai, Shenyang, (Mukden),

Employment of the masses to discover and punish criminal activity continues to bolster the system of justice. In his December 26, 1964, report to the first session of the Third NPC, Chief Procurator Chang Ting-ch'eng emphasized: "The masses know best the background of the cases and the offenders, and the offenders also fear the masses most. By depending on the masses to expose and criticize the offender, the offenders can truly be toppled and suppressed." Chang added that those offenders who refused to admit guilt in regular examinations by judicial departments were forced to "bow their heads and plead guilty" when confronted at mass meetings. A typical example of this form of coercion was sponsored jointly by the Canton Municipal People's Procurators Office and Public Security Bureau in February, 1965. At a mass meeting held in the stadium, announcement was made of the arrest of four "US-Chiang agents" and awards were given to the three informers who "voluntarily reported the secret agents to the authorities"—a commercial worker, a medical worker and a youth. The tactic of mass pressure was given further sanction by Hsieh Chüeh-tsai, President of the Supreme People's Court, in his December 26, 1964, report to the first session of the Third NPC: "In case of need, mass meetings may be called." Hsieh attributed at least part of the credit for the decline in criminal cases since 1959 to the fact that the judges of the people's tribunals had frequently taken their cases to the public: "[They] generally work in a planned manner and bring files with them to the countryside and factories to conduct investigation and study. They ask the masses to state their opinions and deal with cases on the spot."

Furnishing the secret police system with a spy network embracing the population at large, and a source of active auxiliaries for the public security machinery, these urban and rural security committees broaden the base of the police apparatus and greatly amplify its effectiveness. They thus serve as ever-present tentacles, tightening the control of the masses by the Communist Party and state.

Forced Labor

To the continuing campaign for the suppression of counterrevolution, the system of forced labor may be added as a major field of operation for the Chinese Communist public security system. One of the last acts of the GAC before it was superseded by the State Council was the passage,

---

Harbin, Canton, and Chungking, showed that 7,278 incidents had been avoided, 2,039 others had been thoroughly investigated, 1,770 cases of arson, sabotage, theft of public property, and other organized counterrevolutionary activities had been disposed of, and 1,209 escaped counterrevolutionary prisoners had been seized.

on August 26, 1954, of Regulations Governing Labor Service for Reform. The report of Security Minister Lo Jui-ch'ing to the GAC, giving an explanation of these regulations, was published in the *People's Daily* on September 7. It not only provided the most complete exposition to date of the forced-labor system in mainland China, but also constituted an acknowledgment that the system would be continued as a firmly established policy for safeguarding and strengthening the regime.

Outside observers have estimated that several million Chinese are serving out sentences in forced labor camps. The general nature of these camps and the types of "labor" performed in them has been made all too familiar from the accounts of similar cases of human exploitation in Nazi Germany and the Soviet Union. More important for discussion here is the political significance of the forced-labor system as a means of strengthening the state machine, both through enhancing its power, and thereby its prestige in external relations, and through giving it a closer control over its own citizens at home. The political inspiration of the program was reaffirmed, if its full extent remained concealed, in an editorial in the *People's Daily* of September 27, 1954:

A nationwide campaign has resulted in the arrest of large numbers of bandits, despots, special service agents, backbone elements of reactionary parties and groups, and leaders of reactionary societies and Taoist [indigenous religious] organizations. These elements have been sentenced to prison terms, deprived of political rights, and eventually organized in labor corps where they carry out their reform through forced labor.[18]

[18] The Chinese Nationalist government reported that according to incomplete communist statistics of June, 1952, there was a total of 8,020,000 forced laborers in mainland China. Their distribution among the six Greater Administrative Areas into which the country was divided at that time was as follows: Northeast, 1,100,000; North China, 1,700,000; Northwest, 2,430,000; Southwest, 310,000; East China, 1,850,000; and Central-South,630,000. Another early report from communist sources indicated that in Kwangtung province in 1951, 89,701 "reactionary elements" were arrested, of whom 28,332 were shot and the rest—61,369—sentenced to "reform through labor." While not giving the total number of forced laborers, the *People's Daily* of September 7, 1954, revealed that 83 per cent of all "criminals" have "participated in agricultural and industrial production, or have been organized into various engineering corps for the felling of timber, construction of buildings, restoration and construction of conservation works, and the building of railways and highways." It has been estimated from various sources that each of China's more than 2,000 counties contains at least one forced-labor camp. These are known variously as Reform through Labor Camps, Prisoners' Labor Camps, Collective Reform through Labor Camps, Prisoners' Concentration Camps, Beggars' Concentration Camps, and by other names.

Two books on the forced-labor camps in Communist China were published in Hong Kong early in 1954. In the first, *I Came from a Slave Labor Camp in Manchuria*, Pei You-ming, a camp inmate, tells of being subjected to "reform through labor" in the Chatseyao coal mines, after being captured and jailed by the communists. In the second, entitled *The Slave Labor Camp in Northern Shensi*, a former communist executive of the camp, Su Wei-chuan, gives his eye-witness account of the forced-labor projects.

The theoretical basis for the policy of "reform through labor" was stated by Mao Tse-tung in his 1949 report *On People's Democratic Dictatorship*, in which, after promising that "reactionaries" who desisted from counter-revolutionary activities would not be put to death but would be given work in order to "reform themselves through labor so as to become new men," he added the threat: "If they do not want to work, the people's state will force them to do so." Article 7 of the Common Program gave this dictum constitutional status in providing that "reactionary elements" should be "given some means of livelihood and . . . compelled to reform themselves through labor so as to become new men."

Subsequently, the Agrarian Reform Law of June 28, 1950, provided that landlords should "reform themselves through labor." The detailed regulations for the punishment of "unlawful landlords" adopted by some of the administrative area governments in the fall of 1950 provided that such landlords should be punished "with open repentance, labor, or penal servitude" for periods ranging from one to ten years, according to the gravity of the offense and the extenuating circumstances. The laws and regulations for the suppression of counterrevolutionaries, already mentioned, likewise provided for reform through labor, as did the provisions enacted by the GAC on March 21 and 28, 1952, for the Five-Anti and the Three-Anti campaigns, respectively.

During the period of the "Anti" movements and the 1951 campaign against counterrevolutionaries, Chou En-lai reported to the CPPCC National Committee on October 23, 1951, a policy of extending the opportunity to "reform through labor" even to those who had been sentenced to death, if they had no "blood debt" and had "inflicted less serious damages to the national interests." Following the directives of Mao, such persons "would have their execution deferred for a period of two years, during which they would do forced labor on probation." Earlier in explaining this policy, *People's Daily* on May 1, 1951, had pointed out that "to compel them to engage in productive work . . . would benefit the country with certain productive enterprises . . . [and would] punish them at the same time." Needless to say, the adoption of the Constitution did not change the basic policy of the regime in any respect; Article 19 provided that those "feudal landlords and bureaucrat-capitalists" who were deprived of political rights for a specific period should be provided "with a way to live, in order to enable them to reform through labor."

The general system of forced labor in China has been patterned after the model of the Soviet Union, and was in fact set up and maintained at first with the help of Soviet advisers. Minister Lo admitted that during the long period required for the preparation of the August, 1954, regulations on forced labor, "assistance was received from Soviet legal advisers."

And a former communist official of the labor camp at the Yench'ang Oil Wells, southeast of Yenan, has stated that the engineers and technicians for the operation were mostly from Russia, Czechoslovakia, Germany, and Poland, with only 10 Chinese on the staff in command of some 20,000 prisoners.

Not all prisoners under sentence are detained in labor service camps. The regulations on labor service also provide institutes for juvenile delinquents from the ages of thirteen to eighteen, houses of detention for prisoners awaiting sentence or given a very short sentence, and regular prisons for criminals considered too dangerous or for some reason unfit for labor service. But the bulk of the prisoners are organized into the so-called Labor Service for Reform Corps. Depending upon the number of criminals and the needs of production in any given camp, the corps may be organized into small, medium, or large companies, branch companies, and general corps.

There is a certain tendency among outside observers to regard the communist forced-labor system as primarily of economic importance to the regime, because it permits the construction of needed public works and economic development projects at a supposedly minimum labor cost. Yet the political significance of the system should not be overlooked; and indeed, its economic achievements must be viewed in the light of their contribution to the political power of the regime.

In the field of domestic politics, the forced-labor system is a powerful weapon for dealing with internal dissent and unrest. Thus in its statement that "the machineries for labor service for reform . . . constitute a tool of the people's democratic dictatorship, being machineries for the punishment and reform of all counterrevolutionary criminals and other criminals," Article 2 of the August, 1954, regulations has the effect of reaffirming, or in Lo Jui-ch'ing's words, "further defining the political character of the forced-labor system." Furthermore, communist leaders seem to feel that by uprooting hostile or potentially hostile individuals from their familiar environments, where their attitudes might only be reinforced, and by placing them under completely different conditions of hard labor, forcing them to learn a new trade, and to make new ties in order to survive, they will become more susceptible to communist "political education" and "ideological training." Eventually they may be ready to return to society as "new men."

For this reason, Article 4 of the Labor Service Regulations insists upon a strict "policy of coordinating punishment and control with ideological reform, and coordinating labor production and political education." The camp authorities may use their discretion in deciding whether to release a prisoner at the end of his term. If they feel the prisoner has not sufficiently reformed in outlook and behavior, they may submit the case to the competent public security organ for examination, and may obtain a judgment from the local people's court requiring the prisoner to continue in labor service. The number of such extensions of sentence is, of course, not announced.

Meanwhile, whatever the proportion of "new men" among the prisoners, the regulations call for the most rigid security measures to be taken in the camps and other places where forced labor is concentrated. The outer perimeters of the prison or work site are to be closely guarded, as are the prisoners during movement from one place to another. The use of firearms against the prisoners is authorized in the case of riot, criminal or sabotage acts in which the prisoners are armed, attempt to escape, or in other like offenses.

In the field of external politics, the forced-labor system also has its contribution to make to the strength of the state. Any increase in the national wealth and economic potential of the country through the exploitation of forced labor will give the regime a better bargaining position vis-a-vis other countries, and—so long as the price in human suffering is not realized abroad—in a greater prestige and ideological appeal among those peoples who are seeking a rapid economic advance from a relatively low level of development. But there is also a more direct increment to international power and its accompanying prestige, through the use of forced labor on projects having a military and strategic value. A number of such projects have been reported in the case of Communist China. The project of building the Western Hills Tunnel in Yenshi, northern Shensi province, involved 54,000 forced laborers mobilized under the direct command of Russian experts. Similarly, 10,000 laborers were used in the project of enlarging the Yentung Airport. Other projects have included the building of military air bases, military docking facilities, strategic railway lines, munitions factories, and other military installations.

POLITICAL STABILITY AND SUPPRESSION OF COUNTERREVOLUTIONARIES

It may be said of "counterrevolutionaries" under a communist regime, as of "anti-state traitors" under other totalitarian systems, that if they did not exist, the regime would have to invent them. They represent a way of securing total control, while avoiding the risks and penalties of total responsibility, through having scapegoats on whom to blame all mistakes and failures. In the case of Communist China it was not necessary to invent them, since active opposition to the new regime was a legacy from the years of civil strife. However, the violent and ruthless measures taken against counterrevolutionaries shortly after the accession of the new regime had a broader function to perform. In the political realm, not only did they serve to destroy the major remnants of active opposition within the country, but also to discourage, and even to eliminate, centers of potential opposition. Through the use of the weapon of intimidation, they set an example for the public at large of what might happen to those who showed outward discontent over the policies and actions of their new leaders. In the economic realm, at the same time, these measures against counterrevolutionaries also yielded a generous source of forced labor for ambitious programs of economic construction and development. Thus on both counts they served—and continue to serve—as a major disciplinary measure for strengthening the regime. For these reasons, the suppression of counterrevolutionaries has been almost from the first not only the central task of the people's courts, tribunals, and procuratorates, but also the major function of the public security organs and notably of the secret police.

The term "counterrevolutionary" may be broadly interpreted to include all those persons or groups who by action or attitude fail to obey the laws or to support the regime. It can thus be applied to anyone whom the Party and state might for one reason or another consider undesirable. The term is sometimes used synonymously with "reactionary." The list of counterrevolutionary enemies is a long one, including among others spies, traitors, saboteurs, rumor-mongers, bandits, foreign agents, despots, "bad" landlords, and especially former Nationalist officials who withhold active support from the Peking regime.

The theoretical basis for the suppression of counterrevolutionaries, in Mao Tse-tung's 1949 report *On People's Democratic Dictatorship*, has already been noted. In referring to the courts, army, and police as the "instruments of oppression" of the "hostile classes," he promised there would be no leniency toward the counterrevolutionary activities of the reactionaries.

Mao's proposed policy was given constitutional standing in Article 7 of the 1949 Common Program, which authorized the government to suppress and punish severely "all Kuomintang counterrevolutionary war criminals and other leading incorrigible counterrevolutionary elements." Essentially the same provisions are carried over in Article 19 of the 1954 Constitution. These constitutional provisions, in turn, furnish the basis for a series of stringent laws dealing with counterrevolutionary activities, of which the most notable is the set of Regulations for the Suppression of Counterrevolutionaries, promulgated on February 21, 1951.

For the first several months after taking power, the communist regime pursued a "soft" policy toward potential opposition elements, relying more on persuasion than force. But as the new rulers were able to consolidate their power more securely, and as they girded for the effort to carry through a vast land reform program intended to break down the "feudal" economic and social structure of the countryside, a change in official attitude became apparent. In June, 1950, Mao Tse-tung, in a report to the Party Central Committee, called upon the Party and the masses to "raise their vigilance against the subversive activities of the counterrevolutionaries." The outbreak of hostilities in Korea the same month gave added impetus to the campaign against counterrevolution. The following month, the GAC and the Supreme People's Court issued a set of joint instructions on "the suppression of counterrevolutionary activities," and promulgated the statute on the establishment of people's tribunals. Thereafter, newspaper articles and editorials in the Chinese Communist press gave increasing attention to the topic of the suppression of counterrevolutionaries, and the tempo of mass meetings to carry out the campaign was stepped up.

In February, 1951, as noted, the CPGC promulgated the basic Regulations for the Suppression of Counterrevolutionaries. The campaign was maintained at a high level of intensity throughout the year. During the first six months of 1951, according to a report submitted in October of that year by Shen Chün-ju, then President of the Supreme People's Court, the people's courts alone had dealt with 800,000 criminal and civil cases involving the suppression of reactionaries. Huge mass rallies were held in the major cities throughout the country. The opening meeting in Peking on March 24 was followed by others in Tientsin, Shanghai, Nanking, Chungking, Sian, Urumchi, Wuhan, and elsewhere, climaxing in an even larger second meeting in Peking, in May. Other cities also held second-round meetings at which even greater numbers of counterrevolutionaries were denounced and later sentenced to death. The heat of this drive lasted through 1951. Toward the end of the year, however, Mao Tse-tung predicted that victory over the counterrevolutionaries on the mainland was in sight, and his statement was followed by some easing up in the campaign. The problem was by no means allowed to drop completely from sight, however; on June 27, 1952, a further set of Provisional Measures for the Control of Counterrevolutionaries was issued by the GAC, supplementing that of February, 1951, and defining punishment measures for additional lesser counterrevolutionary crimes.

Before noting the extent and severity of the campaign, it is well to examine the way in which it was carried out. The legal basis for it was provided chiefly by the regulations of February, 1951. As originally enacted, this statute consisted of twenty-one articles, in which a great number of crimes were listed, 95 per cent of them punishable in extreme cases by death or life imprisonment. No appeal was granted for sentences under this act, although death sentences given by a lower court were to be reviewed at a higher level. The enumerated crimes were for the most part similar to those outlawed in all communist countries, and included contact with imperialism and revolt against the fatherland, instigating or inducing revolt among public officials or troops, plotting or directing armed revolt among the masses, engaging in acts of espionage, sabotage, or manslaughter, or perpetrating other "acts of instigation and incitement." To broaden the scope of the act even further, Article 16 provided that "all other crimes committed with counterrevolutionary intent but not specified in the law should be punished according to analogous specified crimes."

Provisions were made for reducing or remitting the sentence under extenuating circumstances—if, for example, the accused surrendered voluntarily and showed sincere repentance, or if his repentance were accompanied by "meritorious exploits." But these provisions did little to mitigate the severity of the act. Not only did it apply the principle of analogy to the determination of crime and punishment, but it also was made retroactive in effect, so that individuals could be punished for having committed any of the enumerated crimes before the establishment of the Chinese People's Republic, and even before the founding of the Communist Party in 1921. The law thus gave the rulers of the regime a free hand in dealing with any persons they considered "undesirable" for one reason or another.

The campaign to suppress counterrevolutionaries was directed not only against individuals but also against organized groups, on the assumption that any groups which the communists did not control might become to some degree centers of opposition to the regime. Hence, in October, 1950, the government issued certain Provisonal Rules for Registration of Social Organizations, under which all clubs and societies devoted to literary, cultural, and religious pursuits had to register, and those found to be "reactionary" were to be dissolved. This measure was followed, early in 1951, by the beginning of a vigorous drive against secret societies—those semi-religious organizations which had sometimes in the past played important roles in upsetting dictatorial rule in China—a drive which aimed at their extermination and which continued with mounting intensity down through 1955. Needless to say, the Kuomintang and its affiliated groups came in for special attention. Under regulations issued by the Central-South Military Administrative Committee in August, 1951, for example, all KMT members who had served on party branch committees or higher organs, and all members of similar rank in the KMT youth organization, the Young China Party, and the Democratic Socialist Party were required to register with the government, as were military personnel and government officials above specified ranks and all secret service personnel connected with the former regime.

The enforcement of these various regulations against counterrevolutionaries was by no means left to the courts and public prosecutors alone, but was also entrusted to various non-judicial organs as well. Among the latter, the municipal governments and the public security organs seem to have played the leading roles. The public security forces seem to have done the work of investigating and preparing the case against suspected counterrevolutionaries; their findings were often accepted for all practical purposes as final. The municipal governments, in turn, would call mass meetings at which the alleged counterrevolutionaries would be put on exhibition to hear themselves and their deeds publicly denounced. These were in the nature of accusation meetings rather than trials, and no defense was allowed. Sometimes the number of counterrevolutionaries denounced at these meetings ran into the hundreds, of whom only a token number would be on display at the meeting. Descriptions of such meetings—as published, for example, in the *People's Daily* of March 25, 1951—told of members of the audience shouting, "Shoot the leading special agents!" or "Shoot the despots!" with the mayor replying, "You are quite right; they ought to be shot!" In the aftermath of such meetings, the alleged counterrevolutionaries were quickly sentenced and executed, supposedly to meet the demands of the people.

Not all suspected counterrevolutionaries were disposed of through these public accusation meetings; as already indicated, hundreds of thousands were handled (if not properly tried) through the regular courts. In areas still under military control, cases were turned over to special military courts. Countless others were apparently dealt with by the public security branches without a trial, or with only a secret trial, the courts being used simply to pass sentence on those alleged to be guilty.

Punishment for counterrevolutionary offenses covers a variety of sentences other than death and life imprisonment. Death sentences have been suspended for two years and then, if the prisoner shows the proper spirit at forced labor, have been commuted to a term of labor service instead. Other lesser offenders are given varying terms of imprisonment at forced labor at the outset. In addition, terms of forced labor or "mass surveillance" may be imposed on certain categories of offenders by action of public security organs, even without the sentence of a court. The June, 1951, Provisional Measures for the Control of Counterrevolutionaries provide this kind of punishment for offenders who have not shown adequate repentance for their past crimes, but who have not committed any new crimes to warrant further punishment. Such persons may be deprived of their political rights for periods up to three years or more and may be put on a form of probation, during which they are to be given ". . . ideological education . . . under government control or mass surveillance, to reform them into new men." They are to observe the restrictions placed upon them, to follow an appropriate line of work, and to inform on any others about whose counterrevolutionary activities they may learn.

These measures of governmental control, which may be imposed upon an individual without a court trial, combined with the system of forced labor place the individual citizen very much at the mercy of the governmental organs of the regime, and especially of the secret police. In addition, the methods used and the scope of the campaign against counterrevolutionaries in 1951 undoubtedly have had a considerable deterrent effect upon any who otherwise might want to oppose specific policies or practices of the regime.

It is impossible from the published records to assess the full extent of the campaign of 1951. In Kwangtung Province, for the ten months from October 10, 1950, to August 10, 1951, according to Provincial Vice Chairman Ku Ta-ts'un, nearly 90,000 counterrevolutionary criminals had been arrested, 77 radio transmitters in addition to large amounts of arms and ammunition had been seized, and over 28,000 criminals had been executed, most of them, presumably, for counterrevolutionary offenses. Statistics given by Ma Shih-wu in an article in the *People's Daily* of September 30, 1954, show for Northwest China a total of 38,200 counterrevolutionary cases disposed of by the people's courts in collaboration with public security organs during the 1951 campaign against counterrevolutionaries. In the city of Peking, to take another example, in the year prior to October 1, 1951, nearly 30,000 mass meetings of varying size had been held, with an audience participation totaling nearly 3,400,000 people. The number of accused counterrevolutionaries dealt with at these meetings was not revealed, but as a result of the first big accusation meeting on March 24, according to Lo Jui-ch'ing, then Minister of Public Security, and later PLA Chief of Staff, 199 counterrevolutionaries had been shot to death; and at the second major meeting in May, 221 more were given the death sentence, while over 500 were given other punishment. In Canton, according to the *Southern Daily* (*Nan-fang Jih-pao*), the local military court on a single day in September, 1951, sentenced 704 counterrevolutionaries, 10 of them to immediate execution; somewhat later, the local people's court sentenced another 676 offenders, 22 of them to immediate execution. In Shanghai, according to the second annual report of Public Security Minister Lo Jui-ch'ing, nearly 29,000 counterrevolutionaries had been prosecuted during the year.

These figures can give only a rough impression of the scale on which the early campaign was carried out. Its value to the regime, as a public security measure for deterring potential opposition and for getting its propaganda message across to the masses, must have been considerable. Teng Tzu-hui, reporting to the Administrative Committee of the Central

South China Area in November, 1951, defended the purge as an "enlightened" policy: "Had these criminals not been executed, public wrath could not have been eased, the masses could not have been mobilized, and the remaining counterrevolutionaries could not have been reformed. It would have been a mistake to have adopted a policy of leniency toward those determined counterrevolutionaries."

Mao Tse-tung's action in calling a halt to the intensive campaign against counterrevolutionaries in the fall of 1951 did not mean that the predicted victory over internal enemies and opposition had been won, nor that the policy of ruthless suppression had been abandoned. In sporadic editorials in 1954, the *People's Daily* reminded its readers that the problem of suppressing counterrevolutionaries was still serious. On June 12 it admitted the continued wide prevalence of social unrest in villages and cities alike. It gave examples of "gangs of escaped counterrevolutionaries" secretly in hiding in various places, particularly in the triangular area between Peking, Tientsin, and Paoting. Again on November 10 it urged the people to "resolutely eliminate the activities of rascals and bandits." Again it cited examples, pointing out that the culprits included not only professional thieves and robbers, but also elements of the former landlord class along with "former Kuomintang officers, policemen, and gendarmes, as well as chiefs of secret sects."

Beginning in July, 1955, a new concerted drive against counterrevolutionaries was launched. A *People's Daily* editorial of July 3, entitled "Liquidate the Hidden Counterrevolutionaries," was followed by similar blasts throughout the Chinese Communist press. On July 27, in his speech before the second session of the First NPC, Security Minister Lo Jui-ch'ing presented detailed examples of counterrevolutionary activities throughout the country to show the seriousness of the problem. He alleged that counterrevolutionary elements had even attempted uprisings in some villages.

Under the slogan, "liquidate all counterrevolutionaries resolutely, thoroughly, cleanly, and fully," the communist press called upon the people at large to join the campaign to detect and report counterrevolutionaries. In effect they were asked to join a "nationwide detective network" which would reach "from heaven to earth." They were even urged to "eliminate relatives for the greater righteous cause." Special recognition was given those who were most active in denouncing or informing on others. The Tientsin *Ta Kung Pao* of August 20, 1955, for example, praised one Wu Te-yüan as a grade-A model of treason-preventer and security-protector for having helped the government to apprehend 281 counterrevolutionary and other criminals.

To show the effectiveness of the campaign, the communist press cited examples of the exposure and arrest of counterrevolutionaries in all parts of the country and in all walks of life—in the factories, the farms and agricultural producers' co-operatives, in banks, hospitals, schools, and the like. Some of the cases were as bizarre or exciting as a detective story. One prisoner was finally trapped after hiding out for more than four years in the attic of his brother-in-law's house. Another alleged criminal was discovered after being reported dead for five years.

The drive was directed not only against individuals but also against organized counterrevolutionary groups. Among those reported uncovered during the campaign were the "People's Salvation Army" in the T'angho-Fangch-eng-Miyang area of Honan Province, the "Allied Party of the Chinese Nation" in the Chungking area, the "Light of the Peace" group in the same area, the "Wuhan Underground Working Group of the Chingpu (Progress) Party," various secret religious societies scattered throughout the provinces, and a group of young intellectuals called the "China Humanitarian Democratic League."

This hysterical anti-counterrevolutionary drive had gradually subsided by late September or October, 1955. But it had not entirely ceased, nor was it likely to; anti-counterrevolutionary measures in some form had by now proved useful and essential to the regime. As the *Kwangming Daily* warned on August 18, 1955, "The struggle against counterrevolutionaries will last for a long period. As long as classes still exist, imperialist encirclement will also continue to exist, and there will always be counterrevolutionaries who will seek to undermine our cause."

It is correct to generalize that every case of high treason has been traced to conspiracies originated by the United States or its agents, particularly those on Taiwan. For example, in February, 1964, the Canton post office intercepted a number of parcels mailed from Hong Kong and Macao and labelled printed matter. Concealed within the covers of such magazines as *Hung-Ch'i* were "subversive" magazines. Other periodicals were wrapped so that when the reader unfurled the cover a cap would detonate an explosive. This plot was, of course, attributed to Chiang Kai-chek agents.

On December 29, 1962, the Ministry of Public Security reported that, during the preceding three months, eight groups of Chiang agents had landed by sea in the coastal area of Kwantung province, in Heifung, Waiyeung, Hweilai, Tinpah and Toishan counties, while another group of agents had been airdropped into Yeungkong county. Altogether, 172 agents were said to have been apprehended with the assistance of peasant informers, including two children. These agents were said to be carrying U.S. radios, pistols, codes and poison, as well as counterfeit PLA uniforms and Chinese currency. On November 4, 1963, the Ministry of Public Security announced 9 groups totalling 90 men, had been apprehended. In

February, 1965, Canton Municipality tried another four US-Chiang agents, including Lin Hsin, a former landlord, said to have been trained in espionage in Hong Kong. More frequently, however, the United States and its agents on Taiwan are said to conduct their espionage activities via utilization of military aircraft of the U-2 variety.[19] One means of coping with this form of espionage was the March, 1964, revision of the July, 1962, Instructions for Rewards to Chiang Airmen safely landing planes on the mainland.

Chief Procurator Chang Ting-ch'eng reported to the first session of the Third NPC in December, 1964, that the number of counterrevolutionary cases from January to November of that year was down 34 per cent as compared to the similar 1963 period, and Hsieh Chüeh-tsai, President of the Supreme People's Court, testified to the same body that there were fewer criminal cases in 1964 than any year since 1959. Nevertheless, the work of suppression of criminal activities continues. Since, by extension, any crime in China is considered to be opposed to the revolutionary endeavor, minor infractions, or misdemeanors, have drawn stern censure as evidence of capitulation to bourgeois habit. For example, reports of the prevalence of gambling in the suburbs of Shanghai, including the case of a communal team chief gambling with team funds, were alluded to in the city's *Chieh-fang Jih-pao* (*Liberation Daily*) of January 16, 1963, as "the boldest manifestation of the bourgeois idea of injuring others in order to benefit oneself." When a middle school student admitted: "I was so cor-

---

[19] For example, the Chinese Communists claim to have shot down the following US planes based on Taiwan: February 8, 1958, a RB-57 over Shantung; May 29, 1959, a B-17 over Kwangtung; October 7, 1959, a RB-57D over North China; August 2, 1961, a RF-101C over Fukien; November 6, 1961, a R2V-7 over Liaotung; September 9, 1962, a U-2 over East China; June 11, 1964, a P2V-7 over North China; July 7, 1964, a U-2 over East China; December 18, 1964, a RF-101 over East China; January 2, 1965, a pilotless plane over Central South China; January 10, 1965, a U-2 over North China.

As the cultural revolution has intensified, the Chinese Communist press has alleged that the US has stepped up its spying missions, and even attacked Chinese citizens and destroyed their property. For example, during the first half of 1967, the following allegations were widely publicized: on January 13, 1967, a F-104 fighter was shot down over East China; on February 20, US planes strafed Chinese fishing boats over Hainan Island, with one Chinese killed and three wounded; on March 14, a Chinese fishing vessel was said to be attacked by some 12 US warships, including a carrier, near Hainan Island. On March 15, US planes strafed another fishing vessel in the same area. On April 24, two F-4B US fighter planes intruded into Chinese air space over Kwangsi province, and were said to be brought down by the PLA Air Force. On April 29, the PLA Air Force claims to have shot down a pilotless US reconnaissance plane over Kwangsi. On May 2, four US F-105 fighter planes were said to have dropped several bombs in the Kwangsi area. On June 12, another unmanned US plane was said to have been destroyed over Kwangsi. On June 26, a US F-4C fighter was shot down over Hainan. On June 29, while strafing Haiphong, US planes were said to have attacked a Chinese merchant ship in the harbor.

rupted by bourgeois thought that I sank to the level of a thief," taking goods worth 12 *yuan*, he was advised to open his heart to his school's Party or League committee in order to become "a young man of the Mao Tse-tung era."

Far more serious evidence of the continuation of counterrevolutionary activity has been reported in recent years. Chou En-lai, in his report to the Third NPC in December, 1964, attested that during the period 1959–62 "quite a number of people openly advocated the so-called 3-self and one undertaking" (or extension of plots for private use and of free markets, increase of small enterprises with private control, and the establishment of production quotas at the household level). In addition to this crime of "going it alone" (or working toward the restoration of an individual economy), Chou also reported: "In 1962, under the instigation and direct direction of external forces a group of the most reactionary protagonists of local nationalism staged a traitorous counterrevolutionary armed rebellion in Ining, Sinkiang, and incited and organized the flight to foreign territory of a large number of people near the frontier." During the same period, as mentioned elsewhere, cases of counterrevolutionary activity were discovered in such high circles as the Ministry of Defense (see the account of Marshal P'eng's dismissal).

PROLETARIAN DEMOCRACY THROUGH CULTURAL REVOLUTION

Third among political tasks for 1967,[20] according to the Chinese Communist leadership, is to "fully develop extensive democracy under the dictatorship of the proletariat." Since the cultural revolution represents a new stage of the class struggle, whereby the bourgeoisie are finally to be crushed, the victories of this revolution are to lead to a more perfect form of proletarian dictatorship. Yet, its leaders have become increasingly aware that their goals for state organization will be most difficult to achieve. As Chou En-lai warned the participants at the April 20, 1967 mass rally celebrating the establishment of the Peking Municipal Revolutionary Committee: "it is no easy matter to seize power, nor is it an easy matter to control power, and it will be still more difficult to consolidate this dictatorship of the proletariat." And speaking of the need to transform the machinery of power, Chiang Ch'ing commented on the same occasion that "it is a major task, crucial for the next hundred years."

[20] See the editorial of *People's Daily* and *Red Flag* of January 1, 1967. The first task is to increase production, and the second to integrate the Red Guards and revolutionary intellectuals with the workers and peasants.

Ironically, the revolution to perfect proletarian democracy has been responsible for the intensification of existing controls in the tight inner circles of the leadership. For example, to cope with tendencies to anarchism, the strong arm of the PLA has assumed powers formerly granted to organs of the state or the masses. Thus, while the cultural revolution has so far truly modified the functions and forms of governing, this modification may be described as transitory, experimental, and inclined to promote the Marxist concept of "dictatorship over the reactionaries" with no corresponding improvement of "democracy within the ranks of the people."

Those who plan and direct the cultural revolution have modified their own vision of the role of the masses in bringing about proletarian democracy. For example, in the first months of the cultural revolution, the CPC Central Committee's eleventh plenum determined on August 12, 1966, that "the key to the success of this great cultural revolution is to have faith in the masses, rely on them, boldly arouse them and respect their initiative." Thus, the CC communique continued: "don't be afraid of disorder." By January, 1967, however, through the pages of *Red Flag* (January 1, 1967), the Central Committee was cautioning that "extensive democracy" must be "under the centralized guidance of Mao Tse-tung's thought," and brought about by reason, not force. "It is impermissible to use coercive measures to make others submit." And following the heated battles for control in several of the provinces and municipalities of January-February, 1967,[21] the leaders of the cultural revolution warned against the masses carrying the principles of democracy too far, to the stage of anarchism. As *People's Daily* commented on April 26, 1967; "Anarchism obscures the demarcation line between proletarian mass democracy and bourgeois liberalism. . . . In the final analysis, anarchism is bourgeois individualism. It demands that personal liberation be placed above the liberation of the whole of mankind."

As outlined in the concluding pages of Chapter III, one of the characteristics of the cultural revolution has been the purge of personnel up to the highest levels of Party and state organization because of their "sabotage of the great proletarian cultural revolution and the dictatorship of the proletariat." Of necessity, the leadership has been forced to acknowledge that not only the individual, but even the organizational structure, has been found deficient. In many of the troubled areas, for example, the PLA has

---

[21] According to official reports, power was seized by the revolutionary alliances in Shansi on January 12; in Shantung on January 22; in Kweichow on January 25; and in Heilungkiang on January 31, 1967.

Other provinces where fighting has reportedly broken out include Fukien, Szechwan, Honan and Liaoning, as well as the Sinkiang Uigur, Tibetan and Inner Mongolian autonomous regions.

completely absorbed the normal security forces and functions of Party and state organs. Of the various changes wrought in the state organization, the one most likely to endure is that of the "three in one" committees. [22]

By the end of June, 1967, "three in one" revolutionary committees had been established in Shantung, Shansi, Kweichow and Heilungkiang provinces, and in such municipalities as Peking and Shanghai. Although, with one exception, these committees were formed only after violent struggle against the counterrevolutionary "bad elements" in the respective Party and state committees and councils, the non-violent creation of the Peking committee indicates the regime's intent to eventually establish such organs in most, if not all of China's provinces and cities.

In terms of membership, the "three in one" committees are composed of delegates from the PLA, the former Party and state committees or councils at the respective level, and from the ranks of the activists who support the cultural revolution (e.g., the Red Guards or militant workers organizations). [23] While the leadership welcomes a framework which appears to

[22] As noted elsewhere, the principle of "three in one" committees has also been applied to the creation or transformation of organs in educational institutions, militia units, communes and industries. In the present context, only the committees related to the state government are discussed.

There have been several variations in nomenclature of the "three in one" committees. In Shanghai, the revolutionaries established the Shanghai Commune on February 5, 1967; however, by the end of that month the term commune had fallen in disuse in favor of the title of Shanghai Municipal Revolutionary Committee. In Harbin, the Heilungkiang Red Rebel Revolutionary Committee was established as "the provincial supreme organ of power" on January 31, 1967. In Kweiyang, Kweichow province, the Proletarian Revolutionary Rebel General Headquarters seized power on January 25, 1967. By April, 1967, the Party press was generally referring to all of the "three in one" committees by the simple designation of "revolutionary."

[23] When revealed by the Party press, the leaders of the new "three in one" committees are often found to be veteran Party and state officials, who often served formerly at the respective level or in the same district. For example the Peking committee is headed by Hsieh Fu-chih, who is a member of the Politburo and who earlier was appointed by the CPC Central Committee to carry out the work of purging the city's Party committee of the influences of P'eng Chen.

On April 24, 1967, the leading members of the revolutionary committees of Shanghai and Peking municipalities and Shansi, Kweichow, Heilungkiang and Shantung provinces were personally received by Mao Tse-tung and other Party dignitaries. In addition to Hsieh Fu-chih, from the Peking committee, they were: Chang Ch'un-ch'iao, Yao Wen-yüan, Liu Ko-p'ing, Chang Jih-ch'ing, Li Tsai-han, Ho Kuang-yü, P'an Fu-sheng, Wang Chia-tao and Wang Hsiao-yü. P'an Fu-sheng and Wang Chia-tao lead the Heilungkiang committee. P'an was formerly the first secretary of the provincial Party committee, and retains his prestige after self-criticism of his errors in judgment in carrying out the orders of the eleventh CPC CC plenum. Wang was (and remains) commander of the provincial PLA forces. Liu Ko-p'ing, a member of the CPC CC, formerly was a vice governor of Shansi province and now is co-leader of the Shansi committee. His partner is Chang Jih-ch'ing, who is PLA commissar in take on the nature of a mass or "democratic" organization, it has carefully seen to it that loyal troops and veteran cadres fill the majority of positions. As *Red Flag* has pointed out (no. 3, 1967), veteran cadres should assume leadership posts since "they are more experienced in struggle, more mature politically and have greater organizational skill."

The formation of the "three in one" committees should follow certain set guidelines. Since the cultural revolutionary struggle is regarded as "a contradiction between ourselves and the enemy, not between the people," the CPC Central Committee has emphasized that the seizure of power in an area often cannot come "by dismissal and reorganization from above." [24] Instead, the future components of the "three in one" alliance must wrest power from those in command. But as the forces of the cultural revolution grow stronger and control wider areas, presumably the pattern of Peking will become more common. In Peking, the "three in one" committee was established by direct order of the CPC leadership and "from beginning to end under the kind attention of our great leader, Chairman Mao." However, the character of a mass effort was preserved by the creation of a preparatory Representative Conference of Revolutionary Workers and Staff. [25]

The "three in one" revolutionary committees, as provisional organs of state power, follow the principle of democratic centralism and have generally adopted the structure of bodies which they have replaced. For example, the committee elects its own standing committee, which exercises all powers of the general committee after the latter is no longer in session.

---

that province. Chang Ch'un-ch'iao, of the Shanghai committee, was formerly fifth secretary of the city's CPC committee. He is also a deputy head of the CPC CC's Cultural Revolution Group. Yao Wen-yüan of the Shanghai committee has also been identified as a member of the CC Group. Li Tsai-han of the Kweichow committee has been identified as a deputy PLA commissar. Ho Kuang-yü of the Kweichow committee is a deputy PLA commander of the same military district. Wang Hsiao-yü, formerly the vice mayor of Tsingtao, now heads the Shantung committee.

[24] In Kwangtung province, for example the Provincial Alliance of Revolutionaries claimed to seize power on January 22, 1967. However, this body was denounced as a sham "three in one" alliance which was a willing tool of the Party provincial committee. The Canton *Nanfang Jih-pao* of February 24, 1967, pointed out that the alliance actually represented only eight organizations "and consistently excluded from itself the masses of revolutionary workers and peasants." Members of the former CPC committee welcomed the seizure and continued to hold positions of authority and to dictate orders. This sham seizure was said to be the work of T'ao Chu's associates to carry out his black line.

[25] On March 22, 1967, Chou En-lai, Ch'en Po-ta, K'ang Sheng and other Party leaders presided over the convocation of this Representative Conference. As Chou remarked, this organization "will prepare for the setting up of the revolutionary 'three in one' provisional organ of power." The Peking Municipal Revolutionary Committee was formally inaugurated on April 20, 1967.

The standing committee supervises the activities of its subordinate, specialized branches, such as the departments for finance or security. However, unlike the pre-cultural revolutionary structure, the "three in one" committees presumably do not yet follow a hierarchal pattern from lower to higher geographical unit. Instead, they are directly subordinated to the central leadership, without intermediary executive direction. As stressed by *Red Flag* (no. 3, 1967), the ultimate authority and guide for the committees must be the thought of Mao. Moreover, the leadership has taken measures to ensure that the members minimize their individual roles and promote the solidarity of the general committee.

The style of work demanded of the individual members of the "three in one" committees has been spelled out in some detail by the Shantung Provincial Revolutionary Committee. According to its Regulations on Seriously Improving Style of Work, adopted on June 7, 1967:

> (1) It is forbidden to shower praise on members. . . . (2) No member . . . should make a public speech on behalf of the committee unless it is discussed collectively beforehand by the committee. . . . (3) When members of the revolutionary committees set out for a place or attend mass gatherings, there should be no formal welcomes and send-offs and no applauding. . . . (4) Members . . . must devote a definite amount of time to doing physical labor. (5) Members . . . are not allowed to present gifts in their own name or accept gifts. (6) Generally the names of revolutionary committee members should not appear in the press. . . . (7) Members . . . should live simply. Extravagence is forbidden. . . . (8) Members . . . should set aside a certain amount of time for interviews with the masses. . . . (9) Members . . . should go among the masses regularly . . . call fact-finding meetings and forums to invite people's opinions and criticisms. (10) The revolutionary committee should undertake small rectification campaigns at fixed intervals (for instance every two months). . . .

These Regulations (published in the June 30, 1967 *Peking Review*) have been quoted at length since it is apparent that the strictures contained are meant to be applied universally. As *Red Flag* (no. 10, 1967) emphasizes, they "uphold the great red banner of Mao Tse-tung's thought" and "should be examined and studied by all." Carrying out this imperative, the Peking Revolutionary Committee's standing committee, in enlarged session, passed a decision to study and implement the Shantung Regulations on June 26–27, 1967; the Kweichow Provincial Revolutionary Committee took similar action on June 25; and the Heilungkiang Provincial Revolutionary Committee "drew up similar regulations for itself based on local conditions" on June 26.

The leaders of the cultural revolution have consistently used the adjective "provisional" to describe the new "three in one committees." Moreover, in reporting the seizure of power in Kweichow province and Kweiyang city,

People's Daily of February 23, 1967 observed that, although the committee temporarily exercises "all Party, political, financial and cultural power . . . in the future it will be a supervisory body." Ultimately, the role of the "three in one" committees may be determined by the degree to which their members carry out the strictures imposed by the central leadership and dictated through such regulations as that of the Shantung committee. For, while the leaders have improvised concerning the "democratic" aspects, they have not and cannot change their ideals of "centralism." When the normal state apparatus was found defective, the "three in one" committees were created. Should they, in turn, succumb to the temptations of power, or their members follow independent courses, [26] then the "three in one" committees will certainly reveal their provisional nature, as loyal PLA troops and Party cadres are given increased authority.

[26] *People's Daily* of January 30, 1967, sternly warned against the "tendency to seek the limelight" of some members of the revolutionary committees, as well as the errors of individualism and ultra-democracy. Moreover, this CPC organ emphasized, class enemies will try to split the revolutionary alliance. For an indication of popular opposition to the PLA's authority in the committees see Chapter 8.

CHAPTER 6

Socialist Transformation
of the National Economy:
1949-57

EARLY PATTERNS OF ECONOMIC CONTROLS

In the tradition of Marx, the Chinese Communists profess that economic relations determine the course of development for the entire society. If Communist China is to fulfill its ambitions of becoming a first-ranking world power and spreading communism throughout the world, it must, at the very least, achieve a stage of modern industrial development capable of supporting the logistic burdens of modern warfare. With increasing awareness, the leaders of Peking have also seen that this feat must, in the last analysis, depend upon national economic self-sufficiency. In 1949, when Peking faced the enormous work of transforming the country from a "feudal" and agrarian economy to a modern industrial giant, the immediate need was for the elimination of capitalism in its two major forms—the private sector of industry and commerce and the landlord class's domination of the agrarian economy. To do this, China had to create a comprehensive system of economic planning which could coordinate all segments of the economy under a system of far-reaching and final controls.

The first years, after the communist seizure of power on the mainland, were devoted especially to effecting such controls as would be necessary for the efficient introduction of a central planning system. That a period of "readjustment" was necessary before the "transition to Socialism" could get under way was indicated by Mao Tse-tung in mid-1950, when he warned against the still prevalent "view . . . that it is possible to eliminate capitalism and introduce Socialism at an early date." The concrete task for the next three years, he specified, would be the "proper readjustment" of existing industry "under the leadership of the state sector of the economy." Elaborating on Mao's views, Ch'en Yün, one of the new government's top economic experts, distinguished between a "rehabilitation" and a "reform" aspect of this readjustment effort. In practice, and at a time when commitments to the Korean War precluded any abrupt modifications which might have engendered sabotage, rehabilitation of the war-torn economy consisted mainly in reorganizing the industrial enterprises formerly owned by the Nationalist government and extending state ownership to additional enterprises whenever feasible. The reform efforts were intended to tighten state control over the remaining privately owned industry and commerce: their most conspicious manifestation was the widely publicized "Five-Anti" campaign.

The reorganization of state-owned enterprises was accomplished with relative ease and speed. Many "bureaucratic capitalist enterprises" which had been owned by private investors under the Nationalists provided the communists with a ready made base for the extension of the state sector. In 1949, they were said to account for about 41 per cent of all modern industrial production and major shares of domestic and foreign trade. Most of the communications and transportation networks were also included in this category. Nevertheless, the private sector of the economy still accounted for almost 56 per cent of gross production in that year.

The period of "transition to socialism," therefore, was characterized by an intensification of the drive to control private enterprises and transform them into state-owned or state-controlled enterprises. This was in keeping with the general line laid down for the Party and the state during the period of transition. As noted previously, the "general line" marked the turning point in the shift from the 1949 Common Program to the 1954 Constitution, and was made the subject of a vast propaganda and education campaign. A fairly explicit statement of the meaning of socialist industrialization—and thus of the goals to be achieved in this period— was provided in the December 10, 1953 *Current Events* (*Shih-shih Shou-ts'e*):

. . . On the one hand we must develop state-owned industry which is socialist in nature and expand the system of socialist national ownership; and on the other hand we must carry out the transformation of handicrafts which belong to individual economy, and of industry which belongs to capitalist economy. We must gradually organize handicrafts into handicraft-producer-cooperatives, and gradually turn private industry into state-capitalist industry and finally state-owned industry.

As this quotation indicates, at least for the period of readjustment, the Chinese Communists viewed the entire economy as divisible into five sectors. The "state sector," comprising the state farms in agriculture and the state-owned and operated enterprises on the industrial side, was considered the "leading force in the national economy and the material basis on which the state carries out the socialist transformation." The bridge between state and private sectors for agriculture would be the "cooperative sector," through which the private property of the peasants— after the land redistribution of the agrarian reform program—could be pooled and eventually socialized. In industry, the bridge would be provided by a "state-capitalist sector," in which privately owned enterprises, in effect, would yield a share of ownership and virtually complete control to state agencies. At the level of private ownership, the "petty-economy sector" on the agricultural side included the individual household and farm property. At the corresponding level in industry and commerce there was a "capitalist sector" made up of those firms and enterprises at least nominally still in private hands.

The need to retain private ownership in industry and commerce for a time was recognized by Mao in his *On the New Democracy* in 1940, and later amplified in his 1945 treatise *On Coalition Government*. In his 1947 report on *The Turning Point in China*, Mao gave further assurance that private capitalism would not be destroyed immediately:

> The New Democratic revolution will eliminate feudalism and monopoly capitalism; it will eliminate the landlord class and the bureaucratic bourgeoisie [enriched by government office under the Nationalists]; but it will not eliminate capitalism in general, nor the petty and middle bourgeoisie. On account of the backwardness of the Chinese economy, it will be necessary to permit the existence, for a long time, even after the national victory, of the capitalist economy represented by the broad petty bourgeoisie and middle bourgeoisie.

Private property in the agricultural sphere, as noted in the subsequent section on agrarian reform, was also to be retained temporarily. The ultimate goal in both agriculture and industry, however, remained that of state or collective ownership, preceded by an increasing transformation from the private to a mixed private-public level. At first glance, the temporary retention of private capital and enterprise would appear to conflict with the general objectives. For example, the best known and most direct type of communist control is that of outright ownership of the means of production. It is a basic Marxist dictum that whoever owns the means of production will also hold the key to social, political, legal and intellectual control in any given society. Theoretically, of course, what Marx advocated was ownership "directly" by the proletariat. Communist practice, however, substitutes ownership by the state under the pretext that the state represents the proletariat, or somehow embodies or prepares the way for the final dictatorship of the proletariat. Until the achievement of that final goal, the continued existence of a private sector, together with and closely regulated by the state sector, may be regarded as a marriage of convenience.

The aim of final and absolute state ownership also furnishes a convenient rationalization for any expedient control measure. Thus Peking has instituted rigid fiscal and budgetary procedures, nationalized the system of banking and credit, strengthened its regulation of currency and exchange, and tightened its restrictions on domestic and foreign commerce. Still other controls serve to regulate, directly or indirectly, the day-to-day economic life of the individual as breadwinner and consumer. Such direct measures as food rationing and a host of indirect measures such as increased taxation, forced savings, economy drives, and restrictions on travel and choice of employment give the leadership a powerful economic whip over the head of every individual.

Early in the period of readjustment, pending their transformation into joint public-private enterprises in the state-capitalist sector, private industry and commerce were brought under strict state control. The Provisional Regulations for Private Enterprises, promulgated on December 3, 1950, stipulated in detail the conditions under which such enterprises would be permitted to operate. Statements of plans and business activities had to be submitted to the government for final approval, and the scope of operation was in other ways narrowly circumscribed. Moreover, earnings had to be distributed among dividends, welfare funds and other uses in accordance with government-specified percentages. Subsequently, by requiring large private enterprises to deposit their daily cash receipts in state banks, the government extended its authority over day-to-day operations.

A wider range of state controls served meanwhile to bring the private capitalist enterprises into the state-capitalist sector. One of the most effective devices for this purpose was the stepped-up rate of taxation. In addition, government monopolies over essential raw materials and services made it possible to discriminate price-wise against the private firms. These devices, together with the stringent regulations governing private business in general, the excessive toll in fines and penalties of the Five-Anti campaign, and various other political and social pressures, [1] enabled Peking to

---

[1] Among the social pressures exerted were those of the Federation of Industry and Commerce, which was established late in 1953. In order to induce remaining private firms to join "warmly and enthusiastically" in their own socialist transformation, local chapters of the FIC, through standard propaganda and pressure techniques, "encour-

drive the remaining private businessmen to the wall. Their only recourse was to apply for state loans, which though readily granted, often forced the private organizations to become private-public enterprises as the price of this assistance.

The state's dominant role in the so-called joint enterprises was legally reinforced by the Provisional Regulations Governing Public-Private Jointly Operated Industrial Enterprises, promulgated on September 6, 1954. These reaffirmed the leading position of the socialist sector in joint enterprises and explicitly required that the latter "obey state plans" (Articles 3 and 4). Under Article 9 the operation and management of the enterprise was in effect entrusted to personnel designated by the state. In cases of policy disagreements between public and private representatives, the decision was to be left with the competent organ of the government (Article 10). In order to make perfectly clear where the real power lay, Article 24 placed the "business" of the enterprise under the "industrial and commercial administrative organs of the People's Government " while Article 25 gave the control of its financial affairs to the "financial organ of the People's Government and the Bank of Communications." The distribution of profits was subjected to similarly strict rules, only 25 per cent being taken for dividends to stockholders and managerial salaries, while most of the remainder was assigned to "reserve funds." The latter were, of course, to be reinvested in capital goods and the expansion of state-planned industry (Articles 17 and 18).

All these measures stemmed from Mao's demand, in the 1950 statement, not for a mere limitation of the capitalist sector of the economy, but for a positive improvement of the "relations between public and private enterprises and between labor and capital." In effect, they exemplify what Ch'en Yün called the "adjustment of relations between public and private industry and commerce . . . to enable private capitalist economy to find its rightful place under the leadership of the state-owned economy." And they showed the government's determination, in the words of Article 10 of the 1954 Constitution, to "use, restrict, and transform" private capitalism pending its final elimination.

The extent to which transformation of the private sector was achieved through such control measures is suggested by a few official figures. In 1953, when the period of readjustment was considered closed, the state sector was said to have accounted for 53 per cent of the total industrial production, as compared with 34 per cent in 1949. This proportion was

---

aged" businessmen to form joint public-private enterprises. As Richard Walker pointed out in his *China under Communism*, the state preferred these methods to permitting the private firms to go out of business in order to retain managerial skills; "thus bankruptcy like silence is a privilege which businessmen no longer enjoy!"

even higher in the "modern" industrial sector where the combined percentage of state and state-capitalist sectors by 1952 reached 66, as compared with 31 for the private capitalist sector. According to one Chinese economist, the combined share of the private capitalist and private peasant handicraft sectors in total industrial output declined from 62.7 to 42 per cent in the 1949–52 period. [2] The official figures for 1954 assigned 71 per cent of industrial production to the state sector (which apparently also included the cooperative and state-capitalist sectors) and 29 per cent to the private.

In specific segments of the economy the degree of state control was much higher. The 1952 figures showed the state sector controlling 90 per cent of the total loans and deposits; together with the 8 or 9 per cent in the hands of the state-capitalist sector, this represents a virtual government monopoly of banking and finance. In heavy industry, the state sector reportedly controlled 80 per cent; in foreign trade 90 per cent; and in domestic trade 50 per cent of the wholesale business.

The share of the total product contributed by the private sector might have been even less if the private owners and management had been able to go out of business at will. But for the national bourgeoisie, staying in business had become an obligation. Until the latter part of 1955, the government showed no indication of pressing for the total elimination of private business. Rather, official organs stressed the need to use private business and to remold it along the lines of joint public-private enterprises as the correct path to socialism. Article 10 of the 1954 Constitution specified that this transformation would be accomplished "by means of control exercised by the administrative organs of state, the leadership given by the state sector of the economy, and supervision by the workers."

The campaign to transform private enterprises into joint public-private enterprises entered a new and more intensified phase late in 1955. Mao Tse-tung lent his personal authority and prestige to the campaign by taking an active part, together with other top leaders, in a consultative conference with the Executive Committee of the All-China Federation of Industry and Commerce. In his speech before that body on October 29, Mao was reported to have proposed "more adequate measures for carrying out the socialist transformation of industry and commerce." By the end of the year similar consultative conferences had been held in Peking, Shanghai, Nanking, Wuhan and other cities under the auspices of various branches of the Federation. Through these conferences Party and govern-

---

[2] Chen Han-seng's figures for 1952, in the official source, *China Reconstructs* (January-February, 1954), show 50 per cent of total industrial output contributed by the state sector, 5 per cent by the state-capitalist, 3 per cent by the cooperative, and 42 per cent by the combined private capitalist and petty economy sectors.

ment leaders were able to win the support of the participating representatives of industry and commerce for the government's program of socialist transformation of private business.

The increased tempo of this drive was evident in scattered reports published toward the end of 1955. Statistics of the Central Bureau of Industrial and Commercial Administration published in *Ta-kung Pao* on December 14 showed that by the first part of that month practically all of the 176 large factories which in 1953 employed over 500 workers had since been transformed into joint enterprises. Some 2,000 factories representing industrial trades and about 3,000 commercial establishments underwent transformation during November and early December. In Peking alone, over 16 trades, including 1,549 concerns such as cotton goods stores, general stores, vegetable stalls and restaurants, had been transformed into 121 joint purchasing and marketing units. In Shanghai, over 200,000 similar concerns in 84 trades were similarly reorganized.

These figures point to one of the special features of the intensified campaign—the transformation into joint public-private enterprises not by individual concerns, but by whole guilds or trades. A TASS dispatch from Peking carried in the January 6, 1956 *Izvestiia* gave further details on this process. In Wuhan, for example, 9 guilds with 130 factories were transformed into joint enterprises. Although full details were not revealed, it was reported that by the end of 1957 the transformation of major segments of private industry and commerce should be completed in 27 of the nation's provinces or large cities.

Later it became apparent that this timetable had been drastically foreshortened. On January 20, 1956, Peking announced the completion in the main of its liquidation of private business throughout the entire country. Thus ended some 100 years of foreign investment. The occasion was said to be marked by firecracker salutes, mass rallies, parades, and dancing in the streets. In view of their previously thwarted desire to go out of business, some of the private businessmen undoubtedly "danced at their own funeral." *People's Daily* noted that, while a few of the "commercial capitalists" had committed law-breaking activities and others had adopted a negative attitude, most of them had accepted the transformation willingly.

Chinese Communist controls over the economy, during the period of readjustment and early in the 1953-57 period of the First Five Year Plan (FFYP), were by no means limited to the sphere of private industry and commerce. Every person, for example, was subjected to a comprehensive and rigidly enforced system of food control. According to this pattern, the state purchased the maximum amount of food crops from the peasants (in addition to that part of the yield collected in taxes) at set prices, and then restricted to the minimum the food consumption of the masses.

Thus, there were two phases to this program. In the villages it operated through the "three-fixed policy" (fixed production, purchase and marketing of grain). In the cities and towns it was carried out by the food rationing system.

Although the compulsory purchase of grain by the state had been in effect over a period of years, as had food-saving programs in the cities, these two aspects were formalized in a more comprehensive way in the latter part of 1955. On August 25, Premier Chou En-lai signed and published two regulations: a Provisional Measure for Monopoly Purchase and Marketing of Food in Villages, and a Provisional Measure for Food Rationing in Cities and Towns. The various provinces, autonomous regions, and special municipalities were directed to set the date for these regulations to go into effect, provided it fell within the 3-month period from September 1 to November 30.

The measure for the monopoly purchase and marketing of food covered only two of the "three-fixes"—fixed production being taken care of by the targets laid down under the Five Year Plan. For fixed purchase, Article 14 provided that in households producing a surplus of food over their own needs the state should purchase usually from 80 to 90 per cent of the extra food. This proportion could be raised in the case of rich-peasant households. Moreover, both the quantity and the "concrete purchase rate" were to be determined by the People's Committee (i.e., the government) of the province, autonomous region or special municipality. This government agency would also determine the standard of consumption to be allowed households not producing enough food for their own needs (Article 20). The kind of food, including potatoes, to be supplied to food-deficit households was to be determined by the principle of local availability (Article 22). Food was to be supplied for duly verified current needs, and purchase in advance of need was prohibited (Article 23).

The food rationing measure for cities and towns, in turn, set up seven categories of supply credentials under which food could be purchased: for an established resident, a transfer resident, for industrial and commercial use, or for cattle feed, as well as through a national or local food ticket, or a local feed ticket (Article 4). The supply allotted a given individual depended upon his status and age and the amount of physical labor performed. [3] Residents coming to the cities from the villages were to bring

[3] In July, 1955, *People's Daily* carried an article by Chiang Wei describing the plan. Since supply was to be based upon each household's actual needs, Chiang wrote, every household should prepare a monthly food purchasing plan based on the actual number of persons and amount of food needed. This plan was to be submitted to the proper government food department for approval and all purchases were to be made according to its provisions.

their own food or carry a national food ticket. Restaurants in the cities and towns had to collect food tickets for prepared meals using rice, noodles or processed foods. These tickets were then submitted to the food stores who, in turn, submitted them to the government food control agencies in order to replace consumed supplies (Article 16).

These food control measures were in full effect by November 1, 1955. In the villages, the policy of fixed purchase and marketing was applied directly to each household. Leadership responsibility was assumed by four or five cadres from the county or sub-county district level. In some of the villages, "three-fixed committees," made up of Party members and non-Party activists, were set up to direct the new program. In the cities, the system operated with equal vigor through the preparatory efforts of thousands of Party and government cadres and propagandists.

Very early in the campaign the government was already claiming substantial food savings. Although the earliest date for implementation had been set as September 1, 1955, in that same month *People's Daily* claimed that the inhabitants of Harbin were already able to save 1,500 tons of food a month. Chungking First Steel Factory reported that its workers had reduced consumption from 39.5 catties each in April to only about 29 catties in August. In Nanking, September food purchases were three million catties below the August figure.

The reported successes of elimination of the private sector of the economy and savings on food bear out the thesis that in a communist-controlled country economic development is curtailed only by the limitations of natural resources and the willingness of the people to tolerate and comply with strict and pervasive regulations. Accordingly, Peking's general line of economic development has been stimulated by the goal of rapid heavy industrialization geared to the build-up of military power. The road maps for each leg of the journey are the successive Five-Year Plans. Needless to say, all this requires a vast system of bureaucratic activity.

The CPR's determination to resort to a system of economic planning was recorded in Article 33 of the Common Program, which called for the CPG to draw up, as soon as possible, "a general plan for rehabilitating and developing the branches of public and private economy of the entire country." The first efforts at central planning, however, were rather desultory, involving the drafting of partial plans and targets. The central organ charged with national planning responsibilities at this stage was the Planning Board within the Committee on Financial and Economic Affairs of the GAC. But each of the various government agencies concerned with economic activities had its own planning bureau or section, and one of the main functions of the Planning Board was to coordinate and approve the plans drawn in these separate agencies. But it was never able to produce a comprehensive plan for the whole economy.

Not until the beginning of 1952, when the pattern of state control of the economy was well along, was a more elaborate planning mechanism provided for, in a set of Provisional Regulations Governing Capital Construction. Under these regulations, the cabinet Committee on Financial and Economic Affairs was to adopt control figures for capital construction for the entire economy and issue them in directives to the various ministries of the central and regional (greater administrative area) administrations. The ministries in turn were to issue control figures and directives to their respective lower units, where drafts of the annual plan were actually to be prepared. These would be returned to the cabinet committee via the same route and approved by it and the GAC as a whole. Then the adopted plans were again sent down through the various levels to provide the basis for economic activity for that year.

By the latter part of 1952 the government was ready to embark on a more ambitious planning program, with a Five-Year Plan following the Soviet example. Most segments of the economy were said to have regained their pre-1949 peaks, and the period of readjustment had apparently accomplished its ends. To push the economy ahead required a stronger and more centralized planning system.

An extensive administrative reorganization was the result. Six new ministries were added to the GAC—First Machine-Building, Second Machine-Building, Building Construction, Geology, Food, and Higher Education—while the former Trade Ministry was divided into a Ministry of Foreign Trade and a Ministry of (Domestic) Commerce. Most important was the creation of a State Planning Commission to supervise and administer economic planning on the national level and to integrate the work of planning sections at all levels. The Planning Commission was placed directly under the control of the Central People's Government Council (CPGC), rather than the GAC. Hence the line of control ran from the Council, through the Commission, to the various ministries or departments, and finally down to the individual enterprises.

The inauguration of a series of Five-Year Plans at this juncture showed Peking's great haste to industrialize as soon as possible. In the Soviet Union and most of the East European satellites such plans had been introduced only after the private sector of the economy, at least on the industrial side, had been completely nationalized. Outside the state sector in those countries there remained only the cooperative sector and the petty economic sector of individual peasant and artisan property. Communist China, however, still had a substantial private and an important state-capitalist sector.

The entire Five-Year Plan was not publicized for a long time; indeed, it probably was not worked out before the spring of 1955. A *Pravda* article of September 28, 1953, alluded to general goals, and annual targets for the first year were also published. Other official reports added information about specific projects or targets and fulfillment under the plan. But official reticence persisted until after the second session of the First NPC in July, 1955. In imperfect form the plan was doubtlessly discussed at the National Conference of the CPC in March, 1955. The conference proposed "that the Central Committee undertake to make the necessary revisions in the draft five-year plan on the basis of the opinions stated at this conference, and after making them, submit it to the second session of the first National People's Congress for examination and adoption." The plan was adopted by this latter body on July 30, 1955. Finally, in August, the plan was officially published in book form in Chinese.

Despite the long delay in obtaining specific information, three general characteristics of the plan were apparent from the first: (1) It emphasized the development of heavy industry, machines, fuel and electric power. Light industry and agriculture were relegated to subordinate roles. Consumer wants were virtually overlooked.[4]   (2) It aimed at strengthening Communist China's military power. The reason for emphasizing heavy industry was, in official parlance, not only "to lay a foundation for the development of the national economy," but also "the strengthening of national defense." And (3) it adopted Soviet methods, both for drawing up the plan and seeing that it was carried out. Moreover, the huge quotas and targets assigned revealed the strong, even ruthless determination of the leadership to transform the backward national economy into a modern industrial society at the expense of human welfare.

AGRARIAN REFORM AND COLLECTIVIZATION

The ability to successfully control and manipulate the agrarian sector, as events have illustrated, determines in very large measure the success or failure of all of Peking's economic policies. China must assure itself of an ever-increasing supply of foodstuffs to care for its mushrooming population, to provide raw materials for its expanding industrial sector, and to have a commodity for foreign exchange to obtain essential machinery and raw materials.

To meet these imperative needs, the government must be able, through its control of purchases and sales of agricultural output, to drain off a large

[4] Mao's report of July 31, 1955, on agricultural cooperation (which is discussed more fully in the next section) was probably intended in part to offer a partial corrective to the minimization of agriculture in the plan. Following his directive for a more specific and urgent program some of the provincial plans placed greater emphasis on this neglected sector.

share of the earnings which formerly went to the landlords, money-lenders, and the peasants themselves. To insure an abundant supply of raw materials at favorable prices, Peking early leaned toward some form of collectivization. Collectivization, the ultimate goal of any socialist society for its agrarian field, is also the most certain means to promoting political and social controls over the roughly 80 per cent of China's population who are peasants. Ideologically, this policy is regarded as the working out in practice of the Leninist theory of alliance between advanced industrial workers and the backward peasants.

Ever since the 1920's, the Chinese Communists have faced a twin set of pressures in determining their agrarian policy. From the economic standpoint, they have attempted to control production; from the political standpoint, they have sought to win over the peasants to the revolutionary cause. As a result, agrarian policy has shown a long history of tactical shifts and, at times, reversals. On occasion the Chinese Communists have resorted to the simple expedient of rent reduction to win the peasants' political support. At other times, they have ruthlessly confiscated and nationalized land despite the likely consequence of widespread peasant alienation. On the whole, the oscillation between these two tactical lines has followed no consistent pattern: rather, it has been motivated by expediency, which is sometimes expressed in the Party slogan of "two steps forward, one step back."

The agrarian program developed by the CPC during the period from 1921 to 1927 was generally one of complete moderation. It centered around reduction of both rents and taxes on land. With the establishment of a Chinese Soviet at Ch'aling, Hunan, in November, 1927, largely due to the persuasion of Mao Tse-tung, agrarian policy veered sharply to the left. Basically motivated by a desire to win the political support of the peasant masses, the Party inaugurated a radical policy of land redistribution. In fact, its 1928 Agrarian Law provided for the confiscation of all land in the Hunan-Kiangsi Border Soviet. But this attempt at land nationalization resulted in a dismal failure. The very peasants who the Chinese Communists sought to win were frightened by the radical measures. In an attempt to alleviate this discontent, the Chinese Communists made an abrupt switch in 1931. The land law enacted in that year provided for the confiscation only of "the lands of the feudal landlords, warlords, gentry, temples, and other big private land-owners" and for redistribution among "middle" as well as "poor" peasants. The land of the middle peasants was specifically exempted from infringement. Summing up the new agrarian policy in his report to the Second All-China Congress of Soviets in 1934, Mao declared: "Our class line in the agrarian revolution is to depend upon the hired farm hands and poor peasants, to ally with the middle peasants, to check the rich peasants and to annihilate the landlords." To reassure the well-to-do peasants who feared being lumped together with the landlords, an official classification of peasants was then carried out. In spite of the relative moderation of this program, the Chinese Communists failed to prevent the continued alienation of the rural masses.

The agrarian revolution of the Soviet period continued under this policy until the Party's famous shift to a popular-front policy on the eve of the renewed Japanese aggression in 1937. In an effort to unite all classes against this menace, the CPC suspended its policy of confiscating landlords' property. The irony is that the CPC now pressured the peasants to pay their rents and interest to the landlords. Agrarian reform was watered down to rent and interest reduction. It should be noted, though, that a more advanced program was carried out during the war years in the Shensi-Kansu-Ninghsia border region. In fact, Lin Tsu-han, then chairman of the regional government there, reported that by 1942, 24 per cent of all productive labor in the region had been organized into mutual aid teams and cooperatives.

As soon as the war ended in 1945, and the landlords were of little further use to the CPC, the class struggle against the "feudalistic" landlords was intensified, and the original policy of confiscation and radical redistribution was renewed. The ensuing violence and disorder and widespread resentment among all agrarian segments were once again to force the CPC to abandon its radical approach. By September, 1947, the Party formally approved a basic program which clearly affirmed the right of private ownership. Although sanctioning the principle of confiscation and redistribution, the program rejected the extreme policy of denying any land to the former landlords. They were, in fact, to be given an "equal share" with the peasants. This program culminated in the famous Agrarian Reform Law of June 28, 1950, which was the basis for agrarian reform until 1952–53.

From the outset the basic economic motive of the 1950 law was not to raise peasant living standards, but to strengthen the national economy to facilitate the transition to collectivization and industrialization. Liu Shao-ch'i, in his report of June 14, 1950, made this very explicit:

> The basic reason for and the aim of agrarian reform are different from the view that agrarian reform is only designed to relieve the poor people. The Communist Party has always been fighting for the interests of the laboring poor, but the viewpoints of communists have always been different from those of the philanthropists. The results of agrarian reform are beneficial to the impoverished laboring peasants, helping them partly solve their problem of poverty. But the basic aim of agrarian reform is not purely one of relieving the impoverished peasants. It is designed to

set free the rural productive forces from the shackles of the feudal land ownership system of the landlord class in order to develop agricultural production and thus pave the way for New China's industrialization.

Article 1 of the law stated the aim of the program in almost the same words. Article 2 provided for the confiscation of the "land, draft animals, farm implements and surplus grain of the landlords and their surplus households." But the law also stipulated that landlords were to be given an equal share of the redistributed land "so that they can make their living by their own labor and thus reform themselves through labor" (Article 10). In showing this apparent leniency toward the landlord class[5] the government was again resorting to political expediency. On the one hand, the CPC was ideologically committed to the extermination of the landlords as a class, but on the other it could scarcely afford to alienate any large segment of the rural population. Since it needed the support of the entire peasantry, the CPC also was careful to distinguish even the "rich peasants" from the 4 per cent officially comprising the landlord class. Article 6 specifically protected from infringement "the land owned by rich peasants and cultivated by themselves or hired labor, as well as their other properties."

But the rich peasants—like the national bourgeoisie—were to be allowed such privileges only with the sufferance of the CPC. The economy of the rich peasants was to be preserved, Liu Shao-ch'i admitted in his report, "because the existence of a rich peasant economy and its development within certain limits is advantageous to the development of the people's economy in our country." For political reasons, too, the rich peasant was better tolerated for a time, lest the middle peasants put up resistance in fear that they too would lose their lands and property. Through a policy of toleration, Liu added,

. . . the rich peasant can be won over to a neutral attitude in general and better protection can then be given to the middle peasants, thus dispelling certain unnecessary misgivings of the peasants during the development of production. Therefore in the present situation, the adoption of a policy to preserve the rich peasant economy . . . is necessary both politically and economically.

But the rich peasant did not escape without a foretaste of future deprivations. Article 6 of the Agrarian Reform Law provided that all or part of the land rented out by the rich peasants could be requisitioned by the government. Hence, although the law "preserved" the rich and "pro-

---

[5] In practice, this legal "right" did not prevent the execution of tens of thousands of landlords at the hands of such equally "legal" agrarian reform organs as the "people's tribunals." For an account based on first-hand reports of missionaries and others, see Jean Monsterleet, *L'Empire de Mao Tse-tung* (1949–1954), (Lillie, 1955), pp. 31–45.

tected" the middle peasants, its main emphasis was upon the poor peasants and farm laborers. By far the most numerous class, they were also to be the main beneficiaries of the redistribution policy.

From 1945 to 1947, in the areas under communist control, the organizational structure for implementation of land reform followed the wartime pattern. The *hsiang*, or rural district, was the basic administrative unit. After 1947, local peasant associations organized on the *hsiang* level gradually replaced the formal administrative units in the execution of agrarian reform laws. Under the 1950 law, these "mass organizations" became the principal legal vehicles for requisitioning the property of the landlords, and for carrying out a "unified, equitable and rational distribution" to the poor peasants. For official clarification, these associations could look for guidance to peasant "representative conferences"—then the local organs of the state.

It was the CPC itself which not only set up the timetables for the various regions but also exercised real supervision and control at the local levels. Activation of the peasants and the establishment of peasant associations were initiated in the main by Party cadres specially trained for this work. Only later, when the agrarian program was well advanced, did activist peasants begin to play any significant role in the peasant associations. Throughout, however, the CPC sought to create the appearance of a spontaneous self-actuated movement emanating from the peasants themselves.

The timetable for reform varied considerably according to the date of "liberation" and the physical and psychological preparedness of each region. Basically, however, it followed the same carefully planned sequence. [6] Peasants were not permitted to anticipate the Party schedule. [7]

The agrarian reform program provided many peasants with free land and working capital. They were no longer obliged to pay from 15 to 70 per cent of their crops as rent to the landlords, and their debts to the landlords were cancelled. Yet much if not all of the peasants' financial gain was offset by new agricultural taxes. Another factor was the localized

[6] In the first phase the rural CPC cadres arranged "peasant representative conferences" and organized local peasant associations. In the next, rent-reduction and "anti-despotism" movements were initiated. In the third phase, "reform committees" were established preparatory to actual confiscation, and people's tribunals created to settle any disputes arising from seizure. In the final phase, lands and properties of the landlords were taken and redistributed. The CPR finally issued the title deeds to the new owners, thus completing the "legal" process.

[7] For a detailed picture of the "terror" during this period see Monsterleet, *op. cit.*, pp. 31–33. For an analysis of communist doctrine and practice involved see Karl A. Wittfogel, *Mao Tse-tung, Liberator or Destroyer of the Chinese Peasants?* (Free Trade Union of the AFL, 1955).

basis for administering the confiscated lands. Apart from inequities due to the corruption and irresponsibility of many of the cadres, peasant gain was largely determined by the presence or absence of many rich landlords in their own *hsiang*. The arbitrary classification of the peasants by the cadres also engendered insecurity among the rich and even the middle peasant strata.

From the standpoint of the CPC, it would have been unfortunate if the agrarian reform had improved the peasants' lot to any marked degree, for this would have tended to preserve a small peasant economy emphasizing decentralization and rural conservatism. Actually, the agrarian reform served a dual purpose for the CPC. Politically, it was a transitory measure paving the way for collectivization; economically it was to provide an increase in agricultural production. Both these goals were imperative to the early stage of socialization and industrialization.

So far as the economic objective is concerned, Chinese Communist expectations were not fulfilled. Considerable peasant discontent with the program took the form of widespread desertions and "blind migrations" to the cities. As a political measure, there was never any doubt that the program was but the first step in a long-term drive toward collectivization. It was apparently the combination of political success and economic failure that led Peking, early in 1953, to push on with new programs timed to coincide with the First Five-Year Plan and the drive for industrialization. In an address to the 1953 National Congress of the New Democratic Youth League, Teng Tzu-hui, the Director of the Rural Work Department of the CPC Central Committee, called for an end to the agrarian reform program of the preceding five years and the implementation of a large-scale program of collectivization. The basis for this shift was provided by the Decision on Mutual Aid and Cooperation in Agriculture taken by the CC on February 15, 1953. Teng stressed the importance of "mechanization" in increasing agricultural output. "Mechanized farming and mechanized irrigation," he pointed out, "are not adapted to small plots of land individually owned by the peasants." Thus the shift toward collectivization was made in the name of mechanization according to the familiar dictum of Marx that "a change in the productive forces calls for a change in the relationships of production."

The collectivization program had well-established roots in communist doctrine, both in the USSR and China. In 1929 Stalin had insisted on the need "to merge gradually the different fragmentary peasant households into large farms, that is, collective farms." Stalin observed that "only common and large scale production will make the fullest use of scientific achievements and new techniques, and push forward at a rapid pace the development of agriculture." Mao restated the need for collectivization in terms of the traditional conditions of the Chinese peasantry in a 1943 speech:

> As for the peasant masses, a system of individual economy has prevailed among them for thousands of years under which a family or a household constitutes a separate productive unit; this scattered, individual form of production has been the economic foundation of feudal rule and poverty. The only way to change this state of affairs is by gradual collectivization and the only way to bring about collectivization is, according to Lenin, through cooperatives.

The strategy of collectivization was further elaborated by Mao over a period of years before the 1949 victory. In 1945 he promised that after land reform had been carried out, "by degrees the peasants will be organized on a voluntary basis into agricultural producers' cooperatives or other cooperatives. . . ." In the "New China," he stated in 1947, there would be "an agricultural economy developing step by step from individual toward collective farming." Finally, in 1949, after the establishment of the CPR and while the land reform program was still in full force, he again stressed that "without the socialization of agriculture, there will be no complete and consolidated socialism." Politically, the government believed it would be far easier to supervise the peasants by concentrating them in one place and leading them to rely on collective labor and marketing efforts. Economically, it had the same goal as the land reform—the increase of agricultural production. Implementation was to be gradual. In the beginning there was no fixed timetable or necessary succession of stages. Considerable variation was allowed from one region to another, depending on local conditions and the receptiveness of the inhabitants.

The first and lowest form of collectivization is "mutual aid," which is essentially a seasonal or temporary arrangement. Under this plan the peasants are organized into teams, pooling their implements and working their land in common for a specified period or a particular operation, such as spring planting or fall harvesting. In more advanced mutual-aid teams the members may own some property in common, may map out simple production plans for the team as a whole, and may introduce minor improvements of technique along with some specialization of labor.

The next higher form is the agricultural producers' cooperative. In contrast to mutual-aid arrangements, the producers' cooperatives pool implements and labor and land in what is officially referred to as "the contribution of land as investment." Technically, the peasants still retain the private ownership of their land and may withdraw their "investment." Hence this form of organization is sometimes called a "land cooperative." The producers' cooperatives are in a better position to acquire modern or improved implements and can engage in a more advanced level of planning and division of labor than the mutual-aid teams.

The next step in collective organization, which *People's Daily* of January 1, 1954, termed the "higher and fully developed socialist form of agricultural producers' cooperatives," is the "collective farm." Actually, two categories should be distinguished—the collective farm and the state farm. In the former, the members theoretically own the land in common, rather than "investing" their individual holdings. In the state farms, of course, the land is owned outright by the state. It should be noted that the transition from producers' cooperative to collective farm need not involve any relocation of the peasants (though consolidation into larger units is likely). The change is one of legal title to the land. The Draft Model Regulations for Agricultural Producers' Cooperatives approved by the NPC Standing Committee on November 9, 1955, explicates the nature of this gradual transition:

. . . the cooperative will step by step do away with the dividend for land belonging to members. In accordance with its own needs and with the agreement of its members, at a set price or through other mutual-benefit arrangements, the cooperative will gradually convert the other means of production turned over by its members for common use into communal property—i.e., property collectively owned by all members. In this way, the cooperative will gradually pass from the preliminary stage to the high stage.

Pending this transformation, the government had already provided for the establishment of at least a token number of collective and state farms as model units. The Decision on Mutual Aid and Cooperation in Agriculture of February 15, 1953, called for setting up a certain number of "mechanized or semi-mechanized state farms" and a much greater number of experimental state farms (at least one or two in each *hsien* or county), the latter apparently not mechanized to any degree. The Regulation also called for establishing a smaller number (one or several in each province) of "collective farms of a socialist nature," also on an experimental basis. These farms were to serve as models for the peasants and to demonstrate the advantages of advanced farming techniques in order to promote peasant receptivity to the idea of collectivization. In addition, they were to train personnel for mechanical farming, including operation and maintenance, and in administrative and managerial aspects of the larger farms. [8]

If Communist China had imitated the Soviet experience in collectivization exactly, it would have completed this movement by 1957, the last year of its First Five-Year Plan. In point of fact, the pattern of agricul-

[8] Typical of the organization of these farms was the one established in 1951 in what was then the northeastern province of Sungkiang. Patterned after the Soviet-type col-

tural collectivization shows the same variability as was involved in the first efforts at industrialization under the First Five-Year Plan. In his report to the first NPC session in September, 1954, Chou En-lai stated that one-half of the 110 million peasant households would be organized in agricultural cooperatives by the 1957 completion of the FFYP. Mao did not drastically revise these goals in his major policy report *On the Question of Agricultural Cooperation*, delivered at a meeting of provincial, municipal and autonomous area Party secretaries in Peking on July 31, 1955.[9] By 1957, he said, half of the 500 million peasant population would be in cooperatives or fully socialized collective farms. The remainder were to be so organized by the end of 1960, and the entire process of socialist transformation and technical re-equipment of agriculture was to be completed by the end of the Third Five-Year Plan in 1967. But the intensified drive to form additional cooperatives, touched off by Mao's report, produced such phenomenal results that, by the end of 1955, the entire program was drastically foreshortened. In January, 1956, Mao dramatically announced that the process of forming producers' cooperatives would be largely completed "in the course of the year 1956 alone," while the transformation of these cooperatives to fully socialist collective and state farms would be accomplished as early as 1959 or 1960.

The basis for Mao's optimism was to be found in the official statistics for the collective movement. These show an astronomical growth. From a total of about 14,000 producers' cooperatives at the end of 1953, the number rose to 100,000 at the end of 1954, and to 650,000 by June, 1955. Originally the plan called for a million cooperatives by the spring of 1956. In his July, 1955, report, Mao had called for 1,300,000 by the fall of 1956. But the Chinese Communist press reported that, by November 10, 1955, there were already 1,240,000 cooperatives.

The proportion of the population affected by the collectivization drive also mounted steadily. In 1950, 20 per cent of all peasant households were said to be organized into mutual-aid teams or cooperatives, with the greater share in the former. This figure rose to 25 per cent in 1952, and

---

lective, the farm was made up of some 60 peasant families. Administrative authority was vested in a General Farm Members Meeting, which determined and approved production plans, standards of labor, and rates of remuneration. Actual farm operation was in the hands of a Control Committee. Payment of workers was originally on the basis of a point system which also took into account quality and efficiency; but this was soon abandoned, reportedly because of the resentment of women workers.

[9] Publication of Mao's address was delayed until the October 17 issue of *People's Daily*, which may be explained by the fact that the CC did not confirm Mao's pronouncements with its own Decisions until its October 11 meeting. Mao's report was his first major policy statement on agriculture since July, 1949.

43 per cent in 1953. Later statistics provided only the number of households collectivized. *People's Daily* in February, 1955, placed this proportion at 15 per cent. By November, it was officially claimed to have reached 40 per cent. As noted previously, the original 1957 target had been 50 per cent. But, after Mao's plea, most areas appeared to have more than doubled the number of cooperatives called for in the original plans. [10] Mao himself provided statistics in his December 27, 1955, article on "The Surging Tide of Socialism in China's Countryside":

In the second half of 1955 the situation in China has gone through substantial change. By the end of December, 1955, over 60 per cent of the 110 million peasant households—i.e., over 70 million households—have already responded to the call of the CC of the CPC and joined the agricultural producers' cooperatives of the semi-socialist type. In my report of July 31, 1955, on the problems of agricultural cooperation, I mentioned that 16,900,000 peasant households had joined the cooperatives; thereafter within the short space of several months, over 50 million additional households have joined the cooperatives. This is really an outstanding event. It tells us that in the course of the year 1956 alone, the stage of semi-socialist agricultural cooperation can be in the main achieved. And in the subsequent three or four years—i.e., by 1959 or 1960—the transformation from semi-socialist to full socialist cooperatives can be in the main achieved.

Perhaps Mao and his followers were—to use a phrase Stalin made famous during the height of the Soviet collectivization drive—becoming "dizzy with success." A draft plan for a 12-year agricultural development program, presented to the supreme state conference in Peking on January 25, 1956, with Mao in attendance, revealed that the full socialist stage of collectivization would be principally achieved by 1958, instead of 1959 or 1960. [11]

The narrative of Chinese Communist collectivization should be broken here to point out that there were considerations other than optimism over statistical charts in modifying the original goals. For example, *People's Daily* of August 3, 1954, had acknowledged that less than a third of the

[10] For example, it was reported that in Kiangsu province the number of cooperatives was increased from 35,773 in July to 121,494 by October 4. Needless to say, the pattern varied widely by geographic area. Mao himself pointed out in July, 1955, that the bulk of the cooperatives were then located in Manchuria and North China, with strong development in Chekiang and Anhwei, but only scattered progress elsewhere. The Central Committee's Decision on Agricultural Cooperation in October, 1955, revealed that many mutual-aid teams still existed and even alluded to border areas where "a policy of long-term waiting" would be necessary.

[11] This draft plan specified that at least 85 per cent of the 110 million farm families would be organized into agricultural producers' cooperatives by the end of 1956.

cooperatives formed in that year could be called efficient. Denied incentive under collectivization, the peasants continued their passive, and sometimes active, resistance. The cadres were themselves bewildered by the failures of the cooperatives. Most importantly, in their present form the cooperatives were failing to provide the essential raw materials and capital for industrial expansion. Essentially, then, Mao's call was motivated, at least in large measure, by a desire to avoid further failure on the agricultural front. This required not only an increased organizational tempo, but also that the form itself be modified to promote efficiency. The new form advocated for the cooperatives can be designated by the title "advanced cooperatives."

Fully socialist collective and state farms did not share in the rapid numerical increase. At the end of 1953, China had only ten known collective farms. Their number was gradually increased in line with the Central Committee's decision of February 15, 1953, already cited. In December, 1955, there were said to be about 29,000 Soviet-type collectives in existence, with a high concentration in Manchuria, where over 45 per cent of the peasant households in Liaoning were said to be so organized. As for the state farms, the Peking Statistical Bureau reported that 2,340 had been established by the end of 1953, of which 59 were "mechanized." These latter had at their disposal 1,621 standard tractors, 353 combine harvesters, and many other types of farm machinery. Tseng Chien, in the November 16, 1954, *People's China*, referred to 346,800 acres under such cultivation. He also stated that there were 110 mechanized and semi-mechanized state farms by September, 1954. The First Five-Year Plan called for adding 91 mechanized state farms over the 1952 figure, making a total, according to Mao, of 141 mechanized farms within an over-all total of 3,038 state farms. By 1957, the mechanized farms were to be cultivating about 1,263,-000 acres, while the non-mechanized farms would work an additional 1,500,000 acres. Mao indicated that the major drive for state farms would be postponed until the second and third Five-Year Plans. Total acreage for these farms was to go from nearly 2.4 million in 1955, to over 22 million in 1967.

In his address to the 1953 National Congress of the NDYL, Teng Tzu-hui, then Director of the CPC Central Committee's Rural Work Department, had stated emphatically that "for large scale development of agricultural production, we must gradually realize the mechanization of agriculture." A number of machine and tractor stations of the Soviet type were established at key places to serve the cooperatives—but their number was woefully inadequate. According to Tseng Chien's statistics, only 113 machine and tractor stations existed for the whole country in September,

1954.[12] The First Five-Year Plan called for the addition of 194 stations by 1957, bringing the total to only a little more than 300 for the entire country—a ratio roughly on the order of one for every 10,000 cooperatives or collective farms anticipated for that date. Figures for the number of personnel trained on state farms provide another indication of the embryonic and experimental status of the mechanization program. Tseng revealed that, by the latter part of 1954, these farms had trained up to 50,000 farm workers and administrators, but only 5,000 tractor drivers, mechanics and maintenance men for farm machinery.[13]

Mao's July, 1955, call for a new departure in agricultural policy indicated that the mechanization program was not so much abandoned as demoted. Even under the First Five-Year Plan, the government was unwilling to divert any substantial share of industrial output to production of heavy farm machinery or chemical fertilizer. It chose to rely on more effective utilization of existing agrarian productive forces through the centralization of operations and further coercion of the peasants. In fact, Mao's July report admitted that it would take five Five-Year Plans to complete the mechanization program.

Part of the success of the modified plan for collectivization depended upon strict implementation of the class line advocated by Mao. In essence, this policy called for the leaders and cadres to rely upon the poor peasants as the sinews of the Party; to unite closely with the middle peasants; and to wage a vigorous struggle against rich-peasant tendencies in order to check the development of "rural capitalism." More concrete measures were spelled out in the Draft Model Regulations for Agricultural Producers' Cooperatives adopted by the Sixth Plenum of the CC in October, 1955. Article 11 provided that "poor peasants shall not be restricted and middle peasants shall not be excluded in joining the cooperatives," while "landlords and rich peasants will not be accepted." Continuing, the article provided:

Only after the cooperatives have been consolidated and over three-fourths the laboring peasants in the *hsien* and *hsiang* concerned have joined the cooperatives

[12] Liao Lu-yen, then Deputy Director of the CC's Department of Rural Work and Minister of Agriculture, in an article in *People's China* of April 1, 1954, openly admitted the limited extent to which machine and tractor stations were being used: In Northeast China in 1953, for example, only 104 out of 4,926 producers' cooperatives were practicing mechanized farming with the help of the machine and tractor stations. This represented 2 per cent of the cooperatives in the area.

[13] The "Friendship Farm" which the USSR donated to China, complete with agricultural machinery and Soviet technicians, was, of course, no more than a token contribution in view of China's needs.

348   COMMUNIST CHINA: THE DOMESTIC SCENE

can landlords who have changed their status according to the law, and rich peasants
who have long given up exploitation, be separately admitted into the cooperatives
when they have been considered and approved at the general meeting of members
and by the *hsien* people's council.

Another significant aspect of the modification in the collectivization program in 1955 was that it marked the end of a period of sharp debate
within the Party.   Mao's July 31 report indicates as much:

> Some comrades disapprove of the Party Central Committee's policy of keeping
> agricultural cooperation in step with socialist industrialization, the policy which
> proved correct in the Soviet Union.   They consider that the prescribed rate of
> development in industrialization is all right, but that there is no need for agricul-
> tural cooperation to keep in step with industrialization, that it should, in fact,
> develop very, very slowly.   That is to disregard the Soviet Union's experience.
> These comrades do not understand that socialist industrialization is not something
> that can be carried out in isolation, separate from agricultural cooperation. . . .
> Only when agriculture has been transformed into large-scale cooperative farming
> can such things [as farm machinery, chemical fertilizers, modern means of trans-
> port, and electrical power] be used on a big. scale, or for that matter, used at all.
> . . . In agriculture, under the conditions prevailing in our country, cooperation
> must precede the use of big machinery. . . . We can see, then, that industry and
> agriculture, socialist industrialization and the socialist transformation of agricul-
> ture, cannot be separated, cannot be dealt with in isolation from each other.

In retrospect, one wonders if the worst aspects of the 1959-61 "famine
period" might have been avoided, or at least, minimized, had Mao adhered
to this economic truism that industry and agriculture are mutually dependent!

As the 1953 Decision on the Development of Agricultural Producers'
Cooperatives clearly and emphatically stated, "the basic criteria of the
success of agricultural producers' cooperatives are the increases in their
production."   No reliable information is available on the extent to which
this goal was served by the 1955 acceleration.   Minister of Agriculture
Liao Lu-yen did claim that formation of cooperatives in the Northeast,
up to 1954, had increased production 15–20 per cent.   Mao, in July, 1955,
reported that "roughly 80 per cent of the existing 650,000 agricultural producers' cooperatives have increased output.   More than 10 per cent . . .
have shown neither an increase nor a decline.   The output of the remainder
has dropped."   China's bumper 1955 crop—whether or not it could be
attributed to the cooperatives—doubtlessly influenced the decision to increase the tempo of collectivization.   But there are other indications that,
until at least July, 1955, the program was falling short of expectations.
The NPC session meeting in that month revealed that the First Five-Year

Plan called for a 30 per cent increase in grain production by the end of 1957, based on 1952 output. But Vice Premier Li Fu-ch'un, head of the State Planning Commission, announced at the same time that the 1957 target had been cut back from 30 to 17.6 per cent. [14]

Communist China's collectivization drive, as implied in the foregoing analysis, was beset by several fundamental defects. Three major categories can be distinguished: (1) the traditionalism and apathy of the peasants; (2) weaknesses in the manner of carrying out the program, or personal shortcoming on the part of the Party and state personnel; and (3) defects intrinsic to the collectivization system as such.

Since the Chinese Communists originally won the peasants' support through such slogans as "Land to the Tillers," it was only natural that the peasants should expect to come into permanent possession of their own individual holdings. These aspirations appeared fulfilled when the People's Republic issued title to confiscated farms of the landlords under the 1950 Agrarian Law. Thus the collectivization program appeared as a betrayal and the ensuing disillusionment tended to develop into passive resistance. [15] Even before the modifications of 1955, there had been a growing tendency on the part of some peasants to ignore, withdraw from, or even dissolve the cooperatives. For example, Mao bluntly stated that

[14] Detailed figures on the agricultural targets of the First Five-Year Plan,* in thousands of catties, were as follows:

Item	1952 output	1957 projected output	percentage increase, 1957 over 1952
Food crops	327,830	385,620	117.6
Rice	136,850	163,540	119.5
Wheat	36,250	47,450	130.9
Soya beans	19,040	22,440	117.9
Misc. grains	103,040	109,590	106.4
Tubers	32,650	42,600	130.5
Cotton	2,261,000	3,270,000	125.4
Jute	600,100	730,000	119.7
Tobacco	440,000	780,000	176.6
Sugar cane	960,000	4,270,000	446.4

* See *Chung-Hua-Jen-Min-Kung-Ho-Kuo Fa-chan Kuo-min-ching-chi ti Ti-i Wu-Nien-Chi-Hua 1953–1957* (*The First Five Year Plan for the Development of the National Economy of the Chinese People's Republic 1953–1957*) (Peking, 1955), p. 80.

[15] Many peasants reportedly persisted in engaging in a business or commercial "side line" for personal profit at the expense of the movement. They were said to be reluctant to submit their "excess" crops for compulsory state purchase. At the same time they demanded their full share of the harvest of the producers' cooperative, leaving little or nothing for reserve or welfare funds, or even for purchase of cattle feed. They were slow to repay government loans and resented the presence of "outsiders" sent by the Party and state.

a "fatal mistake" had been made in Chekiang province in the summer of 1954, in allowing the dissolution of 15,000 of its 53,000 cooperatives during a consolidation campaign. Other peasants expressed their resentment by neglecting the commonland to tend their own plots or by destroying livestock to prevent its use by the cooperative. An article in the May 13, 1955, issue of *Cheng-chih Hsüeh-hsi (Political Study)* summarized:

> Since the winter of last year, a very abnormal phenomenon has appeared in some areas, that is, peasants slaughtered and sold livestock massively, felled trees, and became inactive in making production investments. In consequence, difficulties have to a certain extent plagued the spring plowing and production this year. This is a reflection of the low production morale and the fluctuation of thought on the part of some peasants (mainly middle peasants).

After the intensification of collectivization late in 1955, peasant resistance expressed through the sale or slaughter of cattle became a major problem, just as it had been for the Soviets during their collectivization drive of 1929–34. By December, 1955, there were frequent references in the press, although the blame was often placed on a sharp drop in prices.[16] In the face of this critical situation, Peking ordered that cattle could neither be slaughtered nor sold without official permission. Needless to say, all of these acts of resistance were termed traitorous tendencies toward capitalism or egoism opposed to the "socialist transformation of agriculture."

At least until mid-1955, the CPC sought to avoid alienation of the peasants by advising its cadres to use persuasive rather than forceful tactics. The Central Committee's decision of February 15, 1953, explicitly cautioned the cadres against ridiculing, threatening, or applying restrictive measures against those peasants who resisted joining the cooperatives. The Party frequently pointed to the need for improving cooperative management—particularly through consolidation of the existing cooperatives. But the cadres continued to resort to coercive measures to get peasants to join or cooperate in the collectivization program. This coercion included manipulation of state purchases and government loans and the levying of contributions. At times, it could involve outright terrorism. In its question-and-answer column on May 15, 1955, *Cheng-chih Hsüeh-hsi (Political Study)* pointed out that "in some districts . . . peasants . . . joined the cooperatives involuntarily, or not quite voluntarily, or under conditions of compulsion." At another point it alluded to "political suppression and economic restrictions" used by the cadres to prevent the

---

[16] For example, *People's Daily* of December 18, 1955, cited one area in Shantung province where calves were currently selling for 5 to 10 *yuan* (about $2–4) as compared to 20 to 30 *yuan* ($8–12) in the previous year.

peasants from withdrawing. Cadres were also charged with lack of sufficient technical competence. Shocking cases were reported of cadre negligence in the face of approaching emergencies, together with the more common cases of corruption and favoritism and deceit.

The intensification of the collectivization drive in the latter months of 1955 only served to aggravate peasant grievances. While the leaders still claimed that the cooperatives were designed to help the peasant to a better way of life, the program of compulsory state purchases of "excess" produce, for example, often worked injustices. In certain areas too little food was left for local consumption, and to borrow funds meant to court bankruptcy.

Party concern over peasant discontent can be seen in various warnings to the cadres to proceed cautiously and according to local conditions, as well as in the concessions which the CPC offered the peasants from time to time. Measures were proposed to make up shortages in trained personnel. *People's Daily* of February 19, 1955, for example, after admitting that many cooperatives had not yet settled their financial accounts for the previous year, called for the training of additional accountants. On March 9, the same organ reported the convocation by the Central Committee of an All-China (Party) Conference on Basic Organization Work in the Villages. This was clearly an attempt to improve basic Party organization in the rural areas to carry out the struggle for "socialist transformation of agriculture."

But the CPC leadership was quick to reject any suggestion that the basic plan for collectivization be amended or suspended. The view of those Party members who, in Mao's words, "advise us to get off the horse and pause on our journey along the road to cooperation" was firmly condemned. Mao's July, 1955, directive, as noted previously, indicated that the program would be continued. As he stated even more emphatically in a December 27, 1955, article: "Now, among all Party ranks and the people at large, the condemnation of the right-deviationist conservative views in regard to the tempo of socialist transformation of agriculture is no longer in question—this question is already solved."

Having put an end to Party discussion by this fiat, the CPC had to turn its attention to training large numbers of cadres as leaders, accountants and technicians to guide the organization and operation of the advanced cooperatives. These cadres were usually detached from Party organs at the various levels and, after short-term training, organized into working teams for the villages. The number of cadres employed in this "labor-wasting" drive was amazingly large. For example, according to a Wuhan radio broadcast of November 15, 1955, 100,000 new cadres were being trained to staff the 20,000 new producers' cooperatives intended for the Hsiaokan Special District in Hupeh province. In the Hsiangyang Special

District of the same province some 100,000 were to be trained by November 30.

These cadres constituted a vast invading army of, for the most part, nonproductive forces, garrisoned in the villages, living on the produce of the peasants, and serving as watchdogs among them. Many peasants flocked to the cooperatives out of fear, thus defeating the principle of "voluntariness." Meanwhile, the government was definitely discouraging that type of voluntary initiative which occasioned groups of peasants to organize cooperatives on their own, without waiting for the cadres to take the lead. For example, the Chekiang *Daily*, late in 1955, editorially called on the cadres to reorganize these self-established cooperatives in order to strengthen Party control. Rural Party units themselves were told to reorganize in the interests of efficiency.

Fulfilling the terms of Mao's 1955 directives, by the winter of 1956 the cadres had basically completed cooperativization, with the exception of several outlying areas. Peasant households in excess of 120 million had been organized into some 740,000 cooperatives, each containing an average of 160 households. The prosperity of these units widely varied. In areas accustomed to a higher standard of living there was general dissatisfaction with the simple methods employed by the cooperatives. Conversely, in areas with traditionally lower standards of living, unrest existed because the peasants had not prospered as they had expected.

The depths this unrest could reach are indicated by an incident reported in the *Si-An Jih-pao* of August 15, 1957. A counterrevolutionary force called the Chinese Human Life Salvation Army was discovered to have organized in four counties of Shensi province. This body demanded an immediate end to the cooperative movement and a system of unified purchase and distribution. On the morning of May 17, 1957, an uprising disrupted transportation and destroyed two county government seats. At the same time the peasants attempted to withdraw their draft animals from the cooperatives. [17]

Aside from the question of peasant unrest, the cooperatives were failing to fulfill their role in the state's economic goals. The cooperatives were

---

[17] Promises to the peasants joining the cooperatives that they would retain private ownership of animals and farm implements and that they could withdraw at any time were rendered nominal by the fiscal program. The peasant entering the cooperative was expected to contribute his share to the current year's expenditures for animals and implements etc., some of which had previously been turned in by members of the cooperatives. Loans were extended so the peasant could make this "contribution," and no one could leave the organization until all debts were paid. Even if, by chance, this sum could be repaid, the peasant's contributions to the common funds would not be returned should he try to withdraw.

not furnishing the capital accumulation needed for industrial expansion, and even agricultural quotas fell below anticipated minimum levels. At a time when the Great Leap Forward would make tremendous demands for manpower, the cooperatives were not making efficient use of the labor supply. Moreover, tremendous numbers of Party members had to be assigned to relatively unimportant and often duplicated tasks. As will be seen in the following chapter, all of these factors were influential in the Party's 1958 decision to abandon the cooperatives in favor of the commune system.

PROGRAMS FOR INDUSTRIALIZATION

The early principles to guide China's industrialization were summarized this way in a *People's Daily* editorial of May 22, 1953: "Industrialization means that industry occupies a more important sphere than agriculture in the national economy." As noted in the previous section, a necessary requisite for industrialization was the land reform and collectivization program to secure the agricultural sector. Afterwards, the share of the gross national product supplied by the industrial sector was expected to rise from the 20 per cent of 1953 to an ultimate goal of 70 per cent. Since industrialization itself was contingent upon the full development of "heavy industry," the first step would have to center on that objective in accordance with the "socialist method" exemplified by the Soviet Union. Fulfillment of these plans has been regarded as essential to national defense and an improved standard of living. And, as the same Party organ noted, all this would be possible "within our generation, the age of Mao Tse-tung."

This emphasis on industrialization was initially set by Lenin in many statements, including the remark that "there is only one real foundation for a socialist society, and it is large industry." Stalin affirmed the correctness of Lenin's formula that "communism is the Soviet regime plus electrification of the entire country." In this sense, of course, "electrification" involved overall industrialization. Stalin's earliest theory of "building socialism in one country" and his last major work on the "Economic Problems of Socialism in the USSR" both presupposed the importance of converting the Soviet Union into an industrial power.

In applying the Leninist-Stalinist line to conditions in China, Mao has stressed the interdependence of political and economic factors. On the one hand, he said in 1945, "without an independent, free, democratic and unified China, there can be no industrialized China." On the other hand, without industrialization China could never hope to maintain its political independence. Or as Mao insisted when elaborating his concept of the People's Democratic Dictatorship in 1949, "only when her industry has developed and she ceases to rely economically on foreign countries will China enjoy complete and genuine independence."

With the inauguration of the People's Republic in 1949, industrialization ceased to be a remote and theoretical goal and became the subject of concrete planning. The leadership recognized that a number of preliminary steps had to precede any full-scale industrialization program. First, agricultural output, industrial production and trade had to be restored to prewar levels. Second, preparations had to be made for the agricultural collectivization program which would accompany industrialization: Article 27 of the 1949 Common Program specified that land reform was a "prerequisite for industrialization." And third, the state sector of the economy had to be greatly expanded. By the latter part of 1952, these preliminaries were apparently nearly accomplished. Thus the government prepared to move ahead to the task of industrialization through the inauguration of the First Five-Year Plan. But since in China's essentially backward economy, modern industry then represented less than 30 per cent of aggregate output, the shift to industrialization would be a more or less abrupt jolt to the entire economy.

The general principles underlying the First Five-Year Plan have already been noted. The concrete details were finally published in August, 1955, after the plan had been officially adopted by the NPC in July. Under the plan, the major share of state expenditure was to go for capital construction. This involved some 600 major projects of building new plants or expanding existing ones, as well as some 2,000 medium-sized and small projects. Of the major projects, 141 of the most important were to be carried out according to the terms of the 1953 Sino-Soviet agreement which provided for Soviet economic and technical assistance. Of these, 91 were to be new enterprises and 50 were reconstructions or expansions of existing installations: this included modern iron and steel complexes, non-ferrous metallurgical plants, coal mines, oil refineries, heavy machinery plants, chemical works and power stations. The Khrushchev-Bulganin mission to Peking of October, 1954, resulted in a supplementary agreement whereby the USSR would furnish an additional 400 million rubles (about $100 million) of equipment for the 141 scheduled enterprises, as well as another 520 million rubles ($130 million) in long-term credit for building 15 additional enterprises.

In his report to the 1954 NPC session, Chou En-lai stated that the bulk of the Soviet-aided projects would be completed within the first five years, though some would require up to ten years to finish.[18] Upon their completion, Chou added, "we will produce by ourselves metallurgical, power-generating, oil-extracting, as well as forging and pressing equipment. We will produce motor vehicles, locomotives, tractors, and airplanes."[19]

During the period of large-scale construction of new enterprises the burden of meeting annual production quotas necessarily fell to the existing facilities. These quotas are indicated in Table III.

On September 21, 1955, the State Statistical Bureau issued a Communique on National Economic Development and Fulfillment of the State Plan in 1954. According to this and other official reports, impressive successes had been attained under the First Five-Year Plan. In 1954, the total

[18] Li Fu-ch'un's report * to the July, 1955, session of the NPC revealed the production gains to be registered by the construction program under the First Five-Year Plan:

Product	Expected increases entire program *	Expected increases first 5 years
Pig iron	5,750,000 tons	2,800,000 tons
Steel	6,100,000 tons	2,800,000 tons
Electric power	4,060,000 kw	2,050,000 kw
Coal	93,100,000 tons	53,850,000 tons
Power-generating equipment	800,000 kw	800,000 kw
Motor Cars	90,000 units	30,000 units
Tractors	15,000 (in 1959)	
Chemical fertilizer	910,000 tons	280,000 tons

* It should be noted that these figures do not refer to total annual production to be attained under the plan. Rather, they refer to the increases in annual production capacity to be expected from completion of the entire construction program begun under the First Five-Year Plan and from whatever part of the program would be completed during the five-year period.

[19] Geographic location of these capital construction projects reveals certain political and strategic determinants of the program. Priority was given to the Northeast and Northwest areas, bordering on the USSR. The construction of two additional railway trunk lines linking China and the Soviet Union through Outer Mongolia and Sinkiang reinforces the view of a "heartland" concentration of heavy industry within the communist camp. For detailed information on the number and location of these and other projects see the official publication *Chung-Hua-Jen-Min-Kung-Ho-Kuo Fa-chan Kuo-min-ching-chi ti Ti-i Wu-Nien-Chi-Hua 1953-1957 (The First Five-Year Plan for the Development of the National Economy of the Chinese People's Republic 1953-1957)* (Peking: Jen-min Ch'ü-pan-she, 1955), p. 15.

The goals envisaged in some of the regional five-year plans are also worth noting as an indication of diversified plans for different parts of the country. The Kiangsi provincial plan, for example, called for a 38.1 per cent increase in the total value of agricultural and industrial production by 1957, as compared to 1952. Industrial production alone was to increase by 127 per cent in the same period. The Tsinghai provincial plan, by contrast, placed relatively greater emphasis on agricultural production. By 1957, the food production of the province was to rise 74.36 per cent over the 1952 level.

TABLE III

OUTPUT OF PRINCIPAL INDUSTRIAL GOODS ACCORDING TO
THE FIRST FIVE-YEAR PLAN 1953–57*

Item	1952 Output	1957 Projected Output	Percentage Increase, 1957 over 1952
Electric power	7,260,000 KWH	15,900,000 KWH	219
Coal	63,528,000 tons	112,985,000 tons	178
Oil	436,000 tons	2,012,000 tons	462
Pig iron	1,900,000 tons	4,674,000 tons	246
Steel	1,350,000 tons	4,120,000 tons	306
Rolled steel	1,110,000 tons	3,045,000 tons	275
Coke	2,860,000 tons	6,685,000 tons	233
Caustic soda	79,000 tons	154,000 tons	194
Pure soda	192,000 tons	476,000 tons	248
Ammonium sulphate	181,000 tons	504,000 tons	278
Ammonium nitrate	74,860 tons	440,000 tons	588
Motor vehicle tires	417,000 tons	760,000 tons	182
Internal combustion engines	27,600 HP	260,200 HP	942
Generators	746	2,938	394
Electric motors	91,147 units	135,515 units	149
Locomotives	20 units	200 units	1,000
Railway passenger cars	6 units	300 units	5,000
Railway freight cars	5,792 units	8,500 units	147
Merchant ships	84 units	1,347 units	1,604
Trucks	—	4,000 units	—
Bicycles	80,000 units	555,000 units	694
Lumber	10,020,000 cu. m.	20,000,000 cu. m.	200
Matches	9,110,000 units	12,700,000 units	139
Machine-made paper	372,000 tons	655,000 tons	176
Cement	2,860,000 tons	6,000,000 tons	210
Plate glass	21,320,000 sq. m.	40,000,000 sq. m.	188
Cotton yarn	3,618,000 bales	5,000,000 bales	138
Cotton cloth	111,634 bolts	163,721 bolts	147
Gunny sacks	67,350,000 units	68,000,000 units	101
Edible vegetable oil	724,000 tons	1,552,000 tons	214
Sugar	249,000 tons	686,000 tons	276
Flour	2,990,000 tons	4,670,000 tons	156
Salt	3,460,000 tons	5,932,000 tons	171
Cigarettes	2,650,000 cases	4,700,000 cases	177

* See *Chung-Hua-Jen-Min-Kung-Ho-Kuo, op. cit.*, pp. 36–37.

value of industrial and agricultural production was expected to be 2.2 times greater than in 1949: but the value of the "modern industrial" sector was expected to be 4.2 times that of the earlier year. In terms of specific commodities: coal production had increased 9 per cent in 1953, and was expected to increase another 16 per cent in 1954; petroleum production, starting from a 1952 output of 436,000 tons, rose 44 per cent in 1953 and another 32 per cent in 1954; electricity registered a 26 per cent increase in 1953, with a projected 1954 increase of another 20 per cent. Following a 19 per cent increase in 1953, pig iron production was expected to rise another 32 per cent in 1954. For steel, the increases were 31 per cent for 1953, 21 per cent for the 1954 target, and 22 per cent for actual 1954 production. The total output of machine tools and electrical equipment was reported to have increased by a quarter between 1953 and 1954. In the chemical industry, 1953 production was said to have overfulfilled the quota by 14 per cent and was expected to rise another 43 per cent in 1954. The transportation network showed similar achievements. In 1953, 589 km. were added to the railway system for a total of 24,690 km. of tracks, while an additional 760 km. were to be added in 1954. Using this network, freight traffic was expected to increase by 15.5 per cent and passenger service by 14 per cent in 1954.

While agricultural production for 1953 and 1954 fell short of assigned targets, considerable work was reported in irrigation and flood control projects. Irrigation work completed between 1950 and 1954 brought the total to 4.1 million hectares (over 10 million acres) of irrigated area. A rapid rise was reported in the production of cotton yarn to 4.6 million bales in 1954, over 92 per cent above the pre-1949 peak. Production of cotton cloth reportedly reached 1,960 million meters in 1954, or 109 per cent over the pre-1949 peak.

In his report to the 1954 session of the NPC, Chou En-lai expressed satisfaction with the rate of increase in industrial production being accomplished by the Five-Year Plan. Admitting that overall production was still low, Chou was nevertheless able to conclude that "our country is advancing toward the goal of socialism." But, there were indicators that the plan was falling short of expectations in some areas. Even the rate of increase for the prime objective of heavy industry appeared to be tapering off. For example, during the readjustment period from 1949 to 1952, "modern" industrial production had increased at an average 36.9 per cent annually; but in 1953, it was only 33 per cent, and in 1954 had fallen to 17 per cent. Most of the Plan's failures were concealed in the official reports. For example, although 1953 coal production exceeded the planned target by 9 per cent, the target itself had been lowered twice during the year and finally set at 2 per cent *less* than the previous year's output.

Failures were even more glaring in terms of specific cases. On August 25, 1954, *People's Daily* admitted that "each month we still have 15 to 20 per cent of our factories and mines unable to fulfill our national program. . . . Even in terms of value of production, one fifth to one quarter of the factories each month are unable to fulfill the program." In his 1954 NPC report Chou conceded that "if we examine the fulfillment of targets for the four aspects of total production value, production costs, profit and labor productivity, then only 30 per cent of the enterprises completed their plans in all of these aspects."

Coupled with failures to achieve targets must be added the problem of the inferior quality of goods produced and the high rate of waste. The *People's Daily* article just cited also revealed that in the first half of 1954, "the products of a number of the machine-producing factories have a rate of waste as high as 40 per cent, with only a very low passing grade in quality." Numerous articles referred to the waste of manpower. Stories were told of workers waiting idly for adequate water supplies, of overstocking materials needed elsewhere, of machinery and equipment left idle and of whole projects that had to be dismantled when they failed to meet minimum standards. Many complaints referred to poor management practices and outright incompetence. In some fourteen construction units in Szechwan province, for example, actual costs were said to exceed necessary costs by about 20 per cent; in other industrial projects this reached as high as 40 per cent. Other management personnel tried to meet targets by using inferior materials or overpricing the finished product to show a profit for their own unit. [20]

Failure to achieve set standards of quality and quantity can be explained in terms of a variety of factors. For example, the Korean War intervened during the formative stage of the First Five-Year Plan. Moreover, given the society which they inherited, the Chinese Communists launched their ambitious drives with a critical shortage of trained personnel, which existed from the highest planning levels down to the smallest factory. The low level of skills was documented in a *People's Daily* report on the Anshan Iron Works in the heart of the industrial Northeast. There it was discovered that of the 10,000 workers in the building industry of the region

[20] Typical of the many complaints of inefficiency and waste was an article by Chia Ming in the *People's Daily*, in February, 1955, which referred to an inspection of the Second Machine Shop of Shenyang. The inspectors observed that none of the safety devices functioned properly, that some of the drills stopped within twenty seconds of being turned on, that shaft casings leaked oil, and that iron filings, dirt and sand were in the moving parts. All of the drills and drill presses of two models manufactured by the factory were found defective.

only 1.27 per cent could be listed as skilled.[21] This situation also existed in the ranks of management. In fact, the blunders of the leading cadres undoubtedly helped account for some of the worst mistakes of the state planning system. The process of criticism and self-criticism revealed countless cases of delay, waste and corruption. As *People's Daily* observed on August 15, 1954, "a number of comrades" suffered from an "inadequate understanding . . . as to the construction task as a whole."

Utilizing a well worn device, the Chinese Communists traced failures on the part of workers and management to insufficient or reactionary levels of ideological awareness and called for intensified political indoctrination. A *People's Daily* editorial of August 21, 1954, even warned of the presence of undercover subversive agents within the ranks of workers and technicians and urged that "the people's security organs should employ the full strength in investigation work so as to arrest the counter-revolutionaries hidden in the various industrial departments and enterprises".[22]

In 1956, the share of investment to heavy industry under the First Five-Year Plan was further increased.[23] During his April, 1956, visit to Peking, Mikoyan had pledged an additional loan of 2,500 million rubles to construct 55 more enterprises. On August 7, 1958, following Khrushchev's hurried trip to Peking to discuss the Taiwan Straits crisis, Moscow announced plans for the construction of an additional 47 enterprises in China.[24]

[21] See the section on education in Chapter 10 for details on the training of a technical force. The First Five-Year Plan itself recognized this critical shortage of skilled workers and called for the training of 920,000 within the 1953–57 period, including 176,000 for heavy industry, 172,000 for the fuel industry, and 174,000 for the machine-building industry. Nevertheless, these figures would still fall woefully short of actual needs.

[22] As noted previously, during this period the state used direct and indirect methods to liquidate private enterprises. Thus there is reason to suspect passive resistance on the part of individuals caught in the programs, which, in the long run, would thwart industrialization. According to *Ta-kung Pao* of May 11, 1954, some private businessmen desperately withdrew their current capital from the business and purchased excess consumer products.

[23] As noted in the next chapter, the first draft for the Second Five-Year Plan was considered by the CPC Eighth National Congress in September, 1956. Economic programs for that year were coordinated to the plans for the next period.

[24] The total number of Soviet-sponsored projects has undergone numerous adjustments. For example, after Chou En-lai and Khrushchev concluded another agreement in Moscow, in February, 1959, which called for the construction of 78 additional enterprises, top economic planner Li Fu-ch'un announced to the National People's Congress in April of that year that 211 units had been combined into 166. On January 1, 1958, Peking had announced that 57 of the originally scheduled 156 projects had already been completed. However, it might again be mentioned that the significance of these

In addition to loans, the Soviet Union also agreed to provide technical assistance and to train Chinese workers. Thus Appendix II of the 1950 Treaty of Alliance called for some 1,500–5,000 Soviet specialists to assist China in munitions production, 1,000–3,000 to assist in machine-production, and several thousand other advisors to work in other highly specialized capacities. During the First Five-Year Plan period, about 10,800 Russian technicians and some 1,500 other specialists from communist bloc countries aided and trained Chinese workers in on-the-job locations. Another approximately 13,000 Chinese were sent to the Soviet Union for advanced training. Without this increment to the technical manpower source, it is doubtful if Peking could have achieved its economic targets.

According to the official Communique on the Fulfillment of the First Five-Year Plan, by the end of 1957 "the overwhelming majority" of the projects called for in the program had been completed. Of the 156 major Soviet-sponsored projects, 68 were "fully or partially completed and in operation" by the end of 1957, while the increases in annual productive capacity for basic commodities were given as follows in *Peking Review* (April 21, 1959):

Commodity	Unit: 1,000	
Pig iron	3,390	tons
Steel	2,820	tons
Electric Power	2,469	kw
Coal	63,760	tons
Metallurgical and Mining Machines	8.7	tons
Trucks	30	
Cement	2,610	tons
Paper	250	tons
Petroleum	1,312	tons

According to official Chinese Communist statistics, the value of industrial production in 1957 was 21 per cent higher than called for in the original version of the First Five-Year Plan and 141 per cent higher than in 1952. In steel production, a 296 per cent increase was registered in 1957, as compared to 1952; in pig iron a 208 per cent rise; in electrical power, 166 per cent; and in coal, 96 per cent. Still using 1952 as the base year, production of locomotives rose 735 per cent, merchant ships by 338 per cent, internal combustion engines by 2,107 per cent. And similarly dramatic achievements were claimed for almost every target set under the original plan. Agricultural production, however, did not keep pace. For example, yarn production rose by only 28 per cent and edible oils by 12

---

projects is not in terms of numbers, but that they provided the backbone of the industrialization.

per cent. These latter figures point to a significant weakness in the overall economic programs.

Estimating the annual increase in China's population for the years of the First Five-Year Plan to be 2.2–2.5 per cent, the increase in food production was only slightly higher. As noted in the previous analysis of the collectivization drive, the various organizational forms which culminated in the agricultural producers' cooperatives did not significantly increase farm output. In a real sense, the achievements in the sphere of industrialization, particularly in increasing heavy industry's potential, may be said to have come at the expense of the agrarian sector. But a lagging agricultural sector would have to impede industrial development. In its April 5, 1955, issue, *People's Daily* stressed that the final achievement of a modern, industrialized society would require "decades of arduous effort, possibly fifty years." To do this, the Party organ observed, "the people of the whole country must be mobilized." Ultimately, these threads of mass mobilization, more intensive industrialization, and an agrarian sector that could serve industry were woven together into epic theories of the commune system and the Great Leap Forward.

SOCIALIZATION OF TRADE

Any economic programs for the development of agriculture and industry necessarily involve regulation of the functions of distribution and exchange. In Communist China this system penetrates down to the level of the individual consumer. Peking early gave high priority to the development and expansion of a system of state-owned and cooperative distribution and marketing facilities for both wholesale and retail domestic commerce. At the same time, a virtual monopoly was established over foreign trade. The January, 1956, announcement of the major completion of the transformation of private into joint public-private enterprises applied to commercial as well as industrial enterprises.

The result has been a fundamental change in the institutional structure of China's trade. The relative shares of the state and cooperative sectors in domestic wholesale trade in 1950 amounted to 14 and 2 per cent respectively. By 1952, they had jumped to a combined total of 50 per cent, to 70 per cent by the end of 1953, and to about 89 per cent by 1954. According to a report of the State Statistical Bureau dated September 12, 1954, by the previous year the state and cooperative sectors had gained control of 38 per cent of all retail sales in eight major cities. Throughout the country, these sectors controlled 49 per cent of all retail sales in 1953, and about 67 per cent in 1954. In foreign trade, by 1953 the state sector controlled 92 per cent of all imports and exports.

The rapid transformation of domestic trade was brought about by expanding the network of state trading companies (of which there were some 35,000 by 1953) and by the imposition of a system of planned purchase and supply. In effect, planned purchase meant the exclusive right of the state companies to purchase certain basic commodities, thereby controlling and monopolizing the available supply. Planned supply, for all practical purposes, meant a state rationing system. The supply and marketing cooperatives are important adjuncts of the state trading companies. The cooperatives in turn control retail stores and mobile trading units throughout the countryside and in the urban areas.

Planned purchase and supply originally applied only to such agricultural staples as grain, vegetable oils and cotton. With state control over these commodities firmly established by 1953, Peking rapidly began absorbing the other spheres of domestic commerce, both wholesale and retail. The success of its efforts was asserted in a *People's Daily* editorial of February 6, 1955: "In wholesale trade, private capitalism has been basically eliminated, while in retail trade the state trading companies and the cooperatives have won a definite victory, and the supply and marketing cooperatives have achieved firm control over the markets of the rural villages."

Nevertheless, it should be pointed out that the socialist transformation of retail trade and the resulting control over the individual consumer has been a gradual process. In the intermediate stages, private concerns and shops were allowed to conduct business, but only as agents or distributors of the state trading enterprises. They could sell state-owned commodities on a commission basis and at prices fixed by the state. They could purchase goods directly from state companies provided they sold at the prices set by the state retail outlets. But with the transformation of private enterprises, alluded to earlier, the private merchants became state functionaries.

One of the major functions of state control over commerce is to regulate and stabilize prices. This, in turn, requires an end to any form of private speculation. A "correct price policy" entails "timely adjustments" in regional, seasonal, wholesale and retail price disparities, as well as price differentials between industrial and agricultural commodities. Peking has given high priority to this sort of price-fixing. Article 26 of the Common Program provided for "mutual aid between the city and the countryside" and the official press later claimed considerable gains in this direction. For example, the overall totals for shipments of manufactured goods to rural areas of China during the last quarter of 1954 were reportedly 20 per cent higher than for the same period in the previous year. (Ironically, the "statistics" for the quarter were available as early as December 9 of the period covered.)

Closely related to rural-urban trade coordination have been the attempts to encourage trade relations with minority groups. While unifying trade, these efforts also facilitate the political and social integration of otherwise isolated national and cultural minorities.

Despite the zeal with which Communist China approached the question of planned purchase and supply, consumer complaints mounted. To cite but one example, the "letters to the editor" column of the July 2, 1955, *People's Daily* contained a series of complaints concerning the poor quality of a variety of consumer goods distributed by state enterprises, including raincoats, sweaters, radios and shoes. Local press items frequently referred to blunders and mismanagement in the state trading system. The *Anhwei Daily* of April 19, 1953, mentioned a "cigarette incident" which involved a chain of state departments stores in Anhwei province. Through neglect, cigarettes were allowed to accumulate until they became stale. To correct this situation, the stores hired sales promoters to tour the villages distributing the cigarettes by compulsory purchase—twenty packs to each individual, smoker and non-smoker alike.

In the field of foreign trade, the 1949 Common Program, while promising to protect "legitimate" private trading, specifically stated that "control of foreign trade shall be enforced." One of the first steps in establishing control, as in domestic commerce, was the elimination of private speculation and uncontrolled prices. The foremost targets in this phase were the "compradors"—those Chinese merchants who served as agents for foreign commercial establishments. Control of foreign trade had to be achieved at a more rapid pace than over domestic trade because of China's urgent need to secure imports of industrial raw materials and machinery and because of the early ties which bound Peking to the Soviet Union and its satellites. By March of 1950, twelve state companies had been formed to handle foreign as well as domestic trade. The number of these companies underwent continual expansion. By 1955, there were twenty of these monopolistic state companies for foreign commerce alone, each dealing with a specific category or commodity and all under the direct control of the Ministry of Foreign Trade. By the end of 1956, which marked the completion of the transformation of private enterprises, all foreign trade could be said to be a state monopoly. The centralized Foreign Trade Control Office validated or cancelled all import-export transactions and determined final prices.

The pattern of China's foreign trade obviously underwent a profound change under communist direction. Before the Sino-Japanese War, in

1936, 71 per cent of the exports from China proper and 65 per cent of her imports were with Japan, the United States, Germany, Great Britain and Hong Kong. Mainly as a result of the Korean War, exports to China from the West dropped from US$314 million during the first half of 1951, to about US$130 million in the second half. Taking the period from establishment of the CPR to the inauguration of the Great Leap Forward as a whole, Chinese Communist statistics denote almost a fourfold increase in foreign trade. But trade with non-communist countries declined from 66.5 per cent of the total in 1950, to 24.4 per cent in 1958. During the same period, trade with communist countries rose from 33.5 to 75.6 per cent of China's total foreign commerce.

A similarly marked change took place in the composition of commodities involved in Chinese imports. Basically, Communist China must continue to rely on foodstuffs and grains, vegetable oils, and other agricultural products for export. Her imports may be conveniently divided into consumer and producer goods. In 1950, approximately 87 per cent of all imports were producer goods and 12.8 per cent were in the form of consumer goods. By 1958, 93.7 per cent of all imports were producer goods, and only 6.3 per cent consumer goods.[25] These producer goods included machinery, materials for basic construction, heavy manufactured goods, chemical products and some raw materials. These goods, as noted elsewhere, provided the backbone for the program of rapid industrialization called for in the First Five-Year Plan.

During the period 1950–55, Chinese exports to the Soviet Union, then Peking's principal trading partner, fell far below imports. In addition to this unfavorable balance of trade, Communist China was also receiving substantial Soviet credits for the establishment of a heavy industrial base. As noted previously, the first installment for repayment of Soviet loans fell due in 1954. And after 1955, Chinese exports to the Soviet Union exceeded her imports, in order to meet the repayment schedule. As Chia To-fu, former Vice Chairman of the GAC Committee on Financial and Economic Affairs, wrote in *People's China* (June, 1959): "The aim of the nations embraced by this [world socialist] system is not profit, but mutual economic development and fraternal aid." Nevertheless, and as finally revealed in the Sino-Soviet polemics of 1964–65 concerning ideological issues, the Chinese Communists found themselves in a difficult financial situation after 1955. Many of the Soviet-sponsored enterprises were not yet completed or in full operation; thus they provided no immediate capital

[25] At the 1955 NPC session, Foreign Trade Minister Yeh Chi-chuang stated that for the period of the First Five-Year Plan (1953–57) as a whole, the importation of consumer goods would be held to 15 per cent so that priority could be given to the capital equipment need for the 156 Soviet-supported major industrial projects.

accumulation. While long-range plans called for continuing emphasis on building up the industrial base, the purchase of machinery and goods would be limited, at least in part, by the necessity of repaying Soviet loans dating from the period of the Korean War. Consequently, the foreign trade and loan situation of 1955–56 may well have influenced the decision of the Chinese Communist leadership to step up agricultural production—hence increasing exports—while proceeding with industrialization, and at the same time holding consumer goods relatively stable.

ADMINISTRATION OF PUBLIC FINANCE

In Communist China, as in other communist countries, a tightly knit and centralized system for raising and disbursing state revenues provides a powerful weapon of control in the economic, political, and social spheres. Through channeling state funds into particular segments of the economy or placing heavier burdens on other segments the state can carry forward the process of "socialist transformation." Through integrated and coordinated fiscal and budgetary operations at all levels, under strictest control from the center, Peking can provide that no region or province, or even town or village, will follow a preferred policy. And through heavy taxation, indirect levies and an impressive array of other devices, including the exploitation of the state budget for propaganda purposes, the leadership can strengthen its control over every aspect of society.

The Chinese Communists have skillfully and painstakingly sought to conceal the degree and purpose of fiscal control. This is particularly evident in the fact that, ever since the first National Budget in 1950, military and administrative expenditures have ostensibly been minimal, usually registering a decline, while appropriations for reconstruction and social welfare have exhibited a rising spiral. In the 1950 budget, military defense appeared as the largest single item of expenditure, officially accounting for 38.8 per cent of all disbursements. In a report to the Central People's Government Council in February, 1953, Po I-po claimed that military expenses took second place in 1952, accounting for only 26.82 per cent of that year's disbursements. Official budgetary allocations for the military in 1953 dropped to 22.28 per cent, and in 1954 to 21.11 per cent of the total outlay. The 1955 budget, as was also true in the case of the Soviet Union after the Korean War, showed an increase to 24.19 per cent. According to Finance Minister Li Hsien-nien, in his July 6, 1955, report to the NPC, this upswing was necessary "since the imperialists are still encircling China and she has to protect her independence and national construction, liberate Taiwan, and safeguard her sovereignty and territorial integrity."

Although there was a decline registered in military spending in 1957–58, the trend upward was resumed by 1959.

A similar trend can be discerned with regard to the cost of administration. In 1950, this was officially set at 21.4 per cent, the third largest budget item. By 1953, this item was listed at 10.19 per cent. In 1954, the cost of administration was included under "expenditures not itemized," a device probably designed to conceal its rising cost.

An analysis of budgetary trends for this period shows a sharp increase in expenditures for national economic development and educational and welfare services. In 1950, 23.9 per cent of the budget was earmarked for economic construction, and only 4.1 per cent for various social welfare programs. According to Po I-po, appropriations for these combined categories soared to 59.24 per cent in the 1953 budget. In 1954, Teng Hsiao-p'ing officially claimed that allocations for economic reconstruction were six and a half times greater than in 1950 and accounted for 45.49 per cent of all outlay, while social welfare took 14.71 per cent of all expended funds. The figures for 1955, given in a *People's Daily* editorial of July 10, 1955, and summarized in *Pravda* two days later, allotted 47.72 per cent to economic construction and 12.95 per cent for welfare services. This heavy investment in economic construction was necessary to support Peking's industrialization programs of the period.

All of these figures must be subjected to interpretation. For example, the 14.71 per cent in the 1954 budget and the 12.95 per cent in the 1955 budget assigned to welfare programs included substantial expenditures for propagandistic activities; the amount actually spent for cultural or educational programs would, of necessity, have been quite low. More importantly, the share assigned to military spending, consistently under a fourth of the total budget, is deliberately designed to mislead. Many military expenses are concealed under other budgetary items. For example, the cost of many military items is classified under "economic construction." It is generally agreed, that the Second Machine-Building Ministry has been concerned with the development of nuclear weapons, just as it appears that the Third Machine-Building Ministry deals with the production of conventional weaponry. In any case, state factories for production of military goods would be erected by funds assigned to "economic construction."

During the first two or three years after the seizure of state power, the Chinese Communists relied principally on two sources of revenue: a "public grain" tax or agricultural levy imposed on the peasants, and a business and income tax which fell on the urban population. The grain tax accounted for 41.4 per cent of all state receipts in 1950, while business and other taxes contributed another 38.9 per cent, making a combined total of more than 80 per cent. Revenue from state-owned enterprises stood at only 17.1 per cent. By 1954, however, income from state-owned enterprises had shot up to 63.58 per cent of all state revenue. Revenue from the agricultural producers' cooperatives provided an additional 2.56 per cent, and the public-private joint enterprises contributed 2.93 per cent. Thus receipts from state enterprises represented almost 70 per cent of the 1954 revenue, while the agricultural tax dwindled to 13.43 per cent and taxes on private industry and business to 15.4 per cent. In 1955, the share of revenue from state-owned enterprises increased to 76.22 per cent.

The collection of taxes, whether agricultural or business, was not without pitfalls. In a June 15, 1950, report to the National Committee of the CPPCC, Po I-po publicly admitted that peasant resistance had resulted in the death of more than 3,000 grain-collecting cadres. In the urban areas, resistance was occasioned by the policy of apportioning the tax burden of an area by arbitrary, rather than fixed standards. However, to give an appearance of voluntary cooperation, the system of "democratic assessment" was officially used. Under this system, representative members of commerce and industry would hold group discussion meetings to determine a "fair and equitable" apportionment of tax burdens. Even the collection of income taxes followed this procedure, although officially there was a fixed scale of progressive, graduated taxes. [26]

Peking also introduced other tax devices, while reducing or eliminating traditional procedures for raising imports. For example, customs duties were sharply curtailed, mainly because of China's barter-type commerce with the Soviet Union and decline in trade with the West. The salt tax, formerly second only to customs duties in fiscal receipts, declined in importance as the salt enterprises became state-owned. On the other hand, in 1951 Peking introduced a goods tax on handmade cloth. Other devices included a stamp tax on title deeds and other commercial instrumentalities and an exchange tax on marketable transactions, such as the 4 per cent sales tax on heads of livestock. The provinces and municipalities also imposed taxes on urban land and buildings, amusement, restaurant, hotel and tobacco levies, and various license fees.

The sale of state bonds also provided revenue. This anti-inflationary

[26] Theoretically this process of "democratic assessment" was used only until the taxation of private industry and commerce could be based on "fixed rates," i.e., before 1950. Actually, it was used throughout the Three-Anti and Five-Anti period up to the end of 1952 (one of the targets of the latter drive was "tax evasion"). When the "voluntary" reports were suspicious, private businessmen were brought to a "public discussion" and exposed by a close associate or employee for concealment of assets. The guilty party would then be subject not only to heavier taxes, but also to personal persecution. Thus the procedure was useful for disciplining the private businessman who was required to stay in business.

device also served to absorb and control any overflow of circulated currency and to stabilize prices. Bond drives were also useful for heightening "political consciousness" in general and were always characterized by official reports of "oversubscribed" quotas.

During the period of the First Five-Year Plan (1953–57) an additional, and perhaps crucial, source of revenue was provided in the form of Soviet credits. As Khrushchev reminded the 20th CPSU Congress in 1956: "Never before in history has a highly industrial country voluntarily helped other countries to become industrialized." And *People's Daily* of April 9, 1956, pointed out that the 156 Soviet-sponsored enterprises constituted the center of the Five-Year Plan.

In February, 1950, the Soviet Union advanced some U.S. $300 million in credits to Communist China. This first economic assistance agreement provided that the loan be repaid over the ten year period to commence in 1954, in equal installments and at one per cent interest on the unpaid balance. In October, 1954, Moscow advanced a second major credit of approximately U.S. $130 million. Chinese Communist sources place the total Soviet credit for the period 1949–57 at about U.S. $2,200 million. This variation may be explained by the fact that the sum unlisted by Soviet sources was in the form of military assistance and to provide for Chinese purchase of Soviet shares in the joint stock companies.[27] In any case, Soviet credits probably accounted for about 17 per cent of total investment in industrial projects during the 1953–57 period. But the effect of this aid cannot be measured in percentage points. This "fraternal" assistance enabled Peking to industrialize rapidly. By 1957, about 57 per cent of steel production and 50 per cent of coal production came from enterprises constructed with this Soviet aid.[28] Without this aid, Communist China's First Five-Year Plan would have faced greater financial difficulties.

In addition to, and entirely distinct from these enumerated sources of revenue, the Chinese Communists realized large sums of money from sources which cannot be conveniently listed in regular budgetary receipts. These concealed sources include the farm land, livestock, foodstuffs and buildings seized during the agrarian reform campaign inaugurated in

[27] With the intensification of Sino-Soviet polemics over ideological issues, considerable new information on Sino-Soviet economic assistance programs has come to light. For example, in May, 1964, Suslov put total Soviet aid to China during the 1949–60 period at $454 million. But he added that this adjusted figure did not include military assistance.

[28] According to Suslov's May, 1964, report, in China's production 8.7 million tons of iron, 8.4 million tons of steel, 32.2 million tons of coal, 25–30 per cent of power and 80 per cent of lorry and tractor production, on an annual basis, had to be attributed to Soviet-sponsored enterprises.

1950.[29]   Early in 1952, during the "Five-Anti" campaign directed against private businessmen, numerous "big tigers" were found guilty of tax evasion by people's courts.   Hence the government reaped another harvest in fines, confiscations, delinquent tax payments and "restored" state properties.   Likewise, despite repeated assurances of "protection" for remittances from overseas Chinese, the Chinese Communists derived a significant income from what amounted to an outright seizure of these funds.   In his report On the Administration of National Finance in 1951 and Compilation of the 1952 Budget, Po I-po made clear the importance of these various financial sources:

> Particularly in consequence of the gigantic Three-Anti and Five-Anti campaigns this year, the operation of the 1951 National Budget has yielded results far surpassing original expectations.   Not only were receipts and expenses balanced, but also a surplus was realized.   Aside from meeting the required military expenses and insuring complete satisfaction of the needs of national defense, great efforts were devoted to stabilizing the price level.

On the revenue as well as the disbursement side, then, political and ideological considerations enter into the determination of the state budget.   And because of the concealed sources of income and the disguised expenditures, Communist China's finances appear extremely inconsistent and self-contradictory.   Even the fact that the published national budget is invariably balanced—and, indeed, for the years when figures were issued since 1951, has shown a surplus each year—indicates that state statistics are probably more a propaganda device than an index of China's fiscal position.[30]

In reality, it does not particularly matter whether the state budget achieves a hypothetical balance.   Following the Soviet example, the real purpose of Chinese Communist fiscal procedures is to facilitate production and control distribution of goods.   "The general guiding principles under-

---

[29] Hsiao Chi-jung, on the basis of various reports published in the communist press, estimates that well over 700,000,000 mou of farmland (6 mou equal 1 acre), 29,490,000 head of oxen, 147,000,000,000 catties of rice (one catty equals 1.33 lb), and 7,000,000 farm houses were confiscated during this campaign. See Hsiao, *Revenue and Disbursement of Communist China* (Hong Kong: Union Research Institute, 1954), p. 71.

[30] The 1954 budget affords a good example of the way in which the Chinese Communists "balance" their budget or create a surplus.   According to Teng Hsiao-p'ing, the national budget for the year included a total revenue of Y274,708,000 million.   Of this, Y231,880,000 million represented "real total revenue"; the remaining Y42,827,000 million was the "balance from last year."   Total disbursements were placed at Y249,457,800 million, of which Y17,576,200 million was a balance from the previous year.   From this, Teng concluded that there would be a surplus of Y25,250,800 million for 1954.   It is obvious that without the carry-over balance from the previous year, there would have been an absolute deficit.

lying our economic and financial work," declared Mao Tse-tung as early as 1942, "consist of economic development and ensuring supplies. . . . While the merits or demerits of a fiscal policy affect the economy of the state, economics in reality exerts final influence on finance." It is therefore rather ironic that the Chinese Communists should place such great stress on budget equilibrium, while capitalist countries, mainly in the interests of promoting social welfare, have more or less reconciled themselves to the necessity of deficit spending.

Another indication of economic stability in any country is the stability of its currency. When the communists came to power in China, they found themselves in the midst of an economic crisis. An unbalanced budget, soaring prices and the economic ravages of protracted war all threatened the stability of the new Peking regime. At first, Peking resorted to the inflationary expedient of floating additional currency. So far had the process of inflation gone that the 1954 budget, which was equal to about 12 billion US dollars, came to more than 270 trillion yuan. In an effort to stem this inflationary tide and tighten the grip over the general monetary system, on March 1, 1955, the government instituted a major currency reform. All bank-notes in circulation were recalled and replaced with new bills at an exchange rate of one yuan of new currency for 10,000 old-type notes. Despite a variety of inconveniences, the transition to the new currency was claimed to be remarkably smooth as prices and bank deposits remained stable and foreign exchange rates were basically unaffected.[31]   Tsao Chu-ju, Director of the People's Bank of China and one of the main architects of the monetary reform, heralded the new currency as a "sign of further stability and consolidation of the people's currency and a sign of the growing economic strength of our country."[32]

This "smooth readjustment" to a new currency illustrates Peking's total grip over China's economic life. For all practical purposes, China's currency has become "internalized." That is, the rate of exchange, as in the Soviet system, is a computation rate only, prescribed by the state banking authorities.[33]   This high degree of unified control, of course, would be impossible without the nationalization and centralization of the banking

[31] For example, the Shanghai branch of the Bank of China on March 1 announced that the selling rate of 1 pound sterling was 1 to 69,270 yuan old currency, and 1 to 6.83 yuan new currency. At the official rate of exchange, 1 US dollar equalled 2.34 yuan.

[32] That the Chinese Communists had been planning a monetary reform for several years is evident from the fact that the new notes bore the date 1953. However, for "technical reasons," Tsao explained, the final change-over had to be delayed until 1955.

[33] This conclusion may be illustrated by two methods. In the first case, the amount of currency in circulation may have little relation to gold reserves. During the Great Leap Forward (see the following chapter) bank notes were issued at will. On April 14, 1964, the Chinese Communists announced another exchange drive involving the recall of all 10-yuan, 5-yuan and 3-yuan notes in exchange for newly issued 2-yuan and 20

system. Control in this area has been achieved through the People's Bank of China.

The People's Bank, established on December 1, 1948, is the supreme monetary and banking organ in Communist China. From 1949 to 1954 it was under the direct control of the GAC and coordinated with the Ministry of Finance. Under the 1954 Constitution it was placed for administrative purposes under the Finance Ministry. This organization replaces the Central Bank, the Bank of China, the Currency Department of the Ministry of Finance and the Monetary Control Bureau of the Nationalist system; it has also absorbed all private banking establishments in China. In addition to its central office in Peking, the People's Bank operates subsidiary offices in the provincial capitals and other large cities and throughout the rural areas. The Bank even maintains mobile stations in the streets of cities, towns and villages and communes to collect savings deposits and carry on routine banking functions. [34]

The People's Bank alone is empowered to hold state funds. The range of its banking and credit activities is partially revealed by a list of its affiliated banks and agencies. The functions they perform may be regarded as a sort of division of labor in the financial field. The Bank of China issues export licenses, handles Chinese remittances and controls the issuance of foreign exchange. The Bank of Communications provides long-term credit for the government and is also responsible for the control and liquidation of private enterprises. The Chinese People's Insurance Company serves to absorb private and public cash funds and make them available to government enterprises: it is also authorized to issue eighteen different kinds of insurance, including property, personal and agricultural. The People's Construction Bank, which was established in October, 1954, supervises the funds for basic construction projects. The Agrarian Cooperative Bank, which had been established in July, 1951, was replaced by the

cent notes (the former printed in 1960 and the latter in 1962). This exchange was to be completed within the 30-day period commencing April 15, although use of the former notes became illegal effective April 15. (This makes the 2-yuan note the highest presently in circulation.) Presumably, this change in currency was designed to determine the amount of money in circulation and to force the people to turn in any cash they might be hiding in their own homes.

In addition to the problem of black market exchange of the new yuan for foreign currency, the Chinese Communist foreign exchange rate is further complicated by the fact that two rates exist for conversion to currency of a communist country—the official and the non-trade quotation. For example, the official rate for Soviet currency is 100 rubles to 222.22 new yuan. But the non-trade rate is 100 rubles to 129.00 new yuan. See *Shih-shih Shou-ts'e* (*Current Events*), no. 3, February, 1965.

[34] Some indication of the rapidity with which the People's Bank was organized is provided by the following data: In May, 1951, the bank reportedly employed some 160,000 persons; by March, 1953, it had over 300,000 employees. By January, 1960, including its mobile units, the bank had 100,000 offices.

Agricultural Bank of China in March, 1955. This latter organization was absorbed into the People's Bank in April, 1957, and then reconstituted in November, 1963, to handle finances at the village level.[35] The Joint State-Private Bank, which was formed by a merger of private institutions into the state system in 1952, has dealt primarily with the accounts of the overseas Chinese. Despite these divisions of functions, it is the parent People's Bank that assumes all control of currency circulation and funding of public projects.

All cash transactions must be handled through the People's Bank system, which also provides the only agency for the extension of credits. This latter operation has augmented other state controls over the peasant masses and city workers. At the same time, by collecting the deposits of these people, the state has been able to use private capital for the extension of socialism.[36] Through its vast network of branches and subsidiary agencies, the People's Bank has caught all public or private cash resources in its tentacles. The Chinese peasant, having been "liberated" from the ancient curse of the moneylender and the pluralistic private structure of the Nationalists, is now compelled to deal exclusively with this state organ. The worker must entrust his savings to an institution that will invest to further the dictatorship and programs of the communist leadership.

From their first tentative programs for centralized economic planning, through the beginning phases of agricultural collectivization and transformation of private industry and commerce to state enterprises, the Chinese Communists were aided by absolute control and manipulation of the monetary system. These programs, together, accounted for rapid achievement of many economic goals. However, by 1957, for reasons which were fundamentally related to Party and political goals, the Chinese Communists were determined that the pace and extent of economic development must be intensified. Burning ambition and revealed shortcomings collaborated to produce the epic 1958 programs for the commune system and the Great Leap Forward.

[35] As noted in the following chapter, the Agricultural Bank of China was re-estalished in 1963 by decision of the CPC Central Committee together with the State Council to specialize in the accounts of the communes and their component brigades and teams. See *Nung-ts'un Chin-jung (Rural Finance)*, No. 4–5, February, 1965.

[36] The Chinese Communist press frequently alludes to the great increases in deposits held by the People's Bank system. For example, according to a NCNA dispatch of September 19, 1964, deposits in the city of Peking alone rose by 46 million yuan between December, 1963, and August, 1964. Hong Kong's *Ta-kung Pao* of September 8, 1964, noted a national increase in deposits from 1952 to 1964 of 80 per cent.

But, from time to time, other sources have indicated the glaring deficiencies of this enormous banking structure. For example, among the reforms called for at the Third National Conference of Branch Managers, were a simplification of statistical forms, so accountants could understand and properly handle their work.

CHAPTER 7

The Quest for
Economic Self-Reliance:
1958-67

By 1958, as noted in the previous chapter, Communist China's leaders had come to enjoy an unlimited faith in their own ability to transform the backward, agrarian country which they had inherited into a modern, industrial, world power. In their overly optimistic estimations, this transformation need no longer depend upon traditional economic principles. In Mao's vision, the approach to the solution of economic problems or deficiencies is similar to that of a battle waged by a dedicated army of workers. If these workers lack sufficient dedication, this can be remedied by mass political and ideological indoctrination. A politically strong regime, utilizing new concepts within the general framework of Marxism-Leninism, could solve any problem with a lightning speed unknown to the rest of the world. And by so doing, it could set itself up as an example to the newly merging nations who sought a model for their own aspirations of lightning economic development. It was within this context of questing for self-reliance that the CPR, in 1958, announced its plans for two all-encompassing programs of economic reconstruction—the Great Leap Forward and the commune system.

According to these two plans, major emphasis was to be placed on the promotion of heavy industry. Light industry was relegated to a subordinate role. The agricultural sector, essentially, was to hold its own while increasing production of those crops needed to feed the jaws of industry in the form of raw materials. In the final analysis, all of this was contingent upon an immediate and intensive mobilization of the masses.

Many of the accomplishments of the Great Leap have been substantial and lasting. But, by 1960, something had gone awry with the general plans. Newly constructed factory complexes stood idle for want of sufficient raw materials. In the communes, the peasants had come to express their disapproval of militant social as well as economic programs in the form of passive resistance. At the same time, floods and droughts were held responsible for enormous crop losses. Between 1959 and 1962 natural and manmade disasters together spelled widespread famine.

At this juncture, in 1960, to avert an impending calamity of epic proportions, the Chinese Communists were obliged to modify completely their general plan. Agriculture was, of necessity, returned to the leading place in over-all economic development. Light industry's role was promoted over that of heavy industry. Consequently, it is possible to speak of the years between 1960 and 1965 as the period of retrenchment.

By 1965, the leaders of the CPC, now more cautious with the memory of earlier failures, were preparing for their Third Five-Year Plan, to be introduced in 1966, to further the goal of national self-reliance. The following analysis of the major stages of Great Leap and communes, followed by retrenchment, may provide a useful vantage point from which to view China's present stage of development under the new Five-Year Plan.

THE COMMUNE SYSTEM

Background

In December, 1955, Mao Tse-tung intimated in introductory remarks to a book entitled *The Surging Tide of Socialism in the Chinese Rural Areas* that, by 1959, the world might see the peasants of China organized in "a completely socialist way." The decision to organize and develop a commune system did entail a dramatically radical transformation of the nation's entire socio-economic structure. On the economic side, the decision to communalize was prompted by dissatisfaction with the performance of the agricultural producers' cooperatives, and the plan to concentrate on the rapid development of heavy industry in a Great Leap Forward. Politically, the decision was occasioned and facilitated by the anti-rightist campaign which followed the Hundred Flowers period. During this period of rectification, the leadership had sought to mobilize public sentiment against conservative elements and for more active participation in revolutionary policies.

More immediately, the leadership was guided by a growing awareness that the vast water conservancy and industrial programs sponsored early in 1958 were occasioning what would appear to be an impossibility for China—a pressing manpower shortage. In March, 1958, in conference with the members of the CPC Central Committee and delegates from the regional Party committees in Chengtu, Mao announced that the agricultural producers' cooperatives would be combined into larger units. This plan was formally approved by the CC in April. Merger was to proceed according to local conditions and, during this period, the newly expanded cooperatives were usually designated as large cooperatives. Although the term "commune" was not used by the Central Committee until June, and not adopted by the enlarged session of the Politburo until August, this assimilation of smaller cooperatives into larger units actually marked the birth of communalization.

The experimental or model commune popularly referred to as "Sputnik" was first begun in the Sinyang district of Honan province in April, 1958. By June, the 5,376 cooperatives in P'in-yu and Sui-p'ing counties had been merged into 208 people's communes. By the end of August, Honan's 38,470 agricultural cooperatives had been incorporated into 1,378 communes, accounting for 99.98 per cent of that province's peasant households. Finally, by the Peitaiho Resolution of the enlarged session of the CPC Politburo on August 29,1958, the communes were removed from the experimental stage and all China was ordered to adopt the system.

The directive entitled "Resolutions Concerning the Establishment of the People's Communes in Villages" provided a general organizational outline. At a speed determined by local conditions, the cooperatives were to be united into communes, and eventually the communes were to be organized into county units termed a "County Federation of Communes." The resolution advocated collective ownership and stated that within three to six years this would be "transformed into ownership by the whole people." Payment to commune members was to continue to be based on the policy of rewarding labor according to the "three guarantees and one reward" system. That is, the "guarantees" or pledges of production, cost and labor were to be made by the commune's subordinate brigades to the commune in order to obtain from it the "reward" of payment for fulfillment and overfulfillment of quotas. Wage systems were also approved for areas where conditions warranted.

The Peitaiho Resolution stressed that "the people's communes are to become the best organizational form for the construction of socialism and the gradual transition to communism." Compared to the cooperatives which they replaced, the communes were held to be vastly superior in terms of advantageous groupings of people to permit the state to advance its major economic programs, and in the ability of the communes to better accumulate capital for these tasks. The communes could liberate social productive forces better, for example, in freeing women from household tasks required in the less militantly organized cooperatives. Economically,

TABLE IV

PEOPLE'S COMMUNES IN SEPTEMBER, 1958*

	Number of Communes	Number of Households	% of Total Peasant Households	Average Number of Households per Commune
TOTAL	26,425	121,936,350	98.2	4,614
Peking	56	663,124	100.	11,841
Shanghai	23	256,000	100.	11,130
Hopei	951	8,402,639	100.0	8,836
Shansi	975	3,483,564	100.	3,573
Inner Mongolia	812	1,561,023	98.6	1,922
Liaoning	428	3,264,579	100.	7,627
Kirin	481	1,914,547	100.	3,980
Heilungkiang	718	1,946,478	100.	2,710
Shensi	1,673	3,232,904	100.	1,932
Kansu	794	2,006,389	100.	2,527
Tsinghai	144	245,624	100.	2,456
Ninghsia	53	201,815	67.3	3,808
Sinkiang	389	625,151	59.3	1,607
Shantung	1,580	11,347,989	100.	7,182
Kiangsu	1,490	9,127,234	99.4	6,126
Anhwei	1,054	7,219,244	100.	6,849
Chekiang	761	5,697,412	100.	7,487
Fukien	622	2,672,839	95.1	4,297
Honan	1,285	10,272,517	100.	7,994
Hupeh	729	6,040,000	96.1	8,286
Hunan	1,284	8,172,440	100.	6,365
Kiangsi	1,240	3,720,000	92.	3,000
Kwangtung	803	7,905,553	100.	9,845
Kwangsi	784	4,041,944	100.	5,155
Szechwan	4,827	13,676,988	99.1	2,833
Kweichow	2,194	3,101,205	94.5	1,413
Yunnan	275	1,137,148	31.	4,135

* This table was published in *Statistical Work*, No. 20, 1958, p. 23. The numerical revisions in the chapter have been compiled from scattered sources, such as *People's Daily* of February 5, and March 14, 1960, and *Hsin-hua Pan-yueh K'an* (New China Semi-monthly), No. 9, 1959, p. 67.

they would achieve better results through plentiful production, higher speed, less expense and better quality. The union of political and economic interests promised far-reaching results within the framework of a developing communist ideology which calls ultimately for the transition from collective ownership to ownership by the whole people.

Organization of the Communes

The communes generally followed the geographic-physical outlines of the old agricultural cooperatives. As cooperatives were merged into these larger units, no attempt was made to relocate the population or redistribute land. Thus, conformity to local conditions resulted in great variations in size. The largest of the communes embrace an entire county, such as in Ankuo and Hsinhsiang counties, Honan province. Far more frequently, the communes represent a union of one or more rural districts or *hsiang*. The accompanying table indicates the number and size of the communes as of September, 1958. Subsequently, the trend was toward further amalgamation. In 1958, there were 26,425 rural communes. By September, 1959, this number had been reduced to 24,000. This total remained fairly consistent when, in 1959, China abandoned its plan for county federations of communes.[1] However, with the general reorganization of rural areas that took place during the 1959–61 period, when many county units were re-established, the number of communes again increased. Thus, by September 7, 1964, NCNA was referring to 74,000 communes, and this latter total has remained relatively stable.

Communal organization in many instances supplanted or reduced to token importance the existing units of local government. For example, both the administrative functions and the personnel of the *hsiang* were for the most part absorbed by the communes. In the case of the CPC, branches in the communes are the lowest level of rural organization. Party members hold communal offices, but the CPC has jealously guarded its separate identity.

The highest authority of the commune's internal organization is said to be vested in the Congress of the Representatives of the Commune Members, which in some cases can be the People's Congress of the corresponding administrative level. In practice, in the first stage the Administrative Committee was the commune's highest functioning organ. Stated in a *Red Flag* article by the deputy director of the CPC's Rural Work Department, Ch'en Cheng-jen, in January, 1959:

[1] Some provinces merged communes to reduce the total. For example, by March, 1960, Honan had reduced its communes from 1,285 to 1,210. In other areas, however, as communalization was completed, totals rose. For example, Sinkiang's communes increased from 389 to 451.

CHART V ORGANIZATION OF THE HSIANG COMMUNE

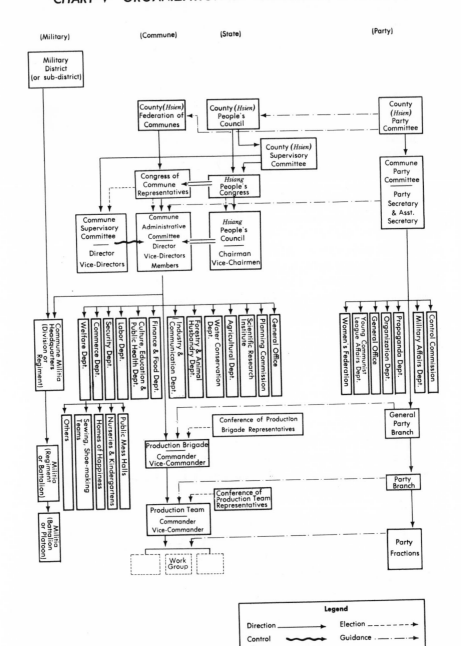

The Administrative Committee of the commune is the organ of united leadership of the commune. All work in connection with the execution of policy, formation of plans, financial control, and management of means of production and the fixing of plans for distribution will be concentrated in the Administrative Committee.

Generally, the Administrative Committee is comprised of a director, several vice-directors and a number of general members. It delegates special functions to departments under its jurisdiction, such as those for agriculture, water conservation, forestry, animal husbandry, industry and transport, finance and food, commerce, culture and education, internal affairs and labor, armed defense, planning and research, and welfare.

The original units of the agricultural cooperatives were reorganized as commune brigades. In September, 1959, there were some half a million of these brigades with an average of 200–300 households. Each brigade, analogous to the congress for the entire commune, has its own congress and administrative committee with a brigade commander and vice-commanders. These officials are elected by the brigade congress, as are the officers of its supervisory committee. The brigade committee reports to the communal Administrative Committee.

Each brigade is subdivided into a number of production teams, the lowest level of communal organization. The team's organization generally parallels that of the brigade, and includes a congress of members which elects team officers. In 1959, there were some three million teams, with an average of forty households.

The accompanying chart illustrates the general organizational structure of commune administration with its parallel Party, state and military organizations.

Since the commune system, which is essentially socialistic in nature, represents only a stage toward the transition to communism, the principal form of distribution is still that of "from each according to his ability, and to each according to his work." The "to each according to his needs" was earlier expressed to some degree in the various social services provided. In the formative period, the communes accepted the system of labor points used in the cooperatives and reimbursed partially in the form of money and foodstuffs, and partially by free services. Since a single pay system was impractical, given the wide variations in economic development among the communes, four systems were approved. These systems differed chiefly in the ratio of wages to supplies. In the first, the commune provided all food and small supplementary wages. In the second system, grain rations were distributed according to stated quotas, and the remaining remuneration, of some 40–60 per cent, was in the form of cash. The third system, more adaptable for the poorer communes, was modelled after the second system, but the amounts of cash payments were extremely small. The fourth system, practiced in the richer communes, provided all daily necessities as well as token cash payments.

Wage scales were first calculated on the basis of the commune's net annual income, minus the expenses of taxes, production and management. The remaining wage fund, in the formative period, represented 25-30 per cent of the total communal income. Wages were distributed according to labor tasks and capacity with a provision that payments be divided into two portions. The first accounted for about 80 per cent of the total monthly remuneration and the second was used for bonus payments. Individual wages were determined by a complex grading system which took into account the peasant's ideological status, capacity for work and actual labor. In the first stage, the teams suggested to their brigades a wage grade for male and female members. The brigade then compared and evaluated the suggestions of its various teams and forwarded its report to the communal administration for final decisions. Wage grades varied from five to twelve, with the average being eight. In the Sputnik model commune monthly remuneration in the early period was provided by the following scale: grade 1-2.03 yuan; grade 2-2.54 yuan; grade 3-3.30 yuan; grade 4-3.80 yuan; grade 5-4.57 yuan; grade 6-5.07 yuan; and grade 8-7.61 yuan.

In addition to the aforementioned arrangements, the commune system also provides for organizations of "collective living" outside working hours. In the first stage, collective housing and dining facilities, nurseries, schools and homes for the aged were promoted to make the most effective use of available manpower. Particularly, this involved freeing about 75 per cent of the woman for regular labor assignments.

The early attempts of the communes to regulate every aspect of human existence are well-known. From earliest infancy, the child would be raised by the state in the communal nurseries. At aged three, the child would be reassigned to a kindergarten, until aged seven, when he would be placed in one of the communal schools. Following his September, 1958 inspection tour of the Honan communes, Liu Shao-ch'i recommended that these resident institutions be extended. As People's Daily said on June 1, 1959, in the nurseries and kindergartens the Party can foster "a habit of love for labor and collectivism" and mold "new men of high communist quality."

Toward the end of his useful life to the commune, the peasant might find himself in a home for the aged, or the so-called "house of happiness." These residences were intended to exploit the eldery person's remaining capacity for labor through lighter assignments for growing vegetables, feeding livestock, sewing and washing clothes. Statistics for 1958 revealed that there were 111,000 of these homes caring for more than two million elderly peasants.

In addition to the labor and welfare organizations, commune members have also been organized along military lines. In implementation of the Every Man a Soldier Movement, Mao Tse-tung, on September 20, 1958, stated the new goal that "the great mass of the people will become workers while in the factory, peasants while in the field, and soldiers while holding weapons." Communal militia units are under the dual direction of the commune leadership and the corresponding military district or sub-district. Since the reorganization of the communes in December, 1958, the militia unit commander has been appointed by the military district and he also serves as a member of the commune Administrative Committee. The Second National Militia Work Conference, held in Peking in February, 1960 and presided over by Defense Minister Lin Piao, called for stricter military district supervision of the commune militia. The military district trains commune militia commanders and senior staff and coordinates these units with the regular armed forces.

Under the commune system, the militia is open to those between the ages of 16 and 50, regardless of sex. By order of the General Staff of the PLA, the national militia is organized into regular military divisions, regiments, battalions, companies and platoons. There are two basic categories within this structure. The ordinary militia of men and women between the ages of 16 and 50 follows a general program of physical and military training. The basic militia is the select core of the organization. Membership is limited to males between the ages of 16 and 30, and females between the ages of 17 and 22, who have a record of activism. Each division of the general militia contains at least one unit of the basic militia, which is responsible for general security and supervision. In times of crisis, the basic units are designed to be coordinated with the regular army for combat service.

The militia units of the communes are useful for internal as well as external security. The discipline and training involved increases the likelihood of the peasant permitting himself to be regimented in labor tasks. In the early days of the commune system, for example, workers were divided into "combat units" and required to observe normal field procedures, such as sleeping and eating on the sections of farmland they were then cultivating.

Development of the Communes

The evolution of the commune system has involved three distinct stages. At its birth, the commune was hailed with fanatic zeal as the answer to China's pressing agrarian problems, and the initial speed of organization further prompted the belief that the realization of communism was just around the corner. By December, 1958, however, the leadership was forced to revise its timetable for the completion of the socialist stage of development. Retrenchment, according to the leadership, meant that it would take some fifteen to twenty years before entrance into the communist milinneum. In August, 1959, the CPC was forced to order still another further retreat.

First Stage: August–December, 1958

By October, 1958, Communist China had established 26,425 communes, representing 98.2 per cent of the rural peasant population. These communes, containing an average 4,614 units, were operated according to the idea of ownership by the people. Consequently, wages represented only 25–35 per cent of individual income, and the peasants were almost entirely dependent on communal organizations for their daily sustenance. The average annual per capita income was about 85 yuan, or the equivalent of $32.40 in U.S. currency.

By November it was apparent that the communes had not fully attained the desired objectives. The level of agricultural productivity remained low. Loss through neglect of harvests and destruction of tools was estimated at 1.5 million yuan, or a per capita loss of 30 yuan, and the responsibility for this was largely due to peasant intransigence. Absenteeism, which reached over 2,000 cases a day in one Canton commune, crippled production. Restive peasants complained about living quarters, food and low wages, and, most importantly, that the traditional solidarity of the family was being undermined.

In their usual way, Party spokesmen sought to place the blame for work slow-downs and inadequate living conditions on reactionary elements. In November, 1958, for example, *People's Daily*, reporting on an investigation of 235 messhalls in Hopei province, placed the blame for poor quality food on the presence of 149 former landlords and rich peasants among the 859 members of the managerial and kitchen staffs. Other organs blamed these same elements for stealing and even poisoning food. But the cadres were also censured for failing to control peasant sympathies. T'ao Chu, then First Secretary of the Kwangtung Provincial Committee, in a *People's Daily* article of February 25, 1959, admitted that departmentalism was a serious problem and that "individual cadres had already degenerated into corrupt elements."

Growing peasant unrest and the gravity of the resultant loss to agricultural production made the CPC acutely aware of the need for remedial action. By November, 1958, editorials in *People's Daily* were directing that conditions in the communal messhalls be improved. At Chengchow, the Politburo convened from November 2–10 to analyze the situation and suggest pertinent corrective measures. In December, the problem was considered by the Eighth Central Committee at its sixth plenum.

The Resolutions on Some Questions Concerning the People's Communes adopted by the sixth plenum on December 10, 1958, marked the transition to the second stage of communal development. This document was at once the most authentic source for admission of failures in the first stage of development, and for the enunciation of a new program which was to constitute the second stage. The resolutions clarified the advantages of communalization in terms of production and distribution and again enunciated the aim of the eventual transition to communism, adding that "it can also be foreseen that in the future communist society, the people's commune will remain the basic unit of our social structure." The errors of the previous months were attributed to popular over-eagerness for the system. Caution was advised in the change from collective ownership to ownership by the whole people. In general terms, the Central Committee recommended that agricultural production be increased by better methods and continued to stress the prime task of industrial acceleration.

Corrective measures form the heart of this CC document. The use of wage scales was fixed and the right to own private property firmly established. Should the commune find itself obliged to use the possessions of the peasants, it must first secure the consent of the owner. This was in no way to involve a change in the owner's title, and such debts accrued by the commune had to be repaid. The peasant was promised such concessions as the reduction of working hours, improvement of the community kitchens, nurseries, kindergartens and homes for the aged, and the increase of educational opportunities. An assurance was added that the commune, rather than seeking to destroy the family, was gradually working to transform it into a more democratic unit. The resolution also provided for a check-up and consolidation campaign within the communes to be concluded by April, 1959:

> The masses should be mobilized to purge the leadership in the communes of those alien class elements who have smuggled themselves into the leadership and the very few who display a very bad style of work and have never corrected their errors even after being repeatedly admonished. . . . Every province, municipality and autonomous region should organize its inspection team consisting of a thousand, several thousands or ten thousand people for the check-up . . . to develop the good points found and overcome the shortcomings discovered, rouse the drive of the people, and find ways of concretely solving current problems and promptly popularizing successful experience.

SECOND STAGE: DECEMBER, 1958–AUGUST, 1959

To implement the decisions of the CPC Central Committee expressed in the Resolutions on Some Questions Concerning the People's Communes the role assigned to the cadres was necessarily augmented. The cadres, who were to carry out the check-up, had to provide an inspiration for the lagging fervor of the peasants. Tens of thousands of Party personnel were chosen to organize and prod the masses according to the CC's directives. These cadres were ordered to identify themselves completely with the commune to which they were assigned by setting an example of selfless labor. Through the efforts of these CPC members from every level of organization the check-up and retrenchment were completed on schedule.

Early in April, 1959, the seventh plenum of the Eighth CC met in Shanghai to study the results. That the drive did not entirely fulfill the Central Committee's expectations is evident by the fact that further modifications were ordered at this session. The most important aspect of the new revisions was the decision to return to the peasants the individual garden plots which had been seized during the first organizational stage. Produce from these plots could improve the peasants' diet. Moreover, they provided space for limited livestock-raising. At the same time, the CC agreed that use of the communal messhalls would no longer be compulsory. In fact, the messhalls had been found to be wasteful: inadequate facilities forced the peasants to walk considerable distances to the halls and then queue for service—time which could be spent more profitably in other activities. The individual communes were to decide when and how they would replace the messhalls. CPC Rural Work Department chief Teng Tzu-hui suggested that the communes might consider mobile dining halls, as well as permitting the peasants to take their food home. By June, at least one commune had decided to distribute foodstuffs to the individual households directly, and let them decide on the method of preparation or what to do with any surplus.

This de-emphasis of communal service organizations, together with permission to the peasant to care for his own private garden plot, marked a significant retreat for the CPC. In essence, the leadership was forced to acknowledge the connection between personal incentive and national increases in agricultural production.

THIRD STAGE: AUGUST, 1959—

The third stage in communal development began when the CPC Central Committee convened its eighth plenum in Lushan, Kiangsi province, in August, 1959. Here the leadership at least temporarily abandoned the former system of commune organization by adopting a resolution to make the brigade the basic unit and to limit the authority of the commune as an entity. In many respects, this retreat returned to the stage and framework of the agricultural producers' cooperatives which the communes had replaced.

Although the Lushan Resolution provided that the commune as such would still retain ownership of large machinery, limited capital accumulations and transportation, yet basic accounting and ownership of draught animals, tools and subsidiary industries were turned over to the brigade.

Since the brigade now assumed the responsibility of planning and meeting its own production quotas, it now had the authority to determine utilization of its subordinate teams. But the teams also profited in the cutback of the central administration's powers. Teams now owned their own means of production, communication and transportation, as well as domestic animals.

The system of distribution was also revised. Beginning with the 1959 harvest, directives ordered that the service and supply portion of remuneration be cut back, and real wages increased. The ideal ratio for supplies was set at 30 per cent, and the maximum at 40 per cent. Rural fairs, abolished when the communes were first organized, were now reopened to aid in distribution.

When this shift of authority between the commune and brigade was ordered in August, 1959, the Central Committee hoped that the setback would be temporary, at most for a five-year period. But, as noted elsewhere, 1960 proved to be a critical year for agricultural production. Although this decline must be explained in part by the unfavorable weather conditions, peasant resistance continued unabated. Beginning in the fall of 1960, the CPC vigorously carried on further rectification in the rural and urban areas. Yet, when no improvement of production or abatement of peasant resistance took place, the Party was forced to consider further concessions.

By mid-1961, in many communes, the authority of the production team, the lowest level of organization, had begun to surpass that of the brigade. In a June 21, 1961 editorial, *People's Daily* told the brigades to base their plans upon the plans of their component teams. By the end of that year the team had become the basic accounting unit. Apart from advancing a share of its income to the brigade and central administrations, the team now retains its own funds and determines how these are to be distributed among the members. Or, as stated in a January 30, 1963 *People's Daily* editorial, the team is "the basic accounting unit of the people's commune and the basic unit directly in charge of organizing production and the distribution of grain." Principally to alleviate food shortages, the CPC has encouraged the team to promote sideline production among its members, as well as the cultivation of the private plots.

Even this retraction of the basic mass-type nature of the communes has not solved all organizational problems. For example, since there are approximately as many teams as formerly there were mutual-aid teams, or about three million units, this places a tremendous demand on the already inadequate supply of managerial and technical manpower. This shortage is particularly critical in the case of the cadres.

The shortage of trained personnel has added to the problem of inequitable distribution of team income. Press organs have repeatedly cited tales of inefficiency and corruption in the handling of team accounts. For example, *People's Daily* of November 22, 1964, admitted that a number of team cadres in Kiangsu squandered team funds after a bumper harvest. Other cadres have been accused of "feudal thoughts of superiority of men's labor" in paying women team members less for the same work being performed by men. Still other cadres have resorted to the practice of giving "real and unreal figures" to manipulate team accounts to their own advantage. Party directives have insisted that the cadres keep their financial records in such a manner that the peasants can understand, and according to the principle of "equal pay for equal work." Moreover, more voice is to be given to the "staunchest supporters of collective farming"—the old peasants. [2]

In 1964, according to *Peking Review* (no. 1, 1965), team income in the people's communes rose 15 per cent, as compared to 1963. Yet, even in the more prosperous communes, members appeared to oppose methods of income distribution. For example, the Canton *Yang-ch'eng Wan-pao* of February 18, 1966, discussed in some detail the situation in the T'aip'ing brigade, Tali commune, Nanhai county. In this prosperous brigade, average income in 1965 was 134 yuan, or a 40 yuan increase as compared to 1964. Nevertheless, members reportedly were unhappy at the arrogance of the cadres, particularly in the latter's refusal to consult the members or show them the books.

Although peasant income from communal labor improved considerably after 1961, many peasants devoted their maximum efforts to sideline production, and only minimal labor to their team tasks. As the September 28, 1962 communique of the tenth plenum of the Eighth CPC Central Committee warned: "There still exists in society bourgeois influences, the force of habit of the old society, and the spontaneous tendency toward capitalism among part of the small producers." Applied specifically to the situation in the communes, the Canton *Nan-fang Jih-pao* of April 6, 1963, denounced those "former landlords and rich peasants in some communes" who were

[2] For example, in his "Notes from a Rural People's Commune," published in the February 1, 1963 issue of *Peking Review*, Wei Chuang reported that three of the six team leaders of one brigade of a commune in Wangcheng county, Kirin province, were in the 40 to 60 age group, and two others were over age thirty. At the brigade level, Wei also noted that the majority of the management committee were older peasants. Recalling that the under-thirty peasants were "mostly teenaged at the time or the land reform," Wei emphatically urged an increased management role for the older peasants—"the paragons of diligence and thrift."

advocating "reserve one's best energies for oneself, and give what is left to the collective." This same source, on August 17, 1963, reported cases of slow-down strikes, poisoning of cattle, and damaging of public property by "bad elements" in some of the communes. Such peasant apathy or resistance was instrumental in the Party leadership's decision to intensify the class struggle in the rural areas. And *People's Daily's* warning of March 25, 1963, of the "struggle in the countryside . . . between the collective economy and the spontaneous capitalist leanings of small producers" signalled the introduction of more intensive efforts to indoctrinate and orientate the peasants to collective labor tasks. Reportedly, in some areas, individual plots were reduced or even confiscated by the communal organization. As noted in a subsequent section, the decision to advance the cultural revolution stemmed in large measure from the need to rectify labor attitudes and practices in the communes.

To help the communes recover from the calamities that beset them between 1959 and 1961, Communist China has increased its facilities for providing financial assistance to the teams—now the basic accounting unit of the communes. From July to September, 1962, for example, 300 million yuan were loaned to the communes, to be repaid interest-free in single or multiple payments over two to five years. [3] The major share of this money went to teams in the more hard pressed areas. In 1963, between March and October, 4,230,000 yuan were advanced to needy communes. According to the Peking *Ta-kung Pao* of October 13, 1963, by August of that year Kirin province alone had received 5,600,000 yuan in long-term, interest-free loans; 4,000,000 yuan were divided among 2,600 communal production teams.

To facilitate the work of the state banks under the People's or Agricultural Banks, the Rural Credit Cooperatives have been strengthened or expanded. These cooperatives adjust surplus and short-supply funds, absorb extra funds deposited in savings accounts from sideline occupations, and help provide the funds in circulation for payment of sideline occupations. The expansion of these cooperatives became imperative when the teams began their own accounting systems. By the end of 1963, they were handling about 60 per cent of the finances of the teams and 100 per cent of the loans to individual commune members. In the December 12, 1963 issue of the authoritative *Red Flag*, CPC Central Committeeman and director of that organ's Rural Work Department Teng Tzu-hui indicated that the services of the Rural Credit Cooperatives would be necessary "for a long time to come." He also pointed out that these organizations were responsible to the branches of the People's and Agricultural Banks which,

[3] This figure can be compared to the total loans advanced by the agrarian banks between 1958 and 1961, which was reported in the May 5, 1961 Peking *Ta-kung Pao* as 12,000,000 yuan.

in turn, were regulated by their Party committees, and called for closer CPC supervision.

Urban Communes

Although the original plan for communalization also called for the establishment of communes in urban areas, these units have remained largely of an experimental nature. In September, 1958, CC General Secretary Teng Hsiao-p'ing conducted an inspection tour in Harbin, Changchun, Szup'ing and other cities and reported that urban communalization "is an inevitable trend." Teng then requested the various city and municipal committees to draft procedures for the organization of these units. The Central Committee's sixth plenum in December, 1958, repeated that urban communalization was inevitable, but cautioned the need of careful planning in view of the complexity of city conditions. Consequently, the drive continued in an experimental stage.

Harbin was the first city to establish communes; by the end of 1959 it had eight units with some 1,270,000 members, or about 70.6 per cent of the city populace. Following Harbin's initiative, the movement spread to other cities. In a January 1, 1960 article in *Red Flag*, Kuan Ta-t'ung pointed out that, in the latter half of 1959, the Party had begun organizing street factories and dining halls in the various cities. Statistics indicated that there were over 20,000 street factories and workshops employing over 750,000 people. By gradually providing household services the way was being prepared for the eventual establishment of city-wide communes. As women were encouraged to take jobs in the street factories, street dining halls, nurseries and kindergartens were opened with great speed.

Because of the basic differences in rural and urban conditions, the city communes developed their own form of organization, which can be distinguished in three categories. In the first, the great state-operated factories, mines or enterprises serve as the center; in the second, offices and schools are the center; in the smallest units, the streets are the center of communal organizations. The first and third became far more prevalent. For example, the Hsiang-fang People's Commune in Harbin was organized around the core of a rural factory complex. It has 18 state-operated factories in addition to a suburban farm—all coordinated by the central communal administration. This commune opened 346 public dining halls, 266 nurseries and kindergartens and some 300 service stations. These centers released over 10,000 women for production, while replacing them with only 3,100 service personnel.

In Shanghai the communes were organized on the basis of street residence. Street residents were organized into units engaged in small-scale industrial production. By 1960, these units accounted for over 70 per cent of the city population, or some 850,000 people in 4,600 units representing the city's 11,000 streets. This required the establishment of 1,667 dining halls providing meals for 400,000 people, and 2,117 nurseries to care for 130,000 children. Another 3,274 organizations provided various services, such as clothes-mending, public baths, banking, etc. The service staff of some 20,000 was recruited entirely from the ranks of housewives.

Since the state owns the major means of production in the urban communes, it alone is responsible for management, production and distribution. The value of these city units consists in the ability to increase production while carefully regulating consumption—all this predicated upon the ability to make the most effective use of manpower. According to official statistics, by the spring of 1960, city communes were providing services for over twenty million people. This included 50,000 dining halls furnishing meals for some 5,200,000 people; 42,000 nurseries and kindergartens caring for 1,600,000 children, and some 66,000 service stations. These impressive totals did not reveal that the urban communes were already suffering from a number of serious problems.

At the second session of the Second NPC, secretaries from the Party committees from five major cities—Peking, Shanghai, Tientsin, Wuhan and Canton—indicated in a joint statement that the city communes were meeting resistance. The "capitalists" and intellectuals had reservations about participation. On April 10, 1960, *People's Daily* cautioned that only those people who genuinely demanded participation in the urban communes should be admitted. Similar to the decentralization process which was taking place in the rural communes, Party directives urged that, at least temporarily, the street be considered the basis of urban communalization.

Urban communes of this type were rapidly expanded. Canton alone organized 22 communes between July and August, 1960. In Peking, the addition of four units in July, 1960 brought that city's total to 37. The smaller cities also participated. For example, the municipality of Hailar, Inner Mongolia, formed three communes in 35 days. In Pangpu, Anhwei province, nineteen junk cooperatives were organized into a single urban water commune. But, as has been shown in the case of their rural counterparts, these urban communes were a far call from the original intentions of the CPC.

The Chinese Communists have had to deal with several major problems connected with the cities in recent years. Not the least of these is the problem of overpopulation or congestion in the urban areas. The Great Leap programs required reassignment of great numbers of persons to industrial tasks, often associated with the urban centers. At the same time, the production failures of the communes, and the food shortages of the 1959–62 period made it increasingly difficult to feed the urban population. As noted elsewhere, the CPC sought to alleviate these problems by sending vast segments of the urban population to work in the countryside. But in his interview with Anna L. Strong, published in the January 15, 1964 Hong Kong *Ta-kung Pao*, state planner Po I-po admitted that, until agriculture becomes mechanized, the urban population would have to be reduced from 130 million to 110 million. At the same time, there is evidence that dissatisfied agricultural workers still dream of bettering themselves by moving to the cities. Thus, the Party press has frequently insisted that the higher living standards and prestige associated with urban living represent only a temporary inequality with peasant conditions. [4]

THE GREAT LEAP IN INDUSTRY

In November, 1957, delegates from 12 Communist Parties meeting in Moscow to observe the 40th anniversary of the Bolshevik revolution issued a common statement of purpose for the development of the world socialist movement. In the area of economic development, the Moscow Declaration announced the communist world's intention to conduct an all-out economic competition with the capitalistic countries. Soviet production was to exceed that of the United States, while Communist China accepted the challenge of meeting and surpassing England's production. At this time, Peking estimated that by 1972 England would be producing

[4] It is unlikely that this propaganda is effective. The Party press itself frequently carries articles on the high standard of living now enjoyed in China's cities. For example, labor insurance was first introduced in 1951 and incorporated into the 1954 Constitution. Expanded provisions for all workers stipulate liberal disability, retirement and death benefits, according to length of service and with all expenses borne by management. A total of 56 days is promised at full pay for maternity leave, with 14 extra days for difficult delivery or the birth of twins. Men may retire at 60, and women at 50 on pensions ranging from 50–70 per cent of full wages. Six months' free hospitalization with 60–75 per cent of pay until the workers returns to his assignment is also called for. Similarly, in the case of housing, according to the Party press, by 1963 Shanghai had over 30 new housing developments, each providing for from hundreds to thousands of families. Each family has its own flat of 2–5 rooms with a private kitchen and toilet facilities. According to the Hong Kong *Wen-hui Pao* of February 21, 1964, modern, low-rent housing with electricity and water and heating in cold areas had already been constructed in 167 cities and industrial districts with state funds. Envious farm workers have been told that the wide variation between rural and urban housing is due to the fact that in the cities industry is owned by the entire people, while in the rural areas collectivization is practiced. Thus, the means to eliminate these differences is said to be through increased urban aid to the countryside and the further development of production and socialist organization in the rural areas. But, to a disastisfied peasant, these arguments are unavailing and the dream of escaping to the city may be expected to persist for a long time to come.

36.46 million tons of steel, yet in 1957 China had produced only 4.44 million tons of steel. Even the target of the Second Five-Year Plan was only 12 million tons. Thus, using this basic commodity as an index, it is apparent that Peking had to devise an all-out crash program if it hoped to achieve its self-proclaimed goals.

The First Five-Year Plan (1953–57) which had one-sidedly concentrated on the expansion of heavy industry, had succeeded beyond expectations in that sector. In steel production, according to the official statistics, 1957 totals registered a more than 300 per cent increase over 1952 production of 1,350,000 tons. But, as noted in the previous chapter, the First Five-Year Plan had not proven an unmixed success. In September, 1956, proposals for the Second Five-Year Plan were submitted to the Eighth CPC Congress, then meeting in Peking. The resultant draft plan was adopted by the State Council at its 42nd session, on February 7, 1957. Had the normal procedures been followed, the plan would have been made official after being detailed by the State Planning Commission and ratified by the National People's Congress. In fact, no formal Plan was forthcoming. Instead, in May, 1958, two months after the First Plan expired, the CPC Central Committee published a revised version of its earlier plan in the form of a dramatic statement that China would exceed England's production within fifteen years. This latter plan is commonly referred to as the Great Leap Forward.[5]

No single factor suffices to explain the 1958 decision to inaugurate the Great Leap and the commune system. But the course of Sino-Soviet relations must certainly have been of considerable influence. Soviet aid to Communist China had declined progressively from the peak reached in the First Five-Year Plan (1953–57). During that period, as reported in the June 30, 1957 *People's Daily*, Soviet loans totalled 3 billion, 120 million yuan. In the single year 1955 over 1.5 billion yuan were advanced. By 1956, however, according to Li Hsien-nien's financial report, this figure was curtailed to 117 million yuan. In the following year loans were further reduced to 22.32 million yuan—a US dollar equivalent of 10 million. Soviet technical assistance was being similarly restricted. Although protocols concluded during Khrushchev's 1954 Peking visit called for technical assistance in the construction of 141 large projects, extended in

---

[5] It should be noted that Communist China, throughout the 1958–62 period, referred to the Second Five-Year Plan. As noted subsequently, after several false starts, Peking now insists that its Third Five-Year Plan became effective in 1966. Thus, it is possible to allude to expenditures, targets, etc. of the Second Five-Year Plan. But since the introduction of the Great Leap and the communes radically revised all existing plans, throughout the text the term Great Leap is used to designate the official plan for industrial development which was released in May, 1958. It should be observed, furthermore, that the Moscow Conference intervened between submission of the draft plan and announcement of the Great Leap.

1956 by Mikoyan's agreement providing for an additional 55 industrial enterprises, these programs were curtailed. [6]

One of the most important factors in the CPC's decision in 1958 to begin the Great Leap Forward and the commune system stems from Mao Tse-tung's firm conviction that national manpower ranks second only to Party leadership as a decisive element in national development. In the past China's vast manpower was usually regarded more as a liability than an asset. While there were some 30 million people engaged in industry, commerce, communications, transportation and education, and many millions of farmers, there were also millions of consumers who played little or no active part in production. The largest single latter component was China's 120 million women engaged in household duties. As Po I-po remarked in a *People's Daily* article of September 30, 1958, the demands of industrialization, irrigation and water conservation, without some drastic compensatory measure, would automatically lead to a point where it would be impossible to provide adequate food supplies. The solution called for organization of the masses for collective production and collective living along military lines. In 1957, male laborers usually worked 249 days annually and females 166 days. In 1959, under communal organization, males worked 300 days and females 250. Communalization meant that China's women were exceeding the former yearly labor contributions of its men. At the same time serious shortages of Party personnel could be met by reducing the number of political units in the villages from 740,000 to 24,000, and better use could be made of technical personnel. By this projected increase in the efficiency of the rural labor forces, in 1958, the leadership deemed it feasible to assign 100 million Chinese to the 1958–59 irrigation drive alone. Another 60 million participated in the ill-conceived backyard furnace campaign. As will be noted subsequently, the belief that China's economic productivity could be increased dramatically by new

---

[6] During the first session of the Second NPC, for example, Li Fu-ch'un reported a reduction of the total to 166 units, or 30 less than the original agreements specified. Although analysis of the rationale for this reduction in Soviet aid is not pertinent to the present subject, several possibilities can be suggested in passing. At the 20th CPSU Congress, in 1956, Khrushchev gave his secret speech damning Stalin for his "cultism." The CPC has never accepted this judgment. Too, the terms of the Soviet loans generally called for repayment in ten years. Chinese debts incurred during the Korean War would, therefore, probably begin to fall due in 1960. The Soviets appeared reluctant to give any more substantial loans. For example, *Peking Review* on January 1, 1966, claimed that total Soviet loans accounted for only 2 per cent of the state revenue during the entire 1950–59 period, with the implication that this was meagre assistance. If the Chinese Communists were to repay their loans, take care of domestic needs, and also fulfill internationalist communist commitments, they had to devise new sources of state revenue. The concept of national self-reliance is implicit in the nature of the programs. For an analysis in depth of the ideological factors involved see Peter S. H. Tang, *The Chinese Communist Struggle Against Modern Revisionism, op. cit.*

labor utilization programs proved disasterously false. Labor reassignment left the agricultural sector seriously undermanned even in the busy planting and harvesting seasons. But in 1958, the policy appeared to be a panacea.

Prior to the announcement of the Great Leap, the Chinese Communists had stressed the economic concept of equilibrium, or the simultaneous development of all sectors of the economy. For example, in his report on the 1956 plan to the fourth session of the First NPC, Po I-po pointed out: "The arrangement of the national economy should as much as possible attain the increase of basic construction corresponding to the increase of production of consumer goods, and make the various branches of the national economy develop in the way of comparative equilibrium. . . ." In reality, as noted previously, the Peking Plan had given priority to heavy industry and capital construction. The theory of imbalance, in keeping with the Marxist hypothesis that balance is only temporary and relative, was utilized even more fully in the conception of the Great Leap Forward.

According to the imbalance approach to economic development, selected productive elements are pushed ahead in continuing spirals of acceleration. At each new, albeit temporary, stage of development, the achievements of these select productive forces become the current target for all secondary productive elements. More specifically, when the Great Leap concentrated primarily on increasing iron and steel production, all other sectors were expected to imitate this progress. While it is possible that, in certain periods, these lesser elements could catch up and balance the economy, in practice this does not occur. This is because as soon as the selected forces reach a new stage of development, higher quotas are assessed and the spiral renews itself.

To promote this economic spiral, two methods could be used. Quotas of the more progressive productive forces could be scaled back, at least until the more backward elments catch up. But, obviously, this pattern would be retrogressive. Consequently, the CPC utilized the alternate method of constantly raising the quotas of lagging forces to correspond with the achievements of the more progressive forces. All of this suggests the importance Peking has attached to the question of variable quotas. A practical example may clarify this pattern.

In the February, 1958 draft economic plan the State Economic Commission fixed the following major quotas:

Pig iron	7,150,000 tons
Steel	6,248,000 tons
Coal	150,000,000 tons
Food	392 billion catties

Compared to 1957, this represented an industrial increase of 14.6 per cent and an agricultural increase of 6.1 per cent. But, after the announcement of the Great Leap, the CPC Central Committee, meeting in Peitaiho, announced the following new quotas:

Steel	10,700,000 tons
Coal	270,000,000 tons
Grain	600–700 billion catties

In December, 1958, the sixth plenum of the Eighth Central Committee again raised quotas. Steel output targets were raised to 18 million tons, coal to 380 million tons, and grain to 525 million tons, or 1,150 billion catties.

As will become clear in analyzing the accomplishments and failures of the Great Leap and communalization, the pattern of constantly raised targets can be regarded as a sort of statistical game, having little bearing on final production figures. But the idea of imbalance was strongly advocated early in these programs, largely to provide incentive and competition.

The water conservancy program of 1958 was probably the most important phase of the Great Leap to agriculture. Finance Minister Li Hsien-nien reported that from October, 1958 to March, 1959, 100 million people daily took part in this campaign. According to the April 24, 1959 *People's Daily*, Fu Tso-yi estimated that some 58 billion cubic meters of earthwork were completed to increase irrigated land area by 480 million mou. Agricultural Minister Liao Lu-yen's report in the same organ on September 26, 1959, testified to the construction of some 60 large reservoirs, each with over a 100 million cubic meter capacity, some 1,200 medium ones, and tens of thousands of small reservoirs. These vast river projects included the transformation of the Hai, completed in 1958, and the harnassing of the Huai, T'ao and Lungchiang Rivers. The Miyun Reservoir, with a capacity of 4,100 million cubic meters, 68 times the size of the Ming Tomb Reservoir, was another of the enormous projects. Coffer dams were constructed across the Yellow River at several points.

These quantitative accomplishments, however, were not matched by qualitative standards. Aside from the policy error of taking manpower from the farms to carry out the irrigation program, much of the work was done hastily and without benefit of adequate surveying. Leaking canals meant that subsoil water rose to the surface. In some areas, then, soil became too alkaline for cultivation. The floods and droughts that plagued China after 1959 were due, in some measure, to 1958's mistakes.

China's electrical power potential is integrally related to the pattern of development of water conservancy. Where rivers were dammed to provide water for the farmlands, a number of hydroelectrical stations were constructed to provide power for the urban and industrial centers. Among others, important networks were constructed at Fengmeng and Shuifeng on the Yalu and Sungari Rivers and at Fushan. The build-up of these electrical power complexes continued unabated during the period of retrenchment, and is still officially termed one of the major economic tasks. In Szechwan province—sometimes referred to as China's rice bowl—in 1949 there were 19 hydro-electric power stations. By 1963, their number had grown to 1,200. The 58 million kilowatt hours of electric power which these complexes supplied to the provincial communes in 1962 represented an 8-fold increase over 1957. Nationwide, Chou En-lai reported in December, 1964 to the Third NPC that rural electric power had increased 22 times over the total for the last year of the First Five-Year Plan, 1957.

The industrial demands of the Great Leap gave even greater urgency to the improvement of the backward transportation network. Communes had to be connected with the factories that processed their raw materials, and the factories had to be linked with the urban centers and great port cities. Thus, programs were launched for the improvement and extension of railways, waterways and highways. As with many other aspects of the Great Leap, unrealistic targets and great haste resulted in many blunders. One notable example was the so-called "native railway" system.

The "native railways" were constructed in various localities to link production centers. They operated on tracks of pig iron, or sometimes of timber covered with sheet iron. Locomotives were usually powered by gas, diesel or automobile engines. According to a May 8, 1959 statement issued by the Ministry of Railways, more than thirty such branch lines were then being built to connect with the main railway system. The system was primitive and inefficient. In 1959, *People's Daily* termed the railways still inadequate and declared the solution to be an implementation of the "walk with two legs" policy which would speed construction of both native and modern rail lines.

The construction of modern railways in the first years of the Great Leap registered far more substantial gains than the "native" lines. The 1,000 km. Paotow-Lanchow line was completed on July 30, 1958. The Lanchow-Sinkiang Railway was extended beyond Hami in 1959, and beyond Urumchi early in 1961. The Lanchow-Sining (200 km.), the Nanp'ing-Foochow (168 km.), and the Kweiyang-Liuchow (605 km.) lines all began operations in 1959. On April 1, 1960, the 256 km. Peking-Chengteh Railway formally opened to traffic. Part of this construction program involved the erection of a number of new bridges. The Yangtze had already been spanned at Wuhan in 1957. In 1959 the Yangtze Bridge at Chungking was opened. About 820 meters long, it provided double-track service. The 3 km. double-track Chengchow Bridge over the Yellow River, begun in 1958, was completed in April, 1960. At the same time equipment needs were met by centers for the manufacture of steam locomotives in Dairen and Changchun. By 1965, the Changchow Diesel Locomotive Works in Kiangsi province was producing a native-design 60–120 horsepower compressed-air diesel engine. This small engine is particularly adaptable to the light tracks in mining and forestry projects.

Another phase of transportation development quickened by the needs of the Great Leap was that of improving and extending existing waterways. Of course, this work went hand-in-hand with the vast projects for irrigation and electrification. In 1958, major waterway projects involved the Hai River in Tientsin and the T'ao River in Kansu. Preliminary surveys were also completed for a grand canal to link Peking with Canton and to chart the Sha River. In April, 1963, China's longest inland waterway was opened to ships of the 2,300 ton class along the Yangtze River. Connecting Shanghai and Chungking, the route reduced shipping time by two-thirds. A February, 1963 dispatch from Nanking reported that 400 km. of the ancient grand canal had already been rebuilt to handle six times the previous shipping capacity. This section, opened to tugs towing a dozen barges apiece, and extending north from the Yangtze port of Yangchow, has electrically-controlled locks. Manufacturing centers in Shanghai and Dairen are engaged in meeting the need for more vessels by manufacturing ocean-going ships of the 5,000–16,000 ton class.

Highway construction, as in the case of railway construction, has been helped by PLA assistance, particularly in the more remote areas. In 1963, for example, soldiers laid 153 km. of standard gauge track and 600 km. of narrow gauge. The PLA also constructed some 400 km. of forest and mountain roads, including bridges and tunnels. In 1964, the PLA Railway Corps added 670 km. of narrow gauge railway track and constructed 420 km. of highways. Although China did not manufacture its first automobile until 1958, by 1961 plants in Changchun were producing 60,000 vehicles annually. In 1964, the Tsinan Motor Vehicles Plant began production of a Chinese-design 8.5 ton diesel-powered truck, capable of 70 km. speeds. As of January 1, 1965, the government reduced the price of petrol 18.6 per cent—the largest cut since the establishment of the CPR—to further improve the transportation situation. Similar efforts have been made to improve inter-city transportation. In 1949, for example, when Peking had only 49 trolleys and 5 buses, rickshaws were a normal mode of conveyance. But by 1962, the city had 1,000 buses and 400 trolleys to carry its urban workers along 99 routes totalling 1,640 km. The government boasted that pedicabs would soon disappear as the rickshaws had done.

These substantial improvements in the transportation system should not detract from the fact that Communist China must still find some way to solve acute shortages. In January, 1964, state planner Po I-po again asked that factories be relocated nearby their sources of raw materials to help alleviate the pressing situation. But the problem of moving goods to factories or consumers was minor. Underlying the transportation shortage was the far greater problem of insufficient agricultural production to feed the population or stoke the factory system. From 1959 to 1961, the Chinese Communists were forced to deal with an economic crisis attributive at least in part to their own manufacture.

SUCCESSES, FAILURES AND FAMINE

The 1958 Great Leap Forward for industry and the commune program for agriculture were intended to transform Communist China into a modern industrial giant with tremendous rapidity. And the first reports for 1958 production appeared to exceed even the epic demands of the quota system. The combination of labor-intensive and modern industrial methods were acclaimed for achieving these goals. For example, steel production, rising 49.7 per cent over 1957 figures, was said to have reached 80 per cent of national self sufficiency. To provide fuel for the vast factory complexes, the number of small coal pits was increased from the 1957 total of 20,000 to some 110,000 pits with an annual capacity of 185 million tons. During the same period, 400 large new mines were opened. Light industry registered similar gains. For example, in his April 22, 1959 report to the first session of the Second NPC, Li Fu-ch'un noted that machine-made paper production had increased from 913,000 tons to 1.22 million tons, and production of rubber shoes from 130 million to 180 million pairs, between 1957 and 1958. Chiang Kuang-nai, Minister of the Textile Industry, placed the increase in cotton yarn production at 31 per cent for the same period. As noted previously, similar improvements were made in water conservancy and electrification, and in transportation. Although the gains in the agricultural sector were less spectacular, general increases were claimed.

Based upon preliminary reports such as these, in December, 1958, the Eighth CPC Central Committee, convened in its sixth plenum at Wuhan, ordered further increases in the various production quotas for 1959. For example, in 1958, steel's quota was set at 10.7 million tons, but 1959 targets called for production of 18 million tons—or a 60 per cent increase as compared to the former year. Coal production was set 40 per cent higher than the 1958 quota, and food grain targets were 50 per cent higher.

By August of 1959, the Chinese Communist leadership was obliged to admit that many of the 1958 production achievements were illusionary. Thus the eighth plenum of the Eighth CPC Central Committee, meeting in Lushan, issued revised statistics for 1958 production of 250 million tons of food grain and 8 million tons of steel. Planned targets for 1959 were scaled downward to reflect this situation. More importantly, to quiet peasant unrest and improve agricultural output, the CC revised the commune structure to give more authority to the component brigades and more freedom to the individual members.

The very fanaticism of the Great Leap and commune programs may have been responsible for the breakdown in statistical work. In April, 1959, Hsüeh Mu-ch'iao, the former director of the State Statistical Bureau, intimated this failure when he warned the cadres that they must abandon their practice of "adding figures at every stage." The unrealistic reports received, which had no correspondence to fact, made it virtually impossible for the Party leadership to obtain a realistic picture for proper planning.

Another mistake made in 1958, and revealed subsequently, was that of striving to achieve production quotas through labor-intensive methods. For example, in the winter of 1958, the peasants had been ordered to collect scrap iron, even including cooking utensils, for melting down and reuse. They were also told to turn in all personal cash assets to be pooled with state funds in financing the Great Leap programs. But the two major labor-intensive drives were those of water conservancy and the backyard furnaces. As noted elsewhere, some 100 million peasants were mobilized for the first drive, and 60 million for the latter. Lacking sufficient experience or trained engineers and supervisors, the peasants engaged in the water conservation drive often constructed faulty canals, dams and reservoirs. The terrible water shortages in some provinces in 1959 and 1960 perhaps best illustrate the deficiencies of this peasant construction. In April, 1960, the Chinese Communists admitted that some 40–60 per cent of the canals were leaky and warned of the danger of vast tracts of arable land becoming alkaline.

The sixty million peasants assigned to tend the two million backyard furnaces (or small, native hearths) were supposed to produce 10 million tons of pig iron a year by 1959. But these furnaces wasted fuel, mineral resources and manpower to a frightening degree, and the end product was usually inferior and unsuitable for further use. Much of the responsibility for this failure can be traced to improper equipment, insufficient skill and planning blunders. More importantly, all of these labor-intensive programs required that peasants be reassigned from their regular agricultural work. Paradoxically, in the most heavily populated country in the world, a labor shortage ensued. According to official estimates, Communist China was short ten billion man-days of labor in 1958. During the fall harvest season, certain areas had a 50 per cent labor shortage, which resulted in great crop losses.

Another example of a major planning blunder was that of advocating a three-field system of farming. Critically short of chemical fertilizers, the planners, at the sixth CPC Central Committee plenum in December, 1958, decided to reactivate this old feudal method of leaving a third of the land fallow each year. In April, 1959, Li Fu-ch'un reported to the NPC that some 299,890,000 mou were then being permitted to lay idle. But this drastic reduction in total farm acreage inevitably had an adverse effect on 1959 agricultural production. Consequently, the three-field system had to be abandoned in the summer of that year, but not before the damage had already been done.

At the grass-roots level, Party cadres sought to fulfill assigned quotas by driving the peasants and workers unmercifully. Stories are told of guards standing over the peasants as they toiled in the fields and of "night campaigns" which deprived the peasants of even minimal sleep requirements. Moreover, many of the cadres were inexperienced, and some were corrupt. All these factors increased peasant unrest and sometimes led to passive resistance. This, too, had an adverse effect on production.

Early in 1959, the Chinese Communist leadership kept up its propaganda claims of production victories. In fact, over-all goals for the Second Five-Year Plan were said to have been reached by the end of 1959, or three years ahead of schedule. But agricultural production wsa already insufficient for human and industrial demands. The CPC Central Committee sought to economize in the former category by ordering a campaign of thrift. Drought and floods—not human factors—were held responsible for the shortages. To combat these natural calamities, by order of the Central Committee and the State Council some sixty million people were mobilized for crash programs in seventeen of the provinces to help salvage the crops. As mentioned previously, the Central Committee, at Lushan, also scaled back production quotas for 1959, although even these targets were unrealistic.

By 1960, the agricultural situation was critical. More than half of the arable land, according to a NCNA dispatch of December 30, 1960, was affected by drought or flood conditions; some areas became absolutely nonproductive. As production declined, Chou En-lai admitted in a November interview with Edgar Snow that "the total value of agricultural production this year may be less that of last year," although he claimed it would still be higher than in 1957, the last year of the First Five-Year Plan.[7] Although it is impossible to establish the level of public health or whether any deaths occurred as a result of starvation, countless reports from refugees fleeing to Hong Kong and Macau testify to a universally inadequate diet and the prevalence of malnutrition. The shortage of raw materials caused the factories to operate on reduced schedules, or even to shut down. In the

[7] It should be noted that Communist China's population increases at the rate of at least 2 per cent annually. Thus, if production remains stable, it is inadequate.

February, 1961 issue of *Red Flag*, Agricultural Minister Liao Lu-yen admitted that twenty million urban workers, presumably now unemployed, were reassigned to rural tasks.

Finally, beginning in 1960, the Chinese Communist leadership came to the conclusion that the entire economy needed to be readjusted to reinforce the agricultural sector. As acknowledged in the January 18, 1961 communique of the ninth plenum of the Eighth CPC Central Committee, the 1960 quotas were not met. Thus the Central Committee ordered a curtailment of investment in heavy industry and stressed that agriculture must become "the foundation of the national economy." As will be described in the next section, retrenchment and readjustment policies replaced the original, fanatical policies of the Great Leap and the communes.

Discounting the exaggerations of Chinese Communist statistics, it must nevertheless be acknowledged that the Great Leap did make some great strides in developing the national economy, and that the communes, in revised form, came to meet the needs of agricultural production. During the period of the First Five-Year Plan, the annual increase in total production for industry was 18 per cent. During the first two years of the Great Leap this was raised to 45 per cent. Agriculture, under the First Five-Year Plan, increased its value at the rate of 4.5 per cent annually. Under the Great Leap this rose to 17 per cent per annum. Evidence exists, however, that the speed of the programs decreased with each year of operation. In the field of investment, for example, while the rate of increase in 1958 was 70 per cent over the previous year, the 1959 increase over 1958 was only 24.5 per cent, and the 1960 rate only 21.7 per cent over the 1959 total. As the rate of investment decreased, so did the speed of the entire program. No statistics can illustrate the tremendous waste of natural and human resources involved in these programs. Yet, the fact that Communist China could weather three successive years of critical setbacks to agrarian and industrial programs is testimony to the strength of the CPC leadership, just as the introduction of a retrenchment and readjustment policy may be said to reflect a certain maturity based on experience.

RETRENCHMENT, READJUSTMENT AND RECOVERY

Agriculture

Nominally, the Great Leap and communalization programs remained effective, but late in 1959 the Chinese Communists were forced to consider retrenchment measures for both the industrial and agricultural sectors. In August, 1958, the eighth plenum of the Eighth CPC Central Committee, meeting in Lushan, ordered a reduction in agricultural production quotas; but even these scaled down goals were unfulfilled. Thus, the ninth CPC CC plenum, meeting in January, 1961 called upon the whole nation to "strengthen the agricultural front thoroughly and carry out the policy of taking agriculture as the foundation of the national economy and of the whole Party and the entire people." As noted elsewhere, the very structure of the communes was adjusted to provide additional incentive to the peasants. By the end of the period of the Second Five-Year Plan, 1963, Communist China had apparently "turned the corner" in its agricultural crisis. Or as phrased in the communique of the Second National People's Congress in December, 1963: "our national economy has begun an all-round turn for the better."

By the end of 1963, cotton production was said to have improved by 20–30 per cent, livestock to have increased by 837,000 head, and grain and soya bean production to have risen slightly, as compared to the previous year. In the rural areas, pork consumption was said to be doubled, while over 90 per cent of the commune workers had a supply of poultry. In addition to the factor of increased side-line production, discussed elsewhere, the state farms had contributed a great share to these production achievements. According to a NCNA release of March 14, 1964, the state farms had doubled their acreage in 1963 and were able to produce three times as much grain as they had in 1957, or 26 per cent more, as compared to 1962. New programs devised at a National Conference on Agricultural Science and Technology were responsible for allocating more funds and manpower to agricultural research centers. Teams from these centers then toured the countryside to instruct the peasants in new seed strains, weed killers and harvesting techniques. One of these centers was described in detail by Li Chin in the February 8, 1963 *Peking Review*. In Shensi province, where nearly every county had its own seed-breeding, veterinary and agro-technical stations, the Changan county station's forty technicians taught area commune members on test plots. A combination of incentives and methods were responsible for the "bumper crop" described by President Choe Yong Kon of North Korea to his Parliament after a prolonged tour of the mainland.

Even more substantial achievements were claimed for 1964. In his December report to the Third NPC, Chou En-lai pointed out that 1964 agricultural production would surpass that of the bumper year, 1957. The state farms claimed a 14 per cent increase in grain and soya bean production and 42 per cent increase in cotton yields, as compared to 1963. Sugar production was said to be 59 per cent over that of 1963. In the January, 1965 issue of *China Reconstructs*, Vice President of the Council for Promotion of Foreign Trade Yung Lung-kwei stated that the number of pigs rose by ten million in 1964. Chou noted that the supplies of pork, mutton, vegetables and non-staple foodstuffs was 30 per cent higher than 1957 totals. In 1965, despite adverse weather conditions in some areas, the Chinese Communists boasted of "an excellent harvest year." And early in 1966, *Peking Review* (no. 6, 1966) reported the Third Five-Year Plan "off to a good start," with grain production again registering increases.

Another way of indicating the growing stability of the agricultural sector is that of evaluating the progress of national and local irrigation programs. After three years of agricultural shortages, officially attributed to flood and drought, the task of more adequate development of the irrigation system was given one of the highest priorities. In his February, 1963 address to the National Conference on Agricultural Science and Technology, Vice Premier and CPC Politburo member Nieh Jung-chen repeated that water conservancy was one of the major targets for national development. The last solid figures for the total land under irrigation were for 1957, and accounted for 500 million mou, or a third of all the arable land. Provisions of the Second Five-Year Plan had called for this total to be doubled, and the goal was presented as fact in the official statistical survey, *Ten Great Years*, published in 1959. But the *People's Daily* editorial of November 30, 1963 mentioned that only a third of all arable land was irrigated and that these systems had malfunctions about 40 per cent of the time.[8]

To improve this situation, the leadership employed a variety of procedures. According to Canton sources, in the winter of 1962–63, some 400,000 commune members in the Chanchiang administrative district alone were assigned to relieve 240,000 mou of farmland through irrigation. Peasants were said to have reclaimed more than 60,000 hectares in the Yellow River area of Ninghsia, Northwest China. Nationwide, 1.3 million hectares were said to have been irrigated in 1963, as commune personnel and state farms concentrated on digging branch canals to join main reservoirs. The crisscross system of drainage canals, totalling 3,900 km. was said to increase the wheat yield per hectare in Northwest China from 0.75 tons in 1948, to 1.8 tons in 1963.

Water conservancy programs continued undiminished in 1964.[9] In Kwangtung province, 90,515 projects provided an aggregate storage capacity of 30 billion cubic meters, pumped by engines of 135,900 horsepower. This brought Kwangtung's total area of irrigated land to 1.6 million hec-

[8] It should be noted that the total area of cultivated land was increased substantially between 1958 and 1963; therefore the 1963 total for irrigated land could be higher than 500 million mou.

[9] Minister of Agriculture Liao Lu-yen strongly reminded the National Conference on Agricultural Production, which met in Peking in February, 1964, of the need to extend the total of arable land through flood and drought control projects.

tares. In Anhwei province, 1,200 km. of main and branch canals irrigated more than 200,000 hectares of land. The dimensions of this latter project can be illustrated by the fact that the main canal was 94 km. in length and 10–20 meters wide. A NCNA dispatch of January 8, 1965, noted that the state farms provided irrigation for an additional 91,000 hectares in 1964. According to a Sian dispatch, the Maowusu desert was pushed back and some 34,000 hectares of land recovered by irrigation.

Despite these statistics, the Chinese Communists admit that the national irrigation system is still deficient. In 1964, in order to curtail state investment, the leadership ordered a concentration on small, local projects which would rely on the labor of the poor peasants. In the winter of 1964–65, in Hunan, for example, some four and a half million peasants were assigned to 510,000 irrigation projects. But *People's Daily* admitted, on February 4, 1965, that some 30–40 per cent of China's large and middle irrigation systems were still not well linked.

Much of the credit for increases in agricultural production in the period of readjustment must be attributed to the side-line production of the peasants. Moreover, the income from side-line occupations has become one of the main sources of rural revenue. According to the *Ta-kung Pao* of December 24, 1963, such work then accounted for about 30 per cent of the peasant's income, although other, non-official sources invariably placed this percentage higher, usually at one-half of the income of the communes, their component brigades and teams, and the individual peasants. Theoretically, as peasant income increases, more consumer goods will be sold: since the state controls consumer goods, the national budget should be greatly augmented.

Goods from side-line production fall into category three of the state plan; that is, they are not included in quotas, need not be sold to the state, and can be disposed of independently. With the exception of the rural fairs or black market activities, these goods are normally sold to the marketing and supply cooperatives run by the state. Statistics show these cooperatives have registered consistent increases. For example, purchases by the cooperatives for the period January–May, 1963 showed a 23 per cent increase over the similar 1962 period. Purchases for January–August, 1965 showed a 15.5 per cent increase over the same months in 1964.

Despite these increases, the marketing and supply cooperatives pose a serious problem for the Chinese Communist leadership. Since more cash can be obtained through side-line than communal production, the peasants are tempted to shortchange their communal assignments. Thus many cadres have had serious misgivings over the land or labor relegated for side-line production. As *People's Daily* observed on August 6, 1965: these cadres "fear that this will influence foodgrain production" and cause a return to capitalist incentives and programs. Moreover, the cooperatives can themselves come to compete with or duplicate the efforts of the state organizations in the rural areas.

The marketing and supply cooperatives also suffer from certain organizational defects. These agencies are often clustered in the towns and cities and there are relatively few in the village areas, where most of their business should be. For example, in 1964 Heilungkiang province had 10,000 workers employed in the cooperatives, but 85 per cent were stationed in the county centers and only 15 per cent in the villages. Moreover, about a third of these units had only two workers each. In view of this unequal distribution, *Ta-kung Pao* recommended, on September 4, 1965, that communal team members be appointed as cooperative agents in areas where there were no cooperatives.

Since the marketing and supply cooperatives must show a profit, they tend to purchase and stock only those goods which have a proven quick resale value. And since the peasant purchasing power is still so low, often items are not stocked, in spite of local needs. When the peasants are unable to procure needed goods and equipment, their purchasing power is further reduced. Moreover, the marketing and supply cooperatives have practically no control over the number or type of goods which the peasants offer to sell them. In the preface to his book, *The High Tide of Socialism in the Chinese Villages*, written in 1955, Mao Tse-tung observed that "the state must have a unified plan, and haphazard aimless production must be eliminated." Consequently, at least some of the marketing and supply cooperatives have sought to control production by signing contracts with communal teams or individual peasants. These contracts are meaningless until some way can be found to make them binding, since no individual is obliged to enter into side-line production. As the peasants increasingly turn to such occupations, to earn much-needed cash, Communist China must device some better means to regulate their activities or side-line production will further promote a return to capitalistic enterprise.

Industry

The Second Five-Year Plan, which was to be launched in January, 1958, was designed to forward industrialization, while holding agriculture at a constant, or registering minor increases. According to this Plan, state investment for heavy industry was to be at a 7:1 ratio, as compared to light industry. As noted previously, the Great Leap Forward favored a similar design for the advancement of heavy industry, and enormous production increases were recorded as the program progressed. However, the failure of the agricultural sector had disastrous consequences to industrialization. Too, the diminishment of Soviet aid and the 1960 recall of Soviet technicians and plans were detrimental to the industrial sector. Thus, in April, 1962, in his report to the third session of the Second NPC, Chou En-lai readjusted the national tasks to give first priority to agriculture, to favor light over heavy industry, and to temporarily retrench state investment in construction of industrial enterprises. Consequently, production figures for 1962 showed increases of from 20 to 100 per cent for light industry, as compared to 1961. These included such commodities as bicycles, sewing machines, footwear, enamelware, synthetic fabrics and plastic products. For example, the Ministry of Light Industry and its related organizations revealed at a national conference held in Taiyuan municipality, Shansi, that by the end of 1962, 560 factories and producers' cooperatives were engaged in the manufacture of plastic products. These plastic goods, such as shoes, film and even furniture, were said to account for about 9 per cent of national sales of sundry goods. As the communique from this conference poetically phrased it, plastic goods were flooding the market "like dandelions springing up in a spring lawn." The Jingwei (Warp and Woof) Textile Machinery Plant, located near Taiyuan, announced that it had singlehandedly produced 56 per cent as many textile machines, between 1954 and 1962, as had been imported to China during the sixty years before 1949.

Encouraged by production figures for 1962, Communist China planned for further increases in the industrial sector for 1963. Again, heavy industry was subordinated to light industry. Wang Yi-chih, Vice Minister of Light Industry, called for the various plants to double output of bicycles for the rural market and to "greatly increase" production of such products as synthetics and plastics by the end of the year. Between January and August, compared to the same period in 1962, production of chemical fertilizer was said to be up 43.8 per cent and tractor production by 30 per cent. By December, the output of certain chemicals, synthetics and plastics was said to be thirty-nine times the value of 1949.

Even more substantial achievements were claimed in 1964. In his December report to the first session of the Third NPC, Chou predicted that the total value of industrial output for the year would be 15 per cent higher than in 1963—including 20 per cent increases in steel, petroleum, chemical fertilizer, cotton yarns, cement and motor vehicles. A January 21, 1965 NCNA dispatch from Peking referred to these estimates as fact. Statistics are also available to indicate 1964 productive increases as compared to 1957: rural electric power increased 22 times, tractor production 4 times, general motor vehicle production 2.7 times, and chemical fertilizer 3 times.

Preliminary reports for 1965 production showed similar advances. Output of textile machinery from January to June was set at nearly double the corresponding 1964 period. According to *Peking Review* (no. 8, 1966), in 1965, some 1.4 million spindles and the same number of looms were installed. Although consumer sales were said to have increased 10–50 per cent, depending on the commodity, in the marketing and supply cooperatives, *People's Daily* admitted on March 4, 1965, that "there is a great gap between the production of cotton on the one hand, and the needs of the national economy and the people's livelihood on the other." Thus, in 1966, the first year of the new Third Five-Year Plan, quotas were set even higher—and universally claimed to be fulfilled ahead of schedule. Gross industrial output was up 20 per cent, as compared to 1965, due to implementing the "thought of Mao Tse-tung."

These achievements can be restated in a different form—that of national self-sufficiency. In the January 15, 1964 Hong Kong *Ta-kung Pao*, Anna L. Strong, an American whose sympathies have long been with Peking, reported a recent luncheon conversation with Po I-po, Chairman of the State Economic Commission. Referring to Khrushchev's 1960 decision to end economic assistance to China, the chairman said this was tantamount to "taking away all the dishes when you have taken only half of the meal." "Today," Po I-po added, "some comrades think that we should present Khrushchev with a medal because he has stimulated us to rely on our own efforts." Stated more emphatically in a NCNA dispatch of December 27, 1964, "the idea of relying on others is to be destroyed, and the idea of self-reliance is to be established."

According to Yung Lung-kwei, Vice President of the China Council for Promotion of Foreign Trade, by 1957 China enjoyed a 55 per cent self-sufficiency in the vital area of machine-building. State planner Po I-po, in an article in *Red Flag*, reprinted in the October, 1963 *Cuba Socialista*, stated that by 1962 China had achieved 85 per cent self-sufficiency in machinery and equipment. In mentioning that the CPR was able to construct its own modern mining complexes, steel mills, etc., the vice premier suggested the goal of national self-sufficiency for all socialist countries. By 1964, according to Yung Lung-kwei, China had reached 90 per cent self-sufficiency in machine-building. On April 4, 1964, *People's Daily* announced the complete self-sufficiency of China in petroleum and petroleum by-products. NCNA, on September 23, 1964, reported an 85 per cent national self-sufficiency in rolled steel and almost 100 per cent independence in the production of rubber, glass and asbestos. When Chou En-lai reported to the first session of the Third NPC, he traced the 1964 economic achievement to the "resolute application" of the principle of self-sufficiency.

Early in 1966, (see *Peking Review*, February 18, 1966), the Chinese Communists announced that the vital textile industries were now supplied entirely from domestic sources.

Yet, isolated reports attest to the fact that Communist China's industrialization programs are still beset by numerous weaknesses. Although, since 1965, China has been producing electronic computers, it has not yet overcome human errors and weaknesses. Thus the Canton *Yang-ch'eng Wan-pao* of December 27, 1964 admitted to the gross mismanagement of its Municipal Corporation of Special Commodity Supply for the overseas Chinese market. By stating that the matter was no more than a "trifling problem," executives of this enterprise allowed cigarettes worth more than 30,000 yuan to get moist and go stale. Other reports indicate that the Chinese consumers are often disturbed by the commodities offered for sale. In Shanghai, for some six months in 1964, the press reminded their readers that "interest in bizarre clothes is a capitalistic tendency." Factories are being induced to standardize parts and measurements in the hopes of improving technical standards and making replacement easier. But perhaps the most revealing indication that industry is still plagued by human and other problems is the campaign, begun in 1964, to intensify political indoctrination in the industrial enterprises. Thus, for example, the National Conference on Industry and Communications, meeting in February, 1964, and presided over by Chairman of the State Economic Commission Po I-po called upon all its workers to emulate the People's Liberation Army in placing men before materials and "comparing, learning from, overtaking and helping."

One of the primary objectives of the post-1961 readjustment period, as noted previously, was to subordinate heavy to light industry, and place both at the service of the agricultural sector. One method of analyzing this assistance policy is that of evaluating production of two commodities of critical importance to the farming sector—chemical fertilizer and mechanized equipment. In his December, 1964 Report to the first session of the Third NPC, Chou En-lai mentioned that tractor production had registered a 4-fold increase since 1957, and output of chemical fertilizer tripled. Yet, an article in *Ching-chi Yen-chiu* (*Economic Research*) of March 17, 1963, had admitted that only about 10 per cent of China's arable land was then being cultivated with the help of mechanization.

As noted in the previous chapter, since the state farms are intended to serve as models for the entire agrarian sector, they have normally received a disproportionally high share of the mechanized equipment available. According to official statistics, in 1964 the state farms employed 11 per cent more tractors and 59 per cent more harvesters than in the year previous. As compared to 1957, by 1964 there were twice as many state farms, cultivating 2.3 times the land. In 1963, they had increased grain production 35 per cent, and cotton by 62 per cent, over 1962 totals. Available, but isolated official reports substantiate claims that mechanization of the state farms registered substantial increases in the period of economic adjustment. For example, an NCNA dispatch from Harbin, referring to the 1962 fall harvest, reported that 60–70 per cent of the work in the area's 150,000 hectares of land cultivated by the 67 state farms was done by mechanical equipment. The more than 400 state farms in the Northeast area attributed much of the credit for raising 1963 production 25 per cent over that of the previous year to the help of chemical fertilizer and mechanical equipment. A dispatch from Shenyang claimed that two times as much chemical fertilizer had been used in the latter year and that most of the cultivated area was tended by machine. This included the addition of 6,000 new 15 horsepower tractors, 350 combines and 200 trucks.

Nevertheless, since *People's Daily* of October 20, 1964, reported that there were some 100,000 tractors, measured in 15 h.p. units, it is evident that even the state farms still suffered from serious shortages. *People's Daily* of January 9, 1965, admitted that "efficiency is low and some farms work with a deficit," but attributed this failure to poor use of manpower.[10] Yet, the admission of shortages in the state farms clearly indicates that the communes must cope with even worse problems in terms of insufficient machinery or chemical fertilizer.

On January 7, 1963, *Ta-kung Pao* noted that 1962 production of chemical fertilizer had increased by 330,000 tons over 1961. By 1963, modern plants were producing chemical fertilizer in Kirin, Nanking, Dairen, Lanchow, Taiyuan and Shanghai. However, since it is estimated that national needs would require some 24 million tons of such fertilizer every year, production is still woefully short. One proof of the still critical shortage of chemical fertilizer for the communes can be found in the continuing mass drives to improve the soil by traditional means. With the slogan "turning low-yielding land into high-yielding," in slack seasons commune members are assigned to moving pond soil and collecting "night soil," or human excrement. According to official reports, nearly a million acres in Szechwan, Kwangtung and Fukien provinces were improved during the 1963–64

---

[10] It might be noted that laborers in the state farms are paid regular wages, like factory workers. Women and children do not necessarily take part in work assignments.

Furthermore, at least 30 state farms established since 1960 have been designed to absorb returning overseas Chinese. As Fang Fang, Deputy Commissioner, reported to the 3rd enlarged meeting of the Third Committee of the Commission for Overseas Chinese Affairs, in September, 1964, these returnees must be taught "to be content with living in the countryside," "to love labor," and "to accept the state's assignments." Presumably, in these centers there has been resistance to production drives.

campaign. Many areas bordering on the Yangtze River reported a 10–20 per cent extension of cultivated land as a result of the 1964–65 mass drive.[11]

One of the most revealing and detailed accounts to date of the shortages of mechanical and hand tools in the communes was published in the Peking *Ta-kung Pao* of March 6, 1965. Researchers from this paper and the Liuyang county supply and marketing cooperative of Hunan surveyed three communal production teams in the county in 1964. These included the Tayüan team of the Taho brigade, the Hsiheng team of the Shihpei brigade, and the Hsinwu team of the T'iench'iao brigade. Since in 1964 the supply and marketing cooperative provided a total of 446,000 farm tools, this would have averaged out to 31 for each team in the county. Collectively, the three teams surveyed possessed 174 tools, or an average of 58 each, while the members privately owned 360 tools, or an average of 11 per household. But, in reality, distribution was most inequitable. For example, the Hsinwu team had only 19 tools needing repairs, and also had one horse-drawn cart for each household. But the Tayüan team had only two carts, or an average of one for each five households. In practice, this means that members of the poorer team were severely handicapped, since they had to rent their tools. Moreover, since only one of the four Tayüan members who had a draft animal for plowing also had a straw coat, the rest had to leave the fields when it rained. Too, members of the poorer team could not compete for high-paying commune assignments.

Supply and marketing cooperatives which provide farm tools to the communes have been critized for emphasizing consumer products at the expense of tools, and for their failure to provide adequate facilities for repair of farm tools. Poor peasants have been assured of the eventual appearance of the "four sets and ten pieces"—i.e., sets of tools for digging, for carrying on the shoulders, for carrying on the back, and for chopping, and "pieces" of rakes, hoes, buckets, straw hats, etc. For the present, and

[11] As with most of its programs, the CPC has found a dual advantage to the "night soil" campaign. Activists and other candidates for Party membership can improve their chances of acceptance, while members can prove their "ideological loyalty" by active support of this odious labor. Thus, for example, the Peking *Kung-jen Jih-pao* of January 29, 1965 reported that over 2,000 college students, and countless PLA members and Party cadres, including two deputy mayors of Peking, were "scooping night soil from cess pits and cleansing refuse pits." The Canton *Nan-fang Jih-pao* of February 11, 1965, alluding to the work of over 7,000 students and professors, cited two college students as exemplary workers. Liu Chin-t'ing of South China Normal College overcame his natural antipathy and fear of his classmates' hostility by realizing that this labor was "an effort toward cleaning out the bourgeois idea of intolerance for filth and stench." Yen Chien-wen was able to overcome his urge to vomit when "suddenly in my ears rang Chairman Mao's remarks: 'peasants, regardless of their blackened hands and their dung-encrusted feet, are still cleaner than bourgeois or petty-bourgeois intellectuals.' "

doubtlessly for a long time to come, the manufacture of sufficient hand tools will be a major problem for Communist China. Given the admission of these shortages, it can only be surmised that the number and supply of mechanical tools lags even further behind.

Several possible remedies have been suggested. One of these is to advocate closer analysis of foreign experiences. An article in *Ching-chi Yen-chiu (Economic Research)* of March, 1963, noted that the Japanese solution of utilizing electric power from the irrigation projects to run appliances linked to overhead tension wires might be studied profitably. But, basically, the government has tried to alleviate shortages of tools by an about-face appeal for the peasants to purchase their own tools, apparently in the knowledge that privately-owned tools will receive far better care and last longer.

Foreign Trade

In Comnunist China, as noted in the previous chapter, foreign trade must fulfill a diversity of duties. At least until recently, China, as a member of the socialist bloc, was expected to coordinate her trade to socialist needs. As Chia To-fu wrote in the June, 1959 *People's China:* "The aim of the nations embraced by this [world socialist] market is not profit, but mutual economic development and fraternal aid." At the same time, in trade relations with non-communist countries Peking must use economic agreements as a means to develop good will, to aid the national liberation movement, and to advance the international communist cause. Yet, these ideological considerations need not—and in fact did not—create a favorable trade balance so necessary for the accumulation of state capital. In China, at least by 1960, national economic programs had come to suffer from the effects of insufficient monetary funds. Consequently, foreign trade adjustments became a matter of vital interest if Peking was to obtain money to purchase grain for famine relief, while also meeting outstanding fiscal obligations.

The year 1959 had marked a critical juncture for Communist China's foreign trade policies. Peking was forced to order a retreat in the communalization programs in order to quell peasant unrest and stimulate agricultural production. Agricultural failures caused grave setbacks to industrialization programs, as factories suffered shortages of raw materials. With substandard production, the factories themselves were unable to provide the goods needed for those domestic and foreign sales which, in turn, should have furnished the revenue needed for actualization of expansion programs. On February 7, 1959, in Moscow, Chou En-lai and Khrushchev concluded a new agreement whereby the Soviet Union met part of the economic slack by pledging to help in the construction of 78 new enterprises. This agreement involved some US$1,250 millions in Soviet aid. In April, Li Fu-ch'un informed the National People's Congress that the 211 units planned for in the various existing programs had been combined into 166 units. Of these, 125 were to be sponsored by the Soviet Union, with construction to be completed by 1967.[12] Although trade with the USSR declined from the roughly 78 per cent of China's total foreign trade in the period of the First Five-Year Plan (1953–57) to only 59 per cent of the 1959 volume, the general view of Sino-Soviet economic relations appeared largely unchanged.

The abrupt reversal of this status which occurred in 1960 may be summarized in the words of the *People's Daily* editorial of December 4, 1963: "We also countered an unexpected difficulty . . . caused by Soviet authorities who, in July, 1960, seized the opportunity to bring pressure to bear upon us and extended the ideological differences between the Chinese and Soviet Parties to the sphere of state relations." In that month, the USSR ordered the immediate withdrawal of all Soviet technicians working on the mainland and, according to Chinese Communist sources, also recalled the various plans and blue-prints for the Soviet-sponsored enterprises. Foreign trade between the two communist powers was necessarily affected by this blow to Peking's industrialization programs. Thus, in 1960, Soviet exports to China dropped to 84.8 per cent and imports to 76.3 per cent of the 1959 level. However, the categories of goods involved did not change substantially. The Soviet Union continued to send China heavy and other industrial equipment, including 1,579 tractors, and to receive agricultural goods, including 416,000 tons of rice. What was vitally affected by this curtailment was Communist China's ability to meet the annual loan repayment schedule of debts to the Soviet Union.[13] According to the April 8, 1961 issue of *Pravda*, the Soviets sought to alleviate pressures on the Chinese economy by rescheduling the approximately US $320 million 1960 installment over a five-year period, interest-free.

In 1961, Communist China's trade relationship with the Soviet Union continued to worsen. Soviet exports to China accounted for only 38.1 per cent of the 1959 level (or 45 per cent of the 1960 total), and imports from China declined to 49.6 per cent of the 1959 level. More importantly, the nature of the commodities exchanged underwent alteration. For example,

[12] One of these enterprises was the Paotou steel complex, which is China's most modern and highly productive center.

[13] Despite the decline in trade volume, Communist China has enjoyed a favorable balance of trade with the Soviet Union since 1956. However, this arrangement may have been in the interests of enabling Peking to repay its debts to Moscow, incurred for military assistance during the Korean War and other aid. In any case, Peking's inability to repay its 1960 installment on time must be attributed to numerous causes other than the question of the withdrawal of Soviet technicians and plans. See, for example, the previous sections on the failures of communalization.

in 1961 the USSR shipped only 33 tractors to China, while it received only 2,300 metric tons of rice. Despite the curtailment of rice shipments to the Soviet Union, Communist China was still obliged to purchase some 6.5 million tons of grain from the West, particularly Canada and Australia. This purchase placed a further strain on Peking's cash assets.

By 1962, Communist China was seeking to replenish its cash reserves through such measures as the distribution of bonus food coupons to individuals who would exchange other currency for the yuan. In Hong Kong alone, some thirteen million food parcels had been mailed to needy relatives and friends on the mainland in 1961. Beginning in the summer of 1962, Peking encouraged the substitution of cash for material gifts by charging import duties of 20–180 per cent on any non-edible contents of gift packages.[14] At the same time, the fourteen Chinese Communist banks in Hong Kong offered free food coupons, redeemable on the mainland, at the rate of 100 pounds of rice for the equivalent of each US $50 exchanged. To accumulate additional cash reserves from the overseas Chinese, Peking also encouraged them to deposit funds in the Overseas Chinese Investment Corporations.[15] A shareholder is promised dividends at the rate of 0.8 per cent per annum, but if he surrenders half of his dividends, he is allowed to have supplies sent to individuals on the mainland.

The 1962 volume of trade for Communist China is estimated to have been about US $2,300 million, as compared to Japan's $10,636 million. China's volume was slightly higher than Singapore's, and smaller than the Malayan market. But, Peking maintained its export volume to the non-communist trading partners at 1961 levels, and in several cases was able to realize a favorable balance which could be applied to grain purchases totalling 4.6 million tons (as compared to the 1961 purchase of 6.5 million tons). However, trade with the socialist countries declined 20 per cent and Sino-Soviet trade probably fell by 25 per cent, as compared to 1961. Apparently, the Soviets continued to withhold heavy equipment. Perhaps for this reason, Peking showed renewed interest in the Japanese trade.[16]

[14] The rules for importation of food grain and nonstaple foodstuffs were revised on January 30, 1963, to provide maximums which could be brought or mailed to the mainland. For example, a person making a round trip could bring in food for his own needs plus 50 kg. of grain, with other limits placed on sugar and oils. See *Ch'iao-wu Pao* (*Overseas Chinese Affairs Bulletin*), No. 1, February, 1963.

[15] According to an item released by the Peking China News Service on January 18, 1963, these Investment Corporations had invested in over a hundred enterprises, including sugar refineries, textile factories, etc.

[16] Since Japan has never recognized Communist China, any trade agreement concluded by Japanese businessmen has been unofficial. By 1958, however, Japanese exports to Communist China had reached $41 million and imports $68.9 million. In May, 1958, the famous "Flag Incident" occurred. Against government approval, a Chinese Communist trade exhibit flew the national flag. When the flag was torn down by Japanese nationalists (again, without

On November 10 an agreement was concluded in Peking with a non-government Japanese trade mission headed by Tatsunosuke Takasaki, a ranking member of the Liberal-Democrat party and former minister of trade and industry. This agreement called for a trade volume of $450 million over a five-year period and ensured China of a source of much-needed machinery and some 450,000 tons of chemical fertilizer.

By 1963, it appeared that Communist China had weathered its foreign trade crisis. As both agricultural and industrial sectors registered slight increases, probably of 3 and 5 per cent respectively, Peking was able to increase its trade volume by about 5 per cent, or to a cash equivalent of about US $2.9 billions. This figure includes some $865 million in imports from non-communist countries (as compared to the Philippine import volume of $587 million for a population of about 30 million) and the purchase of another 5.7 million tons of grain. Trade with the socialist countries accounted for about 43 per cent of Peking's total volume.

In 1964, Communist China further improved its trading position. According to a UN survey, in some sectors this improvement was "spectacular." For example, during the first six months of 1964, Peking sent $137 million in goods to Japan and received $123 million in products. A far better cash surplus was registered in the Hong Kong trade, including profits from the further exploitation of the overseas Chinese market. Communist China maintains some 31 retail sales outlets in Hong Kong. Often food and textiles from the mainland are sold below the world market price. The 1964 exchange of diplomatic recognition with France opened up new avenues of trade, and several Chinese economic missions were sent there and to other western countries to study local enterprises and negotiate contracts. A share of the profits from favorable trade balances was employed to step up aid to underdeveloped nations. While about $100 million dollars was being advanced to such countries as the Congo (Brazzaville), Ghana and Ceylon, Chou En-lai reminded the NPC Standing Committee on April 25, 1964, that Chinese aid had no strings attached, and was intended to help the recipient increase its income and attain independence financially. All products exchanged, according to the Premier, were sold at world prices, and could be returned if unsatisfactory.

In 1965, the Chinese Communists continued to purchase wheat from Canada and Australia, and added such items as artificial fiber from Italy,

---

government sanction), Peking made the question of restitution a major issue. Apparently hoping to force a sort of de jure recognition, Peking demanded an apology from the Japanese government. On May 12, Communist China suspended all trade until such time as Japan should change its "attitude," renounce its "two-China" policy, and cease "interference" in normal trade relations. Gradually, however, the Chinese Communists restored relations on a limited basis with private Japanese concerns.

and copper from Chile. Exports to non-communist countries were about $880 million, and imports about $825 million. Favorable trade balances in several areas permitted Peking to make its final installment on Soviet loans, thus ending one strain on its cash reserves. Figures for 1966, indicate that Communist China's trade with non-communist nations increased by some 20 per cent, as compared to 1965. And the diversification of trading partners competing at world prices, rather than those set by Moscow, should further enhance Peking's position. With the exception of the possible effects of the cultural revolution, any appraisal of Communist China's foreign trade would have to conclude on an optimistic note. If agricultural production can hold its own with population increases while supplying needed raw materials to industry, and if heavy industrial equipment can be secured from non-communist trading partners, then Peking should be in a good position to use foreign trade as a weapon in her arsenal of devices designed to improve her position, aid the national liberation movement, and further the cause of international communism.

Planning and Finance

Two areas basic to Communist China's national economic readjustment are those of improving the central planning and banking systems. Particularly since 1963, the leadership has sought to improve its central planning apparatus at the highest levels. Essentially this has involved extension and specialization of planning organs and the assignment to them of leading, veteran personnel. In May, 1956, annual or short-term planning had been assigned to the new State Economic Commission under the jurisdiction of the State Council. This permitted the State Planning Commission to concentrate on long-term growth. The importance of this latter organization was substantially augmented late in 1963. Until then, its Chairman, Li Fu-ch'un, was the only CPC Politburo member on the staff. In October, 1963, Politburo member T'an Chen-lin and alternate members Teng Tzu-hui, Ch'en Po-ta and Po I-po were named deputy chairmen. Since Po I-po is also chairman of the State Economic Commission, the relationship between the two bodies is immediate. A State Capital Construction Commission, which was established in October, 1958, and abolished in 1961, was recreated in March, 1965, with Ku Mu as chairman. Also under the jurisdiction of the State Council, presumably this commission, together with the Commission for Economic Relations with Foreign Countries under the chairmanship of Chang Hsi-jo, shares in some degree in general economic planning.

The vast majority of the ministries and commissions under the jurisdic-

tion of the State Council participate in some way in economic work.[17]
Here, too, the trend has been toward specialization. For example, in
April, 1963, the State Council established a National Price Commission.
In February, 1965, the State Council divided the Ministry of Light Indus-
try into First- and Second-Ministries. In March, 1965, the Ministry of
Building was subdivided into a Ministry of Building and a Ministry of
Building Materials. With few exceptions, the various ministries, commis-
sions and bureaus of the State Council stand at the apex of networks of
related agencies which exist at every geo-political level.

By decision of this leadership, one major innovation to expedite financial
affairs was the re-establishment of the Agricultural Bank of China in 1964.
By order of the CPC Central Committee and the State Council, the Agricultural Bank then set up branch units at the various levels, often by absorbing the facilities of the lower units of the People's Bank of China.
These Agricultural Bank branches, whenever possible, are staffed by
experienced cadres and all policies are further regulated by the parent
People's Bank. The creation of this specialized system of banking facilities
for the rural areas was motivated by the need to expedite loans to the communes and their component brigades and teams. However, as noted in the
February 28, 1965 *Nung-ts'un Chin-jung* (*Rural Finance*), the Agricultural Bank branches were advised that "loans should be extended to those
who have the ability to repay." By common estimate, only about 30–40
per cent of the peasants would fall into this category; the remaining "poor"
or "middle" peasants could not be regarded as good security risks. Moreover, the facilities of the banks are seriously strained by the need to examine
individually the requests of millions of these peasants and to handle their
deposits from side-line production.

The rural credit cooperatives are designed to reinforce and extend the
facilities of the Agricultural Bank. As low level banks, theoretically owned
by their peasant stockholders, the credit cooperatives are empowered to
receive deposits and issue loans. Since they are under the direction of the
central People's Bank, the cooperatives have no federated structure.
Originally organized in the period of the land reform, the rural cooperatives
were absorbed by the commune structure in 1958, and re-established during
the post-1960 period of retrenchment. According to the *People's Daily* of

---

[17] The exceptions would be such agencies as the Commissions for Nationalities Affairs,
Physical Culture and Sports, Cultural Relations with Foreign Countries, and for the Overseas
Chinese; and the Ministries of Public Health, Higher Education, Culture, Internal Affairs and
Public Security. However, even these bodies may perform economic functions at times. One
example would be the work of the Overseas Chinese Commission in accumulating investment
funds.

July 11, 1963, there were then some 120,000 such cooperatives with total assets of 500 million yuan. By regulation, some 60 per cent of these assets must be kept on deposit in a branch of the People's Bank. A large share of the cooperative's assets comes from the deposits of the so-called rich peasants. However, requests for loans come from all the peasants. Obviously, as in the case of the Agricultural Bank, this creates a particular problem. Although the poor peasants are most in need of financial assistance, their ability to repay is questionable.[18] Many of the cooperatives, in the interests of survival, have therefore been reluctant to advance loans to this needy class.

Communist China must strive continually to improve its central planning mechanism and to make its fiscal agencies more efficient. At the lowest levels, it must see that loans are readily available to needy peasants, for without such state assistance, the peasants cannot substantially increase production. Yet, money circulated in the form of loans is temporarily non-productive in terms of state interest. Furthermore, as noted elsewhere, Peking must jealously guard her cash reserves and may regard any increase in personal loans as detrimental to national investment programs. Yet, if agricultural production—the key to the national economy—is to be raised, more funds must be made available for short-term loans. This dilemma will trouble the leadership for some time to come.

The Third Five-Year Plan should have commenced in 1963. In fact, at a conference in Shanghai in January of that year, Chou En-lai referred to "the nation starting the first year of its Third Five-Year Plan." In the October, 1963 issue of *Red Flag*, Chairman of the State Economic Commission Po I-po mentioned the successful completion of the Second Plan in 1962, "making socialist industry possible." Yet, in the same month, Ch'en Yi observed that a period of readjustment was still necessary before undertaking a long-term plan, possibly of five to ten years. The first session of the Third NPC on January 4, 1965 approved the 1965 Plan for the National Economy, noting that this was preparatory to introducing the Third Five-Year Plan in 1966. This Plan called for increases of 5 and 11 per cent respectively for agriculture and industry. To accomplish this, the state budget for 1965 was increased by 10 per cent over 1964.[19] The order of

[18] According to some Chinese Communist sources, about half the peasant's income now comes from side-line production. Western sources estimate this annual income to average only 60–80 yuan. Yet the purchase of an ox or mule may cost from several hundred to a thousand yuan, and even hand tools are dear in terms of income. Thus the peasant is obliged to seek outside assistance.

[19] As usual, the budget is said to be balanced. As noted in the previous chapter, this claim has been made ever since 1950 and even during the period of the Korean War. The Hong Kong *Ta-kung Pao* of September 8, 1964, however, did admit that prices had risen sharply during the 1959–61 economic disturbance.

priority for state investment remained; agriculture, light industry and heavy industry.

Although the basic cause for postponement of the Third Five-Year Plan was the need to combat ubiquitous economic problems, another factor was certainly that of strained economic relations with the Soviet Union. As economic planner Po I-po informed Anna L. Strong early in 1964, national planning would be delayed until the last of the national debt to the Soviet Union was repaid in 1965.[20] Another reason for delaying implementation of a comprehensive plan can be found in the continued resistance of the populace. Chou alluded to the "ceaseless generation" of "new bourgeois intellectuals and other new exploiters" in his December, 1964 report. More specifically, the Premier said that during the 1959–62 period of economic hardship "quite a few people actively advocated the extension of plots for private use and of free markets, the increase of small enterprises with sole responsibility for their own profits and losses, the fixing of output quotas based on the household, 'going it alone'. . . ." Thus Chou was led to repeat Mao Tse-tung's warning that "socialist society will cover a very long historical period." Yet, rising pressures, political as well as economic, increased the leadership's desire to foreshorten the time for socialist transformation. The cultural revolution became Mao Tse-tung's answer to the "new exploiters."

OPPOSITION TO ECONOMISM THROUGH CULTURAL REVOLUTION

Despite the general improvement in the economy by 1964–65, the Chinese Communists viewed with alarm the manifested and apparently growing tendency to "restore capitalism" as represented by economism.[21] As noted in Chapter 8, the military was given increased responsibility over the economic sector, as part of the socialist education drive to improve

[20] Chou suggested to the Third NPC that Communist China would pay its final installment on the Soviet debt on or ahead of schedule in 1965. He also noted that Communist China had contributed more aid to "socialist and independent countries" in the same period than the total of her Soviet obligation. This would suggest that ideological considerations were given first priority.

[21] In retrospect, it is apparent that the Party opponents of the fanatical policies of the Great Leap and communes who were denounced at the 1959 Lushan Conference of the Central Committee had many supporters who were not then identified. As the denunciation of "Khrushchev revisionism" became more heated, it was likely that the CPC would increase its vigilance against any Chinese adherents of this line. Too, plans to begin the Third Five-Year Plan in 1966, doubtlessly touched off an inter-Party debate over the wisdom or feasibility of restoring the communes to their original status. And the possibility of Mao's passing certainly heightened the convictions of the differing schools.

production by first intensifying political loyalties. Early in 1964, the PLA began to establish political departments in many of the economic organizations. The necessity of this step was indicated by *Ta-kung Pao's* March 14, 1965 reference to the fact that before the PLA increased its activities even in the branches of the People's Bank "for many years it was only at times of great political campaigns that anyone paid any attention to ideological work." The CPC concurrently determined to improve Party contacts with the peasants and workers by intensifying its policy of sending cadres to participate in labor assignments. For example, as part of this 1964 campaign to "take off your shoes and go to the fields," in Szechuan province, Party First Secretary Li Ta-chang announced that cadres at all grades would spend two-thirds of their time in labor on special experimental farms. Yet *People's Daily* admitted on January 16, 1965, that the CPC's re-education drive was progressing too slowly. "At present," the Party organ noted, "some enterprises are carrying out the struggle, but most of them are still in the preparatory stage."

"Socialist education," in 1964–65, meant that every economic organization should promote learning from the thought of Mao Tse-tung. In the trade unions, for example, a general meeting held in Peking under Party supervision in March, 1965, decided that "the trade union officials will learn the thought of Mao." And the improvement in agricultural and industrial production and in foreign trade, in 1965, was attributed to correctly mastering Mao's ideas. But the Party press also stepped up its publication of incidents revealing the failure of economic units to learn from Mao. For example, the Canton *Nan-fang Jih-pao* of December 12, 1965, recited at length a revelation of bourgeois mentality in the Designing Institute of the municipality. By building a three-story tea house with a ballroom, and using excessive decoration in workers' apartments, the designers squandered some 450,000 yuan. By destroying inferior cloth, a knitting factory in the same city was accused on January 14, 1966, of wasting some 50,000 yuan worth of usable goods. These, and innumerable other related incidents, showed that economic planning and development were suffering fron an inclination to restore bourgeois standards at the expense of socialist goals.

The CPC Central Committee's 16 Point Decision Concerning the Great Proletarian Cultural Revolution, adopted on August 8, 1966, to formally mark the transformation of the socialist education drive to the stage of cultural revolution, explicitly indicated the fundamental relationship between political and economic goals and practices. Point 14, "Take Firm Hold of the Revolution and Stimulate Production," emphasizes:

> The aim of the great proletarian cultural revolution is to revolutionize peoples' ideology and as a consequence to achieve greater, faster, better and more economical

results in all fields of work. If the masses are fully aroused and proper arrangements are made, it is possible to carry on both the cultural revolution and production without one hampering the other, while guaranteeing high quality in all our work. The great proletarian cultural revolution is a powerful motive force for the development of the social productive forces in our country. Any idea of counterposing the great cultural revolution against the development of production is incorrect.

The followers of Mao Tse-tung have employed a word previously used by Lenin—"economism"—to designate the principles and practices of that "handful of persons in authority who take the capitalist road" in collusion with the reactionary bourgeois elements.[22] As defined by *Hung-ch'i* (no. 2, 1967), economism is "a form of bribery" which "uses bourgeois spontaneity to replace proletarian revolutionary consciousness . . . and capitalist ownership to replace socialist ownership." Directly counter to Marxism-Leninism and Mao's thought, it is a reflection of Khrushchev revisionism, which employs the "sugarcoated bullets" of economic benefits to sway the masses. It is an attempt to transform the political struggle to the economic plane. Among the practices commonly associated with economism are:

The reactionary elements freely squander the wealth of the state, arbitrarily increase wages and amenities, wantonly distribute all kinds of funds and material and stir up the masses to take over public buildings by force as privately owned dwellings. They instigate violent struggle, create incidents, incite a number of workers to desert their posts in production. . . .

Ambitious to restore capitalism and "the old semi-feudal and semi-colonial path," the practioners of economism reject the dictatorship of the proletariat, propagate individualism and urge class conciliation. The *People's Daily* editorial of April 8, 1967, which denounced Liu Shao-ch'i (although not by name), further indicates that those who now foster economism have long opposed "Marxism-Leninism and Mao Tse-tung's thought." Among their past crimes are those of "singing the praises of exploitation by the capitalists and applauding the rich-peasant economy, opposing the socialist transformation of agriculture, handicrafts and capitalist industry . . . opposing the Party's general line for building social-ism, the people's communes and the great leap forward." They have also advocated the extension of private plots and free markets and fixing output quotas on the basis of the household.

The CPC Central Committee has left no doubt as to the importance it attaches to winning worker and peasant support to the cultural revolution. In its organ, *Red Flag* (no. 1, 1967), the CC called them the "structure"

---

[22] Lenin early used the word to describe non-revolutionary worker organizations, and at least by 1961 (see the Peking *Daily Worker*, July 8, 1961), the Chinese Communists were denouncing "neo-capitalists" with this term.

supporting the "superstructure" of schools and cultural circles. Although the latter are more frequently considered the core groups of the cultural revolution, in Marxist logic the success or failure of the PLA, the Red Guards and allied intellectuals must depend entirely upon the cooperation of the worker and peasant. While the lures of economism are perhaps superficially better suited and more attractive to the worker, the peasant, too, has succumbed to the promise of personal incentive.

Caught up in the frenzy associated with the cultural revolution, peasants have abandoned communal labor assignments, stolen from collective funds and refused to honor state commitments. In January, 1967, peasants stormed the state banks in the Nanchang area of Kiangsi province. In that province, the new revolutionary rebel headquarters was forced to recall all private peddlers' licenses as the peasants refused to sell to the state cooperatives at state-set prices. [23] In the outlying counties of Shanghai, peasants struggled among themselves over the distribution of communal income, as they opposed the setting aside of reserve funds and demanded a personal share in the funds and property already accumulated. Similar cases were reported in Heilungkiang, where, according to *People's Daily* (January 27, 1967), the enemies of the cultural revolution "destroyed the foundations of our country's rural socialist economy," and even in the outskirts of Peking.

Peasants have also waged heated battles against the Red Guards in some areas. Peasant Scarlet Guards (or counterrevolutionaries) resisted the Red Guards in the Nanchang area of Kiangsi, and the surburban areas of Peking. Of even greater consequence, the peasants have rejected the CPC's classification of them as "rural proletariat" to attack urban workers, whom they believe to enjoy better living standards. In Shanghai, in particular, Party sources admit that the three million peasants in the adjacent counties were duped into warfare with the workers. According to the *Wen-hui Pao* of January 20, 1967, "one of the principal leading members of the city's Party Committee" was responsible for this by telling representatives of peasant rebel groups that "the workers are out to rebel against you, you should rebel right back." But it is doubtful if the peasant needed the encouragement of those "who sit on top of the mountain to watch the tigers fight," since there are indications that they have long resented the easier life of the factory worker.

[23] The refusal of the peasants to sell to the state organs is apparently widespread. On February 1, 1967, a "Finance and Commerce System" representing some 17 rebel revolutionary organizations—but not identified with any state body—issued a nationwide order. This directive, if implemented, would virtually destroy all private commerce—called "speculation"—to force the peasant to sell to the state purchasing agencies. Unless implemented, not only will food prices rise, but it will be extremely difficult to provide sufficient food for the urban areas.

The prevalence of peasant upheaval and rebellion was particularly dangerous at the time of the 1967 spring planting. Thus, *People's Daily* (February 11, 1967) cautioned that, since agriculture is the foundation of the national economy, "the 1967 harvest will directly affect the cultural revolution." As PLA forces were rushed to help in the spring planting, the Party leadership determined that the cultural revolution would have to be temporarily suspended in the rural areas. Or as Chou En-lai informed the Conference of Poor and Lower-Middle Peasants in Peking on March 19, 1967: "In the busy spring farming season, power at the production team and production brigade level should not be seized, even in cases where power needs to be seized."

The CPC's suspension of revolutionary activities in the rural areas indicates a basic dilemma. To win the support of the peasant masses, the CPC Central Committee has insisted that the poor and lower-middle peasants are "the main forces of revolution and production" in the rural areas. They are charged with apprehending those "landlords, rich peasants, counter-revolutionary bad elements, rightists and former cadres," and supervising their reform through labor. Even in the cities, the new revolutionary rebel organizations have decreed that the peasants in the countryside should take the lead in reforming bad elements in urban areas. For example, the Shanghai *Wen-hui Pao* of January 20, 1967 declared that "the chief criminals within the city Party Committee should be handed over to the masses in the suburban counties for criticism." On the other hand, without the authority and discipline of the Party the peasants probably will not fulfill production needs. Now suspicious of all cadres, the peasants will find it difficult to accept the Party's directive (such as in the February 11, 1967 *People's Daily*), that even cadres known to have made mistakes (i.e., to have opposed the cultural revolution) should be allowed to "lead the work" in spring planting. Consequently, the PLA will probably have to increase its role as a stabilizing force.

The leaders of the cultural revolution have sponsored a host of orders and regulations to restore order and improve production in the countryside. The "three in one" committees and the PLA local garrisons have directed, such as in the joint order for Kweichow province of February 20, 1967, that all peasants who have gone to the cities must return immediately to their communes; that the local militia protect public granaries and other buildings; that the distribution of seed and grain from public supplies be suspended; and that the slaughtering of draft animals be prohibited. Revolutionary rebel committees associated with the State Council, such as that of the Ministry of Water Conservancy and Electric Power, have promised harsh punishment to anyone who steals state supplies or incites the workers. The State Council itself issued an order on January 29, 1967, to cancel the traditional lunar new year holidays, in order to push the cultural revolution to new heights, and alleviate certain economic pressures. But the leadership has also issued contradictory orders at times, which reveal instability in the rural areas. For example, at the September 15, 1966 Red Guard rally in Peking over which Mao himself presided, Chou En-lai cautioned that workers and commune members must remain at their posts, while students (i.e., the Red Guards) were prohibited from entering factories or communes. As *People's Daily* added in an editorial of the same date, the workers and peasants were perfectly capable of waging their own cultural revolution. Yet, by December, 1966 (see *Red Flag* no. 1, 1967), the CPC urged that students and cultural workers go to the farms and factories "in a planned and organized way" to aid the cultural revolution and abet production. Presumably, the fulfillment of this latter instruction led to the peasant-Red Guard violence already noted. Thus, the leadership may be forced to once again recall its "shock troops," and students have already been ordered back to their classrooms or to other assignments.

Despite the violence and disruption associated with the cultural revolution in several of the provinces, the leaders claim that agricultural production has actually increased. Summarizing the supposedly collective opinions of Communist China's peasants and cadres concerning the effect of the cultural revolution on agricultural production, NCNA noted on December 27, 1966, "there may be ten thousands of factors behind the increased production, but the cardinal one is the holding high of the great red banner of Mao Tse-tung's thought." Although "severe natural calamities" beset many sections of the country, grain and cotton production in 1966 were said to be the highest in China's history. For example, Szechwan province reported total grain output to be 1.5 million tons higher and cotton yield 20 per cent greater than in 1965. Nine Anhwei counties registered a 30 per cent increase in grain crops. By mid-December, the Chinese Communists claimed that an upsurge in procurement and deliveries of grain to state granaries represented over 90 per cent fulfillment of state purchasing plans. On February 20, 1967, the Ministry of Food announced that the annual 1966-67 grain-purchasing plan (which goes from April 1 to March 31) had been overfulfilled by 104.5 per cent.

Production increases and improvement of per hectare yield have been attributed in part to massive reclamation and irrigation programs, which have, in turn, been supported by the PLA. "Taking the country as a whole," NCNA noted on January 6, 1967, "the newly increased area of land assured of irrigation and the area of various kinds of improved low-lying fields are more than those in any previous year." According to a January 13, 1967 dispatch, PLA troops themselves were responsible for reclaiming 40,000 hectares of wasteland in 1966. Similarly, the increased availability and lower price of mechanized equipment for the communal brigades and teams contributed to making 1966 a bumper year. For example, Peking statistics show a 30–40 per cent improvement in the supply of pumping equipment, chemical fertilizer and pesticides, as compared to 1965, and a 60 per cent increase in sales of such semi-mechanized farm implements as hand tractors. Nevertheless, official sources are careful to repeat (such as in a January 8, 1967 NCNA bulletin), that "the good harvests are attributable to machines, but they are primarily a victory of Mao Tse-tung's thought."

The trouble in the agricultural sector associated with the cultural revolution also and perhaps even more crucially has affected industry and communications. In Shanghai, in early January, 1967, virtually all economic activity ground to a halt as counterrevolutionaries shut off electricity at the municipal power plant.[24] With the Northern Area Marine Transport Administration and its subsidiary Shanghai Port Administration in the control of counterrevolutionary forces, dock workers in Shanghai refused to load or unload ships. Although the temporary assignment of Red Guards as longshoremen alleviated the situation at the docks, foreign shippers continued to complain of long servicing delays.

In 1966, movements of bands of Red Guards by railway severely taxed Communist China's already strained transportation system. After November 3, when Lin Piao ordered that the Red Guards should walk to their assignments, bands of "long marchers" were praised by the leadership as models of austerity. By December, the State Council had directed that Red Guards would no longer be transported to Peking by train, in an effort to resume normal railway operations. Yet, by late January, 1967, personnel in the Ministry of Railways were accused of promoting economism, as the leadership sought to recover from a series of strikes on several of the major lines. Peking admitted disruption of service on the Shanghai-Hangchow, Hangchow-Ningpo, Canton-Amoy, Shanghai-Nanking and Ningpo-Peking lines. Although service was later reported restored, as Red Guards defeated and replaced Scarlet Guards, with the controlling influence of the PLA, many of the "three in one" committees were obliged to resort to cancellation of travel permits to ease the strain on the railways.[25]

On January 11, 1967, *People's Daily* admitted trouble in factories in

[24] Shortages of coal, or the regime's inability to transport it to certain areas, probably contributed to this "plot" to stop operations at the power plant.

[25] It should be noted the disruption of rail service is not only critical in terms of domestic interests, but also presents a problem for Peking in its foreign relations. Disruption of service in the Northeast, on the lines controlled by the Harbin Railway Administration, probably affected regular delivery of goods to North Vietnam. This would inadvertently strengthen the Soviet charge that the Chinese Communists have impeded the flow of goods to Ho Chi-minh.

Mukden, Sian, Chengtu, Chungking, Hangchow and Canton. Work stoppages and strikes have plagued such factories as the Peking Number One Machine-Tool Plant, the Shenyang Rolling Mill, and the Sian Number One Auto Spare Parts Plant. These admissions are only representative and symptomatic of similar opposition to Party and state controls in countless other industrial enterprises. They also point to a new factor in Communist China's economic life. Prior to the cultural revolution strikes were practically unheard of in Communist China. Although the Red Guard exodus from the classrooms will certainly have a long term adverse effect on economic development, workers' time off the job can spell disaster to present production quotas.

One of the most appealing mass tactics of opponents of the cultural revolution has been to promote worker demands for higher pay or better working conditions. In Shansi, for example, corrupt members of the provincial Party committee reportedly supplied some workers with cars, houses and money, and then encouraged some 10,000 other workers to strike for equal benefits. In many factories, workers were encouraged to leave their jobs to participate actively in the cultural revolution. Upon returning to their assignments, they found their places taken by Red Guards, hired at higher wages. Understandably, these workers then demanded similar pay increases. In some cases, these demands were not only met, but as in the Shanghai Port Administration, the raises were made retroactive.

In addition to rising discontent and/or expectations on the part of the workers, the practice of granting raises and bonuses to many workers immediately affected distribution of goods in the urban areas. With more money to spend, workers emptied the shelves of many shops, and caused shortages which could not be met immediately by erratic factory or farm sales. But the most serious aspect of this increase in circulation of funds was the drain that it placed on the state banks. Apparently some banks would not, or could not, honor all drafts. Consequently, workers and peasants stormed these institutions and PLA troops had to be assigned to protect state property. Most of the new "three in one" committees temporarily were forced to freeze all circulating funds. The Shansi Revolutionary Rebel General Headquarters ordered all funds to be frozen on January 14, 1967, the same day this "three in one" committee seized power. Similar orders were given in Kweichow province and in Shanghai, although in the latter case the committee was quick to point out that the regulation did not apply to personal savings accounts. Moreover, as the *Wen-hui Pao* emphasized on January 20, 1967, "the signatures of the handful of persons in the Party who are in authority and are taking the capitalist road on papers relating to economic matters are declared null and void as of today." While the revolutionaries of Shanghai were cancelling all previous state contracts, the mass meeting in Peking on January 18, 1967, of revolutionary rebel finance and trade groups attempted to ease the situation. With Chou En-lai, Li Hsien-nien and other leaders in attendance, the representatives determined that all pay raises granted during the cultural revolution, (or, more precisely, as a result of workers' demands), were invalid.

Since the directives of the Shanghai Revolutionary Rebel Organizations have won the explicit approval of Mao, the CPC Central Committee and its Military Commission, and the State Council, these regulations may be taken as representative of the leadership's plan to restore order in the ndustrial sector. A Shanghai directive of January 9, 1967, to be carried out by the public security forces, demanded that the workers restore all public buildings and return to their own homes, and return all stolen goods. Workers, their appetites whetted by previous raises and bonuses, were told to elect their own cultural revolution representatives. The Shanghai committee sternly insisted that all matters pertaining to wages and benefits "shall be discussed at a later stage of the movement," presumably with these elected delegates. In its March 18, 1967 Letter to Workers and Staff and Revolutionary Cadres in Industrial and Mining Enterprises, the CPC Central Committee directed "to firmly uphold the 8-hour day," while carrying out the cultural revolution "outside of working hours."

As workers return to their productive assignments, the situation will remain tense. For example, when the elements who opposed the cultural revolution sought to wreck havoc in the factories by causing slow-downs or stoppages, they told the workers that all who did not leave to participate in the cultural revolution would be suspect. (Similarly, they encouraged other workers to pose as "ultra leftists" by disrupting power supplies and transportation.) Such workers, victimized or duped by the counterrevolutionaries, according to *People's Daily* of December 26, 1966, are to be reinstated and given all back pay. On the other hand, employees who resist the culture revolution are to be punished by salary cuts or, if necessary, dismissal. Although *Red Flag* (no. 15, 1966) warned against the use of force during this readjustment, hostility and violence are bound to occur. Even the "model workers" are now a source of potential danger to the CPC. As *Red Flag* (no. 2, 1967), testified: "some labor models are afraid of mistakes and afraid of losing their honor. For this reason, they appear hesitant . . . and lack the determination and courage necessary for revolutionary rebellion." In short, the CPC has by no means reconciled its twin objective of having the worker both red and expert.

The proponents of the cultural revolution have nevertheless claimed important gains in the industrial sector, similar to those reported for agriculture. In Shanghai, following the January revolution, and despite all the admissions of economic dislocation associated with it, gross industrial output was said to have risen 10.7 per cent, as compared to January, 1966. January targets for forgings, rolled stock, hand tractors, cotton cloth, paint, paper, etc. were reported as overfulfilled. Nationwide, the eleventh plenum of the Eighth CPC Central Committee announced, on August 12, 1966, "on the industrial front, not only have big increases been registered in the output and variety of products, but their quality has also greatly improved." Although the cultural revolution took enormous energies during the second half of 1966, by year's end gross industrial output was said to be more than 20 per cent higher than in 1965, when the iron and steel, machine-building, mining and other enterprises had all surpassed their production quotas. Proudly reporting the achievement of complete self-sufficiency in petroleum products, on December 30, 1966, NCNA declared that, both in quantity and variety, Communist China was now able to build all equipment scheduled under the Third Five-Year Plan (1966–70). At the end of the first quarter of 1967, many enterprises such as the Kweichow Diesel Engine Plant, the Shanghai Number Six Machine Tool Plant, the Shenyang Metallurgical Plant, and other factories located in the troubled areas, reported to have already equalled half of their total 1966 production, while reducing costs by about 10 per cent.

By mid-1967, the cultural revolution had already been responsible for several organizational modifications in the economic sector. Although the basic system has remained intact, and probably will endure, these changes indicate that the regime must improvise to meet current challenges. For example, "revolutionary rebel committees" have been introduced into most, if not all, of the ministries and agencies under the State Council. These committees, such as those of the Ministry of Water Conservancy and Electric Power, collaborate with related mass organizations, such as the State Council's Revolutionary Mass Organization of Water and Soil Conservation Committee. However, any original authority which these committees may have enjoyed, has apparently been reduced. On February 15, 1967, for example, Li Hsien-nien reportedly informed delegates of the Revolutionary Rebel Committee for Central Finance and Trade Systems, which was apparently formed at a January 18 Peking rally of some 100,000 people, that their function would consist solely of transmitting instructions from higher to lower levels and reporting back. The committee, which had assigned some 70 people to two-month investigations of 14 cities, was instructed by Chou En-lai on February 17, to confine its activities entirely to investigation and study. Even so, this committee has fared far better than most similar organizations.

The CPC Central Committee and the State Council have ordered an end to such nationwide groups formed early in the cultural revolution as the

National Rebel General Corps of Red Laborers. This body, which for a time issued directives jointly with the Ministry of Labor and the All-China Federation of Trade Unions, was subsequently accused of fostering economism. Similarly, the ACFTU's role has been greatly diminished, although the organization presumably still survives and will undergo massive rebuilding. [26] The more enduring organizational form would seem to be the so-called "frontline commands" to stimulate production. A form of the "three in one" alliance advocated for state organization, the "front line command" is a loose mass unit of outstanding workers, leading cadres and PLA personnel which was established originally at the county level to take the lead in the 1967 spring planting. It is, of course, subordinated to the provincial revolutionary committee.

The foregoing analysis is meant to indicate, in summary form, that Communist China still has enormous problems to solve before its economic machine can function efficiently to meet national needs. China is still basically an agrarian country and suffers from a shortage of national assets. If no mass movement proves effective in controlling the size of the population, then agricultural mechanization must be developed to a point where the agrarian sector can support food, industrial and foreign trade needs comfortably. The epic plans, and epic failures of the commune system and the Great Leap for industry may have taught the Chinese Communist leadership that economic development requires more realistic programs and will take more time. In this sense, perhaps the much-utilized tactic of "two steps forward, one step back" could be applied to economic development since 1958. For despite the many failures, Peking has made progress and the present situation is better than at any time in China's past. There is a heavy industrial base, foreign trade has been diversified, and Peking is free of its indebtedness to the Soviet Union. If there is no war or major catastrophe, the now experienced leadership may be able to create further economic "miracles." But in the last analysis, Communist China's economic future is tied fundamentally to the Party and State's ability to regiment the population. The cultural revolution indicates that the people are leaning more and more to quasi-capitalistic methods and goals. And Peking cannot, or will not, permit a weakening of the Marxist-Leninist philosophy for economic successes.

The future of Communist China's economic development is, therefore, integrally tied to the leadership's ability to conclude the cultural revolution successfully. Ironically, perhaps the most effective prod the Chinese Communists have for mobilizing the workers and peasants in support of the cultural revolution is the said manifestation of "Khrushchev revisionism."

[26] One sign is that Liu Ning-i, head of the ACFTU, has been promoted to the CC Secretariat.

As worded in *Hung-ch'i* (no. 2, 1967): "The great proletarian cultural revolution must be carried out well before it can be insured that our country will not change its color, before the iron and steel, petroleum, cloth, grain, and cotton which we produce can belong to the people and serve them." In short, Mao believes that the fight against economism, as one of the pillars of the proletarian cultural revolution, is vital to the regime's political survial and economic progress.

CHAPTER 8

The Chinese Communist
Military System

It is hardly necessary to point out that the communist victory on the Chinese mainland in 1949 and the subsequent ascendency of the CPR in Asia and in world affairs are due primarily to the continued growth of military power nurtured by the Party and dedicated to the communist cause. The successful establishment and employment of this power is the result of efficient propagation and skilled implementation of communist militant principles, as advocated by Stalin and brought to an advanced stage of development by the thought of Mao Tse-tung.

In line with Stalin's emphasis on the importance of armed struggle in achieving a communist victory, Mao long ago recognized the indispensability of military strength. "The central task and the highest form of revolution," he wrote in 1938 in *The Problem of War and Strategy*, "is to seize political power by force, to solve problems by war." Much earlier, in his 1927 report on the peasant movement in Hunan, Mao had defined revolution simply as an "armed uprising—the violent action by which one class overthrows the authority of another." Hence Mao's leadership of the Chinese Communist movement has been characterized by sustained military action. Ever since its inception on August 1, 1927, the activities of the Chinese Red Army have accounted in large measure for the record growth of the CPC and its powerful grip on state power. Today, the Chinese Communists possess one of the largest peace-time armies in the world and the greatest potential manpower source. Peking's entry into the nuclear club has added a new dimension to the potential capabilities of the CPR military machine. And the thought of Mao Tse-tung indicates that the militant revolutionary approach will be promoted in Communist China for years to come.

In traditional Chinese society, philosophical, historical and social forces operated to discredit the professional military. As expressed in an old proverb, "just as you would not use good iron to make a nail, you would not use a good man to make a soldier." Even in the 19th century, when the Chinese were faced with the need to defend themselves against the Western powers, there was no substantial national army and the military class had little power and less prestige. The failures of Sun Yat-sen have often been attributed in part to his lack of a trained military force. After a few less significant forerunners, Whampoa Military Academy, established under the general terms of Soviet assistance promised in the 1923 Sun-Joffe agreement, provided the first officer corps with any stature in China.

The birth of the Chinese Communist military forces came only with the expulsion of the communists from the Kuomintang (KMT), or six years after the establishment of the Communist Party of China. On August 1, 1927—the date of the Nanchang Uprising—the Red Army was born out of the defection of units respectively under Chu Teh, Ho Lung, and Yeh T'ing, from the KMT or Nationalist forces. Together this amounted to about 30,000 troops. The Uprising itself was put down, but a substantial force, now called the Chinese Workers and Peasants Red Army, successfully escaped the KMT attack and ultimately reached Mao's mountain stronghold in the Chingkangshan area, Kiangsi province. The details of how this small band began the military exploits that culminated in the victory of communism in China are given in Chapter II. Here it may be mentioned that, when the People's Republic was established on October 1, 1949, the communist military forces—called the People's Liberation Army (PLA) since 1947—boasted a force of some five million men seasoned in the techniques of guerrilla warfare and dedicated to Marxism-Leninism. And it is important to stress that the PLA's power, then as now, rested less in an elite officer corps than in the Communist Party itself. In fact, it may be said that the personnel were interchangeable or identical, [1] and that from the beginning the military was regarded as an important arm of the Party. [2]

---

[1] For a detailed account of how the "civilian" Party chiefs can also dominate high offices in the government and military structures see the chapter on the State machine.

[2] This contrasts sharply with the system in the United States. For example, U. S. policy favors ultimate control of the military apparatus resting with civilians. The Secretary of Defense must be a civilian. Similarly, line officers are not encouraged to engage in political activities.

Less than a year after the end of the revolutionary struggle against the Nationalists, the PLA was, in fact, called upon to wage war in Korea. Several consequences ensued from this confrontation of the Chinese Communist troops called Chinese People's Volunteers with the Allied forces, not the least of which was proof of the "staying power" of the CPR. The approximately half a million Chinese troops who saw action in Korea illustrated again to the CPC Mao's theory of the superiority of men over weapons, and proved to the world that Communist China would have to be reckoned with as the foremost Asian military power. It was not until 1953 (although, as noted elsewhere, the last of the People's Volunteers did not return from Korea until 1958) that the Chinese Communists came to the problem of how to organize and train a peace-time military force.

Following the passage of the 1954 Constitution, in February, 1955, the Chinese Communists took a series of important steps concerning the organization and operation of the military forces. In accordance with Article 103 of the Constitution, the NPC Standing Committee adopted an amended draft of a national conscription law on February 7. Nation-wide discussion of this law was completed at the end of April, 1955, and its final adoption and proclamation followed on July 30, 1955. Secondly, on February 8, the same body adopted the Regulations on the Services of the Officers of the Chinese People's Liberation Army, which was promulgated as law by Mao on the same day.

These new regulations were admittedly based on Soviet practices and were drafted only after consulting "advanced Soviet experience." The reason for compulsory military service, according to General Nieh Jung-chen, was to unify the country and consolidate communist power. Too, the burdens of military service could be more equitably distributed, and the size of the standing army reduced, thereby releasing more manpower and funds for economic construction. But the most important reason was the need for trained men in wartime. Reviewing the state of tension, Nieh declared:

American imperialism . . . continues to adopt a hostile aggressive policy toward the Chinese people. . . . For this reason, we must regain our territory of Taiwan and safeguard our national security. This obliges us to have sufficient reserves whom we can mobilize at any moment to smash imperialist armed aggression victoriously. If we were to continue to follow the voluntary service system, although we maintained a large standing army and had an excess of troops in peace-time, we should certainly have shortages of servicemen when the imperialists started a war of aggression against us, because there would be no reserves.

Together with the reorganization of the People's Revolutionary Military Council (PRMC) into the more professional National Defense Council (NDC), and the creation of the Ministry of National Defense (NMD) within the State Council, these new regulations placed the military system of Communist China on a regular and permanent basis. Moreover, the justification in terms of omnipresent threats from "U. S. imperialism" has remained a constant factor in military planning and policies.

ORGANIZATION OF THE REGULAR ARMED FORCES

According to Article 4 of the Draft Conscription Law, "the armed forces of the CPR are composed of various arms of the Chinese People's Liberation Army." Unlike the Western countries, the Chinese Communists do not maintain separate branches for the navy and/or air force. Instead, these forces constitute components of the PLA, together with the infantry, cavalry, artillery, armored corps, engineers, railway corps, signal corps, technical troops, and public security forces. Article 7 of the Conscription Law differentiated the terms of service for non-commissioned officers and privates as following: 3 years for the army and public security forces; 4 years for the air force, coast guard and seaborne security forces; and 5 years for the seaborne forces of the navy. These terms, it should be noted, are longer than those required in Western countries and even exceed the Soviet term of conscription in some cases. Moreover, on January 19, 1965, recognizing the problem of adequate training, particularly in the case of pilots, technicians and other highly skilled personnel, the terms of required service were lengthened to 4 years for the infantry, 5 years for special forces, security troops, the air force and land-based navy personnel, and 6 years for the seaborne sailors.

The 1955 Conscription Law also provided that non-commissioned officers or privates who had enlisted prior to the Law's promulgation would be demobilized and put on the reserve list or retired by stages (Article 14). *People's Daily* of March 19, 1955, described the send-off given to these demobilized servicemen as they returned to civilian life. By December 10 of that year, according to the *Kiangsu Peasants Gazette*, Nanking, 4,510,000 soldiers of the PLA had already been demobilized. Simultaneous preparations were carried out for the first wave of draftees who, according to Article 19 of the Law, were to be selected from November 1, 1955, to the end of February, 1956. The young men of China were urged to study the Conscription Law, register for military service, and respond to the conscription call.

For commissioned officers, the 1955 Regulations on the Service of Officers established an elaborate hierarchy of ranks and a system of functional classifications to bring the Chinese counterpart closer to the Soviet model. Four grades were provided: (1) marshals, (2) generals, (3) field-grade officers, and (4) company-grade officers (Article 7). "Marshal" was considered more as a state title, while the others were related to a particular service. Thus, one might be a "Marshal of the People's Republic of China," but only a "General" of the Air Force" or a "Colonel of the Public Security Forces." The rank of "Supreme Marshal" was reserved to the Supreme Commander "who has attained particularly outstanding merit in organizing the people's armed forces of the nation and leading the armed forces in revolutionary wars," while the rank of "Marshal" was bestowed on those "who have particularly outstanding merit in organizing and leading the people's armed forces or in commanding armies in the field" (Article 9). Another special feature was the establishment of four levels of rank within each grade below marshal, rather than the three levels common in the west. For example, the rank of colonel general was introduced between that of lieutenant general and general, as in the Soviet system; in the field grade, a senior colonel was placed above full colonel; and in the company grade, a senior captain was introduced. Ranks up to general were further classified in these professional categories: commanding officers and political officers, technical officers, quartermasters, medical officers, veterinary officers, judge advocates, and administrative officers (Article 8).

The proper authority for conferment of rank—or demotion from it, should such a penalty be necessary—varied according to respective levels. The NPC Standing Committee alone could determine the rank of marshal, which was then ordered by the Chairman of the CPR. General grade officers were to be approved by the State Council. The Ministry of National Defense promoted and demoted at the field grade level, while field commanders were given this power for company grades (Articles 18 and 19). In all cases, selection or promotion of officers was to be based on "their political quality and professional ability" (Article 25). The first actual nomination and appointment of officers to fill these newly created ranks took place on September 27, 1955, when Mao, acting on the decision of the Standing Committee of the NPC, conferred the title of marshal on ten military leaders. [3] At the same time Chou En-lai, exercising the appointive power of the State Council, conferred the ranks of General, Colonel General, Lieutenant General and Major General on an undisclosed number of officers. The rank of Supreme Marshal, apparently created for Mao himself, remained vacant.

On May 22, 1965, the NPC Standing Committee, allegedly in the interest of unity, repealed the detailed regulations it had issued in 1955. On May 24, the State Council announced a set of new regulations which abolish

[3] They were Chu Teh, P'eng Teh-huai (now purged), Lin Piao, Liu Po-ch'eng, Ho Lung, Ch'en Yi, Lo Jung-huan (now deceased), Hsü Hsiang-ch'ien, Nieh Jung-chen and Yeh Chien-ying.

most visible distinctions between the various branches of the PLA, as well as between officers and their men. All military and security forces have been ordered to wear only a red star on their hats and a red badge on their collars. Epaulettes or other symbols of an officer's rank have been abolished, including "western style" uniforms. Naval forces have been issued dark grey uniforms similar to those of the army divisions. On June 6, 1965, the Ministry of National Defense issued an order that all reference to military titles was to be abolished. Troops were instructed to refer to officers by using their full name and job titles, or when the latter is unknown, the title of "comrade."

The decision to abolish all distinctions of rank was probably taken as a result of several factors. Some analysts believe it reflects an attempt to disassociate the organization of the PLA from Soviet models, as Sino-Soviet relations have worsened. The principal determinant, however, was doubtlessly a desire to revive and promote the ideal of democracy in the ranks which characterized the Chinese Communist military during the revolutionary struggle. Consequently, the decision would represent an implementation of the earlier thought and practice of Mao Tse-tung. Moreover, the announcement of the NPC Standing Committee and the State Council might be said to mark only a new stage in a trend which has been growing since 1958.

At the time of the Great Leap and commune movements, and akin to the theme that all people should seek to "go to the countryside" or participate actively in manual labor despite their regular working assignments, the General Political Department of the PLA ordered that all officers must spend one month annually in the ranks. Just as the college professor was to learn from the peasants by working in the fields, the officers were to experience new revolutionary fervor by intimate association with their men. By October, 1958, about 10,000 officers, including more than 70 generals, were reported to have already completed their one month service in the ranks.

The concept of promoting good spirit by close union of officers and men, through required service in the ranks on the part of the officer class, continued during the 1959–61 period of economic dislocation. For example, as reported in the PLA's *Bulletin of Activities* (number 2, January 3, 1961), Lin Piao ordered that a third of all cadres in higher offices were to spend some time at the company level.[4] Although *People's Daily* of July 29, 1963, admitted that some objections were still being voiced, the order that

[4] The US Department of State released 29 copies of the *Kung-tso T'ung-hsün* (*Bulletin of Activities*) through the Library of Congress on August 5, 1963. This secret military journal of the PLA General Political Department was issued irregularly and distributed only to selected Party cadres. Some indication of the importance of this source is gained from the sixth issue, which specified that copies were to be given only to higher

officers serve a part of the year in the ranks has remained effective. For example, the Canton *Nan-fang Jih-pao* of January 5, 1966, noted that 83 per cent of the eligible leading PLA cadres spent from two to four months in the ranks in 1965.

Several other policies have been introduced to promote the idea of democracy within the PLA. For example, NCNA on June 7, 1965, noted that, since 1960, each PLA unit at the company level has formed a Committee of Revolutionary Armymen under the Party branch to invite criticism and promote improvement. Similarly, an Economic Committee in each company, comprised of elected men from the ranks, supervises such areas of general welfare as the purchase and preparation of food. A series of orders has attempted to eliminate any cruelty in the conduct of officers toward their men (for details, see "Morale of the Military").

Although the PLA continues to bestow decorations on individual soldiers for meritorious performance, even this sign of personal distinction has been downplayed. More commonly, medals or other decorations are given to whole companies for collective efforts. These rewards are based upon political loyalty as well as performance and apparently have been bestowed generously. For example, the February 1, 1962, *People's Daily* reported that "several hundred thousand five-quality soldiers were decorated." [5] The criteria for distinguishing a good company were set by Lin Piao and reported by *People's Daily* on April 29, 1962, as sound political thought, the three-eight spirit, good military performance and sound management. The policy of recognizing the work of separate companies is intended to encourage competition among the various units, just as individual awards should promote greater personal efforts. [6] Together with the other practices of officers' service in the ranks and the abolition of any symbol of superior rank, this measure is intended to promote the notion of democracy

---

officials in the regiments, or to those of the rank of major or above in the schools, and that the CPD Secret Document Department was to be notified if a copy were lost. Understandably, the US government has released no data concerning its possession of the documents.

The *Bulletin of Activities* was translated into English in 1965, by the Hoover Institution on War, Revolution and Peace of Stanford University, under the editorship of J. Chester Cheng.

[5] The five qualities for individual distinction are correct political thought, good military technique, the three-eight spirit, accomplishment of assigned tasks and good physical condition.

The three-eight spirit refers to Mao Tse-tung's "three sentences and eight characters" enunciated at the establishment of the Resistance to Japan Military and Political University in Yenan. The sentences specify correct political direction, simple hard-working spirit and elastic mobile strategy. The characters stand for unity, alertness, discipline and agility.

[6] It can be added that the Chinese Communists also maintain a complex award system for defectors from the Nationalist military forces. For example, the Revised

in the PLA, which is itself considered as one of Mao's great contributions to military organization. Or as Politburo member Ho Lung boasted in a *Red Flag* article celebrating the 38th anniversary of the founding of the Red Armies on August 1, 1965: "We have created the first army in history which genuinely practices democracy and belongs to the people." It hardly needs to be said that the form of "democracy" advocated for the PLA is similar to the misuse of the term for society in general as summarized in the idea of "democratic centralism." Like the peasants, workers or other professionals in Communist China, the soldiers of the PLA receive all orders through a multi-level apparatus that climaxes in the highest echelons of Party control.

The general structure of the government machinery for handling military affairs has already been discussed in the context of the state organization. The division of functions and formal lines of connecting authority have been set among the Chairmen of the CPR, the NDC, the State Council, and the Ministry of National Defense. The PLA comes under the direct command of the Defense Ministry, although this body is, of course, itself guided by the policies laid down by the NDC, in which the high ranking officers of the PLA are well represented. The headquarters of the PLA is divided into three major branches: the General Political, the General Rear Services, and the General Staff Departments.[7] Two of these are common to all headquarters: the exception is the all-important General Political Department.

The degree of CPC control in the former PRMC and the present NDC has already been examined in connection with the state organization. Needless to say, the same control is maintained in the MND and at all levels of the PLA itself. Lin Piao, since 1959 the Minister of National Defense, is a ranking member of the CPC CC's Politburo and exercises the first position, after Mao, in the CC's Military Affairs Committee. All of the Vice Ministers are either regular or alternate members of the Central

---

Instructions for Rewards to Chiang Airmen Who Bring Planes, as formulated by the PLA staff in Fukien province and published by NCNA on March 15, 1964, stipulated that: Nationalist airmen who return to the mainland will be given jobs, helped to settle, and have their property protected. Cash awards will be based on the type of aircraft turned over to the PLA (ranging from 5,000 gold taels for a F-100 fighter to 8,000 gold taels for a P2V or U-2 aircraft), with additional money given to the flight's organizer.

[7] It should be noted that following the 1959 disclosures at the Lushan conference, this reorganization replaced the more complex division into the following seven departments: General Staff, General Training Department, General Political Department, General Cadres Department, Armed Forces Supervision Department, General Rear Services Department and Finance Department. The General Cadres Department was merged with the General Political Department as a subdepartment; the General Training Department was transferred to the General Staff Department as a subdepartment; and the Finance Department was absorbed into the General Rear Services Department.

Committee. The field armies are commanded by high ranking Party members, and CPC control is carried out at every level through the agency of the political commissar appointed by the Party.

In 1964, Hsiao Hua, then acting or deputy head of the PLA General Political Department (GPD), was named as Director of this most important CPC control agency for the military. He is a full member of the CPC Central Committee and apparently proved his loyalty to the Party's leadership during the shake-up in personnel in 1959, when P'eng Teh-huai was removed as Minister of Defense and Huang K'e-ch'eng as Chief of the General Staff (to be replaced by Lin Piao and Lo Jui-ch'ing respectively), and again in 1962, when the CPC announced that the then Director of the GPD, T'an Cheng, has been removed from the CC Secretariat. Hsiao Hua's Department supervises the appointment and performance of PLA "political guides" or commissars at all levels. According to the Regulation on the Work of the Political Guide in the Company, published by *People's Daily* on November 11, 1961: "The political guide is the company's political worker appointed by the political office. He is subject to the higher-rank political Party office, to a higher-rank military commander and to the company's Party branch," not to the actual field commander. Within the framework of this control structure, the commissar is charged with promoting correct ideological-political loyalties among the troops, determining cases of incorrect thinking, and leading rectification work. His powers exceed those of the regular field commander, should cases of conflict arise, since he is the representative of the Party leadership.

The work of the PLA commissar is carried out through the usual CPC civilian structure, as converted to military use, and by special security agencies. As in the society in general, the basic organization of the Party in the PLA is the branch. CPC cadres and rank-and-file members of these branches are charged with discussing all important questions related to their military units and with carrying out Party work among the troops. For the soldier, as for the civilian, the candidate member must follow certain specified procedures, including examination by the next higher Party organ, before being accepted for full CPC membership. Similarly, and as ordered in the *Bulletin of Activities* of February 20, 1961, preference is to be given to candidates from the national minorities in those areas populated by non-Han peoples. The same source on June 13, 1961, noted that some 7,000 PLA companies still had no Party branch as late as 1959. By way of correcting this situation, in 1960 alone 229,000 soldiers were admitted to Party membership, so that there would be sufficient numbers to organize branches in every company. Based upon the common estimate that there are some three million soldiers in the PLA, this vast increase in the number of Party members probably brought the ratio of Party members to all troops to about one in three.

The General Political Department also has a Youth Work Subdepartment to train progressive young soldiers, supply candidates for Party membership, and collaborate closely with the CPC branches. According to the Regulation on the Work of the Youth Work Branch, formulated by the PLA Political Department in the fall ot 1961, the Youth Work branch is charged with carrying out education in the thought of Mao to raise the level of political consciousness, seeing that strict discipline is observed, and preparing for arduous military assignments. Like the structure of the PLA Party branches, Youth Work branches are formed in every company that has three or more members, under the direction of the Political Department. The general meeting of the branch elects a committee, which in turn elects the branch secretary, subject to the approval of the company CPC branch and the battalion Party committee. Probably about 60–65 per cent of all young PLA soldiers eligible are members of the Youth Work units. [8]

On April 26, 1961, the PLA General Political Department and the CPC Central Committee's Organization Department issued a joint order for the creation of additional Party agencies. Party members in the PLA were ordered to form congresses to elect committees at the county and town level of organization. These PLA Party committees must report to the local regular, or "civilian" Party committee at the same level and their actions are subject to the approval of the higher Party committee of the PLA. Collectively all these Party organs are entrusted with a vital task. As noted in the Regulations Governing Political Work in the PLA, which were issued by the CPC Central Committee, and formally adopted by the All-Army Political Work Conference which met in Peking, February 2–27, 1963, the work of the General Political Department, the commissars and all Party committees within the PLA is to ensure "absolute Party leadership over the army." Ultimately, the success of the military organization in Communist China will be judged in terms not only of professional efficiency but also of the ideological dedication and political loyalty with which these Party organs and the PLA cadres carry out this command.

MILITIA UNITS AND THE "EVERYONE A SOLDIER" PRINCIPLE

Popular in character and military in nature, the militia units in Communist China can be spoken of as the regular "civilian armed forces" to

---

[8] For example, a directive of the PLA Political Department of December 24, 1960, called for 65 per cent of all eligible young soldiers to be admitted on the basis of quality. A January 31, 1961, conference in Peking called for 60 per cent of the army youths not in the CPC to be recruited into the Youth Work branches.

implement and develop the "everyone a solider" principle. In a country whose leadership is firmly committed to the struggle for international communism against its enemy equipped with far-superior military force, the organization of militia units is even more important for safeguarding national survival as well as revolutionary gains and base areas. As Mao said in 1958: "At a time when the imperialists are bullying us in such a manner, we have a powerful regular army, but we still need to organize the people's militia on a large scale. Against a powerful regular army and a nationwide militia, the imperialists would find it difficult to move a single inch in our country in the event of invasion."

The purpose and role of the militia units are clearly evident in their past experience and present practice. Dating back to the Red Protection Corps of the earlier Soviet period in the communist movement in China, the militia units have proven especially valuable as auxiliaries to the regular armed forces. They provide local points of armed support for the tasks of maintaining order and consolidating power on the mainland, and are still the principal ready reserve strength of the PLA. Since these units are scattered throughout the countryside and urban areas, they constitute a valuable subsidiary means to guide the entire population by conducting political indoctrination and promoting agricultural and industrial production. The more far-reaching significance of the militia establishments lies in their stabilizing role in national or international emergencies. Domestically, turning all the people into soldiers guarantees the people's strength against possible careerist usurpers. In a foreign war, the militia can resist enemy invasion and especially reduce the impact of nuclear attacks.

According to Chinese Communist military theory, the militia organization is based on three principles: the "unity of labor and arms," "democracy," and "voluntary participation." The first of these is simply the concept that the members of the militia are at the same time civilians engaged in regular trades and supporting themselves by their own labor. In the rural areas, the members are mostly peasants. In the urban areas, they are drawn from the ranks of the factory workers.[9] The principle itself stems from the logic that the morale of the militia will be higher when the members are organized supposedly to preserve tangible things of vital concern to them. More importantly, within this structure the militia constitutes no great burden on the national treasury.

Under the principle of "democracy," the militia units at each level are governed by "elected" representative organs and committees and commanded by "elected" officers. The size of these units varies according to

---

[9] In the period just after the "liberation," factory protection corps were set up in the urban districts. Later called the Workers Supervisory Corps, these units were comprised almost entirely of factory laborers.

the government area for which they are organized. In the rural areas, the unit at the county level is the detachment; at the sub-county (ch'ü) level, a battalion; and at the rural district (hsiang) level, a company. These companies may be further divided into platoons or sub-companies. In terms of communal organization, the divisions follow the lines of the commune proper, its subordinate brigades and production teams. In the municipalities, units are organized according to place of work or residence.

The highest organ of control in each militia unit is the corps meeting (for the smallest units) or the representatives meeting (for the larger units). This meeting in turn elects a "people's armed forces committee" to act as the controlling body in the interim between its own sessions. There are usually some seven to eleven members on the committee, which is headed by a chairman and one to three vice chairmen. The chairman is also the commander of the militia unit. The dual line of responsibility for the militia units is shown in the fact that the committee members must be approved by the state organ at the corresponding level, and by the militia headquarters two levels higher in rank. In reality, the control and command of the militia is assumed by the CPC-appointed commissar and by the PLA staff in the respective military district. Thus the principle of "democracy" is extremely limited and always subject to the same kind of Party control that characterizes the various organs of the state machine.

Under the third principle, of "voluntary participation," the militia members are supposed to perform their services for their own benefit and that of society in general. These duties include such work as maintaining local order, protecting property, and eliminating counterrevolutionaries. Through various propaganda and indoctrinational devices, the Chinese Communists have apparently overcome the tradition of "dreading to become a soldier," and are able to present the militia as a sign of mass support of Party and state programs.

While many of the duties of the militia are local in character, it also performs a number of functions that are national in scope. Units have been charged with such responsibilities as carrying out the population census, helping the public security organs, transmitting intelligence reports, and protecting state properties. In practice, the militia has been particularly useful in carrying out such measures as the land reform, collectivization, and communal programs, and in leading production drives in both the rural and urban areas. In the event of invasion, these units are to render logistic services and defend their own areas. But perhaps the chief function of the militia has been to lay the foundation for a system of universal military service in conjunction with the PLA.

In 1950, the militia reportedly numbered about 5,500,000. According to a plan formulated in that year, the units were to be increased to a total of about 5 per cent of the population, which, based on present population estimates, would constitute a force of about 37,500,000. In 1952, one report indicated that the force had already been increased to some 12,000,-000 members. Then, in 1956, the Chinese Communists introduced the "Everyone a Soldier Movement," which was designed to transform the entire nation into an armed camp. As Mao has pointed out, the creation of militia units on a grand scale is "a question of having the masses militarize and collectivize their life." As such, the movement represents the ultimate aim of communism.

Although the Everyone a Soldier Movement, by giving elementary training to millions, has tremendously increased China's military potential, its major goal has been economic, rather than strictly military. This conclusion became particularly evident during the 1958 Great Leap and communalization drives. The crisis in the Taiwan Straits of August-September, 1958, served as a great stimulus to accelerate the movement's growth. By October of that year, 2.2 million people in Peking had been organized into 155 divisions, 345 regiments, 392 independent battalions and 453 independent companies. In coastal Fukien, nearly all citizens between the ages of 16 and 50 were mustered into militia units. In Chekiang province and Inner Mongolia, one out of every three persons had begun training, while in Honan province, where communalization had been virtually completed, all commune members were regarded to be worker-soldiers.

The communal militia units accept both men and women between the ages of 16 to 50, although youths between the ages of 16 and 30 form the core of the units, and demobilized veterans the backbone. Training is usually conducted by the PLA, and includes the use of weapons, defense against air attacks, and other field operations, as well as a series of daily exercises. [10] Like their male counterparts, the women militia members participate in all aspects of training. For example, Mao Tse-tung himself

[10] To increase general physical fitness for military service, in October, 1958, the Physical Culture and Sports Commission promulgated its Regulations Governing the System of Physical Culture for Labor and National Defense. As determined by the Commission, there are five basic exercises: (1) 100-meter or 60-meter dash; (2) middle distance race of 800 or 1,500 meters; (3) high or broad jump; (4) weight-lifting, rope-climbing or pole-climbing; (5) weapons firing and grenade throwing. The sixth exercise was to be specified by the physical culture and sports committee of the respective provinces, municipalities and autonomous regions, according to local circumstances and requirements in each classification were to be varied according to age and sex.

Together with political considerations, Mao. Tse-tung's 15 kilometer swim in the Yangtze River near Wuhan on July 16, 1966, was doubtlessly motivated in part by a desire to promote the regular exercise program. Thus he reinforced his 1956 dictum that "you should go into the big rivers and seas to temper yourselves."

witnessed a demonstration of female prowess in Peking when a fisherman's daughter, now a deputy leader of a militia company, reportedly shattered five glass bottles at 100 meters with five rounds from her semi-automatic rifle. NCNA has frequently cited examples of women militia members laying mines, driving tanks, or participating in parachute jumps. Training is conducted after regular working hours, or during free or slack seasons.

In the fall of 1958, the General Staff of the PLA held a series of national and regional conferences to strengthen militia work. Participants viewed militia units to observe the level of military and political training. An October 19, 1958, NCNA dispatch stated that the PLA planned further support of the movement. By the end of 1958, Peking claimed that some 200 million Chinese had already been organized into militia units. At every level, the militia was organized along two general types. Members of the basic units included PLA veterans, Party members and activists. All citizens not listed as "bad elements" were eligible for the ordinary militia units. Leadership was drawn from the CPC committees in the local areas, and committee secretaries concurrently became political commissars and instructors or advisors in the militia units. Political and ideological indoctrination of the militia members antedated actual field training and patriotism was identified with supporting the Party line and the socialist cause.

During the 1959–61 period of economic dislocation, the militia program was seriously disrupted. In addition to the problem of supply shortages, training programs conflicted with the need to increase the time spent in productive labor, and the low level of public health made strenuous field training impossible. Issues of the PLA *Bulletin of Activities* indicate the seriousness of the situation. This source observed that, in some areas, the militia members were terrorizing and robbing the people. In January, 1961 (*Bulletin of Activities* number 5, January 17, 1961), Lin Piao ordered the PLA to dispense rifles and bullets only among proven reliable members. To ensure that the militia would not be allowed to ill-treat the masses, the PLA was commanded to assign militia members to such work as guarding railways, bridges and stores only after prior approval from the local Party committees and PLA units. Before militia could be ordered to participate in the detection of crimes, permission had to be secured from the CPC committee at the county or city level and the higher military offices had to be informed. When conditions failed to improve, in May, 1961, Lo Jui-ch'ing ordered that the PLA units in areas beset by natural calamities were to suspend all training exercises for the communal militia units for the remainder of the year.

The more recent condition of the militia has reflected the general improvement in economic conditions, since 1962. In the fall of that year, there was a general upsurge in militia activity corresponding to the Sino-Soviet border dispute and generally worsening Sino-Soviet relations. However, the current preparedness slogan again appears to be one of resisting a possible invasion from Taiwan or the threat of US—and even USSR—encirclement and invasion. Periodically, the CPC has announced the round-up of agents of Chiang Kai-shek, probably to incite the militia to even more vigilance in their local areas. For example, on March 4, 1966, NCNA-Kunming reported that three officers and 25 troops of the remnant KMT armies had surrendered in Yunnan, after some 17 years of underground subversion.[11]

In keeping with its general emphasis on the need to train properly a new generation of youth, the CPC also advocates that militia units be formed in institutions of higher education. In the spring of 1965, all youths were encouraged to participate in military training exercises to implement Mao's principle that "all are soldiers."[12] One example of the varied advantages to be gained from such a campaign is illustrated by the April 5, 1965, demonstration staged by 7,000 students of Chungking University, Szechwan province. According to the Peking *Chung-kuo Ch'ing-nien Pao* (*China Youth Daily*) of April 17, 1965, the usual demonstrations of military skills were climaxed by the performance of the militia unit of sophomore students from the department of metallurgy. This unit carried out a stimulated bayonet charge to the encouraging shouts of 10,000 spectators to "kill, kill, kill." Although the combat readiness of the college militia units may be open to question,[13] the units themselves are undoubtedly highly beneficial to the Party from the point of view of indoctrination in revolutionary fervor.

Early in 1966, the Chinese Communists urged that the local branches of the Communist Youth League—the CPC auxiliary which was then encouraging all youths to participate in membership—sponsor militia training for their members. The program was similar to those mentioned previously. For example, *China Youth Daily* of February 17, 1966, noted that the CYL branch of the Chih-an brigade, Tsokang commune in Heilungkiang province, was giving instruction in the use of bayonets, rifles and grenades, and running study sessions in the thought of Mao Tse-tung. In praise of its programs, this unit was then recommended as a model for

[11] This emphasis on constant vigilance against subversion or open attack is discussed in detail in the final sections of this chapter.

[12] According to *China Youth Daily* (May 13, 1965), these exercises were in swimming, shooting, grenade-throwing, camping, marching and battle games.

[13] For example, *China Youth Daily* (April 17, 1965) reported that 15,000 middle school and college and university students had learned to shoot in 1964. But since the same source mentions that only 141,960 bullets were used, each student would have fired an average of only about 9 shells—or hardly enough to ensure proficiency.

all CYL branches. Nevertheless, the combat phases of training were largely limited to the hard core militia, while the regular militia's training was confined to indoctrination sessions and drill.[14] However, with increased reports of raids in the Sino-Soviet border regions, Hong Kong sources reported that Radio Peking on February 21, 1967, emphasized that the peasants in the border provinces should cooperate with the PLA to crush all reactionaries—Chinese or foreign. And, as noted subsequently, the troubled situation in several of the provinces and municipalities, associated with counterrevolutionary attacks on the cultural revolution, has brought the work of the militia into greater prominence. Under the direction of the PLA, militia units now constitute a vital force in the "three in one" leadership of many economic enterprises. Or, as worded in the February 24, 1967, Draft Resolution of the Shanghai Municipal Revolutionary Committee, "the armed core of the militia, the PLA and other people's forces are the strong pillars of the provisional organ of power at each level."

It is estimated that at least 15 million Chinese have received training as members of the hard core militia units, in addition to the many, many millions who have been trained in the ordinary militia units. These citizen-soldiers constitute an enormous potential manpower reserve for the regular military forces. Remembering the defeats of the well-equipped Japanese and Chinese Nationalist armies on the mainland, the Chinese Communists know and appreciate the value of militia in total war. With these militia reserves, a set-back to the regular forces would not necessarily lead to a collapse in national defense. And the value of the militia in times of peace is clear as these units have often constituted the shock troops in the development of the CPC's political, economic and social programs. But the Chinese Communist leadership is also aware of the inherent danger in arming the masses, without proper ideological and political guidance. Therefore, it seems likely that the Party's continuing emphasis on the militia and the Everyone a Soldier Movement will be as a means to indoctrinate the masses and use the militia as shock troops for political, social and economic drives, with national defense only as a last resort.

THE MILITARY POTENTIAL

From the point of view of manpower resources, the Chinese Communist military machine is potentially the most formidable in the world. In the

[14] This pattern of instruction is employed in training militia units comprised of returned overseas Chinese. For example, the *Overseas Chinese Affairs Journal* (No. 6, December, 1965) reported this distinction with reference to the Fenyung Overseas Chinese Farm on the Leichou Peninsula, and significantly added that a number of the members had returned from Vietnam.

area of modern weaponry and other military supplies, Peking still suffers from chronic and critical deficiencies, although the growing emphasis on the development of nuclear weapons modifies this situation somewhat. Moreover, as noted in the final pages of this chapter, the Chinese Communist leadership considers it ideological heritage and revolutionary experience to compensate for any material shortage or weakness.

Conventional Forces

In October, 1949, with the establishment of the Chinese People's Republic, the Chinese Communist leadership boasted of an enormous fighting force of veterans seasoned in the anti-Japanese and civil wars. As noted previously, the major task with respect to the military machine, at that time, was the consolidation and reorganization of this force into a regular peacetime army. High on the list of priorities was the development of modern weapons with its accompanying need for technical training of military personnel.[15] Although the transformation of the military into such a permanent peace-time force was delayed by the Korean War, this encounter served to further demonstrate the need for modernization. Until about 1959, the Chinese Communists approached their goal by reliance upon Soviet models and technical assistance. Thus Moscow collaborated to forge the People's Liberation Army into a progressive military machine possessing modern equipment and skills, which would greatly augment the overall armed strength of the single armed camp of the world communist movement.

An authoritative statement of this early Sino-Soviet harmony of interests with respect to the PLA was made by Chu Teh, the veteran commander-in-chief of the Chinese Communist armed forces, on the 25th anniversary of the Chinese Red Army, August 1, 1952. The Marshal, addressing himself particularly to the Russian people through the pages of *Pravda*, explicitly paid tribute to the leadership and example of the Soviet Union in the military field in these words:

[15] In general terms, the CPR's budget for the military tended to show an annual reduction, from more than six billion yuan in 1953, to five and a half billion in 1958. Percentage-wise, in 1953, 28 per cent of the state budget was allocated to the military; in 1955, about 22 per cent; in 1957, about 19 per cent; and in 1958, only 15 per cent. This decrease can be explained in terms of the over-all reduction in the size of the regular army after the Korean conflict, as well as a probable reduction in standards for rations, fuel, and uniforms in 1958. But, the Chinese Communists have always concealed actual military expenditures, often by listing military items under non-military departments of the government. For example, production of military equipment of various types is hidden within the work assigned to the eight machine-building industries; the Ministry of the Interior cares for military dependents and disabled veterans; and the militia are usually locally supplied.

All our commanders and fighters must constantly improve themselves, model themselves on the great, ever triumphant Soviet Army. . . . We must assiduously study Stalin's military science. What Comrade Stalin said to the Soviet Army during the great patriotic war of the Soviet Union is also enlightening and encouraging to us. . . . Owing to our industry in study and our powerful armed strength, we can certainly carry out the glorious task of consolidating our national defense forces . . . and can, together with the Soviet Army, the mighty bulwark of the world peace, defend the cause of peace.

At the same time, Soviet leaders sought to instill in their own fighting forces a respect for the strength and prowess of the Chinese military and a sense of common purpose in defense of a single communist camp. For example, in observance of the 27th anniversary of the Chinese Red Army on August 1, 1954, *Krasnaia Zvezda* (*Red Star*), the organ of the Soviet military, praised the glorious past, the quality, strength and political training of the PLA, and its persistent study of the rich experience and techniques of the Soviet Army.

It is, of course, impossible to determine the extent of Soviet material assistance to the PLA, although some general idea can be deduced from the terms of various Sino-Soviet economic and technical assistance agreements. In the period from 1950 to 1958, the Chinese Communist military probably received a large share of its munitions and other supplies from the USSR, along with the latter's East European satellites, such as East Germany and Czechoslovakia. An example of the manner in which military assistance programs were tied to general economic agreements is provided by the Agreement on Working Conditions for Soviet Experts in China, concluded in Moscow on March 27, 1950. Reportedly, in return for supplying equipment to the PLA, the Soviet Union was to receive from Peking each year a large number of workers, 50,000 tons of soy beans, 5 million tons of rice, 5 million tons of wheat, and 15 million bales of cotton.[16] According to a Hong Kong study, in 1954 the Soviet Union's military aid included 153 tanks, 94 anti-aircraft guns, 117 anti-tank guns, 100 rockets, 107 76mm. cannons, and numerous other supplies.[17] Generally speaking, since the Soviets, like the Chinese Communists, cloak military expenditures under a variety of other economic categories, it is impossible to determine the extent of material assistance, but this aid would appear to have been substantial throughout the early 1950's.

[16] A February 2, 1956, report of the United Nations Secretary-General to the Economic and Social Council publicized a Chinese Nationalist estimate that Peking had sent 1,500,000 slave laborers to the USSR and its East European satellites in exchange for military supplies.

[17] Cheng Hsueh-chia, et al., *Ching-Jih Ta-lu T'ou-shih* (*Today's Mainland in Perspective*), Hong Kong, 1954, pp. 130–32.

Chinese Communist naval forces also profited from early Soviet aid. According to a mid-1953 estimate, the USSR had helped Communist China to develop its naval forces into seven fleets, comprised of 304 vessels with a total tonnage of 78,900. The first three of these fleets were deployed along the coastal regions of Manchuria and North China, while the remainder covered the Eastern and Southeastern waters. Reportedly, the USSR also gave the Chinese Communists anywhere from a "few" to 60 submarines, the number varying with the date and source of the report. In 1954 alone, the USSR supplied Peking with 55 vessels, including four submarines. By September, 1954, the combined Soviet-Chinese submarine strength in the China Sea alone was estimated at more than 100. But in 1966, a Western source recognized only 30 submarines as a currently effective force. Communist China, however, was reportedly engaged in the construction of submarines capable of carrying nuclear-tipped missiles.

Before the Sino-Soviet ideological split, the Chinese Communist navy had also been expanded through the addition of ships built in China with Soviet technical assistance. This category includes a small number of MKV-type torpedo boats. At the same time, the fact that Chinese naval bases were shared by Soviet vessels greatly augmented the Chinese fleet's striking power. For example, although the Russians nominally withdrew from Port Arthur in 1954, they retained control in Dairen, and acquired the new port of Chefoo on the north coast of Shangtung province. Early in 1955, the USSR was reported to have special rights of access to a dozen or more Chinese naval bases, including Hulutao, Port Arthur, Dairen, Chefoo, Tsingtao, Port Lienyün, Shanghai, Chushan, Amoy, Swatow, Whampoa and Yulin.

During the early 1950's, the USSR also supplied most of the some 3,000 planes which constituted the Chinese Communist Air Force. Soviet supplies have diminished probably since 1960. In 1966, a Western observer estimated that Peking had by that time some 1800 jet fighters, mostly Soviet MIG-15's, MIG-17's, and some MIG-19's and MIG-21's, together with about 300 IL-28 light jet bombers. The Soviet boycott has created considerable ill-effects on the acquisition of spare parts and fuel for the Chinese Communist Air Force.

Before the intensification of the Sino-Soviet rift, Soviet military-technical assistance to Peking was evident. By mid-1954, the Chinese Communists were reported to be building and testing their own planes. The pattern of shared naval facilities on the Mainland also applied to air bases, reportedly including those in Peking, Süchow, Nanking, Hankow, Kweilin, Nanning and Kunming. And Russian instructors were reportedly training Chinese Communist pilots in the operation of MIG jet fighters as early as

1949—or a year before the MIG's were encountered by Allied airmen over North Korea. Beginning in 1951, the Soviets were said to be training Chinese paratroops in bases centered around Kaifeng, Changkiakow (Kalgan) and later Peking and western Szechwan. By 1953, these trained units were said to number about 115,000, of whom about a third were women.

Soviet military advisors in China apparently also participated in joint strategic planning, in addition to their training duties. In February, 1954, it was estimated that from 1,000 to 2,500 Soviet advisors were attached to the air force, a similar number to the navy, and from 5,000 to 10,000 to the army. This Soviet force was said to reach down to at least the regimental level in the army. An Advisor's Office in an infantry regiment probably had from 15 to 27 members. Additional reports indicate that, in addition to these advisors, the Soviets also stationed troops in Chinese territory in Manchuria and Sinkiang. In May, 1954, some reports estimated this force as high as 250,000.

Since about 1958, linked to the Chinese Communist plans for national self-sufficiency articulated in the communalization and Great Leap drives, and particularly with the growing antagonisms in Sino-Soviet relations, the Chinese Communists have sought to meet their military needs without benefit of outside assistance. In general terms, the material resources of the PLA have tended to reflect the parallel status of comprehensive economic programs. Thus, for example, during the 1959–61 period of economic dislocation, the PLA suffered from a lack of modern equipment, sufficient supplies, and even adequate foodstuffs. By July 26, 1961, the PLA *Bulletin of Activities* was forced to admit: "The central question today concerning the life of the troops is the question of food."

Although, as noted previously, the troops of the PLA have always been charged with contributing to productive labor, during the 1959–61 period, the military were ordered to augment their own supplies, especially of food, while suspending or cancelling those projects which required state capital investment. In September, 1960, the PLA Central Service Department reported that the PLA then had 1.3 million pigs (or an average of 2.9 men per pig), 50,000 cows, 300,000 sheep, and 2.9 million poultry; that 1.1 million mou of arable land was being farmed by the troops (or an average of 0.4 mou per man); and that in 1960 total production by the PLA should be 42,000 tons of pig iron, 22,000 tons of steel, and 120,000 tons of cement. In fulfillment of central directives, the PLA sought to increase production in all of these categories. Consequently, the July 26, 1961 *Bulletin of Activities* noted that the area of land under cultivation had been increased to 1.66 million mou—or a 45 per cent gain as compared to 1960—and that vegetable production was up 31 per cent and meat production up one per cent. With the general improvement of Communist China's total economic situation, there has doubtlessly been a decrease in the pressures placed on the troops to attain self-sufficiency in food production. However, the policy itself remains operative.

The over-all improvement in the economy has presumably remedied to a large extent the critical shortages of military equipment that existed from 1959 to 1961. This would be particularly easy in the production of small arms and supplies, which do not require enormous capital outlays. Communist China is now manufacturing her own planes, including jets, and building her own naval vessels. However, evidence indicates that the rate of replacement, if not the quality of the new equipment, is still deficient. For example, the PLA air force probably has about 2,500 planes, of which over 2,000 are jets, thus making it the largest modern air force of an Asian country. In addition to the fact that these planes have not been tested in combat, scattered reports show that replacement parts are in short supply, as are skilled mechanics capable of making repairs. The PLA naval forces are plagued by similar problems. For example, as late as 1961, the April 5, 1961, PLA *Bulletin of Activities* acknowledged that 69 per cent of all the transport ships had been constructed between 1940–49, and 10 per cent before 1940. Even if these vessels are seaworthy, and the *Bulletin* admits that "many" were not, it is most unlikely that they have the speed or maneuverability essential for combat service.

In terms of conventional forces, the area in which Communist China exercises the greatest potential is that of manpower reserves. It is estimated that Communist China's regular ground strength is between 2.5–2.9 million trained troops, with an additional half million troops assigned to the security forces. In addition, some seven or eight million demobilized veterans could possibly be recalled to active duty, while several hundred million other Chinese either are serving or have served in the militia units. Indeed, the manpower resources are virtually limitless, since over five million men reach the age of twenty each year. As noted previously, Communist China has had a compulsory military service law since 1955, but the problem is not one of numbers, but rather of selectivity. Only a small percentage of those eligible are drafted annually. Instead, the leadership has encouraged a prolongation of duty, especially on the part of trained leaders and technicians, and, when deemed necessary, military personnel have been ordered to remain in service after the expiration of their original term of duty. Thus, the crucial problem for the conventional military force is one of equipment, supply and training, rather than numbers. Perhaps for this reason, as well as the revolutionary experience, Mao Tse-tung continues to speak of "man," not "weapons" as being the final determining force.

Nuclear Capabilities

Communist China's first detonation of an atomic device, at 3 P.M. on October 16, 1964, in the Lop Nor area of Sinkiang Autonomous Region, immediately required a reassessment of her over-all military potential. Peking's fifth nuclear test, on December 28, 1966, further illustrated Communist China's ability to sustain and further develop its nuclear programs. But these achievements do not negate Mao Tse-tung's continuing pro- testations that atomic weapons are "paper tigers."[18] The Chinese Com- munists have repeatedly declared that "at no time and under no circum- stances will China be the first to use nuclear weapons." As worded in the October 28, 1966, *Peking Review*, the sole reason for acquiring such weapons is "to oppose the nuclear monopoly and nuclear blackmail by the United States and the Soviet Union acting in collusion." Nevertheless, Communist China's entry into the nuclear club is an historical event of major propor- tions. Only time will tell whether her possession of nuclear weapons will invite or deter attack, or give her a better or worse international image.

The process of Communist China's development of atomic weapons can be summarized briefly: a considerable share of this sketchy information has been made available only as an off-shoot of the Sino-Soviet ideological disagreement. In 1949, there were only a handful of nuclear scientists in all of Mainland China, and all were Western-trained. Mao's "lean to one side" policy and the cordiality of Sino-Soviet relations then represented the best avenue to rapid scientific development. In March, 1950, Peking announced the establishment of a joint Sino-Soviet non-ferrous and rare metals company in Sinkiang, as rumors circulated that uranium deposits had been discovered in that province's Takla Makan desert area.[19] At the same time the Chinese Academy of Sciences (CAS), established in

[18] In 1945, only seven days after the Hiroshima blast, in his speech to the Yenan Forum, Mao asked the question "can atomic bombs decide wars?" and emphatically answered, "no, they cannot." During the July, 1946, US tests at Bikini, Mao apparently first coined the expression that the atom bomb was a "paper tiger." Shortly before the outbreak of the Korean War, on May 14, 1950, Kuo Mo-jo declared that "atomic bombs and hydrogen bombs are not formidable." During the course of the Korean War, the importance of atomic weapons was usually downgraded, although the Chinese Volunteers had to prepare for defense against the possible use of such weapons. How- ever, Radio Peking on October 14, 1951, revealed the regime's interest in acquiring such weapons by the statement that "only when we ourselves have atomic weapons and are fully prepared is it possible for the frenzied warmongers to listen to our just and reason- able proposals."

[19] In its Open Letter of February 29, 1964, the CPC Central Committee revealed that the following raw materials which can be used in the production of nuclear weapons and rockets had been shipped to the Soviet Union: 100,000 tons of lithium concentrates, 34,000 tons of beryllium concentrates, 51,000 tons of borax, 270,000 tons of tungsten

1949, made plans to train additional scientists and promote advanced scientific research. [20]

According to the terms of the 1954 Sino-Soviet Scientific and Technical Cooperation Agreement, the Soviets reportedly agreed to exchange atomic reactors and technical assistance for a continuing supply of uranium and other rare metals. In the same year, Peking officially noted the existence of some 36 atomic research laboratories, with a total personnel of 1,725. By 1955, the first Soviet experts were instructing Chinese scientists in these centers, while other Chinese were sent for advanced instruction to the chief Soviet research center for atomic energy in Dubna, outside Moscow. On February 14, 1956, Li Hsien-nien announced that the Soviets would set up a 6,500 kw. experimental reactor in China. An Institute of Atomic Energy was established in Peking. In the same year, the Chinese Communists announced a 12-year comprehensive plan for scientific development in which jet propulsion was assigned priority as one of the 12 major tasks.

On October 15, 1957, a new Sino-Soviet scientific agreement was concluded in Moscow, by which the Soviets agreed to supply samples of nuclear weapons and further advisory assistance. The following year marked the origins of the Great Leap Forward for economic development, as well as the crisis in the Taiwan Straits. Although the first Soviet-sponsored reactor in China began operations in September of that year, there is evidence that Khrushchev had begun to have second thoughts about supplying sample nuclear weapons. As revealed later, the differences at this time centered on Khrushchev's disapproval of the communes and Mao's stand on the ideological questions of war, peace and peaceful coexistence. In 1959, Khrushchev indicated his intention to meet President Eisenhower, while the Chinese Communists reluctantly supported such a summit conference from which they would necessarily be excluded. However, according to reports finally published in *People's Daily* on August 15, 1963, Khrushchev "unilaterally scrapped" the 1957 agreements on June 20, 1959, "apparently as a gift for the Soviet leader to take to Eisenhower when visiting the US in September." In what the Chinese Communists best describe as a form of "blackmail," Khrushchev refused

---

concentrates, 32.9 tons of piezoelectric quartz, 7,730 tons of mercury, 39 tons of tantalum-niobium concentrates, and 180,000 tons of tin. No mention was made of uranium.

[20] The CAS coordinates the work of its Institute for Atomic Energy directed by Ch'ien San-ch'iang (Ph.D. in physics from the University of Paris, 1943); the Institute of Mechanics directed by leading scientist Ch'ien Hsüeh-shen; and the Institute of Automation and Remote Control, which specializes in missile research. But the PLA also maintains its own Scientific and Technological Commission for National Defense, which is directed by Nieh Jung-chen. Nieh, as noted elsewhere, was promoted to membership in the CPC's Politburo early in 1967.

to supply bomb samples or technical materials necessary for the manufacture of atomic weapons.

In 1960, the Soviet Union ordered the recall of its 1,390 scientists and technicians then serving in Communist China.[21] At the same time, Khrushchev expressed his intention to sign a partial nuclear test ban treaty with the western nuclear powers. Although this decision was cancelled and the Soviets resumed testing of nuclear weapons in 1961, Moscow appeared to be considering some form of agreement with the western powers. Chinese Communist negotiators returned from their Moscow trip to attempt an ideological understanding on July 21, 1963. On July 27, Khrushchev signed a limited test ban treaty that had been urged upon him by President Kennedy. Although the treaty did not prohibit underground testing or the continuing production of nuclear weapons, it would seem to hamper any signatory nation from subsequently developing such weapons, without the ability for atmospheric testing.

The Chinese Communists had already intimated their disapproval of the limited test ban treaty. Four days after the treaty was signed, (July 31), *People's Daily* termed it a "big fraud," and emphasized that "it is unthinkable that the Chinese government should become a party to this dirty fraud." Instead, Peking offered a counter-proposal that all countries agree to the prohibition and destruction of nuclear weapons; the dismantling of all bases on foreign soil, and the declaration of Asia as a nuclear-free zone.[22] Chinese Communist delegates to several international conferences then attempted to dissuade other nations from signing the agreement.[23]

As early as September 28, 1958, during the first fervor of the Great Leap, *People's Daily* had commented: "The pursuit of atomic science is not the privilege of a select few and it does not require long training; it can be carried out in wide circles and in a short time." In 1963, Chinese

[21] It is estimated that about 850 Soviet scientists had served in China in the years between 1950 and 1960 while some 1,300 Chinese scientists were being trained in the USSR.

[22] It should be noted that none of these measures was new. The Chinese Communists had long advocated a policy of total disarmament, or barring this, that Asia be declared an atom-free zone. Similarly, the Soviet Union had called for the abolition of atomic weapons in 1946, and Khrushchev had proposed a total disarmament policy before the United Nations in 1959. The charge that the Soviets were now selling out to US imperialism is a characteristic of the Moscow-Peking ideological arguments. Moreover, after the Nationalist government on Taiwan initialled the treaty any Chinese Communist acceptance would be tantamount to an implicit recognition of a "two-China" policy.

[23] At the ninth annual meeting in Hiroshima of the Conference against Atom Bombs, the delegates from Sudan, North Korea, Indonesia, Ceylon, Zanzibar and New Zealand agreed to support Peking's position.

Communist programs for the development of nuclear weapons were further intensified. In his *Scientific and Engineering Manpower in Communist China, 1949–1963,* Chu-yuan Cheng estimates that some 400 senior scientists were engaged in top level nuclear research in the Institute of Atomic Energy and several university centers by 1964. Their numbers included Wang Kan-chang and Ch'ien Hsüeh-shen. [24]

While scientific programs were pushed forward, the Chinese Communists gave indication of their position with respect to nuclear weapons. In the Comment on the Soviet Government Statement of August 3, issued on August 15, 1963, the Peking leadership insisted: "For the Soviet statement to describe all the socialist countries as depending on the nuclear weapons of the Soviet Union for their survival is to strike an out-and-out great power chauvinistic note and to fly in the face of facts." On the day of its first atomic test (October 16, 1964), Peking issued an extended statement of policy:

This is a major achievement of the Chinese people in their struggle to increase their national defense capability and oppose the U. S. imperialist policy of nuclear blackmail and nuclear threats. . . . The atom bomb is a paper tiger. The famous saying by Chairman Mao Tse-tung is known to all. This was our view in the past and this is still our view. . . . The Chinese Government is loyal to Marxism-Leninism and proletarian internationalism. We believe in the people. It is the people who decide the outcome of a war, and not any weapon. . . .

The Chinese Government hereby solemnly declares that China will never at any time be the first to use nuclear weapons. . . . The Chinese Government hereby formally proposes to the governments of the world that a summit conference of all the countries of the world be convened to discuss the question of the complete prohibition and thorough destruction of nuclear weapons. . . .

World reaction to Peking's first testing of an atomic device was mixed. Several western analysts tended to minimize the feat by emphasizing the difficulties that the Chinese Communists will have in converting additional atomic devices into strategic weapons, and in stockpiling and delivering such bombs. [25] The Soviet leadership tended to stress that the great production costs involved in developing a nuclear arsenal were insupportable in Communist China, for capital outlays would be at the expense of total

---

[24] Wang Kan-chang, who received his Ph.D. from the University of Berlin in 1934, was a research associate at the University of California, Berkeley, in 1947–48. Ch'ien, who holds a Ph.D. from California Institute of Technology, was director of the US Scientific Commission of National Defense during the World War II years.

[25] For example, although the PLA could probably convert existing bombers to carry an atomic load, these bombers are slow and highly susceptible to ground and air attack. Even so, most experts agreed that the PLA IL-28 jet bombers could deliver a bomb within a 500–700 mile range, while the propeller-driven TU-4 bombers have a combat radius of about 1,800–2,000 miles.

economic development. Misquoting Mao's remark that, even in the event of a total nuclear war, China would survive, the Soviets have claimed that the Chinese Communist position is tantamount to an abandonment of the "Leninist policy of peaceful coexistence" and "reeks of hopelessness and pessimism." [26] In Japan, fear and anger at the fall-out menace led to mass demonstrations, government protests, and considerable embarrassment for the Japanese Socialist Party, which seeks closer economic ties between Tokyo and Peking. The Japanese Communist Party probably lost considerable popular support when it endorsed the Chinese test as a "defensive measure" for the "prevention of nuclear warfare in Asia." More significantly, the Sinkiang explosion engendered agitation to repeal Article 9 of the 1947 Japanese Constitution, which prohibits any substantial rearmament. The Japanese-South Korea defense treaty reflects a growing uneasiness in Japan over the state of military preparedness.

Peking's first detonation of an atomic device, predictably, had its greatest effect among the "non-aligned" developing nations. The Chinese Communists have sought to win the esteem and raise the hopes of these nations by a variety of measures. For example, Foreign Minister Ch'en Yi, during a September 29, 1965, Peking press conference, observed: "China hopes that Afro-Asian countries will be able to make atom bombs themselves," since "it would be better for a greater number of countries to come into possession of atom bombs." The color-film documentary prepared for international as well as national propaganda purposes, stresses that China's bomb was developed solely by the Chinese and represents the victory of Mao Tse-tung's thought. According to a NCNA bulletin of May 6, 1965, "the rising sun shown suggests China awakening to a brilliant morning," as Chinese scientists "jumping for joy" hail the wisdom of Mao.

Communist China's second test of an atomic device occurred at 10 A.M. on May 14, 1965, also in the "western area" of Sinkiang. It was estimated to be about equal to the first. The third test took place in the same area at 4 P.M., May 9, 1966, and was the first to involve thermo-nuclear materials. [27] The fourth test, on October 27, 1966, was the first to make use of a guided missile with a nuclear warhead. Apparently, the Chinese Communists have been able to leapfrog both the manned bomber and liquid fuel phases in their rocketry program. The fifth test, of December 27,

[26] In the vitriolic words of the August 20, 1963, TASS report: ". . . If China were to produce two or three bombs, this would not mean a solution of the question for her, but would bring about a great exhaustion of the Chinese economy. . . . [But TASS further ridicules Peking's position.] Never mind if half of mankind perishes, if 300 million Chinese die. But imperialism will be erased from the face of the earth, and those who survive will rapidly build on its ruins a civilization that will be a thousand times higher."

[27] The Chinese Communists are producing Uranium-235 by gaseous diffusion at a plant near Lanchow, Kansu province, and plotonium in reactors in Paotow of Inner Mongolian Autonomous Region.

1966, as analyzed by the U. S. Atomic Energy Commission, used uranium-238, as well as uranium-235. The former, which is cheaper to produce, requires far more advanced technical knowledge and equipment. The fifth device has been estimated to be in the 300,000 kiloton range, or fifteen times more powerful than the bomb used at Hiroshima.

Although there is considerable variation, Western sources have been obliged to foreshorten their estimates of Communist China's timetable for stockpiling nuclear weapons, and its ability to use missile delivery systems. For example, in December, 1965, US Secretary of Defense Robert McNamara estimated to the NATO Council of Ministers that the Chinese Communists would have an arsenal of intermediate range missiles with nuclear warheads within two years, and the ability to hit European targets within five years. McNamara calculated that Peking would be able to deliver nuclear weapons anywhere in the world by 1975. Japanese sources report that Peking already has a weapons stockpile, which will grow rapidly. For example, Junnosuke Kishida, of *Asahi's* Association for the Examination of Security Problems, in December, 1965, predicted that Peking would have at least 150–200 atomic bombs by the end of 1967. [28] With the success of Peking's fourth and fifth tests, involving missile systems, some western sources now predict that Communist China will have ICBM's by 1970.

The Chinese Communist leadership has been careful to protect its scientists, who certainly enjoy a higher living condition and are relatively freer from intensive political indoctrination and controls, from the destructive aspects of the "cultural revolution." Thus the August 8, 1966, Decision of the CPC Central Committee Concerning the Great Proletarian Cultural Revolution warns the Red Guards and other revolutionaries in Point 12:

As regards scientists, technicians and ordinary members of working staffs, as long as they are patriotic, work energetically, are not against the Party and socialism, and maintain no illicit relations with any foreign country, we should in the present movement continue to apply the policy of 'unity, criticism, unity.' Special care should be taken of those scientists and scientific personnel who have made great contributions. . . .

[28] For an analogous estimate of U.S. capacities see the article by Dr. Ralph Lapp, who was assistant laboratory director when the University of Chicago began work on the atomic bomb, and later director of the Department of Defense's Committee on Atomic Energy, Research and Development, in *Life*, May 28, 1965.

Lapp estimates that the U.S. is overstocked in atomic bombs (of the 25 megaton variety) and has more than 850 nuclear missiles. He believes that at least 400 of these weapons could be delivered on Mainland targets—or the equivalent of 10 billion tons of TNT, more than 13 tons for every man, woman and child in China's over 750 million population. In terms of destruction, Lapp points out that these weapons would kill 80 per cent of the total population, and that half of the strontium fall-out would remain until 1993. Ingested in food this would cause bone tumors and cancer.

Nevertheless, the closing of the colleges and universities for the academic year 1966–67, in order to promote the "cultural revolution," and the projected revisions of curriculum, will eventually have an adverse effect on the general development of science and nuclear capabilities in Communist China, particularly in terms of replacement of personnel.

The leaders in Peking continue to declare that men are more important than weapons, and Communist China has a virtually limitless supply of military manpower. Yet, any realistic assessment of Communist China's striking power must acknowledge that her entry into the nuclear club may have a profound effect upon military planning and potential.

MILITARY EDUCATION IN THE THOUGHT
OF MAO TSE-TUNG

The PLA *Bulletin of Activities* number 26, July 13, 1961, emphatically states one of the essential keys to understanding military education in Communist China in these words: "Military affairs form the most brilliant facet in the life of Chairman Mao. We are all his students." In assessing the major tasks for the military in 1966, Minister of Defense Lin Piao ranked first and most essential the study and application of the thought of Mao. Among his many claims to greatness as a symbol of the Chinese revolution is Mao's right to be considered as a foremost military philosopher and strategist. And among his many contributions to military thought— particularly in terms of the application of theory to concrete situations— are Mao Tse-tung's ideas on the role of the military and its operational uses. Yet Mao himself has always been guided by ideological principles. In this sense, a distinction may be made between his comprehensive military "strategy," in accordance with and intended to fulfill the tenets of Marxism-Leninism, and his "tactics," of actual organization and manipulation of the People's Liberation Army and the citizen militia.

If Mao's theory may be said to represent the key to understanding the Chinese Communist military system, then the Marxist-Leninist theory of war and peace must be said to constitute the key to understanding Mao. Although this latter area is far too complicated for proper discussion in these pages, certain general principles can be summarized here. In Western terminology, war and peace are antithetic. However Marxist-Leninist theory makes no such distinctions; or as Mao phrased it in his 1937 study *On Contradictions*, "war and peace transform themselves into each other." According to Marxism-Leninism, class struggle must exist as long as the last vestige of capitalism remains, so some form of conflict is inevitable. In the most fundamental sense, war and peace can be regarded, in communist thinking, as reverse sides of the same coin: the temporary prominence of the one in no way negates the likelihood of the other following soon thereafter. The followers of Marx and Lenin believe that, since capitalism must struggle for its own survival, violence is likely and may even be necessary. Although it may assume a variety of guises, war is a fundamental part of the mechanism regulating communism's expansion. Thus Mao has declared that "war is the continuation of politics, in this sense war is politics and war itself is a political action."

The communists add distinguishing norms when interpreting the nature of war and peace. For example, all wars are divided into the categories of "just" or "unjust," usually according to who starts them or who wins the victory. Within the first category, so-called wars of national liberation are regarded not only as just, but also as inevitable. These distinctions can be clarified according to Mao's interpretation in his work *On Contradictions*, which would suggest that the immutable clash between communism and capitalism must lead to at least localized violent efforts, since "imperialism" is by nature predatory.

One of the focal points in dispute between Peking and Moscow in recent years has been the question of revising these fundamental distinctions in accordance with changed circumstances. In the eyes of the Chinese Communists, for example, one of the signs of Khrushchev's "phony communism" was his suggestion that wars may no longer be fatally inevitable, since the communists are now strong enough to curb imperialist inclinations. This interpretation clashes with Mao's idea, which must be regarded as the more in keeping with Marxist-Leninist tradition of the two, that "war can only be abolished through war." "In order to get rid of the gun," he said, "we must first grasp it in our hand." In consequence, the Chinese Communists have been unwavering in their support of "national liberation wars," such as the conflict in Vietnam, just as they have continued to suggest that a clash with the "forces of imperialism led by the United States" may yet be inevitable. Or as expressed in a *People's Daily* editorial of December 19, 1965:

Revolutionary violence is the only language that the imperialists can understand. It is only through armed struggle that the people can destroy the old world dominated by imperialism and create a new one of national liberation, of independence and sovereignty, of democracy and freedom. Under the present circumstances, people's war is the best form of armed struggle waged by the oppressed nations and peoples against imperialism and the most effective magic weapon to defeat US imperialism and its lackeys.

The contradiction between imperialism and its lackeys on the one hand and the oppressed nations and peoples on the other is irreconcilable, involving a life-and-death conflict. Imperialism will never hand independence and sovereignty on a silver platter to the oppressed nations and peoples. The struggle to solve this contradiction may take many forms, but armed struggle is the main and decisive form. This is the universally applicable law of class struggle and social progress.

Moreover, should war with the United States prove necessary, the Chinese Communists have indicated the preferred tactical approach, which was perfected by Mao Tse-tung during the period of the civil war. For example, *Liberation Army Daily (LAD)*, on December 29, 1966, reaffirmed that "war of annihilation is the fundamental policy of our army's military operations." In concrete terms, this means that the PLA must concentrate a superior force against part of the enemy's force, to wipe out the latter completely. And as *LAD* added, this in turn requires luring the enemy deep into Chinese territory, while abandoning areas "in a planned way."

As suggested in the previous pages, Mao's axiom that "political power grows out of the barrel of a gun . . . under the leadership of the Party" has proven true in the Chinese Communist experience. In a real sense, this same relationship may be said to remain true, since the CPC has been able to utilize its military arm to add to its own authority and power. [29] The axiom also has an obvious appeal to leaders of revolutionary movements throughout the world.

The education of the troops in the thought of Mao Tse-tung has been stressed, particularly since 1960. In October, 1960, the CPC Central Committee's military committee ordered that the whole army be re-educated in the thought of Mao, and repeated that political standards were more important than the level of education or skills in selecting cadres or determining promotion. Between December, 1960, and February, 1961, one of the major themes of political education for the troops was to compare conditions under the Nationalists with those under the communists, in order to illustrate the superiority of the latter's system. In January, 1961, PLA regulations provided that 40 per cent of the soldiers' time was to be spent in political and cultural study, based upon a 25–15 per cent respective distribution. By the fall of 1961, copies of a specially prepared volume of *Selected Readings from Mao Tse-tung's Writings* had been distributed to all troops, as required reading. [30]

[29] Field Marshal Montgomery observes that during his 1961 interview, he quizzed Mao about the meaning of this expression, and its continued applicability, and received this response: "What he meant to imply was that you couldn't have a revolution without some fighting and then you needed guns. I asked him if it still held good in these days of so-called peace. His reply was: 'Of course.'"

[30] These selections have been taken from the four volume *Selected Works* and Mao's speech on Contradictions and include: Analysis of the Classes in Chinese Society (1926). An Investigation into the Peasant Movement in Hunan (1927). On the Rectification of Incorrect Ideas in the Party (1929), Strategic Problems of China's Revolutionary

On March 17, 1963, the CPC Central Committee issued Regulations Governing Political Work in the PLA, which concern the work of the PLA General Political Department, and of the PLA commissars and Party committees. During the year, high PLA cadres were ordered to participate in three-month courses to study the thought of Marx, Engels, Lenin and Mao and certain CPC documents. "Four good" and "five good" campaigns were carried on at the company level throughout the PLA to promote political and ideological work. Later, the program of the PLA Changsha Political School received Party endorsement as a model for wide scale emulation. At Changsha instructors live with their students and one cadre is appointed to report on each course to the Party committee by analyzing the thoughts of the individual students. Mao's writings constitute the basic text for all courses, since, in the words of the school's Party committee (reported in *Kuang-ming Jih-pao*, February 27, 1965), "the study of Chairman Mao's works is a short cut to the study of Marxism-Leninism." This line was reinforced at the 20-day conference of the PLA General Political Department, which concluded in Peking on January 18, 1966. Presided over by Hsiao Hua, the participants agreed that "putting politics first" means "putting Mao Tse-tung's thinking first," and called for far greater efforts to apply the thought of Mao. Perhaps the Party purge of the CPC Peking Municipal Committee, beginning in May, 1966, reflects the eagerness of the PLA to fulfill this assigned task. In any case, the thought of Mao provides the basic principles for military training in Communist China.

In terms of military education and operations, three of Mao's most important theories concern "paper tigers," "man-superior-to-weapons," and "people's war." He believes that "imperialism and all reactionaries are paper tigers" because, in fighting the masses, imperialism initially is outwardly strong, but progressively grows weaker due to internal contradictions. On the other hand, once aroused, organized and armed, the masses can grow stronger and defeat imperialism. Mao's "paper tiger" thesis is substantively strengthened by and closely related to his ideas on "man-superior-to-weapons" and "people's war," because of their common revolutionary nature.

War (1936), Combat Liberalism (1937), On the Protracted War (1938), The Role of the Chinese Communist Party in the National War (1938), In Memory of Norman Bethune (1939), Reform Our Study (1941), Serve the People (1944), The People's War (1945), The Army's Production for Self-Support and the Importance of the Great Campaigns for Increasing Production and Rectifying Style in Work (1945), Talk with the American Correspondent Anna Louise Strong (1946), The Present Situation and Our Tasks (1947), On the People's Democratic Dictatorship (1949), Cast Away Illusions, Prepare for Struggle (1949), and On the Correct Handling of Contradictions among the People (1957).

Mao's presentation of the "paper tiger" theme is not intended as illusion, bluff, or deception, either for his supporters or his enemies. In fact, the expression is used to symbolize a well-calculated theory of revolution—to be translated into revolutionary action by bold strategies and meticulous tactical considerations. Fundamentally related to his warning to "despise the enemy strategically," while "taking full account of him tactically," the "paper tiger" theory summarizes Mao's belief that the enemy's total strength—not only militarily, but also in a political, economic, social, cultural and moral sense—must be despised. Thus, in terms of strategy, this disavowal of the enemy's strength serves to justify a determined struggle and instill confidence in ultimate success. But the "paper tiger" theory also carries with it a vital tactical lesson. The enemy's tiger-like destructive power, particularly in terms of scientific and technological superiority, must be heeded. In combining these strategic and tactical considerations, Mao offers a theory to foster dedicated and courageous warfare against the class enemy for the cause of international communism.

Mao's "man-superior-to-weapons" theory is well-known by his maxim: "The outcome of a war is decided by the people, not by one or two types of weapons." This theme meets exactly the needs and conditions of any revolutionary group aiming at the overthrow of an existing political order which is backed by superior force and armed with sophisticated weapons. What the revolutionaries rely on most for winning their victory is revolutionary spirit. What they lack most is any type of superior weapons. Their revolutionary spirit, revolutionary will, revolutionary determination, and revolutionary sacrifice must be so abundant and supreme as to more than make up their inferiority in weaponry. Thus Mao maximizes the active role of men and minimizes the passive role of weapons in this generations-long, hard, and bloody world contest by saying: "The moral atom bomb of the revolutionary people is much more powerful than the material atom bomb and much more useful." (Quoted in *Peking Review*, Sept. 2, 1966, pp. 8–9.)

"People's war" is a political and military strategy to achieve communist ideological objectives initially and principally in the developing world. It devises to defeat "imperialism" by bogging the latter's forces down in world-wide wars of national liberation. People's war is the violent form of the anti-imperialist struggle. It is the military aspect of the communist strategy of anti-imperialist international united front, which has its political and diplomatic aspect represented by peaceful operations.

As a military strategy, people's war strives for mass initiative in the struggle against the "imperialist enemy and its lackeys." Lin Piao describes its invincibility in his 1965 major treatise, "Long Live the Victory of the People's War," in these terms: "You fight your way and we fight ours. We fight when we can win and move away when we can't. . . . You rely on modern weapons and we rely on highly conscious revolutionary people. You give full play to your superiority and we give full play to ours."

As an extension and development of the earlier communist-led guerrilla wars during and following World War II, people's war is to be conducted basically through the tactics of guerrilla warfare by arousing the people against the enemy. These tactics are succinctly summarized by Mao as: "Divide our forces to arouse the masses, concentrate our forces to deal with the enemy. The enemy advances, we retreat; the enemy camps, we harass; the enemy tires, we attack; the enemy retreats, we pursue." By utilizing these tactics, people's war can be made an effective challenge to the United States' world-wide commitment. Thus, the principle and strategy of people's war further strengthens Mao's theories that imperialism and reactionaries are "paper tigers," and that man is superior to weapons.

Although Lin Piao's analysis of "Long Live the Victory of the People's War" refers to the Chinese Communist victory over the Japanese in World War II, most of its some 20,000 words stress the crucial importance of Mao Tse-tung's theories, and Peking's intention to resist every manifestation of US "aggression." The most publicized of Lin Piao's adaptations of Mao's concepts is:

Taking the entire globe, if North America and Western Europe can be called "the cities of the world," then Asia, Africa and Latin America constitute the "rural areas of the world." . . . In a sense, the contemporary world revolution also presents a picture of the encirclement of cities by the rural areas.

In this major restatement, Mao is praised for his theories on use of the peasants in the revolutionary struggle, his ideas concerning the establishment of revolutionary bases, his interpretation of a "people's army," his differentiation between strategy and tactics, and his theory of self-reliance. And these and other contributions of Mao's are put forward as the best theories for revolutionaries throughout the world.

Mao's military thought has been studied carefully in other military organizations besides the PLA. Of the many examples which might be cited, the case of the military organization of the Democratic Republic of Vietnam (DRV) is perhaps most pertinent in the mid-1960's. The struggle of the Viet Cong and North Vietnam is regarded by the Chinese Communists as a "just" war of national liberation. US intervention is considered to be a classic proof of the aggressive nature of US "imperialism." Moreover, since this conflict is in the category of "people's war," as expressed by *People's Daily* on January 7, 1966, the people of North Vietnam "have an inalienable and sacred right to help the South Vietnamese in any form and on any scale." And the North Vietnamese have acknowledged Chinese Communist pledges of all out support. As Radio Hanoi affirmed on February 11, 1964, should the US decide to invade the Democratic Republic of Vietnam, it will "have to cope not only with North Vietnam, but also with China."

The military campaigns of the Viet Cong, supported by Hanoi, have reflected Mao's theories on people's war and guerrilla warfare, and the "paper tiger" strength of the US, just as they probably have provided an outstanding example of the correctness of some of Mao's revolutionary tactics. Paramount among these is the concept of using the peasants in the rural areas to encircle the cities. The similarity in the military tactics of Ho Chi-minh and Mao cannot be attributed primarily to coincidence.[31] The Chinese Communists have been quick to emphasize the value of the Vietnamese struggle in terms of proof of the validity of Mao's concepts. For example, as Chou En-lai pointed out during an April 10, 1966, interview with Ejaz Husain of the Pakistani newspaper *Dawn:* ". . . since the fourteen million people of southern Vietnam can cope with over 200,000 US troops, the 650 million people of China can undoubtedly cope with ten million of them." "No matter how many US aggressor troops may come," the Premier added, "they will certainly be annihilated in China." Lin Piao reflects the same bellicose confidence in his conclusion: "If you want to send [US] troops, go ahead, the more the better. We will annihilate as many as you can send, and can even give you receipts." This confidence comes from the conviction of the correctness of Mao's theories on people's war, man's superiority to weapons, and the nature of the imperialist "paper tiger."

The principles and policies of the People's Liberation Army are firmly rooted in the thought of Mao Tse-tung. When the Red Armies proved successful in China, the strategy and tactics of Mao passed their most critical test. Since revolutionaries throughout the world are apt to follow a proven strategy, which worked under similar conditions of economic backwardness, Mao's military thought must become an even greater influence in the years to come.

[31] Ho is reported to have been in China as early as 1925. When the Viet Minh was established at Liuchow, Kwangsi, China, in 1941, its programs quickly fell under Chinese Communist influence. First Secretary Le Duan of the Dang Lao Dong (North Vietnamese Communist Party) and one of its founders, who is regarded as a likely successor to Ho, was trained at Whampoa. Le headed the resistance movement in South Vietnam from 1946 to 1954, and was again in the south between 1956 and 1958. The subsequent resumption of hostilities followed his plans. On the other hand, it should be noted that Chief of Staff and Minister of Defense Vo Guyen Giap has indicated certain hostility to the CPR, even though his military successes might be attributed to implementation of Mao's strategies for revolutionary war.

MORALE OF THE MILITARY

There are many reasons why the morale of the military in Communist China should be high and buoyant. The PLA has been victorious ever since the tide of the civil war turned in the communists' favor in 1948. The employment of the Chinese "People's Volunteers" in Korea was claimed as a triumph, and was so presented to the troops. The concealed hand in Indo-China, both before and since the 1954 Geneva settlement, is yet another example of success. The military posture of the regime toward Formosa, early in 1955 and subsequently, has been almost arrogant in its confidence of final victory. In the 1960's, the prestige of the PLA has mushroomed as the Party leadership has repeatedly shown signs of approval, even to the extent of calling upon all Chinese to emulate the spirit of the military. Despite the purges of several high-ranking PLA officers, there has been a remarkable solidarity and continuation of military leadership. However, the question of the current status of military morale in Communist China also requires an analysis of several major problems of the PLA.

One approach to the problem of evaluating military morale is that of investigating the feelings or relative degree of contentment of the average man in the ranks. Although the secrecy shrouding the military in Communist China precludes any definitive judgment, certain conclusions can be suggested. General speaking, the Chinese Communist soldier has been well-fed, well-clad and well-disciplined. [32]

The Chinese Communists, of course, have their own explanation for high military morale. *The Chinese People's Liberation Army* listed four such reasons: (1) The PLA is a "people's army led by the CPC . . . entirely different from any reactionary army used by the ruling class as a tool to suppress the revolutionary movement of the people." (2) It is "composed of workers, peasants, and revolutionary intellectuals, with workers and peasants constituting approximately 90 per cent" and is thus "a highly politically minded and class conscious army." (3) It is an army "possessed of lofty ideals," educated in "Marxism-Leninism, and in the teachings of Mao Tse-tung and in patriotism and internationalism," and thus knows precisely "for what and for whom it is fighting." And (4) it is "characterized by its strict discipline which is based on army democracy."

[32] The Chinese Communist soldier has been reportedly subject to Three Disciplinary Rules and Eight Points for Attention. The rules are: (1) obey orders under all circumstances; (2) do not take a single needle or a piece of thread from the people; (3) hand in all booty to the government. The points are: (1) talk to people politely; (2) observe fair dealings in all business transactions; (3) return everything you borrow; (4) pay for everything you damage; (5) do not beat or scold the people; (6) do not damage crops; (7) do not fool around with women; and (8) do not ill-treat prisoners of war.

These points could be summarized under the twin headings of intensive political indoctrination and care for the physical and psychological well-being of the troops. The former stresses the glorious traditions and continuing successes of the PLA, and the latter makes the soldier better off than the average civilian in terms of creature comforts.

In keeping with ideological considerations with respect to the nature of war and peace and the relationship between political power and military strength, the Chinese Communist leadership has always emphasized the critical importance of military preparedness. Although the Chinese Communist military organization has not been committed to any large-scale action since the 1953 Korean truce, [33] the military and the country as a whole have been kept in a state of military preparedness. This policy could be traced back to the establishment of the People's Republic in October, 1949, but can be summarized by referring to several of its manifestations during the 1960's.

The rationale advanced to justify the need of national military preparedness was summarized by the then PLA Chief of Staff, Lo Jui-ch'ing, in his speech marking the 35th anniversary of the establishment of the Red Armies, on August 1, 1962. Pointing to threats in the form of the establishment of SEATO, and the dispatch of military forces to South Vietnam and Thailand, and to over 200 intrusions of Chinese territorial sea or air space since 1958, General Lo emphasized that "all plans of invasion and wars by American imperialism will be shattered." Thus, although at the time the Chinese Communists were involved with India in a struggle over their common boundary, the chief menace depicted was that of US imperialism. The often utilized complementary theme to this stress on the likelihood of US aggression is that the United States will encourage the Nationalist forces based in Taiwan to attempt an actual invasion of the mainland. In the same year, for example, *People's Daily* (June 24, 1962) cautioned "readiness to meet at any time an insidious attack by the Chiang bandit gang." On June 25, Foreign Minister Chen Yi warned: "The Chiang Kai-shek bandit gang with the support and encouragement of American imperialism is now preparing a large scale military adventure, an insidious attack on the coast of the mainland." He added that "this inevitably calls for grave attention and vigilance by the Chinese people." [34]

The Chinese Communists have repeated these twin themes of US threats

---

[33] Notable among the exceptions are the conflict in Tibet and the Sino-Indian border action.

[34] Reportedly, small teams of nationalist guerrillas did harass the coastline in 1962. While the call to all-out effort seems hardly warranted by this insignificant threat, it conforms with the overall principle of "fighting against imperialism and its lackeys."

and Nationalist machinations with increasing frequency and intensity, as they have called upon all Chinese to prepare to defend their homeland.[35] For example, in September, 1965, Peking announced that a US F-104 fighter plane had been shot down over Hainan Island; in October, another US fighter was claimed to have been shot down after four planes intruded over Kwangsi region; in November, US planes were accused of strafing a Chinese merchant ship, the *Nanhai 146*, in the waters off Vietnam, and two "US-Chiang" warships were reported to have fired on escort vessels of a Chinese fishing fleet off the Fukien front. Among the many "incidents of U.S. aggression" reported by the Chinese Communists in 1966, five U.S. fighter planes were said to have intruded into the air space over Yunnan province on May 12, and launched guided missiles which downed one PLA plane.[36] Two other American fighter planes were accused of bombing and strafing Chinese fishing boats on May 28, on the high seas, in the northern Bac Bo Gulf area with the loss of one boat sunk and three damaged, three Chinese killed, and eighteen wounded.

By constantly publicizing the aggressive nature of the United States, in addition to the factors of international influence and importance, the Chinese Communists provide a suitable framework for making greater demands upon their own troops to achieve an advanced state of preparedness. These calls for ever more intensive efforts on the part of the PLA can be divided into two categories. On the one hand, the Peking leadership urges that the military attempt to achieve economic self-sufficiency, and on the other, the higher echelons of Party leadership have called upon the PLA to set an example of advanced political thinking.

As a "people's army," the Chinese Communists have ordered all members of the PLA to participate regularly in productive labor. This policy was strengthened greatly beginning in 1958, as part of the total drive to organize society to strengthen the working force. During that year alone, PLA troops contributed a total of 59,000,000 man-days in different types of construction work. Soldiers built 20,000 water conservation projects and dug 58,000,000 cubic meters of earth. Thousands of army trucks were used to transport iron ore, coke and other materials as part of the

[35] This would appear to correspond with a drive to strengthen and improve the efficiency of PLA troops. For example, in June, 1964, the Chinese Communists issued new and detailed regulations governing commercial ships sailing in the area between Hainan Island—a PLA stronghold—and the Luichow peninsula. Ships must request permission to use these waters 40 hours in advance, sail only in daylight hours, and not use radar without permission. This would indicate a further military build-up in the area. On April 30, 1965, the State Council issued new and more restrictive orders concerning frontier inspection.

[36] *Peking Review*, No. 20 (May 13, 1966), contains pictures of the remnants of U.S. sidewinder missiles allegedly recovered after this attack.

iron and steel production campaign. Other soldiers were sent to work in the mines and refineries or to construct new plants, and air force planes transported equipment. In 1961, official Peking sources stated that the PLA contributed in excess of 22,500,000 man-days to construction tasks, 80 per cent of which were in the rural areas. PLA planes flew over 400 flights to spray crops or attempt to create rain artificially.

Dramatic increases in military aid to civilian tasks were claimed in 1963. For example, NCNA reported that the air force made 1,300 flights to spray crops or drop supplies to flooded areas. Among the 8,000,000 man-days the soldiers gave to the rural communes were included the services of 5,000 technicians, who overhauled machinery and trained local personnel. The PLA railway corps laid some 600 kilometers of narrow gauge track and constructed 400 kilometers of forest roads, with bridge and tunnel facilities. In the area of Peking municipality alone, soldiers were credited with repairing 450,000 meters of canals, building 38 pumping stations, and sinking 197 wells. In 1964, the PLA gave 5.4 million man-days to the rural communes, laid another 670 kilometers of narrow gauge rail tracks, and constructed 420 kilometers of highways. Similar achievements were praised in 1965. For example, NCNA-Canton reported on February 25, 1966, the reclamation in Kwangtung province of 1,000 hectares of coastal lands which had formerly been submerged by tides through the work of PLA troops. By erecting a sea dike and 120 kilometers of canals the soldiers were able to increase grain production by 4,000 tons in a year. Another PLA company on the Yunnan frontier determined to aid the peoples of the Hani national minority there. When the soldiers enlarged the cultivated area from 1,000 to 3,000 mou, grain production rose from 600,000 to two million catties. *People's Daily* of August 4, 1963, reported that over 100,000 soldiers, demobilized or transferred, had been sent to the border area northeast of Heilungkiang for the reclamation of waste land. The troops also ran primary and evening schools for these peoples, some of whom still believed in witchcraft, and trained a local militia.

These reports of military aid to production, in the form of man-hours contributed by members of the PLA, tell only half of the story. Each unit of the regular military forces has been ordered to strive for self-sufficiency in food production, to alleviate the strain on the national budget and prevent taking food from the civilian population. Although statistics are not available, some indication of the importance of this campaign may be gathered from the fact that PLA food output in 1963 was said to be 15 per cent higher than the previous year, and many companies claimed to be already self-sufficient in raising their own vegetables. NCNA on February 6, 1964, claimed that some PLA companies had raised a surplus of food, and were thus able to sell nearly a hundred million catties of rice to the state. [37]

Although the contributions of the regular military to the improvement of economic production must be regarded as a valuable aid to the Chinese Communists, the PLA's most outstanding service to the Party leadership is that of providing a model of correct political thinking for the entire population to emulate. Particularly since 1960, members of the PLA have often been singled out individually or collectively for their correct understanding and implementation of the thought of Mao Tse-tung. The case of model soldier Lei Feng has been mentioned in detail in another chapter, and needs only to be referred to here as an example of this CPC practice of publicizing individual achievements. Similarly, a 21 year old sailor, Mai Hsien-te, has been honored by the Party—including a personal visit by Tung Pi-wu—for fighting three hours, despite serious head wounds. Needless to say, Mai's heroic action against attacking Nationalist gunboats has been attributed to the inspiration of Mao's thought. And Mai enjoys another distinction: unlike Lei Feng, whose exploits were publicized only after his death, Mai is a living hero.

The entire regular military organization has also been cited by the Chinese Communists for having achieved a high degree of political knowledge. In 1963, the Party offered the PLA as a model for a national emulation drive. The various economic ministries under the State Council were ordered to create political departments similar to those in the PLA. In the rural areas, local Party committees urged the various peasant associations to form such units. Gradually, "political guides" or, when possible, political departments, have been created in all economic enterprises. PLA troops and demobilized veterans have been assigned to supervise these departments in factories, banks, rural cooperatives, and other centers. Thus the CPC hopes to remedy the deficiencies in financial transactions by employing the services of soldiers whose political reliability is apparently beyond question.

The CPC Central Committee has itself added a Finance and Commerce Political Department to its own structure. In February, 1965, Politburo member and Finance Minister Li Hsien-nien convened a national conference in Tientsin to further stress the importance of correct politics in business. Li is himself a veteran of the Red Armies. Follow-up conferences were then held at the provincial and municipal levels to implement the decisions concerning the extension of political departments down to the county level. In many cases, this was apparently carried out by transforming the Party committee's finance and commerce department into the

---

[37] These claims must be weighed together with the reports of deficiencies in food production mentioned elsewhere in these pages.

new-type political department.   For example, *Ta-kung Pao* mentioned on June 16, 1965, that about 32 per cent of the political guides were members of the military, and about 54 per cent were former Party branch secretaries, while the remainder came from the administrative bureaus.   On July 31, 1965, the same source noted that in Liaoning province 4,400 demobilized servicemen filled about 70 per cent of the posts of political guides or branch secretaries.

The CPC's decision to assign the regulation of financial matters to the military reflects the Party leadership's conviction of the political reliability of the PLA.   Conversely, the PLA's political reliability stems from the careful training and regulation which the Party provides for the regular military.

As mentioned in the previous sections, the CPC seems to have been largely successful in terms of its political indoctrination of the troops.   But evidence suggests that the problems of physical and psychological well-being have yet to be solved entirely.   The Korean War brought to light certain deficiencies of the PLA which would tend to depress morale. Generally speaking, the Chinese Communist soldier had never before faced really modern fire power.   The cases of desertion and surrender in Korea and the observations of POW's who refused to return to the mainland reflect the strain in the soldier's morale when forced to deal with a technologically superior international force on foreign soil.   Other factors contributing to low morale in the 1950's were the sharp distinctions practiced in the PLA with respect to rank and political reliability.   During the revolutionary years before the seizure of power, officers and men lived together on familiar terms and distinctions of rank were as unnecessary as they were impossible.   But the February, 1955, regulations on officer ranks and services sharply intensified the distinctions between officers and their men.   Reportedly, even meals were graded according to rank.   *People's Daily*, on September 28, 1955, felt it necessary to remind the soldiers that these military differences in status were not to be confused with the "class distinctions" between ranks in capitalist armies.   Other reports indicated that the conferment of honors and rewards favored the politically reliable, and that punishment for crimes or offenses often fell more harshly on those who had no Party affiliation.   Cadres were said to enjoy a safer position in the rear when battle lines were formed, and were the first to be evacuated in time of danger.

Probably the question of faulty morale contributed to the CPC decision in 1958 to rejuvenate, modernize and re-indoctrinate the PLA, as part of the comprehensive military reorganization plan associated with the Everyone a Soldier Movement.   A new combat training program was designed to improve military techniques and coordinate the various army units under the special conditions presented by the possibilities of atomic, chemical or guided missile warfare. It required that field commanders and all personnel at command headquarters study the organization and equipment of all service branches, all types of arms, strategic and tactical capabilities of principal weapons, management of mechanized equipment, and all types of ordinance.

A new Academy of Military Science was established in Peking in March, 1958, with Marshal Yeh Chien-ying as President and Political Commissar, to carry out a research program and accelerate army modernization. At the lower levels, efforts were made to eliminate illiteracy among the soldiers and raise the general level of education for all troops. A directive of the PLA General Political Department, issued early in 1959, encouraged the majority of soldiers to aspire to the cultural standards of a college graduate by 1969. As a first step, secondary education was popularized. It should be noted that the illiteracy rate at the time was very high. In 1958, with the slogan of "wipe out illiteracy within a year," 90 per cent of the illiterate soldiers were said to have mastered some 1,500 characters. Company cadres taught the more advanced; those who knew 200 characters instructed those who knew 100.

Another morale problem which was dealt with in 1958 involved provisions for elderly or disabled veterans. Even before this, Peking reportedly had spent 92,980,000 yuan in payments, compensations, allowances and other benefits for the many demobilized soldiers, and widows and dependents of soldiers, who were visible evidence of the long civil war and the fierce Korean engagement. Until the rural reorganization of 1958, the agricultural cooperatives had adopted a system of support for indigent veterans. On August 1, 1958, the State Council adopted Provisional Rules Governing the Retirement of Regular Army Officers which authorized retirement for: (1) all officers who had completed a prescribed tour of duty and had reached the age of 55; and (2) officers incapacitated by illness or injury. Retired officers were to receive pensions amounting to from 40 to 100 per cent of normal pay, depending upon the value of their service during the revolutionary period. At the same time, the communes inaugurated a system of subsidies to ensure widows and dependents of soldiers the same wage level as that of the working masses, even if their work were curtailed. Some "homes of glory" were built to accommodate aged widows. In urban areas, army dependents were organized to participate in production, but if they failed to earn enough for their own sustenance, they were to receive an allowance.

All of these plans for military reorganization and modernization suffered critical reversals during the 1959–61 period of economic dislocation. The pages of the *Bulletin of Activities* of the PLA General Political Department recite case after case of dangerously low morale. One of the most acute needs of the soldiers was for adequate food. For example, in January, 1961, the Party Central Committee police guard reported that in one company 154 of the 193 soldiers had received news from their villages concerning death, sickness or misery, and that 28 openly manifested discontent. But the soldiers themselves had insufficient food, and some resorted to theft. In one unit, 9 soldiers were charged with petty theft, and most units reported dangerously low levels of health. Apparently, many of the dissatisfied troops took to criticizing the Party. On February 1, 1961, Lo Jui-ch'ing reported that 38 soldiers in the Kunming area were found to be planning to run away.

Some officers and cadres attempted to deal with cases of insubordination of soldiers, during the critical years between 1959 and 1961, by extremely harsh measures. For example, the *Bulletin of Activities* of March 2, 1961, told of eleven soldiers committing suicide from fear of punishment in one military unit during 1960. Of these, two had been charged with political deviation and nine with petty theft. The cruelty of the officers and cadres is evident in the fact that one soldier, charged with the crime of stealing a pair of trousers, killed himself after eighteen hours of intensive interrogation.

Another complaint of the troops stemmed from the Party's decision to lengthen the term of active service. In May, 1961, the PLA reported that 25 per cent of the soldiers in some areas had been retained after their term had expired. Most of these soldiers were heads of sections or technicians: they expressed dissatisfaction with their pay and opposition to their retention. In August, 1961, the PLA decided that 23–25 per cent of troops in the navy and air force would be retained for one or two years, or longer if advisable. With permission of the Ministry of Defense, the PLA was authorized to draft youths under the age of eighteen, in order to begin their technical training early.

As morale reached a low ebb, the military commanders and the leaders of the CPC were obliged to order a number of corrective measures, probably to prevent any overt or widespread sign of discontent by the troops. Lin Piao himself ordered that the soldiers must be allowed sufficient rest. Soldiers were encouraged to sing or participate in games in order to raise their morale. Officers and Party cadres were instructed to be more lenient in their treatment of soldiers accused of crimes. For example, public admonishments for petty theft or sexual relations were forbidden. Troops who were retained after their normal discharge date were given pay increases and promotions, and promised time to go home to marry and one leave a year.

The morale of the military improved, as general conditions improved in

Communist China. But, cases of insubordination or discontent continued. This can be substantiated by the speech of Hsiao Hua to the conference of political departments in Peking, in January, 1966. In his talk, published by *People's Daily* on January 25, the head of the PLA General Political Department noted that "there is a class struggle within the Party and within the army also," and spoke of cadres who claimed special treatment. Therefore, Hsiao advocated, if not ordered, that the troops engage in further criticism and self-criticism to increase their political reliability. In the spring of 1966, the GPD ordered all troops to study Lin Piao's "Long Live the Victory of the People's War," and to work diligently to fulfill the five tasks imposed by Lin for the PLA during the course of the year.

Ever since the establishment of the communist government in China, soldiers have occupied a privileged position in society: this status was granted not only to reward the veterans of the revolutionary wars, but also to attract capable youths needed for a strong modern army. Before the adoption of the Constitution in 1954, the army was active in assisting the Party to rule the country. After 1954, the army retained its prestige, largely because of the ability of communist cadres to promote correct political thinking among the troops. Since 1958, the Chinese Communists have urged a policy of Everyone a Soldier, in terms of political orthodoxy and diligent work especially. Nevertheless, there have been signs of conflict between the military and the civilian functionaries. In 1957, for example, the PLA GPD sent cadres to interview officials in the Central Government concerning their opinion of the army. *Chien-Fang-Chun Pao* of May 23, 1957, revealed that the most common criticisms of the PLA were that the military monopolized too much territory and property, that the soldiers had improper ideas about love and marriage, that some officers and their families led extravagant lives, that the military flounted civil regulations, and that the troops frequently enjoyed greater privileges than civilians.

In long-range terms, the morale of the military and, indeed, the loyalty of the armed forces will depend to a considerable degree on the continued intimate collaboration of the CPC and PLA at the highest echelons of communist power. Militarization of the people must still overcome the traditional Chinese scorn for the military life. Economic programs must be developed and improved to sustain a modern armed force able of utilizing the most advanced of technological devices and equipment. And, as the interval widens from the time of the revolution, and the battle-tested veterans are replaced by a new generation of conscripts, the PLA will have to intensify its political indoctrination efforts. Furthermore, the increasing prominence of the PLA may itself raise accusations that the military is a privileged class in Communist China. Without a strong challenge, it will be difficult for the military to retain the dedication and fervor of the revolutionary generation of troops. The unprecedented challenge came with the increasing role assigned to the PLA in the "great proletarian cultural revolution."

THE PEOPLE'S LIBERATION ARMY AND THE CULTURAL REVOLUTION

In January, 1967, the People's Liberation Army openly assumed the leadership of the cultural revolution in several of Communist China's troubled provinces and municipalities. As the backbone element in the new "three in one" revolutionary committees, the PLA has extended and enhanced its own role in areas more normally considered the prerogatives of Party and state organs. This rising importance of the military corresponds with and reinforces the growing authority of Lin Piao. In turn, both the personal ascendency of Lin and the growing authority of the PLA reflect that the military have been singled out as best understanding and implementing the thought of the "great supreme commander," Mao Tse-tung.

The PLA's tireless ideological endeavor in communist theory and practice strengthens its morale and conviction immeasurably. For it is the process of ideological cultivation which had prepared the PLA as the vanguard and model for all "revolutionary" people in Communist China. But it is equally true that, without such a thoroughly inculcated and dedicated army, there would be no nuclear controlling force for the leadership to charge with leading a mass campaign unprecedented in extent and intensity. Commensurate to its continuously enhanced prestige and increased responsibilities, and with the support of its reinforcements from the Red Guards, the PLA has become the vital vehicle for conducting the proletarian cultural revolution. Therefore, the successes or failures of the military will have a profound impact on the future of Communist China in its struggle against "modern revisionism" both at home and abroad.

The leadership's decision to increase the political responsibilities of the PLA can be traced back to the 1959 Lushan Conference of the CPC Central Committee. Mao's choice of Lin Piao, to replace Defense Minister P'eng Teh-huai and become first vice chairman of the influential CC Military Commission, signalled high trust in the loyalties of both Lin and the men he commanded. As noted in chapter VII, following the severe strain on the national economy in 1959–61, the subsequent recovery was attributed in large measure to the army's loyal support. Thus, the leadership determined that the various economic ministries under the State Council should create political departments similar to those in the PLA, and frequently staffed by military personnel.[38] Gradually, "political guides" or departments were also established in factories, banks, mines and other enterprises. Thus, the PLA added to its experience and accomplishments by performing executive or administrative tasks.

Early in 1966, on the eve of launching the cultural revolution the PLA was given another test, to reassure Mao Tse-tung of the loyalty of his troops. In February, Lin Piao ordered leading army cadres concerned with cultural work to assembly in Shanghai. Under the personal direction of Chiang Ch'ing, the delegates studied films, documents, theatrical performances and related literature, and determined the best means to implement Mao's guidelines for literature and art. As the Forum Summary noted, "the Liberation Army must play an important role in the socialist cultural revolution.[39] Furthermore, the conference cemented a close working relationship between Lin Piao and Mao's wife.[40]

By June of 1967, coinciding with the unfurling of the cultural revolution the PLA was playing a vital, although indirect role. Just as the Red Guards were guided and inspired by the troops, the Chinese Communist leadership made it clear that the PLA's political and ideological stance should become the guideline for all Chinese. Worded in the CPC Central Committee's journal, *Red Flag* (no. 8, 1967): "Energetic emulation of the Liberation Army has become a universal call to action for all the people and all endeavors."

This high trust given to the PLA on the basis of ideological dedication, political loyalty, and professional ability requires constant effort to deepen and improve revolutionary spirit. Therefore, in transmitting Lin Piao's instructions to the PLA in October, 1966, Hsiao Hua, director of the General Political Department, urged even more intensive study. "The army must truly become a great school of Mao Tse-tung's thought," he affirmed. And in its editorial of October 12, 1966, *People's Daily* insisted that the PLA approach applied to all people.

The first task set for the PLA in 1967, and the one upon which all others

---

[38] Red Guard newspapers indicate that personnel of some of the ministries opposed the staffing of political departments with members of the PLA. For example, *Ming Pao* (May 1, 1967) mentioned among the crimes of Minister of Petroleum Yü Ch'iu-li that in 1964 he had refused to accept troops assigned to his ministry.

[39] As noted in Chapter III, it was appearance of this Forum Summary, implying greater PLA control over cultural activities, together with the publication of the P'eng Chen group's Outline Report that marked the coming of the cultural revolution.

[40] According to official sources, Lin Piao personally entrusted Chiang Ch'ing with conducting the conference, and instructed PLA cadres "from now on, the army's documents concerning literature and art should be sent to her." See the Forum Summary, *Peking Review* (no. 23, 1967).

rest, indicates the importance attached to political work. It is: "to firmly apply the spirit of the eleventh plenum of the Eighth CPC Central Committee, hold the great banner of Mao Tse-tung's thought still higher, unswervingly give prominence to politics, take an active part in and stand guard over the great proletarian cultural revolution." According to Lin Piao's orders, soldiers will be selected for training and promotion according to the measure in which they attain these goals. Thus, the three-point criterion for PLA cadres is: (1) loyalty to the thought of Mao; (2) prominence to proletarian politics and close contact with the masses; and (3) revolutionary vigor and drive. This criterion, of course, indicates that rectification is regarded as a constant labor in the PLA. Generally, this follows the normal pattern of criticism and self-criticism. For example, the Canton *Hung-wei Pao* of November 28, 1966, singled out a regiment of the city's armed forces as "a big school for the thought of Mao" and a model for other PLA units to imitate. Its leading regimental cadres regularly spend time with the rank and file troops and subject themselves to the latter's criticisms.

One measure of the leadership's approval of the PLA's political work in the first months of the cultural revolution can be gathered from the increased authority given to the military over cultural work in general. One aspect of this involved the drafting of whole art circles into the ranks of the PLA. For example, at a November 28, 1966 Peking rally of literary and art circles, Hsieh T'ang-chung, head of the PLA General Political Department's Culture Subdepartment, revealed that the CPC CC's Military Commission had instructed the Party Central Committee's Cultural Revolutionary Group to incorporate several leading institutions into the PLA. [41] Thus, the Number One Opera Company of Peking, the National Peking Opera Theatre, the Central Philharmonic Society and the ballet troupe and orchestra of the Central Song and Dance Ensemble were placed under the direct jurisdiction of the military. Since Chou En-lai expressed a hope that many more literary and art circles would join the ranks of the PLA, this course seems preordained by the leadership. At the same time, PLA officers and cadres assumed posts of authority in such organs as *People's Daily* and the offices of the New China News Agency.

The growing prestige given to the PLA's cultural activities was greatly enhanced by the November, 1966 appointment of Mao Tse-tung's wife, Chiang Ch'ing, as "advisor on cultural work to the PLA." In noting this

[41] It should be noted that, in November, 1966, the CPC CC and the PLA had not yet formalized their respective organs for cultural work. Too, Chiang Ch'ing had previously been active in reforming the circles in question. The anouncement of their absorption into the PLA coincided with the CPC Central Committee's revelation that Chiang Ch'ing had been appointed a "cultural advisor" to the PLA.

decision of the CPC CC's Military Commission on November 28, Ch'en Po-ta praised Madame Mao for "having made outstanding contributions" in the struggle of literary and art circles against revisionism.   Chou En-lai observed that the revolutionary achievements of these units were "inseparable from the guidance given by Comrade Chiang Ch'ing." [42]

The relatively "behind the scenes" role of the PLA in leading and guiding the cultural revolution by intensified political activities and extension of control over a host of cultural organs, prevailed until January, 1967.   But, when counterrevolutionary violence broke out in several of the provinces and municipalities, the PLA was ready to assume a direct leading role. Phrased in the January 25, 1967 editorial of *Liberation Army Daily:*

> . . . In the new situation in the present great proletarian cultural revolution, it is not possible for the PLA to refrain from intervening. . . . Our PLA must clearly and actively support the proletarian revolutionary Left.   The demand of all genuine proletarian revolutionaries for the army's support must be met. . . . We must follow Comrade Lin Piao's instruction: enthusiastically support Chairman Mao, zealously support the proletarian revolutionary Left, hit hard at the handful of persons who are in authority and taking the capitalist road, and always keep the banner of our great PLA completely red.

Thus, PLA troops were in the forefront of the revolutionary forces that seized control in the troubled areas.   For example, *People's Daily* of March 3, 1967, observed that in the struggle for control in Shantung province "the PLA played the decisive role at the most critical moment of the struggle to seize power; it made an outstanding contribution."   The Revolutionary Committee of Kweichow province and Kweiyang city similarly noted that "clearcut support from the PLA is a vital link in winning victory."   Although it may be argued that Mao and his followers called upon the army only as a last resort, when Party and state personnel and organizations had been found wanting, the PLA's response lived up to the trust bestowed upon it by the leadership.

In the areas where the forces of the cultural revolution have defeated the counterrevolutionaries, the prestige and authority of the PLA have been increased considerably.   And the Chinese Communisty leadership has ordered major modifications of the Party and state structures to strengthen the political role of the military.   The case of Heilungkiang is representative.   Following the rioting in Harbin, on January 31, 1967, the Red Rebel Revolutionary Committee announced that it had become the "provincial supreme organ of power," replacing the CPC provincial and city committees and the state's provincial and city people's councils.   This

---

[42] Although Chiang Ch'ing certainly served as a "cultural advisor" to the PLA at least as early as February, 1966, her status was unofficial until the November announcement.

Revolutionary Committee is comprised of responsible delegates from: (1) the revolutionary groups, such as the Red Guards and the factory committees, (2) the provincial Party apparatus, and (3) the provincial military command. [43]

"Three in one" revolutionary committees, wherein the PLA often exercises a dominant role, have been established at the provincial and municipal levels as power has been seized by the forces loyal to Mao. In the rural areas, at the commune level and below, and in urban areas in factories and mines, the militia is to constitute the military arm of the triune committees, which also include Party cadres and workers' representatives. Since the militia is under the authority of the PLA, this trend further extends the army's administrative powers.

According to the principle of "democratic centralism," proceeding from the lowest level militia unit, through the PLA's regional commands, the chain of authority for conducting ideological and political work in the army culminates in the PLA's Cultural Revolutionary Group. This organ has apparently replaced, at least temporarily, the Culture Subdepartment of the PLA's General Political Department. On January 12, 1967, NCNA reported the reorganization of the PLA's Cultural Revolutionary Group to include the following personnel: Head: Hsü Hsiang-ch'ien; Advisor: Chiang Ch'ing; Deputy Heads: Hsiao Hua, Yang Ch'eng-wu, Wang Hsin-t'ing, Hsü Li-ch'ing, Kuan Feng, Hsieh T'ang-chung, and Li Man-ts'un; and Members Wang Hung-k'un, Yü Li-chin, Liu Hua-ch'ing, T'ang P'ing-chu, Hu Ch'ih, Yeh Ch'un, Wang Feng, Ho Ku-yen and Chang T'ao. [44]

The PLA's Cultural Revolutionary Group, in turn, was created by and receives its orders from the CPC Central Committee's Military Commission, which is headed by Mao Tse-tung, with Lin Piao as his first deputy. Thus, the army's political indoctrination programs come directly from the highest circle of leadership. It must also be presumed that the PLA's Cultural Revolutionary Group is directed by the CPC Central Committee's

[43] The temporary leadership of the Committee appears to have been vested in the persons of: P'an Fu-sheng, former First Secretary of the Heilungkiang provincial Party committee; and Wang Chia-tao, commander of the provincial military district.

For other examples of the establishment of Revolutionary Committees consult the concluding section of Chapter 5.

[44] As noted elsewhere, T'ang P'ing-chu and Hu Ch'ih were subsequently removed from their offices as editor of *People's Daily* and acting head of NCNA respectively, and may have been dismissed from the Cultural Revolutionary Group.

The conclusion that this Group has probably replaced the PLA's Culture Subdepartment is strengthened by considering the offices held by some of its members. Yang Ch'eng-wu is acting chief of staff; Hsü Li-ch'ing is former deputy head of the PLA Political Department. Hsieh T'ang-chung is head of the Culture Subdepartment. Li Man-ts'un is deputy head of the PLA Propaganda Department.

Cultural Revolutionary Group. The intimate working relationship between these two organs is effected by a policy described at some length in chapter 5—that of having individuals hold simultaneous offices in two or more bodies. For example, Chiang Ch'ing is first vice chairman of the CC's Group and advisor to the PLA's Group while Hsieh T'ang-chung and Kuan Feng are deputy heads of both bodies.

The activities and assignments of the Red Guards may be regarded as inseparable from the leadership and guidance provided by the PLA. The Red Guards not only learned from the PLA's political consciousness and revolutionary experience, but also have relied on the army for orientation and routine services. This close working relationship resembled that of the orbit and the center, or between those who set the model and those who emulate and extend it. It is this integrated strength that has provided Mao and his close associates with the confidence that the Party can be cleansed of revisionist trends or tendencies, and the revolution can be carried to new heights through the "three in one" combination.

PLA troops frequently provide the immediate leadership and inspiration for Red Guard units. For example, *Peking Review* (no. 1, 1967) noted that in the city of Peking alone over 100,000 soldiers "worked, studied and lived with" the Red Guards during the time of the 1966 mass rallies. This pattern has been repeated in many of China's cities and provinces, where thoroughly indoctrinated troops provide the best vehicle for inspiring Communist China's younger generation. Similarly, the Red Guards' organization along military lines follows the example of the PLA. So organized, the Guards are considered as a useful adjunct supplementing the regular military forces.

Worded in the December 23, 1966 *Peking Review;* "The great proletarian cultural revolution now vigorously unfolding in our country is the most fundamental way for the Chinese people to make preparations for war." Although, in a total concept, this refers to the importance of political unity and ideological unity, the statement also implies the relationship between the Red Guard and the PLA, with the former serving as the reserve strength of the latter. This conclusion was stated explicitly by *Liberation Army Daily* in its editorial of January 13, 1967: the Red Guards are "a powerful reserve force of the PLA. In the event of war, they will go to the battlefields and perform new meritorious deeds in fighting aggression." And the Red Guards have been quick to accept this assignment. In February, 1967, when some 10,000 representatives gathered in Peking to establish the Congress of Red Guards of Universities and Colleges, Chou En-lai, K'ang Sheng, Ch'en Po-ta, Hsieh Fu-chih and Chiang Ch'ing personally applauded their resolution that the role of the Red Guards is as a "political shock force" and a "firm and reliable reserve force of the PLA. [45]

Implementing Lin Piao's instruction that "the army must truly become a great school of Mao Tse-tung's thought," the most important work of the PLA after the seizure of power in any area is that of providing correct political instruction. Described by *Red Flag* (no. 2, 1967) as a force "infinitely loyal to Chairman Mao, loyal to the people," the soldiers of the PLA—not the members of the Party—have been designated to lead this vital work of ideological remolding of the masses. At the same time, the people are reminded that their degree of political reliability shall be judged according to how faithfully they follow and imitate the troops. Or, as *Red Flag* (no. 5, 1967) expressed it: "The attitude toward the PLA is actually the attitude toward the dictatorship of the proletariat and it is an important criterion for distinguishing whether a person is of the genuinely revolutionary Left or not."

Throughout the areas now controlled by the forces loyal to Mao Tse-tung, PLA troops now conduct study sessions "to launch the political offensive, to educate and explain" the thought of Mao. As Chou En-lai reminded the delegates to the March, 1967 Peking Conference of Poor and Lower-Middle Peasants, "we trust that with their help, you will be more successful in your study of Chairman Mao's works."

As Chou En-lai reminded the delegates to the March, 1967 Peking Conference of Revolutionary Workers and Staff, the PLA is not only a "fighting force and a propaganda force," but is also a "work force." Thus, along with its heavy political and ideological responsibilities, the PLA is also entrusted with actively aiding, and even leading, socialist construction. [46] This function has become increasingly important due to the dislocation to the national economy accompanying the cultural revolution. As the troops were ordered in the General Tasks assigned for 1967, "while performing our task as a fighting force, let us do well as a work force and a production force."

In the rural areas, the PLA is expected to assist the peasants in routine farm work. For example, on the eve of the 1967 spring planting, the CPC Central Committee issued a Letter to Poor and Lower Middle Peasants and Cadres at All Levels in the Communes. This directive, dated February 20, 1967, emphasized that PLA units should "support and help" the work of cultivation. On February 23, 1967, the CC's Military Commission issued

[45] The Chinese Communists have admitted that some of the Red Guards have refused to honor PLA leadership. For example, on May 16, 1967, *People's Daily* mentioned that soldiers were sent to deal with a Red Guard unit in Peking Teachers University.

[46] As noted elsewhere, one of the errors of the P'eng Teh-huai conspirators denounced at the 1959 Lushan Conference was opposing the policy of troops actively participating in productive labor. But, as *Red Flag* (no. 19, 1959) insisted: "troops should spontaneously and actively take part in the construction of the country and in mass movements."

a Directive to the Army to Give Localities All-Out Assistance, stipulating that farm labor was to be given temporary top priority, with militia members assigned as shock brigades.

Since the militia units are best suited to render special "shock brigade" functions in the communes, the PLA's support to farm labor often may be considered as indirect. That is, the PLA regulates the militia, which in turn directly serves in the rural labor force. This point was stressed in the March 16, 1967 *Liberation Army Daily* reminder that local militia must become "the pathbreakers in revolution" and "models in production." At the lowest levels, the militia constitutes the military arm of the "three in one" alliance with outstanding workers and Party cadres. The Party press has singled out the Hochiachuang militia company of Li county, Kansu province as a "pace setting advanced unit" worthy of national emulation. This company, hailed as a model of organization, political indoctrination and military training, was especially praised by the CPC Northwest Bureau (in an NCNA dispatch of September 20, 1966) for its work as a shock force in restoring and increasing production.

In the industrial sector, the PLA has also guided the militia units comprised of workers. But regular troops frequently also participate directly in labor assignments. For example, on January 26, 1967, *People's Daily* called upon the PLA to protect all state property. In enterprises troubled by strikes, troops have served as replacements in the labor force. Soldiers have also been called upon to take the lead in opening new factories. As defined by the January 1, 1967 *Liberation Army Daily*, troops should "gradually set up some small and medium-size factories." But the most common form of PLA assistance to industry is in the form of guidance and temporary supplementation of the regular work force. In its Letter to Workers and Staff and Revolutionary Cadres in Industrial and Mining Enterprises, of March 18, 1967, the CPC Central Committee stressed its decision that "the PLA should make great efforts to help civilians and support the work of industrial production." Noting that the PLA had sent cadres to enterprises in Peking municipality, Chou En-lai reminded the assembled workers on March 3, 1967, that "this is a very important measure." "The fact that you have their support," the Premier added, "shows that you enjoy the greatest concern and support of Chairman Mao and the Party's Central Committee."

It is axiomatic to conclude that not all civilians have welcomed the growing authority of the PLA. For example, in several of the troubled areas, the PLA has taken over the suspect police and public security forces. As the sole disciplinary organ, the PLA has probably inherited all mass resistance, and increased this hostility by carrying out its reforms. Moreover, specific cases have been reported in the Party press to substantiate this conclusion. For example, in coastal Fukien province, a vital link in the line of defense, after the successful seizure of power, *People's Daily* admitted on February 17, 1967, that there was "deliberate opposition to the correct policy of the 'three in one' alliance." On March 2, 1967, the same source reported that counterrevolutionaries had attacked PLA units in Shantung province.

Based upon the scant reports available, it is also apparent that not all PLA troops are loyal to the cultural revolution. Economic enterprises operated by the military have not been exempt from work stoppages. For example, on January 14, 1967, *People's Daily* admitted that strikes had spread to factories run by the PLA rear services department. In the troubled municipalities and provinces, some officers of the respective military commands have been associated with the counterrevolutionary forces.[47] In Harbin, for example, *Red Flag* (no. 3, 1967) identified one of the dissident groups as the "Demobilized Soldiers' Army," which would presumably refer to veterans of the PLA. The January 12, 1967 announcement of the reorganization of the PLA Cultural Revolutionary Group implies that opposition to leadership policies is a problem which plagues all ranks of the military.[48] As the *Liberation Army Daily* commented in its January 12, 1967 editorial, the new Cultural Revolutionary Team will "launch a new stage in the great proletarian [cultural] revolution of our army to purge the reactionaries' evil influences among the troops."

In addition to the common ideological errors which must be guarded against, the military must also overcome particular tendencies to counter-

[47] Among the confirmed dismissals in the PLA which can be associated with the cultural revolution are those of: Lo Jui-ch'ing, as Chief of Staff (reported a suicide in January, 1967 wallposters); Liu Chih-chien, deputy head of the PLA Political Department, and former head of the PLA Cultural Revolution Group, T'ang P'ing-chu was removed as editor of *People's Daily* and Hu Ch'ih as director of NCNA in January, 1967, and presumably also from their membership in the Cultural Revolution Group. Other military leaders believed purged include Wang Shang-jung, and Lei Ying-fu, chief and deputy chief of operations respectively. Marshals Chu Teh, Ho Lung and Yeh Chien-ying have undergone vitriolic attacks in wallposters and may have lost any position of trust. (Ho and Yeh are vice chairmen of the NDC, while Ho and Chu Teh are also members of the CPC Politburo.)

Japanese and western newsmen in Communist China have also reported the following leaders to have been denounced in wallposters: Admiral Su Chen-hua, head of the Cultural Revolutionary Team in the navy; Wu Fa-hsien, commander of the Air Force and member of the NDC; and Generals Hsiao Hsiang-jung, Liu Chih-chun, Liang Pi-yeh, Ch'iu Hui-tso, Hsü Kuang-ta, Huang Hsin-t'ing, and Li Ta. Among the Party first secretaries who are also: military commanders of their respective regions who have been criticized in the wallposters are Ulanfu, of the Inner Mongolia Autonomous Region; and Wang En-mao, of the Sinkiang Uigur Autonomous Region.

[48] Prior to this announcement, the Chinese Communists had not identified the members of the PLA Cultural Revolution Group. However, wall posters referred to Liu Chih-chien as "the former head" of the Group.

act Marxism-Leninism and the thought of Mao. Although not officially published until 1966 (see the August 1, 1966 *Liberation Army Daily*), in 1958 the Chinese Communist leadership became aware of the existence of a high placed military faction that sought to transform the PLA into "a complete carbon of foreign practice." In 1959, at the Lushan Conference, the CPC Central Committee denounced Defense Minister P'eng Teh-huai and his fellow plotters for opposing Party control over the PLA and the use of troops for productive labor, and seeking to abolish the militia forces. [49] These charges are related to Mao Tse-tung's warning in his work *On Correcting Mistaken Ideas in the Party* against "the purely military point of view."

The "purely military point of view" has become one of the chief hazards to trouble the PLA during the cultural revolution. In its fourth issue of 1967, *Red Flag* published a wallposter of the East Is Red Fighting Group, of the Lu Hsün Corps attached to the Shanghai Revolutionary Rebel Headquarters, terming this analysis to be "excellent." According to this source: "the purely military point of view . . . mistakenly holds that the ultimate purpose of the great proletarian cultural revolution is merely to drag out a number of counterrevolutionary revisionists," without heed to the continuing mission of re-educating and reorganizing society. Minus the jargon, "the purely military point of view" resembles a semi-anarchistic policy focusing on force, and only minimally concerned with political or ideological affairs. It is noteworthy that this error is frequently mentioned in connection with the ideological error of "self-interest," which has, in turn, been used to refer to those individuals or units who have become "dizzy with success." Even while celebrating the explosion of the first hydrogen bomb, the leaders of Communist China took the occasion, in the official press announcement of June 17, 1967, to caution: "It is hoped that the Chinese People's Liberation Army . . . will guard against conceit and impetuosity. . . ." [50]

In the same sense, if not more so, that the Chinese hydrogen bomb was officially hailed as a new victory for the thought of Mao and the proletarian cultural revolution, the various significant roles assigned to the PLA are based on the latter's infinite dedication to Mao's thought and essential

[49] The removal of P'eng Teh-huai, Huang K'e-ch'eng, Hsiao K'e, T'an Cheng and Hung Hsüeh-chih, as noted elsewhere, corresponded with and prepared the way for the rise of Lin Piao. But the actions of 1959 have not been forgotten. Western newsmen in Peking reported that the Red Guard newspaper of the Peking Aviation Institute claimed P'eng Teh-huai was seized by Red Guards in Chengtu, Szechuan province, on December 24, 1966.

[50] On June 17, 1967, having conducted five nuclear tests in less than three years, Communist China announced the successful testing of a hydrogen bomb in the western area. This explosion indicates that, despite the dislocations associated with the cultural revolution, great progress continues to be made in the development of nuclear weapons.

contribution to implementing the cultural revolution and helping the Red Guards. Thus, both the PLA and its administrative chief, Lin Piao, are the means rather than the ends in the cultural revolution. They are serving rather than commanding the Party and Mao. Contrary to a purely militaristic approach, the dismissals of not a few military leaders, including P'eng Teh-huai, Huang K'e-ch'eng, and Lo Jui-ch'ing, and the humiliation of many others, including Chu Teh, Ho Lung, and Yeh Chien-ying, corroborate the long-tested rule of political command over the military. There is little likelihood that new warlordism is appearing above the horizon in Communist China. The PLA and its leaders are both movers and targets of the revolution in this unprecedented proletarian cultural drive.

CHAPTER 9

The Chinese Communist
Social System

THE MASS LINE POLICY

Since its own membership constitutes only a tiny minority of the total population, the CPC must make every effort, not only to place its members in the strategic positions of influence and control throughout the entire society, but also to make sure of the support, or at least the acceptance, of the great bulk of the non-Party masses. It must avoid isolation at all costs. To meet this problem—which, of course, is not peculiar to China—communist theorists and strategists have evolved two closely related lines of policy: the united front and the mass line.

Although purporting to be a working-class party seeking a society in which all other classes will have been eliminated, the Communist Party must, first of all, tolerate the continued existence of other classes pending their eventual extinction. As the party of the proletariat in general, the CPC seeks alliance with other major class elements during the period of struggle and consolidation which marks the transition to socialism. Concrete expressions of this policy include the continued existence of the non-communist "democratic" parties, the inclusion of non-Party personnel from other class backgrounds in the organs of government (particularly those of a representative or advisory capacity), the limited toleration of a private economic sector, and the inclusion of prominent, fellow-travelling non-communists on the leadership rosters of the social organizations and mass movements sponsored by the regime.

As a slightly different expression of the same effort to avoid isolation as a minority group and to heighten its effectiveness, the CPC also attempts (as noted in Chapter 4) to control every organized group and movement in the society. This mass-line policy, it may be presumed, will continue even after the official disappearance of other classes, thus outliving the united front.

The mass-line policy of the CPC stems from the teachings of Lenin and Stalin. Lenin insisted that the Party should constantly strengthen its ties with the masses and lead them. He warned that "without the alliance with the non-communists in various fields of activities, it is impossible to talk about any successful communist construction." Stalin elaborated on this point by saying: "as a rule, when the Bolsheviks preserve connections with the broad masses of the people, they are unconquerable."

As early as March, 1927, according to Stalin, the Comintern instructed the Chinese Party of the necessity of adopting a united front policy through the development of mass movement, or mass line tactics. And Mao fully accepted this Leninist-Stalinist doctrine. He has repeatedly emphasized that the mass line should be applied in all Party work and that Party members, in no circumstances, must isolate themselves from the masses. The Party Constitution stipulates that members must establish, strengthen, and broaden wide connections with the masses of "workers, peasants and all other revolutionary people," and that Party branches must "carry out propaganda and organizational work among the masses."

MASS ORGANIZATIONS

The mass "people's organizations" are the most significant device employed by the CPC to effect its mass line policy. Through these agencies the Party can mobilize and exert leadership over every key group and social activity. The organizations discussed in this section represent only a few of the larger and politically more important of the whole range of these groups. There are dozens of other similar agencies for literary, cultural, scientific, welfare and other activities. In structure, they are much like those discussed here. In importance, they insure that the CPC's tentacles reach every area of the society.

The All-China Federation of Trade Unions (ACFTU)

Because of the revolutionary role and the vanguard function assigned the industrial proletariat in Marxian theory, and because of the urgent needs of industrialization in China, the ACFTU is perhaps the most important single mass organization. Founded in 1925 by the Second All-China Congress of Labor (the First Congress had left no permanent organization), the ACFTU was reconstituted in 1948 by the sixth congress. In May, 1953, when the regime was shifting its emphasis to the industrialization program and the transition to socialism, the seventh congress reaffirmed its broad aims:

... to unite and educate the workers and raise their political consciousness; to consolidate the worker-peasant alliance, and unite with the people of all other strata to actively fulfill the national construction plan; and, on the basis of developing production, to improve the workers' material and cultural life step by step; and to strive for the early industrialization of the country and its transition to socialism.

Since the aims of the ACFTU are international, as well as national, it maintains friendly relations with the communist labor movement in other communist-dominated countries and is active in the communistic World Federation of Trade Unions (WFTU), of whose Executive Committee Liu Shao-ch'i is one of the Vice Chairman. The ACFTU itself is under the chairmanship of Liu Ning-i, a full member of the CPC Central Committee who was also named to the Standing Committee of the NPC at the session of December, 1964.[1]

The trade unions in Communist China offer no exception to the well-known rule that the labor movement under a communist regime is predominantly political in character and subservient to the dictates of party and state. The communists reject the notion that unions should concern themselves primarily with the economic aims of wages, hours, conditions and security and the like. Thus, the ACFTU's former chairman, Lai Jo-yü, warned against committing "mistakes of economism" by becoming "narrow, divided craft organizations." He reminded the delegates to the seventh congress: "in a state led by the working class, the individual interests of the workers and the interests of the state are identical." In practical terms, this means that only those unions approved by the CPC may exist, and that the rights of organization and collective bargaining are restricted by Party directive. Thus the Trade Union Law, promulgated on June 29,

[1] Liu Shao-ch'i, who has been associated with the international communist labor movement since the 1920's is honorary chairman. Until the seventh congress in 1953, the Chairman was Ch'en Yün, another old-time labor organizer and fifth ranked in the CPC hierarchy of command. He has apparently been inactive in recent years, and was demoted from first to second vice-premier in the State Council at the first session of the 3rd NPC in December, 1964. Lai Jo-yü, who replaced Ch'en, was a relative newcomer to the labor movement until he was appointed ACFTU Secretary General in July, 1952. It was he who apparently served as the CPC's spokesman in criticizing the tendency of previous ACFTU leaders, at a level below that of Ch'en Yün, to "deviate from the leadership of the Party." The subsequent appointment of Liu Ning-i would seem to be a return to the earlier pattern of leadership from a high ranking Party official.

1950, requires all unions to report to and be approved by the ACFTU, and defines union rights and duties to include the education and organization of workers "to carry out the policies of the People's Government and to consolidate the people's state power which is led by the working class," and "to organize labor emulation campaigns and other production movements in order to ensure the fulfillment of production plans." The right to strike is not mentioned.

Like the other mass organizations, the ACFTU and its constituent unions perform certain quasi-governmental functions. In cooperation with the Ministry of Labor and other agencies of the state machine, they arrange contracts between labor and management (the state), and participate in the administration of the factories and of such welfare services as social insurance, health plans, maternity benefits and vacations. The ACFTU also engages in a broad program of cultural-educational activities. It operates the Workers Publishing House and promotes sales of its publications; it has organized spare-time schools for workers throughout the country to provide technical and general training, and also runs clubs and sports palaces for worker recreation. But the most important functions of the ACFTU and its affiliates are the activation and mobilization of the workers and the improvement of labor productivity. This most frequently takes the form of "labor emulation" or "new record" campaigns.

Membership in the unions, under the 1950 Trade Union Law, is open to all workers whose wages constitute their sole or chief means of support. Under these terms, engineers, technicians, administrators, and teachers are eligible for membership as well as the common workers. Furthermore, an individual need not belong to a local union in order to join the ACFTU. Thus, by 1953, when this latter rule went into effect, it was estimated that 10,200,000 industrial workers, or over 90 per cent of those eligible, belonged to the 180,000 or so trade unions in the 23 federations comprising the ACFTU (as compared to the 1948 membership of 2,830,000).

The internal structure of the ACFTU follows the familiar communist pattern, but may be discussed briefly here as a prototype of the other mass organizations. It goes without saying that the principle of democratic centralism is basic to the whole structure. Under the ACFTU Constitution, adopted in May, 1953, the supreme organ is the All-China Congress of Trade Unions, which meets every four years. It receives and acts upon reports submitted by the Executive Committee, defines (i.e., rubber-stamps) the policies and objectives of unionism, revises and approves the constitution, and elects an Executive Committee and an Auditing Commission (Article 13). In the interim between congresses, the 98-member Executive Committee is responsible for "implementing the decisions of the Congress and giving leadership to the trade union work of the nation"

(Article 16). The Executive Committee in turn elects a 24-member Presidium and an 8-member Secretariat. The Presidium (which replaces the 14-member Standing Committee of the 1948 Constitution) is the interim body for implementing the decisions of both the Congress and the Executive Committee; the Secretariat, under the direction of the Presidium, conducts routine business. This structural form permits a few leaders to guide the entire trade union movement.

Peasant Associations (PA)

When the Chinese Communists came to power in 1949, they assigned a high priority to the mobilization of the "rural proletariat," largely due to the need to organize peasant support for the land redistribution and other sweeping agrarian "reforms." Hence, in June, 1950, when the Agrarian Reform Law was being promulgated, Liu Shao-ch'i proclaimed the peasant associations to be "the main organizational form and executive organs of the forces of agrarian reform." Some indication of the intensity of efforts to activate the rural masses was given in October, 1951, by Chou En-lai, when he officially reported that membership in peasant associations had soared to 88 million in the four "newly liberated" regions alone.

Unlike the other mass organizations, which are constituted on the principle of democratic centralism, the peasant associations have accomplished their objectives largely through local organizations. Although there are associations on the subcounty (*ch'ü*) and county (*hsien*) levels, the basic organizational unit is the *hsiang*, or rural district. In implementation of the 1950 Agrarian Reform Law, it was the *hsiang* unit which actually confiscated the landlords' holdings and redistributed the lands to the peasants. The practice of decentralization enabled each individual unit to accomodate its program and adjust its timetable to the receptiveness of the peasants in its own locality. However, this in no way implies the absence, or even ineffectiveness, of Party controls. The official CPC policy was clearly and unmistakably set forth in the Agrarian Reform Law and in the General Regulations on the Organization of Peasant Associations, promulgated in 1950. Moreover, it is important to note that the creation of the PA's was initiated mainly by Party cadres, and not by the peasants themselves. Only later, when the program was well advanced, did activist peasants begin to play any significant role in the associations.

The CPC leadership also charged the peasant associations with "re-educating" the "backward and conservative" rural masses to make them conscious of their class responsibility in the world struggle against feudalism, capitalism, and imperialism. In practical terms, this meant peasant indoctrination, through such means as informal "fireside" discussions conducted by trained CPC cadres and the system of spare-time schools organized in conjunction with the Ministry of Education. Nevertheless, since the prime aim was to create working organizations to implement the agrarian reform, it is not surprising that the peasant associations declined in importance as collectivization was achieved. The mutual-aid teams, agricultural producers cooperatives and commune structure (discussed in the chapters on economic development) formed a stair leading to more effective means of peasant organization and controls. It is interesting to speculate that, despite the nature of democratic centralism and the CPC's absolute authority over all the mass organizations, the possibility of the peasant masses using an organization of their own to pressure against official policies may have led to the leadership's decision to abandon the peasant associations.

The All-China Federation of Democratic Women (ACFDW)

The ACFDW was founded in April, 1949, as an outgrowth of the First All-China Women's Congress held in Peking the month previous. Its official aims include "safeguarding women's rights and children's welfare, enhancing the political consciousness and ability of women, securing equality between men and women, and striving for the complete emancipation of women." The more specific general tasks were set forth by Vice Chairman Teng Ying-ch'ao in her report to the Second National Congress of the ACFDW in April, 1953. These include (1) mobilizing women workers in the cities to increase production; (2) encouraging peasant women to participate in mutual-aid and cooperative organizations to increase agricultural production; and (3) liberating women from feudal concepts and social customs.

In accordance with the principle of democratic centralism, the highest organ of the ACFDW is its National Congress. There is also the Executive Committee, elected for two year terms, but the effective control group, per usual, is the Standing Committee. It should be noted, however, that some observers view the permanent Secretariat as the rising power in this and other mass organizations. At the regional level, the federation functions through working committees with branches in the cities and villages. Local conferences directly engage women in the Federation's programs. Like the other mass organizations, the ACFDW performs as an auxiliary arm of certain government agencies. For example, it helped draft, and now helps administer the new marriage law. Also following the pattern of other mass organizations, the ACFDW is affiliated with corresponding groups in other countries. Thus, according to Peking, through the Women's International Democratic Federation (WIDF), the ACFDW allies itself "with all the peace-loving women throughout the world to struggle for world peace."

MASS CAMPAIGNS [2]

The "Resist-America Aid-Korea" Campaign

Both in the implementation of its mass line tactics and in effecting major Party and state policies, the Chinese Communists have resorted to a variety of mass campaigns for the mobilization of the general populace. One of the most important of these earlier campaigns was the Resist-America Aid-Korea movement. To create an appearance of intense loyalty and unequivocal support on the part of the masses, a Chinese "People's Committee to Protect World Peace Against American Aggression" was established. Its purpose was to systematically incite hatred toward America by means of protest meetings, "discussion" groups, parades and other organized measures.

"Documented" charges of germ warfare and inhumane treatment of Chinese POW's were standard matter for study groups and the usual propaganda media. The United States was frequently denounced not only as an "imperialist aggressor in Korea," but also as an imminent threat to China itself. To avoid those "vicious American atrocities," which would surely follow from the invasion of the mainland, the Chinese people were urged to increase production, to cut back on consumption, and to give even their lives if necessary.

On June 1, 1951, the Peking National Committee of the Resist-America Aid-Korea Association formally called for the initiation of three major supportive campaigns: a "patriotic past" movement; a "donation" campaign for the purchase of airplanes and heavy artillery; and a "relief and aid" campaign for military personnel and their dependents. In the first case, all the Chinese people were asked to frame and sign pledges to support the state in its efforts to liberate Korea from the yoke of western imperialism. Statistics for the Northeast, North, East and Northwest regions, published in *People's Handbook* in June, 1952, indicated that more than 50 per cent of the people in those areas had already signed such pacts. In the medium and large cities, the rate of response was given as from 60–90

---

[2] This section has profited from two monographs by Weh-hui C. Chen, "The Resist-America Aid-Korea Campaign in Communist China" and "Mass Movements in Communist China: Nationwide Campaigns in Communist China in Support of the Korean War." These were part of a series of monographs, "Studies in Chinese Communism," prepared at the University of Southern California under the direction of Professor Theodore Hsi-en Chen.

per cent. Mainland newspaper items reported such aspects of this "wave of patriotism" as medical personnel volunteering for front-line duty, merchants parading through the streets to pay their taxes in a body, factory emulation drives, and civilian efforts to uncover and suppress counter-revolutionaries. It should be noted that signers probably often responded perfunctorily, rather than with genuine patriotism. For example, a barber shop signed a pledge to "develop production and stimulate the interflow of goods between the cities and the countryside."

The "donation" and "relief" campaigns antedated the Resist-America Aid-Korea campaign and were useful in meeting economic crises. Even before the complete "liberation" of the mainland, Chinese were asked to give to a fund to support the People's Liberation Army. In the winter of 1949, when famine gripped almost ten million Chinese in Hopei and Anhwei, the people were called upon to save an ounce or two of rice in daily consumption. Again, in 1950, the government initiated a Victory Bond Drive, which reportedly achieved about 70 per cent of its set goal of about US $200 million in the first year.

In the phase associated with the Resist-America Aid Korea drive, the state released purchase price lists for military equipment. A fighter plane was said to cost 1.5 billion yuan, for example, and an artillery piece some 900,000 yuan. All types of mass organizations were asked to raise the purchase price of an article which would then be named in their honor. Thus, the city of Shanghai pledged to provide for 320 planes, while the personnel of fifteen Peking factories agreed to raise the money for 61½ planes. This particular campaign was concluded on December 27, 1951. On February 22, 1952, the official contribution figures were published. A total of 5,024,687,796,521 yuan, equal to the cost of 3,349.7 fighter planes, was said to have been collected. But, on the whole, the response had been uneven. In Hopei, for example, 160 of the 580 villages had failed to organize any donation three months after the call.

The official directive asking for funds for relief of military personnel and their families declared in part:

Our great People's Volunteers . . . left their homes to resist America and aid Korea, to protect our homes and defend our nation. . . . Some gave their lives for us, others are invalid or declining in health. We, the people, must be responsible for their welfare through relief and aid to their families and to the invalid veterans. In the countryside, we must cultivate the fields for them, while in the city we must help their families find employment. In both rural and urban areas we must help their children to go to school and help the families to overcome their difficulties.

Of necessity, the relief campaign assumed a variety of forms. In rural areas, peasants donated fertilizer, seeds and tools and did substitute farming. In urban areas, gifts were presented to the veterans and their families. But of greater significance, Peking found the drive useful in heightening political consciousness.

These various phases of the Resist-America Aid-Korea campaign did not end with the Korean truce in mid-1953. As squabbles continued over the truce terms, the Chinese Communists found continued justification for the economic aspects of the drive.

The "Three-Anti" and "Five-Anti" Campaigns

The Three-Anti campaign was a nationwide drive against corruption' waste and bureaucratism, aimed at cleansing Party and state agencies. In retrospect, it seems to have paved the way for the Five-Anti drive against the "five poisons" of bribery, tax evasion, fraud, theft of government property and theft of state economic secrets. Underneath these professed aims was the greater goal of whipping the merchants, industrialists and businessmen into line in order to carry out the socialist transformation of the economy.

On August 31, 1951, the late Kao Kang, then Party boss in Manchuria, touched off a campaign against "corruption, decay and bureaucratism" in government and Party ranks in Northeast China. In December, 1951, the National Committee of the CPPCC, following Mao's initiative, extended this campaign to the rest of the mainland and issued an order for the mobilization of all mass organizations against the "three evils." Such were the origins of the San Fan or Three-Anti movement.

In its first phase, the campaign was aimed at uncovering specific cases of waste and corruption on the part of Party cadres and government personnel. In a month of preliminary investigations, no less than 1,670 offenders in 27 state departments were "exposed." A report in the *Kuangming Daily* on January 10, 1952, told of an official in the Ministry of Public Security who had mulcted the government of 700 million yuan by forging requisitions. The People's Bank in Honan was accused of wasting 250 million yuan on lavish entertainment. Other officials were accused of accepting bribes and of various forms of gross mismanagement. In view of the prevalence of these abuses, on January 9, 1952, Po I-po, then Minister of Finance and Chairman of the Production and Thrift Supervisory Committee, called upon all organizations to root out offenders as part of their "patriotic duty." After detection, these organizations were to conduct public "trials" of the offenders, or "tigers."

It is difficult to estimate the extent of this purge. Although Po I-po reported on October 1, 1952, that 4.5 per cent of government personnel had been punished for one or another of the "three evils," this figure is regarded to be incredibly low. [3]   Although none of the high ranking members of the Party or state apparatus were accused publicly, the many victims of this drive included mayors, bureau chiefs, local Party executives and regional and provincial officials.   It is clear, however, that the Three-Anti campaign was intended to consolidate the CPC.   Thus, for example, An Tzu-wen declared in the July 1, 1953 issue of *People's China:*

The aim of the movement was to purify our Party organizations and overcome these dangerous tendencies in order to defeat the attacks of the law-breaking elements of the bourgeoisie and to strengthen the leading role played in the state by the proletariat.   This movement was combined with the work aimed at consolidating Party organizations and was regarded as an extremely important and effective measure to put the ranks of the Party in order.

Moreover, the Three-Anti campaign gave the Chinese Communists an opportunity to get rid of such "undesirable elements" as the Kuomintang "turncoats."

The Three-Anti movement was almost immediately joined by the *Wu Fan* or Five-Anti campaign.   Party leaders denounced the "five poisons" as the "sugar-coated bullets" more deadly than enemy planes and tanks with which the bourgeoisie tried to sabotage the new people's government. "Treacherous merchants," for example, were accused of shipping contaminated medical supplies, using spoiled beef in cans, and producing defective equipment, all of which endangered the lives of the "people's volunteers" at the front.

The "five evils" were so all-encompassing as to enable the regime to uncover guilt on the part of virtually any member of the middle class it singled out.   Loudspeakers on main thoroughfares announced the names of "unconfessed" merchants, while accusation meetings became almost a daily occurrence in the larger cities.   Many members of the bourgeoisie, possibly in the hopes of "redeeming guilt by merit," informed on their business associates.   Consequently, it became increasingly convenient for merchants to "confess" in the hopes of lighter treatment.   Since *ex post facto* had long since lost its meaning for the Chinese Communists, it is not surprising that arrests were often made months before the government classified "crimes" or established "legal punishments."   It was not until March 8, 1952, that the GAC adopted a set of Standards and Measures, which was based on those already used in the Peking municipal government.   Five categories were set up for businessmen: law abiding, "basically" law abiding, "semi" law abiding, "serious" law-breaking, and "com-

[3] See, for example, Theodore H. E. Chen and Wen-hui C. Chen, "the 'Three-Anti' and 'Five-Anti' Movements in Communist China," *Pacific Affairs*, v. 26, no. 1, March, 1953, pp. 3–23.

pletely" law-breaking. The penalties ranged from mere restitution of "stolen" funds to the death sentence.

The Five-Anti campaign reached its height in March, 1952, while for the next three months trials were conducted and cases disposed of. On October 1, 1952, Po I-po reported in the *People's Daily* that 76 per cent of the 450,000 businessmen investigated in seven leading cities had been found guilty of one or more of the "five poisons." However, the majority had escaped sentence or been "redeemed by merit." In Shanghai, 1,000 investigative teams had settled accounts with 90 per cent of the city's 160,000 businessmen.

The Three-Anti and Five-Anti campaigns doubtlessly provided added income sources for the Chinese Communists during the critical period of the Korean War. According to a Nationalist Chinese News Service bulletin of June 3, 1952, the two campaigns netted about US $1,250,000,000 in confiscated property, fines, refunds of graft and stolen goods, and delinquent taxes. Non-communist sources have also reported that some 500 prominent businessmen were executed, 4,000 sentenced to prison terms of fifteen years, and 30,000 to terms of over ten years. One report from Shanghai estimated the suicide rate to be about 100 per day at the height of the campaign. Certainly, the drives demoralized and fragmented the bourgeoisie and made it virtually impossible for them to offer any effective resistance to the state's socialist economic programs that followed. Yet the significance of the campaigns was more political, than economic. The transitory nature of the united front was exposed as the campaigns marked a turning point from the New Democratic to the Socialist society.

The "Learn From Lei Feng" Movement

Illustrative of the continuing importance which the Chinese Communists assign to mass campaigns is the "love and learn from Lei Feng" drive presently being carried out in China. On February 8, 1963, the New China News Agency first noted the death of Lei Feng in August of the previous year at the age of 22. Since personal obituaries are uncommon even for ranking Party and state personnel, this delayed observance of the death of an unknown member of the People's Liberation Army and the Communist Party was unusual from the beginning.

In the following days, the *People's Daily* and provincial papers bit by bit released sometimes conflicting details concerning the life of Lei Feng. These may be summarized briefly: Lei Feng had been born in Hunan province of simple peasants. At aged five, he lost his father to the Japanese aggressors; two years later, Lei's mother committed suicide to escape the ruthlessness of the landlord for whom she labored. The youngster fled to the woods, where he was "rescued" by the new people's forces, restored to health and educated. Thus, Lei Feng was able to become a tractor driver aiding the state's plans for rural communalization. In January, 1960, he enlisted in the People's Liberation Army, and in November, 1960, he was received into the Communist Party. In August, 1962, Lei was killed in a freak accident not related to combat duty.

These incidents hardly warrant nationwide laudation: they appear more in the realm of myth, or illustrative of the "Everyman" of the new communist society of China. Rather, it is the character of Lei Feng which has been projected as worthy of mass emulation. This common servant of the revolutionary effort was always eager to take the most odious assignments, to work selflessly for his fellow men while practicing absolute frugality, and to sing the praises of the thought of Mao Tse-tung. A few excerpts from Lei Feng's posthumously published diary indicate his character. "Chairman Mao's words," he wrote, "are like food, weapons and a compass." And "I live for the purpose of serving the people heart and soul, and for the cause of emancipating mankind—the cause of communism."

It seems evident that the Chinese Communist leadership has created its own sort of folk hero to emphasize the virtues essential to the revolutionary society. For example, the first mention of Lei Feng, in praise of his diligence and frugality, corresponds with the growing awareness of the CPC Central Committee that national economic policies and programs would, of necessity, have to be based on a national self-reliance requiring these very same traits. As noted elsewhere, the leadership has also become increasingly fearful that the younger generation lacks the revolutionary fervor of those who survived the years of foreign and civil war. Thus, Lei Feng is the ideal sort of hero for China's youth to emulate. Lei Feng's constant repetition of the fact that the thought of Mao alone was responsible for his industriousness and dedication is, needless to say, put forth as a prod and example to all Chinese. For these reasons, which are inseparable from current propaganda goals, the life of Lei Feng is endlessly referred to in all sort of mass communications.

The campaign to extoll Lei Feng officially began in the spring of 1963, when a special exhibit was opened in Peking. Amid innumerable photographs, the uniform and diaries of Lei were exposed in glass cases to countless schoolchildren ushered through in organized groups. According to official sources, the exhibit ran six months to packed throngs, while similar exhibits were taken on tour of other cities and throughout the countryside. At the same time, *People's Daily* and the provincial newspapers serialized the life of Lei Feng in comic strip form. Wall posters and woodcuts everywhere displayed the image of Communist China's ideal youth, songs were composed, and the PLA's August 1 Studio released a feature movie.

Moreover, classes to study and learn from Lei Feng were organized in all schools and discussion groups and mass meetings were set to analyzing the diaries. In anticipated fashion, the press quickly began to reprint letters to the editor in which individuals claimed to have achieved substantial production goals by emulation of the spirit of Lei Feng, or to have come to a better understanding of the thought of Mao Tse-tung through the words and example of this simple soldier.

Similar honors are endlessly paid to Lei Feng, the mythological hero of the Chinese Communists. It is not surprising that, to date, no one claims to have actually known the young soldier or that the Chinese Communists should put forward a young man in the image of the now venerable Mao. The "learn from Lei Feng" campaign is designed to advance a more readily identifiable image and consequently more appealing subject for mass drives than the impersonal issues of anti-imperialism or anti-corruption. But the movement itself is in the same vein as the other campaigns which have been described. It again affirms that the mass drives and campaigns in Communist China are to promote spontaneous popular emotions and to strengthen the carefully regulated aspects of the CPC's total program for social engineering.

SOCIAL PROGRAMS

Public Health Drives

Summarizing the transformation from town-house living in Los Angeles to residency in a Peking suburb in a September, 1963 article entitled "Why I came to China at the Age of 72," Anna Louise Strong gloated: "I found myself growing younger, healthier, even better tempered." As noted in the chapter on economic development in the post-Great Leap period, not all Chinese have shared Miss Strong's boundless enjoyment of good health. The successive years of poor and inadequate harvests required strict curtailment of food rations. Although it is patently impossible to establish the average caloric intake, all reports would seem to agree that dietary standards fell considerably below the 3,200 calories for males and 2,300 for females advocated as minimal by the World Health Organization. Consequently, although the regime might claim with some degree of veracity that few deaths could be attributed directly to famine, public health was weakened as resistance to disease was generally lowerd. Reports circulated in Hong Kong of peasants collapsing and dying in the fields or along the country lanes, of the widespread afflictions of typhoid, malaria, tuberculosis, and liver disorders, and of the sharp increase in venereal disease as peasant women resorted to prostitution to find money for black market food. By 1962, however, as the leadership's recuperative policies for agriculture began to produce an effect, evidence indicates that the level of general health had begun to register substantial improvement. A comparative sampling examination of children recently emigrating from rural villages in Kwangtung province with children living in rural Hong Kong villages, for example, indicated a parity in nutritional levels, the number of cases of active TB, and the number of children vaccinated against certain diseases. [4] Thus, the contemporary state of the nation's health would seem to lie somewhere between Anna L. Strong's exalted claims and the terrible pictures of mass starvation widely circulated outside China in 1960–61.

Since the state of the worker's health has an obvious effect on his productive capacity, the Chinese Communist leadership has employed a wide variety of means to improve or maintain his physical constitution. One of the most widely publicized of these measures is the exercise program. Beginning in 1951, the State Council's Commission for Physical Culture has issued four sets of radio exercises. Broadcast by Radio Peking every working day at about 10 A.M. and 3:30 P.M., to coincide with the workers' break, the exercises are performed to the accompaniment of minority folk tunes in whatever location the worker finds himself, be it factory or street corner. It should be noted that the musical background represents yet another example of Peking's ability to convert any opportunity for propagandizing. Another ready example of this tactic of combining mass exercise with another advantage is to be found in the emphasis placed on learning to swim well. In the spring of 1965, the Headquarters of the PLA General Staff announced that all soldiers must learn to swim as part of their tactical training for crossing rivers. The army's campaign soon became nationwide as all citizens were urged to emulate the heroes of the PLA. On June 13, for example, 16,000 Young Pioneers, militia members and PLA troops staged an exhibition at Tsinan on the Yellow River. Including the youngest participant, aged eleven, all swam the 1,200 meter distance in full field equipment. Still another example of this two-pronged planning is the current drive to improve rural sanitation by having young students demonstrate their class-consciousness in collecting human excrement for agricultural fertilization.

One of the most pressing needs in the area of public health is for additional trained personnel. Official figures differ widely and seldom provide a

[4] See Robert M. Worth's "Health Trends Since the Great Leap Forward" in *China Quarterly*, no. 22, April–June, 1965. A Professor of Public Health at the University of Hawaii, Worth observed 80 children within 48 hours of their arrival in Macau from Kwangtung, together with 120 Hong Kong children. All the children were between the ages of 5–7 and from the rural areas. All showed marginal protein intake rates.

breakdown by categories. For example, some 48,000 doctors and pharmacists were graduated during the 1949–60 period, according to reports for the latter year. In 1963, Peking claimed that over 110,000 doctors and pharmacists had been trained since 1949. And a November 23, 1964 NCNA bulletin placed the total trained since 1949 at 450,000, of which 120,000 were graduates of medical colleges and the remainder from some 200 secondary medical schools. Accepting the highest figure, and ignoring the question of adequacy of training, it is still apparent that this force is hard pressed to treat a population in excess of 700,000,000. In fact, the training programs are subject to question. Generally, courses of study have been shortened as specialization has become required from the outset of training, with an adverse effect on general knowledge. Similarly, the standards of the secondary centers are inferior.[5]

One means of implementing formal training, in accord with the general principle of "walking on two legs," is the practice of encouraging the practitioners of modern and traditional medicine to learn from one another. In 1958, for example, some 5,000 western-trained doctors were assigned to part-time study of traditional methods, and 400 others to full-time study. Tremendous advancement has been claimed for both branches. Thus, a medical conference meeting in Shenyang, Liaoning province, in April, 1965, announced that 700 of the 1,183 cases of polio treated by the traditional method of apuncture recovered completely. The cure rate for 717 cases of facial nerve paralysis was said to be 66 per cent. At the same time, since 1960, practitioners of modern medicine have been administering live polio vaccine to children. On March 26, 1965, *Peking Review* boasted that polio has been eliminated through the use of modern drugs. The union of traditional and modern is also said to have achieved outstanding results in the field of pharmacology. Since 1955, all private pharmaceutical companies have been absorbed into the state sector. The Chinese Academy of Medical

[5] In its December 10, 1965 issue, *Peking Review* reported on an interview with Vice Minister of Public Health Chang Kai concerning part-time training. Chang noted that "part-time doctors" selected in the rural areas received instruction for two or three years during the slack farming seasons. This force is augmented by the practice of having each communal team select youths "who are politically progressive and who show a love for manual labor," for training courses of two or three month's duration in first aid type procedures. Furthermore, as noted by NCNA on March 3, 1966, nurses with ten years of experience, who attend special part-time courses, are eligible to be promoted as "doctors." These programs still fall short of national needs. Thus, for example, Dr. Huang Chia-ssu, President of the Chinese Medical Academy of Science, after completing an extended inspection tour of three Hunan province communes, was reported in *People's Daily* of August 4, 1965, to have decried the unhygenic conditions, and lack of drugs and trained personnel.

For thorough analysis of the problem of inadequate trained personnel see Chu-yuan Cheng's *Scientific and Engineering Manpower in Communist China 1949–63* (Wash., D.C.: GPO, 1965).

Science and the Research Institute of Traditional Chinese Medicine maintain some 100 research centers. The followers of traditional medicine point with pride to such programs as the restoration and enlargement of the ancient herb garden of Changshuchen, Kiangsi province, where 70 senior technicians now offer one-year apprenticeship training to graduates of middle and primary schools in the healing arts of herbs. Practitioners of modern medicine were informed at the second national conference on oncology in 1965, that the six specialized and two research institutes for the study of cancer have discovered new anti-cancer agents. In November, 1964, NCNA-Tientsin reported that a 32 year old surgeon had rejoined the severed arm of a peasant with full sensation and use of the limb.

In recent years, Peking has claimed success in bringing medical services to the masses of the population. An NCNA-Peking dispatch of September 27, 1964 reported that there were over 10,000 urban hospitals and that each of the 2,000 counties had at least one hospital, in addition to specialized centers for the treatment of TB, cancer and for dentistry. All of the communes maintain their own clinics. These centers are affiliated with the Ministry of Public Health, under the direction of Ch'ien Hsin-chung. Ch'ien is also the president of the Chinese Red Cross, which maintains branches in each of the provinces, including some 50,000 stations and 700 sanitation teams. [6] But the demands upon these limited facilities are enormous. Communist China must take stupendous strides before her public health apparatus can be considered adequate to the national needs. This situation is complicated by the very largess of the program. Insurance for health services is allegedly based on one per cent of a worker's salary. For his first visit to a doctor, the patient pays a registration fee of approximately 20 cents, and 10 cents for each additional visit. Hospitalization, when ordered, is free, and provisions are made for the continuance of salaries. Consequently, many people attempt to avail themselves of these arrangements, and even to "shop around" for additional confirmations or treatments. One western source has concluded that these numerical pressures have created a twofold problem. On the one hand, doctors seldom have more than a few minutes to spend with each patient: on the other, due to the likelihood that the worker welcomes relief from his job commitment, the doctor can excuse only the very serious cases.

Communist China has made considerable progress in the area of public health. The various mass campaigns against flies and spitting have done much to reduce infectious contagion. But, great problems remain. As

[6] It should be noted that, in common with all Chinese Communist organizations, the Red Cross is often assigned tasks nonrelated to public health work. For example, the April 7, 1965 meeting of the Executive Committee concerned itself primarily with a denunciation of U.S. policies in Vietnam and a condemnation of American use of poison gas.

the Canton *Southern Daily* noted in September, 1960, the primary objective of public health services is "strengthening the physique of the laboring people and promoting production," hence, good health for its own sake is regarded as bourgeois. In keeping with this philosophy, terminal cases are probably not permitted to utilize hospital facilities. There is an acute shortage of adequately trained personnel. Doctors do enjoy a quasi-prestigious status, which depends in large measure upon political reliability, rather than talent and dedication. Nurses need have no academic qualifications, and receive on-the-job training from already overworked interns. Thus, the problem of public health will continue to remain a major social issue for some time to come.

Approaches to the Population Problem: Attitudes toward Family and Women

The 1953 census, the first and only nationwide survey conducted by the Chinese Communists, revealed the total mainland population to be close to 600 million, 30 per cent of whom were under the age of fourteen. [7] Based upon a sampling study of some 30 million Chinese, the annual increase rate was set at about 2 per cent. Utilizing these official figures, Communist China's population should have reached the 700 million mark in about 1961, and could reach one billion by 1980. [8] Despite the enormity of these totals, the Chinese Communist leadership in its first years of power either ignored or denounced any efforts at population planning. Thus, for example, *People's Daily* observed on April 25, 1952, that birth control was merely a "means of killing the Chinese people without shedding blood."

The Chinese Communists, instead, concentrated upon remolding society by modifying the laws and practices governing the marriage contract. On May 1, 1950, the new Marriage Law was promulgated and widely publicized through the efforts of such organizations as the All-China Democratic Women's Federation. Replacing the 980th provision of the Kuomintang Civil Code, the new law had a twofold purpose: to provide greater equality for women, while at the same time enhancing state controls over the family unit. For example, the 1931 law had required mutual consent, but it did

[7] This census was ordered to be taken on the night of June 30/July 1, 1953. However, by the following March, only about 30 per cent of the results had been forwarded and tabulated. The official total was 601.9 million, of which 574 million were mainland residents.

[8] The relative accuracy of these official figures frequently has been challenged by the scholarly community. In his *The Size, Composition and Growth of the Population of Mainland China* (U.S. Dept. of Commerce, 1961), John S. Aird concluded that the totals probably erred in undercounting. Earl Pritchard, in his "Thoughts on the Historical Development of Population in China" (*Journal of Asian Studies*, Nov., 1963), estimates that the Chinese population should reach the one billion mark by about 1970. The general problems involved in utilizing Chinese Communist statistics are pointed out in the preface.

not stipulate formal procedures. Consequently, a marriage could be performed by civil or religious officials. The 1950 law requires that the couple procure a certificate from the state which, in turn, permits investigation of the two parties. This investigation is obligatory in the case of Party personnel. As phrased by the January 12, 1957 *People's Daily:* "The application of a Party member for marriage will be discussed by the Party branch, examined by the general branch, and approved by the committee." It should be noted that the ability to investigate engaged couples has become a useful tool in the present efforts to encourage later marriages.

The 1950 Marriage Law also differs from its predecessor on divorce. The Nationalist code had permitted divorce by request of one or both parties for bigamy, adultery, mental illness, or other specified grounds. [9] By failing to ennumerate suitable grounds, the 1950 law leaves the question to the judgment of the individual presiding cadre. This greater flexibility, together with the fact that the new law's promulgation was timed to coincide with the land reform drive, occasioned a rash of divorce proceedings. Some 186,000 cases were approved in 1950, 409,000 in 1951, and 396,000 between January and June, 1952. This frequency represented a challenge to Chinese Communist notions of social stability. For example, one municipality, reporting for a ten month period in 1955–56, observed that 65.9 per cent of all divorces involved couples married less than a year, and 81.8 per cent of the actions were initiated by the wife. Thus, *China Youth* warned in its September 14, 1958 issue that "the advocacy of the freedom of marriage and divorce does not mean that marriage and divorce may be had as one pleases." Nevertheless, the CPC continued to advocate divorce for ideological reasons. Thus the same journal stated in its April 16, 1958 issue: "Nowdays people ask for divorce saying their spouse is a rightist and therefore an enemy, making the couple politically incompatible . . . the reason is sound and the stand correct, and there is nothing to argue about."

The First Five-Year Plan, inaugurated in 1953, took no official notice of the relationship of population growth to economic development. By 1954, however, the Chinese Communist leadership evinced an awareness of the problems created by uncontrolled population growth. Thus, the State Council ordered the Minister of Public Health to "educate the masses on the need of practicing birth control" in order to "better protect the health

---

[9] The grounds for divorce have undergone tremendous change in 20th century China, from the time when a man could get a divorce if his wife failed to bear a son, had an obnoxious disease, or was given to gossip. For example, one Party cadre from Hopei was informed (in the November 3, 1962 Peking *Chung-Kuo Ch'ing-nien Pao*) that sterility should no longer be accepted as grounds for divorce since the socialist society has eliminated the need for children to care for a parent in old age.

of mothers." [10] On December 27, 1954, Liu Shao-ch'i convened a top level conference to analyze the problem. Officially, Peking continued to be reluctant to admit to population pressures, even though its figures indicated an annual increase rate of about 15 million for each year since 1949. By 1956, however, the top leadership appeared more ready to acknowledge that population pressures did, indeed, pose a problem. As Chou En-lai informed a visiting Indian agricultural mission in August of that year, he was "personally strongly in favor of family planning" since "so many people in China are having too many children." In September, Chou pointed out the need for "appropriate control of births" in his report to the Eighth Party Congress.

For about eight months, in 1957, Communist China conducted the first official mass birth control campaign ever ordered in a communist state. One of the leading exponents of the drive was the noted economist then president of Peking University, Dr. Ma Yin-ch'u.[11] Ma published his "A New Theory of Population" in March and addressed the fourth session of the First National People's Congress in July. Using 1956 statistics, Dr. Ma illustrated that 79 per cent of the national income went for immediate consumption, thereby slowing down capital accumulation and investment. He also emphasized that the population increase in 1957 would be about 15 million, although industry would absorb only about one million additional workers in the same year. "Since our population is too large," Ma argued, "it drags down the speed of our industrialization and prevents us from taking big strides forward." Minister of Health, Madame Li Teh-ch'uan, in a March speech, utilized the same argument of realism: "If our population growth is not in accordance with planned childbirth, it will prevent our country from quickly ridding itself of poverty and from becoming prosperous and powerful."

Following this dictum, the national press began a propaganda barrage in favor of later marriages, careful spacing of children, families of three or, at maximum, four children, and the use of birth control devices. In May, all restrictions on abortion were abolished except for the provisions that pregnancy be terminated in the first three months and that no woman have

---

[10] One example should illustrate the crudity of these first efforts. I. Taeuber, in "Population Policies in Communist China," *Population Index* (October, 1956) cites the advice given by NPC Deputy Yeh Hsi-chun, a herbalist: ". . . if a woman swallows fourteen live tadpoles on the first day, and ten more on the following day, she will not conceive for five years. . . . This formula is good in that it is effective, safe and not expensive. The defect is that it can be used only in the spring."

[11] It should be noted that Ma's proclamations coincided with the Blooming and Contending drive, analyzed elsewhere in these pages. Later branded as a Malthusian, Ma was dismissed as president of Peking University, but reappeared in a position of consequence at a 1961 meeting of the Chinese Academy of Sciences.

more than one abortion in any twelve month period. Aside from the enormous problem of overcoming peasant resistance to these measures, the leadership circles themselves appeared restive over the ideological paradox implicit in the campaign. According to Malthusian theory, the means of production never keep pace with population growth; consequently, from time to time, crisis inevitably occurs in the guise of famine, disease, wars or mass deaths. Yet Marxist-Leninists insist that communism can and will provide abundance for all. Related specifically to the Chinese scene, the communists officially claimed that food production would increase 275 per cent between 1949 and 1958. Since, according to their own figures, the population would not increase by more than about 30 per cent, to admit to a problem of inadequate supply would be to give the lie to their claims of economic miracles.

In 1958, as Peking prepared to launch its panacea plans for the Great Leap Forward and communalization, the Chinese Communist leadership reversed its earlier emphasis on planned growth of population. Propaganda in favor of birth control was suppressed as the leadership determined to improve the ratio between populace and the economy by concentrating on super economic planning involving mass mobilization. It might be noted, however, that the communes, as first conceived, might have alleviated population pressures by the enforced barracks-type existence which was attempted. At the Eighth CPC Congress in May, 1958, Liu Shao-ch'i omitted any reference to the 1957 birth control campaign. Instead, Liu reflected the new line of thought by stressing that China's vast manpower reserves were what made it possible "to do anything within the realm of human possibility." If birth control was not entirely abandoned, it was given a vastly subordinate role.

The failure of the Great Leap and communalization and the ensuing economic crisis have been treated elsewhere in these pages. Such fragmentary evidence as exists indicates that the rate of population growth did decline during the 1960–61 period of agricultural upheaval. Near famine conditions adversely affected public health: the number of miscarriages and the infant mortality rate apparently rose rapidly. In a September 5, 1960 interview with British newsman Edgar Snow, Chou En-lai noted that the annual increase rate was still about two per cent, or "in absolute figures, over 10 million each year"—an unaccounted decline of some 5 million annually from previous statistics. The Premier observed that China's population density was considerably below that of Britain, Japan or India and emphasized the potentialities for absorption in terms of "vast territory and rich resources." Nevertheless, Chou stated: "Education on planned parenthood was and continues to be carried on in China, mainly to protect the health of mothers and provide favorable conditions for bringing up children, not because of so-called 'population pressures.' " Similarly, the 12-year program for agricultural development, adopted by the National People's Congress in April, 1960, stressed the need for family planning in all thickly populated areas.

By 1962, and coinciding with the strides in economic improvement, the Chinese Communist leadership was ready to repeat and even intensify its campaign for planned population growth. The ideological dilemma was resolved by stressing the personal responsibility of the individual to the common good, in the best traditions of Lenin. Thus, for example, the September 14, 1962 issue of *China Youth* cited Lenin's belief: "Love concerns the lives of two people, and it leads to a third life, a new life. This makes love bear social relations and in turn a social responsibility." Thus, the good of China requires family planning. Peking has employed all of its mass organizational devices to promote this dictum. The youth, women's and public health organizations have been in the vanguard in sponsoring public forums and exhibitions and in providing field workers. At the provincial level, Guidance Committees for Planned Childbirth have been established under the watchful eyes of the Party and state personnel. These organizations sponsor discussions, provide for the training of personnel, and supervise appropriate instruction in the schools at all levels. At the municipal level, similar agencies perform like functions. As the chief of the Canton Municipal Bureau proclaimed, it is "an inescapable and glorious task to encourage family planning." The city hospitals have become centers for providing information and contraceptives, and as the Canton *Nan-fang Jih-pao* of October 5, 1962, boasted, these units are open without appointment six days a week. The press at all levels frequently propagandizes the campaign. *Chinese Women*, for example, from time to time has offered detailed and illustrated instruction on how to use contraceptive devices.

As in the 1957 campaign, the current efforts center on the desirability of later marriages, small families properly spaced, the use of medical devices, and the permission for sterilization or abortion. In the case of trying to convince the youth of China to postpone marriage, every sort of propagandistic approach has been utilized. For example, *China Youth* (September 14, 1962) insists: "compared with revolutionary work, marriage and love are really a small matter." An article in the September 27, 1962 Peking *Kung-jen Jih-pao* provides an even more unlikely inspiration. Quoting Confucius—"I made up my mind to study at 15, and establish myself at 30"—the paper pleads that youth be celibate in emulation. The letters to the editor columns of the Chinese press provide countless examples of this aspect of the campaign. Thus, one teacher, writing to the Peking paper just mentioned, stressed that young mothers with small children seldom advance in their schoolwork. But another letter reveals the somewhat less than total acceptance of this line by the young. Thus one 26-year old worker expressed his fear of waiting until thirty to marry for "who would marry a man who has already lived half his life?" Perhaps the most convincing aspect of this part of the campaign is the utilization of medical experts to point out the great harm which may occur to the female who marries too young. For example, the superintendent of Shanghai's Gynecological and Obstetrics Hospital (in the March 5, 1963 *Chieh-fang Jih-pao*) detailed the inability of a 20-year old mother to have an easy delivery since her physiological development is not complete. Ideally, and as constantly preached, the planners in Peking would like to have all young women stay single until their middle twenties, and men until about the age of thirty.

A much-stressed corollary to this plea for delayed marriages is the request that parents have "fewer but better children"—preferably two, but certainly no more than three. Such centers as the Institute for Protection of the Health of Women and Children in Kwangtung province have encouraged the use of the rhythm method, but generally the leadership advocates the use of a multitude of cheap contraceptive devices. Since, as will be noted, the peasants have been less than eager in their acceptance of these devices, the family planners have looked with increasing favor on the more certain means of sterilization or abortion.

Although, as noted previously, the Ministry of Public Health relaxed most of its restrictions on abortions in May of 1957, the problems of cost factors, the shortage of hospital facilities, and the need for prolonged recuperation have tended to downplay this surgical answer to the population problem. Or as Chang Hsing-hui, chief of Obstetrics of the Kwangtung Provincial People's Hospital told the Canton Municipal Council— "abortion is a negative approach." Here, many of the items carried by the popular press would surely discourage requests. For example, the *Kung-jen Jih-pao* of September 27, 1962 reported a follow-up to 200 women who had undergone abortions in one Peking hospital, mentioning that only a few suffered no ill effects afterwards. Peking is aware that wholesale abortions have proven successful elsewhere in stemming the population tide. For example, the Soviet Union legalized abortions in 1955, even for such reasons as job plans or overcrowded living accommodations, and limited the fee to $5.50 in state clinics. Since then, the Soviet leadership apparently has had no fear of a population boom. When the Japanese government failed to sell the peasants on contraceptive devices, abortion and sterilization were advocated, again apparently with considerable success. But given the many factors involved, the Chinese Communists have tended to favor vasectomy, or male sterilization, while downplaying abortion. Vasectomy, which can be performed in a hospital outpatient department or doctor's office and requires only one or two days for recovery, has been strongly urged in the press. One sample study, published in *Chung-kuo Fu-nü* (*Chinese Women*) on April 4, 1963, emphasized that there are no physiological or psychological after effects by stating that 72 per cent of the 500 cases had no change in virility, 18 per cent found themselves stronger, and the remainder were either ill, old or fearful. This relatively simple surgical procedure has been advocated for all husbands who are concerned seriously about the welfare of their wives and children.

For a variety of reasons, China's peasants have been slow to accept the ideas or practices involved in the state's campaign for population limitation. Certainly one of the strongest of these currents stems from the traditional or Confucian ethic, rooted firmly in the common personal experience that sanctioned, or even sanctified, large families. Expressed in such popular proverbs as "rear children for protection in old age" and "more children, more happiness," this belief holds that happiness both here and in the hereafter depends upon descendants. As late as February 7, 1958, NCNA acknowledged that more than 90 per cent of village marriages were still arranged by the parents,[12] and the Chinese peasant has stubbornly resisted any Party or state attempts to intervene in the area of familial relationships. Party propaganda that one need no longer fear childless marriage or old age without support, since the state's assumption of responsibility for all, has not dented the peasant's outlook. At the same time, the communists have frequently used the theme of men being more important than machines in their economic and military propaganda. The leadership has assured the Chinese people of its ability to create, here and now, the land of milk and honey and, in such times as the Great Leap Forward, bemoaned a labor shortage. This latter approach may have only confirmed the peasants in their belief in the desirability of large families.

Throughout the mainland, the peasants have resisted scientific solutions to the problem of family planning. Professor Wang Wen-pin of the Academy of Medical Science, noting this tendency, has assured them that the use of contraceptive devices will not have harmful effects. Instead, Wang insists, it is too many children that causes physical and nervous exhaustion. But the peasant is not only reluctant to accept this assistance, he often resents any public mention of personal matters. For example, the Canton

[12] Apparently in an attempt to combat this practice, the Chinese Communists have alluded to archaic approachs in a vein of ridicule. For example, Chou Hsin-min, Deputy Head of the CAS Institute of Law, has pointed to the regulation of Emperor Wu of the Chin dynasty—if the parents of a girl reaching the age of fourteen fail to find her a husband, the government should handle the marriage—as a way of stressing the dichotomy between the old and new orders. (See Peking *Kung-jen Jih-pao*, November 7, 1962).

Nan-fang Jih-pao of December 1, 1963, reported that when health workers visited every street and lane in the city to promote family planning, people remarked behind their backs "what an embarrassing thing to talk about childbirth!" Mao himself went to the heart of the problem in his 1965 interview with Edgar Snow when he mentioned that the peasant has been so slow in his acceptance of any help in family planning.

Given the fact that every drug store now prominently displays contraceptive devices and that the Chinese press continues its efforts in support of family limitation, and given the painfully slow progress in economic development and the human desire for a greater share in this world's advantages, the peasant may eventually be educated to an acceptance of Peking's campaign. But the problem of population planning must continue to loom very large for any Chinese Communist leadership for years to come. It is impossible to delineate the scope of the problem, as it probably affects such matters as the outside world's fear of Chinese expansionism, or the Soviet attitudes toward the common border. The problem or threat of overpopulation grips most of the underdeveloped countries. Should Communist China achieve a working solution, it is inevitable that her prestige will increase enormously in this vital orbit.

Implicitly running through this analysis of Chinese Communist campaigns to control the size of families is the regime's belief that it can create the new communist woman. This woman, guaranteed political and economic equality, will welcome an end to the strict subordinate and submissive role of women in traditional society and become a full and active co-worker in the revolutionary task. As noted elsewhere, this hypothesis was responsible in large measure for the mass labor-intensive programs of the Great Leap and commune era.

To encourage active participation in the Party's various drives, the Chinese Communists have followed a policy of bestowing positions of high trust on women. Soong Ching Ling, widow of Sun Yat-sen, became a Vice Chairman of the People's Republic. Four cabinet posts were given to women: Ho Hsiang-ning, Commissioner of Overseas Chinese; Shih Liang, Minister of Justice; Ch'ien Ying, Minister of Control; and Li Teh-ch'uan, Minister of Public Health. Four other women were elevated to the status of vice-ministers and one, Li Chen, was given the army rank of general. As observed in the Party chapter, four full members of the Central Committee are women as are four of the alternate members. Other women hold posts as vice mayors in the cities, heads or deputy heads of counties and districts, factory managers, commune directors or deputy directors, a wide spectrum of professional posts, and millions of rank-and-file jobs. In 1957, 148 women served as delegates to the National People's Congress, making up 12 per cent of the total representation. In 1964–65, 3,031 delegates were elected to the first session of the Third National People's Congress: 542, or 17.8 per cent were women. On March 6, 1966, NCNA reported that 300 heads or deputy heads of provincial, city, county or district governments were women, and that one in six researchers of the Chinese Academy of Sciences was female. In Peking municipality, 24 per cent of the college faculties, 44 per cent of the secondary teachers and 62 per cent of the primary teachers, were women. Nationwide, 30 to 40 per cent of the work force in the communal brigades were women.

The ensuing economic independence of women has wrought vast alterations in the traditional patriarchial family structure. State nurseries, purportedly established as an aid to career women, assume much of the parental responsibility after the working mother completes her 56-day maternity leave with pay. The whole sum of communal or cooperative type organizations which provide services normally performed by women in the home has permitted women to take full-time employment beside the men of China. Peking-directed propaganda seldom misses an opportunity to emphasize the good results of feminine liberation. For example, NCNA on March 2, 1965 praised the liberation of the Moslem peasant women of Hui nationality who, previously beaten for attending the theatre, are now respected performers of the arts. Seldom does the national press praise the performance of housewifely tasks. During the celebrations associated with the March 8, 1965 observance of the annual woman's day, the editorials and articles of *People's Daily* spoke of the need for women to participate in the class struggle, hard labor, to learn the thought of Mao, and carry out the work of the Party. There was no reference to women's traditional role as keepers of the hearth. Yet, isolated press accounts hint that the leadership recognizes the dangers to social stability related to woman's abandonment of her familial obligations. Thus, for example, *Chung-kuo Fu-nü* carried a lengthy account in its August 1, 1964 issue stressing the need for proper performance of this role. In the words of a member of Nanyang commune: "I would get angry with those who called me a woman . . . that I was now required to do woman's work was repugnant to me." Although this particular woman claimed to have been redeemed through studying the thought of Mao Tse-tung, the repeated emphasis on the importance of also loving "woman's work" would seem to suggest that feminine emancipation has become a mixed social blessing.

Policies for Control of Religion

In the orbit of religious beliefs and observances, communist policy stems from two theoretical considerations. In the first place, Marxist-Leninists regard religion as a form of reactionary idealism, sure to give way before dialectic materialism. Although this process is inevitable, it can and should be hastened to free the masses of the "opiate" of bourgeois design. One useful corrollary in the effort to discredit Christianity, therefore, has become the association of this religion with western, bourgeois intellectualism, particularly as a tool of imperialist expansion in the East. Or as *Hung-ch'i* phrased it in the November 21, 1964 issue: "Many theologians of the West . . . are aware that their theology begins and ends with serving politics." As another part of this drive, the communists seek to promote and use conflicts within the churches themselves by trying to pit foreign elements against Chinese elements, or a "patriotic" against a "reactionary" church. A second theoretical basis for action in the religious field is the tactical principle of change or variation according to which periods of intense persecution are followed by periods of comparative relaxation, or even good will gestures. In any case, particularly after the most outspoken criticism of the Chinese Communists during the period of Blooming and Contending often came from organized religious groups, there can be no doubt that Peking's ultimate goal for the churches of China is eventual extinction.

Generally speaking, the campaign against religion has been gradual, rather than intense. Too obvious interference, as was applied in Tibet, can elicit the sort of resistance the drive is calculated to dismiss. Superficially, Peking has continued to grant certain favors to religious organizations while demanding "purge from within." In 1949, prior to the establishment of the communist regime, the Chinese People's Political Consultative Conference included among its some 600 members eight representatives of religious denominations: five Christians, two Buddhists and a Moslem. According to *Heavenly Wind* (a religio-philosophical periodical) number 433, in a conference with a group of Christian leaders in 1950 Mao announced that, in the stage of the "New Democracy" then in progress, idealism and materialism might coexist: Christianity could exist in a socialist society provided it did so at the wishes of the people.

The 1954 Constitution for the People's Republic states in Article 88 that citizens enjoy the freedom of religious belief. Peking has carefully maintained that no religious leader or organization has ever been persecuted for doctrinal beliefs. However, these declaimers are the thinnest of veils behind which it has sought to hide the fact that the regime has sanctioned the imprisonment of Catholic clergy for being "agents of Rome," and has brought similar nebulous charges of nationalism and imperialism against the missionaries of various other denominations. Among the techniques used to curb religious activities are the usages of relatively minor police harassments. In the Chinese Communist view, freedom of religion also includes the freedom of anti-religion thus in the name of peace and order government must, on occasion, take action to limit religious activities.

Street-preaching and preaching during harvest or other times that might interfere with patriotic duties have been prohibited.

A more serious method for the subtle curtailment of religion has been the destruction of the economic foundations of the various churches. Deprived of properties and revenues in the name of land reform, and prohibited from receiving contributions from abroad, local self-support is virtually impossible. In 1949 there were about one million Protestants and three million Catholics in China: their schools and welfare agencies were closely affiliated with overseas mission-sending churches and orders. The churches they represented were subjected not only to economic isolation, but also to the more insidious tactic for undermining their independence—the forced organization of "patriotic" churches.

In its first stages, the "patriotic" movement proved most successful against the various Protestant sects who lacked the disciplinary unity of the Catholic Church. Communist agents who infiltrated the churches led campaigns for the explusion of all "foreign" elements who were accused of opposing the emerging forces of "progressivism." Once the "foreign" clergy was removed, the communists pressured the native clergy to form "patriotic" churches under the watchful direction of a regime officially committed to atheism. One application of these tactics can be observed in the Chinese Christian Three-Self Patriotic Movement, initiated in July, 1950, by a manifesto signed by more than 400,000 church members. This first major effort to stifle religion indicated the tone to be used in all subsequent campaigns. Rather than destruction from the outside, the churches were to provide their own agencies for eventual annihilation. The three selfs—self-support, self-propagation, and self-government—gave birth to local organizations to carry out the master program. Religious leaders who protested were subjected to powerful attacks.

A similar approach was employed against the Catholic Church. As early as 1950, Catholic university students were attacked by Party-trained classmates. By 1952, following an iconoclast drive, the Legion of Mary had been accused of being an international spy ring and was ordered to be destroyed. Students in Catholic institutions were ordered to attend rectification, or brain-washing sessions. Beginning in 1955, Catholic priests were confined to their rectories under guard, or arrested and subjected to mass trials.[13] Charges centered on the allegation that these clergymen were in

---

[13] One of the more memorable of these arrests occurred on September 9, 1955, when Bishop Kung of Shanghai was arrested together with 27 Chinese Catholic priests and about 300 prominent laymen. After Kung had been conditioned in the matter of Cardinal Mindszenty, two mass trials were staged—both of which proved to be dismal strategic failures. Kung remains in prison, as does the American Bishop of Maryknoll, John Walsh, despite the protests of Richard Nixon (while Vice President) and Senator Mundt against the latter's incarceration.,

the pay of a foreign government—the Vatican—which is commonly referred to as "an imperialist instrument of the US warmongers." In 1956, imprisonments were stepped up: by the end of the year, 2,291 missionaries had been expelled from the mainland. Then, on August 3, 1957, the Chinese Catholic Patriotic Association was organized under the direction of the state's Religious Affairs Bureau. In April, 1958, the CPC demanded that "loyal" bishops be elected by the church members and that the Association supervise all seminary training. Since these measures isolated the Church in China from the Vatican, in July, Pope Pius XII issued an encyclical condemning the Patriotic Association and declaring the Church in China to be in a state of schism. In December, the newly elected Pope John XXIII, speaking to the College of Cardinals, admonished those 18 or 19 priests who had allowed themselves to be "elected" bishops under the aegis of the Association. Despite these disciplinary efforts, the clergy of the Association still claim the validity of their offices in defiance of Vatican regulations. At the second national convention of the Catholic Patriotic Association, January 6–10, 1964, the Chairman, Archbishop P'i Shu-shih, announced renewed fidelity to the CPC, approved of the reform of members by indoctrination and labor, and denounced the reactionary nature of the Vatican as a servant of U.S. imperialism.

China's Buddhist and Moslem people have fared somewhat better than the Protestant or Catholic churches, due to Peking's efforts to woo those Asian or Middle Eastern nations which have a heavy, or majority Buddhist or Moslem population. In 1953, a National Buddhist Conference and its administrative organization led by Shirob-Jaltso declared that China's socialist state was the earthly realization of Buddha's paradise. A Chinese Buddhist delegation participated in the 2,500th anniversary celebration of Buddha's Nirvana in Burma in 1955, and the veneration of the Buddha tooth relic was a major propaganda triumph. The ten million Chinese Moslems, further united by their common Hui ancestry, were organized into the Chinese Islamic Association in 1953, with the double function of guiding native Moslems and making favorable international contacts. Good-will delegations have toured the Middle East. In 1958, the ruling prerogatives and system of contribution of the Islamic faith were abolished and the priestly caste was asked to participate in the labor brigades.

Of the thousands of western missionaries in China on the eve of the communist victory, scarcely a handful remain. Some churches remain open as a display of Party toleration, just as native clergy are still "educated" in the semblance of the traditional order. According to Wu Yao-tsung, chairman of the Three-Self Movement, as reported in *Peking Review* on June 1, 1965, all followers of Christ have the duty as well as privilege of continuing to spread the Gospel. The state has engaged in the reconstruction or preservation of numerous historic shrines, such as the 300 year old Gumbum Buddhist Monastary in Tsinghai, which was recently equipped with lightening rods. It should be noted that this ostensible toleration has certain tactical advantages on the international stage. For example, the October, 1963 Peking Buddhist demonstrations with delegates from eleven countries (including Cambodia, Indonesia, Korea, Laos, Nepal, Pakistan and Thailand) was intended to demonstrate support for fellow religionists in South Vietnam, while reassuring present or potential allies of China's respect for personal beliefs.[14] In reality, no freedom of religion exists in China. By removing the individual from the controls and comforting authority of his family and his God, the Communist Party of China has sought to create an emotional-intellectual vacuum capable of being filled only by the new "divinity" of the thought of Mao Tse-tung and the "clergy" of the CPC.

ENGINEERING SOCIAL REVOLUTION

By determining to eradicate the "four olds" of Chinese society,[15] the leaders of the cultural revolution seek to create the true dictatorship of the proletariat. By creating the Red Guards as a primary instrument for socialist transformation, Mao and his associates seem to have carried the class struggle to a new plane—that of bitter contention between the revolutionary and the non-revolutionary segments of the population. Thus, on the one hand, the young social engineers of the Red Guards are committed to seek out and destroy the old values and customs retained by their older compatriots. But, of equal importance to the leaders in Peking, the establishment of the Red Guards as a mass organization is intended to purge the generation now coming of age of any inclination toward bourgeois values or habits. Party warnings and press admissions indicate that this latter task had much to do with the planning of the cultural revolution.

As Mao Tse-tung himself remarked in his January 9, 1965 interview with Edgar Snow, no Chinese then under the age of twenty had had personal experience of the evils of pre-communist society, or the glory of the revolutionary struggle against the KMT. Youth could be told, Mao mused, but that was far from knowledge based on personal experience. Or, as *Chung-kuo Ch'ing-nien* (*China Youth*) (August 1, 1964) phrased the issue: the younger generation has a tendency to fear hardship, prefer ease, and believe itself superior to the older generation because of its educational

[14] Venerable Thech Thien Hao, president of the Vietnamese Unified Buddhist Association doubtlessly abetted Peking's primary purpose by his recitations of the horrors of 156,000 killed or wounded, and the finding of over 3,000 mutilated corpses.

[15] The "four olds" refer to "old ideas, culture, customs and habits" of the bourgeoisie.

and other opportunities. Despite Peking's exhortations to parents "to resolutely educate the coming generation in the revolutionary spirit of hard and bitter struggle," and despite the indoctrinary aspect of the educational system as sending youths to difficult labor assignments, on the eve of the cultural revolution it was apparent that not all youths were fit heirs to the revolutionary traditions.

Mao Tse-tung had reminded the Chinese students studying in the Soviet Union, in November, 1957, that "the world is yours. . . . All hopes are placed on you." But the warnings and denunciations in the Chinese Communist press reveal that not all young people responded to Mao's call for renewed dedication to socialist objectives. Some failed to appreciate the new communist culture. Readers of the July 4, 1963 issue of *China Youth* were reminded that interest in the traditional Chinese theatre was fraught with danger. Operatic portrayals of the old class society, which often sentimentalized or stressed male superiority, might mislead, since "any attempt to underscore the idea of freedom of love and emancipation of personality will make one find oneself in the mire of the bourgeoisie." But when youths began to favor western music of the rock-and-roll variety over Chinese music, the danger was even more immediate. As one student from Peking Normal University admitted: "because I was bewitched by bourgeois thought, I gradually became a lonely, haughty, arrogant, decadent, sentimental man." Western influence was even more apparent in the manner of "bizarre" new fashions. *People's Daily* of November 22, 1964, sternly admonished those university students who discarded their peasant-styled clothing for the new fashions, while Canton's *Nan-fang Jih-pao* excoriated the young man "whose hair was done in a style not very much different from that of a woman" and had the intolerable nerve to demand that a tailor "make legs of pants of printed cotton as tight-fitting as possible."

While the Party called upon all students to learn the thought of Mao Tse-tung, some young people were said to be "whiling away their time in teahouses," addicted to card-playing in which "the relationship between the players is no longer decent," and engaging in "small talk" in which "laughing and talking become an open invitation for bourgeois thinking to intrude."[16] Even the hobby of keeping goldfish has been denounced unless

[16] The Chinese Communists take the matter of relating jokes and stories very seriously. For example, in an article entitled "Jokes and Idle Chatter," in the January 12, 1965 *Ta-kung Pao*, the case is related of a joke told about a near-sighted peasant who mistakes chicken droppings for jam and consumes them. The article moralizes that the joke is not good since "it shows that our working people were not able to distinguish fragrant smell from foul odor and was an attempt at telling us to despise our class brothers." "Since an assortment of jokes necessarily comes from a class society," the article continues, "they are inevitably stamped with the brand of class." Thus, in the proletarian society, jokes are no longer proper.

the fish are "beneficial to physical and mental well-being." But the most serious mistake of the young Chinese was to engage in personal friendships or love affairs which detract from study and impede single-hearted dedication to Party goals. For example, one young woman, after confessing her close friendship with another girl of similar interests, was reminded by the April 13, 1965 *Yang-ch'eng Wan-pao* that "sworn relationships" are reactionary and friends are no longer needed in China since each individual enjoys the benefits of the whole society. As noted previously, romance and marriage are discouraged until students complete their education, and preferably until after a period of service in the remote areas. Ironically, as illustrated by letters in the September 14, 1963 *China Youth*, more than one student has apparently rushed into marriage to avoid such assignments. However often the Party press has cautioned that "to fall in love too soon will distract from study and affect progress," the Chinese Communists have been unable to completely impose their social norms.

In addition to the strenuous part-work and part-study programs devised for their youths, and employment of the techniques of indoctrination and surveillance, the Chinese Communists have also attempted a rigid organization of leisure time. Thus, the state provides a variety of recreational facilities which are also intended to fulfill semi-political functions. The case of the Loyang Bearings Works may be regarded as typical. Younger workers there reside in collectivized dormitories and are divided into teams for the study of the thought of Mao during off-duty hours. Other urban clubs provide facilities for basketball, volleyball and pingpong, and for "cultural lectures" such as talks by older people on "the miseries of the old days."

Peking's ability to utilize young people as a means to destroy traditional social customs and norms was vastly enhanced by the decision to make the Red Guards into a mass organization.[17] Although the Chinese Communists have not released any membership figures,[18] it must be supposed that all middle school through college students have been encouraged to

---

[17] As noted elsewhere, it is not yet certain whether the Red Guards are intended to replace, supplement or direct and inspire the Young Communist League. Nor have the organizational guidelines for the Guards been formalized. In addition to the obvious fact of mass unrest, which would impede official programming, the delayed decisions of the precise nature and functions of the Red Guards may be intended to allow the utmost flexibility in directing the youths.

[18] One example of the difficulty in establishing membership figures can be gained from the official reports concerning the numbers of Red Guards who visited Peking in the latter months of 1696. According to *Peking Review* of January 1, 1967, "in the last few months 11 million revolutionary students and teachers from all parts of the country came to Peking. . . ." But, the same source on April 28, 1967, reported that "between August and November last year Chairman Mao received more than twelve million young Red Guard fighters. . . .'

join the Red Guards. And since membership clearly represents the way to prove one's loyalties to Mao and his associates and to enjoy educational and job preferment, it must be assumed that China's youths have responded in large numbers.

Yet, whatever the ultimate success of the Party leadership in proper training and indoctrination of the future generation, it must deal with the fact that the present generation of job and office-holders, of teachers and foremen, may be further antagonized to resist the changes of the cultural revolution because of the Party's very success in winning the sympathies and dedication of these young people. If professors have fled from their universities, or doctors have joined workers, or engineers have refused to report for assignments, or veteran cadres have avoided the scrutiny of the Red Guards, the CPC cannot utilize its teenagers to fill the gap. True social revolution always verges dangerously close to civil war. Mao and his followers, however, believe that the communist revolution in China cannot be successfully completed and safeguarded without a thoroughgoing social revolution. With the aid of the Communist-guided mass organizations, mass campaigns, and social drives, they hope to succeed in engineering the fundamental social revolution during the present and succeeding generations.

CHAPTER **10**

The Chinese Communist
Cultural System

A communist regime, as a professed revolutionary spearhead, cannot be satisfied with governing for governing's sake. It has a self-imposed cultural mission to revise value judgments, foster socialist man, and change human nature. Based on their ideology, the Chinese Communists have advanced a new set of ideas and norms of cultural life, led an incessant struggle on the cultural front, intensified the wide use of the mass cultural media and educational channels, and finally encouraged and guided the Red Guards to effect a thorough-going cultural revolution.

Appealing to reason, persuasion is usually more effective than force in spreading ideas and influencing outlook. The Chinese Communists employ persuasion to propagate their ideological beliefs through instruments which they seek to apply with the utmost coverage and penetration. Lenin, indeed, declared long ago that the Soviet state rests on a balance of coercion and persuasion. Mao Tse-tung, too, defines his "Democratic Dictatorship" as simply a combination of force and "democracy." "Toward the enemy," he has said, "it uses the method of dictatorship. . . . Toward the people, it is the opposite; it does not use compulsion, but democratic methods: namely, it does not compel them to do this or that but uses democratic methods in educating and persuading them." Rephrased bluntly, "democratic education" is propaganda in all its dynamic forms. Thus Peking

515

relies not only on the strong right arm of its security forces, but also on the left arm of its propaganda machine to effect a new cultural system,

At the core of the Chinese Communist cultural system are revolutionary propaganda and agitation. "Who is a propagandist?" Mao asked in his 1942 speech "On Opposing Formalism." He answered: "Not only is the teacher a propagandist, the literary writer a propagandist, but all our cadres in all kinds of work are also propagandists." For the Chinese Communists, "propaganda" does not carry the derogatory meaning familiar elsewhere. "Any person talking with another person is engaged in propaganda," Mao insists. Thus, propaganda is not only a pillar of the Peking regime, but also the life work of all Chinese Communists, whose goal it is to bring the whole nation and its posterity into the communist millenium.

CULTURAL IDEAS AND NORMS

Ideological Content of Art and Literature

In non-totalitarian countries, works of art and literature may bear the stamp of national form or flavor, but they are primarily the products of individual expression and aesthetic standards. Masters in the field may teach and inspire, but no one actually prescribes content or form. The Chinese Communists, like their counterparts in the Soviet Union, have transformed art and literature from vehicles of personal creativity and expression into instruments for portraying a set view of life, and rallying support for the leadership and its programs.

In his speech to the Yenan Forum on Literature and Art in May, 1942, Mao Tse-tung clearly indicated that "art for art's sake" must be abandoned:

Literature and art are subordinate to politics, and in turn exert great influence over politics. Revolutionary literature and art are a part of the entire revolutionary enterprise; they are like screws which, in relation to other parts of the machine, may be classified on the basis of importance, urgency, or primacy. But they are the screws essential to the machine, and they are the part essential to the revolutionary enterprise.

If literature and art are "screws," then the writer and artist are themselves little more than identical and interchangeable parts, some better, some worse, but all circumscribed in their individual creativity. Indeed, since the convocation of the Forum on Literature and Art in 1942, Mao has directed that all writers and artists must know for whom and for what they labor. The "whom" is supposedly "the people," but in reality the Communist Party: the "what" is the ideology and other requirements of this Party.

Writers and artists are required to study "Marxism-Leninism and society," for their works must grow out of and reflect the class struggle. To do otherwise is to be held guilty of "individualism," which is a bourgeois error. In the colorful Chinese Communist phraseology, "the red flower is good, but it needs the support of green leaves."

Following these directives, the literary and artistic works produced during the civil conflict after 1945 generally glorified the new hero, the communist cadre who led the masses to revolt against "feudal oppression," "bureaucratic corruption," and "imperialist aggression." The 1949 convocation of a national cultural conference and the formation of the All-China Federation of Literary and Art Circles, which promptly adopted the principles enunciated by Mao at the 1942 Yenan Forum, gave an even wider propagation to the ideas of proletarian realism. And in each subsequent year art and literature have faithfully reflected the Party's current programs. The new hero, model worker, peace fighter, literacy worker, or similar figure, has been praised and glorified ceaselessly.

The Great Leap Forward, launched in 1958, applied to art and literature in quantitative, rather than qualitative, terms. By the summer of 1960, the artistic community was set to an examination of its collective conscience over the degree of fidelity which was being maintained toward Party standards. Invariably, writers, artists and performers reaffirmed that nothing good could come out of a loss of contact with the masses. The June, 1960 Kansu meeting of a provincial dramatic troupe is representative. Young performers, who held that youth was a time for mastering techniques, and old age for politics, were severely criticized and all pledged to work harder to express "the soul of the people." Needless to say, the same approach was taken by the communist leadership. Speaking for the CPC Central Committee and the State Council, Lu Ting-yi congratulated the delegates to the third congress of the All-China Federation of Literary and Art Circles which met in Peking in July, 1960. He acknowledged that the "blooming and contending" policy would continue as the mass line for literary and artistic work and reaffirmed the advantages to the individual and to society which stem from the program introduced in 1957, that the intellectuals spend at least part of their time in "productive" (i.e., manual) labor. Kuo Mo-jo, president of the Chinese Academy of Sciences, orientated his concluding speech to the congress to emphasis the value of "revolutionary romanticism"—or a folklore—which reflects "the present heroic era." Chou Yang, deputy director of the CPC Central Committee's Propaganda Department and vice chairman of the Federation, also used this forum to challenge the intellectuals to form part of the vanguard of the socialist front and to assume the leadership of the mass line.   Professionals and semi-professionals, in the realm of the arts as well as the prosaic, were urged to learn from and to encourage the work of amateurs.

In all essentials, the CPC's plans for artists and writers have not varied from the time Mao ennunciated his principles to the 1942 Yenan forum. But the accomplishments of the program have fallen short of expectations. Among countless examples that might be cited is the pathetically poor quality of the homespun philosophers. *Philosophical Research* No. 6, 1965 was designed to honor those peasants who had applied Mao's thought to their own commonplace experiences in "fresh" articles for the people. Thus Tan Hsien-ping examined the relationship of Marxism-Leninism to automobile driving ("Dialectics in Motor Driving") in these less than inspiring lines:

... Supposing an accident is imminent. If a driver can avoid it by giving the pedestrian violating the rule of the road more room or by stopping earlier, then he should do so. ... It would seem that reason is on your side if an accident occurs while you have faithfully abided by the traffic laws; but if you failed to do your best ... then reason is not on your side and you have failed to do your duty.

There are also hints that the CPC recognizes the inferior caliber of much of the art and literature currently being mass-produced. For example, Canton postponed its Central South China Drama Festival in 1964, for lack of adequate material. During the 1965 Festival, T'ao Chu, then CPC First Secretary of the CC Central South China Bureau, emphasized that selected traditional works must be retained as models for the new dramas and denounced the current dramatic trends of "departing from reality" and the "interpretation of realism as naturalism" (or non-socialist and pessimistic interpretations). Yet, the stress on amateur contributions to a new socialistic culture is being maintained. On November 25, 1965, the Central Committee of the Young Communist League and the Union of Chinese Writers sponsored a Peking conference on the arts for 1,100 activist, spare-time writers. And again, Chou Yang, deputy director of the CPC Central Committee's Propaganda Department, demanded that the amateurs utilize artistic and literary forms to advance the cause of socialism. Since these culturally inferior, but propagandistically effective works serve the demands of the CPC, little change can be expected in official policy.

Language Reform

Among the many problems associated with controls over all aspects of culture and communications, which confront the Chinese Communist leadership, perhaps none is more basic than the question of what to do with or how to manipulate the language itself. [1] Aside from the related difficulties of the variations in spoken dialects, and the fact that the scholar needs to master a few thousand characters, the complicated ideographic form of the written language has hampered the mass literacy drives essential to communist indoctrination efforts. Early in the 20th century, Chinese language reformers led by Hu Shih judged the literary language to be an obstacle to progress because of its rigidity and outmoded vocabulary. To replace the "tyranny of the classics," they advocated the *pai-hua,* or plain-spoken language, based on the vocabulary and syntax of colloquial speech. The Chinese Communists, of course, have had other, more pressing reasons for encouraging language reform. As Wei Chueh, a member of the Standing Committee for Reforming the Chinese Written Language, observed in *People's China* of December 16, 1955, the language is "extremely difficult to learn and does not, under conditions of modern civilization, lend itself easily to practical use in mass education, printing, assimilation of new words and ideas, scientific research, etc." Underlying these pressing needs is the greater, albeit unspoken, demand of indoctrination or control of the thoughts of more than 700 million people.

Two important conferences were held in Peking in October, 1955, to promote language reform. The All-China Conference on Reform of the Written Chinese Language passed a resolution calling for the simplification of characters as a first step toward the final stage of a phonetically written language. In conjunction with the Conference on Standardization of the Chinese Language, then, work was begun to fulfill Mao's 1951 dictum. "The written language must be reformed," Mao said, "it should follow the common direction of phoneticization which has been taken by world languages." This effort involves three stages—simplification, standardization and phoneticization (or the substitution of an alphabet for the ideographs). Simplification entails a reduction in strokes in the more complex characters and the reduction of the total number of characters in use. Standardization involves popularizing the so-called common (or northern China/Mandarin) language. In fact, even before these resolutions were passed, various newspapers and periodicals had already introduced on a

---

[1] Chinese characters are symbolic or nonalphabetic and have changed but little over some three thousand years. This has enabled the scholar of any later period to use the classical models as readily as he might use contemporary sources, thus providing a prime model of historical-cultural continuity. But the spoken language has been modified by time, region and national minorities, so that even a native Chinese must "learn" the literary (or written) language. Spoken differences have hampered oral communication, a problem solved for the upper class and bureaucracy by the official adoption of the Mandarin dialect. Yet, this elite never constituted more than 10–15 per cent of the total population in pre-communist China.

trial basis 141 simplified characters suggested by the Committee for Reforming the Chinese Written Language. In the first stage, 517 characters and 54 radicals were to be simplified; in the second, about half of the 7,000 most commonly used characters would be simplified.

On February 10, 1956, the New China News Agency announced plans for the trial and final adoption of a new 30-letter Latin alphabet. [2] This alphabet was not yet earmarked to replace the Chinese characters, but to help popularize the standardized spoken Chinese in order to abet the mass literary drives. According to Wu Yü-chang, Chairman of the Committee for Reforming the Chinese Written Language, the alphabet would only gradually replace the ideographs; during the transitional period both old and new were to be used concurrently. This policy still prevails, while efforts have been extended to introduce an alphabetical system for the various languages of the national minorities and other groups. At its 63rd meeting, on November 29, 1957, the State Council ordered that the national minorities use the Latin alphabet as the basis for reconstructing their written languages. In 1960, the Uigur and Kazakh nationalities, for example, began using a modified 33 letter Latin alphabet in their schools. Some 20,000 instructors were trained to use the new books in classes for 600,000 primary school students. Meanwhile, at the fifth session of the First NPC, in February, 1958, a phoneticized plan was approved for introduction in the regular primary schools during the fall term. In 1959, the Ministries of Interior and Education, together with the Committee for Reforming the Chinese Written Language, introduced a 26 letter and 4 sets of double consonants manual alphabet for the instruction of deaf and dumb children. But the problem of wide variation in spoken dialect remains. This is particularly acute in the case of draftees into the People's Liberation Army, where misunderstanding of spoken commands can create chaos. Thus, Peking's *Kuang-ming Jih-pao* on October 14, 1964, detailed the methods of language instruction in the p'u-t'ung-hua (common language) or Mandarin pronunciation used by the various Party branches in teaching the military. Each new recruit is paired with a veteran to learn military terms, read Mao's works aloud, sing songs together, and listen to loudspeaker broadcasts.

Any survey of the problems of language instruction in Communist China would be incomplete without some reference to the difficulties encountered in the system of higher education. Scholars trained in the pre-communist

---

[2] The alphabet was said to contain all the letters of the English alphabet except for "v". Five letters were added for common Chinese sounds: the soft "g," "zh," "ch," "sh," and "ng". The letter "y" is considered as a sixth vowel and pronounced like the German "u". The pronunciation of some other English consonants and vowels has been altered for adjustment to Chinese pronunciation.

era often had some proficiency in the English language, since textbooks or periodicals in this language were used in the colleges and universities. But with the 1949 communist victory, English was dropped as a curriculum requirement at both the secondary and college level: as part of the "lean to one side" official policy, Russian became the vital second language, as texts and articles were hurriedly translated and circulated. By 1956, the President of the Chinese Academy of Sciences, Kuo Mo-jo, was claiming that about 70 per cent of the older scientists were able to use Russian texts. Instruction in the Russian language, at least to the point of student reading knowledge, has not been without its curricular and political pitfalls, however. For example, a survey publicized by Shanghai's NCNA branch, on July 4, 1961, admitted that many university students were indifferent to foreign language study. [3] In June, 1962, the Ministry of Education seemed to reflect this situation in its announcement that foreign language testing would generally be omitted from the national entrance examinations for college admission.

Although the importance of foreign language instruction has been greatly minimized by official policy, Peking continues to seek means to train bilinguists—a need, it should be noted, that is often correlated to shifts in foreign policies and tactics. For the masses, there are now a variety of "self-taught" modes, including phonograph records with accompanying texts, readily available in all bookstores. It is extremely doubtful that this particular means has been fruitful. One example of the many defects in the program may be cited. In its October 9, 1962 edition, the Peking *Chung kuo Ch'ing-nien Pao* advised its readers to learn English by purchasing a dictionary and memorizing the idioms! Courses of foreign language instruction are still offered, beginning at the junior high school level, but the leadership has apparently reconciled itself to the obligation of relying upon a corps of experts, rather than millions of poorly trained people. This conclusion would seem to be borne out by the September, 1964 opening of the Peking School of Foreign Languages, under the joint auspices of the Commission for Overseas Chinese and the Municipal Bureau of Education. The first group of 230 specially selected students were offered specialities in English, Japanese or Thai, using the latest advances in instructional techniques, such as tape recorders. In 1965, Burmese and Indonesian were added to the curriculum. According to the Hong Kong *Wen-hui Pao* of March 17, 1965, the returned overseas Chinese students study the language of the country from which they have come, in addition to Chinese. Courses in political theory are also compulsory; five weeks are given over

---

[3] This announcement, timed to a period of growing ill-will in Sino-Soviet relations, may have reflected or anticipated a leadership decision to minimize Russian language instruction for a number of reasons.

to an analysis of the thought of Mao Tse-tung. It is presumably from this and similar schools that Peking will be able to draw upon a corps of linguists essential to carrying out the varied demands of national and foreign policy.

STRUGGLE ON THE CULTURAL FRONT

Brain-Washing through Criticism and Self-Criticism

The Chinese Communists understand that in order to implement their cultural ideas and norms and promote their ideology, they must engage in a determined struggle against those who have the sophistication to distinguish political indoctrination from cultural freedom. The latter is represented by the intellectuals, whose support or compliance is particularly important to the regime. This explains why the stepped up socialization of agriculture, industry and commerce in the latter part of 1955 was accompanied by a drive to "reform the intellectuals." For several consecutive days in December of that year, the *Kuangming Daily*, the China Democratic League's organ, intended for the intelligentsia, carried reports of the meetings of central committees of the various non-communist parties, at which the problem of unity and reform of the intellectuals was given precedence. As noted in the December 6 issue: ". . . As the present agricultural cooperativization and the Socialist reform of industry and commerce have further developed into a new situation, the intellectuals must further reform their thinking so as to fully develop their potential and thereby render more valuable service to the socialist enterprises."

To "reform" the intellectuals, Peking engages in "brain-washing" through the familiar technique of "criticism and self-criticism." While the term "brain-washing" has a derogatory connotation to outsiders, the Chinese Communists use it in a perfunctory way, as they use the term "propaganda." Although the term "thought reform" is more widely employed, the more graphic term was introduced by Mao himself. In the course of the Party Reform Movement in 1942–43, he voiced the desire, in one way or another, to "wash the brains" of those whose ways of thinking were judged inimical toward, or unhealthy for, the new regime. Mao's theory was that the new citizens of the New Democracy had to be cleansed of the "dust" or "burdens" of past poisonous thoughts, such as feudalistic arrogance, bourgeois individualism, worship of foreign cultures, or, and above all, anti-communist inclinations. Thus, "criticism and self-criticism" might be regarded as the washing process.

Edward Hunter's book, *Brain Washing in Red China*, has made the process quite familiar to the western public. At the urging of Mao himself, an "ideological reform study movement" was started in the fall of 1951, with the express purpose of bringing the intellectuals, especially academicians and university professors, into a position of subservience to the Party line. In the usual approach, Party cadres who were also students criticized the past utterances of a particular professor. The professor would then be "invited" to give his explanation, or self-criticism, to a student assembly. Here, the professor might "confess" all his past sins against the Party, or, in the absence of such self-revelation, be subjected to severe criticism and humiliation. Newspapers, academic journals and other agencies might also conduct such procedures until such time as a total surrender was made by the accused. Academicians and professors in the social sciences were especially likely to meet such treatment, with the result that many of these specialists denounced themselves and repudiated their scholastic achievements, sometimes in a quite blatant manner. [4] Hu Shih, the leading Chinese liberal philosopher and scholar, was attacked in absentia; his own son was enlisted to "liquidate" any trace of Hu's influence. Intellectuals with known "leftist" inclinations fared somewhat better, but they too were subjected to close scrutiny before being allowed to join the bandwagon of New Democratic learning.

The Party's handling of the case of the *Dream of the Red Chamber*, China's most popular classical novel written in the spoken language, illustrates a common approach to reform of the intellectuals. [5] Scholarly study of this work has been so extensive that it has become known in literary circles as "the science of the *Dream of the Red Chamber*." Among the most prominent "scientists" in this respect have been Hu Shih and Yu P'ing-po, the latter recognized as an authority for over thirty years. In the fall of 1954, Li Hsi-fan and Lan Ying, two young students just out of Shantung University, attacked Professor Yu's interpretation of the novel as expressed in numerous articles and including his "Short Discussion on the *Dream of the Red Chamber*" which appeared in *Hsing Chien-she (New Construction)* for March, 1954. In joint articles which first appeared in the September issue of the Shantung University publication, *Literature, Philosophy and History*, these critics alleged that Yu had "separated himself from a clear

[4] In a pamphlet entitled *Brain-Washing in Red China*, published in November, 1955, by the Society for the Defense of Freedom in Asia, an anti-communist organization in New Delhi, India, there is a list of 156 top professors, scientists, engineers, artists, etc. who made at least one public confession and recanted their ideological sins.

[5] Ts'ao Hsüeh-ch'in, author of the *Dream of the Red Chamber*, died in 1763, when he was less than fifty, and having completed 80 chapters of his novel. In 1963, the Chinese Communists commemorated the 200th anniversary of his death with a display in Peking's Palace Museum. Throughout the celebration, the Party press emphasized that the permanent value of the novel stemmed from its depiction of the horrors of bourgeois society.

class viewpoint and started from the abstract art viewpoint," and that he had adopted "the viewpoint of the idealism of anti-realism." In short, Yu was judged guilty of having a bourgeois mentality—a condition which was said to stem from his acceptance of the pragmatism of Hu Shih.

An outpouring of similarly critical articles flowed unabated into 1955, while other instruments were also employed to denounce Yu P'ing-po. At the October 24, 1954 forum of the Department of Classical Literature of the Chinese Writers Union, Professor Yu faced his critics and admitted to the embarrassing fact that he had "resorted to the feudal work style exploiting the master-disciple relationship" by having relied on an assistant to prepare some of the recent articles under criticism. He confessed to having "failed to grasp fully the political . . . and ideological nature of the novel, failed to carry out my research with the viewpoint of historical materialism, paying attention to only minor and fragmentary details." But the professor staunchly refused to admit the principal charge of bourgeois idealism. Thus, the press continued to publish stereotyped criticisms and the All-China Federation of Literary and Art Circles and the Chinese Writers Association began conducting a series of joint meetings to condemn Professor Yu's ''bourgeois" stand and question a magazine which had been so tolerant as to print his views. A reorganization of the magazine's editorial department naturally followed. The attack was widened to denounce Hu Shih as the greater target, for Hu was said to have had an "inimical influence" on youth and intellectuals by indoctrinating them with his pragmatic "decadent capitalist view of life." [6]

The Blooming and Contending period only temporarily abated the Chinese Communist program of thought reform. Although less numerous, the intellectuals are still subjected to denunciation and pressures. A typical case in the wake of the decision to abandon the "soft" approach to

---

[6] The case of two other victims of brain-washing during this period may be mentioned briefly. Hu Feng, a veteran communist whose influence in journalistic and literary circles dated back to the early 1920's, ventured to complain in a session of the China Federation of Literature and Art in 1954, that the journal *Wen-yi Pao* (*Literary Gazette*) was reducing the effects of the cultural drive by discouraging young writers. A violent broadside of denunciation followed and by January, 1955, Hu had signed a typically self-degrading confession. Branded a hireling of the enemies of the New China, Hu Feng was expelled from all his public positions. Liang Shu-ming, a prominent authority on rural reform and a leader of the Democratic League, became the victim of a press attack in the summer of 1955. His ideological errors were said to stem from his idealistic Buddhist outlook and included such charges as an under-estimation of the importance of the class struggle and a sentimental advocacy of a slower collectivization policy and industrialization program on the grounds that the peasants had already suffered overmuch. Liang was branded an enemy of communism and of the Chinese people.

For a detailed treatment of the various cases involving brain-washing of the intellectuals, see Theodore Chen's *Thought Reform of the Chinese Intellectuals*.

the intellectuals is that of Feng Yu-lan, who has been recognized as one of China's leading modern philosophers. In 1951, Feng had acknowledged a willingness to follow the philosophic system contained in *The New Principles of Li*. Although he used a Marxist-Leninist viewpoint to reinterpret China's traditional philosophies, he was not above suspicion. Then, following the Blooming and Contending principles, Feng published an article entitled "The Question of Inheritance of the Chinese Philosophical Heritage" in the January 8, 1957 *Kuangming Daily*. In this, he declared that the Chinese Communists had "negated a little too much the ancient Chinese philosophy, thus the legacy that can be inherited is rather small." For this statement, Feng incurred the wrath of the CPC. Consequently, Hu Sheng, deputy director of the CPC Central Committee's Propaganda Department, published a corrective interpretation in the March 29, 1957 *People's Daily*. Hu not only attacked Feng's views and character, but also mobilized several philosophers for a concerted attack to force Feng to publically acknowledge his errors. Nevertheless, Feng continued to challenge the regime. In the June 8, 1958 issue of the *Kuangming Daily* he pointed out that there were a number of philosophical contradictions involved in the Great Leap and that the problems could not be resolved until a real distinction was made between true philosophers and the CPC's "philosophic workers." He also urged the universities to use their departments of philosophy to train theorists.

The attack on Feng began with the statement of six Peking University students on the grounds that the proposal was in opposition to the Chinese Communist principle of combining theory with practice through productive labor. They also noted that this distinction between theory and practice was essentially a bourgeois theory that learning and politics were separate activities. They further emphasized that Feng's theory was "tantamount to the strangling of the life of Marxism-Leninism" and would necessarily lead to "the pitfalls of dogmatism and revisionism on the part of theoretic workers." On July 6, 1958, the Peking *Kuangming Daily* published another article declaring that Feng was still serving the bourgeoise. "As to what he said about systematic study of Marxism-Leninism," the paper added, "it was a pure lie." As his colleagues joined the drive to discredit him, Feng was compelled once more to undergo self-criticism. In an August 3, 1958 article in the *Kuangming Daily*, Feng admitted that "the bourgeoisie of China is dead," and that "the burden of my feudal and bourgeois philosophy is heavy. . . . I want to change for a brain of red stamping." Even so, it must be assumed that Professor Feng will be watched vigilantly for further signs of bourgois relapses from the truths of Marxism-Leninism.

Among the more highly publicized of recent cases involving thought reform is the controversy concerning the philosophical issue of whether "two can merge into one." As Mao Tse-tung stressed in his *On Contradictions*, the concept that "one divides into two" is basic to the Marxist-Leninist dialectic. That is to say, two aspects of a unified force struggle against one another to reach a higher stage. But beginning with the May 29, 1964 issue of the *Kuangming Daily*, the CPC violently criticized elderly philosopher and Party official Yang Hsien-chen for suggesting that, in fact, "two merge into one." Yang, who was made an alternate member of the CPC Central Committee in 1956, and promoted to full membership in 1958, had apparently suggested that two opposites are prone to enter a union in which they then become essential to one another, even though their basic differences remain. This rather abstract debate is actually fraught with tremendous consequences to the Chinese Communists. At a time when Peking is dedicated to its campaign against revisionism in the international communist movement, and has bitterly accused the Soviets of collaboration with United States "imperialism," Yang's conclusion is clearly untenable. If his "two into one" position is held, it would eliminate the very nature of the class struggle and lead to class reconciliation; it would also eliminate the antagonistic contradiction between capitalism and communism in favor of a working arrangement whereby each would become vital to the other. Whereas Mao has insisted that union is only transitory and relative, Yang would have it a permanent condition.[7] Thus the CPC has marshalled every agency to denounce Yang. Class notes taken by his students at the Higher Party School have provided ample ammunition for criticizing his views and accusing him of forwarding the revisionist line. The press attack has continued without respite and Yang has apparently been stripped of his offices.

Another case involving a high-placed Party official is that of Professor Feng Ting. Feng, a member of the department of philosophy of Peking University, was chief editor of *K'ang-ti Pao*, the organ of the New Fourth Route Army, during the War of Resistance against Japan, and after 1949 held posts of vice chairman of the Culture and Education Commission of the Government Administrative Council and deputy director of the CPC East China Bureau's Propaganda Department. In June, 1954, he was named vice chairman of the Culture and Education Bureau of the East China Military and Administrative Commission. He is also the author of three major works, *Communist Philosophy of Life, Commonplace Truth*,

[7] Evidently, Yang first stated his "two into one" theory in 1961, and repeated it at the Higher Party School in 1963. The concept would apparently explain such actions as the Communist-Kuomintang United Front against the Japanese, or Peking's first efforts at accommodation of the bourgeoisie in the early years of the communist regime in China. The fact that the CPC's denunciation dates only from the spring of 1964, seems to indicate that the nature of the Sino-Soviet debates made it imperative to denounce any possibility of adjustment to the so-called revisionist position.

and *The Historic Task of the Working Class.* This highly respected teacher and Party official was first attacked by the official organ of the CPC Central Committee, *Hung-ch'i* in its April 29, 1965 issue for misleading youth to forsake the communist revolution and attempting to popularize bourgeois pragmatism. One example of the innumerable press articles that then appeared in criticism of Feng Ting will indicate the tone of the campaign. The January 25, 1965 *People's Daily* carried an article by Chiang Hung-tai, a technical cadre, describing the effects of his having read *Communist Philosophy of Life* in 1963. Chiang admits that during the period of economic hardship he wavered in his dedication to communism, since Feng made it appear that true communism is only for the distant future; he therefore spent all his income freely on himself and despised his fellow workers for being uncouth and vulgar.

The Chinese Communists must also protect the unlettered masses from the evil effects of bourgeois intellectuals or unorthodox literary and art forms. One example of this "protection" involves the case of the popular movie, "Early Spring in February," which is based on the 1929 novel *February* by Jou Shih. Jou joined the CPC in 1930, and was killed in 1931. His novel related the story of Hsiao Chien-ch'iu, who, tired of urban life, began teaching in a rural middle school. [8] The movie version proved highly popular until the CPC intervened, in the September 15, 1964 *People's Daily*, to term the movie a "storm in a teacup." The hero, Hsiao, is accused of being a bourgeois coward who seeks to appear as a "saviour" to Sister Wen, while the movie directors are castigated for deliberately expurgating those literary passages which deal with Hsiao's "affection" for the widow. In the September 17, November 8, and later issues of the same organ, the movie is repeatedly denounced for not clarifying the point that poverty is due to capitalistic exploitation and can only be alleviated by destroying capitalism.

A similar appraisal of another popular movie has been responsible for a shake-up in the Ministry of Culture. In 1922, Shen Yen-ping published a novel, *Lin's Shop*, which was adopted by Hsia Yen for the movies in 1958, and first shown in 1959, with favorable comments. Shen (whose pen name is Mao Tun) was removed as Minister of Culture by the first session of the Third National People's Congress; Hsia was fired as a vice minister of Culture by the State Council at its 155th meeting on April 30, 1965. Following their removal, "Lin's Shop" was again released so that the CPC might

---

[8] Basically, the plot turns on Hsiao's love for T'ao Lan, who is being courted by the son of a member of the local gentry. Hsiao also encounters Sister Wen, the widow of his classmate, Li Chih-hao, who had died a revolutionary martyr. To support the poverty-stricken widow, Hsiao must sacrifice his love for T'ao Lan. However, his close relationship with Sister Wen creates village gossip and she commits suicide.

illustrate its "prettyfying of the bourgeoisie, covering up of class exploitation, and obliterating of class contradictions," particularly by depicting the hero, the shop-owner, as "honest and good."

The instances of thought reform of the intellectuals in 1964 and 1965 are cited to indicate that there can be no end to Chinese Communist brainwashing of the intellectuals, and that these efforts will presumably be intensified at such times as the CPC deems the need acute for communist orthodoxy and solidarity. Thus, the continuation and degree of intensification of thought reform are contingent upon the far wider areas of mass acceptance of Chinese Communist policies and programs, and Peking's continued role as the vanguard in the international communist movement's drive against revisionism. In either case, the need for thought reform may be presumed to increase with the passage of time. And the tactics, having proven effective, will be retained. [9]

The Blooming and Contending Policy

In the early months of 1957, the Communist Party of China launched what it termed a socialist-revolutionary movement on the political and ideological fronts. This was the "blooming and contending" campaign, and represented a response to a variety of needs. As Chou En-lai had reported to the CPC Central Committee's Conference on the Problems of the Intellectuals, convoked on January 14, 1956, the factionalism that had developed among the intellectuals had to be eliminated. Chou estimated in the 1956 *People's Handbook* that 40 per cent of China's superior intellectuals supported the Party actively; another 40 per cent were cooperative, but not sufficiently active; and 20 per cent were backward and counter-revolutionary, or hostile to the CPC.

The inauguration of the "one hundred flowers" campaign was first revealed by Mao Tse-tung in an address to the Supreme State Conference on May 2, 1956. On May 26, Lu Ting-yi, then director of the CPC Central Committee's Propaganda Department, defined the purpose of the movement to a group of intellectuals assembled in Peking in these terms:

The Chinese Communist Party advocates one hundred flowers blooming for literary works and one hundred schools of thought contending in the scientific

[9] One interesting example of Peking's emphasis on criticism and self-criticism is found in the Sino-Soviet dispute. The article "On the Question of Stalin," which was prepared by the editorial offices of *Red Flag* and *People's Daily* and represents the highest kind of official attitude, notes: "When Stalin did something wrong, he was capable of criticizing himself. For instance, he had given some bad counsel with regard to the Chinese Revolution. After the victory of the Chinese revolution, he admitted his mistake. . . . Khrushchev . . . simply doesn't know what self-criticism is."

field . . . to promote the freedom of independent thinking, freedom of debate, freedom of creation and criticism, freedom of expressing one's own opinions. . . .

Expressed by the Department's vice director, Hu Sheng, artistic and scientific work would take place in "big gardens with abundant flowers, where all intellectuals who really have special talents in certain fields can make their useful contributions."

As initially conceived, the Hundred Flowers campaign was confined to the fields of literature, art and the sciences. But, with the news of the Hungarian uprising of 1956, popular unrest increased. Anxious to avoid any mass demonstrations on the mainland, Mao Tse-tung determined that the intellectuals must be allowed more freedom of expression. At the second plenary session of the Eighth Central Committee, in November, 1956, Mao appealed to the Party to launch a struggle against the persistent tendencies toward subjectivism, factionalism and bureaucratism. He also expressed the hope that the various democratic parties and non-partisan individuals would lend their criticism to the CPC's rectification campaign. Thus, the scope of the Hundred Flowers was widened to include politics.

An analysis of official Party documents reveals that the Blooming and Contending movement was directed toward a twofold objective. First, it was to solve the problem of internal contradictions. Admitting the presence of individuals antagonistic to CPC programs, the leadership hoped to eliminate these pockets of discontent by encouraging participation in the rectification campaign. At the same time, by bringing this discontent into the open, the Party would be better able to deal with it. The campaign itself followed three rough stages: the formative, from May, 1956 to February, 1957; the blooming and contending phase from March to June, 1957; and the anti-rightist campaign which followed.

During the formative stage, most of the intellectuals were suspicious and hesitated to speak. As Lo Lung-chi observed in the March 23, 1957 *People's Daily* few flowers bloomed and few schools were contending. Shaken from their apathy by the incidents of the Hungarian revolt, many of the intellectuals began to hazard doubts over the future of communism. As Tang Ch'u-min pointed out in the March 8, 1957 *Kuangming Daily*, some people began questioning the comparative strengths of the socialist and imperialist camps, and "renounced the leadership of the Party and even suspected the superiority of the socialistic system."

It was to reveal the sources and areas of discontent that Mao convoked the Supreme State Conference on February 27, 1957, and lectured on the correct handling of contradictions among the people. Mao advocated, in place of suppression, that the dissident elements be encouraged to express their doubts, so that they might be appropriately criticized and corrected.

Consequently, in April, the Central Committee conducted a conference for propaganda workers: this marked the official inauguration of the Blooming and Contending phase. Under the direction of the United Front Department, various forums were organized so that every segment of society might have an opportunity to air its opinions, while Party organs faithfully reprinted these statements.

Erroneously believing in the sincerity of the movement's alleged objectives, a number of intellectuals began to speak out against Party policies. Both the volume and the depth of the criticism were shocking and even omnious to the CPC. Accusations were flung at even the most sacrosanct Party policies. For example, Ch'u An-p'ing, editor of the *Kuangming Daily*, denounced "Tang T'ien Hsia," or Party monopoly, while Hsü Teh-heng, chairman of the academic Chiu San Society, attacked the slow-death tactics employed against the democratic parties. Wang Thou, lecturer at the People's University, criticized the methods of socialist transformation. And even Marxism-Leninism itself was challenged as outmoded by such individuals as Li Hai-tsung, professor at the People's University, and Lei T'ien-chu, vice director of the Institute of Mechanical Science.

Inspired by the higher intellectuals, the general public took up the attack. Student unrest grew and strikes occurred. During the first weeks of June, 1957, such centers of learning as Peking University, the People's University, Tientsin Nankai University, Shanghai Futan University and Nanking University became involved in the anti-Party criticism. As reported in the June 6, 1957 *People's Daily* by Tseng Chao-lun, vice minister of Higher Education, and Ch'ien Wei-ch'ang, deputy president of Tsinghua University, the emergence of a popular leader at this critical moment might lead to all-out rebellion.

The urgency of the situation demanded *de facto* abandonment of the blooming and contending policy—an action that transpired on June 9, 1957. On that date *People's Daily* acknowledged that the unexpected popular expressions were no longer "in conformity with the interests of the people and the interest of the Party rectification campaign." Although unrest persisted, as is testified by the student strikes in Hupeh province several days after the announcement, the anti-rightist campaign was thereupon launched with great vigor.

Now, all those who had spoken out against the regime were branded as rightist elements. The leaders were further accused of belonging to the "Chang-Lo Alliance" allegedly headed by Chang Po-chün, vice chairman of the Democratic League, Chairman of the Chinese Peasants and Workers Democratic Party and Minister of Communications, and Lo Lung-chi, vice chairman of the Democratic League and Minister of the Timber Industry. More than a hundred leading intellectuals were numbered among the "alliance" membership. [10]

Although the Party attack was carried to every area of the mainland and every citizen was expected to reaffirm his loyalties, a special drive was initiated during the latter months of 1957 to root out rightist elements within the Party. [11] Many of the Party members attacked had had considerable experience in the CPC.

The rectification campaign also included a re-education drive to teach the intellectuals that the terms "red" and "expert" are synonymous and that knowledge is only a tool to serve the Party. One important tactic was to force conformity through the instrumentality of the labor program. At the same time, the stature of the intellectual was reduced by a vast enlargement of the propaganda and indoctrination facilities, and by encouraging the proletariat to assume the work of the educated classes. Thus, in the first months of 1958, according to official sources, more than a million cultural clubs and 430,000 spare-time art troupes were organized, and some 473,000 libraries were opened. Newspaper circulation increased from 3.4 million copies in 1951 to 15 million in 1958; magazine sales rose from 900,000 to 17 million. As noted elsewhere, this extension applied to the television, radio and film industries.

The Blooming and Contending movement had enormous implications for the Party's general programs. By revealing the deep contradictions between the Party and the intellectuals, it reminded the CPC leadership that its ideological remolding techniques had been critically unsuccessful. By showing how many so-called rightists were employed in the various propaganda media, the campaign seriously challenged the CPC's effectiveness in educating the masses. In the publishing field alone, for example, the important agencies of *Wen-yi Pao*, People's Publishing House, Popular

[10] This included Tseng Chao-lun, vice minister of Higher Education Fei Hsiao-t'ung, Vice Director of the Nationality College; Ch'u An-p'ing, editor of the *Kuangming Daily:* Ch'ien Wei-ch'ang, Vice President of Tsinghua University; Ch'ien Tuan-sheng, Director of the Peking Political and Legal College; Yeh Tu-yi, Deputy Secretary General of the Democratic League; Shu Chu-cheng, publisher of the Shanghai *Wen-hui Pao:* Lu Yi, Deputy Editor-in-Chief of the Shanghai *Hsin-wen Jih-pao:* Lung Yün, Deputy Chairman of the Revolutionary Committee of the Kuomintang; Huang Shao-hsiung, T'an T'i-wu and Ch'en Ming-shu, of the latter's Standing Committee; Chang Nai-ch'i, Vice Chairman of the China Democratic National Construction Association and Minister of Food; and T'ao Meng-ho, Vice President of the Chinese Academy of Sciences, as well as thousands of less prominent critics.

[11] Included in this action were such well-known figures as Ting Ling, Chinese Communist woman writer and winner of the Stalin Literary Prize, Tseng Yen-hsiu, Vice Director of the People's Publishing House, and hundreds of representatives from the fields of education, journalism and business. For a more complete account of the Party rectification movement see the chapter on the Party.

Readers Publishing House, the Current Events Handbook, and the New China News Agency were found to have harbored rightists in high positions.

The Third Plenum of the Eighth Central Committee, meeting in September, 1957, initiated a comprehensive plan to rectify the situation. Five measures were adopted. Party cadres were sent to leading schools, scientific institutes and publishing houses. Party members began lecturing in the institutions of higher learning.[12] Party committees at all levels began sponsoring their own periodicals for the ideological remolding of members. In addition to *Hung-ch'i*, the semi-monthly issued by the CPC Central Committee, the various provinces and municipalities began publishing such noteworthy journals as: *Tung-feng* (*East Wind*), by the Hopei Provincial Committee; *Shang-yu* (*Aiming High*), by the Szechwan Committee; *Chieh-fang* (*Liberation*). by the Shanghai Municipal Committee; *Hsü yu Shih* (*Abstract and Concrete*), by the Anwei Committee; *Ch'un-chung* (*Masses*) by the Kiangsu Committee; and *Ch'i-yi* (*July First*) by the Hupeh Committee.

Individual punishments of rightists included demotion, removal, imprisonment and execution. Following the Hanyang student uprising of June, 1957, during which more than a thousand youths wrecked Party and state offices and demanded Mao's resignation, punishment was meted out to all those accused of stirring the riot. The dean of studies and vice principal of the Hanyang Middle School were among the seventy persons reportedly executed, and student leaders received prison sentences of from five to fifteen years. Student conformity was strengthened by the administration of political examinations and investigations, with the "failures" being assigned to hard labor. The regulations of the State Council issued on July 17, 1957, provided for the assignment of summer work on the basis of a student's degree of political loyalty. Similarly, writers and teachers were subject to reform through labor. Over 560 faculty members from Peking University and 229 from Tsinghua University were demoted in rank. According to the November 17, 1957 *People's Daily*, some 21,000 intellectuals had been demoted by that date.

Despite the harshness of the anti-rightist struggle, the CPC continues to profess adherence to the Blooming and Contending policy. In the name of the Party Central Committee and the State Council, Lu Ting-yi reaffirmed its continuity as being "devised by Comrade Mao . . . for the development of our sciences and arts" and to set "the political criteria of socialism and communism." The harsh measures employed against the

[12] Among the high-ranking CPC members who participated in this phase of the CC program were Lu Ting-yi, then director of the CC Propaganda Dept., and vice directors Ch'en Po-ta and Chou Yang, as well as numerous first secretaries of municipal and provincial committees.

intellectuals indicates that many have not yet been reconciled to Party ideologies. As Theodore Chen notes in his scholarly analysis of the *Thought Reform of the Chinese Intellectuals*, the community of scholars in China "have not lost entirely their mental alertness or sense of values." And it is even possible that the very severity of the anti-rightist campaign widened the breach between the intellectuals and the communists, to the point where a "cultural revolution" was deemed essential.

THE MASS CULTURAL MEDIA

In view of the importance of cultural guidance and influence, control and manipulation of the mass media of communications by the Chinese Communists is a foregone conclusion. The most familiar of these controlled media are radio and press. Others include books, periodicals, films, theaters, music, cinema, and even "whisper campaigns."[13]

In China, radio plays an important part in reaching the scattered masses. The Hsinhua (New China) Broadcasting Station, the first "people's" radio installation, was established in Yenan in September, 1945 amid "numerous technical difficulties." During the civil war, KMT stations were seized, and by 1949, the Chinese Communists operated 49 such units, including 38 set up that year alone. By 1950, 58 stations were operating; by 1952, there were 71. Today, these facilities include the Central People's Broadcasting Station, or Radio Peking, and numerous regional networks around such metropolitian installations as the Shanghai station in East China, or the Mukden station in the Northeast. Initially, there were also a number of government-controlled private stations (32 in 1950), but these shared the fate of private business in general.

Domestically, these stations air national and international news and provide educational and entertainment programs. The regular broadcast of exercises has been noted elsewhere, as have the introductory foreign language instructions. More recently, since 1964, Radio Peking has sponsored televised instruction in Peking municipality in conjunction with the University of Peking. Thousands are enrolled in courses in mathematics,

[13] Among the other common methods of mass communication, Peking claims great progress in developing the telephone system, which, at times, is also used to relay radio broadcasts. In 1949, according to NCNA of January 17, 1965, the city of Peking had only 20,000 phones. Since then, the system had proliferated, a fourfold increase being reported during the 1958–62 period alone. Early in 1965, a 6-figure dialing system was introduced, since the 5-figure system was deemed obsolete. In May, 1963, 95 per cent of the rural communes were said to be linked by telephone service. Nevertheless, this method of communications is still inadequate. Most of the communal production brigades must still rely on mail service for Party and state directives, and NCNA, on May 8, 1963, hinted that not even all the brigades had regular mail service by that date.

beginning physics, chemistry and the Chinese language; they report regularly to designated centers for testing purposes. But the most important of the various educational phases of Radio Peking is in the area of political and agricultural instruction for the rural masses. In February, 1964, a special department was organized to prepare programs on scientific farming methods to be beamed throughout the countryside.

Although Communist China still suffers from a shortage of radio equipment, maximum use is obtained from available sets. Foreign observers have frequently commented on the plentitude of street corner loudspeakers, and "collective listening" reaches an enormous audience. NCNA noted, on November 20, 1964, that 95 per cent of the cities and counties, 80 per cent of the communes, 60 per cent of the brigades, and 40 per cent of the teams already shared in the advantages of over six billion loudspeakers located in rural areas. For the national minorities, trained radio monitors translate broadcasts into the native language. And the manufacture of transistors means that even the most remote areas can now be included in the national network.

In addition to its role in contacting the Chinese masses, Radio Peking has been assigned the task of providing regular programs of a propaganda nature which are beamed to many international areas. Earlier, most of these programs were aimed at the overseas Chinese and their host countries in Southeast Asia. Now, the voice of Radio Peking is heard on every continent. By March, 1967, for example, approximately two or three hours of daily programs in the national languages were beamed to North and South America, and Europe, as well as to the African areas of Capetown, Salisbury, Dar'-es-Salaam, Monrovia, Accra, Freetown, Lagos and Cairo.

Next to radio, in terms of direct contact with the entire population, is the press. Liu Tsun-chi, vice director of the Information Bureau, affirmed that the press in Communist China has a key role. "Its duty is to promote social progress, to help with the economic development of the country, to expand the basis of democracy, to stir the people's national consciousness and develop their spirit of internationalism." The New China News Agency—Peking's version of TASS—is a prime instrument in carrying out this mission. By 1950, in addition to its headquarters in Peking, NCNA had already established 12 branches and 57 sub-branches on the mainland, and 8 foreign branches. By 1966, NCNA had units in at least 46 countries.

The roster of newspapers in Communist China is headed by the Peking *People's Daily* (*Jen-min Jih-pao*), the official organ of the CPC Central Committee, which is followed by scores of provincial and municipal newspapers and such specialized organs as the highly influential *Liberation Army Daily*, *The Daily Worker* (*Kung-jen Jih-pao*) or *The China Youth* (*Chung-Kuo Ch'ing-nien Pao*). There are papers of special interest to workers, peasants, the army, and the national minorities, but even those which are nominally run by the non-communist parties or mass organizations take their editorial cue from the Party's central organ in Peking. Since literacy is now common for the under-thirty Chinese, these papers enjoy a wide, if not almost universal, circulation. The production teams, or the basic level of organization in the rural areas, each subscribe to the daily papers. Since discussion is expected, the members follow the press.

Typical of the political control exercised over the news services were the decisions taken at the National Press Work Conference of March–April, 1950. All newspapers were charged with "enlightening the people so they could actively promote New Democracy . . . thus strengthening the relationship between the people and the government." Therefore, the press claims to have "replaced tedious reports on meetings, trifling items about personal activities and academic discussions which have no bearing on actual conditions, with a new type of news." This "new type" news is no more than the current Party line and consists primarily of polemics against China's enemies, particularly the United States, and in praise of production contests, PLA achievements and the ever-repeated thought of Mao Tse-tung, and such topical events as the regime wishs to popularize. As a principal source of communist education through propaganda and indoctrination, the *People's Daily*, for example, is daily "required reading" for all CPC cadres.

The CPC exercises rigid censorship of all publications in Communist China. According to the Regulations Governing the Control of Book and Periodical Publishing, Printing and Distributing Trades, adopted late in 1951, all manuscripts must be submitted for strict scrutiny. This law holds that no one may "print or distribute books or periodicals that violate . . . the decrees of the government; they shall not publish words or charts disclosing state secrets." The publishing houses must also provide copies of their publications to designated government offices and state libraries. On the other hand, the "people's publishing houses" enjoy considerable privileges and facilities. In their respective areas, they have absolute monopolies. The state-operated Hsinhua Bookstore, for example, with branches throughout China, thrives on publishing required readings for Party cadres—the works of Marx, Engels, Lenin, Stalin and Mao—school textbooks, government documents and the like. The rural supply and marketing cooperatives have also been charged with distributing books to the peasants. According to incomplete figures printed in *People's Daily* on September 10, 1964, these cooperatives were operating over 10,000 such book-selling centers. In 1963, they distributed over 120,000,000 publications; in the first six months of 1964, they circulated over 100,000,000 books or pictures.

Since the early 1960's, the Chinese Communists have shown more interest in publishing translations of western literary masterpieces. For example, in 1962, the Literature and Art Publishing House of Shanghai issued a new translation of Chaucer's works. In Peking, the plays of the Spanish dramatist, Lope de Vega, were made available. In 1963, the Chung Hua Publishing House commissioned a series of "Histories of Foreign Countries" (including volumes on "The Pyramids," "The Munich Intrigue," and The Paris Commune") and a "Concise Geography Series" for the reading level of a junior high school student.[14]

The film industry and the theater furnish two more important avenues for mass distribution of communist culture or propaganda. Because of its traditional popularity with the Chinese, the theater had only to be "reformed" to fit its new cultural assignment. For example, the traditional operas, which often portrayed national legends, had to be purged of such "bourgeois vestiges" as spitting to express contempt (in conflict with the national anti-spitting laws), and of any portrayal of courtesans or of supernatural elements. The new story theme seeks to glorify "heroes of the masses."

Music, in general, possibly because of the emotional effect it conjures, has been conscripted into communist cultural service. In March, 1964, the departments of Peking's Art Institute and the Central Conservatory of Music organized the Conservatory of Chinese Music in Peking "to develop socialistic, national music," including the new type operas. The Central People's Broadcasting Station and the editorial departments of two music magazines collaborate annually in sponsoring an opinion poll to select that year's popular song hit, in order to "encourage creative song-writing." The propagandistic nature of this popular music may be gathered from the opening bars of one of the hits, "Socialism Is Good:" "The reactionary group is toppled. Imperialists are scurrying away with their tails tucked in between their legs."

In the cinema, communist efforts to inject propaganda date back well before the establishment of the new regime. Even under the Nationalist government's censorship, motion pictures with thinly concealed communist themes kept emerging from the studios, thanks to communist infiltration of the industry in the 1920's and 1930's.[15] Since the 1949 victory, state-

---

[14] It should be noted that the publication of western literature is strictly supervised and orientated to reveal the class struggle, and discredit capitalism. For example, the monthly anthology, *World Literature*, concentrates on reprinting articles by fellow communists in other countries. A reference to Shakespeare's *Merchant of Venice* stresses the evils of usury in a capitalistic society, etc.

[15] One of these pictures, "Song of the Fisherman," won a prize at the first Soviet Film Festival in 1934. During the War against Japan, activities of the Yenan government and the Eighth Route Army were well propagated. Documentaries turned out during the civil conflict depicted the "revolutionary heroism" of the PLA and the "corruption" of the Nationalists.

owned studios have been established in several areas to produce films on a planned basis. These are heavy with documentaries or educational films. Minority languages are dubbed in.[16] The "academy award" winner of the second annual "Hundred Flowers Film Poll," organized by the movie magazine *Popular Screen*, is illustrative of the nature of the "entertainment" films. Chou En-lai, Chen Yi, and other top-ranking communist leaders attended the awards ceremony for the producers of "Li Shuang-shuang," a "comedy" about a young peasant woman and her husband in a rural commune.

Mobile 3–4 man projection units now bring these films to the entire Chinese population. In 1954, of the 800 million Chinese who saw a movie, only 300 million were in the rural areas. Ten years later, in 1964, peasant attendance at the cinema was given as 2,000 million, or a daily average of six million.

The dissemination of propaganda in Communist China relies upon unconventional, as well as conventional, channels. One of the more effective of these avenues has been the skillful use of organized "whisper campaigns." These have great impact because of their word-of-mouth communication, but their effectiveness depends upon the careful use of the mass organizations and campaigns discussed elsewhere. Notable in this connection are the mass "petition" drives. In 1955, for example, the Appeal against Atomic Weapons, sponsored by the World Peace Council, secured a reported 355 million signatures, including 60–70 per cent of the population in certain areas. Wall posters have become a favored medium in recent months. Cartoons are another popular means of spreading propaganda. These sometimes crude line-drawings relate the current Party line in very elemental form. For example, "Dream of the Gold-Eaters," drawn by China's leading cartoonist, Hua Chun-wu, illustrates the story of a "dollar club" whose wealthy members are full of gold dollars and human blood, the latter obtained by "General Gun" and "Mr. Mosquito" from the poor of the world. Even children's toys now convey propagandistic messages. Dolls of twenty national minorities, such as the "golden-skinned Han girl in satin jacket and trousers," are intended to teach a love of all Chinese peoples. Building kits make miniatures of the Yangtze River Bridge. Mechanical toys are designed to promote a "love of serving others;" for example, a dark-haired girl doll bearing a tea serving tray, when wound, "starts walking toward you, nodding and smiling, and stops only when the

[16] In late 1953 and early 1954, the Central Cinema Bureau of the Ministry of Cultural Affairs adopted two important policies for the film industry: one concerned the "strengthening of film production work" and the other "the building of a film projection network and a film equipment and supplies industry." Films were to be planned 2–3 years in advance and to be examined and approved by the ministry. Projection priorities were given to the urban over the rural areas.

cup is taken from the tray." Collectively, all these agencies and instruments represent the world's greatest effort to indoctrinate an entire people in the line approved by the select few who constitute Communist China's power nucleus.

EDUCATIONAL POLICY

Educational Goals and Methodology

Education is a concentrated form and systematic channel of cultural transmission. On October 1, 1949, the Chinese Communists inherited an educational system which had always been inadequate to population needs, and which had been further and critically taxed by the long years of foreign and civil war. Yet, if the CPC's programs were to work, the educational system would be a vital instrument to instruct and transform the people. Communist China has boldly admitted that all education is of an uncompromisingly political character: if "red" and "expert" sometimes conflict, the primary importance must be acknowledged for the former. Thus, to the outsider, the only thing that permits the Chinese Communist form of indoctrination to be dignified with the label "education" is that it is associated with formal institutions and trained professionals.

In 1951, Vice-Minister of Education Ch'ien Chün-jui defined the goal of education in these terms: "for the present, China's educational policy is primarily serving the working class and the peasantry, not the people in general." At this stage, the institutions of higher education were busily studying Russian models and attempting to master the Russian language in order to utilize Soviet texts. But the major emphasis of the national program was to provide a sort of crash plan to eliminate illiteracy. As in countless other examples of the role assigned to education by a new totalitarian regime (Castro's Cuba being a close example), the CPC was aware that, minimally, a people must be able to read official propaganda if indoctrination is to proceed effectively. Moreover, the elimination of illiteracy is the first step in any training program. Mao Tse-tung observed this fact as early as 1945. "To eliminate illiteracy among 80 per cent of the population," he said, "is an indispensable step in the building of a new China." [17]

---

[17] The models for the literacy drive, according to the Ministry of Education, were the examples of the Soviet Union and other "People's Democracies." In the USSR, the literacy drive was combined with the land collectivization drive. According to Chinese Communist statistics, by 1933 81.9 per cent of the formerly illiterate population in the Russian Republic and 85.3 per cent of the formerly illiterate people in the Ukrainian Republic had met minimum Soviet standards of literacy.

In 1950, the CPC defined literacy as the mastery of 1,000 characters—a goal which was increased to 1,500 in 1956 for the peasants, and to 2,000 for the urban workers.[18] Party directives charged the trade unions in the cities to serve as conveyor belts to educate the workers. In the rural areas, various mass organizations collaborated to reduce the about 70 per cent rate of illiteracy. Then, in December, 1955, the Ministry of Education issued instructions to the provincial and municipal governments to establish associations for the eradication of illiteracy according to targets ranging from two to seven years, and based on age and location and occupation of the students.[19] One reason for the quickened tempo of the literacy drive was that the CPC anticipated greater efficiency in the rural areas as the land collectivization drive proceeded apace. It is evident that the Party's aspirations have not been entirely fulfilled, since Chinese Communist sources, as recently as 1965, have admitted to a continuing 20 per cent illiteracy rate among the urban workers.

The anti-illiteracy drive, together with technical and general instruction, was chiefly administered through spare time teaching institutions. Beginning late in 1949, the regime opened many night schools and spare time schools for both workers and peasants. By mid-1950, there were some 14,000 of these centers in the urban areas, with an enrollment of about 700,000, and some 10,000,000 peasants were receiving similar type instruction. Many of these courses, however, were also designed to meet Party indoctrination goals; as much time was assigned to political course work on "revolutionary theory and government policies" as on actual practical instruction.

With respect to the regular school system, Chinese Communist statistics showed that there were 227 colleges with 134,000 students by mid-1950, and 3,690 secondary schools with 1,090,000 students, as well as 16,000,000 pupils enrolled in the 212,890 primary schools. Although this rise in enrollments was substantial, it soon became apparent that additional facilities were imperative if the various economic programs were to succeed. For example, in 1952, the dean of Peking Normal University noted that, at the rate of development then prevailing, it would take 1,100 years for teacher training schools to produce the number of graduates required in the next five years. To meet these needs, in November, 1952, a Ministry of Higher Education was organized within the GAC and the entire educational system was incorporated into the framework of the First Five-Year Plan of 1953–57.

During the period of the First Five-Year Plan, approximately 7 per cent of the total national budget was earmarked for education. Schools of all

[18] *People's Daily* uses about 2,000 characters.

[19] Each province was to submit its own timetable for the achievement of mass literacy.

types and at all levels sought to increase their enrollments and great achievements were reported, although facilities remained inadequate. For example, by 1954, 252,000 students were matriculating in institutions of higher education, at least 94,000 of whom were new students. This repre-

TABLE V
CADRES TO RECEIVE HIGHER EDUCATION 1952-57*

Classifi-cation	No. of students entering in the five-year period	% by class-ifica-tion	No. of grad-uates in the five-year period	% by class-ifica-tion	No. of students in school in 1957	% by class-ifica-tion	% in-crease 1957 over 1952
TOTAL	543,300	100.	283,000	100.	434,600	100.	227.4
Engineering	214,600	39.5	94,900	33.6	177,600	40.9	268.8
Agriculture & Forestry	41,800	7.7	18,800	6.6	37,200	8.6	240.7
Finance & Economics	16,400	3.0	25,500	9.0	12,700	2.9	57.9
Political Sci-ence	10,600	2.0	4,800	1.7	9,300	2.1	242.3
Health	57,600	10.6	26,600	9.4	54,800	12.6	221.4
Physical Ed-ucation	6,000	1.1	2,800	1.0	3,600	0.8	1,107.7
Pure Science	32,600	6.0	13,800	4.9	27,100	6.2	283.4
Liberal Arts	29,300	5.4	21,600	7.6	20,400	4.7	150.9
Teaching	130,700	24.0	70,400	24.9	89,000	20.5	282.0
Arts	3,700	0.7	3,800	1.3	2,900	0.7	79.3

* See *Chung-Hua-Jen-min-Kung-Ho-Kuo Fa-chan Kuo-min-ching-chi ti Ti-i Wu-Nien-Chi-Hua 1953-1957 (The First Five-Year Plan for the Development of the National Economy of the Chinese People's Republic 1953-1957)*, p. 120.

sented a 60.6 per cent increase over 1947 figures. At the high school level, 1,190,000 new students were expected to swell the total enrollment to more than 3,600,000, or a 23 per cent gain as compared to 1953, and double the highest figure reached by the Nationalist government in 1946. Based on these figures, the Chinese Communists anticipated that there would be 430,000 students in the institutions of higher learning by the end of the

First Five Year Plan in 1957. Tables V and VI indicate a breakdown of the type of training to be given under the Plan:[20]

Meanwhile, as Minister of Education Chang Hsi-jo reported to the NPC on July 22, 1955, a total primary school enrollment of 59,500,000 was

TABLE VI
CADRES TO RECEIVE TECHNICAL SCHOOL EDUCATION,
1952–57*

Classification	No. of students entering in the five-year period	% by classification	No. of graduates in the five-year period	% by classification	No. of students in in 1957	% by classification	% increase 1957 over 1952
TOTAL	1,005,700	100.0	888,300	100.0	671,800	100.0	105.6
Engineering	346,300	34.4	186,400	21.0	244,000	36.3	219.0
Agriculture & Forestry	121,600	12.1	82,900	9.3	98,800	14.7	148.3
Finance & Economics	51,000	5.1	52,700	5.9	33,300	5.0	63.7
Teaching	360,500	35.8	465,500	52.4	218,500	32.5	63.3
Health	118,500	11.8	98,700	11.1	70,900	10.6	119.3
Physical Education	4,100	0.4	800	0.1	3,500	0.5	—
Arts	3,700	0.4	₋1,300	0.2	2,800	0.4	385.1

* Source same as for Table V, on p. 540.

expected for the year—or a 7.5 per cent increase over 1954. Too, the number of adults registered in part-time classes in the urban areas alone was planned to increase from 2,587,967 in 1953, to 10,000,000 by the end of the Five Year Plan in 1957. Since a similar rise was expected in spare-time classes in the rural areas, it might be said that nearly half of China's vast population was enrolled in some type of regular instruction during this period.

[20] It should be noted that the plan also provided for 10,100 students to be trained abroad between 1953–57. Of these, 9,400 were to be sent to the Soviet Union, and 700 to other "People's Democracies." By year, 700 were to be sent in 1953, 1,500 in 1954, 2,400 in 1955, 2,600 in 1956, and 2,900 in 1957.

These astronomical demands taxed an already strained system. Industrialization programs created an insatiable demand for skilled laborers, without the funds or facilities to meet the problem. And shortages at every level meant that many were assigned to teaching with inferior knowledge or abilities. At a joint work conference on spare time education for industrial workers sponsored by the All-China Federation of Trade Unions and the Ministries of Education in December, 1955, it was declared that the education being provided "lagged far behind the needs of industrial construction, agricultural cooperativization and technical reform." Another indication of the glaring weaknesses and inefficiciencies of the educational system came to light during the 1956 period of the Hundred Flowers. *People's Daily* of October 5, 1956 admitted to widespread complaints from teachers concerning the poor quality of facilities, and particularly of the constant interference of untrained Party cadres in educational matters. (See the section on the Hundred Flowers campaign).

In 1958, (as discussed in detail in the following section), the CPC sought to alleviate the strains on the educational system, while providing additions to the labor force, by a series of "Great Leap" measures. Although these programs may have made many students "red," few indeed could qualify as "expert." Of course, since part time education was the order of the day, enrollment figures boasted tremendous advances. For example, NCNA of December 25, 1959, reported that some nine million workers had already gained some middle school education, and 400,000 had studied at the college level. In the regular institutions, the State Statistical Bureau claimed in *Ten Great Years* (published in Peking in 1960), that in 1958, 72,000 graduated from institutions of higher learning; 191,000 from technical middle schools; 1,313,000 from regular middle schools; and 16,225,000 from primary schools. This represents a "great leap" as compared to 1957 totals for these categories of 56,000, 146,000, 1,299,000 and 12,307,000 respectively.

As with other phases of the Great Leap, these figures do not give a true picture of the actual situation. By 1961, both the general economy and the educational system were suffering critically from the unrealistic demands imposed by the Party. Officially, Peking continued to boast of heroic achievements. For example, on April 8, 1960, a report delivered to the second session of the Second National People's Congress acclaimed the fact that over 19,000,000 city workers alone were enrolled in courses at all levels from literacy classes through university training. But the deficiencies of the part-work and part-study approach, as well as the major role assigned political instruction, were responsible for producing students with little or no grasp of the knowledge and skills normally associated with educational programs. By September, 1961, the CPC itself acknowledged the failures of its programs. In a speech meant for that year's graduates, Party leader Chen Yi called for a de-emphasis of political courses and a reduction of the innumerable educational institutions, preferably by combination into larger units.

In the fall of 1962, the CPC resurrected the old "meetings of immortals," or brain-washing sessions wherein the intellectuals were expected to engage in criticism and self-criticism concerning their deviation from Party lines. This time, the sessions were called "forums of higher intellectuals," and the teaching profession was particularly subjected to this form of rectification. Thus, for example, countless college professors came forward to "surrender their hearts to the Party" (i.e., admit errors) and to pledge personal academic goals, such as the rewriting of textbooks, or "voluntary" assumption of additional teaching assignments. Experienced teachers at all levels were charged with helping the novices or those with poor teaching records. For the students, the CPC advocated greater care in selection and assignment to labor camps for those with poor academic records.

In fact, as the CPC ordered a series of economic retrenchment measures, such as the shift in the level of authority in the communes, and shortened hours or even closing for those factories which suffered from a lack of raw materials, and as the economic situation still appeared to be undergoing a critical test, most of the educational programs were administered chaotically. In the cities, for example, the constant reshuffling of workers made it virtually impossible for them to attend classes with any degree of regularity. In the communes, production requirements, backyard plots, and stepped up indoctrination left little time for regular instruction. Not until late in 1963, did the various newspapers resume their plaudits of the educational system. By 1964, the emphasis was on better quality instruction in the regular schools—if necessary for fewer students—and amalgamation of the various part time schools so that trained instructors could be better utilized.

These retrenchment policies can be best illustrated at the college level. Under the provisions of the First Five Year Plan, college enrollment was to increase about 134 per cent between 1953 and 1957. The Great Leap called for a 700 per cent increase by 1963. [21] To meet this demand, the number of colleges and universities was increased from 236 to 840; however, many hardly deserved the designation of college or university, since the level of instruction was about that of a secondary school. But after the January, 1961, decision of the ninth plenum of the Eighth CPC Central Committee, which called for a general retreat in the economic sector, many

[21] In 1963, the Chinese Communists reported the college graduating classes to total over 200,000, as compared to the 56,000 graduates in 1957, but this figure includes graduates of the part time "universities."

of these institutions were closed or merged. By the end of 1962, there were only 400 colleges and universities.[22]   Although course requirements in political theory, or communist policies, were curtailed, generally speaking the college student was still subjected to endless forms of indoctrination. Students are still required to contribute manual labor during the vacation periods, most college students participate in some form of militia training, and all are constantly pressured to fulfill the needs of the Party.[23]

Statistically, Communist China can claim great achievements for its educational system, despite the admitted defects.   Although figures have been very scarce since 1958, some comparative standard is available.   For example, the student publication *Evergreen*, in its October, 1964 issue, listed about one million college graduates for the period 1949–63.   In 1956, approximately one-fourth of the graduating class continued their education in university centers.   In the past few years, college enrollment has tended to decrease.   It was about 955,000 in 1961, but only 819,000 in 1962.   Yet, this numerical decrease may mean that the level of instruction has been improved as the Party leadership has sought a more realistic adjustment of resources to enrollment.

Communist China's progress in the area of higher education must be examined in terms of quality, as well as quantity.   Here, the view is less overpowering.   On October 5, 1962, the vice president of Peking Geological College, Hsiao Ying, observed in a *Kuang-ming Jih-pao* article that "efforts must be made to approach the international level in those courses in which we have made relatively good achievements."   By insinuation, even the strongest departments have inferior standards, to say nothing of the many weak departments and courses.   The substandard nature of college instruction can be traced to the beginning step of student admissions policies. National entrance examinations are administered in major cities and other designated areas annually.   Prospective students must first pay a testing fee and then pass a physical examination to prove their ability to endure the rugged college programs.   The entrance examinations are open to all

[22] During this period, a number of new institutions of higher learning were opened to deal with special minority groups.   For example, the University of Overseas Chinese in Ch'uanchow, Fukien province, was founded in September, 1960.   The fact that new centers were opened even while existing institutions were being closed is due to the needs of foreign policies.

[23] Several examples are mentioned in the chapter on the social system.   Assignment after graduation is primarily determined by a student's degree of political reliability, with the choicest assignments going to the faithful.   One example of the indirect form of political pressure can be gained from the following advice given by the Peking *Chung-kuo Ch'ing-nien Pao* of March 30, 1963, to college students who might be thinking of falling in love: "Only those who have given serious importance to their obligations to the people and to the state, and only those who have paid serious attention to their studies and who avoid talking about the question of falling in love and marriage until after they have acquired skills and taken up their work properly have really not spent their youth in vain."

graduates of a middle school or those with an equivalent level of instruction who are under age 25. In the case of PLA veterans or workers, the age limit is 27. In special cases, and with a letter of recommendation from a Party cadre, others may also take the national test. The test itself includes questions in the area of political knowledge, the Chinese language, mathematics and sciences. [24] There have been few hints as to the relative difficulty of these examinations, or the rate of failure. In 1955, however, about 75 per cent of the Party cadres tested failed to achieve a satisfactory score. The examination grade is also based on a preferential system in which special concessions are given to such groups as CPC cadres, overseas Chinese, national minorities and the children of socialist "martyrs." [25]

Instructional testing procedures for the students admitted to the colleges and universities also indicates a low performance level. Beginning in the 1964 academic year, experiments have been conducted in "open" testing at such centers as Szechwan University and Chiaot'ung University. Rationalizing that the standard testing merely measures rote learning or memorization, these institutions permit the student to consult books, notes or even one another during the examination. Moreover, test questions are often distributed in advance to "foster independent thinking." Fantastic results have been credited to the "open" system. For example, the vice president of Chiaot'ung University observed contributions to the "all-round development of the students, morally, intellectually and physically," while the chairman of the physics department lauded a quite understandable situation in which "nine out of ten students gained between 80–100 per cent in their marks under the new system." As *People's Daily* commented on September 10, 1964, the students' "tension and fear of examination is greatly reduced or removed, and their spiritual burden is lessened." Given this approval by the CPC's authoritative organ, the method of "open" tests will doubtlessly be expanded throughout all the institutions of higher education, despite what would seem the encouragement of inevitably lower standards.

For the varied services which it provides to the Chinese Communist leadership, the teaching profession in China is held officially in "high esteem." [26] In addition to the hundreds of thousands of Party cadres, model workers and peasants and other activists who may be said to be

[24] As noted previously, foreign language requirements have been suspended, and even when enforced could be omitted for workers, veterans or other desirable candidates.

[25] Statistics for the 1963 graduating classes indicate only that 54 per cent were of worker or peasant origins.

[26] Given the fact mentioned by NCNA-Peking on June 10, 1965, that only "the deaf, stammerers or the physically deformed" are rejected for normal school training as future teachers, the esprit de corps of the teachers must be something less than is implied by this suggestion of a privileged status.

engaged in teaching on a part-time basis, by January, 1962, some three million full-time teachers were instructing over 100 million Chinese youth at all levels. In the twelve years between 1950 and 1962, the ranks of middle school teachers increased 4.5 times, while the faculties of institutions of higher learning registered a ten-fold increment. Peking University's faculty, which numbered nearly 2,000 in 1963, reflected a 12-fold growth, as compared to 1949, while that municipality's 17 engineering institutes accounted for over 10,000 full-time teachers.

These statistics are as incomplete as they are unreliable, but they do indicate one of the major problems confronting the teaching profession in Communist China. The vast majority of the teachers have received their own education in the schools and colleges established after the 1949 victory —and these institutions have shared the common and critical problems of inadequate facilities and textbooks, a scarcity of trained instructors, and a curriculum dominated by political considerations. It must therefore be reasoned that the national teaching corps suffers from the defects of this system, and that their own teaching is less than satisfactory in many cases. Moreover, aside from the relative academic freedom of the Hundred Flowers period, the teachers have been hampered by the ideological overlordship which is physically manifest in the presence of Party watchdogs or commissars in all educational institutions. Since the teachers represent the Party's greatest arm to reshape the minds of China, their political reliability is of more concern than their intellectual abilities or performance. Harassment is constant, from Party cadres and activist students. The latter are trained to denounce their instructors for questionable presentations or personal conduct, to the extreme of one student turning in a professor for the "bourgeois" habit of bathing with soap!

In the colleges and universities particularly, Party restrictions tend to create serious problems which, in turn, weaken the calibre of instruction. Professors are expected to teach assigned courses, not necessarily in their specialities, and to participate regularly in manual labor projects, Party work and administrative duties. Peking's *Kuang-ming Jih-pao* of October 5, 1962, implied the detrimental effect of overburdening faculty members by advocating that teachers be guaranteed that $5/6$ of their duties be confined to professional activities. The CPC has shown cognizance of the inferior training and knowledge of the great majority of younger teachers by stressing that "old" or veteran professors must tutor the young teachers on their own time. The seasoned professor may then expect some assistance in his research and writing projects from his charges.

The Chinese Communist leadership has from time to time found it wise to implement or vary its educational methodology. Its goals, however, are changeless. As phrased by Canton's *Nan-fang Jih-pao* on December 18,

1964: "We must educate and influence the younger generation with proletarian thinking and socialist trends and splash bright red color on the pure souls of children." Should the educational system achieve this end, this and any future Chinese Communist leadership can rest secure.

Education Combined with Productive Labor

Of the many changes introduced to coordinate Communist China's educational system with her economic or political programs none has been as important as the work-study plan. The January, 1958 Nanning meeting of the Central Committee's Politburo took up the question of reorientating education; later in the same month, the Central Committee of the Young Communist League issued a report which first advanced a program providing for student labor. This work-study plan, the report emphasized, constituted the best way to combine the interests of the intellectuals with those of the workers.

The program was given nationwide introduction at the fifth session of the First National People's Congress, on February 3, 1958. Po I-po, Director of the State Economic Commission, announced to the delegates that the plan would immediately be put into effect. Subsequent affirmations of the work-study program were then issued by the All-China Conference on Educational Work, convoked by the CPC Central Committee in May, and by publication of a theoretical work by Lu Ting-yi, then director of the Central Committee's Propaganda Department. On September 19, 1958, the CPC Central Committee itself issued a directive that all schools include productive labor in the regular curricula. The plan was to be implemented by schools opening their own factories and farms, and by factories and cooperatives launching their own schools.

Seen chiefly as a practical expedient designed to solve or ease the labor shortage, the plan actually had its ideological roots in Marxism-Leninism and the works of Mao Tse-tung. Accepting Mao's postulate that the educational objective of complete knowledge is best served through training in productive labor, the resolutions of the CPC Eighth Congress stressed the need to coordinate both cultural and technological revolutionary aims. As Liu Shao-ch'i commented during an inspection trip of Hofei, Anhwei province, in the fall of 1958, the new program was designed to produce an ideal society in which the individual would spend half his time in work and the remainder in profitable study.

The ambitions of the work-study program required the introduction of several measures. For example, all students had to be organized into labor teams, with provision for specialization where possible. During the 1958 steel production drive, over 27,000 teachers and advanced students in the fields of mining and metallurgy were asigned to the backyard furnaces. But the vast majority of the students were formed into farm teams and shared regular peasant conditions. Peking Agricultural University, for example, sent its entire faculty and student body to the villages for a year.

During the 1958–59 period, there was a great upsurge in the establishment of farms and factories adjacent to schools. An official survey attested that 21,000 schools above the middle level had opened 150,000 factories, while 14,000 schools were organizing more than 10,300 farms cultivating two and a half million mou. Wuhan University alone boasted of organizing 140 factories and workshops. At the same time, the Party encouraged factories to open their own schools. On September 1, 1958, the *Kuangming Daily* reported that 23,500 spare-time "red and expert" "universities" had been opened. Generally, the factories provide skilled laborers as instructors and the students contribute their labor to the factories. Eventually, the program hopes to wield factory and school into a single unit.

After two years of experimentation, the most obvious result of the work-study program was the tremendous increase in the total number of students. According to official Party reports for the 1957–58 period, there were 7.6 million middle school students and 441,000 in institutions of higher learning. During the 1959–60 period, middle school enrollment reached 15.9 million, while there were 810,000 students in the higher institutions—or almost double the previous record. There were, however, certain glaring difficulties. Time spent in student labor meant time away from academic pursuits. Liu Hsiu-hsuan, vice president of Tsinghua University, admitted that many professors complained of the detrimental effects on quality of teaching and research. Workers, required to leave routine duties for further instruction or to teach, noted the interruption to production and complained of the inferior quality of teaching.

By the autumn of 1959, the Party sought to remedy these deficiencies by advocating a reduction in student labor hours and re-emphasizing the importance of learning. The Chinese People's University, for example, then limited teacher participation in productive labor to two to three months annually. On April 8, 1960, Yang Hsiu-feng, then Minister of Education, announced further reforms to the National People's Congress. This included a downgrading of courses at all levels: for example, the mathematics and physics courses taught at the college or university level were to be simplified and included in the senior middle school curricula; courses previously offered at this level were to be modified for introduction at the junior middle school level. When feasible, courses were ordered to be combined. Thus, at the elementary level, courses in history, geography and natural science were combined into a "common knowledge" course. Science courses were added to fill the curricula and introduce the student early to those areas essential to technology. At the same time, the revised curricula, often simplified, permitted the student more time for productive labor.

With slight modification, the work-study program remains the key to educational plans in Communist China. In December, 1965, the Ministry of Education and the CPC Central Committee jointly sponsored a National Conference on Urban Part-Work, Part-Study Education. Among the high Party leaders who instructed the delegates, Liu Shao-ch'i and Chou En-lai affirmed that the program was introduced in 1964, apparently in an effort to disavow the mistakes made in the earlier 1958–63 period, and called for a master schedule of five more years of experimentation and then ten of popularization. At that time, 17 million children were reported to be studying in part-work and part-study primary schools, or an 80 per cent increase over 1964 figures for part time schooling, and a 14 per cent increase in the total of primary school students. Student enrollment in part time middle schools was up 87 per cent, as compared to 1964. In the area of advanced education, 4,000 graduated from the part time regular colleges and 10,000 from the work-study agro-technical institutions by 1965.

The renewed emphasis on work-study education represents a dual objective—to alleviate pressures on already critically inadequate regular school systems, while at the same time enlisting more children in the labor force. In the rural areas, schooling can be confined to the slack farm seasons. In Kiangsu province, for example, the communal brigades, singly or jointly, operate classes which are integrated with farm practices. Teachers, who are graduates of secondary schools, are paid on a point system based on the number of days engaged in teaching and farm labor. The same pattern applies to the cities. For example, according to NCNA of January 26, 1964, Shanghai had 350 part-time schools for 50,000 children. Peking has provided for all the Chinese youth in such programs. Thus, the 3,000 fishermen's families living on boats on the shores of Lake Taihu, in Kiangsu province, now can send their children to day or night schools in the port cities and villages. About 86 per cent of the children attend classes intermittently, as their progress is recorded on special cards. The adult population of China is encouraged to continue education through correspondence schools, which, to quote an official publication, are "well adapted to the mass training of specialists." [27] In four to six years, the correspondent can receive a college degree from such institutions sa the Chinese People's University or Amoy University. The courses themselves vary in length

[27] In 1914, the Commercial Press in Shanghai began offering correspondence courses in the Chinese and English languages, mathematics, and commercial subjects. This practice was re-introduced by the Chinese Communists in 1952, and greatly intensified after 1958.

from six months for logic, to five years for a certificate in factory management. Local centers test and answer questions by mail, and a nominal charge is involved for participation and use of textbooks.

As the pragmatic solution to Communist China's educational demands, the part time schools, reinforced by continued study, will doubtlessly continue to enjoy high Party favor. Thus, the leadership continues to emphasize that quantity has not come at the expense of quality, despite the patent questionability of such claims. For example, in reporting the previously mentioned national conference on urban part-time education, *Peking Review* of December 17, 1965 boasted: "Facts produced at the conference showed that, though students in work-study schools spent only half of their time in classroom studies, what they learned was not less than those studying at full-time schools." Perhaps this quote stands as the best testimony to the different standard of education in general in Mao's "socialist paradise."

CULTURAL LIFE AND THE CULTURAL REVOLUTION

Although the cultural revolution launched by Mao and his associates is intended to transform every aspect of Communist China—political, economic, social, and military—it pertains in a special way to the cultural life of the nation. The elimination of the "four olds" would, indeed, mean the creation of a new communist culture which would, in turn, promote and sustain the other aspects of national existence. This ambitious goal requires major modifications of the educational system and propaganda vehicles to eliminate any vestige of the bourgeois mentality and train a new breed of communist, who is best personified now by the dedicated member of the Red Guards. Given the enormity of its goals, the cultural revolution would predictably have to overcome many obstacles. For a nation proud of its thousands of years of cultural contributions, and for a people thoroughly subjected to indoctrination, the inevitable conflict may ultimately decide the relative successes or failures of the entire communist program.

In the long run, just as the transformation of culture may be said to be the key to making China into the ideal Marxist-Leninist state, the key to this transformation depends upon the effectiveness of the CPC's education programs. As noted previously, in its broad sense education now means a thorough indoctrination in the thought of Mao, so that all Chinese can emulate his ideological dedication in their daily tasks. Early in the cultural revolution, rank-and-file Party members and peasants and workers were organized into teams to study the works of Mao, in emulation of the programs of the PLA. By mid-summer, 1966, for example, 70–80 per cent of the adult peasants in Kwangtung province and over 800,000 Party cadres were organized; in Shansi province, over 180,000 study groups were formed for nearly three million students of the thought of Mao. Among Mao's works, the following are considered obligatory reading for all: "On Correcting Mistaken Ideas in the Party," "Combat Liberalism," "In Memory of Norman Bethune," "Serve the People," and "The Foolish Old Man Who Removed the Mountains." [28] For cultural workers, "Five Militant Documents" by Mao have been selected for special attention: Letter to the Yenan Opera Theatre, January 9, 1944; "Give Serious Attention to the Discussion of the Film 'The Life of Wu Hsun' " May 20, 1951; Letter Concerning Studies of 'The Dream of the Red Chamber,' October 16, 1954; and Two Instructions Concerning Literature and Art, of December 12, 1963 and June 27, 1964. To meet the demand for materials imposed by these strictures, publishing houses have greatly accelerated production. Thus, between January and May, 1967, more than 29,000,000 sets of Mao's *Selected Works* were printed. Photographic services reproduced more than 840,000,000 portraits of Mao from July, 1966 to May, 1967.

Of all the areas and aspects of education, however, none has been so vitally joined to the path of cultural revolution as that of higher education. The Red Guards were born in the college and university centers. Student demonstrations in May, 1966, against the administration of Peking University by its President, Lu P'ing, occasioned the first wall posters, and led directly to the leadership's announcement of June 4, that Lu P'ing had been removed as President and CPC First Secretary of the University, and that the Peking Party committee was being thoroughly reorganized, in part to punish the protectors of Lu. Lu P'ing, like President K'uang Ya-ming of Nanking University, had been exposed by the students for favoring gifted students, "treasuring book knowledge over the practical" and reducing the time spent on political study and productive labor, and favoring a bourgeois admissions policy. [29]

[28] This list was published in *Red Flag*, No. 3, 1967, and reprinted in *Peking Review*, February 10, 1967.

[29] These first attacks marked an abrupt departure from the Party line for higher education which had been followed since 1961. Following the August, 1961 pronouncement of Ch'en Yi in the name of the Party and state, the colleges had tended to emphasize the role of "expert," Although part time study programs were retained, the stress on scholarship obviously had an adverse effect on politics and labor. Thus, the June, 1966 decisions indicated a return to the earlier emphasis on "red" over "expert."

In contrast to these first attacks on college administrators for favoring students of bourgeois origins or inclinations, in April, 1967, the Red Guards launched a bitter attack on Party officials who had granted special favors or concessions to children of Party cadres. The special boarding schools for children of cadres dated back to the years of the war against Japan. Although the Party leadership determined in 1955 to gradually close these centers, their numbers reached about thirty by the 1960's. According to the Red Guards' *Ch'un Lei (Spring*

On June 13, 1966, the CPC Central Committee announced that admission to institutions of higher learning was to be postponed for six months to carry out "the sharp and fierce struggle" of the cultural revolution. In effect, this sanctioned the closure of these institutions so that the more militant students could be organized into Red Guard units and be free for total dedication to political tasks. At the same time, college administrators were ordered to reform entrance requirements, curricula and grading procedures. Middle school students awaiting acceptance to college were urged to obtain "ideological diplomas" by participating in productive labor and politics to develop "outstanding moral, intellectual and physical qualities."

Point Ten of the CPC Central Committee's August 8, 1966 Directive indicates several of the leadership's demands for reform: it urges that schooling be shortened, courses be fewer and better, and that students actively participate in productive labor. On August 2, 1966, *People's Daily* published a July, 1965 speech by Yeh Chien-ying, which further hints at the nature of reforms. Yeh praised the early educational policies advocated by Mao and Lin Piao at the Chinese People's Anti-Japanese Military and Political University. This school was established in 1936, and operated at Yenan during the anti-Japanese war to train some 100,000 revolutionary cadres. With Lin Piao as president and political commissar, and Mao as chairman of the educational committee, the center was run with "self-reliance, industry and thrift" to bring politics to the fore. Since the students remained only 6 to 8 months, courses were concentrated and condensed according to the unusual theory that "the time required [in study] should not be too long . . . the more one studies, the more ignorant he becomes, and he becomes divorced from reality."

Since the Anti-Japanese Military and Political University has been upheld as a shining example, it may be predicted that the leadership has determined to drastically condense the usual curricula. This approach was reinforced when the July 12, 1966 *People's Daily* published in full the recommendations of seven college students to Mao and the CPC Central Committee. These students of the China People's University pointed out that the average college-bound youth enters school at age 7 or 8, and doesn't complete his training until he is 25 or 26: "Seventeen years of hard academic study really wastes one's youth and leads the young generation astray" since "the content of study material is diffuse and repetitive . . . [and] the longer students study the more muddle-headed they become." Urging that the period of education be cut in half, the students point out a telling

---

Thunder) No. 4, April 13, 1967, Liu Shao-ch'i, Teng Hsiao-p'ing, and Lu Ting-yi protected these special schools as "hotbeds of revisionism" to foster a new class of "spiritual aristocrats," as their own successors.

advantage: teachers, already scarce and now suspect by the cultural revolution, could train twice as many pupils.

Primary as well as secondary schools have also been affected by the cultural revolution and its associated Red Guard movement. In urging that these schools re-open as soon as possible, *People's Daily* of March 7, 1967, indicated the necessity of reform at this level. "Cultural revolutionary committees" are to be elected by revolutionary pupils, teachers, administrators and ancillary staff and cadres "for making concrete arrangements for the operation of classes." "The lessons will consist mainly of the conscientious study of Chairman Mao's works," while the middle school courses in mathematics, foreign languages and the sciences are revised, and the primary schools reform courses in arithmetic and general scientific knowledge.

Anticipating that the cultural revolution's effect will cause much unrest in re-opening educational institutions, the March 7, 1967 *People's Daily* cautioned that "the spearhead of the struggle must never be directed against the pupils." Moreover, the Party leadership has sought to prevent any reoccurrence of violence in these centers by assigning remolding and training of teachers and students to the PLA. According to a directive issued in the name of the CPC Central Committee and the State Council on December 31, 1966, Mao determined that PLA cadres should instruct teachers and students, during the period from January, 1967 to summer vacation, in politics (or the thought of Mao) and military preparedness (or regular drill exercises). This policy of training groups for a 15–20 day period, according to the CC, "should become a regular system" in the future carried out during summer or winter vacations. In K'ung Chiang Middle School, some 300 soldiers of the PLA were sent to train the 1,800 students in mid February, 1967, and, as noted elsewhere, countless troops have been assigned to Red Guard units in a supervisory capacity.

As a result of the concern of the leadership and the care of the PLA, the students in Communist China have continued to exercise a major role in the cultural revolution. Yet, it is also apparent that the picture is not one of total success. For example, in reminding the delegates to the March, 1967 Congress of Red Guards of Peking Middle Schools that "it is our hope that you will modestly learn from the PLA," Chou En-lai also denounced "the phenomenon of our schools being dominated by bourgeois intellectuals." Particularly, Chou castigated the members of the United Action Committee, a pseudo-revolutionary student group said to follow the Liu-Teng line. But the most telling sign of the continued unrest is the fact that, despite Party orders, many of the schools and colleges closed during the cultural revolution had not reopened for the 1967 academic year. For example, the

CPC CC's Provisions of March, 1967, published by *Hsin-pei-ta* on March 14, 1967, ordered that "all revolutionary students and teachers . . . return to their schools before March 20," to form provisional organs of power for conducting the cultural revolution from those centers. But, later reports showed that many failed to respond to the order. The boycott by the bourgeois elements, who doubtlessly fear for their own safety, and the more militant Red Guards who prefer active participation in the struggle, means that the educational centers cannot function in the prescribed manner. Thus, even if the ordered reforms do not destroy the already questionable educational standards, the fact is that over a year has been lost already in training skilled manpower to meet enormous national needs. Part of this deficit can be met immediately by graduating students early. But, in the long run, the current and most likely future practices will cause untold difficulties.

The cultural goals of the leaders of the cultural revolution and the line advocated by their opponents present a sharp conflict which reflects the basic nature of the class struggle. In the words of the August 12, 1966 Decision of the CPC Central Committee, the cultural revolution is meant to "transform educational, literary and art and all other parts of the super-structure that do not correspond to the socialist economic base." Chiang Ch'ing further commented on this point in her November 28, 1966 speech to the Peking rally of literary and art workers. "A nation must have its own forms of art, its own artistic expression," she said. Thus, it would be impossible for the Chinese Communists, as atheists and Marxist-Leninists, to "critically assimilate ghosts, gods and religion," or any of the other themes and some of the forms of western art and literature. In her July, 1964 address to the Forum of Theatrical Workers in Peking, Chiang Ch'ing gave a concrete example of the differences in Chinese Communist literature. Criticizing the new plays for their failure to depict conditions correctly, she cited the play "Great Wall Along the Southern Sea" as a revolutionary model. "First the leadership set the theme," she said, "and then the play-wrights went three times to acquire experience of what life was really like. They even took part in a military operation to round up enemy spies."

The literature and art representing and by and for the masses which is advocated by the leaders of the cultural revolution might be considered as the "red" aspect of "red and expert" goals. By contrast, the followers of the counterrevolutionary black line have tended to favor "expert" aspects. Thus, Liu Shao-ch'i is said to have advocated the development of profes-sional, rather than peasant or worker, writers who would be free to follow their own creative urges. According to *People's Daily* of April 23, 1967, in early March, 1956, Liu called Chou Yang and other counterrevolution-aries to his home to promote this black line. He urged that the Chinese

Writers Association provide special funds and subsidies to provide comfortable facilities for professional writers, and give them the leisure to pursue "a good knowledge of history and world literature and at least one foreign language." He also insisted that the writer be free from Party strictures so that he could create his own works. In short, Liu apparently urged that the promises of the Hundred Flowers literally be realities. Similarly, T'ao Chu is said to have insisted: "We must respect the freedom of writers." He "openly opposed and resisted Chairman Mao's directive urging writers and artists to go among the masses" and "wanted writers to carry out self-remoulding on the basis of their sense of responsibility."[30]

One of the foremost exponents of the general line for art and literature in the years immediately preceding the cultural revolution was Chiang Ch'ing, the former opera star who became Mao's wife. Chiang Ch'ing offered her own reason for heightened cultural work in her November 28, 1966 speech: "A few years ago [probably late in 1963] I was ill. My doctor advised me to spend more time in cultural pursuits so as to restore the functions of my organs of hearing and sight." It was most natural that Madame Mao, who previously had played no active political role, should first turn her attention to Peking opera. By July, 1964, Chiang Ch'ing was addressing opera and theatre personnel on the specifics of reform. She pointed out that there were some 2,800 companies specializing in opera out of about 3,000 theatrical companies then active in entertainment, and that these companies represented an excellent opportunity to carry the Party's message to the masses. However, the traditional operas would only undermine socialist goals, so new workers must be trained in Marxist-Leninist themes.

In 1964, these admonitions did not seem unusual. In retrospect, however, Chiang Ch'ing's role as a cultural critic occasioned serious difficulties which ultimately led to the inauguration of the cultural revolution. According to *Red Flag* (no. 6, 1967), Liu Shao-ch'i was "the biggest obstacle to the revolution of Peking opera." He spread the idea that "old operas have much educational value" and impeded Chiang Ch'ing's efforts. In contrast, at the same time Lin Piao was vigorously urging the cultural workers of the PLA to carry out the reforms recommended by Madame Mao. By 1965, the wedge had widened between the reformers, as represented by Chiang Ch'ing and Lin Piao, and the traditionalists, as personified by Liu Shao-ch'i, Chou Yang, and other advocates of the so-called black line. As noted in Chapter 3, Mao's call in the fall of 1965 for intensified cultural reform led to the creation of two separate reports which, in turn, reflect this division between the two factions. The Outline Report of

[30] These and other charges are contained in the lengthy January 14, 1967 criticism of T'ao Chu prepared by the Canton Liaison Center of the Wuhan Revolutionary Rebel Headquarters of the Red Guards and published in their organ, *Tung-fang Hung*.

February 12, 1966, claimed to be the personal work of P'eng Chen, stood in sharp contrast to the February 20 Forum Summary prepared on the orders of Lin Piao and under the personal direction of Chiang Ch'ing. On May 16, 1966, the CPC Central Committee ordered the Outline Report to be revoked and the Group of Five in Charge of Cultural Revolution dissolved. The new Cultural Revolution Group, created by the CC to be under the direct authority of the Politburo's Standing Committee, gave the office of First Vice Chairman (second only to the Head, Ch'en Po-ta) to Madame Mao.

During the interval between Mao's 1965 call to greater efforts and the CC's Decision to reorganize the Cultural Revolution Group, two currents should be noted. On the one hand, cultural work teams were sent throughout the mainland. Under the direction of Teng Hsiao-p'ing, and the protection of Liu Shao-ch'i, many of these teams were later branded as rightist in their approach. As Chiang Ch'ing stated in her November 28, 1966 speech, the teams "turned the spearhead against the revolutionary students." It may be recalled that when Mao returned to Peking on July 18, 1966, after consulting with Ch'en Po-ta and K'ang Sheng, Chiang Ch'ing reported the situation concerning the teams to her husband. Presumably, this information reinforced Mao's decision to promote the Red Guards as a leading force to carry out the cultural revolution. It is significant that, at the first Red Guard rally in Peking, on August 18, 1966, Ch'en Po ta, K'ang Sheng and Chiang Ch'ing shared the platform with Mao. During this same time, apparently many cultural workers attempted to save their prestige and offices by resorting to hurried confessions. The most publicized of these cases was that of Kuo Mo-jo's self-criticism. After an April 14, 1966, meeting of the Standing Committee of the NPC, the respected President of the Chinese Academy of Sciences and Chairman of the All-China Federation of Literary and Art Circles delivered an extempory speech in which, as he says, "I made a frank self-criticism to express my sincere feelings." Comparing his past writings to those produced by worker and peasant authors, Kuo Mo-jo suggested that all his work should be burnt.[31]

[31] Kuo Mo-jo's confession received much attention outside of Communist China, since it hinted that another campaign to reform the intellectuals might be in the offing. In the late summer of 1964, debate began in earnest in the Party press concerning the principle of "two in one," which can be traced back to Taoism. This philosophical concept had been advanced by Yang Hsien-chen, a member of the CPC CC and president of the Higher Party School from 1958, until his replacement in September, 1961 by Wang Ts'ung-wu. Yang's theory was condemned by the August 31, 1964 issues of *Red Flag* and *People's Daily* for obviating Mao's theory of contradictions and minimizing the nature of the class struggle. The apparent reluctance of many intellectuals to enter into the "two in one" debates probably heightened the leadership's interest in carrying out further reform among the intellectual community. In referring to his self-criticism, Kuo Mo-jo told the delegates to the Afro-Asian Writers Emergency Meeting in Peking on July 4, 1966, however, that "it is absolutely normal in our country for a revolutionary writer who is responsible to the people constantly to remould himself and to make serious self-criticism from time to time."

The drive to reform culture and cultural circles had reached a new stage on November 26, 1965, when the Shanghai *Wen Hui Pao* carried an article by Yao Wen-yuan "On the New Historical Drama 'Hai Jui Dismissed from Office.' " Prepared under the "direct guidance of Comrade Chiang Ch'ing," this criticism attacked playwright and Vice Mayor of Peking Wu Han who, in January, 1961, had first published "Hai Jui" in the journal *Peking Literature and Art*. The play, which deals with the legendary 16th century mandarin, Hai Jui, who withstood the emperor to protect the peasants against cruel exploitation, had earlier been regarded as a correct interpretation according to Mao's dictum that certain things can be absorbed from history. However, on December 21, 1965, Mao explicitly stated that the crux of "Hai Jui" was the question of dismissal from office. At Lushan, in 1959, he had dismissed P'eng Teh-huai; therefore, the play was a veiled criticism of P'eng's dismissal and those of other rightists.

While the influential *Liberation Army Daily* and other newspapers began to insist that Wu Han was part of a conspiratoral gang bent upon opposing the leadership of Mao and the CPC Central Committee, in Peking municipality the P'eng Chen "counterrevolutionary revisionist clique" forbade the city papers to reprint Yao Wen-yuan's article. (Later, it was revealed that Wu Han and his associates were being encouraged to produce literature intended to create opinion favorable to the overthrow of the dictatorship of the proletariat by Liu Shao-ch'i himself.)[32] Wu Han's closest coconspirators were identified as Teng T'o and Liao Mo-sha. Teng, a secretary of the Peking CPC committee and editor-in-chief of its organ *Frontline*, had abused his offices to advance the revisionist line.[33] Liao Mo-sha had collaborated with Wu Han and Teng in writing *Notes from Three-Family Village*. He headed the Peking committee's United Front Work Department.

In the December 30, 1965 issue of *People's Daily*, Wu Han attempted to salvage his reputation as a respected scholar and propagandist by issuing a 10,000 word self-criticism. However, this confession was regarded as a cunning example of seeking to avoid criticism by assuming the initiative. Moreover, as meetings of "immortals" were swiftly organized, other self-confessions revealed the extent of sympathy for views similar to those held by Wu Han. For example, T'ien Han, chairman of the Union of Chinese

[32] *People's Daily*, April 17, 1967.

[33] According to the May 10, 1966 Shanghai *Chieh-fang Jih-pao*, Teng used tales from history and myth in his essay collection *Evening Talks at Yenshan* to discredit the general line. For example, in his essay "From Three to Ten Thousand," he commented: "If a man with a swelled head thinks he can learn a subject with ease and kicks his teacher out [apparently apropos Peking's attitude towards Moscow] he will never learn anything." *Economic Research* No. 5 (May 20, 1966), called Teng the boss of the "Three Family Village" anti-Party group, and accused him of opposing the commune system and seeking to restore land to the peasants in 1961.

Drama Workers, was found guilty of having depicted a "good" mandarin in a 1961 work. Hsia Yen, playwright and Vice Minister of Culture from 1954 to 1965, was accused of favoring "humanism" (or non-communism). While *People's Daily*, now often reprinting editorials of the *Liberation Army Daily* on its first page, called upon all readers to "expose the authorities and open fire on them," the finger of guilt increasingly pointed to Chou Yang.

Among his other offices, Chou Yang was the First Vice Chairman of the All-China Federation of Literary and Art Circles, an alternate member of the CPC Central Committee, and a deputy director of the latter's Propaganda Department. According to the charges levelled at a meeting of the CC Propaganda Department which was presided over by Deputy Director Chang P'ing-hua, and reported in *People's Daily* of July 29, 1966, since the 20th CPSU Congress Chou had followed Khrushchev's revisionist line and attacked the CPC leadership. "Waving the red flag to oppose the red flag," he openly encouraged academic circles to oppose the thought of Mao. Most seriously, as "chief ringleader of the black line in literary and art circles," Chou Yang used his Party and state offices to form a clique in the Ministry of Culture and the CC Propaganda Department. Among his favorites were: T'ien Han, a Vice Chairman of the All-China Federation of Literary and Art Circles and Chairman and Party secretary of the Union of Chinese Drama Workers; and Yang Han-sheng, also a Vice Chairman of the ACFLAC and its Party secretary. T'ien Han was attacked for his veiled criticism of the CPC general line dating back to 1961, while Yang Han-sheng was accused in the December 27, 1966 *People's Daily* of supporting Chou Yang's black line as early as 1956.

The anti-Party plotters in the Ministry of Culture are said to include former Minister Lu Ting-yi, whose purge has been discussed elsewhere, as well as Vice Ministers Hu Yü-chih, Lin Mo-han, Hsiao Wang-tung (who for a time was Acting Minister after Lu's downfall), and Hsia Yen. Hsiao Wang-tung's case may be considered as representative. His appointment as Vice Minister of Culture in May, 1965, came upon the nomination of Lo Jui-ch'ing and was approved by Teng Hsiao-p'ing and Liu Shao-ch'i. From that office, and later as Acting Minister, Hsiao issued propaganda extolling the achievements of P'eng Chen, Teng, and Liu and demeaning the thought of Mao.[34] Given the vital function which propaganda plays in Communist China, the presence of conspirators of the Liu-Teng line in the Ministry of Culture represented a real threat to Mao and his associates. But, even more importantly, the conspiracy spread to and included the CPC Central Committee's own Propaganda Department. This situation stemmed at least in part from the CPC's normal practice of dual offices in

[34] See, for example, *Mao Tse-tung Chu-i Chan-tou Pao*, No. 2, February 23, 1967.

the Party and state apparatus. For example, until his purge, Lu Ting-yi was both Minister of Culture and Director of the CC Propaganda Department; Lin Mo-han was a Vice Minister of Culture and Deputy Director of the Propaganda Department.

With the June, 1966 CPC CC decision to name T'ao Chu Director of its Propaganda Department, a purge was carried out within that organ to eliminate the followers of the Chou Yang line. Among the Deputy Directors denounced were: Hsü Li-ch'ün, who was accused of subverting the cultural revolution at Peking University and being a friend of P'eng Chen; as well, of course, as Lin Mo-han and Chou Yang. Of necessity, the purge extended out to the Propaganda Department's agencies in the Bureaus, provinces and municipalities. Among those dismissed were: Hua Chia, deputy director of Canton's propaganda department; Wang K'uang, director of the CPC Kwangtung provincial committee's progaganda department and of the Central-South Bureau's propaganda department; Sung Yü-hsi, director of the Honan provincial committee's propaganda department; and Tseng Tun, director of the similar organ of Hupeh province. At the same time, T'ao Chu named new appointees to assist him in carrying out the Party's propaganda. These included men such as Chang Chi-ch'un, a member of the CPC CC, and Chang P'ing-hua, an alternate member of the CC. The latter served as T'ao Chu's deputy and, like his mentor, was later purged for subverting the cultural revolution. Another Party veteran purged was Hu Ch'iao-mu, a member of the CPC CC and alternate member of its Secretariat and author of the official history of the CPC. Hu was accused of supporting P'eng Teh-huai at Lushan, of criticizing Mao's ability as a writer, and of infiltrating the Union of Chinese Writers with agents of the Liu-Teng line.

The All-China Federation of Literary and Art Circles and its various specialized unions have already undergone numerous changes in personnel as a result of the cultural revolution's disclosures. For example, Chou Yang, Hsia Yen, T'ien Han and Yang Han-sheng—all Vice Chairmen of the Federation—have been denounced and purged. The Union of Chinese Writers had undergone practically a complete reorganization, with the purges of Vice Chairmen Chou Yang, Shao Ch'uan-lin and Liu Pai-yü. T'ien Han has been removed as Chairman of the Union of Chinese Drama Workers. Thus, the mass organizations for cultural activities have shared the same fate as the Party and state propaganda organs.

The downfall of T'ao Chu and his associates by January, 1967, as a result in part of the disclosures of the Red Guards, again emphasized the CPC leadership's inability to transform the CC Propaganda Department into an effective instrument for carrying out the cultural revolution. But, like the "three in one" alliances that are considered provisional organs of power, the Cultural Revolution Groups of the Central Committee and the PLA may be regarded as at least provisional, if not permanent, organs to supervise and conduct work that might formerly have been considered the special prerogative of the Propaganda Department. This conclusion is reinforced by the fact that Ch'en Po-ta, who has long been first deputy director of the Propaganda Department, is also the Head of the CC's Cultural Revolution Group. But it might be added that even if this expedient practice proves effective, the crisis in the CC's Propaganda Department indicates a major failure of the CPC and its central leadership.

The press in Communist China, as an instrument of the CPC's propaganda network, has been greatly affected by the difficulties and breakdowns cited above. As editorial staffs of the regular press have been found guilty of counterrevolutionary activities, the various journals of the Red Guards have flooded the market. Some newspapers have been suspended, others have gone through name and personnel changes to clear their reputations. The PLA's *Liberation Army Daily* has come to rival, if not surpass, *People's Daily* as the foremost exponent of the Party line. Yet one thing has remained entirely consistent: the leaders of the cultural revolution recognize the fundamental importance of the press as a means to indoctrinate the masses. Thus, seizure of the newspapers is regarded as a vital part of the seizure of political power.

On the eve of the cultural revolution, careful readers of the Party press could spot the relative decline in the *People's Daily* as a vehicle of foremost authority. It was the *Liberation Army Daily* that took the lead in exposing the plot of the "Three-Family Village," and later revealed the corruption in the Peking CPC Committee.[35] Its editorials (particularly of April 18, May 4 and June 6) reprinted by *People's Daily*, *Kuang-ming Jih-pao*, and *Wen Hui Pao*, also set the main points for conducting the cultural revolution and upheld the supreme importance of Mao's thought. With the dismissal of its editor-in-chief, Teng T'o, and the appointment of T'ang P'ing-chu to that post, *People's Daily* regained much of its stature by early June, 1966. T'ang, who had formerly been a deputy editor of *Liberation Army Daily*, and was respected by T'ao Chu, appeared the ideal choice to insure the paper's orthodoxy.

The mouthpieces of the Peking CPC Committee fared less well. On June 7, 1966, the newly reorganized Peking committee announced that the editorial boards of *Peking Daily* and *Peking Evening News* had been dis-

---

[35] As noted elsewhere, the Shanghai *Wen Hui Pao* first published Yao Wen-yüan's article attacking "Hai Jui Dismissed from Office," which led to the exposure of the Wu Han clique. The condemnation of Teng T'o and the Peking municipal papers was first printed in the *Kuang-ming Jih-pao*. However, it was the *Liberation Army Daily* that then broadcast these incidents with the voice of authority.

missed for their association with the "Three-Family Village" line. The new editorial board to serve both papers was placed under the direction of Chai Hsiang-tung. *Frontline* suffered a more drastic punishment. Its board was dismissed and publication suspended for, as *People's Daily* had forewarned on May 21, 1966, sheltering a person or persons with "mad ambition." Peking *Ta-kung Pao*, an old and respected organ, ceased printing in its usual format on September 10, 1966. On September 15, renamed *Ch'ien-chin Pao* or *Progressive Daily*, it reappeared with the professed intention of being a loyal mouthpiece of the cultural revolution. *Chinese Youth Daily*, the organ of the Young Communist League, made a similar pledge; by August, 1966, however it had apparently suspended operations. Its place was taken by the various Red Guard papers. In early September, observers in Peking reported that the *Peking Daily* had also been placed under "temporary suspension." On September 10, the *Yang-ch'eng Wan-pao* (*Yangcheng Evening Paper*) of Canton appeared under the new title of *Hung-wei Pao*, or *Red Guard Daily*, apparently in a gesture to illustrate its loyalties.

Throughout these early months of the cultural revolution, T'ao Chu was responsible for guiding the Party press. His opinions on the function of the daily paper, as revealed in the attacks made on him after his downfall, indicate yet another problem for the newspapers during the second half of 1966. While he directed the CPC's Central-South Bureau, the *Yangcheng Evening Paper* was his special mouthpiece. Yet Red Guard disclosures, made on January 14, 1967, by the Wuhan Revolutionary Rebel Headquarters, claim that as early as 1959 T'ao Chu had insisted that the role of the evening paper should be as much for entertainment as for indoctrination, or education in "proletarian politics." According to the *Hung-wei Pao Leaflet* of February 18, 1967, T'ao Chu's *Yangcheng Evening Paper* had opposed the thought of Mao for ten years. Renamed the *Red Guard Daily*, it continued to commit anti-Party crimes according to T'ao's directions. "Their purpose," the *Leaflet* claimed, "was completely to kill and silence witnesses and destroy incriminating evidence." When T'ao Chu fell, yet another round of purges and reorganizations began. For example, in January, 1967, T'ang P'ing-chu was removed as editor of *People's Daily* and Hu Ch'ih as director of NCNA for their association with T'ao.

The upheaval associated with the fall of T'ao Chu and the violent seizures of power in several of the provinces in January, 1967, resulted in efforts of the rebel revolutionary groups to wrest control of the local newspapers from the anti-Party elements. For example, in Heilungkiang province, rebels took over the newspapers and radio on January 12—an example termed entirely correct by the February 10, 1967 *People's Daily*. On January 4, in Shanghai, the "Spark and Prairie Fire" Revolutionary Rebel

Headquarters seized control of the *Wen Hui Pao*. Speaking in praise of this victory in its February 1 issue, *Red Flag*'s article, "Power to Exercise Leadership Over Newspapers Must Be Seized," pointed out that this paper had lost the leading role it exercised in denouncing "Hai Jui" when the board has been reorganized by revisionists within the Shanghai CPC Committee.

The film industry, which is another popular means of mass indoctrination, has also been charged with fostering an anti-Party line. The most publicized of the films found defective is that of "Inside Story of the Ch'ing Court," adapted from a 1949 play by Yao K'e, and shown repeatedly since 1950. It is now found to be a glorification of national betrayal and capitulationism. Termed "patriotic" by Liu Shao-ch'i, the film depicts the weaknesses of China and suggests the advantages to be gained from learning from the west. Another film found to be counterrevolutionary is "The Prairie Fire," which was first shown in 1962, amid much favorable criticism from the Party propaganda network. Now, the film is denounced for extolling the role of Liu Shao-ch'i as a "hero" and "big saviour." Like other theatre personnel, the workers of the film industry will be expected to learn from the reforms of the Peking opera. As *People's Daily* mentioned on April 19, 1967, the opera, as reformed through the influence of Chiang Ch'ing over the last three years, is "the pace-maker of revolutionary change in the sphere of ltterature and art." And this point was inferred by Mao himself when, on June 22, 1967, he and his close associates attended an opera performance and honored the case.

Perhaps because of the myriad difficulties concerned with proper control of the normal propaganda media, such as the press or the theatre, the leaders of the cultural revolution have encouraged massive use of the big character or wall poster. The wall poster has been utilized on previous occasions, such as in the Hundred Flowers campaign, but never with so total an endorsement from the leadership. Mao personally indicated the importance of the wall poster by using this medium at the time of the eleventh CPC CC plenum to call for an attack on those leading comrades "adopting the reactionary stand of the bourgeoisie." His August 5, 1966 poster is officially regarded as a landmark in the cultural revolution. In its Directive of August 12, 1966, the CPC Central Committee followed Mao's lead by urging: "Make full use of big character posters and great debates to argue matter out . . . in this way the masses will be able to raise their political consciousness in the course of the struggle. . . ." And Lin Piao stressed at the November 3, 1966 Peking rally of Red Guards that the use of such posters is an important manifestation of "extensive democracy" as practiced by the dictatorship of the proletariat. He said: "the Party is fearlessly permitting the broad masses to use the media of freely airing their views, big character posters, great debates and extensive exchange of revolutionary experience, to criticize and supervise the Party and goverment, leading institutions and leaders at all levels." In fact the wall poster, which is the chief source of news-reporting by foreign correspondents in China, is an ideal vehicle to serve Mao's thought. It conveys the impression that it is the masses themselves who are demanding the reforms of the cultural revolution and thus reinforces the strategy of the mass line.

It should be apparent from the foregoing analysis that the guidance and control of cultural life in Communist China is the spiritual foundation of the Party and state consolidation of power, more important though difficult than harnessing the political, economic, military, and social forces of the nation. If the CPC is to gain national and international support, and if the prestige of its leadership is to be enhanced, much of the burden and perhaps a large share of the success or failure depends upon its crucial policies and programs to convince the Chinese people in leading a communist-orientated cultural life.

CHAPTER 11

Conclusion

Communist China is now undergoing a gigantic and historically unprecedented experiment which is meant to involve directly the bodies, minds and hearts of one quarter of the world's population. If successful, this struggle will affect all mankind. On the surface, however, the present turmoil seems primarily to be a desperate power struggle between pro-Mao and anti-Mao forces. And the prominent role assigned the PLA and Red Guards, and reports of disturbances and suppressions in their ranks, strengthens the impression that the current disorder is in the tradition of military rule, or revived warlordism. Yet, the present uproar, centering around the "great proletarian cultural revolution," had its own unique, ideological character which has, in turn, caused striking political, economic and social dislocation and efforts at reconstruction.

In seeking to better understand the unique nature of this struggle, a series of crucial questions arise. Was Mao's authority as leader of the Party and state challenged or threatened? Were his ideas and programs diluted, compromised, sabotaged, or betrayed by those whom he called his trusted associates? Did either Mao or his critics anticipate the enormous consequences of their open disagreement? Who initiated the struggle? Who reacted? Who has come to benefit from it, and who to suffer? Who has the better assurance of final victory? And in what possible form? Although answers to these questions cannot be authoritative, they can be meaningful in terms of understanding Communist China today and tomorrow.

Mao has symbolized Communist China ever since his forces seized power on the mainland in 1949. In fact, Mao has exercised *de facto* control of the communist movement in China since November, 1931, when the Chinese

Soviet Republic was established under his chairmanship, and *de jure* control, since his January, 1935 election as Chairman of the CPC Central Committee at the Tsunyi Conference. His position in the history of the Chinese Communist Party and state, similar to Lenin's status in the Soviet experience, appears assured. For example, although Mao resigned as head of state in 1959, in favor of Liu Shao-ch'i, his action was not that of a supplanted ruler or "victim," but rather as a "king-maker" or "father of the emperor." Since in the communist system, the Party controls the state, as full time chief of the CPC Mao's stature became loftier, if not literally elevated. This conclusion is corroborated by the absence of any accompanying move to make Liu Chairman of the CPC Central Committee, or to have Mao "kicked upstairs" as the CC's honorary Chairman.[1]

It can be said with certitude that Mao's leadership of the CPC was not seriously threatened or challenged from within after 1935. There have been several instances of disagreement between Mao and some of his prominent associates in matters concerning Party line, strategy and leadership—such as those of Chang Kuo-t'ao in 1938, Ch'en Shao-yü (Wang Ming) in 1942, Kao Kang and Jao Shu-shih in 1953–54, P'eng Teh-huai in 1959, and P'eng Chen in 1965. But none of the dissidents actually hoped, or more truly was in such a position, to replace Mao.[2] It is also true, to a large degree, that anti-Mao leaders since 1935, including Teng Hsiao-p'ing or even Liu Shao-ch'i, are far outdistanced by Mao in the mastery of communist revolutionary ideology, in the accomplishments of communist revolutionary practice, or in the attainment of the communist revolutionary vision. They have been disturbed by certain of Mao's decisions—such as the organization of the soviets, the route of the Long March, the implementation of the anti-Japanese national united front with the KMT, ranking of the leaders, the Great Leap and the commune systme, and relations with the CPSU and the USSR as well as other communist Parties and states, etc. But it is significant that the tactics of Mao's critics have been described as "waving the red flag to oppose the red flag." That is, even Mao's opponents have so far been unwilling or unable to operate outside the general confines of Mao's theories and practices, or to attack him directly. This is illustrated by the recent strife between rival groups of the Red Guards, where even the anti-Mao factions have deemed it necessary to still pay tribute to Mao's leadership.

[1] Differing from the 1945 version, the 1956 CPC Constitution innovates a provision that "the Central Committee may, when it deems it necessary, have an honorary chairman." This post was obviously intended for Mao when he retires from active political service.

[2] Recent Party literature referring to P'eng Teh-huai's "vain hope of overthrowing the leadership of the Party Central Committee headed by Chairman Mao"—an expression that could be applied to others of the dissidents—is probably more a perfunctory than a substantive allegation.

A man who has become a legend in his own lifetime as the celebrated symbol of communism in China, Mao enjoys the sort of well-established and secure position that seems to defy the ambitions of knowledgable contenders. Unlike the proverbial house of cards, or the cases of such leaders as President Kwame Nkrumah of Ghana, Prime Minister Abubakar Tafawa Balewa of Nigeria, or President Sukarno of Indonesia, Mao's authority is not likely to be toppled easily. Should he wish it, Mao could spend his remaining years as a hero, in a sort of splendid glory far overshadowing that of some prominent founders of powerful Chinese dynasties. But, as a dedicated revolutionary, Mao cannot settle for personal well-being or power; instead, he must strive for mass acceptance and application of those theories to which his life has been dedicated. In this respect, his service to international communism contrasts sharply to that of Stalin in his declining years. Stalin is now recalled for his many grave blunders in dealings with his associates and followers as well as fraternal parties and states, instead of his efforts to secure a legacy of communist revolutionary theory and practice for future generations. Ironically enough, though, Mao's very commitment to revolutionary goals stands in sharp contrast to the lagging revolutionary efforts of many of his followers and associates. Many veteran members of the CPC apparently have become more concerned with their own vested interests, associated with position, power, prestige and bodily comfort, than with the defense or enlargement of the fruits of revolution. Many have inclined to seeking temporary abatement of the revolutionary struggle, through compromising such principles of Mao's as "letting politics [revolution] take command." For them, it is his thought, far more than his person, that creates problems, gaps or contradictions between themselves and Mao.

While it is unlikely that his opponents would seriously threaten Mao as the paternal leader, it can be anticipated that disloyal followers would seek to undermine or betray his thought. Of course, just as Mao the man can be artifically flattered, lip service can be paid to his thought. But, lip service alone cannot long suffice, for true respect for Mao's thought requires one to master his revolutionary outlook, to be equipt with revolutionary spirit and dedication, and to practice revolutionary struggle daily in personal as well as Party life. Yet, token professions of respect and support can temporarily conceal dangerous critics. Thus, P'eng Teh-huai is now accused of being "an out-and-out big bourgeois warlord, careerist and conspirator who, with a speculator's mentality of 'investing in a share,' wormed his way into the Party and the army." P'eng Chen is called the representative of a "counterrevolutionary revisionist clique for the undermining of the great proletarian cultural revolution in a futile attempt to restore capitalism." Liu Shao-ch'i is identified tacitly as the "behind-the-scene boss" of P'eng Teh-huai and P'eng Chen, and "the Khrushchev of China" who heads "the counterrevolutionary revisionist front," "attacks the socialist system," and "spreads the ideas of 'the dying out of class struggle'."

The threat to Mao's thought is implicit in the nature of the accusations made against his critics. Mao has emphasized that the struggle between socialist and capitalist roads, "it seems, will continue in China and in our Party [the CPC] for at least 20 years and possibly half a century. In short, the struggle will cease only when classes die out completely." In his big-character poster "Bombard the Headquarters," dated August 5, 1966, Mao exposed the nature of those who oppose his thought:

Adopting the reactionary stand of the bourgeoisie, they have enforced a bourgeois dictatorship and struck down the surging movement of the great cultural revolution of the proletariat. They have stood facts on their head and juggled black and white, encircled and suppressed revolutionaries, stifled opinions differing from their own, imposed a white terror, and felt very pleased with themselves. They have puffed up the arrogance of the bourgeoisie and deflated the morale of the proletariat. How poisonous! Viewed in connection with the Right deviation in 1962 and the wrong tendency of 1964 which was "Left" in form but Right in essence, shouldn't this make one wide awake?

Clearly Mao and his faithful associates understand the danger to his thought. Thus, his fervent adherents have intensified their efforts on his behalf in direct proportion to the challenge. This probably explains in large measure the current energetic demands to study his thought carefully and ceaselessly. Via a press now almost totally dedicated to praising Mao's ideas, this study campaign's degree of success should promote respect for Mao as well as his theoretical contributions. Such reverence for Mao, especially in the form of pledges to "read his works, follow his words, and implement his instructions"—as called for by Lin Piao—would, in turn, further popularize, emphasize and enhance Mao's thought.

It is, of course, impossible to define precisely the distinction between Mao the man, and Mao's thought. But it is certain that the man must perish, for all men are mortal, and the aged and infirmed are particularly vulnerable. To popularize Mao's thought simply to encourage blind obedience to him is a case of personality cult of the first order. To so stake the future of the Party and state on one old leader is reminiscent of the negative lesson provided by Stalin during his last years. In any case, given Mao's age, the advantages would be very temporary. It would be utterly unwise for a successor-designate to permit, let alone to promote, such blind cultism for a failing or falling leader. Should Lin Piao seek to use Mao the person as political capital to defeat his competitors, he would be at a total loss—not unlike the case of Malenkov, after the leader is gone. In an oriental sense, this would be to look like a "son-emperor." Even by western standards, such a maneuver would only magnify his problems by creating unfavorable contrasts between him and his renowned predecessor. On the other hand, Mao's thought represents a positive advantage to Lin and Mao's other followers. With it, they will inherit the role of standard-bearer and will be readily equipt with a tested contemporary ideological weapon. It is important to note that Lin Piao is officially hailed as Mao's "best student and closest comrade-in-arms": "He always puts into practice Chairman Mao's proletarian revolutionary line most faithfully, most resolutely and most thoroughly. He sets the best example of creative study and application of Chairman Mao's works and he always unswervingly defends and propagates Mao Tse-tung's thought."

To both supporter and opponent, Mao's thought outweights and will outlive Mao's person. With his thought embodied in a system of theory and practice and used as a guideline for mass action, Mao's personal usefulness is primarily to symbolize, defend and develop his thought. Mechanically speaking, Mao can be considered as the means; his thought as the end. In more simplified terms, the acute conflicts and fighting in mainland China today are over Mao's thought, rather than Mao's person.

Understanding, then, that the principal issue involved in the present struggle in Communist China is that of basic ideological principles,[3] it follows that the side which is ideologically stronger would have an advantage in initiating action or carrying out the struggle. To Mao and his followers, ideological struggle within the Party for purposes of rectification, unity and education is a constant factor in daily life. In his August, 1937 treatise "On Contradiction" Mao said: "Opposition and struggle between ideas of different kinds constantly occur within the Party; this is a reflection within the Party of contradictions between classes and between the new and the old society. If there were no contradictions in the Party and no ideological struggles to resolve them, the Party's life would come to an end." On September 7, 1937, in his thesis "Combat Liberalism," Mao added: "We stand for active ideological struggle because it is the weapon for ensuring unity within the Party and the revolutionary organizations in the interest of our fight. Every communist and revolutionary should take up this weapon."

By contrast, the critics of Mao's thought appear ideologically weaker, or less prepared. They seem to have avoided struggle by offering pretensions to orthodoxy. Yet, they have constantly suffered from inconsistencies in their theoretical and practical performances. Speaking of this sort of element, Mao noted in his "Combat Liberalism":

People who are liberals look upon the principle of Marxism as abstract dogma. They approve of Marxism, but are not prepared to practice it or to practice it in

[3] This ideological struggle is similar to that between Moscow and Peking. For details see Peter S. H. Tang's forthcoming book entitled "Sino-Soviet Relations: Issues and Analysis."

full; they are not prepared to replace their liberalism by Marxism. These people have their Marxism, but they have their liberalism as well—they talk Marxism but practice liberalism; they apply Marxism to others but liberalism to themselves.

The opponents of Mao's thought today are said to pay similar lip service to Marxism-Leninism and the thought of Mao, while having lost faith or interest in promoting proletarian revolution and dictatorship at home or abroad. Mao and his followers often describe the action of these ideological opponents within the Party as "waving the red flag to oppose the red flag." Like Khrushchev, these opponents, including Liu Shao-ch'i, are inclined to put tactics before strategy, and strategy above ideology. Consequently, they are indifferent to compromising ideological requirements on the pretext of strategic or tactical advantages. In "Combat Liberalism" Mao further stated: "Liberalism rejects ideological struggle and stands for unprincipled peace, thus giving rise to a decadent, philistine attitude and bringing about political degeneration in certain units and individuals in the Party and the revolutionary organizations." The tactics of the opposition are, therefore, less ideological than organizational, less open and direct, and more clandestine and zigzag. They may well hope to be in the majority in the struggle through general inertia and corrosion.

It must be remembered that it was not his opponents, but rather Mao himself and his faithful associates who initiated the present mass campaign in the form of cultural revolution to rectify the Party and to educate the people with Mao's thought. Mao's call to action in November, 1965, and his encouragement to the Red Guards, as evidenced by his eight meetings with some eleven million "revolutionary teachers and students" between August and November, 1966, are in line with his earlier use of mass campaigns such as the Three-Anti drive of the early 1950's and the Blooming and Contending campaign of 1957. His approach to ideological and social rectification has been basically in agreement with the attitudes of Lenin and Stalin. For example, Lenin said: "The dictatorship of the proletariat is a persistent struggle—bloody and bloodless, violent and peaceful, military and economic, educational and administrative—against the forces and traditions of the old society." Stalin also suggested that the maintenance and expansion of the proletarian dictatorship mean, among others, "creating among the proletarian masses a cementing force and a bulwark against the corrosive influence of the petty-bourgeois elements and petty-bourgeois habits." Likewise, on June 30, 1949 Mao said in his "On the People's Democratic Dictatorship":

The people's state protects the people. Only when the people have such a state can they educate and remould themselves by democratic methods on a country-wide scale, with everyone taking part, and shake off the influence of domestic and foreign reactionaries (which is still very strong, will survive for a long time and cannot be quickly destroyed), rid themselves of the bad habits and ideas acquired in the old society, not allow themselves to be led astray by the reactionaries, and continue to advance—to advance towards a socialist and communist society.

Thus, the cultural revolution led by Mao and his faithful associates today cannot be regarded simply as a desperate expediency, but rather represents a fundamental communist program of far-reaching significance. It is to rectify the Party by the way of changing human nature in conformity with communist principles. In turn, those who are rectified or remolded demand a most dedicated and uncorruptible Party to lead the proletarian revolution and dictatorship to fruition. Mao's timing of such a combined move of cultural revolution and intra-Party ideological struggle is to meet needs at home and to resist the "revisionist" trends in the international communist movement. Apparently, Mao hopes to make another major contribution to the communist cause during his life time by solving the problems of Party degeneration and retrogression of the revolution. If successful in this, Mao believes that the solutions to economic, technological, social and military problems will then be close at hand, to say nothing of the possible impact on the international communist movement.

So far, Mao's opponents seem to be reacting primarily with measures other than ideological—such as sabotage, strikes, demonstrations, organization of pseudo-Red Guards units to challenge Mao in the name of Mao, battles, armed clashes, kidnappings, and even mutinies. Apart from some self-criticism in public and in writing, these dissidents contribute few ideological deliberations in print which would systematically repudiate the thought of Mao.[4] Their lack of effective initiative appears to stem from their own inconsistency in theory and practice. Preoccupied with tactics, their appeal tends to be limited in scope and private in nature. By contrast, in promoting the communist system, Mao's emphasis on a public concept and interest and the destruction of private ambitions tends to have a mass appeal. Thus, the dissidents, including Liu Shao-ch'i and Teng Hsiao-p'ing, are generally being revealed and repudiated out of the public limelight with the exception of limited examples of self-criticism. As of this writing, it appears that Mao's opponents are losing their battle

[4] Two of Hong Kong's over 40 newspapers—*Hsiang-Kang Yi-pao* (*Hong Kong Night Gazette*) and *Hsin Wu Pao* (*New Noon Paper*)—have been considered to be mouthpieces of the Liu-Teng faction. While praising Liu and Teng, they have tended to slight Mao. But they do not systematically repudiate Mao's thought. Another little red book, modeled on *Quotations from Chairman Mao* exactly in form, under the title of *Liu Chu-Hsi Yü-lu* (*Quotations from Chairman Liu*), was edited and published by Tzu-Nien Ch'u-pan-she in Hong Kong in June, 1967. Many of the quotations from Liu refer to the all-people Party, all-people state, material incentives, peaceful transition, peaceful transformation, peaceful competition, and peaceful coexistence. Liu was quoted as saying that the great weakness of the CPC is its poor and childish state of ideological preparedness, as "no great work has yet been published."

in the intra-Party ideological struggle. Barring unforeseen developments, they will probably go down in Chinese Communist historical accounts as companions of Chang Kuo-t'ao, Ch'en Shao-yü, Kao Kang, and the like. They may retain their membership in the CPC, and even in its Central Committee and Politburo, as has happened in the case of P'eng Teh-huai since 1959. But they will serve only as negative examples, like Khrushchev, in the eyes of Mao and his faithful followers.

In the long run, the criticized and repudiated in the intra-Party ideological struggle are expected to be its greatest beneficiaries. They should be saved from their errors or from being victimized by sugar-coated bullets. But the Party and state and the very ideological foundations of Marxism-Leninism are also anticipated to profit immensely through Mao's thought. Through a series of successful ideological struggles, the communist system in China can be free, at least temporarily, from the "corrosive which eats away unity, undermines cohesion, causes apathy and creates dissension." In connection with the communist efforts based on the formula of unity-struggle-unity, Mao said in April, 1945: "Communists must be ready at all times to stand up for the truth, because truth is in the interests of the people; communists must be ready at all times to correct their mistakes, because mistakes are against the interests of the people." With these efforts he hopes to see an invigorated Party composed of members genuinely dedicated to the revolutionary cause. As he suggested in September, 1937: "A communist should have largeness of mind and he should be staunch and active, looking upon the interests of the revolution as his very life and subordinating his personal interests to those of the revolution."

As of this writing, the struggle between the supporters of and opponents to Mao's thought is still going on. Many cases of abuses, brutalities and unnecessary bloodshed have been reported. Mao and his close associates recognized some of these mistakes, as they admitted earlier certain "transitory and partial shortcomings" occurred during their vigorous drives to carry out the Great Leap Forward and the commune system in 1958. However, as they said, some of the transitory and partial shortcomings in major mass campaigns are difficult to avoid. The proletarian cultural revolution and the Red Guards' activities are conducted under the slogan "to learn revolution by taking part in it." These movements are like a revolutionary war, to which Mao referred in December, 1936: "A revolutionary war is a mass undertaking; it is often not a matter of first learning and then doing, but of doing and then learning, for doing is itself learning." So far, as confusing as it is, the struggle can still be measured in ideological terms. As the symbol of his thought, rather than the founder of a personal dynasty or a Stalin-type ruthless dictator, Mao is not likely to be defeated by the ideas or actions of his opponents. If the present major surgery of the cultural revolution in China should succeed, its repercussions will be enormous in the communist world and beyond.   If it should fail, future revolutionaries will probably look toward the cultural revolution for inspiration as another historical landmark like, although many times more significant than, the 1871 Paris Commune with which Marx was closely associated.

In short, since 1949 Communist China has been and remains an active laboratory or a dramatic stage for Mao's thought or communist revolution and dictatorship in action on a nation-wide scale.   Judging from the continuous chain of action-reaction-action in Communist China, as directed and analyzed through the thought of Mao which is conveniently digested in the popular handbook of *Quotations from Chairman Mao Tse-tung*, Mao's thought is the vital center of national collective thinking and endeavor. To Mao and his followers his thought is the foundation of their Party, state, economic, military, social and cultural life.   It has become the national goal of the Chinese Communists and their international show piece.   The foundation of the collective national will and the weapon for revolutionaty struggle, Mao's thought is relied on for national defense vis-a-vis both "US imperialism" and "Soviet revisionism."   It is a challenge to people both at home and abroad offered by Mao's followers who are convinced that such a vigorous ideological challenge is superior to and immune from the threat of nuclear bombs or ICBM's.   As long as this conviction remains, the so-called era of Mao Tse-tung will survive Mao himself in China.

Selected Bibliography

A Decade Under Mao Tse-tung— Hong Kong: Green Pagoda Press, 1959.

AI, HAN-SUNG, *Tsen-yang-tso I-ko Kung-Ch'an-Tang-yüan* (*How To Be A Communist Party Member*), Hankow: Chung-nan Jen-min Ch'u-pan-she, rev. ed., 1952.

ARNOL'DOV, A. I., *Kul'tura Narodnogo Kitaia* (*The Culture of People's China*), Moscow: Izd-vo Akad Nauk SSR, 1959.

ARTUROV, O. A., *Gosudarstvennyi Stroi Kitaiskoi Narodnoi Respubliki* (*The State System of the Chinese People's Republic*), Moscow: Pravda, 1951.

ASAHI SHIMBUN TOA BU (comp.), *Chugoku Kyosanto* (*The Chinese Communist Party*), Getsuyo Shobo, 1946.

BARANDOV, G. V., *Kitaiskaia Revoliutsiia i Bor'ba Kitaiskoi Kompartii* (*The Chinese Revolution and the Struggle of the Chinese Communist Party*), Moscow: Otdel Izd-va Nar. Kom. Oborony Soiuza SSR, 1934.

BARNETT, A. DOAK, *China after Mao*, Princeton, N. J.: Princeton Univ. Press, 1967.

——, *China on the Eve of the Communist Takeover*, New York: Praeger, 1963.

——, *Communist China: The Early Years 1949–55*, New York: Praeger, 1964.

——, with Ezra Vogel, *Cadres, Bureaucracy, and Political Power in Communist China*, New York: Columbia University Press, 1967.

BOORMAN, HOWARD L. (ed.), *Men and Politics in Modern China: Fifty Preliminary Biographers*, I, New York: Columbia University Press, 1960.

BRANDT, CONRAD, SCHWARTZ, BENJAMIN, and FAIRBANK, JOHN K., *A Documentary History of Chinese Communism*, Cambridge, Mass.: Harvard University Press, 1952.

BRANDT, CONRAD, *Stalin's Failure in China 1924–27*, Cambridge, Mass.: Harvard University Press, 1958.

Buck, John L., *Land Utilization in China 1929–33*, Chicago: University of Chicago Press, 1937.

Buck, John L., Wu, Yuan-li, *Food and Agriculture in Communist China*, New York: Praeger, 1966.

Chandrasekhar, Sripati, *China's Population*, Hong Kong: Hong Kong University Press, 1959.

Chang, Chia-Sen (Carsun), *The Third Force in China*, New York: Bookman Associates, 1952.

Ch'en, Hsi-hao, *Ko-ch'ü San-shih-wu-nien chung chih Chung-Kuo-Kuo-Min-Tang (The Kuomintang in the Past Thirty-Five Years)*, Shanghai: Commercial Press, 1929.

Ch'en, Jerome, *Mao and the Chinese Revolution*, New York: Oxford University Press, 1965.

Ch'en, Po-ta, *Stalin and the Chinese Revolution: In Celebration of Stalin's Seventieth Birthday*, Peking: Foreign Languages Press, 1953.

Ch'en, Shao-yu, *Liang-t'iao Chan-hsien (The Two Fronts)*, no place, pub. by the Publication Bureau of the CPC CC, distributed by Wu-ch'an-chieh-chi shu-tien, 1931.

Chen, Theodore Hsi-en, *Thought Reform of the Chinese Intellectuals*, Hong Kong: Hong Kong University Press, Distributed by Oxford University Press, 1960.

———, *Teacher Training in Communist China*, Washington, D.C.: U.S. Dept. of Health, Education and Welfare, 1960.

———, *Chinese Communism and the Proletarian-Socialist Revolution*, Los Angeles. Univ. of So. Calif. Press, 1955

Cheng, J. Chester (ed.), *Politics of the Chinese Red Army: Bulletin of Activities*, Stanford: Hoover Institution, Stanford University, 1966.

Cheng, Chu-yuan, *Communist China's Economy 1949–62: Structural Change and Crisis*, S. Orange, N.J.: Seton Hall University Press, 1963.

———, *Scientific and Technical Manpower in Communist China*, Washington, D.C.: National Science Foundation, 1965.

———, *Income and Standard of Living in Mainland China*, 2 vols, Hong Kong: Union Research Institute, 1957.

———, *The People's Communes*, Hong Kong: The Union Press, 1959.

Cheng-feng Wen-hsien (Documents on Reform of Party Spirit). Hong Kong: Hsin-min-chu Ch'u-pan-she, 1949.

Chiang, Kai-shek, *Soviet Russia in China*, New York: Farrar, Straus and Cudahy; 1st ed., 1957, 2nd ed., 1958.

China's Revolutionary Wars, Peking: Foreign Languages Press, 1951.

Chinese People's Republic, Ministry of Internal Affairs (comp.), *Chung-Hua-Jen-Min-Kung-Ho-Kuo Hsin-cheng Ch'ü-hua Chien-ts'e (A*

Sketch of the Administrative Division of the Chinese People's Republic, Peking: Ti-t'u Ch'u-pan-she, 1960.

Chinese People's Republic, State Statistical Bureau (comp.), *Wei-ta ti shih-nien: Chung-Hua-Jen-Min-Kung-Ho-Ku Ching-chi ho Wen-hua Chien-she Ch'eng-chiu ti T'ung-chi (Ten Great Years: The Statistics of the Economic and Cultural Construction of the Chinese People's Republic)*, Peking: Jen-min Ch'u-pan-she, 1959.

COHEN, ARTHUR, *Communism of Mao Tse-tung*, Chicago: University of Chicago Press, 1964.

CHOU, EN-LAI, *Ti-erh-ch'i K'ang-chan chi Chiang-lai (The Second Stage of the War of Resistance and the Future*, no place: Chieh-fang Pub. Co., 3rd ed., 1938.

CHOW, TSE-TSUNG, *The May Fourth Movement: Intellectual Revolution in Modern China*, Cambridge, Mass.: Harvard University Press, 1960.

———, *Research Guide to the May Fourth Movement: Intellectual Revolution in Modern China, 1915–1924*, Cambridge, Mass.: Harvard Univ. Press, 1963.

CHU, TEH, *K'ang-Jih Yu-chi Chan-cheng (Guerilla Warfare in Resisting the Japanese)*, Hankow: Hsin-hua Jih-pao, 1938.

———, *Lun Yu-chi-chan (On Guerrilla Warfare)*, Shanghai: Chien-she Pub. Co., 2nd ed, 1938.

———, *On the Battlefronts of the Liberated Areas*, Peking: Foreign Languages Press, 1952.

———, *et al., Ti-Pa-Lu-Chün Chiang-ling K'ang-chan Hui-i-lu (Memoirs on the War of Resistance by the Generals of the 8th Route Army)*, edited by Ch'en Cho-ai, no place: Nu-hao Co., 1938.

———, *et al., Wo-men Tsen-yang Ta-t'ui Ti-jen (How We Defeat the Enemy)*, Hanknow: Hsin-hua Jih-pao, 1938.

CHUGUNOV, V. E., *Ugolovnoe Sudoproizvodstvo Kitaiskoi Narodnoi Respubliki (The Criminal Procedure of the Chinese People's Republic)*, Moscow: Gos. Izd-vo IUrid Lit., 1959.

Chung-Hua-Jen-Min-Kung-Ho-Kuo Fa-chan Kuo-min-ching-chi ti Ti-i-ko Wu-Nien-Chi-Hua 1953–57 (The First Five Year Plan for the Development of the National Economy of the Chinese People's Republic 1953–57), Peking: Jen-min Ch'u-pan-she, 1955.

Chung-Hua-Jen-Min-Kung-Ho-Kuo K'ai-kuo Wen-hsien (Literature on the Founding of the Chinese People's Republic), Hong Kong: Hsin-min-chu Ch'u-pan-she, 1949.

DALIN, SERGEI ALEKSEEVICH, *Ocherki Revoliutsii v Kitae (Sketches of the Revolution in China)* Moscow: Moskovskii Rabochii, 1927.

DOOLIN, DENNIS, and NORTH, ROBERT C., *The Chinese People's Republic*, Stanford: Hoover Institution, 1966.

ECKSTEIN, ALEXANDER, *Communist China's Growth and Foreign Trade*, New York: McGraw, 1966.

ELEGANT, ROBERT S., *China's Red Masters, New York:* Twayne, 1951.

EUDIN, XENIA JOUKOFF, and NORTH, ROBERT C., *Soviet Russia and the East, 1920–27: A Documentary Survey*, Stanford, Stanford University Press, 1957.

FAIRBANK, JOHN KING, *The United States and China*, new ed., Cambridge Mass.: Harvard University Press, 1959.

FEIS, HERBERT, *The China Tangle: Pearl Harbor to the Marshall Mission*, Princeton, N. J.: Princeton University Press, 1953.

GEORGE, ALEXANDER L., *The Chinese Communist Army in Action*, New York: Columbia University Press, 1967.

GITTINGS, JOHN, *The Role of the Chinese Army*, New York: Oxford University Press, 1967.

GRANQVIST, HANS, *The Red Guard*, New York: Praeger, 1967.

GRIFFITH, SAMUEL B. II, *Peking and People's Wars*, New York: Praeger, 1966.

——, *The Chinese People's Liberation Army*, New York: McGraw-Hill, 1967.

GUDOSHNIKOV, L. M., *Vysshie Organy Gosudarstvennoi Vlasti i Gosudarstvennogo Upravleniia Kitaiskoi Narodnoi Respubliki (The High Organs of the State Power and State Administration of the Chinese People's Republic)*, Moscow: Izd-vo Akad. Nauk SSR, 1960.

HALPERIN, MORTON H., *China and the Bomb*, New York: Praeger, 1965.

——, and PERKINS, DWIGHT H., *Communist China and Arms Control*, Cambridge, Mass.: East Asian Research Center and Center for International Affairs, Harvard Univ., 1965.

Handbook on People's China, Peking: Foreign Languages Press, 1957.

HSIEH, ALICE L., *Communist China's Strategy in the Nuclear Age*, New York: Prentice-Hall, 1962.

HSÜEH, MU-CHIAO, SU, HSING and LIN, TSE-LIN, *Socialist Transformation of the National Economy in China*, Peking: Foreign Languages Press, 1960.

HU, CH'IAO-MU, *Chung-Kuo-Kung-Ch'an-Tang ti San-shih-nien (Thirty Years of the Communist Party of China)*, Peking: Jen-min Ch'u-pan-she, 1951.

HUNTER, EDWARD, *Brain-washing in Red China: the Calculated Destruction of Men's Minds*, New York: Vanguard Press, 1953.

International Commission of Jurists, *The Question of Tibet and the Rule of Law, Geneva,* 1959.

———, *Tibet and the Chinese People's Republic,* Geneva, 1960.

ISAACS, HAROLD R., *The Tragedy of the Chinese Revolution,* Stanford: Stanford University Press, 1951.

ISRAEL, JOHN, *Student Nationalism in China, 1927–37,* Stanford: Hoover Institution, Stanford University, 1966.

JAN, GEORGE P. (ed.), *Government of Communist China,* San Francisco, Calif.: Chandler, 1966.

JOFFE, ELLIS, *Party and Army: Professionalism and Political Control in the Chinese Officer Corps 1949–64,* Cambridge, Mass.: Harvard University Press, 1965.

JOHNSON, CHALMERS, *Peasant Nationalism and Communist Power: The Emergence of Revolutionary China, 1937–45,* Stanford: Stanford University Press, 1962.

LENG, SHAO CHUAN, and PALMER, NORMAN D., *Sun Yat-sen and Communism,* New York: Praeger, 1960.

LETHBRIDGE, HENRY J., *China's Urban Communes,* Hong Kong: Dragonfly Books, 1961.

LEWIS, JOHN W., *Leadership in Communist China,* Ithaca: Cornell University Press, 1963.

———, Major Doctrines of Communist China, N. Y.: Norton, 1964.

LI, CHOH-MING, *Economic Development of Communist China: An Appraisal of the First Five Years of Industralization,* Berkeley: University of California Press, 1959.

LIU, SHAO-CH'I, *Internationalism and Nationalism,* Peking: Foreign Languages Press, 3rd ed., 1952.

———, *Lun Kung-Ch'an-Tang-yuan ti Hsiu-yang (Training of the Communist Party Member),* Hong Kong: Hsin-min-chu Ch'u-pan-she, 1949.

———, *Lun Tang (On the Party),* Peking: Hsin-hua Shu-tien, 1950.

———, *On Inner Party Struggle,* Peking: Foreign Language Press, no date.

MACFARQUHAR, RODERICK P., *The Hunderd Flowers Campaign and the Chinese Intellectuals,* New York: Praeger, 1960.

Mao's China: Party Reform Documents, 1942–44, trans. by Boyd Compton, Seattle: University of Washington Press, 1953.

MAO TSE-TUNG, *Mao-Tse-Tung Hsüan-chi (Selected Works of Mao Tse-tung),* 4 vols, Peking: Jen-min Ch'u-pan-she, 1951–1960.

———, *Mao-Tse-Tung Chu-tso Hsüan-tu (Selected Reader of Mao Tse-tung's Works),* 2 vols, Peking: Jen-min Ch'u-pan-she, 1964.

————, *Mao-Chu-Hsi Yü-lu* (*Quotations from Chiarman Mao*), Peking: Hsin-Hua Shu-tien, 1966.

————, *Quotations from Chairman Mao Tse-tung*, Peking: Foreign Language Press, 1966.

————, *Selected Works*, 4 vols., Peking: Foreign Language Press, 1961–65.

————, *On Correct Handling of Contradictions Among the People*, Peking: Foreign Languages Press, 1960.

————, Chu Teh, *et al.*, *Pa-Lu-Chün ti Chan-lüeh ho Chan-shu* (*The Strategy and Tactics of the 8th Route Army*), Shanghai: Shenghuo Pub. Co., 1938.

————, and LIU, SHAO-CH'I, *Lessons of the Chinese Revolution*, Bombay: J. Bhatt, 1950.

————, WANG, MING, DIMITROV, GEORGI, *et al.*, *China: The March Toward Unity*, New York: Workers Library Publishers, 1937.

————, *et al.*, *Hsiang-ch'ih-chieh-tuan ti Hsing-shih yü Jen-wu* (*The Situation and Our Tasks during the Stage of Stalemate in the War*), 2 vols., no place or publisher, 1940.

————, *et al.*, *Hsin-Min-Chu-Chu-I Kung-shang-cheng-ts'e* (*The Industrial and Commercial Policies of the New Democracy*), Hong Kong: Hsin-min-chu Ch'u-pan-she, 1949.

————, *et al.*, *Min-tsu Ko-ming chih Lu* (*The Way of the National Revolution*), pub. by Hsing-hsing and distributed at Hankow by Hsing-sheng T'u-shu Kung-ssu, 1938.

————, *et al.*, *Mu-ch'ien Hsing-shih ho O-men ti Jen-wu* (*The Current Situation and Our Tasks*), Hong Kong: Hsing-min-chu Ch'u-pan-she, 1949.

McLANE, CHARLES B., *Soviet Policy and the Chinese Communists, 1931–46*, New York: Columbia University Press, 1958.

MEISNER, MAURICE, *Li Ta-chao and the Origins of Chinese Marxism*, Cambridge, Mass.: Harvard University Press, 1967.

MIF, PAVEL ALEKSANDROVICH, *15 Let Geroicheskoi Bor'by. K 15-Letiiu Kommunisticheskoi Partii Kitaia* (*15 Years of Heroic Struggle: In Celebration of the 15th Anniversary of the Communist Party of China*), Moscow: Partizdat, 1936.

————, *Kitaiskaia Revoliutsiia* (*The Chinese Revolution*), Moscow: Partizdat, 1932.

————, (ed.), *Strategiia i Taktika Kominterna v Natsional'no-Kolonial'noi Revoliutssi na Primere Kitaia; Sbornik Dokumentov* (*The Strategy and Tactics of the Comintern in National-Colonial Revolution as Exemplified in China: A Collection of Documents*), Moscow: Izd. In-ta MX i MP, 1934.

MU, FU-SHANG, *The Wilting of the Hundred Flowers*, New York: Praeger, 1963.

MYRDAL, JAN, *Report from a Chinese Village*, New York: Pantheon, 1965.

NORTH, ROBERT C., *Moscow and the Chinese Communists*, Stanford: Stanford University Press, 1953.

PAYNE, ROBERT, *Mao Tse-tung, Ruler of Red China*, New York: Schuman Inc., 1950.

People's Communes in China, Peking: Foreign Languages Press, 1959.

RHOADS, EDWARD, J. M., *Chinese Red Army 1927–63: An Annotated Bibliography*, Cambridge, Mass.: Harvard University Press, 1964.

ROSTOW, W. W., *et al.*, *The Prospects for Communist China*, New York: John Wiley and Sons, 1954.

RUE, JOHN E., *Mao Tse-tung in Opposition, 1927–35*, Stanford: Hoover Institute, Stanford University Press, 1966.

SCHRAM, R. STUART, *The Political Thought of Mao Tse-tung*, N.Y.: Praeger, 1963.

———, *Mao Tse-tung*, New York: Simon and Schuster, 1967.

SCHURMANN, FRANZ, *Ideology and Organization in Communist China*, Berkeley: University of Calif. Press, 1966.

SCHWARTZ, BENJAMIN I., *Chinese Communism and the Rise of Mao*, Cambridge, Mass.: Harvard University Press, 1951.

SNOW, EDGAR, *Random Notes on Red China (1936–45)*, Cambridge: Chinese Economic and Political Studies, Harvard University; distributed by Harvard University Press, 1957.

———, *Red Star Over China*, New York: Modern Library, 1944.

STALIN, JOSEPH, *O Perspektivakh Revoliutsii v Kitae (On the Prospects of Revolution in China)*, Moscow: Gos. Izd-vo Polit. Lit-ry, 1954.

———, *Stalin on China*, Bombay: People's Pub. House, 1951.

TANG, PETER S. H., *Communist China Today: Domestic and Foreign Policies*, New York: Praeger, 1957.

———, *Communist China Today: Vol. II: Chronology and Documentary Supplement*, New York: Praeger, 1958.

———, *Communist China as a Developmental Model for Underdeveloped Countries*, Washington, D.C.: Research Institute on the Sino-Soviet Bloc, 1960.

———, *The Training of Party Cadres in Communist China*, Washington, D.C.: Research Institute on the Sino-Soviet Bloc, 1961.

———, *Communist China Today: Vol. I: Domestic and Foreign Policies*, rev. ed., Washington, D.C.: Research Institute on the Sino-Soviet Bloc, 1961.

———, *The Commune System in Mainland China*, Washington, D.C.: Research Institute on the Sino-Soviet Bloc, 1961.

————, *The Chinese Communist Struggle against Modern Revisionism: Theory and Practice*, Chestnut Hill, Mass.: Research Institute on the Sino-Soviet Bloc, 1964.

————, and MALONEY, JOAN M., *Communist China: The Domestic Scene 1949–1967*, South Orange, N.J.: Seton Hall University Press, 1967.

TENG, HSIAO-P'ING, *Report on the Rectification Campaign*, Peking: Foreign Languages Press, 1957.

TREADGOLD, DONALD (ed.), *Soviet and Chinese Communism*, Seattle; University of Washington Press, 1966.

TROTSKII, LEV, *Problems of the Chinese Revolution*, trans. by Max Shachtman, New York: Pioneer Publishers, 1932.

U. S. Congress, Senate, Committee on the Judiciary, *Nature of Communism in Occupied China*, Washington, D.C.: U.S. Govt. Print. Office, 1957.

Union Research Institute (ed.), *Who's Who in Communist China*, Hong Kong: Union Research Institute, 1966.

VANDERVELDE, EMILE, *A travers la revolution chinoise*, Paris: L'Eglantine, 1931.

Voprosy Kitaiskoi Revoliutsii (Problems of the Chinese Revolution) (Articles by Stalin and Bukharin in a collection of materials and documents of the Party and the Comintern on the Chinese problem from the 7th plenum of the Executive Committee of the Comintern in Dec., 1926, up to the "Feng Yu-hsiang betrayal."), Leningrad-Moscow: Gosizdat, 1927.

WALKER, RICHARD L., *China Under Communism: The First Five Years*, New Haven: Yale University Press, 1955.

————, *The Continuing Struggle: Communist China and the Free World*, New York: Athene Press, 1958.

————, *The Chinese Danger*, Chicago: American Bar Association, 1966.

WANG, SHIH; WANG, CH'IAO, MA, CH'I-PIN, and CHANG NIN (eds.), *Chung-Kuo Kung-Ch'an-Tang Li-shih Chien-pien (The History of the Communist Party of China: A Short Course)*, Shanghai: Shang-Hai Jen-min Ch'u-pan-she, 1958.

WATSON, FRANCIS, *Frontiers of China*, New York: Praeger, 1966.

WILBUR, C. MARTIN and HOW, JULIE LIEN-YING (eds.), *Documents on Communisn, Nationalism and Soviet Advisors in China 1918–27*, New York: Columbia University Press, 1956.

WITTFOGEL, KARL A., *From Marx to Mao*, Seattle: University of Washington Press, 1960.

————, *Oriental Despotism: A Comparative Study of Total Power*, New Haven: Yale University Press, 1957.

WU, LI-P'ING, *Lun Wo-kuo Jen-min Nei-pu Mao-tun (On the Contradictions Among the People in Our Country)*, Peking: Jen-min Ch'u-pan-she, 1957.

WU, MIN, and HSIAO, FENG (eds.), *Ts'ung "Wu-Sze" tao Chung-Hua-Jen-Min-Kung-Ho-Kuo Tan-sheng (From the "May Fourth" to the Birth of the Chinese People's Republic)*, Peking: Hsin-ch'ao Shu-tien, 1951.

WU, YUAN-LI, *An Economic Survey of Communist China*, New York: Bookman Associates, 1956.

————, (ed.), *Realities of Communist China*, Milwaukee: Institute for Asian Studies, Marquette University and the Bureau of Business and Economic Research, Robert A. Johnston College of Business Administration, Marquette University, 1960.

————, *The Economy of Communist China*, New York: Praeger, 1965.

YAKHONTOFF, VICTOR A., *The Chinese Soviets*, N.Y.: Coward-McCann, Inc., 1934.

YU, TE-CHI, *Mass Persuasion in Communist China*, New York: Praeger, 1964.

YUAN, TUNG-LI, *Russian Works on China 1918–1960 in American Libraries*, New Haven: Far Eastern Publications, Yale University, 1961.

ZHDANOV, M., *V Boiakh za Sovetskii Kitai (In the Battles for Soviet China)*, Moscow: Molodaia Gvardiia, 1932.

Index

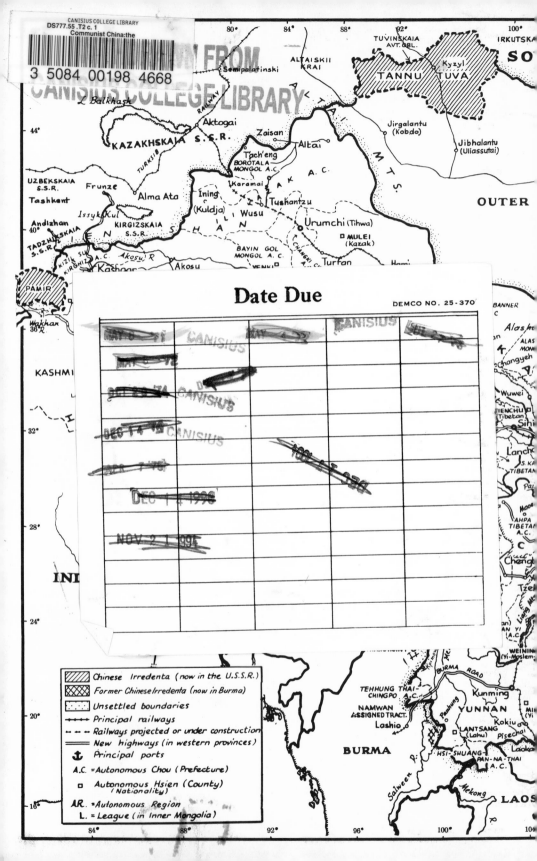